20

EDMUND WILSON

LEWIS M. DABNEY

EDMUND
WILSON

A Life in Literature

Farrar, Straus and Giroux

New York

Farrar, Straus and Giroux
19 Union Square West, New York 10003

Owing to limitations of space, all acknowledgments for permission to reprint previously published and unpublished material appear on pages 599–602. Illustration credits appear on pages 641–642.

Library of Congress Cataloging-in-Publication Data
Dabney, Lewis M.
    Edmund Wilson : a life in literature / Lewis M. Dabney.
        p. cm.
    Includes bibliographical references and index.
    ISBN-13: 978-0-374-11312-4
    ISBN-10: 0-374-11312-2 (alk. paper)
    1. Wilson, Edmund, 1895–1972. 2. Authors, American—20th
century—Biography. 3. Critics—United States—Biography.   I. Title.

    PS3545.I6245Z594 2005   2004057148

Designed by Jonathan D. Lippincott

www.fsgbooks.com

1   3   5   7   9   10   8   6   4   2

For Sarah, my love and my literary ally
For Elizabeth and Lewis, our wonderful children

Keep going; never stoop; sit tight;
Read something luminous at night.
—Wilson, "A Message You'll Expect, My Friends"

Though grave-diggers' toil is long,
Sharp their spades, their muscles strong,
They but thrust their buried men
Back in the human mind again.
—Yeats, "Under Ben Bulben"

Contents

Preface

Edmund Wilson had influenced several of my professors at Columbia University, whose enthusiasm led me to him. I thought his prose in all its clarity and strength wonderful and his elucidation of literature through personality and history brilliant. I decided to do my doctoral dissertation on his early work. During that time Lionel Trilling and F. W. Dupee suggested to me that there ought to be a book that would tell the story of this life in which art and ideas played so large a part. When I began to teach English at Smith College, Helen Muchnic was teaching Russian literature there, and through her I was fortunate to meet Wilson at her home in Cummington, Massachusetts.

Before dinner that evening, Wilson, known for quizzing people about their specialties, grilled me on American writers. Perhaps self-conscious with an admirer, he spoke with a pronounced British accent. As an old-fashioned republican Wilson had bristled at Britain's imperial politics and class snobberies, but I was aware that his formal education before World War I and before the American literary revival of the 1920s was British in tone. In one of his books Trilling described how the shy and slender young editor he'd called on at *The New Republic* in 1929 came in midlife to resemble "a British ship captain closely related to Henry James." James defines the artist as "one of those people on whom nothing is lost," and when Wilson stopped questioning me and sank back into his chair, he was alert to all the currents in the room.

Wilson liked my 1962 review of *Patriotic Gore* in the *Columbia University Forum*, and the following summer he invited me to Talcottville for four days. He was editing *A Prelude* and the subsequent journals, but his wife, Elena, drove us on expeditions, and he allowed himself long talks accompanied by white wine. We discussed the Civil War and its literature as well as Dos Passos and Hemingway, my mother's friends in France during the twenties, whom I had met as a boy. Wilson was intensely curious, and would slap his thigh in laughter, but his standards were stern. He lacked respect for politicians who lied about major issues, and when I spoke as though from knowledge of some aspect of his life I knew little about, the old-fashioned reporter said, "You must train yourself never to make an assertion that is not based on positive evidence."

Wilson spoke of his boyhood, of the sense of America his father had given him, and related this to the open, upstate landscape and the old stone house. At Princeton, he said, "I had a very pleasant time except when my reforming zeal came to the surface," an allusion to his attack on the selective eating clubs. Wilson mentioned a novel he was planning to write in the form of a round of visits among "the blasted young men" of his college circle. When I asked what separated him from them, he replied that during World War I he had escaped his class by serving as a private in the hospital corps.

He was suspicious of what he called "the Ph.D. octopus." Twenty years before he had written of becoming uncomfortably aware, at a professor's house in Princeton, "that this all-absorbing scholarship was after me." In this essay, "Thoughts on Being Bibliographed," he presents himself as a literary worker of the 1920s trying to keep alive the fire, feeding sticks into the flames and attracting the interest of creatures who seem eager "to thrust him into a throne and have him an object of veneration," though others "would feel safer if they could eat him." When late one night of my Talcottville visit I encountered Wilson on the way to the bathroom, with a darkly glaring look, echoing a theme of "Thoughts on Being Bibliographed," he said, "You should be writing your own essays and stories instead of annotating mine." But if someone was going to write about him, he wanted that person to be accurate. The next afternoon, when we had separated for a while, there was a knock at my door and he stood there with one of the journals in his hands. "When did I write this?" he queried, pointing to a passage. Unsure whether he didn't know or was testing me, I produced a date that satisfied him.

On the morning we said goodbye—I wouldn't see him again, though we exchanged letters—Wilson, discounting the elegance and wit of some of his early pieces, told me that in his opinion he hadn't written well until 1925. Now, he said, he was doing his best work in the journal. As on the preceding days, he handed me a glass of orange juice before we sat down to breakfast, and swigged his down after pronouncing the Hebrew words, *Hazak, Hazak, Venit-hazayk*, translating them, "Be strong, be strong, let us make ourselves strong." When I mentioned his well-known rejection of religion he explained that the ritual worked—"It helps me jack up my waning powers."

Two decades later, with the cooperation of Malcolm Cowley and Roger Straus, I edited the Viking *Portable Edmund Wilson*, later to become the *Edmund Wilson Reader*. I began this biography with extensive interviews in Wilson's circle, and when, at Roger Straus's request, I turned aside in 1990 to edit his last journal, *The Sixties* (1993), I talked with every figure in that volume I could find. I needed to make sure that any inaccuracies of fact in Wilson's manuscript were not legitimized, but this was also an opportunity to fulfill the biographer's curiosity and know the man through the eyes of friends and associates. *Edmund Wilson: Centennial Reflections*, which I edited four years later, emerged from symposiums in Wilson's centenary year at Princeton and at the Mercantile Library in Manhattan. This book frames a dialogue between an older and a younger generation of scholars and literary journalists—on one hand Daniel Aaron, Jason Epstein, Elizabeth Hardwick, Alfred Kazin, Mary Meigs, Neale Reinitz, Arthur Schlesinger, Jr., and C. Vann Woodward, on the other Paul Berman, David Bromwich, Andrew Delbanco, Wendy Lesser, Louis Menand, Jed Perl, David Remnick, and Sean Wilentz. Their commentary on Wilson rounds out a rich critical literature. In addition, I am indebted to details in Jeffrey Meyers's account of Wilson and Frances Kiernan's of Mary McCarthy, as well as to Tim Page's editing of Dawn Powell's letters and journals.

At the Mercantile Library symposium, Morris Dickstein mentioned the need for a book about Wilson, as had Trilling and Dupee. He observed that the literary world had been flooded with information about Wilson the man—his diaries and letters, McCarthy's memoirs, and the biographies of her in which he figured "more or less as the villain," a biography of Wilson, by Meyers, that focused "too much on the almost clinical lover, the difficult husband, the distracted, intermittent father, the imperious personality." Dickstein spoke for those who wanted "a scrupulous and detailed intellectual biography" of the critic in his times and the perspective of our own. I hope to have met this challenge and, insofar as it is possible, to have created a true account of Wilson's turbulent life at the center of the period in which modern American literary culture took form. In his case biography is literary history.

EDMUND WILSON

Introduction

On a brisk afternoon in September 1922, a conservatively dressed young man with red hair sat on the upper deck of a Fifth Avenue bus in Manhattan, engrossed in a manuscript. A friend at the literary magazine *The Dial* had put a long poem into his hands. *The Dial* was interested in publishing it, and the editors hoped that the young man—Edmund Wilson— would write an essay to elucidate the poem. By the time he reached Greenwich Village, Wilson had completed a first reading of T. S. Eliot's *The Waste Land*. Decades later he would recall being "bowled over," and his essay called the poem "simply one triumph after another." This recognition of Eliot followed Wilson's account, in *The New Republic*, of Joyce's *Ulysses* as a masterpiece fusing naturalism and symbolism, re-creating the mind "straining always to perpetuate and perfect itself" and the body "always laboring and throbbing to throw up some beauty from its darkness." He believed the general reader could absorb these works that challenged existing literary forms and commandeered in new ways the powers of language. Both Eliot and Joyce, he thought, occasionally tried one's patience, but he was committed to making them more accessible.

Edmund Wilson was twenty-seven. He was fortunate to come on the scene as a critic when he did, but he had trained for this moment. At fifteen he had been sure of his literary vocation, and he absorbed all that liberal education had to offer both at the Hill School and at Princeton, where extraordinary teachers encouraged his curiosity and enthusiasm for books and about ideas. He emerged from his parents' uncongenial marriage with emotional scars, but his confidence in his abilities was strong, and he was seasoned by a year as a hospital orderly in France during World War I. Though he hated the suffering he saw, he liked being on a footing of relative equality with Americans of diverse backgrounds, and returned to his country skeptical of institutions and of rank and social privilege. He joined *Vanity Fair* as an editorial assistant, immediately became its managing editor, and began publishing criticism there as well as in other magazines.

The generation of the 1920s was brought up on the best of the Old World and hoped to equal it, applying the work habit—even as they broke away from Victorian mores—that Americans traditionally brought to commerce. Wilson was indebted to the men of letters of eighteenth- and nineteenth-century England and France as well as to Emerson, and at the beginning of his career owed much to H. L. Mencken and Van Wyck Brooks. While these critics shied away from the transformation of literature after the war, he became the spokesman of writers bringing this about. He found a podium at *The New Republic* in 1925, and for ten years his work appeared in almost every issue, often twice, a running account of books and of American culture, alternating with the studies of the new international literature that became *Axel's Castle*. The Depression deepened the perspective on his class attained in the army, and he largely put aside criticism to be a reporter on the labor front. He absorbed Marxism while doing the studies reprinted in *The American Earthquake* and overcame his naiveté about the Soviet Union. As the 1930s ended, he came into full possession of his powers as the biographer-historian of revolutionaries in *To the Finland Station* and the post-Marxist, neo-Freudian critic of *The Triple Thinkers* and *The Wound and the Bow*.

In Greenwich Village of the jazz age Wilson explored the newfound freedoms of booze and sex. He was sexually innocent until twenty-five, then lost his virginity and his heart to one of the most desired women of the period, the poet Edna St. Vincent Millay. His private life became as chaotic as his professional life was disciplined. Wilson was the only well-known literary alcoholic of his generation whose work was not compromised by his drinking, but alcohol undermined his marriages. In addition to four of these—his third, to Mary McCarthy, providing fodder for gossip, attacks, and counterattacks, which survive in their writings—he had many affairs and sexual encounters. As he aged, the once handsome man became physically unattractive, but still had no difficulty as a seducer. When asked how he got "all those dames" into bed, he answered that he "talked them into it" by discussing subjects in which they were interested.

Jason Epstein described Wilson as "by nature a pedagogue. He was always in search of a promising student. And this, I believe, is what his love affairs were really all about."

The early forties were his dark period, a midlife crisis not of identity but of morale, due not only to his failing marriage to McCarthy—he was sexually faithful, she not—but to the deaths of friends and the grim spectacle of a second world war. A resilient temperament, a new literary platform, and marriage to Elena Mumm Thornton enabled him to recover and achieve a second career. In *The New Yorker* he progressed from reviews to long essays and reportage, again trying out the materials of his books in magazine form. He brought a single-minded concentration to everything from nineteenth-century American writing and the Russian classics to Native Americans, Israel, and the ancient texts of the Dead Sea Scrolls. His contemporary Malcolm Cowley wrote that one followed *The New Yorker* "to see what in God's name he would be doing next." He turned his literary journalism into chronicles, began editing his diaries, created *The Twenties* and *The Sixties* as well as his book about American character and culture in the Civil War, *Patriotic Gore*. Wilson's experience as a free-living man of the twenties meant more to him as it became memory and history. In later life he came full circle, embracing "the old provincial America" that the family home in Talcottville, New York, represented.

Wilson's story—in the words of Paul Horgan, who knew him in various settings—is that of the artist "searching for a rational design in the world through his own life and the act of writing." This story is carried by his letters, verse, fiction, and memoirs, and reflected in his criticism, history, and reportage. It is the autobiography of his generation, the *confession d'un enfant du siècle*—a child of the century—that Christian Gauss suggested he write but Wilson himself could not see as a whole. His multivolume journal, a record of American life from 1914 to 1972, looks outward from the self to the world. Yet the glimpses of Wilson are accurate, though he sometimes gets a detail wrong when he retells the anecdotes of others. Just as he does not spare the women with whom his sexual experiences are eventually made public, he never tries to make himself look good. He describes an outburst in a drunken quarrel with his second wife, Margaret Canby, in 1932 exactly as this was overheard and recalled by a neighbor in their building in a memoir published after Wilson's death and before the appearance of his journal for these years.

The stories of others—Fitzgerald, Hemingway, and Dos Passos, Malraux, Nabokov, and Auden, along with Millay and McCarthy, Louise Bogan and Dawn Powell—who helped define the literary and intellectual life of Europe and the United States over these fifty years are interwoven in this biography. Their voices in the correspondence complement Wilson's, and so do those of non-authors—Stanley Dell, an early friend, Margaret Canby, Mamaine Paget Koestler—who have their own eloquence on paper, the mark of an era that, though culturally narrower than ours, was in many ways more literate. But it is Wilson whose voice is dominant.

It is tempting to explain Wilson's powers in terms of the pain and psychic struggle of his life, which was his method in portraying writers and historical figures. He wished to have made better connections with his father, who died when Wilson was twenty-seven. His youthful affection for his mother faded as, impressed neither by her son's career nor by what she saw of his private life, she doled out on her terms his share of the estate left by his father, while Wilson haggled with magazines and publishers for money. The critic, journalist, and portraitist never had the success he wanted as a fiction writer or playwright. His first three marriages were failures. One can see Wilson—Edgar Johnson, the Dickens scholar, seems first to have suggested this—as the wounded archer of his account of Sophocles' *Philoctetes*, a play that offered him metaphors for the tension between the writer and society as well as the relationship of art and neurosis. Philoctetes has a suppurating ulcer and a magical bow, a gift of the gods on which the conquest of Troy depends. But if Wilson projects himself as Philoctetes, in his portraiture he is also young Neoptolemus, who, sent to acquire the weapon, realizes it will not work without the willing presence of the exiled, sick, irascible warrior.

Isaiah Berlin integrated these two figures in his view of his friend. Thinking Wilson by nature "disharmonious," Berlin linked this to his profound understanding of the artists and public figures he wrote about. "He was always worried about whether he thought this or that was true or false," Sir Isaiah said. "He was an uncomfortable man, uncomfortable with himself; and that's what caused the friction, and the friction caused the genius." In proposing Wilson as the most important critic of their century, Berlin accounted for his staying power in terms attractive to a biographer: the other critics mostly wrote "just intelligent sentences," but "everything Wilson wrote was filled with some kind of personal content."

His writing reveals a figure full of contradictions: a rationalist and classicist who was also a restless romantic, questing for more books and writers to investigate, ever more scenes in which to re-create himself; an empiricist who kept coming back to questions of belief and faith; a man of ideas for whom abstractions lacked the validity of individual figures and particular scenes; someone self-absorbed in relation to his family, vulnerable to romantic entanglements, endlessly generous with literary friends. Wilson was an explorer, "bold enough"—as he remarked of someone else in one of his late self-interviews—"to open up a whole new geography of the intellectual world." Restless and tireless, doggedly thinking through subjects, expanding and recycling his work in some thirty-two volumes that still entertain, instruct, and inspire, this determined man gave to books and writing their full weight in the human struggle.

PART ONE

Edmund Wilson, Jr.

1

12 Wallace Street

A Nest of Gentlefolk

Born May 8, 1895, Edmund Wilson, Jr., was a shy boy, the only child of Edmund and Helen Mather Kimball Wilson. He grew up in Red Bank, New Jersey, thirty-some miles south of New York, near the ocean. Though accessible to the city by the North Jersey Coast train, the town then had a Southern flavor. "In the spring," his daughter Rosalind recalled, "old men would appear on the streets selling soft-shell crabs from baskets of seaweed. The summers were long and hot and full of mosquitoes, bred in the Jersey swamps." Twelve Wallace Street (one day to be renumbered and renamed 100 McLaren Street) was a three-story house on several acres, with barns and coops, fences, and a vegetable garden. A dark house with large ground-floor rooms all opening into one another in the style of the 1880s, it was set off by a bright, ever expanding garden that won the boy's mother first prize in a Monmouth County competition. Three servants lived with the family. Jennie Corbett, the maid and housekeeper, had emigrated from Ireland at age fifteen. Almost six feet tall, with "beautiful Irish blue eyes" and "the soul of a saint," she was there to help young Edmund take his first steps, and the Wilsons grew to depend on her. Gerda the cook was part Indian, silent and proud. Her mulatto husband, Oscar, served as coachman.

Wilson's large head had damaged his mother during what was a difficult birth, and when he learned this, presumably from her or from Jennie, he would associate it with her distrust of intellectual men. Yet she doted on the cherubic baby with the dark eyes, the reddish hair and complexion of her people, calling him Bunny, since he looked, she said, "just like a plum-bun." Mother and son visited back and forth within the family, and a snapshot shows them driving down a lane in a pony cart, she wearing a long dress with a bustle and he, six or seven years old, a straw boater. Physically alike, they appear equally intent and determined.

Perhaps they were on their way to the nearby town of Sea Bright, where he played with his cousins, including Reuel "Sandy" Kimball, Jr. The boys delighted in childish pranks, cut wax phonograph cylinders on a machine, played checkers, and put on puppet shows, a diversion Wilson later shared with his children. Sandy and his sister Esther, whose mother was Wilson's socially ambitious Aunt Caroline, always had a French governess. "At Sea Bright," Wilson recalled in a memoir, "the lawns were ironed smooth." The Kimballs were doctors, and Uncle Reuel was the pillar of the clan. "Thick-set and short, with a bristling square-cut mustache," he was "a terrific worker," a diagnostician who cared enough to sit up all night with patients who needed him. Like Edmund he had red hair, and like Mrs. Wilson he was gruff in tone.

Twenty miles south, at Lakewood, their Kimball grandparents lived in a home that seemed a temple of Victorian tranquillity. Wilson's grandmother, also named Helen, grew flowers in her conservatory and wrote pious verse, while his grandfather, Walter Scott Kimball, a homeopath who due to ill health no longer practiced much, was usually found among his stuffed owls (one of them later Wilson's) and his chessmen in his library. Wilson's and Sandy's Aunt Laura, then still living with her parents, recorded the cousins' first stories in paper pamphlets she sewed together. She took them on nature walks with a guidebook, a source of the colorful anatomies of flowers and landscapes in Wilson's journals. Uncle Paul, a dashing playboy as well as a surgeon, had an intriguing deadpan manner and did tricks with dimes, performing song and dance routines like "The Man Who Broke the Bank at Monte Carlo." Wilson recalled of his family that "I knew almost nobody else, that my relatives were extremely varied and that most of them seemed to me interesting."

Differences between the Wilsons and Kimballs helped to shape the future critic. His grandfather Thaddeus Wilson was a Presbyterian minister, though "a very moderate one." His parents went to church at Shrewsbury, and on "bleak and severe" Sunday mornings his formidable paternal grandmother, a Calvinist of Dutch background, instructed the child in the Scriptures. His mother was proud to be a collateral descendant of Cotton Mather, but her people "had scrapped the old-time religion and still retained a certain animus toward it." She forbade the use of a catechism that threatened eternal damnation, remarking that her mother-in-law had "a 'queer' and morbid side." Edmund, however, "stood very much in awe of" his Wilson grandmother, who amused herself by studying mathematics, and the respect for the Bible she instilled would flower in his studies of the Old Testament and the Dead Sea Scrolls. Although in youth he identified with his mother's family, the values he absorbed through his father's had the deeper hold.

He enjoyed visiting his Wilson connections in Virginia. His Uncle John died when the boy was four, and after Aunt Susan took their children back to Charlottesville his father regularly went down to pay her debts, taking the son along. On balmy nights Edmund Jr. explored Jefferson's campus with his cousin Susan Wilson, a friend all his life, and her brother Edmund Minor Wilson. Lincoln was Wilson's father's hero, and when one of his cousins called Lincoln "a bloody tyrant," the future author of *Patriotic Gore* was shocked to realize that there was more than one view of American history.

Such conflicts were muted by the shared family background in New York State, whence his four grandparents had migrated to New Jersey after the Civil War. Though his name implied a connection with the British magistrate and dramatist Edmund Wilson, his true Wilson ancestor had emigrated from Londonderry into central New York equipped, according to family legend, "with nothing but a fishing-rod and a silver onion watch." The Kimballs, once yeomen farmers among the high medieval walled towns of East Anglia, were early settlers in Massachusetts Bay. As the nineteenth century began, the first Reuel, Edmund's great-great-grandfather, a preacher—in Hebrew his name meant "friend of God"—and his Mather bride drove ox teams through the Berkshires into the wilderness, settling on the high plateau between the Mohawk Valley and the Adirondacks. But in that "new America, now forever for a century on the move" the fire-and-brimstone faith lost its hold. Reuel was put out of his pulpit by his congregation, and his grandson, Wilson's grandfather Kimball, read Herbert Spencer and John Stuart Mill and went to medical school.

Dr. Kimball came home to find a bride, Helen, one of the eight daughters of Thomas Baker, a Jacksonian democrat who had a stone house in the tiny town of Talcottville in Lewis County, New York. Edmund Sr. eventually bought the place from the surviving Bakers, allowing his wife's Uncle Tom and Aunt Rosalind to go on living there. Built by Tories in flight from the Revolution, the old house survives with its foot-thick walls and beams secured by handmade nails, carved mantels over the fireplaces, a front gallery the length of the building, a large front door with a fanlight over it and on either side a long pane of glass that, with its white filigree of ironwork, reminded the boy of ice over winter ponds. While Uncle Tom occupied a downstairs room, upstairs lived Great-Aunt Rosalind, eldest of the Baker daughters, receiving visitors by special arrangement, elegantly dressed but "so bloodless and shrunken as dreadfully to resemble a mummy" to young Edmund, who was also reminded of Miss Havisham in *Great Expectations*. In this "pocket of the past" his father was comfortable and Wilson would one day return to retrieve his roots and don the role of country squire.

Summer family reunions at Talcottville were an idyll for an only child from suburban New Jersey. On the milk train north from Utica young Wilson would gaze through the window at "the widening pastures, the great boulders, the black and white cattle, the rivers, stony and thin, the lone elms like feather-dusters" in the clear light of late afternoon. Sandy and he, usually staying with the Collins family down the road, were reunited with Talcott, Baker, and Kimball cousins from as far away as Iowa and Wisconsin—"we fished and swam in the rivers, had all sorts of excursions and games." During chilly evenings after college, Edmund would sit by a woodstove with his mother to read Michelet's multivolume *History of France*. At Talcottville, too, he read Maeterlinck and was impressed by his vision of the literary life—"first the dedicated toil, then the orgy." Northern New York was associated in Wilson's mind "with the first moments of my being conscious that I was capable of imaginative activity and some sort of literary vocation." At seventeen, arriving for a solitary week of fishing and reading, he would recall, in *Upstate*, a new sense of his identity. "I said suddenly to myself, 'I am a poet,' then after a moment corrected myself with, 'No: I am not quite a poet, but I am something of the kind.'"

The conflict between his genteel clan and the new class of millionaires helped shape Wilson's social attitudes. In a memoir of Lakewood he describes how bachelor Uncle Paul took him, age nine or ten, to play at a showy estate whose owner is here called James Finch—echoing Jay Gould, cornerer of gold during the Grant administration—and characterized as "the son of a great grabber and wrecker of railroads." A mural of the Canterbury Tales, sixteen feet high and eighty feet long, adorned the main hall of the house, and among the outbuildings was a theater, used not, as Edmund first assumed, for amateur theatricals, but for musical comedies imported from New York. He tried not to be impressed by all this or by young James's toys, including cowboy and Indian suits, hung on hangers in a special closet, and a custom-built miniature automobile. This millionaire's son, who seemed to the young Wilson totally uneducated, surprised him by a greater understanding of physics, winning an argument over whether a log would float in a large puddle. Wilson reestablished a sense of superiority by rejecting his playmate's behavior with one of his many servants as they rode in a pony cart about the grounds. James commanded the footman to get some fruit from a nearby tree. When the man hesitated, the English governess explained that the fruit was unripe and inedible. The young master repeated his order, declaring, "These men must do their duty, Anna!" Edmund told himself he wouldn't "have been allowed to behave like that," would never "speak like that to or about a servant."

It was midlife before Wilson recognized that his family "had been drawn into the orbit of the power represented by the Finches." This understanding was triggered as he savored memories of the Kimballs' Lakewood house with its books and flowers and oriental rugs. He recalled the water running from nickel-plated faucets into porcelain basins unlike the old wood and tin ones at Wallace Street, and he remembered his father saying that to build this new house had strained the doctor's finances. His physician uncles died relatively young. Uncle Reuel wore himself out on behalf of his wife's ambitions while Uncle Paul, a ship's doctor on the yachts of the rich, became an alcoholic and was often depressed. In retrospect, Wilson believed it was through his gentle Kimball grandparents that "the superior virtue and value of certain things" had come down to him—"of the spirit that studies and understands against the spirit that acquires and consumes; of the instinct to give light and life against the lethal concentration on power; of the impulse that acts to minimize the social differences between human beings instead of trying to keep them up and make them wider." In this form the snobbery of the professional class and the gentry became part of Wilson's intellectual enterprise, that of an American democratizing Matthew Arnold's idea of culture.

Father, Mother, Son

Wilson's rejection of his playmate's world and attitudes also mirrored his father's idea of the American community, a man living among neighbors for whom he felt some measure of responsibility. The senior Edmund was a conundrum—a distinguished local lawyer who served a term as attorney general of New Jersey and a neurotic who regularly collapsed under the weight of a mysterious, terrifying mental ailment. Born in Shrewsbury in 1863, "Ed" attended Andover and Princeton. At Princeton he edited the newspaper with his brother John and excelled in the struggle between the debating societies, Whig and Clio. In his senior year, after leading a student rebellion against the faculty, he was "rusticated," made to live in the town of Kingston ten miles north of campus. He took his law degree at Columbia and went into practice in 1891. In both corporate and criminal cases he relied upon "learning, logic, dramatic imagination and eloquence," says Wilson, naming important tools of his own work. His father would cause the jury "to live through the events of the crime or supposed crime, he would take them through the steps of the transaction, whatever this was, and he would lodge in their heads a picture that was difficult for his opponent to expel." Well paid when representing corporations, he enjoyed the chance to oppose them and would work for little or nothing for local people whom he thought had a case, but almost never undertook a case he didn't think he could win. Rehearsing his arguments at home, "he would pace back and forth through the rooms, go nervously up and down stairs, and all other operations would have to be suspended."

Wilson Sr. was a charismatic man who dressed well, drove fast horses, and whom women found attractive, but a colleague noted that he "retained to the end some of the rigid Calvinistic views in which his childhood was reared." Wilson says that he refused to invest in the stock market, considering this a form of gambling. Although this kept him from becoming a rich man in circumstances where that would have been easy, it gave him a moral advantage in a state "dominated by corporations." He had aimed for a political career in the tradition of New England magistrates who served God within the world and of Lincoln, who rescued the Union. When Wilson declares in *A Piece of My Mind*, "The Republic has thus had to be saved over and over again, and it continues to have to be saved," it is with his father's Calvinist urgency. A lifelong Republican, as New Jersey's attorney general his father took a stab at reform when challenged by Woodrow Wilson, the Democratic governor-elect (no relation), to go after the Republican rackets that controlled Atlantic City. Said to have avoided entrapment by several beautiful blondes, he unearthed a little used law that allowed him to bring in jurors from another county and send several hundred men to jail, including the boss of Atlantic City, who went to prison with aplomb, in a fur coat and a limousine. The prosecutor explained to his son that this man would only be replaced by another, but Woodrow Wilson saw the conviction as a triumph and later offered Edmund's father various Washington posts.

Such gentlemen reformers were uncomfortable in an age of business dominance, of party bosses and machine corruption. Their moral snobbery was always collapsing into cynicism, as when a seasoned attorney in another state destroyed the illusions of a Harvard Law graduate then opening his practice by observing—in language worthy of Mark Twain—"You think you're a lawyer. Son, you ain't a lawyer. You ain't nothin' but a incipient commercial instrument." These resentments contributed to the Progressive movement. Though Wilson's father's ambition for elective office faded, he counseled the Republican Party, befriended the socialist editor of a local paper, and allied himself with a businessman named Sigmund Eisner—the great-grandfather of Disney's Michael Eisner—to improve the Red Bank school system.

He was a popular public speaker, delivering lay sermons on politics and such subjects as "Duties of Educated Men" and "The Power of a Lie," as well as an encomium upon his moral debt to a teacher at the Shrewsbury Academy. The texts of these talks are old-fashioned in diction, with what Wilson came to regard as "a silvery quality of clearness." A favorite subject was Lincoln, the rail-splitter and grave humorist whom he called "the Great Commoner," a self-made American who vindicated the national ideal. Meanwhile Wilson's father grew bored with the law. Although he had to provide for his younger brother John's family as well as his own, he declined offers of partnerships in New York firms—his wife persuaded him this would be too hard on his nerves—and practiced from an office permeated by "a casky vinous smell" from the liquor store below—amusing to his son, since he never drank.

His hypochondria was precipitated by the fate of John, also a lawyer, who had moved to Pittsburgh, failed in his practice, and succumbed to Bright's disease, a kidney condition worsened by nervous tension. The doctor was delayed by a blizzard, and the senior Edmund was alone with his brother when he died. After this, he would experience attacks in which he imagined diseases affecting one organ or another, the symptoms invariably requiring immediate attention. Following the successful conclusion of a case, he'd retreat behind a felt-lined bedroom door, where his fears multiplied. Edmund Jr. grew up accompanying his parents "for desolating drives or walks" in the course of which his father endlessly described his ailments. Alternately—in an instance used in the novel *I Thought of Daisy*—he would "freeze us with prophetic looks and announce that the household was 'hurtling to ruin!' because he'd just gotten a caterer's bill or something." Rosalind heard stories of trained nurses "going quite mad, rushing downstairs to beat up sofa pillows or to scream uncontrollably"; she reports that the doctor who had the most success with her grandfather prescribed a cup of chamomile tea "that was made a certain way involving twelve steps and almost as many people." He had several unnecessary operations, including the removal of his gallbladder. Sometimes he signed into a sanitarium. By the time his son was in college these eclipses "were lasting for months and years."

Wilson later speculated that his father's malady "may partly have been a form of the Calvinist fear of damnation," a fear to which the son thought himself on some level subject. His father's mother, Dutch in background, had raised him on the fundamentalist catechism according to which the majority of the human race are consigned to eternal torment. On his deathbed he murmured, "What does the doctor say about my condition?," restating complaints about nonexistent illnesses, now apparently anxious about the state of his soul. Insofar as the ancestral quest for salvation entered into his vision of public service, to withdraw from a corrupted world intensified his nervousness, and in a materialistic age this may well have shown itself as corruption of the body. Wilson Jr.'s determined rejection of Christianity and the refusal to fear death that would keep him from having a pacemaker when this would have prolonged his life owed something to his father's obsession with his physical condition.

Helen Mather Kimball Wilson, who abbreviated her name to Helen M. K. Wilson in letters to her son rather than sign them "Mother," became equally formidable and difficult. Nelly, as she was usually called, was only five feet tall and, in her youth, very pretty. An extrovert who liked horses, dogs, and the garden club, she admired money and social position, was a member of the Daughters of the American Revolution. Although her doctor brothers, Reuel and Paul, were members of the professional class, a third, Wilson's Uncle Win, was the family's first businessman. A successful bachelor, he left her money in his will. One of her older sisters eventually married an impoverished farmer, while the other chose the wealthy owner of a slaughterhouse, who took good care of her until he abandoned her and their four children. Helen had known Edmund Sr. since boarding school. He fell in love with her when he was thirty and her father's chess partner. Though she later called herself fortunate to have caught such a dashing man, for a time she resisted him, perhaps intuiting a deeper incompatibility.

The onset of his hypochondria devastated Mrs. Wilson's nerves, and her brother Reuel persuaded him to consult a neurologist in London. On the boat trip home she became deaf overnight. Her son believed this was because the doctor had suggested that his father was "mad." Diagnosed as having gout of the ear, she henceforth depended on people shouting or on an ear trumpet, described by Rosalind as "a three-foot job with a hose in the middle, a horn mouthpiece on one end, and a tubular piece she inserted in her ear." Mrs. Wilson spoke loudly, and would hold forth on the porch about her neighbors' shortcomings, without regard to what they might overhear. But she had a good business head and, no longer able to hear her husband's complaints, was a bastion of sensible support for him. With a rueful sense of his limitations, Mr. Wilson told people, "I would have sunk many times without the rock which is my wife." When persuading him to take on another case, she'd go to his room and announce, "There's no money in the bank!"

Wilson describes the collision of their tastes and temperaments. Red Bank's leading citizen dispensed advice—with a certain condescension and restrained impatience—to a wide range of acquaintances. His wife disapproved of some of his friends—the Jewish Eisner and the socialist editor, who wasn't allowed to enter the house because he "did not wash." The couple disagreed about 12 Wallace Street, which Mrs. Wilson thought gloomy, urging him to build a better-designed home with the larger grounds she wanted for her garden. He was attached to the house and refused to spend the money. They also quarreled about traveling. She wanted to go to places that were "lively and gay," while his father, she told the boy, "simply visited cities, systematically informed himself about their populations, politics and products, inspected their public buildings and looked in on the proceedings of their legislatures." Wilson recalled that as soon as his father arrived in a new city "he began asking people questions, beginning with the driver of his cab." In a surviving photograph of the couple, at an Austrian spa in 1908, the handsome man in glasses has shoved a newspaper into his pocket and stands behind his wife, one hand on the back of the chair where she sits stiffly erect with a slight, complacent smile, gloved hands folded in her lap.

Edmund, in youth his mother's ally, agreed with her about their home.

In the poem "A House of the 'Eighties" he remembers looking down from the window on a rainy night, upon a scene that seemed

> sunken out of time or drowned
> As hulks in Newark Bay are sunk and slowly drown,

Perhaps he had been reading Poe's "The Fall of the House of Usher," or a story about wizards:

> —The ugly stained-glass window on the stair,
> Dark-panelled dining-room, the guinea-fowls' fierce clack,
> The great grey cat that on the oven slept—
> My father's study with its books and birds,
> His scornful tone, his eighteenth-century words,
> His green door sealed with baize—

This door dramatized the father's isolation and the son's exclusion. When the house was sold after his father's death and his mother bought a large white wooden house not far from her brother Reuel's home at Sea Bright, Wilson often walked over to 12 Wallace Street. Magnified in memory and imagination, in his middle years it became the setting of not only this poem but a play as well as a story.

A shy boy could try to command the family stage through conjuring. In *The Sixties* Wilson recalls his mother taking him to Martinkas, a magic shop in a dubious neighborhood on New York's Seventh Avenue. "I was fascinated and a little frightened by the devils and mysterious objects of which I did not then know the secrets." As a magician he would work for a skill with his hands which in other respects he lacked, and he was well-known among friends for his not always successful efforts with cards. He sometimes calmed his nerves by practicing magic tricks in front of a mirror. The rationalist who rejected religion but loved ghost stories and mythologies could try to produce the illusion that he was in control.

He owned the standard children's books—*Lorna Doone, Bob, Son of Battle*, Hans Christian Andersen, and the *Arabian Nights*—and in his grandfather's library at Lakewood he found the ghouls and vampires of Ralston's *Russian Fairy Tales* as well as "those long, old-fashioned, form-less books full of amusing or curious things," like Robert Burton's *Anatomy of Melancholy* and the *Noctes Ambrosianae*. Mrs. Wilson hoped he'd follow her brother Paul in liking sports, but when she took him to watch polo he could not ignore the horses' bloody sides. She is said to have presented her son with a complete baseball outfit that he took to the ball field and gave away piece by piece.

Margaret Edwards, a childhood friend, recalled that they would put on plays—"he would write the story and I drew the scenery and figures." His cousin Sandy and he wrote and illustrated a series based on Sherlock Holmes. The critical temperament, however, already stood in the way of imaginative invention. In the schoolboy hand that Wilson soon abandoned there survives a revealing page headed "What I would like to Write [*sic*] about." In fact he tells what he doesn't want to do with what may have been an assignment: he will not make the story "too sad" or "make much plot to it," or make the schoolboy hero "too successful" or "too good." Discouraged by his own strictures, he concludes, "I don't believe I shall ever write this story."

Wilson's travel diary of a trip to Europe in 1908, when he was thirteen—set down in a leather-bound journal that was Margaret's gift—would be innocuous without his interpolations when publishing it half a century later, at the beginning of *A Prelude*. This was the age of Baedekers and the Grand Tour, of American pilgrims going to Europe to drink culture at its source. In an essay of the 1930s Wilson recalled the "amazement, a wonder that became exaltation" with which he "had come upon the Apollo Belvedere when I had first visited Rome as a child—how I had turned back to stare at its beauty." In his childhood diary, as the family group goes north through Italy to Germany and France, he dutifully names the ancient buildings, calling the museums and their contents, "interesting" or "very interesting." The prose comes alive when he is actually interested. The conjurer and future skeptic notes how the priests at Pompeii make Apollo appear to talk by speaking through a brass tube in the statue. Setting the torture instruments at Nuremberg in an effective series, the boy leads us to "a wheel with a knife blade on it which cut the victim up very small and very slowly, a cradle full of spikes in which the victim was rocked to death," and "a pear which when put in the mouth swells up to four times its ordinary size, thus slowly cracking the victim's head open." In decrescendo he adds "a flute of iron which was fastened to the fingers and mouths of musicians who played badly."

The thirteen-year-old who is distanced from the purposive human cruelties here catalogued omits the explosive tensions of his family life. At

Karlsbad he mentions skipping up and down the hills and eating huge crackers. In a bracketed interpolation in *A Prelude*, Wilson explains (as he put it in a letter to his old friend Margaret) "what was really going on" at Karlsbad. Uncle Reuel had persuaded his father to join them at the resort in order to try to relax. There Edmund Sr. grew positively cheerful after sitting with the doctor at outdoor cafés, listening to the ubiquitous waltzes and—with no experience of alcohol—consuming quantities of Pilsner beer. Alcohol, however, the son now learned, was Uncle Reuel's private vice. The respected physician regularly escaped the demands of his wife and his two practices on benders, and drinking with Edmund's father set him off on "one of his sprees," a solitary trip to Prague, which on his return he pronounced to be indeed a beautiful city, and then collapsed in a stupor.

Literature could neutralize the skeletons in one's family closet. In one of his last articles, Wilson recalled that Richard Harris Barham's versified *Ingoldsby Legends*, with their gruesome anecdotes and jocose humor, had a "fetishistic" power as he entered his teens. There he learned that "the murders and mutilations, the ordeals and the outrages of life are real, but it is possible to laugh about them." Barham's expression of Victorian unease prepared Wilson for the "small, squat, much-used volumes" of the old Globe edition of Dickens. His portrait of Dickens in *The Wound and the Bow* subordinates the jolly, sentimental novelist to the dark symbolist. He enters into young Dickens's sense of abandonment at the blacking factory, drawing on his relationships with his own parents. "Lasting depressions and terrors," the critic writes, "may be caused by such cuttings-short of the natural development of childhood."

Within the Family Triangle

At Karlsbad Wilson felt sorry for his mother, under strain before his father arrived, then let down by the brother she counted on. Through boyhood he was her sympathetic companion. The habit of speaking loud enough for her to hear left the mark of a "boom" in his high-pitched voice, the voice a friend affectionately recalled as the treble that sounded as if he were repressing a belch. When he went off to Hill, Mrs. Wilson, in a not fully successful effort to get him to write home, gave him a book called *Letters of a Japanese Schoolboy*, and it survives, with the inscription in Wilson's schoolboy hand, clearly modeled on hers, "From his mother" and, also in his hand, "You are the nicest girl I know." He must have shown her the compliment instead of shouting it.

Most of the girls he knew were cousins, a circle of sublimated flirtations anticipating his relationships with women writers. Upstate in summers was "my pretty, dark cousin Dorothy, whom I was always hoping to kiss." His second cousin Adelaide Knox, who lived next door to the Kimballs at Sea Bright and was a few years older, was an object of his devotion from their European tour through college, while another, Helen Vinton, had a crush on Wilson that would burn long after she'd married. In adolescence he and Sandy satisfied their curiosity about sex in Havelock Ellis. At Uncle Reuel's second residence in Manhattan, a house on East Forty-first Street off Fifth Avenue, they surreptitiously explored the set of brown volumes of the *Psychology of Sex*, then available only to doctors. The case histories in fine type at the back of these books—"the versatile British officer" whose preference extends "through the vegetable and animal worlds and persons of both sexes, beginning with a humble melon and ending with 'a woman, a friend and lady of my own class'"—were liberating to boys growing up under Victorian strictures. They were part of Wilson's preparation for the journal entries in which he'd one day celebrate sexual experience.

The Oedipal plot of his first published story, "The Conjuring Shop," written at Hill at fourteen, has a transparency possible only in the work of a young person who had never heard of Freud. A boy inventor tries to sell his mysterious device at a magician's store, and though the stingy shopkeeper will pay him nothing, his wife gives him twenty-five dollars and pronounces the apparatus "a great success." As her husband inspects it in the basement, preparing to market it as his own, she locks the door, and when the man lights a match he is consumed by explosive flame. In the subplot of a subsequent skit, "The Sane Tea Party," Edmund Sr. is brought onstage as a "hopeless hypochondriac" named Elgrim Sexton, whose face is "lined with the worry and anxiety of dying many deaths." Sexton dies, leaving a long suffering daughter. "You're a great girl!" the young male observer tells her, echoing Wilson's phrase written to his mother in the book that was her gift. As a college senior Wilson would set himself against the father figure in a story in which a stables manager who wants to get rid of his wife bribes an alcoholic jockey to run away with her. In California they fall in love, but when their cash runs out they return. The jockey shoots his boss in the arm and is immediately captured, while the woman abandons "this world of lust and treachery and murder" for a convent.

The lovely gardens of Wilson's mother revealed an instinct for warmth and light that her married life denied, and when his father's self-absorption made her lot intolerable, the son encouraged her to leave him. After she had a slight stroke, his father grew more attentive. One night, however, he heard his mother, from her bedroom, ask his father whether he loved her, hearing no reply and unable "to imagine him answering" such a question. In college Wilson read something of Freud's *Interpretation of Dreams*, and after graduating he'd have "a dream about going to bed with my mother," relieved to learn, from the chorus of Sophocles' *Oedipus Rex*, that such dreams were not uncommon. Attraction to his mother and rivalry with his father were heightened by the shyness, the awkwardness with girls that caused him to be named "most likely bachelor" by a number of his classmates. His mother remained for a few more years "the nicest girl I know." During World War I he would write her hundreds of pages chronicling aspects of his life as a hospital orderly in France and afterward at general headquarters.

Meanwhile his father passed on intellectual habits and values. When the boy's grades were undistinguished he was warned against "weltering around in a Dead Sea of mediocrity"—this was "the worst fate with which he could threaten me." In the metaphor, the old Calvinist anxiety about Election has become a fear of descending to the average. At dinner, with his mother at her end of the formal table too far away to hear anything his father said, the boy had the benefit of Mr. Wilson's conversation, which "mostly consisted of either asking people questions in order to elicit information or telling them what to think." His father was given to "asking my view of some question, then immediately squelching this view and setting me right on the subject, or of explaining at length, but with an expert lucidity, some basic point of law or government." Wilson believed that "a permanent antagonism existed between my father and me, that I was always, in tastes and opinions, on the opposite side from him." He looked to Uncle Reuel and Uncle Paul as models, then to his teachers. Yet he would quiz people and hold forth just as his father had and, like his father, would "read up" on subjects when traveling.

Through the two years in the army, on which he reported to his mother, Wilson wrote his father just half a dozen letters, discussing a possible transfer to Intelligence or expounding his political views. Yet to step from the ivory tower into a real world that both shocked and excited him led to a change in his allegiances, and he came home to find he was "no longer afraid" of his father, that he actually admired him. Mr. Wilson had urged him to learn about Lincoln, often recommending William Herndon's biography, with the result that he "made, automatically, a point of knowing as little as possible about Lincoln." At the graves of American soldiers in France, however, he ironically invoked the Gettsysburg Address in an epitaph questioning Woodrow Wilson's crusade "to make the world safe for democracy." After the war his father and he began to have satisfying talks. This man whom he'd thought of as a reactionary had the same opinion of the Palmer raids and the Red scare that Edmund did. He did some post-war legal work for the president, whom he confided had sounded him out about a Supreme Court appointment if a vacancy appeared during the balance of his term, saying he'd agreed to accept. The son's pride must have been enormous.

By then the young critic was busy beginning his career in New York, preoccupied with one woman and eventually committed to another. The conversation between father and son was forever suspended when Edmund Sr., opening the unheated stone house at Talcottville in the spring of 1923, developed pneumonia and, upon returning to Red Bank, died. Freud believed the most significant day in a man's life to be that of his father's death, and this may have been so in Wilson's case. In a poem of the mid-thirties he wrote,

> When dead I saw you, silent, straight and lean,
> The film of age's tarnishment effaced,
> Life's heaviness refined—
> Looking, I knew at last that I had seen
> The man of whom old Princeton teachers told—

continuing,

> That youth by age and honor left behind,
> By manhood's melancholy languished for.

His father's perceived weaknesses died with him, and the rebalancing of the family triangle that was overdue came all at once, when Mrs. Wilson, as they went downstairs from the bedroom, paused to declare, "Now I'm going to have a new house!" It was the frankness of a deaf person used to

speaking her thoughts, and she had long been frustrated, but her eager-
ness to move on was plain. Remembering how often his mother "made
him choose" between his parents, in effect forcing the child to take her
side (as Wilson described this emotional turnaround to Mary McCarthy),
he made a different choice for himself. When reading over his father's
speeches and legal papers he discovered he was already emulating his father's style. "My methods in writing had seemed to me personal," he recalled. "Though I had imitated Shaw, Henry James and a number of other
writers, I had consciously corrected these tendencies and was unconscious of my principal model. I must have picked up his style mainly from
his dinner-table lectures."

Though Wilson looked up to and fostered intellectual women, in his
work he interpreted the struggles of male artists and public figures, playing his part in the generation produced by World War I, who challenged
the Victorian deference to the feminine. He followed his father's example
within the field of literature, outside the moneyed society with which Edmund Sr. was at odds. When he read Herndon during the 1930s he found
the explanation of his father's interest in Lincoln: "a great lawyer who was
deeply neurotic, who had to struggle through spells of depression, and
who—as it followed from this portrait—had managed, in spite of this
handicap, to bring through his own nightmares and the crisis of society—
somewhat battered—the American Republic." Wilson was shadowed by
his father's neurosis, in consequence, perhaps, of this identification. He
would have a breakdown at the exact age when the elder Wilson's
hypochondria had descended, and for years afterward suffered spells of
depression. Liquor, which could lift him out of these, became the equivalent of a felt-lined door behind which he could withdraw from his wives.
He must have experienced a shock of recognition when Margaret Canby,
the generous-hearted second wife who died in an accident after only two
years of marriage, declared (as he wrote in his journal), "You're a cold,
fishy, leprous person, Bunny Wilson."

His mother lived to be eighty-six, both a support and a trial. When
Mary Blair, Wilson's first wife, couldn't reconcile motherhood with her
career on the stage, his mother would step in to raise Rosalind, who loved
and was loyal to her. Through the 1920s and '30s Mrs. Wilson maintained
what amounted to a second home for him, his retreat from Manhattan.
Met at the station by her driver, Oscar, in her latest custom-made Cadillac, he'd find a flask of brandy tucked in the side pocket and, at his bed-

side, sharpened pencils and the yellow legal pads on which he wrote. But she never revealed any interest in his work, though Rosalind reports that she read for several hours every evening. Her son's books were placed "in the lower shelf of her bedroom bookcase behind locked glass doors." That his articles usually appeared in the back sections of magazines rendered them, in Helen Wilson's view, a bit suspect. In a story the critic told to more than one friend, when going through the house after her death he found at the back of a closet a roll of his familiar yellow legal sheets wrapped in a rubber band. Momentarily believing it was a manuscript of his that she had cherished, he uncovered instead a roll of favorite recipes.

Recalling Wilson as "a man of great brain power," Stephen Spender wrote, "one felt his brain revving behind the great frontal box of his forehead." What soured his relationship with his mother, however, was less her intellectual limitations than the will his father had made many years before. Seeing his wife and son as allies, instead of leaving Wilson a portion of the estate he left them the money together, and Mrs. Wilson, with her good business head, in charge of it. "She was sort of a man of business for him," Mary McCarthy drily recalled, protecting their capital, which survived the crash intact and, though reduced by FDR's Bank Holiday, would be enlarged by what Uncle Win left her. But by nature Helen Wilson was stingy. What she gave to her Talcottville retainers, McCarthy said, was always "'Plenty good enough'—that was a sign-off line, meaning it was all the recipient had a right to expect." Wilson's *New Yorker* friend of the later years Edith Oliver spoke darkly of "the silver umbilical cord," and Rosalind has documented its workings. When her father came to Red Bank, where he had to ask for money, she remembered him making "scenes." Later on, her grandmother told her and Reuel, the son of McCarthy and Wilson, that she'd bought their house at Wellfleet—one he actually bought with money borrowed partly from her but mostly on a mortgage—and, alternately, that she was "supporting that house." In old age Mrs. Wilson would complain that, with their wrangling over his finances, his visits upset her nerves—she insisted she didn't want him to come, even as, Rosalind says, she planned "what she'd give him to eat." Wilson had a temper, was irritable when interrupted at work, irascible when he drank. He rarely drank at Red Bank, but would burst out in tirades at his mother, then catch himself and pat her hand.

Leon Edel, who edited four volumes of his journals, sees the critic damaged in boyhood by a cold woman isolated in her deafness. In a

Freudian reading of the bond of Neoptolemus and Philoctetes in Wilson's essay in *The Wound and the Bow*, Edel ascribes a latent homosexuality to this inveterate womanizer. In fact, though there are references to homosexual fantasies among the heterosexual ones in Wilson's accounts of his dreams, he was driven by the need for more intimate relationships with women than his father had with his mother. He was damaged not by the pretty young woman whose photograph he had in his bedroom at Wellfleet, but by the battle-ax he depended on and resented. Her place in his psyche was a dark one. In a dream that he recorded in 1934 she tells him, "Nobody will ever love you." One must allow for the impact on his mother of the turning of his allegiance toward his father after his father's death. The situation was no easier for her than for her son. But her spoiling and controlling had consequences in his family life. Wilson expected his wives to have his mother's management skills without her means, and when they failed in such respects he could be petulant and contentious. Mary Blair told Rosalind that the psychiatrist who briefly treated him after his breakdown, in 1929, said "he had a mother complex and should never marry anyone."

When writing "The Author at Sixty" he recorded a nightmare in which he was back "alone, at night—in the old house at Red Bank (which I dream about constantly, not the one Mother bought after Father's death), with the corpses of two people I had killed. I propped them up at the dining-room table in the walnut-stained paneled dining room. I had turned off the lights, and the room was pitch-dark, and I lay back, a little way from the table, in the kind of chair in which one reclines. The body of the woman was facing me." Wondering if he was in Hell, he looked around for a drink, and had gone through the front door down the steps to the lawn when his mother appeared and led him back into the house. She turned on the lights to show there was nothing there, then opened a corner cabinet to reveal "large puppets of mine that I had put away, laying them on their sides. What I had thought was the corpse of a woman was simply a puppet-queen." Even in this dream, he has his mother reassuring him. On awakening he persuades himself that "the woman was Margaret," not his mother, the other body being "my father."

The resentment of his father was a wound of youth, a product of the sealed green door, the nervous self-absorption that, among other things, kept his father from attending his college graduation. The ache and burden of the man's duality did not fade. "The victim of a malodorous disease which renders him abhorrent to society and periodically degrades him and makes him helpless is also master of a superhuman art which everybody has to respect and which the normal man finds he needs," Wilson writes in his essay on Sophocles' *Philoctetes*, done at the midpoint of his career. He could be describing the emotional cripple and the legal wizard who got clients acquitted of murder charges, put the Atlantic City crooks in jail, was mourned by people of all classes at his funeral. Here too, perhaps, is Uncle Reuel, the dedicated diagnostician periodically laid low by liquor. When Wilson's mother said, "These brilliant men always had something wrong with them," she made her son fear that fate and strengthened the drive to prove her wrong. Implicit in his interpretation of Sophocles' play is the wish to have reached out to his father sooner, somehow drawing him from his isolation. "In taking the risk to his cause which is involved in the recognition of his common humanity with the sick man," he writes of Neoptolemus in the last sentence of *The Wound and the Bow*, "he dissolves Philoctetes' stubbornness, and thus cures him and sets him free, and saves the campaign as well."

2

"School-Days and Early Influences"

❧

Though Wilson's literary training is usually associated with Princeton, he acquired his vocation and the intellectual discipline that sustained it at the Hill School. He was a greenhorn when his mother brought him in a carriage from the railway station to his rooming-house on an autumn day in 1909. She called him "Bunny" in front of the other boys. He tried to fight everybody who then took up the refrain, but there were too many of them and the nickname stuck. To his future New York apartment-mate Ted Paramore, he seemed "a slender stalk of a boy with vermilion hair, pale, translucent skin, and brown, frightened eyes."

Looking back, Wilson related the school's academic pressure to the industrial grimness of Pottstown, Pennsylvania, where gray slag pits and blast furnaces were then close enough to light up certain dormitory rooms at night. The boys' lives were regulated by bells. They were graded each week in all their courses, and anyone with more than one D confined to campus. He entered in the fourth form (tenth grade). Like his father he had attended the Shrewsbury Academy, but he was poorly prepared for Hill, and it was the following spring before he could boast in a letter home, "I didn't get any D's this week." At year's end he was barely passing Latin and algebra and, even with high marks in English, ranked in the middle of his class.

The evangelical intensity was also daunting. The school had been founded by the Congregationalist minister Matthew Meigs, whose son John, called "Professor," was headmaster in 1909. While Professor raised money and built up the plant, "Mrs. John" took charge of the moral tone. "We had to go not only to chapel, but also—under irresistible pressure—

to the meetings of a school YMCA; and we were always being called together to listen to special exhortations." A schoolmate remembered Mrs. John's warning lecture—for later Hill boys it would become a film—to the matronly types who cleaned the dorms about the dangers of harassment and rape by the boys. Any indulgence of the flesh was frighteningly taboo. Assembled in wooden seats beneath the penetrating electric light of study hall, surrounded by busts of classical writers and confronting a picture of Jesus called *The Light of the World*, one was warned of dangers that awaited the weak during the approaching Christmas holiday. Pictures of a "fallen woman" illustrated what might flow from the fatal impulse to flirt with a waitress, and any erotic hopes that might survive the fear of ruining a young woman's life were destroyed by graphic accounts of venereal disease.

At twenty-five, in *Vanity Fair*, Wilson would look back on "Youth" as a time of "agonizing shyness, of introspective morbidity, of callow religious hysteria." The well-educated men who were his teachers steadied him. In his memoir of Alfred Rolfe, he recalls the evening when, resenting the Greek master's sarcasm in class, he sought Mr. Rolfe's private help and waited his turn in an attractive bachelor apartment which resembled that of his Uncle Paul. On the table Wilson noted several plays of Shaw, whom he'd heard of as a wicked cynic, and though he left still resentful he could picture Mr. Rolfe reading in bed as he loved to do.

An Englishman from the Lake District, John A. Lester had the task of correcting his comma splices and misspellings, and gave him a number of Ds, at least one, he assured his mother, assigned "from force of habit." Wilson recalled with approval, "He drilled us in sentence structure, grammar, the devices of 'rhetoric' and prosody, as if we had been studying a foreign language." Mr. Lester was more than a grammarian—it turns out that his use of English had been formed by his father, a miller who insisted that nothing but verse be spoken while they made deliveries. He invoked "the Great Trinity: Lucidity, Force, and Ease," a metaphorical adaptation of the Holy Trinity suggestive of how, in this period, literature could for some ally itself with religion and for Wilson, take its place.

In school and college Wilson was never part of the mainstream. From the first he avoided team sports. When he writes to his mother of a strange boy who retreats to the bathroom at night to read, whom the gang are going to lock in from the outside, one wonders whether this might have been the boy said to have given his baseball outfit away in order to return to his book. On "dark and drizzly" days when he felt "dreary and dyspeptic" he haunted the old library, finding that the card catalogue had little to do with what was on the shelves, going through piles of books in the corners in search of "recondite gems." It was a good place "to calm one's nerves" while awaiting the results of an exam. But that first spring, when he published "The Conjuring Shop" in the *Hill School Record* he found what he'd longed for back in Red Bank, friends with whom he had something in common. Stanley Dell, a year ahead, had lived in Italy and Switzerland and was fluent in French and German. Because he took a year off after graduating, he and Wilson would go through Princeton together. Alfred Bellinger, whose Congregationalist family were British in their tastes, was a class behind and went to Yale, yet Wilson and he established an epistolary relationship that lasted through their college years. After pining for home for six months, Wilson was soon having so much fun that he no longer looked forward to vacations.

Half a century later Bellinger, who became a noted classical historian, debated with Wilson the sources of their little group's passion for literature in the alumni bulletin. Though Wilson stressed the beginnings of the American literary renascence of the 1920s—he'd been reading or hearing about Mencken and Dreiser and delivered his senior year oration on O. Henry—his friend remembered a curriculum full of Carlyle and De Quincey and Boswell. Wilson credited their teachers' encouragement, but Bellinger called Wilson their spark plug, being much "better read," "more independent of thought," and "more of a literary person" than the other boys. Bellinger recalled their fun experimenting with literary techniques: "We were fascinated by learning to use the language in prose or verse. We wrote sonnets and French forms; we imitated Pepys and Dr. Johnson; we read our work aloud to each other, not in public after the modern fashion, but attempting to find out if it was any good."

At this time writing was taught through imitation of styles, and the other boys were impressed by Wilson's Browningesque monologue dated St. Valentine's Day and called "Valentine's Apology." Imitation easily shaded into parody, and when he lost a suitcase at the railroad station during his first year at college, he parodied Browning's verse novel *The Ring and the Book* in ten verse pages called "The Case and the Studs." In the fall of 1911 the schoolboy was guest contributor to the column of the journalist F.P.A. [Franklin P. Adams] in the *New York Evening Mail*, writing a parody called "The Decadence of Modern Literature." Adams sometimes wrote in Pepys's manner, and Wilson would imitate Pepys in letters to Alfred from Princeton.

For the *Record* he produced social satire, essays on Sterne and Aphra Behn, critiques of the magazines of other schools, and a good deal of fiction. In the story "Adventures of a Gentleman," he considers that literature may be a romantic delusion. A middle-aged writer worn out by his struggles and dying in a shabby boarding house is in his own mind the hero of his novel, dying "in a handsome house after a brilliant career." When he dies his manuscript is sold to "a publisher of cheap novels." The man's name, Edgar Saffron, makes him an artistic son of the hypochondriacal Elgrim Sexton of Wilson's "Tea Party" skit. A career of a different kind but ending in the same fashion is described in the essay "The Successful Mr. Sterne." Laurence Sterne, the author of *Tristram Shandy*, was no failed dreamer like Saffron—"He saw for himself immortality, and unlike other conceited men, got it." Yet his moment of fame in London's fashionable world led straight to his death of pleurisy: "The book that made Sterne, and sent his name down through the ages, was his ruin as a man. We should never have heard of him if he had not written the book which became so popular, but if he had not become so popular, he might have continued to be the quiet, eccentric, kindly parson of York," the young Wilson writes, anticipating his use of the myth of the wound and the bow, the distance that may exist between the life and the life-accomplishment.

This was the beginning of his debt to Hippolyte Taine, whose *History of English Literature* he discovered in his father's library and read when his English class was going through the eighteenth-century novelists. He relished the start of the chapter on Sterne, who is envisioned taking the reader on a long journey, equipped with a pair of marvelous magnifying spectacles that make "a hair on his hand, a spot on a tablecloth, the shifting fold of a coat" so interesting that "he will never get out of his room." It was Taine, rather than Sainte-Beuve, whom Wilson considered his primary model among the French historian-critics, more for his methods of presentation than for his famous formula of the moment, the race, and the milieu. "He had created the creators themselves as characters in a larger drama of cultural and social history, and writing about literature, for me, has always meant narrative and drama as well as the discussion of comparative values."

The boy's first evaluative criticism was a column about the literary magazines of other schools. It is natural, he says, to learn from published writers, not the same thing as copying whomever one has most recently read. Already he claims the role of supporter-critic of his comrades that would lead him to be called Old Doc Wilson. Citing Burke's ability to detect in a poem by George Crabbe "some qualities which had escaped the other great men" to whom the starving poet had sent it, he writes, "If we had the fine perceptions of Burke, we might be able to read our exchanges and gauge correctly who among their authors would some day become famous." He predicts that "a few of these contributions to prep-school magazines" will one day appear in the appendix of Mr. _____'s "Complete Works" as "Youthful Fragments."

When he returned to study Greek with Alfred Rolfe in the sixth form, the luminosity and subtlety of the language stirred Wilson. The first time Mr. Rolfe read aloud a passage from the *Iliad*, "you knew what Homer was as poetry, and no amount of construing and syntactical analysis could blur the effect of that rhythm." The class rapped out with pencils on their desks, "Clearly the rest I behold of the dark-eyed sons of Achaia," a line from Hawtrey's translation of Helen's speech when looking for her brothers from the walls, that Matthew Arnold took as a standard. It was not the empty drudgery of learning the dates of the Peloponnesian Wars for ancient history. One was always made to feel "that there was something worth having there behind the numbered paragraphs and paradigms of Goodwin's Greek grammar, the grim backs and fatiguing notes of the Ginn texts 'for the use of schools'—something exhilarating in the air of the classroom, human, heroic and shining."

Outside class, as one learns from the quaint volume *Mr. Rolfe of the Hill*, the teacher was a genial citizen of this community of boys and men, turning out school songs and rhymes that helped one learn the names of English kings and American presidents—"John Quincy Adams of Puritan stock / A notable chip off a notable block," and "Andrew Jackson who didn't propose / To give all of the plums to political foes"—as well as after-dinner speeches, limericks, and doggerel. A solemn memoirist of the school notes that Rolfe "could rouse Professor's displeasure by an entirely innocent but unfortunate display of apparent levity," as when, presiding at morning exercises, he suggested that Sunday breakfast be delayed until eleven and morning chapel moved into the afternoon. The master's wit helped Edmund begin to smile at the rotation of visiting evangelists who "worked on" the Hill boys, from the "reformed debauchee and bad egg" who proclaimed a respectability that "looked precarious" to the sophisticated preacher from New York who pretended to sympathize with work-ingmen to "Weeping Bob," so known for his "lachrymose and mealy-mouthed virility," who "used to read us Kipling in a way that did much to disgust me with that writer."

Thus the forms of Christianity that flourished at American prep schools, even into the 1950s, undermined the respect for religion in-stilled at Wilson's Calvinist grandmother's knee. "Under the constant stimulation of the Hill School," he recalls, "I tried hard to keep God in my cosmos, endeavoring "to translate my moments of exalted or expansive feeling into terms of the religious illumination about which I was con-stantly hearing." But he'd "never known what it was to feel faith as some-thing vital," and "what had at first been a certain awed respect for this side of the activity of Hill" gave way "to the conviction that it was all in awful taste." The skeptical Kimball side of him took over, and he per-suaded himself that his teachers agreed with him. In verses set down in his school copy of the *Ancient Mariner* one "John A. Leicestair"—the name spelled with what Wilson thought a North of England accent—disputes what a Coleridgean has termed "the sacredness of all life." In fact, Mr. Lester believed in a "mysterium tremendum" and a not neces-sarily rational power behind it, as he explained to "Ed" in a letter forty-five years later.

Wilson had discovered Mencken, whose specialty was ridiculing preachers, and was following the gospel of reason he found in Shaw. The plays that he'd first seen on Mr. Rolfe's table he bought when changing trains at the Philadelphia railroad station during vacations. He would recall how Shaw turned the world into "a vividly lit stage full of small, distinct, intensely conceived characters explaining their positions to one another," combining intellect and aesthetics in "an explanation that burned like a poem." On the train back to Pottstown in February 1912, near the end of the polemical preface to *Major Barbara* he "came to the following words: 'At present there is not a single credible established religion in the world.' For a moment," he says, "I was jolted a little; but I looked out the window at the landscape, rather muddy and sordid with winter, and had to recognize that this was true, that I knew perfectly well it was true, and that I ought to have admitted it before."

What he calls a revelation in reverse was solidified at the last Sunday service in the spring of 1912, when the speaker, a minister famed for his associations with Henry Ward Beecher and Theodore Roosevelt, proclaimed that the boys would consider life after death "ve-ery impo-ortant indeed" once they were as old as he. "This finished immortality for me," Wilson decided, for if your reason told you that there was no evidence for the existence of the soul, "it was an act of weak-mindedness and cowardice to give into this primitive myth when you had got to the end of your rope and were about to be extinguished yourself"—a view he'd hold to the end. Bellinger argued that it would be fatal for the human race to take the belief in immortality away from people. At seventeen, Wilson considered himself able to put truth above utility, uncompromised by "the official morality of Hill." Yet in his own way he was orthodox enough, for the school motto (supplied, of course, by Mr. Rolfe), was Whatsoever Things Are True.

When he lost his faith he complacently reflected that he was free of the "struggles, earnest labors, sleepless nights" from which the boy, a Christian athlete, sitting beside him as he read Shaw on the train would, Wilson was sure, continue to suffer. The school evangelism, however, maintained its hold on him. Each spring Mrs. John interviewed graduating seniors in a room on the top floor of her house called the Sky Parlor, ferreting out future leaders who might one day need to be rescued "on the edge of the abyss." When his turn came she rather disappointed him by seeming to believe a literary boy in no danger of sin. Over a long life Wilson would successfully prove her wrong, and in some verses on the deaths of friends he'd see himself weighed down by temptation—"Between the bottle and the bed / Dull morning and tormented night"—redeemable only by "This little work that buys the light." Literature became the source of light in Wilson's Protestant ethic, the aura of guilt and sin setting off the vitality of books and ideas.

His vocation came to him within a class training he both absorbed and prepared to subvert, on behalf of an intellectual standard taken over from the British public school. Harold Hoskins, of the class behind him, recalled how Bunny refused to attend the big football game, preferring to read in bed beneath an elaborate poster of *The Ingoldsby Legends* that he'd brought from home. The rambunctious boys squeezed the narrow cot through the door and carried it to the game with him in it, still reading. In a lengthy jingle sent from college to Alfred, however, he plays the affable alumnus, nostalgically recalling the bells and anthems and athletic events that had been hard to bear. Much had changed since "With Mother, rather fearfully, / I first drove up inside a hack," he writes, and of his alma mater sternly declares, "It is *not her fault if we fail.*" In a note accompanying this verse Wilson jokes of it as a great work that he'll allow to be published "in that forthcoming biography of me—'Wilson: The Man and Author,' by A. R. Bellinger, PhD. I should suggest inserting it at the end of the chapter, 'School-Days and Early Influences.'"

Alfred and he had agreed to give each other a book twice a year and evaluate each other's selections in letters, occasions that, for Wilson, became critical exercises. To his friend he sent the first of many letters to comrades that, with a saving humor, take the role of evangelist for literature. In it, Wilson urged his successors at the *Hill School Record* to keep faith with all those who had or would work for the magazine and to enjoy themselves.

3

Literature Among the Playboys

Princeton was a radically different experience. The boarding school discipline that created the cocky litterateur gave way to an ostensibly easygoing, neo-aristocratic life in a playground of lush green lawns and brand-new gothic buildings. There was an evangelical minority, but the pressures most students experienced were social rather than moral or intellectual, as F. Scott Fitzgerald shows in the novel *This Side of Paradise*, with its celebration of step-singing on spring evenings and the football team. Yet the line between the playboys and scholars was less sharp than at Harvard and Yale, and Fitzgerald absorbed the values of the intellectual minority on campus and its leader, Edmund Wilson. Wilson, uncomfortable among the moneyed elite whom he struck as a grind, found models in professors who, on their side, responded to his energy and precocious learning. Woodrow Wilson, the university's president from 1902 to 1910, had remade the college intellectually, creating the system of precepts or tutorials and recruiting such men as Christian Gauss, who taught Dante and French literature, and the philosopher Norman Kemp Smith, two professors who had a lasting impact on the future critic.

His cousin Sandy Kimball, a year older, was already at the college. At first Wilson lived in a dormitory financed by his father's class, and he and his next-door neighbor, Sterling Carter, the son of one of his father's classmates, helped each other out as their fathers had, Wilson acting out the speeches in Shakespeare for Carter, who did math with him. Coasting through the academic requirements for freshmen, he and Stanley Dell survived the rush, a sometimes brutal battle with the sophomore class for control of the gym doors. They took the train to Boston for the Harvard

game, and threw peppermints at the actors in a bad performance of
H.M.S. Pinafore in Trenton. The heading "Playing chemistry in the Lab"
in the journal he began before his junior year depicts a misadventure in
which he attached a Bunsen burner "to the water pipe instead of the gas
pipe" and got "a fountain of water in the face," also breaking a lot of glass.

Fitzgerald, other friends, and one or two professors figure in this record
of landscapes, anecdotes, and conversations, including the efforts at sophisticated wit with which college boys impressed each other in the absence
of the girls who were often on their minds. Wilson studies and savors experience upon the page. Though the material is light, the prose is "meticulous," as Anaïs Nin, herself a journal keeper, noted when these jottings
appeared in *A Prelude* (1967). The author was solemn in his ambitions.
When he forged an alliance between the *Nassau Literary Magazine* and
the student newspaper his father had edited thirty years before, he opined
that "the progress of the college follows closely in the footsteps of the *critical protestants* of the *Princetonian's* pages and our own." In this period
students responded to Shelley's literary idealism, and in midnight conversations with friends Wilson echoed *Prometheus Unbound*, taking art and
reason as the fire entrusted to man. He wanted to be "a soldier" in Voltaire's "Liberation war of Humanity"—"such phrases," he would recall, "were
often in my head." He wrote a poem in which the campus by night, apparently "The Sleeping College," is a stage "where learning lives and human souls find birth."

National Traditions and Classroom Mentors

For all his later attacks on British pretension, Edmund Wilson was the
last great critic in the English line. Course work in college hadn't much to
do with this. Their English professors often bored him and his friends, as
those at Harvard and the University of Pennsylvania had Eliot and Pound
a few years before. When the stuffy Henry Van Dyke published a magazine story called "Fisherman's Luck," the Princetonians were delighted to
find that the two capital letters had been transposed. Fitzgerald would recall that the enthusiasm one lecturer created for Romantic poetry was
nullified in tutorials led by preceptors without much interest in literature.
In the *Lit* Wilson parodied the survey course—"Dr. Johnson was a very great
man who had a very great influence on his age. Tomorrow, gentlemen, we

shall take up Wordsworth, Byron, and Burns. For the preceptorial, read Congreve's *The Way of the World.*"

His British enthusiasms were various. As a freshman, he published a parody of Shaw that anticipated the dramatist's views on education in the preface to *Misalliance.* When this volume came out, the student sent his piece to Shaw and had the satisfaction of a reply—a postcard with Shaw's picture addressed to "Edmund Wilson, Jr, Red Bank, N. J., U. S. America," bearing the message, "Yes: you seem to have been among the prophets." Soon he was reading De Quincey and Arnold. In the *Lit* he regularly reviewed the Edwardians, recommending Max Beerbohm's parodies, promoting and then repudiating Masefield, discriminating among the novels of Bennett and Galsworthy. He liked eighteenth-century British writers. Taine had interested him in the "poor scholar, awkward and queer, with hard blue eyes" named Jonathan Swift, who, when refused his degree ostensibly because of errors of logic, passed after he "presented himself for a second time without having condescended to read the subject up." In letters to Bellinger, Wilson notes Boswell's novelistic skill at biography and the "Scotch honesty [that] compelled him to tell the truth" about himself, "even when his part was a ludicrous or mean one." He admires Macaulay's "scrupulous thoroughness, his sound literary conscience, and his knowledge and acceptance of his own limitations."

In the British tradition he studied Latin and Greek. With a friend he took a reading course that bypassed Caesar and Cicero for Latin poetry, and as an upperclassman he worked away at Homer, Plato, and Aristophanes. From an old lexicon of his father's, about which he wrote a sentimental quatrain ("On a Rose Found in a Greek Dictionary"), he graduated to the huge, elegant Liddell and Scott lexicon, and wouldn't forget how he brought this back from the bookstore on his English bike, swinging the book with one hand. Liddell and Scott had been used, he knew, by Browning, Arnold, Pater, Wilde, and Thomas Hardy. After midnight, momentarily distracted by the drunken songs of collegians on their way back to the dorms from the Nassau Inn, he identified with a storied British lexicographer said to have strangled to death a stranger by whom he was interrupted, who returned to his work and, because of its quality, was not prosecuted.

When he arrived by ship with Dell and others for a summer bicycle tour in June 1914, Wilson would recall breathing "England!" in "awed ecstasy." They rode from Edinburgh through the Lake District—he studiously reading Wordsworth's *Prelude* in the evenings—and on through the cathedral towns to Wales. He left the group to seek out Meredith's home in Surrey, and there, looking up the hill toward the tiny cottage "where half a dozen great novels were written," he began the journal he'd keep for almost six decades. Going on to London, he wrestled with a battered suitcase that more than once burst open, and in a shirt borrowed from one friend and a tie from another explored the city—Westminster Abbey, the bookshops, the music halls, the Baker Street of Sherlock Holmes, the Oxford Street of De Quincey, and a theater where he twice saw *Pygmalion* with Beerbohm Tree and Mrs. Patrick Campbell. Staying at the old Langham Hotel, he observed a vista of Portland Place that reminded him of Henry James's *Golden Bowl*.

The friends thought they were on their way to France, but the declaration of war on the August 4 bank holiday kept them from crossing the Channel. Wilson saw people "riding on top of taxis, cheering in the crowded streets; a mob around Buckingham Palace calling for the King and Queen—'Mary! we're wyting!'—making them come back to the balcony over and over again." He wondered whether "the war was all going to be a tremendous bank holiday." Glad to have a president who promised to keep America out of war, he sailed home to a land more remote from the first campaigns and the bloody deadlock in the trenches than can be imagined today. A 1916 editorial in the *Princetonian* titled "Armageddon" referred not to the carnage overseas, but to the battle for the Ivy League's basketball championship.

In this sheltered scene Wilson told a graduate student that he thought of "working our own field," though to the other this was too much like being "a big toad in a small puddle." He was stimulated by the boisterous Mencken of the magazine *The Smart Set*, with his lists of pet peeves and catalogues of daily experiences. Mencken recommended *Huckleberry Finn* and *What Maisie Knew*, calling James's novel a "passionless masterpiece." To Bellinger, Wilson announced that he had discovered "two masterpieces—Henry James' *The Turn of the Screw* and Edith Wharton's *Ethan Frome*." Their generation had been brought up on Longfellow, Lowell, and other New England poets, but the same professor who introduced Fitzgerald to Keats impressed Wilson by bringing Whitman into his course on the Romantics—he roared out, "Born on Long Island, died in Camden—found life beautiful!" in defiance of those who, Wilson recalled, "living close to Camden, assumed that it was too far away from the localities mentioned in 'The Scholar-Gypsy' to inspire the right kind of poetry." Wilson discovered Emerson, and echoed his account of the American poet when turning a piece of literary tourism to evangelical use. "At Oxford and Cambridge," he wrote in the *Lit*, "you walk along a street, cross a little stream, stand in the quad of a college, or come suddenly upon some unexpected meadow traversed by shady paths, and, following close on the joy of discovery, as soon as you have learned its name, you begin to remember the great ones of fiction and history who have stood exactly where you have stood." Complaining that Princeton lacked such a nimbus, he declared that the only remedy was "to bring about the celebrated events and become the great men ourselves, with a view to our successors." His generation's task was "living up to our posterity."

Two professors helped Wilson form his first intellectual ideals. Norman Kemp Smith, a Scotsman of Calvinist background, then in his early forties, was an authority on Descartes and later known for his translation of Kant's *Critique of Pure Reason*. "Swaying from side to side and regarding us from under that solemn brow," in his lectures he explained "in his full deep Scotch, the closely linked chain of philosophic thought through the centuries." Kemp Smith was encyclopedic—interested "in literature, science, ideas, and news—in everything that men were doing." He sometimes invited students for Sunday dinner or a country walk, occasions when he seldom spoke except with a carefully formulated reflection. He believed in God, yet reinforced Wilson's contempt for conversions through personal weakness—one couldn't allow oneself to be persuaded of immortality by the death of "a favorite daughter." Kemp Smith left Princeton to be part of the war effort in the United Kingdom, and afterward assumed the chair of logic and metaphysics at Edinburgh, but they stayed in touch. He would introduce Wilson to the work of A. N. Whitehead, the mathematician turned philosopher whose *Science and the Modern World* is a point of departure in *Axel's Castle*. Wilson's essay "The Historical Interpretation of Literature," included in the second edition of *The Triple Thinkers*, cites Kemp Smith's view that aesthetic judgments are based on the satisfaction of the emotional need for order and meaning. A trained taste will be satisfied by more highly organized and deeper work.

Christian Gauss's lectures on Dante and Flaubert gave Wilson an enduring standard. Gauss used to come into the Dante class "without looking at us, and immediately begin to lecture, with his eyes dropped to his notes, presenting a mask that was almost Dantesque and leveling on us only occasionally the clear gaze that came through his eyeglasses." It was a gaze Wilson would associate with Gauss's injunction to be loyal to the truth "no matter where it led or whom it hurt." Gauss demonstrated the poet's classical "objectivity" and the "significance of his every stroke," the "vividness of the scenes and characters," the "tremendous intellectual power" that organized the world on behalf of "a reasoned morality." He suggested that the English lacked such control of their material—his sketch of Browning as a tone-deaf beefeater concocting facile moral dramas in Italy while Dante's ghost looked on with wry disdain led Wilson to remove the poet from his pedestal. The lectures on Flaubert in Gauss's course on French literature made Wilson, as a senior, want "to write something in which every word, every cadence, every detail, should perform a definite function in producing an intense effect." These two European writers were also touchstones for Pound and Eliot and contemporaries of Wilson's like Allen Tate. The American literary moderns would take over the ideal of a seamless, impersonal art in which every word counted toward a single impression.

Like his contemporaries, the young man had learned of continental artists and composers from James Huneker's *Egoists* (1909) and its successors, seeing them as excitingly immoral. But in a sophomore independent study he discovered the arch-decadent writer Joris-Karl Huysmans to be "too artistic in the sense that he is too appreciative of a certain field of art to the exclusion not only of all other art but of almost all life," the judgment Wilson would be tempted to make of the writers in *Axel's Castle*. Huysmans's hero Des Esseintes illustrated "the second-rate tragedy of a man perverted by too much culture and bored to death by civilization." Gauss, both moralist and aesthete, mediated between the young author of these roundly Johnsonian sentiments and what became his second culture, that of France from Voltaire and Rousseau and the Romantics through the nineteenth century.

Wilson sensed the essence of a national culture in Voltaire's ironic wit, and his own mix of "dialogues, fables, political pamphlets, serious discourse, masses of criticism" would echo the philosophes, as the critic George Steiner has noted. His taste for French historical criticism having been stimulated by Taine, in college he discovered Sainte-Beuve's *Causeries du lundi*, which he wanted to emulate until its gossipy journalism sent him back to Sainte-Beuve's master, Arnold. In class, Gauss's criticism combined an encyclopedic range with a neoclassical aesthetic and an interest in literary personalities. He laid out the map of nineteenth-century literary history Wilson brought up to date in *Axel's Castle*'s opening chapter, and the influence of his lectures colored the characterizations of Taine, Ernest Renan, and Anatole France in *To the Finland Station*. While writing these books Wilson would correspond with the professor, sometimes asking for a reference or the source of a quote.

Though Gauss later served as Dean, he was an outsider at Princeton when Wilson first knew him. Known to have shared drinks with Wilde, he walked the campus accompanied by his shabby mongrel dog, Baudelaire. "He was good with people who were different," Dell recalled. When one day he asked where beauty, justice, goodness, etc., came from and Wilson answered, "Out of the imaginations of men," he abandoned his Socratic manner to say, "That is correct," allowing the student to take him as a secular humanist. Wilson was impressed when he suggested that the impulse to conceal a harsh judgment of a friend's manuscript would be not kind but dishonest. The record of Gauss's lectures later made by another student includes an emphasis that would have registered with Wilson. "Without the belief in the efficacy of his own will," Gauss declared, "no man has ever accomplished anything worth accomplishing." As Wilson began his career after World War I, he'd picture his mentor in a Promethean role, "a last champion of man's divine pride of reason and imagination / Against all that tumult and stone." Less feverishly, writing in middle age, he quoted another student to whom Gauss stood for the view of language and literature as the "never-ending flow of man's struggle to think the thoughts which, when put into action," constituted "the advance of civilization." Wilson took him as a voice of "that good eighteenth-century Princeton which has always managed to flourish between the pressures of a narrow Presbyterianism and a rich man's suburbanism."

"Blasted Comrades of My Youth"

"The shy little scholar of Holder Court," as Fitzgerald called Wilson, didn't smoke or drink coffee or alcohol, except for a glass of champagne at the annual banquet of his club. In a photograph of the *Nassau Lit* board he looks worn, as though studying more than was socially desirable in a campus governed by the gentleman's C. He had other pleasures, including biking through the autumn lanes and, in winter, "moonlight skating through the level country solitudes of Stony Brook." But when he found himself fiddling with an eraser instead of applying himself to the page of Homer before him he appealed to his Puritan heritage, in a show of grandiloquent despair writing, "Calvin, I understand you; Jonathan Edwards, you are justified."

By day Wilson lived in the *Lit* office, into which an older editor and he dragged a large wooden bench which they painted black, sawing holes in the back and setting it against the windows so as to observe the campus without being seen, in "the semi-godlike role of the critic." In an editorial he ridicules talk of the golden days when college customs went unchallenged. How wonderfully naive and merry life had been when "a procession was held at midnight to celebrate Halley's Comet; a doctor's excuse could be had for a quarter; when one did not like a lecturer one prevented him from talking; when one was bored by a preacher one cut him short by coughing." Indeed, these were "the days of boyishness, fresh and unaffected: that is, they were days of prevalent drunkenness, cheating in examinations, intellectual cowardice and repression, indiscriminate mockery, general ignorance and the branding as a 'sad bird' of anyone who tried to rise above it." This brisk, sarcastic prose vents the resentment of the minority at conditions that had by no means disappeared.

He objected to the selective clubs—which as university president Woodrow Wilson had failed to dislodge—not as elitist, but because the selection, unlike that of the Yale senior societies, had nothing to do with merit. After excitedly going into Charter as a sophomore, he found that all he did there was eat and read the papers. At dinner he often sat next to John Wyeth, the class aesthete and something of a sad bird, who remembered Edmund firmly maintaining his literary talk amid a crowd of men as they discussed their dates at the next prom or party after the game. His last editorial termed the club elections "arbitrary and unfair," leading people to "behave with one accord like a lot of fools, cads, and snobs." If this angered those he remembered as "the debonair young men who were planning to be bond salesmen and brokers," the next year "the children of serious republicans" asserted themselves when a quarter of the sophomores, led by Dick Cleveland, the son of former President Grover Cleveland, refused election to any club.

Alongside these "Shawesque" editorials on campus issues, Wilson turned out poems, criticism, and short stories for the *Lit*. He admitted to Bellinger that, in poetry, he hadn't "much distinction in the art of words," a discovery that did not keep him from verse celebrations of his artistic heroes—"Swift: The Dark Hour," "Whistler at Battersea." An essay about Henry James has an undergraduate's reservations, missing in the novels Mark Twain's native flavor and Meredith's love interest. But his friend Wyeth helped him understand James's mannered periodic style and the indirection of his dialogue as literary conventions, and Wilson admired the tight dramatic staging, "the impression of real human relations with all their complexities of motive and cross-motive." Writing when James was still alive and at work, the youth defines his "fine Puritanism" as a dramatic opposition of imagination and urbanity to the moral sense. *Paradise Lost* is, he says, no more real a "struggle between the spirits of good and evil than *The Turn of the Screw*."*

His voluminous college fiction, imitative of James or H. G. Wells or Meredith, reveals his emotional and sexual inexperience. He reported to Bellinger that a friend "came in and burst into roars of laughter at the sentence I had written, which was 'My God, girl!' said the doctor, 'We don't wear wigs in America,' and really one can hardly blame him, because it is certainly a little startling, out of its context." An interpolation in Wilson's college journal notes, "I never went to dances, since I had never been able to learn to dance," and he confesses that as a senior, he consulted a doctor after having an emission. By this time he could imagine seducing women on the strength of his writing, though he didn't delude himself that his fiction would bring such success. In a late night reverie in a letter to Bellinger, he confronts an imagined Princetonian literary ancestor, Sir Simeon Wilson (author of *A Proper Digest and Inquiry into the Laws of Franchise of New Jersie*). When this comical figure says that Edmund will never match his achievement, the youth cheerfully predicts "a great future for myself." He then finds himself at the top of the Campanile in Venice, looking out over the city with the *Divine Comedy* in his hands. A mysterious, beautiful woman stands nearby, with "a book before her on the railing—my last novel!"

"'How do you like that book? It's pretty darn good, is it not?' I blurt out.

"'No,' she replies, in a lovely voice, 'It is the saddest stuff that ever I read.'"

---

*This essay contains Wilson's first statement of the idea that James would have been more direct and masculine had he experienced the Civil War, an idea developed in *Patriotic Gore* half a century later.

His daunting anima figure remains unimpressed when he reveals it is his work, yet she grants the hero his boon. "Looking for strength to the sky," she exclaims, "Never mind, I'll marry you just the same."

Wilson's mother remained "the nicest girl" he knew. Indeed, Stanley Dell remembered her as pretty and kind, but she was deaf and not literary—at some point she acquired the idea that Gauss was a bad influence, turning her Bunny into an intellectual snob. During vacations he visited friends' families, often the Bellingers or the Carters in the small town of Washington, Connecticut. Though Alfred's stiff Victorian grandmother took offense at what seemed a disparaging reference to Wordsworth, his mother shared Wilson's interest in such dark writers as Hardy and Housman. Sterling's family lived in an old-fashioned "rather Spartan" way, with no central heating, and he camped with them on Mount Tom in western Massachusetts during the summers. A New Hampshire classmate, Edgar Woodman (whose grandson, half a century later, would be the partner of Wilson's artist daughter Helen), had a cousin named Charles Walker, an editor of the *Yale Lit*, whom Wilson met when the boards of the magazines exchanged dinners. Walker, a poet who'd write a novel about the 1919 steel strike and go left in his politics, would be a friend for life.

Among the campus writers Wilson was scarcely the shy scholar. "Red-haired, eager, tireless, he bubbled with ideas and threw them out by the handful," Gauss recalled. Editorially snobbish about the Triangle Show (such musical comedies being "largely futile and uninspired"), he was competitive enough to write the book in 1915, Fitzgerald doing the lyrics. He loved a joke and sometimes set up literary hoaxes, as three and four decades later he'd send Leon Edel on an endless Freudian paper chase through the stacks of the Harvard Library or direct Vladimir Nabokov to a book from which, when opened, a mechanical butterfly flew forth. He identified himself with the group whom the college walls, as Dell put it for them all after graduation, "had held together in a bond of easy interchange and intimacy." Among them "Old Doc Wilson" would be a literary elder brother, cheerfully commenting on their manuscripts and suggesting publishers, advocating art for its own sake and as a way of coming to terms with life's problems. He later extended this pattern of friendship to women writers—Elinor Wylie, Louise Bogan, Peggy Bacon, Dawn Powell. Once you'd got experience into a satisfactory aesthetic form, he'd tell Bogan, you could "thumb your nose at the world."

While such Harvard contemporaries as Cummings and Dos Passos fulfilled their promise, the Princetonians were, in Wilson's view, side-tracked or wrecked. Bill Mackie, with whom he'd discovered Latin poetry, was a prototype, fading even in college. Bill's brilliance appears in a spoof about his summer reading, written as a gentleman about town in eighteenth-century London. His Pepys *Diary* style is so plausible that this letter has been catalogued at Yale as that of one William, Lord Mackie, although Shelley and the Pre-Raphaelites, James's *A Small Boy and Others*, and Max Nordau's *Degeneration* are included on his list. To Wilson the disorganized piles of books on the floor of Bill's room seemed "something immoral." He became a campus drunk and flunked out by failing astronomy—"I had no idea," he said, "I was going to suffer a total eclipse." Regretting the squandering of such talent, the aging Wilson wrote, "I have never known anyone droller or more sensitive to literature."

Stanley Dell, his closest friend, had lived much abroad, his mother being confined to a TB sanitarium in Switzerland. He kept what was described as a wonderful diary, and Wilson deemed him a future novelist. As the war drew closer, Dell wrote eloquently against plans for military training at Princeton, but an acute sense of duty led him into the ambulance service attached to the French Army. Afterward he would try journalism in New York and, a sure critic of French writers, could have followed Gauss into a distinguished academic career. Yet his wealth made earning a living unnecessary—in its way as much a handicap as would be Wilson's struggle to support himself—and after spending his college years, as he wrote to Wilson, getting rid of Christianity, he didn't replace his faith with a literary credo.

John Peale Bishop, class of '17, brought to college a technical skill at English verse the others lacked. A Southerner with an aristocratic air, his sense of living in a post-heroic age made the fin de siècle congenial. As he walked the rainy Princeton lanes reciting Swinburne and Rossetti, he saw himself welcomed to the company of noble alums like Aaron Burr and "Light Horse" Harry Lee, literary ancestors with, however, an intimidating aura Wilson's comical Sir Simeon lacked. Wilson's successor at the *Lit*, Bishop would follow him, after the war, to *Vanity Fair* and be his rival in love for Edna St. Vincent Millay. As a poet he would never find his own voice, remaining largely imitative.

It was Bishop who famously brought Fitzgerald into the group. Too small for football, Fitz, as he was called in college, wrote for the humor magazine *The Tiger* and aimed to be a campus star by writing the yearly musical comedies for the Triangle Club, spending little or no time, in his roommate John Biggs's words, on "the courses so generously made available by the University." At their first meeting Wilson recognized his self-assurance, his penetrating "hard green eyes." Wilson corrected the spelling and syntax of Fitzgerald's lyric drama *Shadow Laurels* and published it in the *Nassau Lit*, followed by the story "The Ordeal." In a letter about their Triangle Show, *The Evil Eye*, Wilson purports to be overwhelmed by "the increasing bitterness and cynicism of my middle age," hoping the younger man can infuse into it some of his celebrated effervescence. Through the fall of 1915 Dell, Bishop, Fitzgerald, and he made up one of Gauss's tutorial groups in the French course, and Wilson can be imagined illustrating for the others the value of precise language, the importance of aesthetic form. The gulf between a senior and a junior was larger then and, given Wilson's authority and Fitzgerald's intellectual immaturity and enthusiasm, they stepped easily into the roles of mentor and mentee.

At Princeton Fitzgerald was not yet the genius of legend, and when at Christmas 1916 he withdrew from college under cover of illness to avoid academic dismissal, Bishop and Wilson wrote an exasperated satire in which they have their friend depict his fall as that of a self-promoter who made his scattered reading "go further than most people do with the reading of years." Seven months later Fitzgerald returned and took over *The Tiger* with John Biggs. In a letter to Wilson, working in New York and living in Greenwich Village, with characteristically mixed vulnerability and confidence he asks, "Do you realize that Shaw is 61, Wells 51, Chesterton 41, [his friend Shane] Leslie 31, and I 21?" remarking that there should be a better man for 31 and, Wilson would doubtless say, for 21. Fitzgerald's development would be strikingly discontinuous. What he and Wilson shared was their ambition. When he said, "I want to be one of the greatest writers who ever lived, don't you?" Wilson couldn't share this fantasy "because I had been reading Plato and Dante," while Fitzgerald was still absorbed by Booth Tarkington, Compton Mackenzie, Wells, and Swinburne. But Wilson observed of his friend that "when he got to better writers his standards and his achievement went sharply up, and he would always have pitted himself against the best in his own line that he knew." A competitive awareness of Fitzgerald's gift was to feed Wilson's preaching of standards, nagging his friend to do better. He would ridicule the first draft of *This Side of Paradise*, comparing it to Daisy Ashford's *The Young Visiters*, and his review of the published text was almost as savage.

Looking back, Wilson wondered whether his attacks, in college, on the church might have weakened Fitzgerald's allegiance to the Catholicism on which his moral controls depended, bound up as this was with what he ashamedly considered a "lace-curtain Irish" strain. In *A Prelude* Fitzgerald is quoted as saying, "I can go up to New York on a terrible party and then come back and go into the church and pray, and mean every word of it, too!" Wilson may well have called this too porous a conscience. Yet in *This Side of Paradise* Amory is saved from fulfilling his lusts in the apartment of some New York girls when the man following him turns out to be the Devil. Wilson and Fitzgerald were equally distressed on the warm commencement night when Bishop and Alec McKaig left them to go off with two "hookers," a word Wilson hadn't heard before. "That's one thing that Fitzgerald's never done!" the younger man avowed, already in the habit of referring to himself in the third person. After almost two years in the army Wilson would still think it wrong to pick up a French prostitute, and in a letter to Fitz he recurred to that "ghastly" evening "when you and I sat alone upon the darkened and deserted verandah of Cottage" (Fitzgerald's club) and "let John Bishop take the shabby whoring of the Princeton streets for the harlotries of Rome and the Renaissance."

The war brought the first fragmentation of the group, marriages a second. Dell and Bishop would marry socialites, Dell's wife sweetly but boringly conventional, Bishop's possessive and, in the eyes of his friends, destructive of his poetry. Fitzgerald's meteoric rise from *This Side of Paradise* to *The Great Gatsby* in five years would be undermined by his alcoholic demoralization and Zelda's illness, and his struggle for perspective on their marriage is reflected in the bitterness that enters into *Tender Is the Night*. Wilson came to think his friends too vulnerable to the Princeton ambience of "country-house social prestige," from which the professional tradition in his family insulated him. He thought them prone to be seduced away from art, as when John Biggs gave up writing realistic novels to become a lawyer and in the end a judge on the U.S. Court of Appeals, a career that Wilson (who liked Biggs and believed they had much in common) deemed second best. He had explanations for everyone's failings and hesitations.

In conversation as he approached seventy, Wilson mentioned an unwritten work—he feared he might not live to do, and in fact did not—to consist of a round of visits among "the blasted comrades of my youth." The

fin de siècle was real in pre–World War I Princeton. Gauss "never got out
of the nineties," Dell believed. Wilson absorbed Ernest Dowson and Wilde
and Pater (whose "gem-like flame" he would echo in a poem), and all his
life he produced pen-and-ink drawings, some of the best of these in
Beardsley's vein. The conceit of "blasted comrades" recalls Yeats on the
Rhymers' Club in his *Autobiographies* and *Trembling of the Veil*. Yet Beardsley, Arthur Clough, and the others Yeats had in mind actually drank
themselves to death, while no such explanation is required to explain the
burnt-out talents or altered paths of most of Wilson's companions. Fitzgerald was the one who lived out the legend. In the spring of 1916 Edmund and some friends invented a doomed Pre-Raphaelite poet named
Edward Moore Gresham, telling his story and publishing fragments of his
supposed work. Wilson's "The Last Remains of Edward Moore Gresham"
would lead to a job when it caught Dorothy Parker's eye at *Vanity Fair*. In
a haunting echo two decades later, he'd begin the dedicatory verses for
his collection of Fitzgerald's literary remains, "Scott, your last fragments I
arrange tonight."

In "Thoughts on Being Bibliographed," distinguishing their college
generation from later ones whose ambitions turned professorial, he recalled, "You read Shakespeare, Shelley, George Meredith, Dostoevsky,
Ibsen, and you wanted, however imperfectly and on however infinitesimal
a scale, to learn their trade and have the freedom of their company." For
four years Princeton had given Wilson models as well as an audience for
whom to write. A classical standard and the training at reading literatures
in their own tongues, begun with Latin and Greek, prepared him to find
his way around not only among French and then Russian writers, but also
in Hebrew and Hungarian. It was a purely humanistic education in the
tradition going back to Erasmus, though absorbed within a country club
environment. His last piece for the *Lit* reviews the true story of a man
who put himself through Princeton (at that time rare), honoring the
school while, in Wilson's possibly naive opinion, acquiring values that
would insulate him from a commercial society.

Upon entering the army Wilson wrote nostalgic verse about his alma
mater. But the war years made it seem that "more things are dead in
Princeton than the leaves," and afterward it was impossible to have "sentimental emotions" about any institution. He wrote up a drunken class reunion in a 1927 *New Republic* piece on his generation's lost illusions.
This was the last reunion Wilson attended. As a socialist during the 1930s
he saw Princeton as a pseudo-aristocratic façade of capitalism:

I too have faked the glamor of gray towers,
I too have sung the ease of sultry hours,
Deep woods, sweet lanes, wide playing fields, smooth ponds
—Where clean boys train to sell their country's bonds.

He was taking off on an alumnus named Struthers Burt, a Wyoming rancher and novelist who thought the *Alumni Weekly* ought to praise alumni authors more, and who wrote poetry about returning to his alma mater with "the keen swift faith that God is good." Wilson characterizes Burt's God as "a big beneficent trustee / Who asks well-bred professors in to tea." The undergraduate pieties thus disowned were not reasserted when Wilson's Marxist allegiance had faded, though his visits to Gauss and their correspondence continued.

In 1943 the university's *Library Chronicle* would publish "Thoughts on Being Bibliographed," an essay that for literary journalists has a weight like that of Emerson's "American Scholar," and after participating in the Christian Gauss seminars a decade later Wilson was awarded an honorary degree. But to the aging critic, Harvard—despite "what is bad about it"—seemed a much more valuable place, and no professorship was ever named for Princeton's most distinguished graduate in the humanities. This generation at Princeton liked making fun of Yale, with what they half-envied as its success code and Wall Street connections, and Wilson sometimes fell into the habit. Yet when he chose to sell his papers, it was Yale's Beinecke Library that purchased them.

4

World War I:
"The Others Stayed with Their Class"

❦

As a college senior Wilson was restlessly eager for the outside world but had no idea how he would support himself. Stanley Dell and he had studied sociology and labor problems at Columbia summer school following their junior year and when, not long after graduation, he discussed his future with his father he talked of trying his hand at political journalism in Washington. Forty years later Wilson purported to remember their exchange verbatim. "Don't you think you ought to concentrate on something?" his father asked, to which he replied, "Father, what I want to do is to try to get to know something about all the main departments of human thought." His father judiciously observed, "That's a possible ambition. Go ahead if you're really serious." Wilson would become ever more serious after (as he put it in some postwar verse) he'd observed Europe "with her barbarity lying bare," had "seen the anatomy of society / Performed under my very nose / Without the assistance of ether."

During the summer of 1916, while President Wilson campaigned for reelection by promising to keep America out of the European conflict, Edmund enrolled at a summer preparedness training camp in Plattsburgh, New York. As a boy he'd never wanted his father to teach him to shoot, and on the rifle range he was "so nervous" that "I don't think I ever hit the target." At once Wilson "loathed the Army," learning that he could neither command men nor imagine killing strangers "in cold blood."* He

---

*With friends after the war he'd burlesque training camp in the role of a red-faced, bespectacled Major Waldron barking out instructions. Fitzgerald especially liked the lecture on "places of concealment: If you climb on a roof of house, be sure to keep on side that's hidden—side

was used, however, to surrounding himself with like-minded individuals in what might otherwise be a hostile situation. Charley Walker, his *Yale Lit* friend, helped them through long dusty hikes by reciting his verse and listening to Wilson's many ideas about novel writing. Edgar Woodman was one of their roommates, another a "brilliant" and "amiable" man named Sakolsky, whose qualities, Wilson wrote to Bellinger, helped him get rid of "a kind of instinctive snobbishness" toward Jews and interested him in Hebrew thought and literature.

That fall he moved into an apartment at 15 West Eighth Street in Manhattan with three Yale acquaintances. To Fitzgerald their rooms were mellow and sophisticated, and a glimpse of Wilson walking down the sidewalk in his already "inevitable" brown suit and carrying a cane, absorbed in his thoughts, evoked the metropolitan spirit. Wilson liked the winding streets and low-roofed houses, the slummy bohemianism of the Village, but the postcollegiate social scene his friends were part of was alien to him, and in the evenings he sometimes sat down to study Homer, his Liddell and Scott propped before him on the dining room table.

After he futilely visited a number of newspaper offices with letters of recommendation, his father persuaded the owner of the *New York Evening Sun* to take him on as a cub reporter at fifteen dollars a week, a sum Mr. Wilson occasionally supplemented. He started work at four in the morning, telling Alfred he was busy "writing up little stories about people being almost killed under trucks, being fined for buying partridges, attempting suicide in hospitals, and things like that—or rather, rewriting most of them." That witnesses always saw the same events differently taught him the unreliability of human testimony, the need to check up on everything for oneself. His style turned out to be unwieldy—"I could not write about any subject without striving for the well-modelled sentence and the impassive Flaubertian irony, so I never made anything sound exciting." When allowed to do an editorial about the Princeton clubs, the city editor warned him not to sound like Dr. Johnson, to which Wilson gamely replied he wished he could. Occasionally allowed to review books, he promoted *A Book of Vassar Verse*, taking note for the first time of the work of one Edna St. Vincent Millay.

The European conflict hit his family and friends early. In 1915 his

---

that's away from enemy . . . Scout that gets on side exposed to enemy can be seen by enemy and shot. Scout must keep from getting shot. Scout's no good if he's dead."

cousin Adelaide lost her dashing French husband, André Cherronet-Champollion, who was killed at the front. Dell wrote to Wilson of his French ambulance unit's nighttime rescue of three hundred badly wounded men. "Some died on the way. None of them complained. Some of them joked. The only purpose in the joke, and the only possible justification of the courage to grit the teeth and pull through somehow, is that when the surgeon was through they would be out of the war." But where Hemingway's heroes would make a separate peace, Stanley thought "a little deprivation and responsibility" might be "character building," writing that "when you add the necessity of caring for others, you have as good an experience as a man would ask for." A few weeks later he received the Croix de Guerre "for recovering a wounded non-commissioned officer in broad daylight under circumstances of great danger."

When the United States entered the war in April 1917, Wilson was confused about his own course. After Plattsburgh he didn't want to enter officers' training alongside his friends, yet if he failed to enlist he could be drafted and sent to fight anywhere. Indecision was the only thing that could panic this determined advocate of reason and will. He was rescued from what was becoming a nervous crisis when David Hamilton, one of his apartment-mates, decided to join the hospital corps. Wilson got his parents' permission to do the same, telling himself he could nurse damaged soldiers. Though not in other ways comparable to the dangerous course that Dell had chosen, a year as a private at a base hospital in eastern France would be decisive in enabling Wilson to speak for a larger America than that of his privileged boyhood.

He enlisted that June and was described in the U.S. Army records as five foot six and one-quarter inches with brown eyes and a fair complexion. By midmonth David and he were encamped at the Detroit State Fairgrounds amid rumors they'd leave for France soon. But ten weeks of boring busywork followed—guard duty, latrine cleaning, repeated training exercises. Submerged in the "profanity, obscenity, and pure stupidity" of the army, no longer in rational control of his life, and with no one around who could speak "the real language," Wilson was depressed by the habits and manners of his fellow soldiers, by the animal nature that he shared with them. When his unit paraded through Detroit streets "the crowds were incredible: the roofs were bristling with people and the roads were so full that four soldiers abreast could hardly get through." Not much happier when spending weekends with David's conventional family in

Grosse Pointe, to Stanley he cited the Latin motto beloved of the Renaissance, *Nihil humani mihi alienum est*,* signing himself, "Yours for sweetness and light."

The narrative that can be constructed from Wilson's correspondence, journal notes, fiction and verse of 1917–1919, and details recollected later on, charts the nation's and his loss of innocence. Scores of genial and chatty reports to his mother, all signed "Yours lovingly, Edmund," convey his army life. The brief wartime journal contains encounters and anecdotes he didn't want to share with her, beginning with his view of the class structure from below when finally sent overseas on a troopship out of Montreal. Assigned a berth in an abandoned steerage because his name began with W, he resented the denial of empty first-class cabins to the ordinary soldiers. He escaped in books, reading Joyce's *Dubliners* on the train to New York, and on the voyage the romantic comedies of Shakespeare that he didn't already know. He wrote editorials for the newsletter of Base Hospital 36, glad at last to have a job that required some intelligence.

At Southampton, where it rained steadily, flooding their tents, he found Chesterton's *History of England* and James's *The Sense of the Past* in a bookshop, and read in the papers about the upheaval in Russia "with men named Lenin and Trotsky coming to the top." The troops were shipped by train to an estate in the south of England turned into a camp, then crossed the channel to Le Havre, where they were loaded into boxcars on which signs specified "40 men, 8 horses, lengthwise." He entertained his mother with an account of the men singing and carrying on while pocketing the utensils and goblets at the restaurants where the train stopped for food en route to northeastern France. To Charles Walker he wrote of bawdy verses and of soldiers reciting Shakespeare and Tennyson. But in Wilson's car a private became delirious with fever, and a soldier in another car died of pneumonia, incidents that led to a protest story about military negligence, "The Death of a Soldier," which was held up by a censor and published in *The Liberator* after the war.

Called "Woodrow" or "Ed" in the unit, by the time they reached the resort town of Vittel in the Vosges he was more at ease with his fellow soldiers. "I had flopped with my company on narrow army cots in a palatial and freezing chamber, where our breath went up as steam," he recalled three decades later. "When one came to in the morning in the chilly air, to

* Nothing human is alien to me.

the curses and obscene shouts of one's equally uncomfortable companions, one looked up at the high painted ceiling full of the muses and floating goddesses held appropriate to such places in Europe." The crude army language that oppressed him in Detroit became a form of solidarity among countrymen thrown together in difficult circumstances on foreign soil.

Wilson was introduced to a multi-ethnic America and to the reasons that people left the Old World. John Andersen, a lab assistant, was self-educated in several languages. Born in Denmark—his "fine and sober smile" recalled that of Erasmus—he described a countryside where people ate with wooden spoons and believed in trolls. An Irish-American sergeant named Holland reported that in Tipperary, when a woman claimed to be possessed by the devil, the villagers tried to exorcise him by forcing her to stand naked over a fire. Some of these new friends were artists. A painter from Michigan, whose forebears had been hereditary farriers in the family of an English nobleman, admired Whistler and commented wittily on art and sex. Initially liking their officers, Wilson encountered another sort when detailed to carry wood for the stove and keep the water pitcher warm in the office of a military dentist who turned out to be "the worst kind of horse doctor"—fracturing instruments in people's mouths, pulling their teeth instead of fixing them, and once, in his presence, beating a dazed recruit who resisted. Wilson must have had this in mind when telling his father that "on one or two occasions, I see that I should have chosen the guard-house rather than to stand by."

Off duty he explored the town with its cafés and shops and a park on the main street leading toward the gloomy winter country. They ate "soup, French-fried potatoes, beefsteak, jam, bread, and cheese for about sixty cents apiece," and he found that a glass of wine or brandy warmed him up. A generous allowance from his father made it possible to buy scores of books from Paris, which he read at the café, where he also wrote letters and conducted a literary flirtation with the owner's daughter. Ninette Fabre appealed to his romanticism, with "her black hair, her green eyes under delicately penciled black eyebrows and her perfect oval face." She had pale skin and burning cheeks and was being treated by the American army doctors for tuberculosis. Her bearded and bad-tempered father threw out any soldier who made advances to her, but Wilson was given a goodbye kiss when he left Vittel, and he sought Ninette out on his return to France in 1921.

He wrote compellingly to his college group in letters, to Walker predicting a collective burst of intellectual energy after the war and telling Fitzgerald he had "decided to resume the writing of my forthcoming books, war or no war." Dell, discharged from the French ambulance service because of weakening health, was back in the States, engaged to Grover Cleveland's daughter Marion and trying to pass the physical tests for various branches of the American military. He'd told Wilson, "At first you're all cut up at the sight of the wounded, but you soon get used to it," adding, "Nothing gets exhausted so quickly as human sympathy."

As an American, Wilson had moments of believing that his president's intelligence and idealism might prevail. But he explained to Stanley how these months in "the hospital business" had changed him, with "men dying (in large numbers) through pneumonia and improper care, before they so much as see the front, and being buried perfunctorily before their families know they are dead." Despite the "piles of British propaganda" Kemp Smith was sending from a ministry in London, "the illusions of nationalism," like the ignorance of the fighting men, made "the ideals which are said to be the goals of this war seem as dubious as the ideals which we know to have proved false in earlier wars." So Wilson would believe when resisting American entry into World War II, a popular war, and the Vietnam War, which turned unpopular. Debating the relationship between artistic and political commitments, he told Dell that "although my single aim has been literature, my great men have never been Pater and Symonds but Dante and Socrates and Voltaire, who can certainly not be said to have been indifferent to politics." Although skeptical of military crusades, he feared that one day—as happened during the 1930s—he would be tempted "to extinguish myself in a political cause."

He wrote also to Sandy Kimball, who, because his mother refused him permission to enlist, had settled for the Reserve Corps. Wilson worried about his cousin. Pushed by Aunt Caroline to follow in Uncle Reuel's steps, Sandy had enrolled in the College of Physicians and Surgeons at Columbia, but couldn't keep up, and when he reported that his mother thought his problem mere selfishness and lack of will, Wilson wished he'd move out of the house. Proposing to a woman who turned him down further diminished his confidence, and in December 1917 Sandy reported a "terrible contracted and haunted feeling," a severe neurosis that, by February, had been ascribed to thyroid deficiency—he explained that "thyroid extract, exercise, rest, and good advice" from a doctor were curing him. A March letter claimed he was much better, invoking the end of "my self-imposed incarceration" and "my chrysalis life," but when he declared,

"My sepulchre is broken and I am stepping forth into the sunlight," Sandy was halfway between a religious conversion and a breakdown. Wilson was troubled.

His duties left time for country walks and bike rides on roads to little towns in the darkness, the poplars, and the mist, with "the unseen, unrealized reality" of the war always in the background. Hearing of a château in the remote woodland near the German border, David and he trudged through snowy fields to find the place and were hospitably received and included in a Christmas party for the village children. Back at Vittel they were told that the dapperly dressed little man who owned the château was a cross-dressing lesbian rumored to hold wild champagne parties, throwing the empty bottles into the dungeon, where prisoners had once been abandoned. Sometimes Wilson went as far as Nancy, not far from the front and under threat from the Germans. The houses on its eighteenth-century square had a "sober loveliness," and on one corner was an art museum with works of the local painter Georges de La Tour and the engraver Jacques Callot. An art dealer fleeing the town to Vittel's relative security sold him a copy of Callot's popular *Tentation de Sainte Antoine* and some prints made from the original plates of the series *Miseries of War*, which would give the orderly, in his own words, "a certain support" in experiences to come.

When he and a companion hired a man with a cart to drive them back from a long walk they picked up a French soldier worn out after three years of the constant cannonading. "Boom! boom! boom! Death! death! death!" the Frenchman said with bitter helplessness: "Two million men! Men that you've never seen! But what can you do?" The soldiers, he said, killed their officers if they remained behind instead of leading the attack, though these officers were at once replaced—"*On se débarrassé de celui-là, on a autre*," Wilson set down this long speech in French, noting that it was the time of the French mutiny and that the soldier said the English army was in much the same frame of mind.

In the spring of 1918 everyone he talked to impatiently expected the end of combat. Weary of the hospital routine of waiting, he applied for a transfer to the Intelligence service, where he thought he might make some use of his mind. When he learned that instead of forwarding his application to Washington his commanding officer destroyed it along with a number of others, he enlisted the help of an officer who'd been a professor, then of his father, who wrote that he'd approach their New Jersey senator. Briefly he was distracted by the task of historian of the unit, or rather the enlisted man who did the work while the credit went to a committee of officers whose names appear on military memo No. 86, which he drily enclosed in a letter home. The job allowed him the use of a typewriter for his letters.

In June the first victims of mustard gas were shipped in by train and taken on stretchers to the hospital. The gas attacked throats and genitals, and the men's swollen, raw penises had to be carefully bandaged. Patients began arriving day and night, among them wounded British soldiers "all over mud and blood." A few weeks before, hearing nightingales singing outside in the park had made Wilson appreciate Keats's ode, but literature could not screen off the horror of mutilated men, and a "New Ode to a Nightingale," dated June 8, 1918, contrasts "those tones flung glowing to the dark" with "the sharp lament of dogs that bark," sounds of a world drained of affirmation by the soldiers' dying.

Wilson's responses as a wound dresser have been likened by Edel to Whitman's. In fact he lacked the poet's spiritualized feeling for the soldiers, but to see a doctor roughly rip bandages from unhealed wounds angered him, and he was moved by those who couldn't articulate their pain. Half a century later he recalled a syphilitic soldier who "seemed unconscious and could not talk: he could only make a clicking sound." In a journal passage also used in a short story, a German American traumatized by having bayoneted a German soldier is seen "densely immured in some impregnable stronghold of stupidity or dazed by some great transplantation." Yet he nervously wandered the halls and when roused one night for his medicine, "woke up with a shriek that was like a green gash in the dark and dashed the glass across the room with a wild panic-stricken gesture." At the beginning of August 1918 Wilson goes so far as to tell his mother of the effects of bullets that explode within the body and "arsenic that damages the lungs." Several weeks later he tells Bellinger of spending "my nights for a month dressing gas burns." In the journal he notes, "One patient had three-quarters of the surface of his body burned and his lungs partially destroyed. His face was purple. At intervals during the night, he would whistle hoarsely and, when I came to him, ask: 'Are you ready to move yet, Sergeant?' He thought he was still on the march. In the morning he died."

The flu epidemic followed, and a literary letter is interrupted by an account of a hectic night among the patients, "patrolling a hall in white cap and gown (supposed to protect against infection), to keep the wild men from jumping out the windows. One of them was evidently telling someone at home all about his initiation into the trenches; another was groaning, 'Blood! Blood!'" Wilson adds, "I kept awake by means of what Doc [Charles] Walker [now a burial officer in England] used to call 'shrapnel-like thoughts' snatched from H. L. Mencken's *Damn!* (an excellent book which I commend to you; it is very short)." Looking back in another story, he would reflect that "no one who has ever watched an army doctor trying to deal with a flu epidemic will ever get over his impression of the miserable impotence of the human race at the mercy of multiplying bacteria." He realized that, left to itself, "humanity was a raving madhouse," and that only through long effort could any order be brought into it at all.

He had to assist at deathbeds and lay out the dead, working alongside "an elderly undertaker, who went around in felt slippers, with a lantern and a kind of nightcap on his head. He knew just how to handle dead bodies. We would put them on a stretcher and carry them down to a basement room, where we sometimes had to pile them up like logs. They were buried in big common ditches." One was that of a hospital nurse, for whom he wrote the epitaph included in *Night Thoughts*. When the worst had passed and he collapsed and was put to bed for a day or two, Wilson made a vow—as he recalled this when moving left after the Crash—that if he survived he'd never live "indifferently or trivially again." The youth who'd felt something human, heroic, and shining in his Greek classroom and taken seriously his prep school's motto, Whatsoever Things Are True, resolved to "stand outside society" and devote himself to "the great human interests which transcended standards of living and convention: Literature, History, the Creation of Beauty, the Discovery of Truth."

By coincidence, only a day or two after the break from routine enabled him to take stock, he learned that General Headquarters wanted him as an interpreter, and the colonel in charge was allowing the transfer. Though Wilson didn't know it, his father's pressure on their New Jersey senator had led to a reply from General Pershing, stating that he'd be commissioned when his experience warranted. Joy at escaping the base hospital was tempered by regret at leaving his companions, but he resolved to help John Andersen achieve an educated man's career, despite John's awkward, self-taught English, and wouldn't forget the integrity of such a seemingly simple man as the cook's assistant Joseph Mroch. Mroch and the mess crew had a farewell party for him. Regaling his mother with it, he says that "Holland came in and, after a riotous argument about the prospects of peace, presented me ceremoniously with a set of his Sergeant's stripes," since at GHQ he was to be raised in rank. "Ye'll have learned something," he said, "from these roughnecks, these bloody hypocrites and prevaricators!" Wilson adds that "outside of John and the rest, the messmen were certainly my best friends," something he couldn't have expected "when I had to work in the mess at the fairgrounds in Detroit."

The last ten months in the army were anticlimactic. At Chaumont, his first job was to sign passes, which he issued to everyone who asked for one. On Armistice Day he was transferred to a three-man unit absurdly called the Department of Exterior Fronts, their job being to analyze the military and political situation outside France and Germany. With Europe "in a state of revolution and dissolution" and the Paris Peace Conference soon to convene, for ten days he sifted reports of conditions in Poland, then the conflict on the Dalmatian coast, which Italy sought to annex. This working group was suddenly dissolved and he was reassigned to an able captain named Blankenhorn, a former editor at the *Evening Sun* who was supplying information to Colonel House, President Wilson's aide. Edmund hoped that the United States would be able to restrain Britain and France, now jockeying for power and territory, spurred by a popular press that wanted Germany punished. Only the President could "enforce different social and international conditions from those which made the war inevitable," he wrote home, objecting to Theodore Roosevelt's attack on Wilson for going to France as a peacemaker, to which his father also objected in a letter that crossed with the son's.

To be back in his social class was strange. Officers astonished him by inviting him to dinner, and the ex-reporters writing propaganda were interesting to talk to, bitter as they actually were about the war. On the other hand, the smug Yale man who headed Intelligence liked to say the masses needed guidance from above. Although Wilson respected General Pershing, he detested the regular army martinets who with great dash "administered a filing cabinet," lobbied for promotion, and when not speaking of the need to keep the Germans down might talk eagerly of the next war. This first encounter with bureaucracy helped to radicalize him.

In a typical army snafu he was sent as interpreter to the occupied town of Trier (Trèves) on the Moselle, on the assumption that he spoke German. Traveling through the ruined border country to an attractive city filled with people subdued and in mourning, in his letter home he stresses their "bitterness, grief, bewilderment," adding "the Christmas celebrations are like gasps of air by someone who is suffocating." He didn't enjoy being part of an occupying force, but sometimes visited an amiable Princetonian who represented the allies in a little town three-quarters of an hour down the river, the model for the "Lieutenant Franklin" who is played off against the martinets with their petty ambitions in Wilson's story of this name. Another character in the story is an engineer major with "square-tipped mechanic's fingers," whose American pragmatism might prevail were he not an outsider eager to go home. In the silence of a huge, depressing German military barracks the narrator contemplates "the death to which all those men had gone out" and "in which their cries and commands, their groans and howls of laughter, were extinguished": "All the discipline, the energy, the labor, all the hammering of human beings into soldiers only in order to have their old training-school turned over to a young American who was hardly a soldier at all!"

Back at headquarters Wilson was granted a leave to Paris, and when he returned to Chaumont the Intelligence center was breaking up, with some people sent on to the peace conference and others going home. Assigned by Blankenhorn to analyze the military situation in Russia, as he digested reports during the spring of 1919 he wrote to his father that the allied intervention in the civil war there was a mistake, for encircling these people would solidify them behind the Communists, as the French had been united in their revolution by the threat of external enemies. Food aid would be a better weapon against communism. Anticipating *To the Finland Station*, he took the Russian Revolution as a product of Lenin's "strength of mind and will"—"his confreres" were "a motley crew, ranging from the kind of academic idealist that Wilson was supposed to be and isn't, to real hell-fire bloodthirsty scoundrels," but Lenin had "carried his plans out as the result of a long and intensely held political ideal and, although coldly, without vindictiveness."

National and class hatreds engulfed Europe from Portugal to the Urals in 1919. Class distinctions had collapsed on French trains; people frankly voiced communist sympathies or hopes for the American president at the conference. Discerning a sense of brotherhood between the soldiers of the allied armies, in another letter Wilson told his father of his good fortune to have had, in the enlisted man's uniform, a passport "to the vast debate of the people of the Western World on the conditions of their life and the hopes of their future." To Dell he declared himself a socialist who expected to live in Greenwich Village and find a job in journalism, perhaps at *The New Republic*. Walter Lippmann, one of the editors, was too close to the administration from Wilson's point of view, but there was a good literary section, with reviewers allowed to go their own way.

To Bishop, who wrote of perhaps studying at Oxford, Wilson replied that he preferred the University of Paris, but his superiors denied him permission to enroll there on the grounds, he told his father, that he was indispensable, though soon afterward announcing that their work was done. The headquarters unit prepared to leave Chaumont June 1 and for once in his experience the army met its schedule, because Pershing arrived and, seeing that nothing was going on, cleared everyone out. "Lieutenant Franklin" closes with the sentiment that "there's only just one country to go back to—and to stay in and to never leave!" When the cruiser *North Carolina* steamed into New York harbor as the sun set on a calm evening in July, Wilson was glad to have left "the dry tempered fields of Champagne, ploughed over with so many conflicts." He took in the "rotten salty smell of the river, the grease, the sour heat and the smoke of the factories," the rankness of the summer grass, the sounds of American voices, "the swift shuffling sounds of an American train." This sketch—incorporated in the Coney Island chapter at the end of *I Thought of Daisy*—strikingly anticipates Fitzgerald's tribute to "the fresh green breast of the new world" at the end of *Gatsby*. Wilson catches his breath in the lyrical appreciation of "my own, my native land" that bound modernists of the 1920s to the American past and has separated them from their successors in a more fragmented culture.

Although he was physically unscathed by the war, what he found at home completed the dark aspect of his experience at Vittel. Uncle Reuel had regressed into a second childhood and been hospitalized, and he died the April before Wilson's return. Wilson was eager to see Sandy, from whom he'd had an intelligent, cheerful letter. Declining to go back to medical school, Sandy had lived for a while in Washington, only able to get work at a military hospital lab and then in the Chemical Warfare Service. He returned to New York and found a place around the corner from his sister and her new husband and a job in Putnam's bookstore, where Fitzgerald and Dell bought books from him. In his letter Sandy wishes there was a more genuine spiritual morality and tells Wilson not to "be surprised if when you come home you find me a Christian." Mischievously, he warns his cousin, "Please don't sit down and write one of those long styleless serious essays about what is wrong with the world or I will endeavor to see that you are detained at Ellis Island," closing, "I miss you most horribly in spite of my failure to write, as there are so many things to talk over that can't be talked over with anyone else." As children they'd been inseparable, and this letter suggests what a wonderful companion Wilson would have had had things turned out differently.

When Mrs. Wilson visited the discharge camp on Long Island she told her son that Sandy had been institutionalized following a mental breakdown. In *The Twenties* Wilson recalls this as "a shock that I had difficulty absorbing." Going to see his cousin when demobilized and again in August, expecting that he'd soon be released from the hospital, the second time Wilson found Sandy "much worse," much more depressed. Attributing to his cousin his own capacity to be gripped by indecision, he wrote to his mother, "It was partly, apparently, that he was worrying about what he was going to do when he got out, which made him gloomy." Yet Sandy "partly retained his intelligence," writing "a story in which he figured as the inadequate son of a great old king" which suggests that Uncle Reuel's death had pushed him over the edge. He was transferred to a hospital in Riverdale "for discipline," and on a visit by his sister and his friend Eberhard Faber was described as "quite cheerful now." Wilson, intuiting the worst, learned he'd been sent for observation to the state hospital at Wingdale, where he was diagnosed with schizophrenia—what doctors then called *dementia praecox*—and soon "passed into eclipse," Wilson's pain implicit in his rare use of euphemism. Mental illness had appeared on the seemingly stable side of his family, and this "amputation of a whole relation" was for long "felt as something of a trauma." The loss would be renewed each time he visited the grim state hospital over the years, meetings sketched in the diaries. On one such occasion in 1952, when there'd been flickers of Sandy's "old smile and characteristic little giggle" beneath the coarsened manner and expressionless face, Wilson "wanted to weep as I was walking away."

In mid-August 1919 he moved into a place on West Twelfth Street in New York with his old apartment-mates. Stanley, now married to Marion Cleveland and working on the *Evening Sun*, was living at his father's house in Greenwich, Connecticut, and through the couple Wilson met John Amen, a longtime friend eventually to be—unfortunately for Wilson—his tax lawyer. John Andersen, his army buddy, came to town and was taken down to Princeton to see Gauss, who wrote a letter to Columbia on his behalf. Nothing would come of this, and Andersen eventually became a farmer in Canada, writing numerous books that Wilson recommended to his contacts, one of which was published.

At Vittel he had longed for the peace that made literature possible. During the fall of 1919, leading a quiet life and going to the Yale Club daily for dinner, he wrote steadily and, not letting rejection slips unnerve or discourage him, made a list of magazines and systematically circulated everything he'd written. Certain pieces were never printed. In a dialogue indebted to Shaw and Renan, set at GHQ, the Angel Raphael is a private who has been mapping Europe's chaos and summons mankind to the struggle to become the rational and moral beings they claim to be; then the officers lock him up as crazy. The published work includes the quatrains, after Simonides, at the graves of soldiers in France. The one that echoes the Gettysburg Address in a skeptical take on the nation's purposes in World War I is the germ of Wilson's questioning of Lincoln's cause in *Patriotic Gore*. The scathing verses called "The New Patriotism" attack the postwar Palmer raids and the Red scare of 1919–1920. Theodore Roosevelt's son, a lieutenant colonel active in the American Legion, proposed that war veterans be involved in "Americanizing" the foreign-born of New York State. Wilson doubted that men "who only yesterday / Learned not to ask but to obey, / And, netted in a narrow mesh / Opposed the guns with living flesh," could forget

> The strands of that steel-woven net—
> How they were bullied and inspected,
> Court-martialled, censored, and suspected;
> How they said "sir" and snapped their hats
> To save the world for democrats.

That he found his father's position on these subjects to be much like his own helped bring about their rapprochement. At the discharge camp he'd been "unexpectedly proud" when Wilson Sr., grumbling about the bureaucratic mess and informed by an officer that this was subversive talk, retorted, "The inefficiency of you army people is an outrage against the taxpaying citizens." Having typecast his father as a reactionary, Wilson was gratified when he attacked the arrests without warrant and the indiscriminate expulsion of radicals, stating, too, that socialism in Europe and Russia was no threat to the United States, where the law protected individual rights and opportunities.

The war years created a gulf between Wilson and Bellinger. Alfred had been in charge of a troop train where the soldiers were in boxcars and the officers in third-class carriages, and outraged Wilson by remarking that the officers suffered grievously from the cold. Wilson put him into a story as a smug man excessively pious about Yale (he was Skull and Bones), then sent the manuscript off for permission to publish. Bellinger responded reasonably enough, accepting the satire while noting it was risky to confide to Wilson things one didn't want to see in print, a thought that would occur to more than one friend when the journals appeared posthumously. Alfred complained that "these last half dozen years I have felt myself being carefully, dispassionately, and thoroughly analyzed by a man who was determined that no phase of human experience should escape him"; he thought it "too awful if you've no other use for people than making of clever analyses which are almost tragic from being so nearly right." With this letter he sent on what purports to be a preface, written after Wilson's death, to his "History of the Literatures of the World," attributing the author's dogmatism to the lack of intellectual competition at Princeton, where "he not unnaturally dropped into the habit of considering himself infallible." So Bellinger burlesqued the role of biographer Wilson had assigned to him on leaving Hill, in a context unforeseen by either of them.

Loyalty to the men he saw suffer and die had changed Wilson and made it impossible to accept this friend's complacent assumption of privilege. The allegiance that, at the end of the flu epidemic, he'd sworn to literature and history, beauty and truth, was high-flown, but these years, he would recall at seventy-two, had separated him from "the habits and standards of even the most cultivated elements of the world in which I had lived," a world that now appeared "too narrowly limited by its governing principles and prejudices." To know he could get along with ordinary people was liberating. From France he had written to his father that everybody in the army, if not too old for it, ought to be an enlisted man for a certain length of time—"It enables all kinds of people to meet on an absolute social and financial equality, and, while it lasts, at least, eliminates snobbishness and self-consciousness completely."

Wilson's portrait of Justice Holmes in *Patriotic Gore*, written in his sixties, contains the observation that "for a young man who has always lived comfortably and accepted the security of convention, it may be an educational advantage for him to see his society with the bottom knocked out, its most honored institutions threatened and its members, irrespective of class, thrown together in conflict to the death or in obligatory cooperation." Among Wilson's contemporaries were those, like his New York apartment-mates, who left the old universities with the same grounding in the classics and the Enlightenment, as eager as he for careers in the arts, but soon enough returned to a family business or profession, and to the country club. At the stone house in Talcottville in 1963 Wilson dismissed the idea that he was abler or had cared more about writing than his college circle. He'd benefited by the professional code of his father and his Uncle Reuel, and had been seasoned by viewing the war as a private. "The others," he said, "stayed with their class."

PART TWO

The Twenties

5

Vanity Fair, Mencken, and Edna St. Vincent Millay

Vanity Fair, with its clever drawings, stylized photographs of actresses, singers, and writers, and reports on the New York artistic scene amid glossy advertising for clothes, cars, customized cigarettes, diamond necklaces, and European tours, was the most successful of the "smart" magazines of the 1920s, its circulation sometimes as high as 80,000. Like *The New Yorker*, which would be created by Harold Ross and William Shawn, it published distinguished writers, including Conrad, Cocteau, Eliot, and Arthur Symons. Talented young people, taken on to read manuscripts and do compressed, ironical captions for the photographs, as Wilson was in 1919, were allowed to write for the magazine. They were never paid much but—like Clare Boothe Luce, for example—often left "to be important somewhere else."

A monthly, *Vanity Fair* mirrored the personality of the editor. Frank Crowninshield, the product of a distinguished Boston family, a childhood among artists in Paris and Rome, and the New York literary trade, was tall and dapper—he always wore a carnation in his buttonhole—with an elegant mustache and watchful brown eyes. Crownie was master of what Robert Benchley, then managing editor, called "the Elevated Eyebrow school of journalism. You could write about any subject you wished, no matter how outrageous, if you said it in evening clothes." His office was resplendent with flowerpots and books on the shelves, drawings and stacks of photographs around the base of the walls. He cultivated celebrities from European writers to Charlie Chaplin and Houdini, and was attentive, too, to the New York debutante who dreamt of getting into the kickline at the Follies. The magazine was "a crazy place, with everybody laughing all the time." Regularly the editor tore up the slips of paper on which an efficiency expert hired by Condé Nast set down exactly how many minutes each staff member was late arriving at work. Yet working for Crowninshield had its tensions.

When Wilson submitted his collegiate parody of literary biography and the fin de siècle, "The Last Remains of Edward Moore Gresham," Dorothy Parker, then making a name with her drama criticism and light verse, liked the wit and took the piece to her boss, who asked its author to drop by the offices at the Berkeley Building on West Forty-fourth Street. He "was apparently not over eighteen," though with all the presence of "an ordained and fully accredited acolyte" of literature. A storied office upheaval gave him a much better job. Parker, Robert Benchley, and their friend Robert Sherwood were agitating to get their salaries raised. Told not to discuss this, they wore placards around their necks that on one side said "Don't ask," on the other spelled out what they earned. Sherwood was soon fired, and when Parker wrote that the actress Billie Burke had "bad ankles" and threw herself about the stage like a burlesque performer, Burke's offended husband, Florenz Ziegfeld, went to Nast, who made Crowninshield stop her from further drama reviews. She resigned in a huff, Benchley, in sympathy, followed, and Wilson was offered the job of managing editor at $45 a week, considerably less than Benchley's salary of $100.

John Bishop was soon brought in as Wilson's assistant, and within a year the two were rotating in the position, each thus able to continue his writing and find time for a private life. Jeanne Ballot, who became Crowninshield's secretary in 1920, admired the Princetonians, who among other things wrote notes to each other in Latin. She had a crush on Bishop, who dressed immaculately and seemed to her a gentle dandy. Wilson "had a wonderful profile, like a statue," Ballot said sixty years later, adding "I was learning too, and every morning he would fix my ignorance. He would sit down and educate me." In an unpublished memoir she elaborates: "'Miss Ballot'—we were all very formal—'who was Henri Bergson?' he would ask, and I'd say, 'Wasn't he the fingerprint man?'—thinking of Bertillon—upon which he would give me a little lecture on Bergson." The proper secretary, whose father escorted her to work every day, was thrilled by one of Crowninshield's games with the staff, the daringly flirtatious routine called "The Rape of the Sabine Women": "Mr. Bishop would pick me up and dash across the room and Mr. Wilson would pick up another girl and dash madly at us. The word *rape* was tabu in those days and I never told my family about this. Once, Mr. Bishop threw out his shoulder during this game, and we were all panic-stricken."

At the Algonquin, where Parker and Benchley introduced Wilson to the celebrated Round Table, Alexander Woollcott was at first brusque. But when he learned that the Doctor Kimball who'd delivered him was the young man's grandfather and the "Lawyer Wilson" who had rescued an uncle from bankruptcy was his father, he was welcome among the wits wisecracking at the table in the Pergola room. Often the talk was of Ring Lardner, at the peak of his fame as a writer of humorous short stories. A morose and saturnine figure, Lardner kept his distance in Great Neck, reminding Wilson (in a Calvinist metaphor) of an invisible, unforgiving god who regards his followers with a certain scorn. Wilson came to regard the Algonquinites just as sternly. He never liked literary cliques and, in a retrospective emendation in *The Twenties,* Heywood Broun is characterized as a phony and George S. Kaufman as a self-promoter, whom many thought a plagiarist. There Wilson recalls suggesting that Benchley try serious satire. He may have been jealous of Benchley, who was Dorothy Parker's companion, her partner in what the sign on the door of the office where they proposed to write identified as the Eureka Nut and Bolt Company.

Parker was Wilson's first female writer friend. Petite and well-dressed, with intense eyes behind her horn-rimmed glasses, she delivered her wicked remarks in a gentle voice, but the way she doused herself in perfume kept him from "paying her court." She is the "partly Irish" Kay Burke of the short novel Wilson wrote in 1941–1942, published in 1998 as *The Higher Jazz.* Kay "had a great nose for social class and always dropped her Broadway manner and gave a passable imitation of something else when any breeze from Park Avenue was sniffed." At their parties her group "drank highballs, talked show and magazine business and exchanged the kind of jokes they esteemed—from lunch at about two to four o'clock the next morning." After that she'd sober up for a week and "sit up all one night at her typewriter" producing a monthly article "which her admirers would read with raptures." This was not the balance Wilson envisioned between the toil and the orgy, but in *The Twenties* he returns to Dorothy's gossip and her puns. Like so many whom he'd know over the years, "she was beglamored by the idea of Scott Fitzgerald," and a meeting was arranged with Scott and his bride, Zelda. In the tone of the period she characterized the four of them on a long bench beside a table at the Algonquin as "a road company of the Last Supper."

John Dos Passos remembered meeting Wilson by the elevators at *Vanity Fair*, a "slight sandyheaded young man with a handsome clear profile" who accented their introduction "by turning, with a perfectly straight face, a neat somersault." Wilson's criticism in the magazine was spritely, the reviews ranging from Paris and Bloomsbury to the new American writers, the essays setting European freedoms against the Victorian mores of his own country. James, though he "understood Europe with the last intelligence," is seen inhibited by the fetish of refinement among educated Americans of his time, while Hawthorne determinedly prefers William Wetmore Story's statue of Cleopatra in a toga to the naked beauty of the Venus de Milo. Freud had grown fashionable, and Wilson promoted the *General Introduction to Psychoanalysis*. Against the irrationality of World War I and the multiplying neuroses of his patients Wilson sets "the Freud whom Havelock Ellis has described as essentially an artist, the extraordinary Viennese Jew with his rare equipment of combined creative imagination and scientific passion for truth." Marx would be similarly described in *Finland Station*.

In other early pieces Wilson echoes Mencken's *Prejudices*, stating an aversion to afternoon tea, ocean cruises, Eddie Cantor, youth, the artistic possibilities of the movies, summer, weddings, motoring, crocheted ties, and the country ("I am not one who has been able to find books in the running brooks"). Smuggling criticism into this format, he promotes "underrated" Edith Wharton and balances Kipling's strengths and limitations. He was excited to meet the man whose defiance of genteel provincialism had opened the way for the writers of the twenties. At college, reading Mencken had inspired his wish to work in "our own field," and in France, Mencken's account of the broad, square-syllabled speech he called *The American Language* led Wilson and a friend to compile a glossary of army slang, which Mencken drew on in a subsequent edition. The older man generously took Wilson under his wing. In shirtsleeves and with his feet on his desk, a bottle of gin at hand, he suggested how to improve Wilson's radical antiwar stories and encouraged the tale of schoolboy sexual initiation called "Galahad," though the bedroom scene was too explicit for Mencken's journal *The Smart Set*. He got the young critic freelance reviewing at the *Baltimore Sun* and offered to get him a job there.

In a June 1921 sketch in *The New Republic* Wilson values the color and force of Mencken's prose and his saturation in American life. He was "a genuine artist and man of first-rate education and intelligence" for all his remoteness from James, Wharton, and Henry Adams. Likening Mencken to the Puritan preachers he lambasted, Wilson states that in his work Puritanism and American manners had come of age, going halfway to meet the larger world. He made poetry of the democratic scene "which absorbs and infuriates him." Wilson contrasts Mencken's comic inventory of ignorance and exploitation to some lines from *Song of Myself*, the expansive poetry of a fresher pastoral America. This article delighted its subject, who—in a letter Wilson showed off to friends—said, "No one has ever done me before on so lavish a scale, or with so persuasive an eloquence. A little more and you would have persuaded even me."

By mid-decade, when Walter Lippmann called Mencken "the most powerful personal influence on this whole generation of educated people," Wilson would not be so reverent, saying that his raillery against the boobs let conventional readers enjoy an easy feeling of superiority. When *Notes on Democracy* appeared in 1926, its confused Nietzscheanism made Wilson wonder whether the strength and superiority Mencken celebrated were those of Beethoven or of the heavyweight champion Jack Johnson. In the meantime, unlike the older man, Wilson was giving major figures of the American twenties their place on the literary stage while absorbing Joyce and Eliot, Proust and Yeats. Wilson would push for a radical transformation of American society during the Depression, while the German affiliations that had helped Mencken break the hold of Anglophiles on the culture took him to the Right. But Wilson carried on Mencken's work of making prudery and naiveté unfashionable. Both rejected Christianity— Dos Passos kidded his friend as Dr. Anti-Christ, a role Mencken had pioneered—and believed that intellectuals should stay at their native posts while alert to art and ideas from abroad.

To Mencken's account of the mediocrity of American culture and conviction of the need for something better, Wilson would recall that Van Wyck Brooks added "historical perspective and an analysis of the causes of what was wrong." Brooks stirred Wilson's idealism in the last words of *The Ordeal of Mark Twain*, calling Americans "to put away childish things and walk the stage as poets do." In *America's Coming-of-Age* he had deplored both the narrow refinement of New England and a commercial society's effects on the life of the mind. Following this model, which set Jonathan Edwards against Benjamin Franklin, Wilson contrasted James and Henry Adams to Mark Twain and Dreiser in an article called "The Gulf in American Literature." He corrected Brooks's influence as he did Mencken's. In

"The Delegate from Great Neck" (1924), one of several staged intellectual conversations in which he puts words in the mouths of opposing figures, Brooks the moralizing highbrow confronts Fitzgerald, cast as eager, trendy spokesman for the younger generation. Fitzgerald invites him to a party, but he is unable to "come down." A published piece of his biography of James seemed to Wilson perverse: arguing that James was ruined by expatriation, it converted the story of a great novelist "who happened to be an American" into "the tragedy of an American who was rash enough to try to become a novelist."

As Bishop and Wilson settled into their jobs, they collaborated on a collection of verse and prose about death in the modern world called *The Undertaker's Garland*, a talky version of the somber themes to which Eliot gave lasting expression in *The Waste Land*, which appeared later the same year. Typed by Jeanne Ballot and published by Knopf, the book was illustrated by the Beardsleyan drawings of Boris Artzybasheff, and Bishop's lush romantic poems echo the nineties, though he has also read Eliot. Wilson's exuberant verse recalls that of the unfortunate Gresham. His preface moves from slaughter in the trenches to the failure of love and devaluation of art in the business world. His bitter story "Death of a Soldier" is followed by "Emily in Hades," which signalizes the moment when debutantes turned conventional wives took off their shoes to dance on tabletops. Emily misses out. She dies young and wakes in the underworld, one of those "souls buried in sullen shadows underground / That reach forever toward the shores of light," these last words a translation of Virgil's *ad luminas oras*, a phrase Wilson also used in a poem about Edna St. Vincent Millay.

Nearing twenty-five, the precocious intellectual had had no sexual experience. Ever since Millay's famous poem "Renascence" had reached him in France, he had wanted to meet the poet who portrayed herself as buried alive, yet embraced the world with passion. Reciting her defiance of Apollo's arrows in the shower, he thought he might be worthy "to deal her the longed-for dart." Wilson's memoir in *The Shores of Light* looks back to the April evening when Millay dropped in on a Greenwich Village party after a performance with the Provincetown Players. "She was dressed in some bright batik, and her face lit up with a flush that seemed to burn also in the bronze reflections of her not yet bobbed reddish hair. She was one of those women whose features are not perfect and who in their moments of dimness may not seem even pretty, but who, excited by the blood or the spirit, become almost supernaturally beautiful." When she threw back her head to recite that night, she had "a beautiful, long throat" that "gave her the look of a muse," and a voice with a thrilling timbre. Millay was not, as her biographers claim, the woman Wilson loved most, but her dramatic presence would resonate in his mind for thirty years, portrayed in poems, a novel, his journals, and his memoir. In *The Twenties* he states, "Edna ignited for me both my intellectual passion and my unsatisfied desire, which went up together in a blaze of ecstasy that remains for me one of the high points of my life."

She had grown up in a world of female affection. The strongest relationship in her life was with her mother, a matriarch who to Wilson resembled a New England schoolteacher but with something "almost raffish" about her, which showed itself in such startling remarks as "I was a slut myself; so no wonder my daughters are." Cora Millay, who divorced when Edna was eight, lived through her eldest daughter, who was herself devoted to her sisters, Norma and Kathleen, as well as to classmates at Vassar. After graduating from college at the advanced age of twenty-five Edna moved to the Village, where she acted in Floyd Dell's plays and became his lover. There is an image of her "running around the corner of MacDougal Street, flushed and laughing 'like a nymph,' with her hair swinging" and Dell, also laughing, in pursuit, figures from Keats's Grecian Urn come to life. She corresponded with the poet Arthur Davidson Ficke, and when they finally met on his way to France as an officer, they fell in love. Ficke was married, and she later offered to marry his homosexual friend Witter Bynner. By 1920, established as the rakish princess of the world below Fourteenth Street, she was shamelessly flirting on the page and sleeping with one man after another. The carefree verse of her *A Few Figs from Thistles*—"We were very tired, we were very merry, / We went back and forth all night on the ferry"—defined a cultural moment when everything seemed possible.

For Wilson, Millay gave feminine form to the heroic voice of literature. He responded to the tones of English romanticism from Keats to Housman and Hopkins in her work. They were deepened by her art of performance—"The Poet and His Book," on the page melodramatic and inflated, stirred him. He got to know her by promoting her poetry at *Vanity Fair*, and his memoir credits Crowninshield with bringing her to a larger public. Bishop too was soon smitten, and Crownie liked to complain of the difficulty of having both his assistants in love with one of his most

brilliant contributors. It wasn't easy for them when, on a Fifth Avenue
bus, she recited a sonnet about a more successful lover, "Here Is a Wound
That Never Will Heal, I Know." Wilson, however, thought poetry her real
passion and credited her with a "disarming impartiality" among her suitors. She called these two "the choirboys of Hell," innocent votaries of the
goddess of fallen love, and protested that their "both being in love with
her" hadn't set them at odds.

One night at the beginning of June the trio did self-portraits in verse.
Edna's lines—which her sister Norma thought too "lewd" to be circulated—
are provocative, moving from "A large mouth, / Lascivious" to

> A small body
> Unexclamatory,
> But which,
> Were it the fashion to wear no clothes,
> Would be as well-dressed
> As any.

The handsome Bishop is less pleased with his appearance, having a forehead too broad, "eyes meaningless and grey," and a "torso" that seems
"maladroit and charged with lust"—a phrase that in Millay's handwriting
has been corrected to "eagerly male." Wilson accents his historical intelligence. Writing on the back of a note from Fitzgerald asking him to cash a
check and wire the money ahead to Greenville, South Carolina, he makes
himself an heir both of Romanticism and of the Age of Reason:

> He could have been happy in the XVIIIth century,
> Before the Romantic Revival . . .
> But now Byron has spoken
> And the damage has been done;
> He cannot rest quietly among his books
> For thirst of dramatizing himself.

Briskly self-critical, he confides that he loves to attack the forces of reaction because he thinks he has a gift for invective. But through this playful
exercise Millay was deciding which one to bed first, and the intellectual
approach didn't win the day. Edna and John very soon thereafter became
lovers.

Without any idea of what he was getting into, the sexually more experienced Bishop was emotionally crippled by this affair, something Wilson, himself for the better part of a year "demoralized," never understood. In a letter tendering his love on Millay's terms Bishop believes "that your desire works strangely like a man's. And that desire has few secrets from me." Yet he sees that it will be difficult to have her "come to me from someone and leave for someone else," wonders whether she doesn't "hurt for sheer pleasure in hurting," fears something in him "may be wounded or shattering in the process." Toward the end of the month John was cordially invited to the Cape for the Fourth of July weekend. Meanwhile Edna spent a day or two at Lake Placid and three weeks at an artists' colony at Woodstock, New York, where she had her hair bobbed and had an affair with the tenor Luigi Laurenti, who had a "divine" voice.

At the office Wilson received a business note with a flirtatious ending, thanking him for his sweetness to someone who was "after all a weaker vessel." Late in July, apparently between assignations with Bishop, Edna proposed a meeting with him in New York. Perhaps it was at this time that, believing he'd been "innocent long enough," he awkwardly bought a condom from a druggist on Greenwich Avenue, who to demonstrate its virtues inflated one until it burst, an omen, Wilson would one day reflect, of disasters to come: "abortions, gonorrhea, entanglements, a broken heart." On the last point he did not exaggerate. Remembering, in *The Sixties*, "when I had made love to her for the first time in my life to anyone," he recalls Edna's summation: "I know just how you feel: it was here, and it was beautiful, and now it's gone!" At any rate, she was soon gone herself, without saying where.

Over the next weeks, in seven urgent notes and letters long buried in the archives, Wilson reveals himself as a man obsessed. The first day he urges her to come back to town, ending, "I love you," and in a second note asks, if she is still in New York, to "please be decent and call me up. Otherwise, you'll leave me pretty flat." He then addresses her at the Cape—where Bishop was arriving for the weekend—asking when he can come up: "I suppose all this is pretty casual to you, but it's not to me, as you know." Having been unable, he says, to talk with her about his feelings, he can now only "stupidly" write them, saying he spends the time "composing arguments" to convince her to marry him. In reply Millay calls him "false" to expect more than she had offered, but ruefully says, "I have thought of you often, Bunny, and wonder if you think of me with bitterness." His final letter insists she is necessary "to the deepest part of me—the part that has always been lonely before, the part that has scarcely ever felt dependence on another person." He had stood apart from life—which compared to art "already filled me with contempt and with impatience at its stupidity," he declares as if he were Henry James—and fears his concentration will be impossible to recover. Though he may someday be "the lover of a hundred women," her memory will continue to "hurt my heart." He adds, "You have taken down the prison where my flame was burning and how, if you leave me or forget me, shall I ever get it back in its prison again and make it burn steadily alone?" The letter breaks off without a signature.

Wilson's memoir recollects with self-deprecating humor his weekend at Provincetown before Labor Day. Arriving in his turn on the slow, shuffling train, he gets lost in a field and drags his suitcase across the dunes "through scrub-oak and sweetfern in the breathless hot August night" until he sees the light of the house the Millays rented from the liberated Greek professor Jig Cook and his feminist wife Susan Glaspell. He recalls the impression made by Edna's mother, thought Norma and Kathleen very pretty, and admired the three sisters' jolly song about male faithlessness. Though Edna later encouraged him to drink, saying he was more attractive than when sober, either Kathleen or Norma told friends that Wilson refused coffee, a cigarette, and a drink, declaring that "he never drank." The couple repaired to the porch swing, where, tormented by mosquitoes, they remained long enough for him formally to propose and her to decline. It would "haunt" him that she said something like, "That might be the solution." The next morning they walked on the beach, and in *The Forties* he recalls stealing a kiss behind a bush. "By the time we're fifty years old," he suggested, "we'll be two of the most interesting people in the United States." Millay, the apostle of spontaneous youth, replied, "You behave as if you were fifty already."

"Modern Sappho, 18 love affairs, and now Bunny is thinking of marrying her," Alec McKaig wrote in his diary in September, suggesting Wilson's ignorance of Edna's openness also to lesbian experiences. Wilson first told this urbane classmate that Edna might possibly marry him because he had a small income, then that John and he were unpleasantly at odds, eventually that he couldn't work nights anymore and spent hours doing magic tricks before the mirror. He had no idea that, according to the biographer Daniel Epstein—who perceives Bishop's centrality in this triangle—she was now sleeping with three other men and, along with

drinking heavily, used morphine. Her stance of reckless bravado, however, collapsed before Wilson's eyes that fall. She took a two-room apartment with her sister Kathleen, where she was exposed to her suitors'
constant demands, then moved to "a wretched cold little one room,"
forced to share a bathroom with other tenants. He helped care for her
through one or two "depressing illnesses," bringing her a heater and typing for her when she couldn't get out of bed, evidence that he might indeed have been the solution. In a robe and under her shabby covers she
listened while he read aloud "immortal page after page conceived in a
mortal mind." Millay depicts this scene in the poem "Portrait," where the
nameless lover is bitter she won't marry him.

In fact she was pining away for Ficke, himself now in love with someone else—that "malady of the ideal" which Proust would sum up for the
1920s—and she continued to have assignations with Bishop, who pursued her desperately as her interest waned. In November, when "farcical
mishaps" had disrupted their schedule, John, knowing she was "dis-
traught for someone else," finally said, "It's no good. The lie is played out
as far as I am concerned." He would never know that, perhaps by him,
she'd become pregnant. Nancy Milford, for her biography, was informed
by Norma that in December Edna had a "botched" abortion, leaving her
"bloody and weakened." Whoever had been her partner, she had every
reason not to want to make love with John.

When a doctor recommended she go abroad, Crowninshield made
the trip possible by paying her to leave behind a series of light pieces for
Vanity Fair written under the pseudonym Nancy Boyd. Wilson helped
produce these on memorable nights of bootleg gin and exhilarating talk.
His journal depicts a reunion with John on "our old high and festive basis" before she sailed for France in January 1921. Wilson writes, "After dinner, sitting on her day bed, John and I held Edna in our arms—according
to an arrangement insisted upon by herself—I her lower half and John
her upper—with a polite exchange of pleasantries as to which had the
better share." Epstein converts this into an image of simultaneous lovemaking ("the three wound up in the bed together") and—via Millay's
famous quatrain about burning the candle at both ends—into a "*ménage-
à-trois*" that had been going on since May. In fact, she was orchestrating a
symbolic embrace, with their different attractions carefully neutralized,
and the choirboys seem to have been as innocent in their behavior that
last evening as each was of what she'd been through.

Wilson's heartbreak is documented in bad romantic verse he warns readers of *The Twenties* to skip. Yet the following spring he was seeing another woman, and he had some perspective on Millay when he took a vacation in Paris that June. Crowninshield had called on her there—giving her introductions to Edith Wharton, Dorothy Thompson, and G. K. Chesterton among others—and thought her run-down, but when Wilson showed up she seemed healthy and soignée, receiving him "in a serious black dress" before "her typewriter and a pile of manuscripts," speaking of her writing projects and her resolve to cease "breaking hearts and spreading havoc." It soon turned out she was happily occupied with the British journalist John Slocombe, who was in process of abandoning his wife and children for her. In *The Twenties* Wilson recalls that they walked and talked in the Bois de Boulogne, and that at a later meeting Edna asked him to take her to the South of France. He declined, knowing she "would leave me for anyone who seemed more attractive." To Bishop he declared that it was all over—"When I looked at her, it was like staring into the center of an extinct volcano"—adding, "These are old Dr. Wilson's last words on the chief maelstrom of his early years."

The volcano was scarcely extinct, though all three married within the year. John was first to fall away. When Wilson wrote to Edna with this news she replied with some pseudo-Chaucerian verses "on the occasion of John the Bishop's *triste perditioun*." Wilson's "*douce billet*" by her pillow, with its "courteous words" and "salty wit," had, she added, turned her "herde heart into milk," leaving her with "no evyll thought, but many a wystful onne." She then offered up (what seems an "evyll thought") the "pious pagan prayer that one of these days you'll become a dirty inveterate souse, and bully your wife and beat your kids and kick your dog, and think of me with steadfast love."

The next year Edna married urbane, protective Eugen Boissevain, widower of the feminist Inez Milholland. On her wedding day she entered the hospital for an operation—"on her intestines—for congenital stoppages," Wilson later reported to Bishop, saying she still seemed unwell. He had "found her drinking gin and reading William Morris on the top floor" of the narrow house on Bedford Street, the smallest house in the Village, which the Dutch importer had bought for them. She was "all alone and with really an air of having allowed herself at last to be attended to and put away and forbidden to see people." If she needed the tolerant Boissevain's protection, that year she won the Pulitzer Prize for *The Harp Weaver* and some poems from *A Few Figs from Thistles*, the first woman so honored for poetry. Her reading tour was a triumph, and she and Gene returned from a six-month world cruise to acquire their 435-acre farm 110 miles north of the city, refurbishing the old farmhouse they called Steepletop. A letter to Wilson upon moving in—"This is just a snowball at your window—I can't write letters"—sketches their country scene and insists, "I'm getting stronger, Bunny."

He would rationalize his inability to win her in *I Thought of Daisy* (1929), characterizing the poet Rita as beyond the ordinary happiness of men and women, her work derived from her sexual compulsions. "Any great strength or excellence of character must be, by its very nature, incompatible with qualities of other kinds," he proposes here, anticipating the portraiture of *The Wound and the Bow*. This account of Edna was colored by the romantic ending of Taine's *History of English Literature*, which, Wilson remembered, around that time so absorbed him that he read it while walking down the street. Here the French critic chooses the bohemian poet Musset over lordly Tennyson ensconced on the Isle of Wight, in a passage that affirms the creative role of pain and suffering.

If too much of Millay is sentimental and shallow, evaporating on the page, she could rely on him for support as well as honest criticism when she became a victim of the radical shift in taste brought about by Eliot and other moderns. "Your verdict was like an Imprimatur to me," she writes when he likes some poems, agreeing that others are second- or third-rate. It was Wilson who introduced her to three women poets who became loyal friends, Elinor Wylie, Louise Bogan, and Leonie Adams. She would justify her admirers' faith in *Fatal Interview*, distilling a vision of life and love and loss within the constraints of the sonnet form:

> Love is not all: it is not meat nor drink
> Nor slumber nor a roof against the rain,
> Nor yet a floating spar to men that sink
> And rise and sink and rise and sink again;
> Love cannot fill the thickened lung with breath,
> Nor clean the blood, nor set the fractured bone;
> Yet many a man is making friends with death
> Even as I speak, for lack of love alone.
> It may well be that in a difficult hour,
> Pinned down by pain and moaning for release,
> Or nagged by want past resolution's power,

I might be driven to sell your love for peace,
Or trade the memory of this night for food.
It may well be. I do not think I would.

Wilson thought the sequence that contains this sonnet and the lavish tribute to eros, "Oh, sleep forever in the Latmian cave, / Mortal Endymion,
darling of the Moon!" the finest ever written by an American. Attempting
to couple her with Yeats as great lyric poets of an age of prose, he over-
praises his old love, but his memoir helps one correlate such verse with
the intoxicating effect Millay had on people and the magnanimity that,
despite her narcissism, they saw in her. It lessens the danger that, in a
world in which her formalism remains out of style while her private life
has a lurid appeal, she will be reduced—as a reviewer of two biographies
of Millay suggests—to "a resplendent casualty of sex, drugs, and fame."

What Wilson's desperate letter calls the breakdown of his solitude
would cause their relationship to reverberate in his mind and thus in literary history. When they met during the mid- and late-1920s he rose
again to her allure. Two decades later, visiting Millay with his new wife,
Elena, at Steepletop, the middle-aged critic scarcely recognized the heroine of his youth, and her dependence on her husband was childlike. "The
whole thing was like one of those dreams that I had never quite ceased to
have, in which I found myself with Edna again—though in these dreams
she had sometimes seemed faded and shrunken, never ruddy and overblown as I saw her now," he'd write in his memoir, and in the journal
reflect that to live only in the moment, whether for passion or art, "produced dreadful disabilities and bankruptcies later." In the darkened living
room he asked her to recite "The Poet and His Book," which had once
moved him with its "rushed phrases and powerful images," its "deep sonori-
ties of sorrow and wonder," and when she did so she again seemed heroic,
"groping back *in luminas oras* from the night of the underworld." What
she'd said of their love so many years before—that "it was here, and it was
beautiful, and now it's gone!"—had not proved true for him.

6

Coming of Age

The dream of the college group making careers together was fading. After Bishop accepted the hopelessness of his situation with Millay, he wearied of *Vanity Fair* and New York. In the spring of 1921 the heiress Margaret Hutchins began pursuing him. Wilson disapproved of the match. Acknowledging a "strong physical passion" between the pair, to Dell he characterized Hutchins as "a prime dumbbell" whose "passionate gentility and correctitude" would thwart their friend's freedom to write, and to Fitzgerald he predicted she might "lead John around by the balls." But John, having abased himself to Edna, was prepared to be taken over by someone who loved and wanted him. In an extraordinary love letter to Millay in December 1921, he confessed that her image continued to stand between him and other women, yet he married Margaret seven months later.

Dell had married first. For a while he and Marion Cleveland lived in Princeton, but when high mountain air seemed indicated for what he believed was a case of tuberculosis similar to his mother's, they moved to a resort hotel in Colorado Springs. "Stanley is so brave and shows such a lovely spirit," Marion enthused to Wilson. A new acquaintance had given her "bookish" husband "the most beautifully bound volume" of *The Spell of the Yukon* by the inspirational writer Robert Service, now, ironically, a subject of gleeful satire among Wilson's New York friends. Stanley wrote that he was bored by "zealous disciples of the Great Healthy West." Reading widely and introspectively brooding, he complained that "the ratiocination of a New Englander irritates like a hair shirt," adding that, like water that boiled without cooking anything on Pikes Peak, "in this intellectual vacuum, my mind boils and boils, and yet, I fear, produces nothing palatable." This letter ends with the remote, even sad formality of "Yours always, Stanley Dell." Three years later the self-styled child of the Puritans would be redefining himself as a product of "the gauzy olive groves of Italy," disappearing into expatriation and neurosis.

Wilson met Zelda Sayre when she came up from Montgomery for her wedding to Scott Fitzgerald in April 1920. She was reclining on a couch in a languid pose, just as Daisy and Jordan do in *Gatsby*'s opening chapter. Wilson appreciated her "astonishing prettiness" and ersatz, sexy talk, as when she said that hotel bedrooms "excited her erotically," yet he worried she might be a disastrous choice. Writing to Gauss three weeks after the wedding, he hoped she would "seize the opportunity to run away with the elevator boy or something." His journal soon reports that "Zelda rushed into John's room just as he was going to bed and insisted that she was going to spend the night there," then "cornered Townsend [Martin] in the bathroom and demanded that he should give her a bath." However, he saw no shadow of madness in her, as would Hemingway. To Bishop in France in the fall of 1922 he cheerily says that the Fitzgeralds have stopped drinking and are behaving rationally, in "wonderful form." They've made a pact that neither will go out alone with a member of the opposite sex, and Scott is again working.

Fitzgerald and Wilson were the only two of their group still determined to succeed as professional writers and, as the decade began, they exchanged friendly gibes about each other's abilities and plans, a little like racehorses eyeing one another prior to the bolt from the gate. "No *Saturday Evening Post* stuff, understand!" Wilson wrote when inviting Scott (as he was called after college) to contribute to a proposed collection of war stories. "Brace up your artistic conscience, which was always the weakest part of your talent!" Three months later, poking fun at the sloppy self-indulgence of the first version of *This Side of Paradise*, he declared that (Joyce's *Portrait of the Artist* being an exception) "this history of a young man stuff has been run into the ground and has always seemed to me a bum art form." Scott wearied of these lectures, and when Wilson pressed him to "make something really beautiful," he responded by indicating the kind of comment he'd prefer:

    p. 10x   I find this page rotten
    p. 10y   Dull! Cut!
    p. 10z   Good! Enlarge!

p. 10a. Invert sentence I have marked (in pencil!)
p. 10b. False [crossed out] Unconvincing!
p. 10c. Confused!

———
——— Ha-ha!

Wilson would approach this kind of criticism in his reading of *The Beautiful and Damned*.

Scott was sometimes concerned for Wilson's welfare. "I have heard vague and unfathomable stories about your private life," he politely wrote a year after the pursuit of Millay ended—"romantic stories" that "make me wish to God you were not so reticent." The allusion was to Wilson's affair with Mary Blair, whom he first saw onstage in February 1921, as the desperate Emma Crosby in O'Neill's play *Diff'rent*. Slim and intense, Blair had auburn hair and large, expressive eyes, and her powerful low-pitched voice was effective in O'Neill's theater. In her publicity pictures she sometimes has a Mary Pickford look, with penciled eyebrows and bright, full lips. A caption below the photograph in *Vanity Fair*, perhaps Wilson's doing, describes her performance in *Diff'rent* as "intense and exceedingly intelligent," while a reviewer thought her best in scenes where the old spinster "is determined to have a man whether or no."

Two years younger than Wilson, Mary was from Pittsburgh and Irish in background. She had wanted to be an actress since childhood. Raised a Swedenborgian, she went to high school with Kenneth Burke, philosopher of literary form, and the historian-critic Malcolm Cowley. Cowley remembered her as a liberated schoolgirl who wore grown-up dresses, "a pre-flapper—cigarette smoking, free in her language, not giving a damn about her studies." After graduating from the new Carnegie Tech drama school she married a classmate, Charles Meredith, and Rosalind Wilson informs us that "they did some exhibition dancing together." But Meredith left her, and she got a divorce in Reno before coming to New York to join the Provincetown Players.

Offstage she had a zany humor, a relief to Wilson after Edna's nervous intensity. She favored lighthearted street slang—"It's all applesauce to me!," "I want that in writing," and "you dirty lizard" are listed among her expressions in *The Twenties*. Otherwise Mary rarely appears in the journals, but Wilson saved her letters. At the beginning of their relationship these are zesty and vibrant. She'd like to see "all of our best politicians," including President Harding, "lured" to Tahiti "under a fake illusion of the seductive powers of the South Sea Island maid." She begs to differ with Pound, who has called her friend Mina Loy his idea of a brilliant woman—Mina, she says, "loved speaking of God when swallowing two raw eggs and gorging all the food in sight."

That spring she and Wilson discussed the theater and did a good deal of drinking, and in April he wrote to Dell that he might propose. In June from the Connecticut shore, where she was performing that summer, she invokes their lovemaking: writing "in a Cinderella attic," she warns that "any strange rhythmic sensation" he may receive is an illusion, for here is "no decadent seductive atmosphere, no room with rose-colored curtains," but at the head of her bed a man's gift of "pure and white" cherry blossoms. Having fled her admirer to this virginal chamber, she assures Wilson, "I thought of you and I thought of me and I thought of love." It was what he had yearned to hear from Edna. Mary was equally reassuring when she freed him of obligation after their "happy times" together, saying, "In any event we mustn't worry about each other." When he planned a trip to France that summer he invited her to join him, apparently to counter Edna's attractions, and she had her passage booked and passport ready, then couldn't come because of an operation for what she vaguely called "a tumor."

His job at *Vanity Fair* gave Wilson a foothold in the literary world. He could speak for the cultural heritage and the young writers back from the war, could review friends as voices of the new generation and sometimes publish them. His boss was a lively character. At a banquet Crowninshield introduced the aging matinee idol John Drew as someone he had come upon outside "a deluxe cathouse" in Marseilles, apparently disputing the bill. Pretending to write to Wilson from his deathbed, he anoints the young man his chosen successor and implores him to use commas a little more often. A professional charmer, he was always sending people presents and received scores of letters in feminine handwriting, which he'd sniff in case they were scented and sort according to the implications of the perfume. Yet Crownie's favorite word was "serendipity," and he was inclined to assume that whatever sold was good. Wilson aspired to a more serious milieu, as Fitzgerald did for him.

In the spring of 1921 he tried out at *The New Republic* while Bishop held the fort at *Vanity Fair*. Walter Lippmann told him the magazine was considering hiring a managing editor. They were losing subscribers, and Lippmann confided that Herbert Croly, the founding editor, who had been an ally of Theodore Roosevelt, was sometimes out of touch. Wilson was sequentially taken to dinner by the half-dozen members of the board, each of whom confided that all the rest were "timid old maids," an opinion he shared and privately extended to the speaker, hoping they would decide they needed him. "When you become a regular editor," he wrote to Dell, "you draw a large salary and never go near the office, but stay at home and write books." However, he told Stanley it was difficult to liven up the magazine because each member of the board could veto any material that offended his prejudices, and what remained was of interest only to those die-hard readers he characterized as Unitarian clergymen. Lippmann left *The New Republic* for the *New York World*, and Wilson— irritated with another editor, who snubbed his army friend John Andersen—decided to stay at *Vanity Fair* when Crownie granted him a six-month leave to go abroad.

Worn out by the year of emotional strain, he felt that, like Edna, he needed a furlough in Europe. He worked nights to build up a backlog of pieces to leave for publication, and his father advanced him some money. During the voyage he was drained, and in Paris Wilson—whom Mary McCarthy characterized as something of a stage-door Johnny—followed the aged chanteuse Yvette Guilbert from one café to another where she sang of youth and love, jotting down lyrics that moved him. He didn't miss Blair much, writing to Dell that for too long he had been "occupied with women at the expense of everything else" and adding, "I am anxious to find a *modus vivendi* which will enable me to live and let live. I really don't want to marry—but—but I can't go into this subject here."

The Paris literary scene was restorative. Crownie had provided introductions to luminaries ("Through Walter Berry you will meet Mrs. Wharton. They are great friends," etc.), informing each that Wilson was of high character and would be an important critic. He met the art critic Madame Picabia and, over lunch, enjoyed Cocteau's witty remarks about the styles of Flaubert and Stendhal, comments he later found that Cocteau was repeating from his own writing. He observed his American contemporaries. In his notes, bisexual Djuna Barnes discusses her liberation from her husband and mentions she'd advised Pound (lifting this, Wilson noted, from Thoreau), "Be simple, Ezra, be simple." Paris seemed to Wilson a more civilized place for writers than Manhattan, yet to Fitzgerald on June 22 he signed himself "Yours for the shifting of the world's capital of culture from Paris to New York." A tension between patriotic aspiration and deference to the Old World would characterize his work until well after World War II.

Ten days later he preached the value of the Continental aesthetic to Scott, who had written pronouncing all Europe "of merely antiquarian interest." It seemed that Zelda had tied the elevator ("one of those little half-ass affairs," Wilson reported to Bishop) at their floor with a rope while she dressed for dinner, and they'd been put out of their hotel. In response to his letter, Wilson insisted on the grace and measure of every French writer from Racine to Anatole France. At home, he said, "the intellectual and aesthetic manifestations" had to "crowd their way up and out from between the crevices left by the factories, the office buildings, the apartment-houses, and the banks." Half-parodying the scare tactics of preachers going back to Jonathan Edwards, he described America as "simply not built" for artists—"if they escape with their lives, they can thank God, but would better not think they are 100 percent elect, attired in authentic and untarnished vestments of light, because they have obviously been stunted and deformed at birth and afterwards greatly battered and contaminated in their struggle to get out." The good news was the vitality of the American idiom and of New York as a literary center. The danger was complacency: "every American savant and artist" should beware of "the ease with which a traditionless and half-educated public (I mean the growing public for really good stuff) can be impressed, delighted, and satisfied; the Messrs. Mencken, Nathan, Cabell, Dreiser, Anderson, Lewis, Dell, Lippmann, Rosenfeld, Fitzgerald, etc., etc." should remember that (as John Stuart Mill had said of himself) "they all owe a good deal of their eminence 'to the flatness of the surrounding country!'"

Notebook in hand, Wilson went south from Paris into Italy, reversing the family tour of his boyhood. Though he hadn't wanted Millay to accompany him, he tried to get Djuna Barnes to go along, but she refused because—she would tell him thirty-five years later—he preached to her of Edith Wharton's virtues and she hated *Ethan Frome*. At Cannes he tracked down Ninette Fabre, whose father now had a café there as well as in Vittel. When he tried to kiss her she lightly put him off, saying that one kiss of his had lasted her two years. Ninette soon married, but for over a decade they exchanged affectionate letters, remaining friends as

Wilson often would with former lovers. In Venice he looked at beautiful medieval texts of Homer and got a letter from Djuna hoping her "dear E.W." wouldn't be found, à la Shelley, "in any body of water great or small." In Florence he had an epiphany to which, he wrote to Bishop, as a secular humanist he couldn't do justice: "I arrived there on a day of crystal fire just on the edge of autumn and coming out into that square along by the Uffizi Gallery heard the public band playing some gay piece of Italian trumpery and saw the pigeons riding the surf of sound on joyous and serene wings against the diamond light of the *Paradiso*—such a moment, in short, as Mr. T. S. Eliot would carry about with him for years as a fetish against Bleistein and Sweeney, as an indemnification for the horrors of Lloyd's Bank or whatever it is, but which I, since it had no moral significance for me, can do nothing more than utilize incidentally in a private letter like this."

In a journal passage at the elegant Boboli Gardens Wilson dramatized his refusal of the temptation of Europe for the American writer. This led to a first-rate lyric contrasting leisure-class extravagances—fountains where dolphin statues preside and goldfish "drift idle in the eternal sun," pathways that wind "through velvet glooms or golden light" until "a marble youth . . . stops the alleyway with white"—to the origin of American letters in the "bare-swept houses, white and low; / High stony pastures, never ploughed" of early New England:

> There, setting bare feet on bare wood,
> They came who late in silks had gone;
> Dim candor by your desks they stood,
> Austere to wake the winter dawn.

Another piece, called "Night Thoughts in Paris" though completed back in New York, reiterates the theme that "the barbarity of the background gives dignity to those who struggle against it."

At home, as he absorbed this trip he found it ironic that the artistic standard Europe afforded Americans was threatened by Dadaists and futurists in their naive enthusiasm for "the machines, the advertisements, the elevators, and the jazz" of the United States. He advised those who had gone to Europe "to drink culture at its source" to warn their hosts not to abandon eighteenth-century harmonies. Yet too much inherited tradition evidently weighed hard, and in "Night Thoughts in Paris" Wilson—again anticipating *Gatsby*'s last pages—contrasts European trains ever moving over the same worn tracks to the freshness and freedom of American trains rushing across vast spaces between nameless towns. Summoning himself and others to the task, he concludes with a mock-epic echo of Blake's "Jerusalem": "I shall not cease from mental fight nor shall my sword rest in my hand" until "the time-clock has been beaten to a punchbowl!"

At the beginning of 1922, with a raise to seventy-five dollars a week, he was back at "the old madhouse," as he called *Vanity Fair* in a letter to Fitzgerald. He was dismayed when Crownie, who liked to talk about being and behaving like a gentleman, borrowed from Putnam's bookstore below them "a volume of an expensive and splendidly printed edition" of Voltaire, cut out the pages containing a letter that he wanted to print, and returned the book. But Wilson stayed at the magazine through the spring of 1923, and his eclectic writing there defines the first phase of his criticism. He is international, circling from a new edition of Byron's letters through Bloomsbury to reprints of Maupassant or Octave Mirbeau or Huysmans. He looks into a collection of American folk ballads and into the survey *These United States*—to which he'd contributed "New Jersey: The Slave of Two Cities." He calls the dialogue of O'Neill's middle-class characters stale and repetitive but the speech of others like the protagonist of *The Hairy Ape* poetic, racy, and real. He would reprint little of this writing, which can be exuberant, even sentimental. James Huneker's essays on European writers and musicians are likened to "floral bombs and the close-packed rockets of fireworks," that left their color "in our hearts." Yet as the critic Daniel Aaron says, this early work sometimes attains a Mozartian lightness and elegance.

Wilson's strongest early pieces appeared in other magazines, and in one of them he plays off Fitzgerald's work against his knowledge of the man. First published in *The Bookman* and reprinted in *The Shores of Light*, "F. Scott Fitzgerald" begins by stating that the author of *This Side of Paradise* and *The Beautiful and Damned* "has been given imagination without intellectual control of it; he has been given a desire for beauty without an aesthetic ideal; and he has been given a gift for expression without very many ideas to express." Wilson, of course, had all he claimed the other lacked, yet knew it didn't make him a novelist. Fitzgerald possessed "an instinct for graceful and vivid prose which some of his more pretentious fellows might envy." *This Side of Paradise*, Wilson wrote with the standard of James, "does not commit the unpardonable sin: It does not fail to live. The whole preposterous farrago is animated with life."

Scott wasn't fazed by the severity of Wilson's critique, saying that "like everything you write it seems to me pretty generally true. I am guilty of its every stricture and I take an extraordinary delight in its considered approbation." He was fascinated by the personal sketch, which adapts Taine's categories of the moment, the race, and the milieu. Wilson links his Irish romanticism and cynicism with the pleasure-seeking rebellion after World War I, and calls him a voice of the comfortable houses and country clubs of the Middle West, of new money that is genial rather than sophisticated or snobbish. Fitzgerald persuaded his friend to take out a reference to his drinking. "The most enormous influence on me in the four and a half years since I met her," he ominously stated, "has been the complete, fine and full-hearted selfishness and chill-mindedness of Zelda."

The hole in Wilson's life left by the others' marriages was for a time filled by Elinor Wylie, who joined the staff at *Vanity Fair* after her success with the poetry of *Nets to Catch the Wind*. She was ten years older than he, and her life had been beset by tragedies—two siblings committed suicide, as did her son and her first husband. She embodied the bohemian legend, having deserted husband and child for someone who left his wife and children for her. She had been a beauty. In an episode that illustrates Virginia Woolf's view of Americans as well as the limits of Woolf's feminism, when Elinor was in England with Horace Wylie, Leonard and Virginia had them to dinner and, in a letter to Vita Sackville-West, Virginia, jealous of Elinor's looks or her style and always the snob, called her "a solid hunk: a hatchet minded, cadaverous, acid voiced, bareboned, spavined, patriotic, nasal, thick legged American." When Wilson knew her, she had aged and in some ways resembled Woolf's caricature. She was "almost skeletally thin," with "the harsh voice of a peacock," which she is said to have acquired by identification with Shelley, the subject of her novel, *The Orphan Angel*. But with Wilson she was well-balanced and affectionate, as reassuring as he found her formal furnishings and old-fashioned literary culture.

The samples of Wylie's wit in Wilson's journal suggest a more refined, less volatile Dorothy Parker. At a gathering where the talk turned to Whitman, Christ, and Kahlil Gibran, on being asked her favorite poets she answered, "Why, Milton, for example." Someone cried with horror, "You haven't been influenced by *Milton*!," to which she replied, "Well, why should I be?" and then, "You admire Jesus Christ, but you don't behave like him, do you?" Characteristic of her verse is the well-known lyric "Wild Peaches," celebrating the ease of life on Maryland's Eastern Shore. There in the spring, she writes,

> every little creek
> Is shot with silver from the Chesapeake
> In shoals new-minted by the ocean swell,
> When strawberries go begging, and the sleek
> Blue plums lie open to the blackbird's beak.

The poem turns from sensual temptation to Wylie's ancestral New England. She had what her biographer calls a "need for romance, preferably without much sexual expression." Wilson wrote teasingly to her as one Roscoe N. Wingo, a lovelorn literary hack seeking "my spiritual sister, my passionate playmate, my mental mother," language expressive of Wilson's own needs. Christening him "Bunnius Augustus," Elinor declared that "among members of the sterner sex you are my favorite friend in N. Y."

Leaving the bachelor ménage to which he'd returned after the war, he took a place with the bon vivant E. E. "Ted" Paramore, Jr., grandson of a New England railroad millionaire and son of a Santa Barbara yachtsman. A younger boy at Hill and at Yale a leader of his class, Ted had gone to Russia at the end of the war and during the Revolution guided a trainload of 128 American refugees to safety through the snows of Siberia. Wilson thought he might make a career in political journalism, but he had plenty of money and, instead, settled into a routine of drinking and "wenching," while contributing parodies, burlesques, and satires to *Vanity Fair*, *The Smart Set*, and *The Freeman*. He was famous for "The Ballad of Yukon Jake," a raucous parody of the Robert Service verses so admired by Marion Dell. From Santa Barbara Ted regaled Wilson with sexual triumphs on the Pacific's golden shores, and when they moved in at 777 Lexington Avenue, above a furrier's shop, he set out to teach his bookish friend the strategies of seduction. One technique was to hand a woman the pioneer sex manual of old Dr. Robey, "which aimed to remove inhibitions by giving you permission to do anything you liked."

Wilson was still seeing Blair. Now sometimes called "the O'Neill actress," she opened as the spoiled, neurotic heiress of *The Hairy Ape*, "outfitted with a snowy white crepe de Chine gown, white cloak and white hat with flowing veil, to point up the contrast with the grimy, coal-blackened stokers in their glowing inferno." When the producer moved the play to Broadway, however, he replaced Mary, over O'Neill's protest, with stunning Carlotta Monterey, later the playwright's wife, since, as one of O'Neill's biographers noted, "Mary was not enough of a personality for uptown—not luxurious enough." Another reports that her acting "could vary from one evening to the next; it all depended on her emotional state and frame of mind at the time." Wilson consoled her in the railroad flat, which was divisible into parts with a bathroom between, giving each man privacy "to entertain our girls." The couple did a lot of drinking.

After some months, in a mock-Puritan confession, he proposed to Fitzgerald to escape this routine. "I go, I go to the high cold hills of New England," he declared, "where my ancestors served the altars of learning and committed murders in the name of God. My stomach is rotted with bad gin, my tonsils are riddled with ulcers, my soul is laid waste with contemplation of my own and others' sins. . . . Pray for my soul!" In September 1922 he reported to Bishop what would be a recurring ambition "to buy a little house in the country whither I can retreat and derive strength from contact with the classics." For the present he'd "move downtown" and "live alone," perhaps near Elinor on University Place. At the end of November he parted with Ted and told John he had moved "into a large corner room with bath" in Elinor's building.

Mary and Wilson, however, spent at least one evening together in December, when she became pregnant. They were married on Valentine's Day 1923 in a hopeful frame of mind. In March, when she was two and a half months along, they took the train to her hometown of Pittsburgh. After the journal's three-page anatomy of the industrial city, one Verna Tolley is quoted saying, "We *must* get some clean towels. I'll get some at the Hotel Pennsylvania tonight." In an interpolation of the 1950s Verna is identified as "someone that Mary Blair knew, a trained nurse available for other purposes." It seems they were setting up an abortion. Wilson would one day tell his daughter Helen that he "hated abortions," having gone through a number of them. This one, however, did not occur.

He didn't mention Mary's pregnancy when he told his parents he was going to marry her. Although his mother disapproved of a divorced actress, his father said that "any woman Edmund married would be accepted completely," as loyal on this score as he'd been tolerant of Wilson's over-arching intellectual ambitions after college. Mr. Wilson came into town to talk the matter over with, of all people, Frank Crowninshield, on some antique assumption of an employer's responsibilities. The ensuing scene strengthened the son's resolve to leave the magazine. "Crowninshield," he reports, "handled this interview with the usual lack of tact." He "told my father that my being married might have the desirable effect of stimulating me to more serious effort." Being affably confessional, Crownie explained that "the failure of his brother Edward had had the effect on him, Frank, of stiffening his moral backbone and spurring him to work and make money." "Ed-ward," he added (pronouncing it in the proper Bostonian way), was a confirmed drug addict. Wilson says that his father heard Crowninshield out "with the polite silence of someone to whom this kind of man was alien."

That spring Wilson departed *Vanity Fair*, and in the summer they were living on Long Island where, he informed Bishop, "Mary is working on a baby," adding, "I am glad enough to have one, though all these bonds and responsibilities appall me sometimes." He hoped to support his family as a freelance writer. This letter proclaims the delights of country life, citing Virgil's pastoral eclogues. In the journal, alongside precise sketches of the seashore in mid-August, is a naturalistic account of turtles copulating in the backyard, the male, as if in resignation to biology, "leaning at an angle of forty-five degrees" with glazed eyes.

From Long Island the couple moved to the Brooklyn apartment of Wilson's cousin Carolyn Link, who was out of town. A letter to Mencken complains of "the execrable food, the fumes from a nearby confectionery factory, and the demoralizing effect of the inhabitants," but the location was convenient to the hospital where Rosalind Baker Wilson—named for her great-great-aunt Rosalind and the first of what Wilson is said at one point to have hoped would be seven daughters—was born on September 19, 1923. Mary had a small part in a play called *The Lullaby*, but listed herself on the birth certificate as "housewife," while the critic, *Vanity Fair*'s former managing editor, checked the box for "plant manager." From California Ted Paramore entered his "formal candidacy for godfather, promising to teach her the Lord's Prayer, the catechism, the apostles' creed, the Communist Manifesto, Mother Goose, the constellations of the Zodiac, the secrets of alchemy, the art of making good gin, and Descartes's Law of Signs, as befits a responsible and self-respecting godfather, aware of the seriousness of life, the need of sound morals, and the pitfalls that await a maiden unpanoplied with the armor of faith and holy grace." Wilson established the family at University Place, where instead of his old corner room he took half a floor.

His father had died in March, as he told Bishop in the letter relating his marriage and Mary's pregnancy, "but left me nothing, his will having been made ages ago." Their joint inheritance was to be managed, as has been said, by his mother, and she would manage it well, but Wilson knew she planned on another house and travel. The magazine criticism he wrote produced little income, and he had an inkling that, in Melville's phrase, he would be "damned by dollars"—always pressing publishers for advances and haggling over contracts, doing reviews that distracted him from larger projects, reusing magazine pieces in book form. Until the 1950s his lifestyle would be far from his parents' comfortable Edwardian one.

A decade later, Wilson wrote to a friend whose father had died, "Your father's death makes a big psychological difference to you, I think—robs you of something and gives you something new at the same time—at least it did in my case." In the poem "When All the Young Were Dying, I Dwelt Among the Dead," he attacks the social world in which the senior Wilson's abilities and ideals had served to isolate and defeat him. In the letter to Bishop, Wilson speculates that his father's "melancholia" may have resulted from "an insufficient capacity for dissipation." Edna had teased him for his sobriety, said he had sex appeal when drunk, and to Bishop he resolves "when I waste time in the future to waste it only in dissipation." He preferred Uncle Reuel's vice of going on an occasional bat to hypochondria, and like Edna and Mary, his second wife, Margaret Canby, would be a drinking companion. His father, however, Wilson adds, "got more results with his nervous energy than I have yet got with mine, and it is high time for me to even the balance."

7

Private Life

A Failing Marriage

The circumstances of Wilson's alliance with Mary Blair scarcely brought out the best in either party. He proposed to her when she became pregnant, but after she had set up an abortion, they decided to have the child. Mary "preferred her career to her maternity," recalled a Cape Cod woman friend. Another said, "at home she was a Calamity Jane. Everything went haywire and she was the complaining type." For two years Wilson worked at home, his only regular job as press agent for the Swedish ballet. His personal needs were modest—he could get along on fried-egg sandwiches, supplemented by Limburger cheese and gingersnaps—but he was incompetent to help with a baby. His mother paid for Rosalind's Jamaican nurse, Stella, whom she came to love. In the evenings Mary was at the theater and Wilson often on the town, after which he might make notes for a reportorial piece or in his journal. He came to find it difficult to be married to an actress, but until 1926 the couple stayed together with their baby. When Mary began going on the road she more than once took Stella and the baby along, though they usually remained with Wilson.

His first two plays are products of this marriage. He wrote *The Crime in the Whistler Room* for Blair. She was in the habit of asking people to write plays for her (Sherwood Anderson being one), and Wilson, who loved the stage, was willing to believe he could write for it, an illusion shared by prose stylists from James through Dos Passos and Mailer. "Bill" McGee, the Blair character in *The Crime*, like Mary from Pittsburgh, has her coloring and boyish figure and uses some of her expressions. Her lover, the breezy alcoholic writer Simon DeLacy, is superficially based on Fitzgerald but holds forth about the effects of industrial capitalism on the soul of man as Wilson did. The plot is masked autobiography—it turns on pregnancy and the decision to have the baby. Respectability and convention are represented in a decayed country-house family who cannot even rearrange the room that houses their priceless Whistler paintings, much less accept Bill and Simon. All the conflicts of the time have been seen in this play—"East vs. West, rich vs. poor, old vs. young, Anglo-Saxon vs. immigrant, refinement vs. vulgarity, etc." Harold Clurman, later codirector of the Group Theatre, liked it, but Alexander Woollcott found it talky—"No knife," he said, "could cut deep enough to whittle this text down to the essential idiom."

Wilson cheerfully planned to do better. *A Winter in Beech Street*, as he initially called his next play, was started with Mary in mind but became a dramatic reconstruction of the breakup of the Provincetown Players. Some of his characters are deadbeats, others tempted by Broadway glitter, and their devotion to art is undercut by their jealousies and changing alliances. At the climax a character based on Harry Kemp, a celebrated drunken guru of the creative, momentarily holds them together by reciting Keats's sonnet that affirms those "silken ties, that never may be broken." The theme of secular communion gave Wilson the title *This Room and This Gin and These Sandwiches* when he completed this play a decade later. In the actress Sally Voight he nostalgically conflates Mary with Edna, who occasionally acted with the Provincetown group. Sally is carried off by the Wilson figure at the end.

Though Eugene O'Neill produced *The Crime in the Whistler Room* for Mary's sake, he did not encourage Wilson to try again. Wilson, however, tells in the journal of giving the playwright drinks one night in their apartment, determined to see what lay behind his morose façade. A torrent of talk was unleashed—about Sophocles, the homosexuality of sailors, the uninhibited ways of old-time actresses—turning into a disoriented monologue as O'Neill consumed everything he could put his hands on, finally leaving at four a.m. Wilson judged his plays with the detachment he summoned for all his male contemporaries. He considered them to be sometimes labored naturalistic drama, overly influenced by the "poison-spitting" quarrels between man and woman in Strindberg. What saved the early O'Neill was his capacity "for drawing music from humble people."

Mary's career as the O'Neill actress brought her headlines but not stardom. Her most famous part was opposite Paul Robeson in *All God's Chillun Got Wings*. That she kissed Robeson's hand in the play earned her the wrath of the Ku Klux Klan (which Wilson heard was also after him), while Robeson received the good notices. She was long remembered for her harangue in the one-act play *Before Breakfast*, directed at a man who remains offstage and ending with a "piercing scream" when she finds he has killed himself. At one point Mary reported to Wilson, "Agnes O'Neill endeavored to tell me I was neurotic and I told her I never had been till I met her husband." When preparing for *Strange Interlude* she warned him, "I'll be falling into one of those O'Neill moods."

From the beginning Wilson had a bad conscience in this marriage. The guilt-ridden verses "To an Actress" state that his first affirmations of love were false ("I knew myself a liar from that day"). At some point Mary and he began to quarrel when they drank, and apparently their lovemaking turned sour—in these lines he accuses himself of "cold tenderness and trumped-up ecstasies." Mary more than once came home from the theater to find him and Millay reading poetry together, with "a Do Not Disturb sign on the door." She mocked them for taking verse so seriously. Language, however, had always bound these two, and Edna's voice stirred the old emotions. A letter from her, long buried in the files, suggests that Wilson confided he found it difficult to love his wife. "I'm sorry you're in such a mess," Edna says, and teases, "As you say, you were never meant to be human." She hopes "the summer will straighten things out somewhat," and observes, "Of course trying to compel yourself to emotions you don't have makes it worse." Early in 1924 she writes that she loves him enough to go driving with him in an open carriage in Central Park "in a howling blizzard in a muslin frock," but will settle for a glimpse before she leaves on a poetry reading tour.

E. E. Cummings, who defied the conventions, described the Wilson of this period as "the man in the iron necktie," but by 1925 he was taking off his tie and, apparently, his shirt as well. One man's wife made an assignation in order, it turned out, "to talk in a goofy way about her emotions and philosophical concepts." When he told her he "couldn't do it," she snapped, "Then why do you think I had you in my bed?" Hazel Rascoe, the wife of the critic Burton Rascoe, was a former nightclub dancer with "melting" brown eyes and an extraordinary sex appeal, who confided she was full of appetite and a connoisseur of men. Making comedy of his awkwardness, Wilson records that on the night when Hazel (Belle Gifford in the journal) surprisingly phoned him up, "I told her, full of hope, to come right around. But in spite of the fact that I performed the at that time for me heroic feat of carrying her into the bedroom, it turned out that she only wanted to tell me how worried she was about [Burton's] drinking." One evening he arrived at the Rascoes dressed in tails with Zelda's childhood friend Tallulah Bankhead on one arm and Mary Blair on the other in pajamas, and put on a magic show. On another occasion he and Rascoe got into a drunken fight, which neither of them could remember afterward. There were different versions, but Dawn Powell, whose friend Coby Gilman was there, believed that Rascoe bit Wilson on the nose when he was "overadmirous" of Hazel.

In January 1926 he was at Red Bank with tonsillitis when Mary, who complained that she had to compete for good roles, wrote that she and Rosalind were poring over family photos in the apartment, awaiting his return. Wilson's poem "Infection" (beginning "Five days in fever thus I lay") broods on the gray, debilitating urban literary routine—"bad whiskey, manners, plays, / Bad talk abroad, bad work alone, / Bad damp apartments on bad days, / Have poisoned me from brain to bone"—only to conclude it is "the bad heart that poisons all." His zest for life revives in a recorded dream in which he is one of a troop of marching soldiers entering a marvelous green countryside, singing a song echoed by feminine voices from beyond the trees. Mysteriously released from duty, he looks forward to an evening with a cultivated, attractive woman for whom he once had a passion, and there is a large car, with a chauffeur who has acquired some Scotch. Yet an obstruction separates him from the dream woman as the magic moment passes.

When visiting Sherwood Anderson in New Orleans in March 1926, Wilson had sex with a prostitute. "The dirty floor—green oilcloth—of the anteroom to the bathroom—the horrible stink of the broken closet, in which an unused condom floated," and "the picture of Christ in the room below" set off the starkness of the act: she "simply threw herself on her back across the bed with her feet hanging down at her side and pulled her skirts up over her stomach." Trying to humanize the situation, he prompted the young woman to talk—about hustling, about her family, her best friend, about being unwelcome with her respectable family at Christmas. The journal doesn't insist on his sympathies—"I wiped [her tears] away with the red quilt and they came again. I wiped them away again, and that was the end of it." In New York that August, on a smothering night amid crowds "keyed down by the heat," Wilson hired another prostitute, and he had her return more than once, as much to talk about her life as for sex. The futile aspect of his life is evident when he notes that after she'd gone "I read, shoving my mind along against lassitude with effort but not without pleasure (if one can speak of pleasure at a time when the capacity for pleasure of any kind seems all to have been spent), a page-and-a-half paragraph of Matthew Arnold."

That September from a Denver engagement Mary wired, not very coherently, "MANAGEMENT CHANGED HANDS LEADING MAN CAN GET SOMEONE CHEAPER PLAY EVERY WEEK STRENUOUS SO REFUSE TO PLAY FOR ANY SMALLER SALARY CHEERYO SORRY I WILL BE BACK ON YOUR HANDS BUT THINK IT JUST AS WELL." Wilson gave her their apartment and took a furnished room on West Thirteenth Street, which would be his base for years. It was a dingy place with a common bathroom on the floor below, which T. S. Matthews, an assistant at *The New Republic* (where Wilson had at last become an editor), remembered as "a perfect picture of helpless, squalid bachelorhood: an unmade bed, empty gin bottles on the dirty floor, no carpet, one naked electric light bulb." But he could easily look in on Rosalind, and when one day he found her in her crib under an open window in the rain he took both her and Stella to his mother's. Though Mary and he didn't divorce until 1930, this, he'd tell McCarthy, was the end of the marriage.

He began spending long weekends and vacation time with his mother and daughter at Red Bank, during the week staying in apartments of friends who were out of town or in his furnished room. When in Red Bank he'd read to Rosalind in the evenings—a few years later it would be Dickens or the Old Testament stories. On weekends when he didn't come down, her nurse would take her up to New York City to see one parent or the other. Wilson was to her reassuringly solid. She observed his abstraction—when a beggar asked him for a quarter he gave the man a ten-dollar bill and asked him to go get it changed—but "felt secure with my father, that somehow he'd continue to exist." She "hated" visiting her mother in New York, for Mary's friends seemed to have nothing to do but chain-smoke and curse.

Rosalind declares she "never loved" her mother. Tragically for the two of them, Wilson's mother, who took over the child's care, would lead her to believe that Mary had abandoned her at birth. Rosalind begins the memoir *Near the Magician* by saying she was "taken from the hospital where I was born" down to Red Bank and stayed on with her grandmother, for "my grandmother felt, 'Rosalind is my child.'" She elsewhere states that she spent less than six weeks with her mother, who in fact looked after her for almost three years. Mary apparently never knew how Mrs. Wilson cut her out, but to Wilson after her separation she wrote, "I am in such a state of depression over my whole life and the way it has turned out I haven't the mental capacity to struggle or cope with my situation and I feel that someone else will have to do it for me." A scrawled, undated note reads:

Dear Bunny:
You left me without any money and thinking I was to have dinner with you and talk things over.
I'm absolutely weary of existence this way.
I feel perfectly useless in my position and am wandering about like a lost hen not even wet.

Mary

In "To an Actress," urging the unnamed woman to believe in her craft, Wilson compliments her on "the deep heart, / The will that keeps it for the shapes of art," and says it is he who has "played / The falsest part in that ill-favored piece," their life:

How many times, remembering faith betrayed,
At thought of you alone through fault of mine,
     With loneliness and darkness all around,
     I've waked at night in horror and, half-drowned,
Spat bitterly as bathers choked by brine.

He had thought he could make himself love her, had reassured her that he did when he didn't. The memory of his falsity with Mary would lead him to hold out against Margaret Canby, who once begged him, "Say that you love me—lie to me!"

After the separation he had one or two encounters with Edna. In November 1927 she seemed "well and normal again," had gained weight, though her looks were coarser. In a passage from the journal that was excluded, after his death, from *The Twenties*, he adds, "When we kissed and embraced it was very strange, almost as though she had forgotten the things she had taught me." Her mechanical lovemaking was a letdown to one who in the early poem "Lesbia" had imagined her seducing Satan. Another time she was in a different frame of mind: "She was all burning and lit up when I came in" and "she put her arms around me and kissed me," and "it was I who was too stiff and unresponsive."

Two attractive Greenwich Village women encouraged his attentions. Petite, long-legged, and elegant, the Hungarian Magda Johann, called Katze Szabo in *The Twenties*, was a regular on the party circuit, and Wilson recognized her as a model for the drawings of German-born Hans Stengel, her boyfriend, a caricaturist whose suicide is described in a later article included in *The Shores of Light*. For months Magda let Wilson think he might win her, but when yearningly walking with her hand on his arm he wearied of the game, feeling "as if I had acquired some precious and desirable *objet d'art* rather than as if I were having dinner with a human companion whom I liked and desired." Belatedly aware of the age gap between them, he admitted to himself that he needed a stable life while she naturally wanted to flirt and meet people. A comic situation arose when another suitor, a literary Englishman studying law at Harvard named Sylvester Gates (in *The Twenties* Gerald Jenks), wrote her a love letter that she shared with Wilson. It brought back "all my adoration" of Edna, and his effusion to Magda about the value of love and moral seriousness sent her rushing off to give herself to his rival.*

Florence O'Neil reminded Wilson of Scott Fitzerald in her wit and self-preoccupation. A showgirl who was blonde and short, she dyed her hair with Golden Glint and used an expensive carmine rouge to avoid, she coyly claimed, looking like "Daniel Webster or someone of the kind." He set down her wisecracks, shoptalk, and personal history. There was insecurity behind Florence's comic mask, and during a taxi ride she matter-of-factly said "she didn't know whether she had ever been happy." Wilson liked her spunk, and she genially flirted with him without ever getting into bed. When, on a semidate, she suggested they hadn't much time to lose, that she was only there "for a limited engagement," she likened him, as he rushed to the charge, to Rudolph Valentino, saying, "You kill me in your sheik role!" Florence may have been the woman who wittily kept him at bay—"I wanted to kiss her inside the thighs, but she said, 'Closed for the day'"—and whose feet Wilson held "like two moist little cream cheeses in cloth cases."

He used these bits of dialogue and observation in *I Thought of Daisy*, the novel he began after a sunny June day with Florence at Coney Island gave him an upbeat ending for a tale of lost innocence. Daisy is derived

---

*Wilson never knew the upshot, but sixty-five years later, Isaiah Berlin informed the present writer of learning from a friend of Gates that he had been successful with Magda, "for half an hour."

from Florence and made to represent the ordinary American life that, in reviews of the late twenties, Wilson urged writers to connect with. It is Daisy/Florence to whom his protagonist turns on the rebound from Edna, rather than to Mary Blair.

Frances, Margaret, and Leonie

Wilson's first book after *The Undertaker's Garland* with John Bishop was *Discordant Encounters: Plays and Dialogues* (1926). This little-known collection includes *The Crime in the Whistler Room* and two "Imaginary Conversations" between opposed literary figures, the exchange between Paul Rosenfeld and Matthew Josephson defining a different cultural battle than that between Brooks and Fitzgerald. Here one also finds the text of *Chronkite's Clocks*, whose hero is Charlie. To John he called this "a great super-ballet of New York" intended to feature Charlie Chaplin, "a Negro comedian, and seventeen other characters, full orchestra, movie machine, typewriters, radio, phonograph, riveter, electromagnet, alarm clocks, telephone bells, and jazz band." Leo Ornstein agreed to do the score, but apparently never got around to it. Three years later Wilson satirized himself when imagining a Village production he called *Fire Alarm*, the work of a dilettante he names DeGross Wilbur, whose gimmickry was later turned to use by someone else—just as Chaplin, who laughed appreciatively when shown Wilson's ballet, might have been stimulated by it when he made *Modern Times*.

Taking a break from his failing marriage and the New York winter, Wilson went to California to recruit Chaplin, who politely explained that he always created his own material. After a few days with Ted Paramore, now a screenwriter in Hollywood, Wilson enjoyed the hospitality of Ted's family in Santa Barbara and the storytelling of his father, "Mr. Ed," whose fame as a raconteur had reached Henry James twenty-five years before. Ted introduced him to Margaret Canby, who had grown up with one sister in a large cluttered house on a nearby estate. Like Wilson she had been born in 1895. Her father, I. G. Waterman—who was painted by Mary Cassatt—was a financier with artistic tastes, her mother a member of a prominent Scottish Canadian family. A charming woman, Margaret had been educated abroad, knew languages, was musical like her parents and sister. Ted had taken her to dances at New Haven and fallen in love with her, though unable to make up his mind to propose. Now he was trying to get her away from her husband, who, he said, "beat her up when drunk" and manipulated this sweet-tempered woman "with the clever gesture of sobbing, sulking, melancholia, and threats of suicide." Margaret and Wilson swam and spent an afternoon at the beach, she wittily sketching the local society. Ted swore that Margaret (whom he called Maggie) was the center of his life and sent bulletins about her situation to Wilson back in New York.

In his journal Wilson set down Margaret's remark that "if a man so much as goes out and cracks the ice himself in a girl's apartment, they assume that he's her lover." He noted a "joke in *New Yorker* about girl who wouldn't tip taxi driver because he didn't have sex appeal." His desires to experience life more deeply and to write about it better were both satisfied after he met, in February 1927, Frances Minihan. She was the woman to whom he was closest during his thirties and with whom he formed the habit of recording his intimate relationships. As he re-creates the beginnings of their affair fifteen years later in *Memoirs of Hecate County*, he was restlessly walking on Fourteenth Street one evening and climbed the dirty marble steps up to the Tango Gardens, where a "headlong and demoniac" band of black musicians played beside a crowded dance floor alternately lit by blue lights and darkened. After dancing with a woman who earnestly pressed against him in order, she explained, to earn a larger tip, he sought out one with a round face "with gentle modelling and bluish-gray eyes" that resembled "little fine-sepalled flowers," a mouth he could imagine kissing. She wasn't heavily made up, nor did she seem eager, but she agreed to have a drink with him afterward. Pale-skinned, with copper reddish hair that smelled of cigarettes, Frances—called Anna Lenihan in *Hecate County*, a name that Leon Edel maintained when doing editorial work on *The Twenties* and *The Thirties*—was petite, even tiny, no more than a hundred pounds or so. Her "deep husky city voice" and Brooklyn accent overlaid something foreign—the language of people who had come from Lemberg, then a city in Austrian Galicia, eventually Lviv in western Ukraine. They met a second time and, though shy, she was as ready to exchange a kiss as he. A waitress as well as a taxi dancer, on the night they became lovers she told him she was married, had a daughter, and a husband who was in Sing Sing for car theft.

In April or May, following a fever and depression, Wilson was diagnosed with gonorrhea. He was cured with silver nitrate, a risky process. The genial Viennese doctor warned, "If you come back again, I'll cut it off." Wilson said nothing to Frances, assuming she'd gotten the disease from her husband, Al, without knowing it, but in *Hecate County* describes "the snap in my sympathies" that followed, a mark of "the instinctive suspicion of people who talk differently and live differently from us" and "the fear of the poor and the humbly employed, about whom we so often feel guilt." After spending two summer months with Rosalind and Stella in an old Coast Guard station in Provincetown, which O'Neill let him have at a nominal rent (reminding him there were "three quarts of raw Belgian alcohol in the outside toilet"), he was back in touch with Frances. The burst of journal notes that describe her life and their lovemaking are at once joyous, uninhibited, and methodical.

Frances's sexuality was natural, neither crude nor embarrassed. "Her pale little passionate face in the half light with that mouth moist, and always ready, more like a sexual organ than a mouth, felt the tongue plunging into it almost like intercourse—liked to cuddle up at night—cuddled up with her mother when she slept with her—her mother would push her away—I don't know what I do to her.—Responds so easily with that rhythmic movement—quickly catches the rhythm—to any stimulation—." He recorded the carnal exhilaration of "the night when she had on a red dress and I was drunk and kissed her, just rubbing my mouth against her wet lips, again and again, till it was almost like some kind of intercourse— meaty effect like lips below." He described "how lovely she looked in the dull light of the half dark—her eyes Slavic and rich and deep with shadows and her mouth rich and dark red." The "little narrow lozenge of her cunt" was "so pretty it would make me linger and preoccupy me so that I almost forgot to do anything else."

Writing in a private journal, Wilson was impelled to explain how bodies worked, to demystify this subject, as one day he would try to demystify war. As graphic as are this and his other accounts of sex over the years, one might conclude that he exploited women by describing his experiences with them in print. During his affair with Frances he had no intention of publishing anything about her. In 1927 he made a will that largely consists of distributing his books, his only property, to friends. His executor, John Amen, is here charged "personally to destroy by burning certain notebooks kept by me from year to year during my lifetime." What he was doing in these journal scenes was radical. They preceded *Lady Chatterley's Lover*, which broke the taboo against intercourse in a novel. Wilson's *New Republic* review of *Lady Chatterley* (reprinted in *The Shores of Light*) calls the book "vigorous and brilliant," its author deserving of a medal from the republic of letters. Yet he pokes fun at Lawrence for rhapsodizing over certain familiar English words and causing his lovers "to decorate one another with forgetmenots in places where flowers are rarely worn." Wilson too was a romantic, but he was influenced by Joyce and the French naturalists as well as Havelock Ellis's case histories.

Over the next years he would try to capture Frances's personal history on the page, in passages that can be hard going because her life was so difficult. When her father, whom she couldn't remember, had died of TB, she was placed in a Catholic charity home, where the sisters brutally punished the girls. She escaped when her mother remarried and was sent back to school, but found it hard to keep up because of the uproar at home. At fourteen she took a job at the National Biscuit Company and at seventeen she married Al, attempting to spend her wedding night wrapped in a blanket on the couch until her mother told her she should go in to bed. Al's family were middle-class, churchgoing Irish Catholics in the insurance business in Oswego, New York. They accepted her when he told them she was a Russian violinist—she had delicate hands and had played the violin when growing up—but decided she was not to be tolerated when they found she couldn't play bridge. Now she and her daughter, Adele, lived with her mother and her stepfather, in whose household she did all the cooking and nervously tended the furnace in the basement, near which she slept. Fatty, her Russian stepfather, a small-time crook, was trying to turn her mother's two rooms into a combination speakeasy and whorehouse.

Wilson's account of all this is flavored by Frances's short, exclamatory phrases and sentences—"didja ever hear ov'um?"; "loved'um just the same." She loved Al and their sex life, and for many months felt guilty betraying him with Wilson. When he read to her Yeats's lines,

> He that made this knows all the cost,
> For he gave all his heart and lost,

she said, "Like me with Al, for instance." She declared of Fatty, "Honestly it's an awful thing to say, but I'd rather have my mother dead than livin' with a guy like that!" He sometimes tried to get Frances into bed, and her mother became jealous, calling her a whore in Ukrainian—"and oh, that sounds terrible in Ukrainian, you know."

It is clear from the forty-some letters and notes he saved that Frances loved Wilson, almost from the first. She was not a kept woman. She continued to earn her living, though he found money for her when she needed it. He was gentle and loving with her, and she learned what it was like to be doted on. She gave him "his deferred manhood," John Updike observed of Anna in *Memoirs of Hecate County*. "After we had finished making love the second time," Wilson says, "I came back from the bathroom and put my arms around her in bed and told her that I'd been so happy with her. I lay over on my back, and she touched me several times lightly on the cock." When the subject of marriage arose, Frances laughingly suggested she wouldn't be able to trust him out of her sight at night, and he found it hard to imagine her in the role of his wife, despite his class-leveling experience in the hospital corps. He wouldn't realize what she meant to him until he gave her up to marry someone from his circle.

He tried hard to fall in love with Margaret Canby, who had finally divorced her husband. With Ted now married to another woman, whom he had gotten pregnant, Margaret came on to New York, where her father lived. Walking with Wilson on Broadway early in 1928, she talked of her family, of a relative who "had invested in $10,000 worth of fireworks and set them off in the Bois de Boulogne, and then killed himself." Later Wilson learned that her father had separated from her mother and lived with Daisy Green, of the Floradora Sextet of the 1900s. When he married her later on it was the match of millionare with showgirl that Floradora and, afterward, the Follies fostered. But the Depression would leave his family little—there is a glimpse in *The Thirties*, expanded in *The Higher Jazz*, of a home on Philadelphia's Main Line and Margaret's "cousin Watty," an alcoholic relic with fine manners. Photographs suggest the range of Margaret's temperament: a full-face shot appears pensive, even sad, while the snapshots from a photo booth show her humorous side, and in a three-quarter pose she is jaunty. Malcolm Cowley remembered her as "always beautifully turned out."

They went to bed on April Fools' Day 1928, after Wilson boasted of his "amorous adventures." This athletic, upper-middle-class woman lacked Frances's melting, playful eroticism. The journal notes include her "hard pointed chin (sticking in my back)," "her amiable face—her Scotch matter-of-factness and composure," and the "discrepancy between ordinary manner and way of talking and passionate enjoyment (groaning)." When they made love again a few days later "it had almost the violence of some accident from which it took a long time to extricate ourselves—a muscular crushing embrace—we lay stunned when it was over." The barriers, however, were down. "When I said how sorry I was about not having been able to give her a better time, about having had her come down late to my house, etc., I was astonished to see tears come into her eyes." Glimpsing his reflection in the mirror, Wilson remarked that he "looked like an old ruined chestnut worm," and with her reassuring wit Margaret answered, "Well, who are you arguing with? I never said you were an Adonis."

T. S. Matthews thought the critic brought out a maternal streak in women, who "felt that while his mind was roaming (occupied with very serious matters and in awesomely select company)," he needed someone to guide him in out of the rain. Wilson was someone with whom Margaret could drink and have the kind of wisecracking fun she'd had with Ted and, once upon a time, Jim Canby, and unlike them he was serious about life—he was the first man she'd known who worked for a living, and that impressed her. Before sailing for Europe on the *Majestic*, she told him with a certain bitterness she "was beginning to miss me" and that was "one reason she thought she ought to go." From shipboard she reported, "My health is beyond worry," the twenties euphemism for getting her period. She soon was back in New York, and they spent a day at Montauk Point before she returned to Santa Barbara and her son, Jimmy. Claiming she owed Wilson money, she mailed him ten dollars and invited him to "go and debauch yourself as far as you can on it," poignantly adding, "pray for me if you have any pull with God."

She urged Wilson to visit her, offering to find him a guest house near her on the beach. Flattered by her interest, and convinced that in a season by the Pacific he could radically improve *I Thought of Daisy*, he took the fall of 1928 off from *The New Republic*, promising to return for at least six months. "It will cheer me so to have someone I'm fond of to damn life with," Margaret wrote from a ranch in Wyoming, and said she had two gallons of gin stashed away in Santa Barbara against his arrival. Meanwhile Wilson, a bicyclist who'd never driven a car, quixotically acquired a motorcycle, and initiated it in Red Bank, where it ran away from him, careening through his mother's shrubbery. When he sent Margaret a snapshot she replied, "a side car for me would be the final touch—Don't kill yourself."

While she was in Paris, however, he'd become involved with another woman. Carefully raised within an old and staid Episcopalian New England family, Leonie Adams had graduated from Barnard, where she roomed with Margaret Mead. What some have called her obscure and overwrought

but mellifluously romantic verse Wilson found elegant, and in the anony-
mous survey "The All-Star Literary Vaudeville" he declares that the language of *Those Not Elect* "seems to branch straight from the richest
seventeenth-century tradition." Indeed, there are echoes of *The Tempest*
as well as Housman in such a piece as "Lullaby." Leonie seemed to him
pretty, with a "touch of Spanish sensuality," and they shared a passion for
Proust.

After asking him in for tea and conversation, in 1925 Leonie enthusiastically informed Louise Bogan (as Bogan passed this on to the poet
Rolfe Humphries) that "the Great Wilson" had called on her and "made
some hearty passes at her, inviting her to stay at his house." To the critic
and novelist Judith Farr, her student at Columbia in 1958, she recalled
how, that April thirty years before, Wilson held forth on "what the great
love was all about" and persuaded her to go to bed. A virgin and religious,
in the journal (where she is called Winifred) she argues that it's a mistake—"I'm not sure it's right to make love!" Yet she was prepared to be initiated and Wilson, belatedly fulfilled with Frances at thirty-two, enjoyed
being the experienced one. The next day he told himself he wouldn't have
led her on if he hadn't been drunk, and in his journal he writes, "She was
so sweet, so dear." Adams's letters of the next weeks are sweetly solicitous
about his health, his mood, his struggle with *I Thought of Daisy* in the ugly
room on West Thirteenth Street. She assures him she enjoyed the experience and he shouldn't worry about her; repeatedly, she looks forward to
seeing him.

In fact she was ashamed of what she'd done and bewildered because
it seemed to mean so little to him, bitter that "I never could understand
how Edmund could attach so little importance to the mingling of the
flesh," as she put it to Farr. The mindset she brought to this experience
is that of the early lyric "April Mortality," included by Harold Bloom in his
Best Poems of the English Language:

> Rebellion shook an ancient dust,
> And bones, bleached dry of rottenness,
> Said: Heart, be bitter still, nor trust
> The earth, the sky, in their bright dress.

The poet speaks of the anguish she must bear at the expense of "the drifting race of men" and of her frustrated wish to have had a meaningful, enduring experience:

And if thou dreamest to have won
Some touch of her in permanence,
'Tis the old cheating of the sun,
The intricate lovely play of sense.

Be bitter still, remember how
Four petals, when a little breath
Of wind made stir the pear-tree bough,
Blew delicately down to death.

Yearning for a deeper communion, Leonie was also afraid she might be pregnant, and would eventually tell Wilson she had always wanted a child. He took her to the theater on her last day in New York before leaving for Europe on a Guggenheim Fellowship, but put off talking about their relationship until just before she sailed, whereupon she made a scene, "delivering a number of preachments," as she apologetically put it from France. In this letter she says, "My health is all right, I think," and in her next letter, "my health is now quite all right." She sent him her poems and he sent her a draft of *I Thought of Daisy*. He gave her an introduction to Bishop and she met up with Allen Tate, also in France on a Guggenheim. They all stayed at a pension in Brittany, where another guest was young Leon Edel, who six decades later recalled how Leonie talked about the beauty of Edmund Wilson's mind.

With Margaret back in California and Leonie abroad, in *The Twenties* Wilson sadly observes of these adventures, "The days when we embrace many and love none." On the same page he celebrates lovemaking with Frances as a "perfect feeling of possessing her completely." He saw her several times before leaving for California. "I'm happy now!" she declared, despite the misfortunes she sometimes had to report, and when he asked why, said, "Because I'm sure I don't love my husband any more." She added, "I wanted affection—I suppose that's why I went so crazy about Al." As he packed in his room on West Thirteenth, while her daughter, Adele, discreetly waited on the steps across the street, Frances said, "I don't like to see you go." She'd never talked this way, never kissed him so fervently, he thought without seeing it as a statement of love or request for him to respond with the words that Margaret and Leonie longed for. He presented her a fifty-dollar bill, and she ambivalently remarked, "I didn't think you'd ever do that!," adding, "I don't see why you go so far away!—You're the only person who's ever been nice to me!" Wilson's letters to Frances have disappeared, but a letter to "Dearest Ed" on the Coast wishes he'd written sooner and asks whether anyone else "is taking up your time," adding "I'm so lonesome without you there's no one to fuss over me or love me the way you did."

He enjoyed autumn in Santa Barbara: "the dry, fawn-colored mountains" and "the aromatic smell of the light eucalyptus logs burned in the fireplace," as well as the watercolor effects—the blues, reds, and garnets of the flowers and the women's dresses, the beach with the pink and blue water and the distant islands against the sunlight. The New Yorker likened the movements of the sandpipers to chorus girls: "all make for the waves, then all right turn, then all stop and simultaneously stick their bills in the sand." This "earthly paradise" was, however, "a little soft and cloying." A letter to the editor Maxwell Perkins states that to think "isn't necessary out here and the natives regard it as morbid." Yet the "calm Pacific spaces" were conducive to work, and there was "scarcely one word" of the original version of *Daisy* "left standing." He wasn't flattered when Perkins reported that Fitzgerald, who had yet to see any of the book, offered to review it favorably. Sending the editor an outline of the study of the international literary movement that would be *Axel's Castle*, Wilson said he worked on this as a way of loosening up for the novel—such criticism was "easier to do and in the nature of a relief from *Daisy*," which "in long stretches gets on my nerves." To recognize that he was a better writer about literary and historical figures than of fiction would take even longer than to admit he loved Frances.

In *The Twenties* Wilson detours around these California months with Margaret. Stepping back into the third person he writes, "he never loved her more than when he'd called on her at night, flashing a searchlight through her window, and saw her in that imperfect light, piling out of bed with her thick, brown, and naked legs." They lacked an easy intimacy. When asked to fasten her bathing suit he broke off "all the little hooks and eyes." After a shaker of cocktails and a long walk on the beach to the amusement park at Sandyland they had a staged picture taken in a wagon behind what may be a bighorn sheep, Margaret genial, Wilson uncomfortably looking down. On the way home he remained awkward, unwilling to overstate his feelings: "Stepped on her toes and hurt them rather badly when I tried to kiss her, stopping her, standing among the stones, on our strenuous but exalted return. I kept saying that I didn't know whether I had told her how much I liked her, how fond I was of her, etc." That wasn't what she wanted to hear.

He went home December 22 to spend the holiday with Rosalind—on Christmas Eve they always visited Kimball relatives who had a big house in Rumson—and after seeing him off, looking over the solitary ocean on a lovely day, Margaret didn't "feel like singing a hymn of praise." In a not so veiled reference to her aspirations, her letter to Wilson adds, "I hope something cheerful happens by this time next year. In the meantime I'll try to get over feeling like Madame Butterfly." If he didn't tell Margaret he had a girl in New York, Ted said something about it, for in her tragicomic way she wrote of imagining him New Year's Eve "walking down Broadway blowing a trumpet—or trailing a strumpet." She thought of coming east in April and wished "I didn't care about you and miss you so much." Wilson may have wished the same.

8

Literary and Cultural Criticism

A Critic Among Writers

In Wilson's pragmatic, post-Darwinian aesthetic, artists are antennae of the race, registering its difficult effort to move ahead. "With each such victory of the human intellect, whether in history, in philosophy, or in poetry," he states in "The Historical Interpretation of Literature," "we experience a deep satisfaction: we have been cured of some ache of disorder, relieved of some oppressive burden of uncomprehended events." For a literary critic, "this relief that brings the sense of power, and, with the sense of power, joy," is the positive emotion marking first-rate work. Those who make such judgments, whatever their standard, are, he says, individually self-appointed and collectively self-perpetuating. Such arbiters of taste of course make mistakes, but they are corrected in time. By the mid 1920s Wilson had the authority in his generation he'd acquired among school and college friends. As a reviewer he knew how to orient the reader to a book's story line and texture, rather than to "let out a whoop" of approval or condemnation or hang one's own essay on the work, in his opinion also amateurish. A good deal of his account of his contemporaries survives as what Clive James, himself a reviewer by trade, calls permanent criticism.

His review of *The Waste Land* appeared in *The Dial* a month after the poem was simultaneously published there and as a book by Boni and Liveright. Eliot created a museum of past literature, "piling up stratum upon stratum of reference, as the Italian painters used to paint over one another," yet his vision of our world "of strained nerves and shattered institutions" did not depend on knowing his arcane allusions. To Bishop in France Wilson refers *The Waste Land* to "Eliot's own agonized state of mind during the years which preceded his nervous breakdown." The poem conveyed "the sufferings of the sensitive man in the modern city chained to some work he hates and crucified on the vulgarity of his surroundings." It would reverberate in Wilson's harrowing "Jumping-Off Place" during the Depression, as it does from the burned-over country of "Big Two-Hearted River" to the valley of ashes presided over by T. J. Eckleburg's enormous eyes in *The Great Gatsby*. Yet Wilson was enough of a romantic to think that Eliot made the young poets old before their time. With Elinor Wylie's help, he produced a lighthearted parody of the despairing writer called "Air for Vitriol and Demi-Virginal," complete with footnote padding and an epigraph from Jonson's *The Alchemist* with what was already a signature line, "Thou looks like antichrist in that lewd hat."

He was among the first to judge Yeats the great modern poet. The Irishman challenged the boundaries between spirit and body, self and world, and refined the language without becoming insular or cloistered. Maintaining the noble voice in an age of commerce, science, and democratic education, Yeats integrated romanticism with techniques the critic was beginning to call symbolist. In the poems of *Responsiblities* he had chastened his style "to write for my own race / And for the reality." In 1925 Wilson noted that a volume of Yeats's lyrics, eclipsed in the book reviews by the novels of James Branch Cabell, Aldous Huxley, and Joseph Hergesheimer, was "probably comparable only to the very greatest of its kind in the world." Such poetry "could afford to wait and lie idle: it was written for a long life."

He didn't know that Ezra Pound had influenced both Yeats and Eliot, and thought Pound scattered, at his best in short lyrics and fragments. Bishop reported on an evening in Paris when "the great Amurricn Poet went big and thoroughly enjoyed himself," getting tight and promoting his version of a multicultural American language, including black, Jewish, and Western accents, "which he employs to wearing excess." Yet Wilson's friend saw "something rather noble and certainly very sensitive" when he recited Dante and Arnaut Daniel. Wilson's later twenty-three line portrait in anagrams upon Pound's name honors the poet for opening doors on Europe and the world, but contains the line "A NUD POZER / AND PURE OZ." He underestimated three other Americans of the older generation. Too much the urban intellectual to respond to Robert Frost's pastoral music, too committed to rhyme and meter to appreciate William Carlos Williams, he was unmoved by Wallace Stevens's decorative ironies and missed the passionate affirmation of mortal life in "Sunday Morning." He praised the "melting music" and spontaneous feeling of his contemporary E. E. Cummings though wishing the poet would trade typographical experimentation for a tighter discipline. Wilson's reservations about Hart Crane's first book infuriated Crane, who—himself of a wealthy family—attacked the critic as a privileged elitist, though later was glad to have his help in winning a Guggenheim. Wilson admired several women lyric poets. Leonie Adams, Louise Bogan, and Elinor Wylie were singers like Edna Millay, in touch, their friend believed, with their emotions. They used the regular forms on which he relied in his own alternately earnest and amusing verse, with its old-fashioned metrics and rhyme schemes.

When he looked at American fiction Wilson went back to James. He preferred the middle period of the novelist's English residence, when he had come "into the full possession of his language and form" and hadn't yet "lost any of the vividness of his youthful imagination." James interpreted individual character in the tradition of classical French drama and of Shakespeare, and Wilson defended him against Van Wyck Brooks's biography, which attacked his expatriation and took him as a failed social prophet. Yet James's inhibitions and renunciations put off the new writers. Both Hemingway and Fitzgerald took the famously "obscure" hurt, through which James explained to himself his non-participation in the Civil War, as a cause of impotence. In *The Sun Also Rises,* Bill Gorton jests of "Henry's Bicycle," while sexually disabled Jake Barnes says James "was riding horseback." Louise Bogan's friendship with Wilson began with a letter in which she wondered about the novelist's lack of passion. In some verses published in *The New Masses* Wilson sets the master's art against his famous lament to Howells for the unlived life:

> So he the scrupulous, the chaste, the great,
> Blower of prose to perfect forms of glass
> That elegantly bottle human fate,
> Grown old, confessed a soul dry-rotted with regret,
> Having ever vainly fingered ladies' lace,
> But never slept with Lison or Lisette.

That was no longer true for young Wilson when these lines appeared, yet one of his recollections of the year with Ted in their high-flying bachelor pad consisted of sitting by the gas heater reading a perfect form of glass, *The Wings of the Dove.*

Edith Wharton's technique and her subject seemed to him well matched. There is no better summary than the young critic's of her "swift manipulation of social groups and the punctual sardonic Providence which always arranges that the characters should meet each other unexpectedly at just the wrong time"; of the "gusto" with which she describes worldly people and her inability to interest us in shabby people whom she admires; of "the aloof spiritual sensitiveness to which all the chances of life appear as irony because man's habits and follies and necessities do not accord with his purest dreams." Wharton's polished style and mastery of form, her contrasts of the glittering and sordid, reflected New York City's hardness and insistence on material things, yet she was "a bitter intellectual snob" who saw both money and society strangling the superior person "in an all-embracing net of idiotic conventions." While *The Custom of the Country* and *The House of Mirth* attacked nouveau riche America from the cultivated upper class, *The Age of Innocence* condemned the failure of that class to follow through on its artistic instincts and its yearnings for freedom.

Gertrude Stein's genius, "conscientious and sane," excited Wilson, though she gained the world's attention with the problematic book *Tender Buttons. Three Lives* (1909) had improved on Flaubert's "A Simple Heart," for the style of "Melanctha" and "The Gentle Lena," unlike Flaubert's, took on the accents and rhythms of the minds it recorded. Stein was—as Wilson would become—a portraitist of character. Yet the effort of *Geography and Plays* to detach words from ordinary meanings and associations seemed to him misguided, as did her direct application of principles from cubism to writing. The French rightly thought that painting ought not to be literary, but, he quipped, there was no reason "why literature should not," and literature was "inevitably founded on ideas," a conviction marking Wilson's distance from post-structuralists who would one day judge words to be unhinged from their signification. In a thank-you letter after one of his reviews Stein embraced his premise, while stating that she liked "people and politics and painting." She was "awfully awfully pleased" with Wilson's "feeling and understanding and appreciation of her work," she said, carefully adding, "I don't believe that you do me more than justice but you do me a whole lot of justice."

Sherwood Anderson's legend as the small-town American turned bohemian artist had reached its height when the two men met in 1921. Escaping the life of a paint manufacturer and advertising man, he'd published *Winesburg, Ohio* in 1919 and the novel *Poor White* in 1920, then won the *Dial* award, and moved from Chicago to Greenwich Village. Established in New York, he wrote to Wilson, "I have come to think of you as a man of very sensitive good sense and I hope I may talk with you now and then." Characterizing Anderson's haunting strength in a review, Wilson spoke of being "soothed as well as disturbed by the feeling of hands thrust down among the inner organs of life—hands that are delicate and clean but still pitiless in their explorations." To Dell he declared that the stories in *The Triumph of the Egg* (1921) made Sinclair Lewis's realism seem shallow, to Bishop that Anderson's "gift for making a local story seem of universal significance" might enable him to become their generation's best novelist.

Anderson's story as an artist was about to sour. In person this literary elder brother of Faulkner and Hemingway had "a humorous racy quality" Wilson took as "very Southwestern" and vast quantities of "anecdotes, adventures, queer characters" whom he talked of always entertainingly. His conversation when writing *Many Marriages* made the novel seem a "wonderful erotic nightmare full of strange symbolic scenes reared on the old circus ground of American life." But in *Vanity Fair* Wilson had to pronounce the book a flat narrative of a man who left his wife to marry his secretary, its poetic repetitions merely boring. In subsequent novels Anderson would sacrifice the authenticity of small-town constraint and yearning to the role of a Lawrentian apostle of bohemia. He turned self-conscious and stilted when, as Wilson put it, he "took pen in hand," falling into the dreamlike solemnity that, apparently inspired by Brooks and Stieglitz, he deemed appropriate to a fabulist. In one of Hemingway's first letters to Wilson, in the fall of 1923, he observes that Anderson's work has "gone to hell, perhaps from people in New York telling him too much how good he was."

Hemingway's emergence owed something to Wilson, something to the fact that during the 1920s a new literary style could be mainstream news. Burton Rascoe's column in the *New York Herald Tribune*, drawn from a round of publisher's luncheons, theatrical openings, and cocktail parties, had informed Hemingway that Wilson liked his stories in *The Little Review*. He sent *Three Stories and Ten Poems* with a request for names of possible reviewers, and in a follow-up letter asked for a joint review with *in our time* (the Boni and Liveright edition of 1925, containing fifteen rather than eleven stories, was titled *In Our Time*). Declaring Wilson's opinion the only one "in the States I have any respect for," Hemingway denied the influence—which Wilson's letter politely notes—of Anderson's racetrack stories on "My Old Man." He was forthright about his debt to Stein, whose method was "invaluable for analyzing anything or making notes on a person or a place"; she had, he said, "a wonderful head." Wilson's *Dial* review in 1924, the first notice of Hemingway in the United States, grouped him with Anderson and Stein as well as Twain in *Huckleberry Finn*—and, he'd soon add, the best of Ring Lardner—as a "distinctively American development in prose," marked by a naiveté of language that could convey deep feelings and a complex personal psychology.

Wilson's experience piling bodies in France made real to him the dying Italian soldier's decision to make a separate peace, and what he saw at Chaumont of Europe's chaos in 1919 showed the truth of such paragraphs as that in which the six cabinet ministers are shot in the rain against the wall of the hospital. *In our time* had for him more "artistic dignity" than anything else their countrymen had yet written about the war. On a visit from Toronto not long afterward, Hemingway seemed "one of the glibbest and slickest and most knowing young newspapermen" he had ever met, yet was professionally objective about his work. Several years later, admiring the classic tale of wounded veterans, "In Another Country," Wilson felt free to suggest that in "The Killers" he'd given "the thugs a line of banter which sounded a little too much like the hero of your novel and his friend on their fishing trip—that is to say, a little too sophisticated."

His understanding of Hemingway's premises was incomplete. Reviewing *The Sun Also Rises* as "The Sportsman's Tragedy," he noted that the pleasures of hunting, fishing, and bullfighting embodied life's cruelty. The scenes at the Irati River made one "feel, behind the appetite for the physical world, the tragedy or the falsity of a moral relation," a malaise that infected the brilliantly painted landscapes. Yet as an heir of the Enlightenment Wilson could not absorb the weight of trauma, death, and meaninglessness in Hemingway's writing. He praised this artist as "not a propagandist even for humanity," but a propagandist for humanity is certainly what Wilson was. Though he too could perceive the abyss, he was temperamentally unsuited to believe that literature was not an instrument of human progress.

In the anonymously published tour de force assessment called "The All-Star Literary Vaudeville" Wilson summed up scores of American writers, many new and difficult, with what Morris Dickstein calls "a no-nonsense directness that would become his hallmark." Even when "wrong-headed or rudimentary," he engaged each figure and book "with the full weight of his own experience and sensibility." Faulkner had yet to emerge, and he found no one who could be called a major novelist, though looking as far afield as Jean Toomer's *Cane*. *Babbitt's* ogre hero almost equaled the "three-dimensional ogres" in Dickens, yet Lewis's mechanical satire swamped his narrative. Cather was a better artist, but the grandeur and loneliness of her prairie landscape were more convincing than some of her people. Dreiser, with his "newspaper narrative of commonplace scandals and crimes," told the truth about American society in a style verbose and leaden. The best of Wilson's contemporaries seemed to him isolated eccentrics like the nineteenth-century classics—Poe and Whitman, *Walden* and *Moby Dick*, all "independent one-man turns," he wrote in the language of vaudeville.

Two promising writers, he said in this piece, had yet to mature. John Dos Passos's early novels were overly documentary and "ridden by adolescent resentments." Everybody lost out, as Wilson would later put it— those who were on the side of the angels had to suffer, if they were not "snuffed out," while the pleasures of those who succeeded in bourgeois society were made repulsive. When he plunged into *Manhattan Transfer*, however, he was impressed "by what seemed to me the wonderful handling, in the first fifty pages, of the New York of the period of my childhood." Here people of their generation talked "as they actually did." Dos Passos already showed the moral concern for the country as a whole that would lead Wilson to consider *U.S.A.* their generation's most important fiction. "From the point of view of its literary originality and its intellectual interest," he would think *The 42nd Parallel* (published in 1930) "by far the most remarkable, the most encouraging" American novel since the war.

Fitzgerald was Wilson's other instance of an immature talent. In the dialogue "The Delegate from Great Neck" (1924) he is portrayed as a lightweight who regrets having to write "a lot of rotten stuff" because he can't afford his establishment "on less than thirty-six thousand a year." This is the persona Scott assumes with friends in a passage from *The Twenties* headed "Great Neck, mid-April [1924]." He falls asleep while Ring Lardner and Wilson talk, finally getting to baseball and literature as the "deep blue patches" of dawn appear at the windows. When he wakes up he characteristically asks whether they've analyzed him "ruthlessly." Lightly, he declares he is going to live abroad until he has "accomplished something important and then come back and have people give him dinners." It was in a different tone that Fitzgerald entered in his April ledger, "Decision on the 15th to go to Europe," a course Wilson had more than once suggested would benefit his work. On that very day he wrote to Max Perkins, "I feel I have an enormous power in me now." In a thought Wilson would have admired, Fitzgerald added of the book that became *The Great Gatsby*, "I cannot let it go out unless it has the very best I'm capable of in it, or even, as I feel sometimes, something better than I'm capable of."

In August from his perch above the Mediterranean, he enthused to Perkins that in *Trimalchio*, an early version of *Gatsby*, he had produced "about the best American novel ever written." To Wilson in October he more modestly described it as "wonderful." Perkins gave Wilson the text, and he wrote to Fitzgerald, "It is very thrilling and in the end truthful and beautiful," echoing the "Ode on a Grecian Urn" of Fitzgerald's favorite poet. Though he couldn't gauge an account of a world beyond his own experience, the book contained "unforgettable phrases that I have loved." By this time Fitzgerald was transforming *Trimalchio* into *Gatsby* in Rome. Six months later, when Wilson received the published book, which more than achieved Fitzgerald's aspirations, his enthusiasm was qualified. This was "undoubtedly in some ways" the best thing his friend had done—"the best planned, the best sustained, the best written," accomplishing what "people" had "scolded" him for not doing. The judicial tone becomes a stammer of enthusiasm as Wilson adds, "It is full of all sorts of happy touches—in fact all the touches are happy—there is not a hole in it anywhere." Yet Gatsby's activities as confidence man were not plausibly spelled out. And Wilson, applying a standard he didn't to *The Sun Also Rises*, found the characters unsympathetic, the story unpleasantly bitter—"you will admit that it keeps us inside the hyena cage." In 1926, a year after T. S. Eliot wrote to Fitzgerald that *Gatsby* was the first step the American novel had taken since James, Wilson called him a writer of "inspired imagination and poetic literary brilliance" at last acquiring control over his material.

Wilson would do everything to produce a happier vision of his country in *I Thought of Daisy* (1929). His Daisy is a generous pal who helps the narrator mature, not Fitzgerald's destructive "golden girl," and his narrator an idealistic intellectual, not a bond salesman who will go back to his Midwestern family's hardware business. Wilson drives his book to an upbeat conclusion. Yet when going through the page proofs, he would write with characteristic honesty to the novelist Hamilton Basso that *Daisy* lacked "the vividness and excitement, and the technical accuracy" of *Gatsby*, noting "how much better Scott Fitzgerald's prose and dramatic sense were than mine." That Fitzgerald "had to pass through several immature and amateurish phases before he arrived at that one" gave him hope.

The man whose career was to unfold over five decades would never be free of the need to measure himself against his wonderfully talented friend. Their relationship was strained in the course of Scott's long struggle with *Tender Is the Night*, begun as a novel about matricide, a subject that, Wilson thought, "might well have taxed Dostoevsky." As the book dragged on and was reconceived while Fitzgerald's life fell apart, his guilty sense of accountability to Wilson increased, though Wilson tried to dismiss the mentor role as "highschool (Princeton University) stuff." Looking back, he credited Gauss's lectures on Dante and Flaubert with prompting Scott's development from "a loose and subjective conception of the novel to an organized impersonal one." It was the young critic, however, who hammered home this lesson from 1919 to 1924, sharpening the novelist's awareness of the temptation, for him, to be facile, and the need for artistic form. After Fitzgerald's early death, Wilson's influence would be carried on through his work with *The Last Tycoon* and *The Crack-Up*. At this point, he'd justify Bishop's observation—noted in Alec McKaig's diary—that of the Princeton group only one man truly believed in another—Wilson in Fitzgerald.

New York and the Arts

Like his early criticism, Wilson's panorama of jazz-age New York is characterized by its concreteness, its glinting exactness. He incorporated the popular stage in a monthly column in *The Dial* in which he wrote also of everything from Hemingway's stories to a reprint of Horace. He sketched the Follies and the circus, the music hall singer Alice Lloyd, and the Italian-American impersonator Farfariello, who "originates all his own ideas, writes all his own songs and even makes his own wigs." As *The New Republic's* cultural man-of-all-work, beginning in 1925, Wilson circulated through the arts of the metropolis, from Stravinsky conducting *Pétrouchka* to Houdini, nightclubs and burlesque shows, Charlie Chaplin in *The Gold Rush*, the painting of O'Keeffe and George Bellows. A reader who admires these vivid pieces, reprinted in *The American Earthquake*, will find passages of equal interest in his journal *The Twenties*.

Vaudeville drew him from a listless Broadway scene—the American plays mediocre, the Shakespeare and Sheridan not up to British standards—and for four or five years he followed the fashions at the Follies. Ziegfeld's mix of stand-up comics and beautiful women caught the "fantasy" and "harlequinade" of the busy well-to-do New Yorker's life. Documenting a dress rehearsal of the chorus line, Wilson tells how "the ponies" are organized by Ziegfeld according to the color of their costumes (*"You've got two white ones together! Put somebody between them. You go over on the end, Gladys. Now, begin again!"*) and come swinging in, kicking and cracking their whips in unison. The tenor's song states the theme—"You'll find it rough but gentle, Romantic, sentimental . . . I would LIKE to corRAL a very merry necessary little gal!"—while Will Rogers throws his lariat around the milling women. "The new woman" was also glimpsed at the Follies. In Wilson's journal, sumptuous Gretta Nissen appears "as a female Bluebeard, with a complacent Scandinavian smile," who "slowly decapitates her lovers and shoves their heads out the door with her foot." When you take the subway home after these shows, he writes, "it speeds you to your goal with a crash, like a fast song by Eddie Cantor."

At her midtown speakeasy Texas Guinan presided over her version of mechanized sex. "In the windowless compact room under the great glowing peony of the ceiling that melts from pink through deep rose to orange, swollen and hypnotic to drunken eyes, among green and red carnation panels that frame bogus senoritas," Wilson shows "this formidable woman, with her pearls, her prodigious glittering bosom, her abundant and beautifully bleached yellow coiffure, her bear-trap of shining white teeth, her broad back that looks coarse and raw behind its velvet green grating, the full-blown peony as big as a cabbage exploding on her broad green thigh," introducing her "little girls" to her customers. Like Cummings, Dos Passos, Robert Benchley, and Frank Crowninshield, he'd choose the Minskys' burlesque instead, unless the purity crusaders had shut it down. He loved their *Antony and Cleopatra*—the joking with Antony's "I am dying, Egypt, dying," the transformation of Cleopatra's asp into a property phallus called the "wassup."

It was the age of "The Daring Young Man on the Flying Trapeze," and at the circus Mlle. Leitzel, costumed in silver, hung at a rope's end high above the arena without a net and threw her body about like a bacchante.

She was "the free-est and least self-conscious of performers, and the performer most distinguished by style." Houdini the daring escape artist also soldiered in the cause of the Enlightenment, using his craft to deflate the claims of spiritualists, telepathists, and mediums. At the Hippodrome he robbed the marvelous of its pretensions, producing effects that a blindfolded subject on stage assumed to be supernatural while the audience saw how they were achieved. Through Mary Blair, who'd once been on the same bill, Wilson became acquainted with this "short strong stocky man with small feet and a very large head," "wide-browed and aquiline-nosed" like idealized busts of Roman consuls and generals. A rabbi's son and "scrupulous and serious-minded" professional, when Houdini died in a freak accident, the sometime parlor trickster and manipulator of mechanical devices paid tribute to the master magician. Of a biography, Wilson wrote that to follow Houdini's early life "among the East Side cabarets and the dime museums" stirred one "as one can always be stirred by the struggle of a superior man to emerge from the commonplaces, the ignominies and the pains of the common life, to make for himself a position and a livelihood among his less able fellows at the same time that he learns to perfect himself in the pursuit of his chosen work."

When Gilbert Seldes, a friend at the highbrow *Dial*, brought out a book celebrating what he termed the lively arts, Wilson praised his ability to describe what he'd seen, but objected that he tried to build up the comic strip *Krazy Kat* at the expense of Dr. Johnson. Anatole France hadn't, Wilson said, found it necessary to denigrate the legitimate theater while praising the *café chantant*. Seldes and Wilson would go in different directions after radio took up the popular arts for its expanding audience, when the spontaneity and the individualism these two writers valued began to fade.* Seldes made a career in radio and television while Wilson focused his energies on Joyce, Proust, and other modern classics, then after the Crash on political issues.

His film reviews contrast the distinction of Chaplin and other actors and directors from the Old World to the mechanical gags and the lack of aesthetic focus of the entertainment industry now established in Hollywood. On the page he conveys the slapstick violence of the cabin scene on the edge of the cliff in *The Gold Rush*. When he went to California (as

---

*Seldes would one day tell Wilson he was foolish to judge popular culture by the quality of the individual artist. Yet in the same letter Seldes declares, "I often read a paragraph of yours about someone we both admired, and it says more than I say in five pages."

mentioned above) to try to recruit Chaplin for *Chronkite's Clocks,* he perceived the actor as a highbrow-lowbrow, "the inequalities of his personality" embodied in those of his face, "the upper part imaginative and full of intelligence whereas the lower part was square-jawed and coarse." Fearing Chaplin wouldn't be able to compete with a less subtle comedian, he was delighted when Buster Keaton and Harold Lloyd began imitating their colleague.

Alfred Stieglitz's photographs achieved something of the freedom of plastic art in cloudscapes that conveyed effects "of a feathery softness or of a solidity almost marmoreal." Stieglitz, in a fan letter to Wilson, had said that O'Keeffe and he admired the "genuine sparkle" of the critic's work, and Wilson wrote up the Stieglitz exhibition in 1925. Reprinting his account of that day at the Anderson Galleries in *The American Earthquake,* in a postscript he recalls how the impresario piloted him around telling him what to see and how to see it in an endless "ribbon of talk" maintained in a nasal voice and through the sniffles of a cold. Wilson reflects that he'd been a child when Stieglitz set up the "little bird refuge for artists" called Gallery 291 at a time when the city was "as bracing, as electrical and full of light, as San Francisco had been." He took O'Keeffe's blazing colors, conventionally enough, as a lyrical expression of the feminine. Influenced by modern painting, he used its primary colors to satirize a Greenwich Village interior in 1927 and to document a suicide attempt during the Depression. Jed Perl has noted, "He almost turns the Dimiceli home into an interior by Matisse." *The American Earthquake,* which embeds these accounts of the arts within the metropolitan scene, is full of painterly effects—the sweaty haze of Broadway in August, a wintry scene on the bus futilely searching for a place to live ("old servant's bedroom on Ninth Street turned into four-room apartment; two rooms without air, two rooms without air or light," Wilson writes in "It's Great to Be a New Yorker!").

Music was part of the mix in twenties New York, partly through the efforts of his friend Paul Rosenfeld. Taking up where James Huneker left off, Rosenfeld, a portly little man with a mustache like Chaplin's, wrote of composers and their musical personalities, promoting the European moderns and hoping to inspire an American school of composition. At soirees in Paul's apartment poets read and composers performed their work. Wilson calls up a glimpse of "the bespectacled figure of [Aaron] Copland, at that period gray-faced and lean, long-nosed and rather unearthly," leaning over the keyboard "as he chanted in a high, cold and passionate voice a poem of Ezra Pound's—'An Immorality'—for which he had written a setting." Looking back, the French-trained Copland felt indebted to Wilson for his conviction that one could "make something of America," could "make an American Culture." There was a general impression that classical and popular music might achieve some fusion. While Wilson says that Rosenfeld could only accept jazz "transmuted by the style of a Stravinksy or a Copland," he promoted Schönberg, who evoked for Wilson the beat of New York, the ragged texture of American life. In "The Problem of the Higher Jazz" (1926) Wilson speculates about the musical possibilities, and he'd return to this theme in the short novel whose protagonist is partly drawn from the German-Jewish Rosenfeld.*

His commentary on architecture marked his loyalty to Greenwich Village, where cheap rents, Italian food, and a café culture sustained many whom he knew. His apartments with Mary Blair, his furnished room, and the places he borrowed from friends like Elinor Wylie were in this district or on its margins. Though the Village seemed past its heroic days (as has been true ever since, each generation convinced it has arrived too late), it afforded human scale in a city otherwise governed by the speculative vertical expansion of real estate in skyscrapers. Not many years had passed since architects designed such aesthetically pleasing structures as the Woolworth Building and the Flatiron Building, but the apartment construction of the twenties boom hemmed Wilson in—"upright rectangles of drab or raw yellow brick" that were "perforated, as if by a perforating machine, with rows of rectangular windows"; "blunt truncated meaningless towers"—a bleak cubistic setting that conveyed the reproductive efficiency and stultifying uniformity of the machine aesthetic. His nostalgia for the architectural past was stimulated by the endless cacophony of jackhammers. He and his friends, like many others before and since, fled the city either to recover or to work or both, and it was depressing to return from Cape Cod in the fall of 1927 and find Washington Square dwarfed by symbols of corporate capitalism—two "huge coarse and swollen mounds—blunt, clumsy, bleaching the sunlight with their dismal pale yellow sides and stamping down both the old formal square and the newer Bohemian refuge."

---

*He never stopped making judgments of the exhibitions and concerts he attended. In the 1960s, when *Patriotic Gore* had made Wilson prominent, in one of his self-interviews he would unload all his accumulated opinions about painting and drawing, especially of a satiric kind, and about music, particularly opera, opinions he could no longer venture as a professional reviewer. "I'd never dare to write such stuff today," he said, looking over his shoulder at his early reportage.

Whatever the odds, he believed in the struggle for a better American society. "The People Against Dorothy Perkins," a report on a seventeen-year-old girl's conviction for an accidental murder, anticipates Wilson's defense of countrymen out of work, starved, or beaten down during the Depression. Dorothy Perkins had shot a suitor when she was infatuated with another man, drunk, and struggling with her father over a gun. The young reporter sketches the courtroom scene, with "the Stars and Stripes over the judge's desk, hanging crooked and nearly black, as if tarnished by decades of fumes from the cases of the criminal courts," on the witness stand his jazz-age heroine, her slim figure with "long adolescent's arms like broom-handles," her red-gold hair and her face that "burn the assemblage at a single point with an intensity of passionate life." Also vivid are the slick prosecutor, the jurors (four of whom turn out to have wanted Dorothy electrocuted for first-degree murder), and a judge who sentences her to five to fifteen years because "women have done too much killing" and male jurors let them get away with it. Wilson's bitterness that his article could do nothing for the girl took him to another literary form. In the poem "To a Young Girl Indicted for Murder" he condemned the ineffectuality of literary men who failed to put the idealism of the page into action—"those praisers of the past, accepters of defeat, / The ghosts of poets—violent against God / no longer in my day."

In apartments and in "iridescent" speakeasies he absorbed more than his share of Prohibition booze, its bitter taste ingeniously disguised by colorful fruit juices. He had a strong constitution, could get by on little sleep, seldom had hangovers, and got back to work at nine in the morning. By 1927, however, liquor seemed to have become a destructive social force. His "Lexicon of Prohibition," a catalogue looking back to Franklin's *The Drinker's Dictionary*, sets over a hundred terms for drunkenness in a list that leads from mild incapacity to helpless intoxication. Words like "sprees" and "toots," which connote "an exceptional occurrence," were used less as "fierce protracted drinking" became nearly "universal." In a 1929 letter to Allen Tate he mentions a Saturday night party at which, "about midnight, the guests began very slowly breaking phonograph records over each other's heads." The writer who captured this, without knowing, he said, what it might mean, sometimes doubted that the arts could flourish in such a scene. His last piece for *Vanity Fair*, published as these developments first made themselves felt, was called "Wanted: A City of the Spirit."

At The New Republic: *Culture and Society*

In 1925, Robert Morss Lovett, one of those who had interviewed Wilson four years before, gave him two books to review for *The New Republic*. He brought the work back the same day, and Lovett hired him as a reviewer and a reporter. In November 1925 Wilson became a contributing editor, and a year later was one of eight editors nominally sharing direction of the magazine. Until September 1931 he "ordered all the articles on cultural subjects in the back of the magazine and supplied the middle of the magazine with articles by myself and others." This podium enabled him to become adept at "pursuing a line of thought through pieces on miscellaneous and more or less fortuitous subjects," like the reviewer-critics on whom he modeled himself: so Shaw, in his weekly chronicle of the London theaters, had been able, without boring readers, to impose gradually his values as an artist and citizen, while Poe's creative pieces were sprinkled "into a rapid stream of newsletters, and daily reviewing that was itself made to feed his interests and contribute to his higher aims." Wilson, like these forebears, was a historian, moralist, satirist, and entertainer as well as a judge of quality. He would one day reflect, that, with this platform at *The New Republic*, he finally began to write well, and a young Lionel Trilling attributed the lucidity and ease of his prose to addressing the same educated readers week after week.

Supported by the fortunes of Willard Straight, an idealistic partner of J. P. Morgan, and his wife, Dorothy, the magazine occupied two old brick houses painted yellow in a shabby-genteel neighborhood on West Twenty-first Street not far from the Hudson, across from a theological seminary and near a home for girls in trouble with the law. Malcolm Cowley describes the offices as furnished with heirlooms and things picked up in secondhand shops. People worked hard, but the tone was easygoing and familial. Along with Lovett, a literary historian and a patron of many good causes (FDR would make him secretary of the Virgin Islands), Wilson's associates at "the back of the book" included his longtime friend Stark Young, the drama critic, who was homosexual, and would write the Southern romantic novel *So Red the Rose*. They left politics to Herbert Croly and the economist George Soule, who were likely to be focused on tariffs or war reparations. Wilson got Cummings, Bogan, and their fellow poet Rolfe Humphries as well as Hemingway to write for him, and when he read a good book by the young historian Allan Nevins, solicited a review.

Calling himself "a concision fetishist," he urged R. P. Blackmur to be clear and concrete and not overly academic—one could avoid "the impressionistic criticism of the day before yesterday" without reducing literature to its "philosophic or psychological" content or to "a sort of literary scholasticism which limits itself to putting things into categories." Blackmur, subsequently a leading New Critic, soon earned praise. Cowley remembered how Wilson launched him at the magazine by accepting an essay on Valéry after another editor had turned it down.

T. S. Matthews, who started out at *The New Republic* and would become editor of *Time*, pictures Wilson "at thirty already inclining to stoutness and baldness, with pale, blinking eyes and a high, strained-tenor voice"; his profile was "regular as a plump Roman emperor's and his expression like an absent-minded, cantankerous professor's." Ascending the creaking stairs, he'd sometimes stop to look over the papers and magazines, "then, collecting himself, cry, 'Well, see you presently!' and dart out." A fellow Princetonian who lived in Princeton and commuted in to Manhattan, Matthews hoped this connection would forge a bond with Wilson. But Wilson had no small talk or clubby loyalty. After a visit to the college, he might say simply that he'd seen Gauss, or if he hadn't been there, limit himself to asking whether there was enough ice for skating on the lake. In conversation he rehearsed his work, irritating Matthews, who wanted to offer his own ideas. "When he was holding forth, as he sometimes did, on a subject that interested him, he seemed perfectly oblivious of his audience, and would go on and on in his rapid-fire high-pitched voice, gesturing mostly by jerking back his head or wagging it from side to side," pausing only "at the end of a paragraph." One was mistaken to interpret this pause as an invitation to speak, for Wilson then "broke ruthlessly in at the exact spot where he had left off."

Wilson could type with two fingers, but his copy was generally produced with a pencil on a legal-sized tablet. Matthews noted his "peculiar way of holding a pencil: he seemed to bunch his whole hand about it, using his middle finger and his forefinger to guide the point." He was an inveterate reviser. "Anything he wrote was likely to be rewritten several times before he was satisfied with it; he would cross out paragraphs on his galley proofs and paste in new passages, typewritten, if there was time; if there wasn't, he would crowd the margins with his small but legible handwriting, in pencil." He'd make "drastic revisions" even in page proof, angering the printers.

His best *New Republic* pieces put his imagination at the service of social criticism. Several of these—including Wilson's first historical portrait, perhaps his best short story, and the dramatic monologue "A Preface to Persius"—were written during three exhilarating weeks with Frances in the fall of 1927. Though the singular instance was always more real to him than generalization or theory, he went in for credos, and "A Preface to Persius" joins a classical aesthetic to a romantic view of the creation of literature from pain and dislocation. At a secondhand bookstore on the way to dinner the narrator picks up an eighteenth-century British edition of the Roman satirist, a volume that, in its fine leather binding, appears as "a little casket in which something precious was kept." While eating dinner over a bottle of wine he reads the preface by William Drummond, M. P., and is touched by this urbane Englishman's fellowship with a writer of rough-hewn verses in Nero's Rome. At another table is Cummings, who stops by to deliver one of the high-speed monologues Wilson considered as remarkable as his poetry. Enraged at the executions of Sacco and Vanzetti, he wonders how the condemned men had stayed alive for so long—"Why, I've seen them shoot people first and search them afterwards—and if they've got any bullets in them, they arrest them for carrying concealed weapons!" His closing anarchic burst, "Be a fine thing to blow the subways up!" irritates the Wilson figure, who then reminds himself that the artist must submit to the pressures of a chaotic reality, that the critic too must absorb its shocks if he is to supply a judgment and perspective that complete the work.

As Wilson loftily envisions art's effort to impose meaning on "the mysterious flux of experience which escapes beneath our hand," the marginality of serious literature in America is brought home in the "loud sour laughter" of a nearby party of men and women "all pink and of huge size." The narrator, linked to Drummond's eighteenth century by the book in his hand, reflects that when that culture was destroyed by industrialism and moneymaking, beneath it had opened up the social void, and into this "Europe heavily and dully sank, not without some loud crackings of her structure"—boozily he adds, "America, in a sense, was that gulf." Allied with the writers of the past, he resolves to go on writing on behalf of a different vision of his country, but is banged into by two of the bulky pink people on his way out of the restaurant. Self-pity is not an option, for these "rude collisions with reality"—as they are similarly described in *The Twenties*—are the impetus of literature.

Thus Wilson Americanizes Arnold's *Culture and Anarchy*. He updates

Arnold's "Function of Criticism" in "The Critic Who Does Not Exist." Like his Victorian predecessor, he values a sophisticated intellectual culture on the French model, in which schools and theories contend with one another in a debate that involves artists and readers. American factions, he notes, speak mostly to themselves—each produces "a certain amount of criticism to justify or explain what it is doing, but it may, I believe, be said in general that they do not communicate with one another; their opinions do not really circulate." Identifying these groupings (one can supply one's own within the cultural marketplace of the moment), he believes that Mencken and Sinclair Lewis, Eliot and his disciples, such neo-romantics as Fitzgerald and Millay, and the socio-biographical critics would all gain if their assumptions were considered by a neutral eye. It is Arnold's faith that true criticism, though arising from the interests of political factions, will manifest "a free play of mind" and be "not the minister of these interests, not their enemy, but absolutely and entirely independent of them."

One notes that Wilson does not claim for himself the role of neutral arbiter, though he had shrewdly assessed the work of different camps, and in the staged confrontations called "imaginary dialogues" he had set tradition against the energy of the new and outlandish. He'd contrasted the literary personalities of the 1920s to such solid craftsmen as Wharton and James, while in their eccentricities and independence linking them to the mid-nineteenth-century classics. But he does not want to be a full-time literary critic, aspiring to be a writer of poetry, drama, or fiction who also writes criticism, or someone whose literary criticism feeds a larger historical project.

His subsequent historical portraits emerged from arduous research, but he could draw on information from his father and Gauss for "Woodrow Wilson at Princeton." The president's failure to complete his reforms first of New Jersey, then of the United States, and to win American support for the League of Nations, was anticipated, the critic proposed, when he failed to understand how the Princeton alumni would fight for their eating clubs. President Wilson had been conditioned by his early life among parsons and schoolmasters in a familial circle of sweetness and light. The orator's conviction of the triumph of the word didn't prepare him to grasp the values of worldly antagonists, and the straitlaced moralist couldn't understand people who would defend their right to freedom and fun. Those whom he angered "had no doubt never known the ecstasy of transcendent moral conviction, of the triumph of the personal will which knows also that it 'conquers in this sign,' of the shaping of God's institutions from the baser habitations, however gilded, of the children of this world." Edmund Wilson was on both sides of the issue. He shared his generation's taste for such freedom and fun but, as the party of the twenties wore on, Bishop discerned "the ghost of Cotton Mather plowing under his conscience like a mole." Wilson would remain in Arnold's sense a Hellenist, yet his evocation of the shaping of God's institutions from the things of this world marks the Hebraism that would be liberated when it appeared to him wrapped in the flag of Marx's scientific socialism.

The decades of cultural history do not always respect the calendar, and as the 1960s didn't really begin until Kennedy's assassination, so the leftward swing of literary opinion Wilson would lead in the early 1930s started with the trials, in 1927, of Sacco and Vanzetti, anarchist immigrants convicted of murder. Vanzetti's famous testament had convinced Dos Passos, Millay, and others that he was indeed "innocent of these two harms." Dos Passos lost his voice when speaking before crowds against their execution, and Edna was arrested. A trial lawyer's son, Wilson wasn't sure both men were innocent, though no one then knew that ballistic evidence would one day confirm Sacco's ownership of the murder weapon. Instead, his first political editorial charged that an Anglo-Saxon establishment, backed by the Boston Irish, ignored the rights of immigrant Italian Americans. Half a century before his time, he argued that a more pluralistic American literature would articulate the diverse heritage of "A Nation of Foreigners." He drew on his army experience, and perhaps on Randolph Bourne's idea of a transnational America. But when Croly, his boss, praised him for not pushing a Marxist view of class conflict he was ashamed not to have done so.

When it was all over Dos—as his friends called him—observed to Wilson that "during the last days before the executions" it was "as if, by some fairy-tale spell, all the different kinds of Americans, eminent and obscure, had suddenly, in a short sudden burst of intensified life, been compelled to reveal their true character in a heightened exaggerated form." Wilson feared he had revealed his, for on the August weekend before the sentences were carried out he was partying in Boston with the flappers Louise and Henrietta Fort, driving around the tense city and the suburbs to the shore and then to Beacon Hill, where their foursome drank a gallon of alcohol and ate lobsters. From his journal account came a story that is a paean of liberal guilt, first called "Lobsters for Supper," published in *The American Earthquake* as "The Men from Rumplemayer's." In the background are editorials, cartoons, a newspaper headline declaring that the Massachusetts Supreme Court will not intervene. Liquor is an anodyne, as are the two women's charming songs and well-bred slang, the solid Beacon Hill house with its flavor of old literary Boston. The Wilson figure takes ironic note of the lobsters trapped in a paper bag on the floor of the car, the "condemned clams" at polluted Revere Beach. Returning to the Cape with the first fine taste of autumn in the air, he receives two telegrams, one signed "FORSAKEN," urging him to rejoin the party, the other saying, "PICKETERS AND SPEAKERS NEEDED FOR LAST PROTEST" (Wilson received an almost identical wire from Dos Passos). The tale ends with a metaphor of bankruptcy like those Fitzgerald would use after the Crash: "But I had used up my extra money, so I couldn't answer either summons."

In half a dozen brilliant reviews in 1929 Wilson took the measure of a literary scene not yet overwhelmed by politics. He urged the opposing American camps to resist myths that solaced the imagination. Dos Passos seemed to envision a sturdy army of workers eschewing the temptation of new cars and radios in order to build socialism, and Eliot a world of highly literate seventeenth-century churchmen. In the polemic *For Lancelot Andrewes*, Eliot declared that civilization depended on the church, assuming that Christianity remained persuasive to most first-rate minds, while in the play *Airways, Inc.* Dos Passos made middle-class American life more ugly and bitter than it actually was, "even under capitalism and even in a city like New York." So Pound wanted to see writers as late medieval troubadours, and Mencken (no longer to Wilson so bracingly American) took society as "a sort of German university town, where people drink a great deal of beer and devour a great many books, and where they respect the local nobility." In a skeptical letter, Allen Tate called Wilson naive if he thought anyone could negotiate "reality" without imagined alternatives, and shrewdly suggested he had his own unexamined American mythology. But Wilson's article insists our writers stand on their own two feet and make sense of commercial society, for their world was quickly becoming "everybody's world."

When Trilling met Wilson at *The New Republic* in 1929, "he seemed in his own person, and young as he was, to propose and to realize the idea of the literary life," the life of a man of letters in the cultural capital. "One got from him a whiff of Lessing at Hamburg, of Sainte Beuve in Paris."

While challenging contemporary writers, he championed them against the conservative academics who called themselves New Humanists. In this bitter early culture war, Irving Babbitt, a Harvard professor known for his critique of Romanticism, and Paul Elmer More, whose *Shelburne Essays* expounded Greek philosophy and early American literature, attacked the "new morality" of modern letters, proposing a moderation and restraint ostensibly drawn from the classics. With his classical training Wilson faulted Babbitt for translating Antigone's "unwritten and unfailing laws of the gods" as "in the heavens," thereby making Antigone's act into one of Christian conscience. This ideologue was said to have a map of the country in his study marked by pins wherever Humanist centers had sprung up. He pronounced that "in 'dealing with error,' we are no longer obliged to be moderate," on which Wilson drily commented that "as Professor Babbitt, in his writing, hardly ever deals with anything but error, he is rarely obliged to be moderate." Paul Elmer More foolishly equated Joyce's ability to follow the confused nature of consciousness with a denial of free will; he patronized A. N. Whitehead's attempt to overcome the dualism of man and nature; denouncing art for art's sake instead of trying to comprehend it historically, he preached restraint "to a people bound hand and foot." Yet Wilson respected More's learning and moral seriousness, wishing they were made relevant to the "often only semi-literate" twenties. This scholar should bring to his own century the same care he brought to the acts of the Council of Chalcedon in the fifth.

More had retired in Princeton, and Gauss took Wilson to call on him one Sunday afternoon in 1929. The conversation is recalled in "Mr. More and the Mithraic Bull," so titled because a student had that week asked Gauss a question about the Near Eastern god that he brought to the philosopher. Published in *The Triple Thinkers* after More's death, Wilson's memoir is one of the lasting markers of the long forgotten Humanist controversy, the other being Hemingway's comments in "A Natural History of the Dead." Like "A Preface to Persius" this is a semidramatic piece. More, a plain-spoken Midwesterner, condemns Eliot and Baudelaire, Joyce and Dos Passos, with the same stiff-necked righteousness with which Woodrow Wilson denounced the city bosses. He is contrasted to Gauss, an exponent of the Enlightenment and the Romantic heritage that remained Wilson's point of departure. More's deaf sister punctuates their talk when she walks through the room wondering what to do with "all that old stuff" in her bureau drawers, finally deciding to "burn it up."

Taking a politely deferential role, at the end of the piece Wilson brings

his own views in, when the future reporter on varieties of religious experience seeks out a statue of Mithras in the Princeton museum. A naked
youth clasping the sacred bull that he will sacrifice, though Darkness and
Evil threaten "its throat and its balls," this pagan revelation rooted in "all
the multiform life of the earth" is contrasted to More's view of Christ
above the world, as in the Perugino *Crucifixion*. Wilson evokes the artist's
struggle to extract the meaning of life from the process of living. When he
returns, this time with Gauss, the building is closed and they are left
standing at the door, peering through a glass darkly at the enigma of the
statue.

9

Between the Acts: 1929

Wilson lost his first close literary friend in 1928, when Elinor Wylie died at only forty-three, two months after suffering the last of several strokes. They had spent less time together in the last few years. Possessive and paternalistic toward his women writer-friends, Wilson did not think any of their husbands really worthy of them, and this included William Rose Benét, whom Elinor had married. As Mrs. Benét, however, she had written ebulliently to him of her love for life and poetry. The memoir he published six weeks after her death leaves its author, like the author of "Dover Beach," among "doubtful human creatures, all quarreling or herding together, knowing little and thinking less, vague, pig-headed, purblind and violent."

Herbert Croly too had had a stroke, and when Wilson got back to New York from Santa Barbara, the partially paralyzed editor brought up the future of *The New Republic*, where the editorial board ostensibly had equal powers. He did not believe that Bruce Bliven, who'd been hired as managing editor, was the right man to take his place. Wilson's salary was raised and Cowley, by now a half-time editor, had the impression his mentor was Croly's preferred successor. As literary editor Wilson had made *The New Republic* the primary organ in the United States for people who loved books, and he was Croly's moral heir, his aspirations for his country dovetailing with those of the author of *The Promise of American Life*. Wilson, however, was not the man for such a management post. Two years later Croly would be dead, and the board were left to collaborate, while Wilson moved the magazine to the Left through his own writing.

After his long struggle with *I Thought of Daisy* he was still unsure of the manuscript. In January he sent the new draft to Edna, hoping she wouldn't mind her portrayal as the poet Rita. He didn't hear from her for a month, then received an urgent note that the book was "very uneven" and "not a whole," still unfinished, though she liked "much of it tremendously"—he owed it to himself to make it better. She wasn't at all offended by the characterization of Rita, but begged him not to let the novel go to press that spring, setting up a meeting in New York to which she said she'd bring her notes. But she didn't come. At the time Millay was struggling to keep alive her affair with the poet George Dillon, while engaged in the sonnet sequence of *Fatal Interview*.

Wilson retreated to his "narrow, stale-smelling" room on Thirteenth Street during the cold winter evenings to work up the symbolist background of modern poetry. Frances occasionally came to see him there, but he cryptically recalls "it was difficult for her then"—she knew he'd spent three months with another woman. From California Margaret kept up her pressure, assuring him that Ted thought they made a fine couple. She reported on her reading and encouraged his work in letters that are loyal and yearning. In partnership with a friend named Miggs she was opening a hat shop that should pay for her stays in New York. Wilson wondered whether they had enough in common to marry. He felt "some sort of obstruction" against marrying her, identifying this as loyalty to Mary Blair, who after three years of separation wasn't ready for a divorce, and concern for Ted, "who was still to have hopes of Margaret."

Leonie Adams sent further regrets about having "moped and quarreled" on the day she sailed for France, along with entertaining gossip about the London literary scene. She offered a trenchant report on her Paris encounter with Gertrude Stein: "She had written a command: You will come, quite simply—and she said she is a pure California product. She even gave a resume of American literature bringing it down from Emerson to herself as the consummate flower of American genius. That is, for abstraction and pure intellect." Shrewdly Adams adds, "It may be all right as regards Emerson, James, and Stein, but she put in Mark Twain, Whitman, Poe, and in fact every considerable figure, in the abstractionist hierarchy. With poor [Ford Madox] Ford a yard away she pointed out how he had absorbed and misapplied James, as Joyce had herself, since in their low European way they are caught by experience." It must have amused Wilson to picture Stein condescending to Europe à la the early James while she presented herself as the brilliant creator of Joyce's stream of consciousness.

   Disarmed by Adams's mind and wit, he wrote to her that Margaret and he had talked of getting married. Whatever his expectations, he woefully misgauged her response. The affronted poet shot back a furious claim that he had made her pregnant. Implying she'd had a miscarriage—though confusedly stating that a "torn membrane" had been "healed" by a London doctor in October—Leonie excoriated his "fiendish" behavior. Later that same day she penned an apology for having "worried" him, and, also on January 22, she wired *The New Republic* warning him not to tell any of this to Allen Tate. Wilson's responses haven't been found, but he must have been rueful, for three weeks later she wrote, "You mustn't hate yourself on my account." Explaining how much she'd wanted a child, she claimed to have had the miscarriage "about August," which the doctor allegedly discovered in October. Her next letter calls Wilson "on the whole the best person I have known" and assures him she has grown up emotionally by accepting the fact that she is totally alone and that "hostility must underlie every human contact." Robert Frost, who had become interested in Adams's work, is said to have remarked that "she sought a mythic love" and "required the misery that came to her instead of this."

   When the third letter arrived, Wilson wasn't in New York. He was in a sanitarium after a nervous breakdown. The onset of the experience can be found in *The Twenties*, where he recalls that he was unable to "work at my book in that ghastly little room," and "I took to drinking and going alone to Noel Coward's current revue, which would appear to me at the time amusing but, when I was sober, come to seem disgusting, as the silly little tunes ran through my head. *Teach me to dance as Grandma did* has always been associated in my mind with the nauseating smell of my room." With guilt over Leonie's charge added to irresolution about Margaret, he found that he couldn't bounce back from a night's drinking at the beginning of the working day. When he set out for Red Bank for a weekend he was "seized with panic" when he got into a taxi. The symptoms were worse than they had been "at the time of my anxiety about the war: I began to tremble violently, and I realized that I could not go down to my mother's. I called up Aunt Caroline and asked her to recommend a doctor. She sent me to a young G.P. who simply thought I had been drinking too much and had me spend a couple of days in the hospital, putting me to sleep with a shot of morphine." Blair believed that he was drinking ethyl alcohol, the cheapest, crudest liquor available, and if so the diagnosis was plausible, yet after his release the symptoms returned, and he feared he "was going insane," having long "had a fear of this kind, on account of Father and Sandy." On his most recent visit to Sandy at the state hospital, his cousin, looking out onto a "green slope, beyond the barred windows, all golden-green in the late afternoon sun," had said, "Life's all right if you can stand it."

Alarmed that he couldn't get himself under control, Wilson telephoned John M. McKinney at the Neurological Institute in upper Manhattan, and the Freudian psychiatrist received him late at night at home in his bathrobe. McKinney noted that Wilson was almost thirty-five, his father's age when the latter's morbid hypochondria began. Reassuring him he "was not going insane," he said, "Neurotics are strong people. It's like polarization in physics. The neurosis is the other side of a positive assertion of will." This clearly hit home to the future author of *The Wound and the Bow*. It confirmed Wilson's observation of both his father and Edna. McKinney kept him functioning during this period when he sometimes "thought there was a pencil writing for him all by itself." As he recalled these weeks to a friend decades later, he "couldn't get over the idea that I was being followed. Eventually, every time I had this feeling, I would turn around as though to confront my follower. By doing this repeatedly I convinced myself that it was an illusion." In *The Twenties* he adds that "the panics and depressions continued" until "it seemed to me I was condemned, by some power I could not control, to destroy myself in some violent way." McKinney persuaded him to go to the Clifton Springs sanitarium west of Syracuse. "It was the dreariest point of the winter, and the bleakest part of northern New York," he writes. "The spell I spent waiting in a reception room that has a plain wooden clock on the wall was something I cannot describe."

That wooden clock has remained on the wall of the old building (the hospital having moved to newer facilities nearby) where in 1929 the Lehigh Railroad's Black Diamond express from New York made a special stop and patients disembarked, signing themselves in for a minimum of a month. According to Mr. Irving Hubbard, the former chief pharmacist who had been there since World War II, Clifton Springs pioneered by treating alcoholism and neurasthenia without drawing a clear distinction between them. Drinkers and nonviolent mental patients were housed in the same ward. McKinney must have known that, instead of threatening Wilson, this would reassure him he wasn't crazy. Put on a drug called paraldehyde, he liked its "exhilarating relaxing effect" and read poetry to the night nurse in the belief that he could con her into giving him more. They undoubtedly wanted him to consume as much as he would in order to wean him from alcohol. An addiction to paraldehyde was easily broken, Mr. Hubbard said—among other things, the drug made one continually flatulent. Wilson felt secure in the hospital, though its routine was boring. In a cheery letter Mary Blair reported that Rosalind was on an extended visit to her family in Pittsburgh, and offered her apartment whenever he was released, a gesture for which he'd remain grateful.

Resuming his work at a table amid the patients in the stark, high-ceilinged room, he polished and typed up his accumulated verse for the book to be called *Poets, Farewell!* He told Millay where he was and asked for her notes on *Daisy.* Belatedly she sent them just as he left Clifton Springs at the end of the first week in March, with a cover letter that calls Rita's conversation "terrible." Edna writes, "The moment she opens her mouth, she doesn't exist, she dies on your hands," and in "the long speeches where she dilates upon the economic status of woman" Rita "talks like a page out of Queen Victoria's girlish diary." Edna genially rewrote some of these lines, but Wilson didn't get her suggestions until after her death, for instead of being forwarded to him from Clifton Springs to New York her suggestions were returned to Steepletop, while she rushed off to Paris to meet Dillon. He sent *Daisy* to Perkins as it was. He wrote to ask if he might dedicate his forthcoming "book on modern literature" to Gauss, who had been a journalist in the Paris of Mallarmé, and remembered Villiers de l'Isle Adam's drama *Axel* as "a central document in symbolism." He picked up the first chapter of *Axel's Castle* where he'd broken off in New York. Wilson knew he was recovering when able to revise "the passage in which I tried to explain symbolism," so thoroughly was his sense of rational control invested in his ability to write critically.

Though Hubbard recalled that no one was ever released from Clifton Springs in less than a month, Wilson insisted on leaving after three weeks. The retired pharmacist classed him with those alcoholics whom the staff, not wholly facetiously, dubbed "the geniuses," people who had liquor functioning so well in their working lives that they could never give it up, and more than one of Wilson's friends would view him this way. He took his paraldehyde prescription to the city and kept using it until Dr. McKinney warned him not to take too much, whereupon Wilson returned to alcohol, for life. The doctor also tried to help him confront his neuroses, and, when recommending psychoanalysis to a friend a few years later, Wilson spoke of having been "psyched." But he told Rosalind that McKinney "tried to get me on the couch" and in *The Twenties* declares, "I hate the sense of dependence" and thus "detached myself." During the first years after his collapse Wilson would suffer a "sense of floating in a void outside the world of other human beings, where one's ties are not felt as binding, the dreadful feeling of not being real, of not being a part of society through either purpose or relationship, the strain of associating with people combined with the fear of being alone." It was some time before he "recovered from what I suppose were manic-depressive 'mood swings': moments of liveliness or heartiness would be followed by a despondency and silence that people did not understand and that made me, I am afraid, at the time, a rather uncomfortable companion."

Leonie responded to his breakdown with a bitter self-absorption. When he brought her up to date from Clifton Springs she replied that she too had difficulty concentrating, "and it would do some kind of good to see you, although you may not understand about that now." She wired: "I AM TOO UPSET TO WORK UNLESS YOU ARE CERTAIN YOU CAN SAY NOTHING TO MAKE ME FEEL BETTER I WILL COME TO TALK TO YOU." He was evidently certain; two weeks later she wired him at *The New Republic*, "I AM IN A BAD WAY AND MUST AT LEAST UNDERSTAND." In the journal he recalls having to face "Winifred," who had quickly come back from Europe and with whom he had "harrowing interviews." He would one day tell Mary McCarthy, "the thing that I like about you is that you don't make me feel guilty," as Leonie "always did" (in recalling this McCarthy added, "This irritated me, because my whole ambition was to make him feel as guilty as possible"). It was an effect that in her later years this imperious woman had on others: for Judith Farr, Adams was "a beautiful spirit" who could make you "feel guiltier than anyone else could ever do. You always felt you hadn't done enough, hadn't tried enough, hadn't understood enough."

Leonie's confidante, Louise Bogan, ended his torment. During an early summer visit to the Hudson Valley farm where Louise lived with her husband, Raymond Holden, a minor poet and Wilson's college classmate, she revealed that Leonie's pregnancy had been imagined. In a new burst of angry letters Leonie would accuse them of betraying her, yet her intellectual friendship with Wilson soon reasserted itself, and when he persuaded her they hadn't made fun of her confusion, she reconciled with Louise. Wilson's relief glows in the account of that weekend at Hillsdale in *The Twenties*. Swimming in a deep quarry, with its "warm gusts and icy veins of springs," he envisions "against the white lights of the setting sun, the bodies of the bathers, like spirits drawn by Blake, outlined in the light, as if half-transparent and radiant themselves."

Margaret had been distressed to learn what happened, hoping he wouldn't "get tied up in knots again my dear." She urged him to press Mary for a divorce, an alternative being, as he'd suggested, that they find small apartments across the hall from each other if she was able to come east the next January. He'd recall making up his mind to marry her on return from Clifton Springs, but in fact remained gripped by indecision, for his relationship with Frances was deepening. "She was lying at the foot of the bed—I at the head. I saw her eyes over her hips—soft-hard and round—like cunning burrs—burrs like agate marbles—with their unexpected depth, especially when the rest of her face was hidden." He recalled that "though I tried to conceal my collapses, she always knew at once what was happening, and this made me feel a little better, for it meant that my solitary experience, my frightening isolation, was being understood, and hence shared, by another human being." Margaret was able to pay him a surprise visit in June, which included a day at Coney Island, but no mention of this appears in *The Twenties*, and Frances and he are passionately reunited the moment it is over. "I still loved her so I kissed her till her mouth was bruised," he writes, and she defines love the same way—"I like it, being made love to! I could be made love to forever!" A week later, she models for him the new red dress he has bought her. "Her nose was all swollen from my whiskers kissing her—her hair, which was almost smooth, only slightly waved, smelled clean of tar soap," he writes with an openness of feeling new for the journal.

In August, he was settled comfortably with Frances when Margaret offered to "come and valet" him the next winter, asking where he expected to be living, but during the second week in September—as is clear from her letter in reply—he urged Margaret to come on at once and committed himself to a divorce from Blair. On some level he knew he wasn't in love with her—there is a note from these days for a story about a fictional character whose impulse is to strangle the woman whom he is "determined to marry." The journal suggests why he suddenly jumped at Margaret's offer, for on September 5 or 6 his lover, perhaps testing the waters, teases him about the possibility of getting pregnant. "I think I'm swelling up down there—I don't know whether it's because I eat a lot and have been drinking a lot." She says it might be "funny to have a little Edmund running around the house." Her period may have been late, and she mentions the abortions she and a friend had once obtained for thirty-five dollars, though there is nothing to indicate she was pregnant or that she "aborted Wilson's child in September 1929," as Wilson's first biographer asserts. The distressing prospect of Frances in the hands of a back-alley hack moved the man who "hated abortions" to try to end the affair. This was the only way he could express his love for her.

Margaret attempted to heed his summons. Chiding him for his impulsiveness ("You must admit you are sudden—after not hearing from you for about a month you present a scheme which would barely give me time to buy a ticket"), she made plans to rent her house, arranged to leave Jimmy with his father for the year, and broke the news to Miggs, her business partner. The child-care arrangements, however, were threatened when Canby lost most of his money in the October Crash, and Margaret's mother begged her to stay until Christmas. That Wilson wanted her back was almost enough for her. Reminded of "the many times I stumbled across the sand at five a.m. returning from your house" and seeing "everything the same," she wrote, "I am looking forward so to being with you again that the spark of life in me is being nursed along by the knowledge." But on the same day she invoked these romantic memories he persuaded Frances to spend the night, and the next morning the sight of the "capable young woman, in her green dress, ironing her apron on the card table" evoked her "sweetness and dearness," his own "affection, satisfaction." When he left Cummings's flat on Charles Street for a small place of his own in November, he imagined Frances cozily lounging around there in his spare pajamas. He was still surprised to know she cared for him. Worrying about her family, "she put her arms around me and kissed me as if I meant something to her—as if to embrace me and be embraced brought her some relief."

At a discouraged moment in his journal of these years Wilson states that the "sober judgment" for which he had been praised and "which, by an effort, I was sometimes able to muster in print was nothing more than compensation for the disappointment and humiliations of a life which never hit the mark or suited the means to the end." Before and after his breakdown his cultural antennae were particularly acute. "I begin to wonder whether the time hasn't arrived for the intellectuals, etc., to identify themselves a little more with the general life of the country," he suggests in a letter to Tate. In a digression when reviewing the diary of

Dostoevsky's wife, he objects to importing European attitudes of futility and despair "into a country full of money and health." Americans, like the nineteenth-century Russians, needed "simultaneously to adapt European culture to the alien conditions of American life and to cultivate from our own peculiar and un-European resources an original culture of our own." *Axel's Castle* would reflect these concerns just as *I Thought of Daisy* did. The introduction to symbolism that was finished at Clifton Springs appeared in *The New Republic* at the end of March 1929; the Yeats, Valéry, and Eliot chapters followed during the fall, the Joyce in December. He wrote them late at night, then went to Julius's bar in the Village to drink and listen to fractious arguments from the Right and Left.

Gratified by Mary Blair's loyalty during his breakdown and seeking her cooperation in the divorce, Wilson, perhaps with money supplied by his mother for some other purpose, paid for her trip to Europe in 1929. She wanted to see Paris and hoped to work out a theatrical connection there. She wired for more cash, and her letters show her trying to enjoy herself (Paris for her was a Coney Island "without the roller coaster"). She sailed back from London and that fall made her last efforts onstage, citing the usual problems with the play or the company from Wilmington, Detroit, Chicago. One evening when Mary phoned and Wilson sounded tight she urged him to stop drinking, claiming she'd quit for good. From Chicago she wrote of consulting a lawyer about the settlement, hoping "we can get things fixed up all right so it won't be too long till you can have some new foundation."

On his return to New York from the sanitarium, Cummings's rakish second wife, Anne Barton, had wired him an invitation to call on her— "LITTLE BIRDIE OUT OF THE WEST WILL YOU FLY IN TO MY LOVE NEST APRIL 15 WOULD BE BEST RSVP." He apparently passed this up, but accepted one from the couple for an August weekend at Silver Lake in New Hampshire. Afterward he told Tate that Cummings was shrewd about the world yet interested only in the gifted individual, the artist. He was "the pure romantic," a type that might not survive much longer, "though perhaps I think this merely because the romantic in myself has recently been giving up the ghost." The title poem for *Poets, Farewell!* is, however, flagrantly romantic. "Farewell, gay pastorals!" he writes; looking back to the weekend with Louise Bogan at Hillsdale. He concludes, "We have rhymed under gray skies in the stubble grass— / Sped plunging motor-rides with drunken song— / Had Wyatt with breakfast, Yeats with the final glass." What was dying was belief in his own poetry—as early as college, he'd known he had no "distinction" in the use of words "for poetic purposes"—and the last line of "Poets, Farewell!," "I leave that speech to you who have the tongue," is a bow not just to Louise but to all those he'd cavalierly treated when starting out as a reviewer, including Stevens, Frost, and Cummings himself. Entwined with his farewell to verse was a growing confidence in the power of his prose.

Events were about to provide Wilson a new role, a political one. He'd been troubled by the bitter textile workers' strike dragging on in Gastonia, North Carolina. *The New Republic* had elected not to send down a reporter—Dos Passos, who wanted the assignment, was judged too far left, and young Matthews, in Asheville for a wedding, was asked to stop by Gastonia instead. On the same day that Ella May Wiggins, a young widow active in the Communist-organized union, was killed during a conflict between an armed mob and the strikers, Matthews reported that nothing much was going on. Again the liberals seemed in default of their responsibilities, the political point of Wilson's savage and self-contemptuous story of partying the weekend before the executions of Sacco and Vanzetti. Black Tuesday took him by surprise—he hadn't "exercised enough insight," he said, "to realize that American 'prosperity' was an inflation that was due to burst"—but he'd recall being "exhilarated at the sudden unexpected collapse of that stupid gigantic fraud." In a droll movie review he had described desert prophets inveighing against Mammon, "the gigantic finger of God" writing out "its warning on Belshazzar's wall." Wilson likened the Crash to "a rending of the earth in preparation for the Day of Judgment." The social earthquake that followed made literature for a time an insufficient faith, and he was drawn to the Marxism of which only a year before he'd thought Dos Passos naively credulous.

In November and December he documented what he called his last days with Frances, doing so not in the journal but on separate pages he could stash elsewhere, twenty-some sheets interweaving stories of her life with scenes of them together. Though his account of their sex is scarcely mechanistic, the detachment that carried over from his criticism into writing about his own sexual behavior helps immobilize him. There is something disquieting in his passivity as he relates the difficulties from which one wishes he would rescue her. The class gulf between them remained—"She didn't think of writing as work—didn't think of me as working because I didn't work with my hands"—and to know they were soon to part left him silent and moody. In December, when Margaret wired she'd be on the train in a week, Wilson finally told his lover the truth. "So you were thinking of marrying somebody else all the time!" she exclaimed. She then confessed she had tried to get involved with another man, and boasted "I'm going to get someone who can do it eight or nine times," then warned him "not to cheat on Margaret." On Christmas Eve he found out Frances had given him crab lice, and this malady, like the gonorrhea when they were first lovers three years before, made it easier to accept Margaret's arrival.

Margaret had written she hoped his troubles were about over, though divorce court would be hard on him—"Just take a drink and you won't mind," she said. They spent two wintry January weeks at a country inn in Riverton, Connecticut, reading in bed and listening to the radio "bringing incongruously the wavering gold fluid of Debussy, the music of old Victor Herbert operas, and the St. Louis Blues," but Margaret appears only once in four or five journal pages, apropos her "brindled hair." She is unmentioned in a letter to Bishop on the anniversary of Wilson's breakdown, which begins "I've come up here to get away from New York and do some work," then surveys the intellectual scene from the dogmatism of Babbitt and More to the problems in a Marxist reading of American conditions. He takes brisk walks in a landscape whose majesty helps him convert inner sorrow into resolve. In verse that came from this experience and was completed several years later Wilson echoes Pater to mourn the fading gemlike flame of those like Scott and Edna. He pleads for the skill he will employ, in prose, as memoirist and curator of reputations:

> They flicker now who frightfully did burn
> And I must tell their beauty while I live.
> Changing their grace as water in its flight,
> And gone like water; give me then the art,
> Firm as night-frozen ice found silver-bright,
> That holds the splendor though the days depart.

His wife filed the necessary charge of adultery, and they were divorced February 3, 1930, the decree, according to form, forbidding Wilson's remarriage except with the judge's permission. She showed up at court drunk and weepy, but they parted on good terms, with "a look of understanding between us on a level away above our wrangling." Mary briefly tried to intrude into his relations with Margaret, but she remarried immediately after Wilson did. *The Twenties* concludes with a thought appropriate to more than one of his romantic relationships that ripened into affection: "I could count on her, she counted on me."

One day Wilson would observe that Mary McCarthy was "acting out a novel when she should have been writing one." In 1929 he had been living a tale he couldn't write, though its fragments are here pieced together with the help of the memories of friends and the letters of the women involved. His breakdown and recovery paralleled the end of the jazz age, a period "in which nonsense and inspiration, reckless idealism and childish irresponsibility," he'd recollect, "were mingled in so queer a way." Like Fitzgerald, he was attuned to the times, but the critic had an intellectual confidence the novelist's private life with Zelda eroded. In his journal, as in the poems, Wilson is determined to move on. "When all our ideas of honor and loyalty, derived from our social class, from our Renaissance education, from our foolish early fantasies of ourselves, have been broken up and carried off by the currents in which we find ourselves drowning," he writes, "we are at a loss as to what to fall back on, but we are bound to fall back on something; and this is perhaps where the real conscious solidarity of the human race begins." He would come to maturity as a writer during the 1930s, and his study of history in *To the Finland Station*, though eventually disillusioning him and darkening his politics, deepened his perspective on literature and society. In *I Thought of Daisy* and *Axel's Castle*, completed as the ground of American life shifted beneath his feet, Wilson seeks to reconcile the work of the artistic avant-garde with the claims of human community and action.

10

From Whitehead and Proust to Marx:
I Thought of Daisy and *Axel's Castle*

I Thought of Daisy and *Axel's Castle* were written in sequence, and to read them side by side is to see Wilson the critic thoroughly eclipse Wilson the novelist. When she read the second edition of *Daisy*, the poet Marianne Moore noted its virtues—"pungent, pithy, direct, fresh. Unspoiled perspectives of revery and a real love of what is human and charming." Yet the novel was mechanically derivative of its models and schematic, the five-part structure a procrustean bed imposed on the story. Edna told him it was not a whole, and Ted Paramore kiddingly detected "a certain prolixity in your later manner, which I can only ascribe to your subsisting too long a stretch upon a diet of Proust and grain alcohol." *Axel's Castle* remains a brisk, broad-gauged introduction to the modern classics. Wilson filters an aesthetic nourished in Europe—"that remote diamond mine of the fine arts," as he calls it—through a practical American idealism. Returning us to a time when Proust, Joyce, et al. were new and fresh, he presents them through the eyes of a reporter for the general reader.

Both books are indebted to A. N. Whitehead, whose *Concept of Nature* Wilson had read on the return train from California in 1924, and to Kemp Smith's pamphlet explaining how, in Whitehead's philosophy, the new physics of relativity replaced bits of matter by overlapping events in time and made aesthetic and moral values natural realities alongside color, sound, and taste. The next year Wilson looked into the forbidding text of the *Principia Mathematica*, the work of Whitehead and Bertrand Russell, "compounded of the Roman, Greek, and Hebrew alphabets; excessively large exclamation points; defective signs for equations of proportions." He went on to their popular writings. Not drawn to Russell's Voltairean ironies—among other things, human beings were seen "blowing ourselves to smithereens through releasing the energy of the atom"—he seized on the perspective upon literature of Whitehead's *Science and the Modern World*. Here, Romanticism was understood as a rebellion against the scientific mechanism of Newton and Descartes, and Wilson described another swing of the pendulum in the mid-nineteenth century, to a neo-classicism backed by Darwinian biology. This, he thought, was followed by a second romantic reaction in the French symbolism of the period of Rimbaud and Mallarmé, a source of the techniques and attitudes of Yeats, Eliot, and Proust. *Axel's Castle*'s first chapter adds these antecedents of the moderns to a map of the nineteenth century acquired from Gauss's lectures.

Whitehead had moved to Harvard, and early in June 1927 Wilson had a stimulating talk with the Englishman. Having edited John Dewey's essay on Whitehead's philosophy in *The New Republic*—the pedestrian prose of the benign pragmatist and liberal led Wilson to think of him as John Doughy—he offered his own impression. In person Whitehead was dry, dispassionate, witty, and urbane, with a taste for paradox that was distinct from the "earnest intensity" of his thought. For this physicist and prophet, God became the ultimate harmony and creative purpose of the universe. Normally Wilson wasn't much interested in metaphysics, considering it "the poetry and fiction" of people who don't think in "concrete images," but Whitehead's metaphysics reassured him that art could give durable meaning to what sometimes seemed a life of reflex and blind instinct.

Whitehead's argument made more plausible Proust's theory of involuntary memory—the flooding back of the past through experiences that expressed a person's central truths—and Proust is the other source shared by *I Thought of Daisy* and *Axel's Castle*. The last volume of *In Search of Lost Time* (*À la recherche du temps perdu*, initially translated *Remembrance of Things Past*), appeared early in 1927. Robert Linscott, the editor, who had dinner with Wilson one summer at the Cape, recalled his total fascination with the novel: "As Edmund was raising the first spoon [of soup] to his mouth, I asked him a question about Proust," whereupon he "lowered the spoon and started to talk. Now and then he would pause, lift his spoon, then under pressure of another thought, lower his spoon and continue his talk." While a servant brought in courses of fish and dessert "he was all the time raising and lowering his spoon but never getting it to his mouth." As his guest finished the meal Wilson appeared to be "coming down to earth," and glancing over, he exclaimed, "Why Bob, she hasn't given you anything to eat." The ardent thirty-page re-creation of the seven volumes that is a high point of *Axel's Castle* was written in just such a frame of mind and creates something of the hypnotic effect on the reader that Proust had on Wilson.

Six months before this "Short View of Proust" appeared in *The New Republic* he was beginning to write a novel with a flavor of the cork-lined chamber. Wilson, too, reconstructs life through the process of memory, and he attempts a formal eloquence like Proust's. Using the *Daisy* notebook in the Wilson papers at Yale's Beinecke Library, Neale Reinitz documents how intricate is his debt to *À la recherche*, from the party scenes that bring characters together to the images that recur in the narrator's mind like musical motifs, causing breaks from the present into a reverie about literature and life. Wilson's way of absorbing the great novelist was to emulate him. He also does this with Joyce, who fused symbolism with the naturalism Proust rejected. In an effort to overcome the limitations of "this history of a young man stuff," which to Fitzgerald he had called a "bum art form," he tries to combine first love and painful maturation with an intellectual's search for purpose in a series of "symphonic movements."

He started with journal notes about his day with Florence O'Neil at Coney Island in 1927. The blonde chorus girl who had "clear pink skin and pretty coral lips, under her little brown bell hat," was kindly, fun, upbeat about life. The character drawn from her is neither innocent Daisy Miller nor the Daisy Buchanan who carelessly destroys Gatsby, nor yet the Daisy of "A Bicycle Built for Two"—this Daisy's first husband took her to Atlantic City on a motorcycle on her honeymoon, successfully bringing on a miscarriage as they jolted down the highway. As a voice of the real America, she helps the narrator hold his own with two more compelling characters, the poet Rita, based on Millay, who had magnetized Wilson at the beginning of the decade, and the novelist Hugo, based on Dos Passos, who increasingly impressed him at the end. "Resolutely" thinking of Daisy gives the Wilson figure a certain insulation from Rita and Hugo.

The portrait of Rita doesn't ring true. Wilson told Bishop he'd written "more or less real" descriptions of Edna, then nervously changed them. His version of her declamatory feminism—as she said in the letter he didn't receive—is stilted, and though an account of promiscuity as her creative wound relieves his feelings, he would get their encounter right only in the memoir in *The Shores of Light*. A similar problem exists with Professor

Grosbeake, in whom Whitehead's exposition of the regenerative implications of electrons, atoms, durational events, and quanta is crossed with
Gauss's understanding of literary history and his fatherly role for Wilson.
Wilson arbitrarily awards Grosbeake Frieda Lawrence (whom he had met
at a party for D. H. Lawrence) as a wife.

Perhaps the best thing in this book is the portait of Hugo Bamman,
the young Dos Passos seen as the type of the 1920s-style subversive establishment intellectual. Wilson catches Dos's manner and convictions—
the stuttering, bubbling rush of speech, which masked the authority of
his mind; his myopia, and the piercing gaze when eye exercises enabled
him to discard glasses; his inability to be comfortable with the stridently
emancipated women of whom he approved; his need to leave his hat
where he could get it quickly at a party. Fiercely independent, sick of the
complacency of American culture, Hugo travels light, leaving for the
Middle East with nothing but a musette bag just as Dos had, hitching a
taxi ride to the docks without letting friends see him off. Not yet well informed about Dos's background, Wilson makes Hugo's father a Republican of Puritan stock and takes his appearance and manner from John Jay
Chapman, the subject of a future portrait. In the account of Hugo's radical-
ization during World War I, details from Dos Passos's *Three Soldiers* and
Cummings's internment in *The Enormous Room* are merged with memories from the base hospital in the Vosges. Wilson plausibly conflates the
rebellions of these three writers against the gilded age that had frustrated
their fathers. Like Wilson and Cummings, Hugo has applied himself to
literature "as to one of the old-fashioned professions, Medicine, Law, or
the Church." He seeks to purge the American upper-middle class of
weakness and corruption through novels that are "sober, even morose,"
just as Dos Passos did.

Daisy gives us the curve of Wilson's relationship to bohemia, from the
quick electrical clicking of a door that lets his narrator into a fashionable
party to the wearing of this life on his nerves, when a Victrola beside an
open window high above the street emits a mesmerizing shriek that becomes "an unending wire of sound" that is "worn away so that it seemed
almost snapping." At a party liberation turns anarchic. There is a flavor of
Hogarth, whom Wilson admired, in the man in a green and orange kimono
whose mascaraed eyes are "cadaverously closed," and in the advertising
man who, infatuated with Dostoevsky's nihilistic heroes, shoots up his
wife's plaster cast of the Winged Victory. A poet drunkenly reads verses

about Daisy's lovely hands, following which she leads the narrator upstairs to the servant's bedroom, where they have sex on a pile of coats. When Rita sweeps into the party on the arm of a cynical newspaper editor, along with a local Italian bootlegger and two prostitutes looking for business, the half-drunk, jealous narrator throws a punch at the bootlegger and wakes up lying on the floor.

In this chapter, Wilson attacks the illusion of the classics as "a fortress of absolute beauty and wisdom" in a disillusioned, proto-deconstructionist monologue. But in the book's upbeat finale, an old jukebox version of "American Patrol" wakes memories of the Fourth of July as Daisy and the narrator wait at the Battery on a summer day for the ferry to Coney Island. Once aboard, Wilson evokes the romance of the night when his troopship returned from the war. At Coney Island the couple stroll the boardwalk, swim and eat seafood, visit "Noah's Ark" and the waxworks display. He finds himself face-to-face with a young man whose pockets bulge with foolish-looking gifts and prizes doubtless carried for a woman,— "Mr. Suburban American, at the seaside, with packages and a straw hat." It is himself in a mirror. Instead of quailing, this intellectual enthuses about "the fluidity of manners in America, the plasticity of social position." Recalling the "new accent, half agonized and half thrilling," of a jazz piece Wilson may have taken from *Rhapsody in Blue*, he hears it in the city sounds while detecting echoes, too, of the Old World—the orchestras and open squares of Europe, the Hebrew tongue the composer's father had chanted as a rabbi or cantor.

As *Daisy* ends, the friendly kiss that in Wilson's journal concludes his day at the beach with Florence O'Neil is wrested into a sexual union supposed to signify the narrator's coming of age. Two years earlier, writing of Frances in the privacy of his journal, Wilson had captured their lovemaking with feeling, but this moment with Daisy is set down as "hot, moist, mucilaginous and melting." It enables him to celebrate rebirth "from the fears and snobberies of youth, from all our preconceived ideas, from all those foolish abstractions we learn, all those things that we think we think," yet the speaker of this enunciamento is victim to what he himself identifies as a "gulf between the self which experiences and the self which describes experience!"

While this book was a commercial disaster—Wilson told Cyril Connolly that when a woman said she'd purchased and enjoyed the book, he replied, "Oh, it was you who bought it"—*Axel's Castle*, published by

Scribner's in 1931 in a form revised from the *New Republic* serial, has seldom been out of print. From Santa Barbara during the fall of 1928 he'd
told Perkins it would include Yeats, Proust, and Joyce, contemporary classics, and Valéry, Eliot, and Stein, all "very fine." Wilson makes their work
compatible with twentieth-century science, even as he contrasts their assumptions to those of prewar progressives like Shaw and Wells. He has
reservations about what he was first to call the Alexandrian tendency of
authors "warming their hands at the fire of their predecessors' lives, as we
burn coal to release the sunlight stored up by ancient forests." He rejects
the fear of life and incapacity to deal with it in Proust, the ineptitudes
matched to the crowded consciousness of Joyce's Bloom, the resignation
and impotence of Eliot's personae, and predicts that literature will return
to the life of action. As he promised Perkins, however, he writes "popular
accounts" of these writers that "persuade people of their importance and
persuade people to read them." His achievement is to have identified
what Arnold called the master-spirit of an age.

Before *The Waste Land* appeared, Wilson had sketched the Jersey
landscape in an Eliotic vein, seeing "life grown heavy and sordid in those
thousands of brick-walled rooms behind those dirty windows." His cultural
nationalism and the liberations of liquor and sex had turned him in a different direction than that of the man who went on to *For Lancelot Andrewes* and "Ash Wednesday." In *Axel's Castle* Eliot is called a Jamesian
Puritan driven by "the horror of vulgarity and the shy sympathy with the
common life, the ascetic shrinking from sexual experience and the distress at the drying up of the springs of sexual emotion, with the straining
after a religious emotion which may be made to take its place." Wilson
predicts that the poet's dramatic imagination will lead him to write plays.
Although his effort, as a literary critic, to detach aesthetic values from all
others is called misguided, Wilson admires the essays in which this fellow
American reshaped the British canon and gauged English, Irish, and
American writers in relation to one another and to the Continent. Eliot's
critical prose has for him "a sort of sensitive charm in its austerity—
closely reasoned and making its points with the fewest possible words, yet
always even, effortless and lucid."

In an early article Wilson had cited Yeats's Blakean meditation on the
beauty of a seagull thrown upon the plowed land by a storm. The hard
images, the plain, even prosaic, yet "luminous and noble" language of
Yeats's second phase made him "one of the few genuine masters alive—
perhaps the only poet of the first magnitude." In *Axel's Castle* Yeats is

compared to the Dante who could "sustain a grand manner through sheer intensity without rhetorical heightening." Clive James singles out this remark as permanent criticism. But the chapter on Yeats makes too much of the French connection, blurring fin de siècle symbolism with Irish myth. Wilson, repudiating his own poetic, lyrical self, turns to Yeats's prose as to Eliot's. The *Autobiographies* were "the product of some dying loomcraft brought to perfection in the days before machinery," yet they contained a modern terseness and unexpected juxtapositions, as when Yeats writes of Oscar Wilde, "He had been almost poor and now, his head full of Flaubert, found himself with ten thousand a year." Wilson expounds the astrological system of *A Vision*, on which Yeats built major poems. But neither *A Vision* nor French fin de siècle symbolism can help Wilson the rationalist explain the ineffable spiritual claims of the poem "Among School Children."

In an evangelical vein Wilson had opined that "Joyce was sent not to delight us but to put the fear of God into our hearts." Yet he produces a happy, morally expansive account of *Ulysses*, more tolerant of the master's arcana than was his 1922 review, more aware of Joyce's purposes. He follows the Homeric parallel, savors "Dublin, seen, heard, smelt and felt, brooded over, imagined, remembered," regards the triad of Stephen, Molly, and Bloom as an homage to the human family, shows how the master's naturalism neither satirizes nor sentimentalizes humanity. Joyce had transformed the rules of novel writing, rejecting "solid institutions, groups, individuals," and even "solid psychological factors," dualisms of good and evil, flesh and spirit, instinct and reason, as well as the conflict of duty with passion or personal interest, but he created substantial, believable characters. With a psychological insight greater even than that of James, he was the poet of that new phase of the human spirit which Proust, Freud, Whitehead, and Einstein charted. *Finnegans Wake* had begun to appear, and this essay concludes with the first published version of the "Anna Livia Plurabelle" passage, the music of the women's voices blending in that "of the river itself, light, rapid, incessant, almost metrical, now monotonously running on one note, now impeded and syncopated." Wilson is excited by a dream-novel reaching into myth, though wary lest Joyce overindulge in allusions, jokes, and linguistic games.

The remarkable account of *À la recherche* first published while he followed Proust's lead in *Daisy* distills the plot and identifies major themes. The novel was composed of "social episodes (often several hundred pages long), enormous solid blocks, cemented by, or rather embedded in, a dense medium of introspective revery and commentary mingled with incidents treated dramatically on a smaller scale." Proust revealed character through personalities whose shapes keep changing, and undermined the social hierarchy on which his web of human relations was based. A periodic sentence takes this merciless moralist from "the shimmering reveries of boyhood" to "the chatter, the sociability and the vivacity of young manhood" and "the realization of human corruption and cruelty" in "a nightmare of the passions, which at its climax . . . seems blasted with the dry breath of Hell." Wilson describes the Albertine section with clarity and delicacy of comprehension, identifying the subjectivity of love (a theme, he notes, of such lesser novels of the period as *Gatsby* and *The Sun Also Rises*) with the belief that one can neither know nor master external reality. In the postmechanistic, relativistic world of twentieth-century science, Proust constructs reality by turning memory into art that will endure.

This affirmation is set against a disenchanted sketch of the novelist's life. Where in the Joyce portrait Wilson praises the artist through his work, Proust proves to be unworthy of his creation—a hypochondriac racked by perversities and unable to confront the world, who sells his mother's furniture to a bordello, someone with the misogynistic homosexuality of his character Charlus. Wilson exposes Proust's neurotic maladies without the sympathy he'd later have for Kipling and Dickens as childhood victims of oppression. The reader discovers the deep division in this chapter and in *Axel's Castle*. The critic's personal history contributed. His analysis of this multivolume work had first appeared in 1928 and the account of Proust's personality in 1930, a year after the collapse that linked Wilson to his father, whose felt-lined door opened, as it were, upon Proust's chamber. Writing long before his breakdown became public knowledge, the scholar Sherman Paul sensed in his disgust with Proust a "refusal to be neurotic." Wilson tries to reconcile the man and his work through Proust's strength of mind and the heroism with which he retrieved the failure of his life in art. In the passage that, on his deathbed, he dictated about the death of the novelist Bergotte, Proust set forth obligations "which seem to be derived from some other world," laws "based on goodness, scrupulousness, sacrifice" and "to which we are brought by every profound exercise of the intelligence," including the duty to do one's work as it should be done. Wilson would make this passage a moral touchstone, pointedly citing it even to Russian Marxists, but he never explained how a self-indulgent neurotic lived up to such a code.

He had become impatient with Valéry and Stein. If he'd known German, Rilke would have been a better choice than Valéry, who had long since left off writing verse to pontificate about the intellectual life in prose. In 1923 Wilson had done "a whole lot of justice" to Stein, but by 1927 the "psychological truth" of her work had come to seem in "a solution of about one percent to the total volume of the dose," and the volume of the dose "enormous." Instead of removing her from the book he pads out her chapter with notes on the suggestive basis of all language and the "systematic comic nonsense" of Dadaism. An exhausted avant-garde is summed up in the contrasting figures of "Axel and Rimbaud": the aristocratic hero of a fin de siècle drama, who rejects life as vulgar and commits suicide on a pile of jewels; and the poet who achieves a visionary art of disorientation of the senses, then gives up writing to turn African trader. In such grand emblems Wilson put this literature behind him as the Depression began.

His contemporary Kenneth Burke—himself about to become a Communist—was distressed by "the shift in *Axel's Castle*," the rejection of the contemplative life, the ivory tower. And while the figures of Axel and Rimbaud have a certain application to Stein and Valéry, they are reductive of the others who are not escapists, Yeats owing as much to Keats and Blake as to the 1890s, Joyce to Flaubert and James, Proust to Balzac and Dickens. Wilson is surer of the artist's duty to society than how society molds the artist, and his historical criticism is as yet immature. The young man who divided his time between books and romantic affairs attributes first Yeats's and then Valéry's withdrawals from the world to an affair that went bad, something the author of *The Triple Thinkers* and *The Wound and the Bow* would have judged only a catalyst.

In his journalism, as he told Tate, he was "going further and further to the left all the time." He recommended Dos Passos's *42nd Parallel* as a lesson in bridging the gap "which constitutes a perpetual problem in American literature and thought, between the special concerns of the intellectual and the general pursuits and ideas of the people." He applied his first reading of Marx to reporting on the midterm elections of 1930. He inserted a passage on the collapse of the boom and the social experiment in Russia into the proofs of *Axel's Castle*, and wedded a ringing call "to make a practical success of human society" to his celebration of abstruse masterpieces. Having it both ways, through such a populist, pragmatic standard going back to the distrust of the unsanctified imagination by the Puritans, Wilson made serious literature compatible with radical politics for the writers and, as they soon called themselves, intellectuals of the new decade.

Criticism was no longer defined as in "A Preface to Persius," where the artist is engaged with reality and the critic stands back for perspective. In *Axel's Castle* he is reality's spokesman, bringing the work of the saints of art into the mainstream.

While he struggled for perspective on Proust, he helped get the Marxist Mike Gold's attack on Thornton Wilder as an escapist printed in *The New Republic*, and when Wilder's admirers wrote angry letters Wilson weighed in on Gold's side—Wilder was Proust's disciple, and his exotic locales might indeed be "a sedative for sick Americans." To *Axel's Castle* he added a famous summation of Proust as the last great historian "of the Heartbreak House of capitalist culture," saying, "the little man with the sad appealing voice, the metaphysician's mind, the Saracen's beak, the ill-fitting dress-shirt and the great eyes that seem to see all about him like the many-faceted eyes of a fly, dominates the scene and plays host in the mansion where he is not long to be master." In *Starting Out in the Thirties* Alfred Kazin would recall what this passage meant to him at the beginning of his career: "I felt myself to be a radical, not an ideologue; I was proud of the revolutionary yet wholly literary tradition in American writing to which I knew that I belonged, and would say over to myself, from *Axel's Castle*, the last, woven sentence of Edmund Wilson's chapter on Proust."

A generation discovered modern literature in this book. Though its sales amounted to no more than a thousand copies a year, it had soon gone through four printings and made Wilson known well beyond his literary contemporaries and *The New Republic*. In 1936 he joked to Bogan that he wanted to sell it to the movies, "with Adolphe Menjou as Proust and the Marx Brothers as Joyce." After World War II, in the pigeonholing account of criticism called *The Armed Vision*, Stanley Edgar Hyman condescended to Wilson as a popularizer, yet credited *Axel's Castle* with "an effect in our time, in opening up a whole new area of literature to a wide audience, second only to T. S. Eliot's *The Sacred Wood*." As a survey the book is incomplete, for most of the writers had significant work ahead of them. It has been dated by the New Critics' close reading and by the major biographies. Criticism has not, however, improved on Wilson's approach to these writers as living beings, his integration of art with personality and intellectual history. Frank Kermode speaks of his ability to proceed from "passionate identification with the work under discussion" to "detached appraisal" and to "historical inference, which does not neglect the primary response." While the argument of *Axel's Castle*, involving Wilson's own contradictions and his experience in his times, remains unresolved, through its process he reconciles what is sometimes called the "Voltairean I" of the Edwardians and their Victorian forebears with "the modern I" of Rimbaud, Joyce, Proust, Eliot's *Prufrock*. He asserts the continuity of past and present within what was still a manageable literary history, and creates for later readers a bridge between the American 1920s and '30s.

As he made his way in a less exciting literary age, when the role of interpreting these writers was appropriated by the academy even as the avant-garde itself dissolved, Wilson would be put off by the categorizing of these masters of his youth as something called "modernism." Donald Hall, poet and editor, tells a story of the unfortunate effects of using this word at a party given by the critic and editor Harry Levin during the '50s. Hall had read *Axel's Castle* at sixteen or seventeen, and later *The Triple Thinkers* and *The Wound and the Bow*. Finding himself on the couch with "the great man," he nervously told him he wrote poems, and Wilson replied that "when he saw my name on a poem in a magazine he would look at it with especial attention." Emboldened, Hall added that he was working on the prosody of modernist poetry, to be explosively interrupted, "Never use that filthy disgusting word in my presence!" Hall continues: "For a moment I did not know but what 'prosody' was the offending word, but I soon discovered that it was 'modernist.'" Wilson, who'd been drinking heavily, indulged in a brief tirade, among other things saying that "no one who used such an obscene term could ever write a decent line of verse." With seeming compunction, the poet remembered, "he then reached over and patted my knee, and said something like, 'Of course I may be entirely wrong. You may be quite good.'" But he later resumed his attack on the word, eventually silenced by a combination of liquor and Levin. "Harry said, more or less, 'Why, Edmund, I believe it's in the O.E.D. Why, Edmund, I believe I've used that word. Why, Edmund, I believe you've used that word.'"

He never did so, at any rate on the page. Near the end of *Axel's Castle*, he is hostile to what would be called postmodernism, resisting Valéry's prediction that, in cultures dominated by radio, movies, and television, literature would become purposeless in its endless introspection and quest for novelty, its tendency toward esoterica and pure play, an art "based on the *abuse* of language." Wilson's conviction is that an elite art can serve human betterment, and need not be closeted and marginal. He maintains the classical premise that literature delights and teaches, invigorating the life of society and the language of ordinary men and women. As the 1930s begin, he chooses a Shelleyan vision of the poets as legislators of the world over the dream of aesthetic perfection. His last sentence foresees the end of "the whole belle-lettristic tradition of Renaissance culture perhaps, compelled to specialize more and more, more and more driven in on itself, as industrialism and democratic education have come to press it closer and closer." Against this fear Wilson sets the work of those who can "break down the walls of the present and wake us to . . . the untried, unsuspected possibilities of human thought and art."

PART THREE

On the Left

11

With Margaret Canby:
Political Commitment and Tragedy

❧

Wilson's own life revived with the spring in 1930, as the gray buildings of the Village opened "to the freedom of wind and light as if they had been the virgin hills of the island." Margaret and he were starting over with the new decade. Two days after his divorce became final, on his thirty-fifth birthday, they were married at the Washington, D.C., home of John Amen, then Assistant Attorney General. After spending their wedding night in a hunting cabin on the Potomac, on the way home they called on Margaret's Cousin Watty in his barren splendor at Chesnut Hill, near Philadelphia. Wilson's novel *The Higher Jazz* contrasts the old man's deterioration with the vigor of his Margaret character, who looked "stronger and more dominant than I had ever known her to do: her young compact and sinuous body contrasting with his thin-skinned and pulpy one, decaying in its bag of clothes." Back in New York, they paid a visit to Rosalind and Wilson's mother at Red Bank, and in June they returned to stay at an old resort hotel on the coast called the Peninsula House. They went out in a boat at night and got lost among the islands. He couldn't manage the outboard motor in the current and would proudly recall rowing into Monmouth Beach with a broken oar.

Wilson, Margaret, Jimmy Canby, aged twelve, and Rosalind, aged seven, spent the summer in the O'Neills' old Coast Guard station on the Cape. Perched on the edge of the eroded dunes at Peaked Hill Bars, the place was spacious, with a pleasant blue and white decor, a master bedroom, and a tiny dormitory. The ancient bathroom no longer worked, but its tub had acquired a new use as a container for homemade, lime green booze, a ladle hung over one side. Visitors, when they'd had enough to drink, climbed the watchtower and slid down its roof into the sand. Harry Kemp, the drunken idealist of Wilson's *This Room and This Gin and These Sandwiches*, lived in a shack on the dunes. Representative of this unpublished poet's verse are lines in which an overnight wind builds the waves to burnished heights and clears away "the sick distrust of the embattled nations." Not far away, in another shack, lived Blair's friend Hazel Hawthorne. She had left her first husband and was trying to write, though unwilling to leave her children behind when Wilson offered to help her get a Guggenheim in Europe. Years later, as an old lady in Provincetown, Hazel remembered her impression of him moving in—a "strange, inept man" trying to pry loose the storm shutters with a hammer. After giving Wilson a hand, she brought him some ginger ale to go with his whiskey.

It was a charmed summer. He and Margaret trekked the half hour into town for groceries, which they brought back in knapsacks. They swam in the surf and walked the beach, dragging back driftwood for the fireplace, and when no one was around made love in the sunlight on the dunes, ignoring the flies and the heat. She'd urge him, "Stay in me! Keep in me!" and he did his best to make his "large pink prong" obey. He liked to contemplate the distinguished cast of her features and her soft figure, tiny hands and feet. Rosalind Wilson adored her stepmother, who "was always thinking up treats for Jimmy and me." Jimmy was full of Wild West ideas, and the children had their own pony. The Coast Guard personnel gave them cakes and cookies, and at night, when patrolling the beach with huge flashlights, occasionally joined their parents for an illegal drink. One adventurous night Wilson went out on the bay with the Portuguese fishermen to visit their traps, watching nets pulled in with butterfish and the exotic, richly colored squid.

Margaret wasn't free to make a home for her son in the East, even if Wilson could have provided it. Her divorce agreement stipulated that Jimmy attend school in California, living half the school year with each parent. In September Wilson put the two of them on the train for California. But Margaret found that (as she hadn't been able to do the year before) she could leave Jimmy with his father and rent her Santa Barbara house, and in a month she returned to the Cape. Wilson had stayed on, correcting the proofs of *Axel's Castle* while he discussed the consequences of the Crash with Dos Passos. Now married to Katy Smith, the witty sister of Hemingway's friend Bill Smith, Dos had bought a house and small farm in a hollow among the ponds.

When the Wilsons took an apartment in New York at the end of October, 20 percent of the adult workforce was unemployed. Wilson regarded the political scene through the magic lantern of Marx's *Eighteenth Brumaire of Louis Bonaparte* and *The Class Struggles in France*. In *To the Finland Station* he declares, "Never, after we have read *The Eighteenth Brumaire*, can the language, the conventions, the combinations, the pretensions, of parliamentary bodies, if we have had any illusions about them, seem the same to us again," for "now we can see for the first time through the shadow-play to the conflict of appetites and needs which, partly unknown to the actors themselves, throw these thin silhouettes on the screen." Dwight Morrow, a J. P. Morgan partner and a millionaire, was campaigning for the Senate in New Jersey, and apparently being groomed to succeed Hoover as president. Morrow praised the moral fiber of the people. In a report on the "nice little man" whose voice was amplified by the megaphone at a Newark rally, Wilson noted that in the bitter weather "the men in the bread lines, the men and women beggars in the streets, and the children dependent on them, are all having their fiber hardened."

Herbert Croly had died in May, and the board of *The New Republic*, politically adrift, debated their editorial position. Matthew Josephson, a new assistant at the magazine, recalled that Wilson's January 1931 "Appeal to Progressives" to "take Communism away from the Communists" and apply it to American conditions did more to move opinion to the Left than any other polemic of the time. "Money-making and the kind of advantages which a money-making society provides for money to buy are not enough to satisfy humanity," he insisted, restating Emerson's "Things are in the saddle and ride mankind." He wedded this traditional humanism to the need for central planning and government ownership of the means of production.

While enthusiastic young writers deluged *The New Republic* with letters, he and Margaret went back to the wintry Cape to get their things out of the Coast Guard station, which two weeks later was destroyed in a storm. On the train they briefly resumed being free spirits of the twenties: "Love-making with gusto just before taking train—she took a douche with Angostura bitters by mistake—in lower berth together sat up till late talking and laughing—conversation punctuated by stopper blowing out of gin bottle to our great hilarity (stopper blew out of other gin bottle in suitcase and saturated clothes with gin, violet border to colorless stain)." Dos pronounced the "Appeal" a "battle cry very neatly oiled to slip past mental obstacles," and joked that Wilson's program might be sold to the public through advertising, which he sometimes tried to envision in the service of good. Katy reported that store clerks in Provincetown were reading the article. She told Margaret that before she took over the state "on a white horse" it might be necessary to stab each of these literary revolutionaries in his bath, calling her husband by his pet name Muttonfish and Wilson by the nickname Dr. Anti-Christ that Dos had given him, one which, a few years later, he would redefine by sending Katy and Dos some anti-Marxist sayings.

Margaret and he wintered at the Berkeley, an apartment-hotel on Fifth Avenue. Though the place was not really to her taste—"full of elevator boys and old ladies"—she decorated the living room with red brocade curtains, and they made love every night until she insisted it was too much. She didn't like his always afterward urging her to "go in and fix yourself up." He didn't want them to have a child, though he later regretted that decision. Margaret lacked Wilson's enthusiasm for what people were beginning to call the masses; class lines were not, she thought, shrinking away as rapidly as her small income from the Pennsylvania coal mines. He'd remember holding forth on politics while she "would smoke her cigarette with perfect poise, saying nothing, serious-looking," until her well-bred manner "drove me into asserting my intellectual advantage of her in satire on and comprehension of the social structure, sense of the futility of worldly privileges and distinctions."

In the spring of 1931 Josephson began to see Wilson in a revised uniform, his dark suits accompanied by "a broad-brimmed black Stetson, which I came to think of as his political hat." He chronicled the toll of bank failures, layoffs, and demonstrations. In the first part of an article initially called "Progress and Poverty," as the radical economist Henry George had named his tract, then called "May First" for the international labor holiday, he etches the elegant lines and proportions of the just completed Empire State Building, its harmony with light and sky. It was built in less than a year, and he reports, "forty-eight men were killed in the process (One man, who lost his job, could not find work elsewhere and came back to be again turned away; he jumped off the seventy-second story and went through a one-inch tile on the sixth)." On the unfinished fifty-fifth floor a pencil drawing of two figures having sex and "a gigantic vagina with its name in four large letters under it" reminds Wilson the building is sometimes known as "Al Smith's last erection." Gazing through the windows, past other office buildings that will have to be emptied if all this new space is to be occupied, looking over the expanding circles of the industrialized urban community, he turns to the tragedy, near the polluted Passaic River, of a laid-off auto worker named John Dravic. In better times Dravic had taught his two older sons to play the violin and the cello, performing trios in the evening, but he abandoned hope after he failed to make a go of a little corner store he'd bought for three hundred dollars. Wilson focuses in on his three sons, carefully tucked into bed, their heads "blown out with point-blank revolver shots," and the father, having shot himself, still "straining the upper part of his body as if he were trying to grab something to pull himself up from the floor."

Cultural institutions reflected the crisis, were vitiated by the lack of community, the stark ugliness of industrial capitalism. The brand-new functional building of the New School for Social Research on West Twelfth Street, its walls adorned with revolutionary murals by Thomas Hart Benton and José Clemente Orozco, seemed the mask of a bankrupt society. The curriculum was a trendy hodgepodge, from lectures on Marxist sociology to "Native Players on Their Own Instruments." At the Metropolitan Opera a "brassy proscenium arch" and "expensive disproportionate settings"—in stark contrast to the failing New York neighborhood outside— cut the audience off from the gaiety and heartache of *La Bohème*. The irrelevance of the performance is brought home in Wilson's one-paragraph notice, which mentions a friend so drunk he thinks the opera is *Manon*. This and other short interludes, like those in Hemingway's *In Our Time*, are interspersed within the 1932 volume Wilson assembled from this reportage and called *The American Jitters* after "Got the Jitters," a popular song.

In his world, it was among the women, few of whom in that period had the political outlets of their men, that the jitters were most visible. Rambunctious Anne Cummings, frustrated with her role while the men talked revolutionary politics, asked the wives in the ladies' room, "Now can't we make some trouble here? Let's go downstairs and say 'Piss, shit, fuck.'" Margaret confessed to Wilson that she too sometimes wanted "to break things, kill people, say dirty words," but she held herself in check, turning to liquor when he became totally absorbed in his writing and his political cause. "There were party drinkers and there were all-day sippers," Malcolm Cowley recalled, Anne being one such and the new Mrs. Wilson another. "Don't you like to sip?" she'd ask?

Zelda Fitzgerald had been institutionalized—Scott told Wilson she was "off her head"—and Louise Bogan had collapsed from the effects, she said, of hatreds, fears, jealousy, and self-contempt as well as alcohol.

Placing herself in the hands of Dr. McKinney, who had rescued Wilson, she signed into the Neurological Institute. In the vein of her anthologized "Evening at the Sanitorium," she wittily versified her grim routine:

> My God, what was the crime? Did I deserve
> Therapy, out of possible punishments?
> What the betrayal, that the faded nerve
> Must bloom again by means not making sense?
> O, I shall mend! Even now I grow quite well,
> Knitting round wash-cloths on the paths of hell.

In an eloquent buck-up letter, Wilson located their generation between the Victorian age and an uncertain future: "Everything is changing so fast and we are all more or less in a position of having been brought up in one kind of world and having to adjust muscles, socially, sexually, morally etc. to another which is in a state of flux."

Eager to learn what was happening around the country, he turned over the literary desk at *The New Republic* to Cowley and gave up his editor's salary to be a roving reporter for the magazine. It was an alternative to producing what Dos called prose made up in the office, springing from "neither experience nor observation but from sheer intellectual whoopee." The long article "Detroit Motors" opens with a panorama of the assembly line at River Rouge. In a pioneering effort at interview journalism Wilson presents auto workers, engineers, and union types through their own words, a style soon to be emulated by young Studs Terkel and that would lead to that of the "new" journalists. A woman at a press describes the speedup and its effects, the sudden hush when someone loses a finger. A Scottish labor organizer complains that the Communists don't "talk the language of the American worruker." The Model T and vaunted five-dollar-a-day wage had made Henry Ford's seem a capitalism that could democratize, but Wilson found him politically incoherent and ineffectual. Wilson contrasted the individualist who defeated the bankers, the idealist of the World War I peace ship, to the tyrannical CEO whose instability matched his ignorance. Ford's empire now reeled from the economic contraction—the work force cut to a fifth and an ever lengthening line of old cars waiting to be smashed and recycled.

For close to three months Wilson was on the road in the mid-South. Accompanying a Red Cross worker and a county agent on their rounds in rural Kentucky, he documented poverty, malnutrition, the collapse of community. He sketched the idealized Anglo-Saxon features of a starving family much as Walker Evans would photograph the Gudgers in *Let Us Now Praise Famous Men*. In West Virginia twenty thousand miners were armed and on strike. "Frank Keeney's Coal Diggers," as Wilson christened them, had once owned the land where they lived in company towns and made $2.60 to $3.60 a day, and had seceded from John L. Lewis's United Mine Workers under the leadership of Frank Keeney, a former associate of Eugene Debs, the socialist jailed by Woodrow Wilson during World War I. The odds were against the miners, but their vigor and resolve were heartening.

At Chattanooga he confronted the barrier of race. In a lynch-mob atmosphere in a small town just across the Alabama line, the nine young black men called the Scottsboro boys had been convicted of raping two white women in a freight car. The testimony was suspect and the verdict was on appeal, the defense split between the then ever cautious NAACP and the Communists, who were out to make martyrs, peddling their doctrine to Southern blacks as a form of revivalist religion. It was one of those situations "from which nobody emerges with credit," as Dos Passos put it.

In Tennessee, Wilson also visited Tate, who had written to him of the isolation of "the Southern literary man in the South: a preference for life here in the ordinary sense, with a decided weakness for 'foreigners' for intimate society." The Fugitives were in the process of releasing their manifesto, "I'll Take My Stand," and Wilson momentarily envied writers who could retreat to a family farm and a regional mythology, escaping "the deadening of feeling, the social insulation, which impoverish life in industrial communities." Yet he thought it foolish to pass resolutions limiting the growth of industry, and much irritated his host by reporting that such Southerners made a religion of ancestor worship.

Margaret was left behind on these expeditions, but they devised a three-month holiday together, first at a ranch near Santa Fe and then in California. "JITTERS UNDER PERFECT CONTROL," she telegrammed on her way to pick up Jimmy, and from Santa Barbara she sent a cheerful account of dropping in on Ted Paramore one night, finding him "in bed alone reading 'The Wet Parade' and Art [Carey] in the other twin bed with a buck-tooth blonde—nice and chubby." While awaiting her in New Mexico Wilson explored the cliff dwellings, which suggested how much better these long vanished tribes' religion and social organization had fit

them than did the institutions of twentieth-century Americans. He satirized his contemporaries flocking to the Hopi ceremonies, from the socialite Mabel Dodge Luhan, who sought to identify her "wanton promiscuity"
with the Indians' sexual code, to a Harvard poet who apparently yearned
for the role of Christ in the next Penitentes crucifixion rite. Years later,
Wilson, his vision no longer focused by Marx's magic lantern, would return to the Southwest to fortify his morale at the Zuni Shalako dances.

The couple hoped to re-create the happiness of the previous summer
at the Cape, and en route to Santa Fe Margaret wired that "FROM HEAD TO
FOOT" she was "IN THE MOOD FOR LOVE," using German in her shyness
with the telegraph operator. Somehow their romantic holiday backfired.
When trail riding, they tied their horses to trees and she took down her
riding breeches, "which was strange and very sensual," but he found himself fantasizing about "a blonde Follies girl with a fleshy red mouth." As
he'd recapitulate the moment at the end of *Hecate County*, the grand
mountain scenery only brought home "the strain of our wrong relation." A
dark intuition in this scene of Margaret's fate is recorded in one of Wilson's best poems, "The Voice." The melancholy undertow of great literature is his backdrop:

> All Virgil's idylls end in sunsets; pale
> With death, the past of Dante opens deep.
> The men of Shakespeare do not break, they fail;
> And Joyce's dreamers always drift asleep.

Thinking of his cousin Adelaide, who had been in and out of sanitariums
since her husband's death in World War I, and of his own breakdown,
again he hears "This voice that always says, 'Farewell! Sleep well!'":

> I heard it, dulled with love against your breast,
> I heard it in our peace of summer suns;
> I heard it where the long waves of the West
> Retard the dark with loud suspended guns;
>
> And even in the white bark of that wood,
> Those mountains roped and broken by our race,
> Beside those high streams where the horses stood
> And watched our strange and desperate embrace.

They moved on to her home for the late summer, but at some point Margaret declared, "You don't like Santa Barbara—or don't like me," and he does seem uncomfortable in the garden-party photograph in which he squints into the sun as she leans forward to talk, perhaps to the photographer, a cigarette in one hand, the other clutching her husband's arm. He tried to fit in with her crowd, who as one woman said were "making the best of the last twenty-four hours of capitalism." Margaret enjoyed the sparkle of her former life. Rosalind would remember when her stepmother "went to a dance and a man stepped on her evening dress. He gave her fifteen dollars and she bet him fifty dollars she could get three evening dresses for that, which [in that summer of 1931] she did." Ted had lent them an automobile, and Wilson admired the "very Californian" daring with which his wife and his friend negotiated the unfenced coastal road to Los Angeles. One midnight after an argument, this man who had never driven a car and wouldn't again decided to drive down in order to hash something out with Ted. "Of course, it was less difficult at night when there were few other cars, and I had only a truck or two to pass," he notes; "but when I got to Ted's house in Hollywood, I didn't know how to stop the car and kept driving around and around the block. I can't remember what I finally did." On the way home he "got stalled on the Canejo Grande and started to back off—in the way of other cars." When he got back, he says—"I can't remember how, I can't have driven myself—Margaret greeted me with, 'My lone eagle!' (that was what Lindbergh had been called)."

Dos Passos's friend John Howard Lawson, then a politically uncommitted screenwriter, later one of the Hollywood Ten, remembered the author of *Axel's Castle* convincing him of the need for "an American form of Communism" during a drunken two-day discussion of art and politics in Santa Barbara. At one point Wilson went to sleep on the dining room table, then fell off "with a crash." He hadn't written of the movies since the mid-1920s, but when in Hollywood he saw Eisenstein's unfinished epic about the Mexican revolution, he wrote it up for *The New Republic*, using a staccato impressionism to detail a sequence of rushes many of which have disappeared. Upton Sinclair had mortgaged his house to fund this film, and Wilson tried to put him in touch with donors. When Wilson's piece appeared, however, Eisenstein felt obliged to protest this account of his film, because it stated that he was happier as an artist in Mexico than in the USSR.

To Gauss Wilson decried the "sour situation" of their "wonderful country," and the California chapters of *The American Jitters* mirror the despair that Nathanael West and, a generation later, Joan Didion, found in the golden land. The people of Los Angeles were "cultivated enervated people," lovers of "mixturesque beauty," as their architecture showed, and they were pious folk, each denomination having its "cheery little odd-boxes, god-boxes." He recounts the entrepreneurial styles of three fore-runners of the electronic ministry, Aimee Semple McPherson, the young Reverend Bob Shuler, and Shuler's ex-lieutenant, an educated Calvinist named Brieglieb, as they battled for the support of the transplanted Mid-westerners who had added to the city's appetite for media scandal. He in-tuits the coming of a uniquely American fusion of Eastern religion with ersatz sex, picturing a "roguey old yogi" in a garden where "pink clematis or purple clitoris rises or droops in rhythm to the movement of the mystic's fingers."

The most powerful piece in *Jitters* emerged from Wilson's journal, where a list of suicides from the coroner's records in San Diego with the apparent causes and the means ("July: family trouble—ant paste; health—shooting; no work—gas; deranged—shooting; no work or money—drowning") is placed next to a vignette of the elegant Coronado Beach Hotel, built in the 1880s at "the last luscious moment just before the power of American money, swollen with sudden growth, had turned its back altogether on the more human comforts and ornaments of the old non-mechanical world." "The Jumping-Off Place" integrates the hotel and the suicides. We pass through rooms occupied by coupon-clipping ladies and gentlemen into the banquet room where a federation of women's clubs are "solemnly reading aloud and debating, one by one, the amendments proposed to their innumerable by-laws," then celebrate their money raising to the tune of "The Battle Hymn of the Republic":

> Twenty-thousand dollars by nineteen-thirty-four!
> Our fund is marching on!

It is a version of Eliot's "In the room the women come and go / Talking of Michelangelo." A concluding one-sentence catalogue of people who have killed themselves, their occupations and races, conveys the exhaustion of the American dream of the West. Among other ways of ending their lives, these Gadarene swine "throw themselves into the bay, blue and placid, where gray battleships and cruisers guard the limits of their broad-belting nation—already reaching out in the 'eighties for the sugar plantations of Honolulu." Wilson marries an apocalyptic vision like that of *The Waste Land* to a lament for the republic owing something to Gibbon's *Decline and Fall*.

As he envisioned the imperial expansion of this morally enfeebled people, the lure of suicide made itself felt in his private life. He returned to the East, but Margaret stayed on the West Coast through October. Uncomfortable in her girlhood room, she was planning to move in with Miggs, her old partner in the hat shop, who was in bad shape after a failed love affair, then discovered her "half-dead in the kitchen" with the gas turned on. Thereafter, when despondent, Margaret sometimes remarked that she might "do a Miggs."

Wilson was in Lawrence, Massachusetts, to report on immigrant textile workers who picketed in the cold, rainy New England autumn, confronting the prospect of a hungry winter. The leaders of the various unions seemed to him more competent to run the mills than management. Between the American Federation of Labor and the Communists, he was drawn to an independent union led by decent young men willing to be beaten up for their views, products of A. J. Muste's Brookwood Labor School. Like Keeney's Coal Diggers and the Wobblies leading a strike at Hoover Dam, they were anticapitalist yet free of the Communist lingo of "ideologies" and "liquidating" class enemies. The Reuther brothers and others in the early history of the Congress of Industrial Organizations would share this native radicalism. The strike, however, failed, apparently when the gentlemanly negotiator for the owners broke his word to the organizers, and Wilson castigated the managerial elite of which "Mr. X" was a specimen. For all their genteel pretensions he and his wife were "only individuals on the make," part of a huge machine for moneymaking, for the creation of consumption and consumers. Such people could no more challenge capitalism than their grandparents could religion, and if they preferred to have a good time—like the swingers of a later age—their liquor and their sterile affairs turned self-indulgent and sour. Alternately, they would become increasingly "insipid, fatuously cheerful, two-dimensional, spic and span," falling victim to their own advertising.

Jitters proceeds to "The Case of the Author," where Marx's account of the workings of selfishness and self-deception in the human psyche is applied to Wilson. A harsh self-assessment results. A petit bourgeois with a self-image derived from the professional tradition in his family and from

the resistance of his father and others to "the life of machinery and enormous profits," he'd entered the army as an enlisted man but hadn't, as
he'd resolved in France, afterward seceded from conventional society in
the cause of Beauty and Truth. During the 1920s he had made as much
as $7,500 a year—in 1929 he made $5,400 from The New Republic.—
with small family inheritances (one from a Talcottville great-aunt) affording the luxury of travel and a margin for "classical reading, liquor, and
general irresponsibility." To subject his individual development to this
analysis brings Wilson's book to the point of a conversion narrative. In the
USSR, he believed, a classless society was being created by a disinterested vanguard in charge of affairs, who could impose better methods and
ideas on the masses than they would have attained on their own.

What little Wilson then knew about Russia came from the illustrated
magazine U.S.S.R. in Construction. Sidney Hook, the future philosopher
of pragmatism and vehement anti-Communist, recalled being similarly
magnetized by photos of tractors and electric power dams when American
society "seemed to be coming apart." Hook had shared, he said, Wilson's
view of Marxist theory as "an engineer's technique for analyzing society
and its various forces," an instrument of reason and will. To Wilson the alternative seemed "the creed of one of the churches." When Jitters appeared, Hemingway wrote to Dos Passos, "Bunny's book was wonderful
reporting—wish he had kept on reporting and not to have had to save his
soul." So the historian Charles A. Beard accused Wilson of accepting
communism as a faith. Perkins, his editor at Scribner's, found him "so
completely committed to Communism now that it's hard to see how he
can ever get it off his mind, even if it comes to seem something remote as
it probably will."*

For the Communist Party, he would have been a big catch. Mike Gold,
who wrote for The Daily Worker, thought snobbery the cause of Wilson's
resistance, remarking that he "ascended the proletarian 'bandwagon' with
the arrogance of a myopic, high-bosomed Beacon Hill matron entering a
common streetcar." It was true that he was marked by the class consciousness of Hill and Princeton, along with the shared loyalties of the

---

*When commenting on Hemingway's Stalinism in The Wound and the Bow, Wilson attributes
the same need to the novelist. "In the moment of seizure," he writes, the convert "saw a scroll
unrolled from the heavens" explaining history. Now the skeptic Wilson says that one would get
over this "phase of snowblindness and learn to see real people and conditions." After Hemingway's fatuous assertions he had "sobered up" in his stories of the late thirties and "largely
sloughed off his Stalinism" in For Whom the Bell Tolls.

literary world. Wilson, however, had never been a joiner. He was good at resisting churches, and when he looked into the enthusiastical church of the Party, it turned him off as had the evangelical preachers at school. He remarked to Cowley that communism might be the right thing for him, and Cowley, later for some time stuck in Stalinism, recalled Wilson as "the bellwether of the flock who leads the sheep into the pen and walks out unharmed on the other side." This was somewhat the role he played for Lawson and, apparently, for young W. H. Auden, who read *Devil Take the Hindmost*, the British edition of *Jitters*, alongside Marx while at Oxford.

He wasn't much good as an agitator, for he couldn't give a speech. Matthews remembered a dinner party, thrown by Hart Crane's patron Otto Kahn, at which Dos Passos was the guest of honor and Wilson was expected to speak in praise of him. Belatedly, he caught the toastmaster's eye and "in his high voice, in a breathless rush and with heavy pauses," declared: "I've recently been—in California. I was very much—struck—by the domestic—architecture there. Many of the—buildings—have extremely—fancy—façades. I was told that—they are so jerry-built—that frequently—the front—falls down—before the back is—finished. And I just want to say—that in my opinion—the work of Mr. Dos Passos—is not like that." The observation and writing in *Jitters* have also lasted, surviving the author's revolutionary convictions. Wilson documents industrial oppression, rural disasters, the cultural elite, employed and unemployed immigrants, as well as every region of the country at this moment between the Crash and the dawn of the New Deal. Conveying what he looked back on as the exhilaration as well as the sadness of "those desperate days when nothing worked" but everything seemed possible, the book is reprinted as history in *The American Earthquake*.

Wilson's one direct engagement in the labor wars is not chronicled here, for it took place the following February in backwoods Kentucky, where he was part of a group delivering food and clothing to striking miners in a Communist-run district union. They included Cowley, the labor reporter Mary Heaton Vorse, Quincy Howe, later prominent in radio news, and young John Hammond, radical heir of the Vanderbilts and future impresario of jazz and blues. Hammond, who'd driven down, seemed someone who had steeped himself in Proust, "then received an injection of Communism," a characterization also applicable to Wilson. The writer Waldo Frank, later his neighbor at Cape Cod, was elected leader. Wilson regarded Frank as dismayingly naive when he pronounced that after the radicals won everyone in the cabinet "is going to be an intellectual," from

the president "all the way down to the postmaster general," but at Pineville
he had a moral force the critic credited to his Jewish heritage. The Party
people on the other hand, included Allen Taub, a flashy lawyer, and his
wife, Doris Parks, an enthusiastic soapbox preacher of the Communist
line. Wilson had been brought up in the atmosphere of his mother's anti-
Semitism, and this Jewish couple, pushy to the point of courting danger
for them all, awoke a prejudice he thought he had overcome at the Plattsburgh training camp.

An organizer had been shot and died the day the New Yorkers arrived.
When they drove into Pineville—"entering war zone," he noted—they
were told not to sit with their backs to a window, and the square where
they met with the mayor, the coal-company lawyer, and the deputy sheriff was surrounded by machine guns. In the thirty pages that are our only
source for this episode, Cowley, known for his physical courage, is seen
protecting a truck full of sugar against a crowd of deputies, at one point
with a gun in his back. Hammond races his car out of town with film that
a cameraman, Ben Leider, throws to him over a deputy's head. The others are arrested and taken to court, and though the charges are dropped,
the anti-union crowd at the hotel send the women out of town in a taxi
that night, then drive the men to the state line and shove them across.
Someone threatens to kill Taub, and Wilson sees his face "covered with
blood in the darkness." Like Preacher Casy in *The Grapes of Wrath*, Frank
refuses to concede that no one has been hurt, saying, "You can beat me
up, but that's a lie." A day later, a picture of Taub's bandaged head was
printed all over the country.

In *The New Masses* Wilson labeled this episode a "class-war exhibit," illustrating the repressive nature of capitalism in a company town, but to
Dos Passos he wrote that "if the literati want to engage in radical activities,
they ought to organize or something independently—so they can back
other people besides the comrades and so that the comrades can't play
them for suckers." The conflict between the literary Left and the Communist Party would resurface after Wilson's death, when Matthew Josephson repeated the charge of a man named Colman of the "Committee for
the Defense of Political Prisoners" that during the confrontation Wilson
"disappeared." Howe told Leon Edel that "it was logistically impossible for
any of us to 'run out' at any time." Cowley—who Josephson cites making
the same charge—assured the present writer that "Bunny's behavior was
perfectly honorable," though he didn't "play a speaking part." On his death-

bed Hammond remembered his satisfaction that someone who wrote as well as Wilson "had kept a record."

With Frank and Lewis Mumford, Wilson drafted a manifesto in which the economic chaos became a "crucial symbol" of the need for "a new cultural order." Agreeing to sign this high-flown document, Dos wondered, "What are you going to do with it? post it up on billboards? it might go well on toilet paper like ex-lax advertising—or is it going to be laid on Mr. Hoover's breakfast table?" Wilson developed his own position in the pamphlet "Culture and the Crisis," published, ironically, by the League of Professional Workers for Foster and Ford, a Communist front during the 1932 election. He argued for a protest vote for William Z. Foster, the only presidential candidate who seemed to have a plan and a will to carry it out, and got the signatures, among others, of Hook, Lincoln Steffens, Langston Hughes, and Countee Cullen, as well as Leonie Adams, one of five women among "the famous fifty-three."

Major portraits were to emerge from the short pieces in which, on more solid ground, he took Marx, Flaubert, and Shaw as "Critics of the Middle Class." Flaubert attempted to stand "outside the bourgeois psychology," as Wilson was trying to do. In *L'education sentimentale* he showed the dilettante Frédéric Moreau paralyzed between women of opposed classes, exactly the tension Wilson experienced between Frances and Margaret and would explore in his best-known piece of fiction, "The Princess with the Golden Hair." In contrast to Flaubert, Shaw now seemed to him an opportunist, popularizing a compromised Marxism in the establishment, endorsing Mussolini and Stalin as strongmen. Wilson found the illumination Shaw had once provided in *Das Kapital*. In a sentence reused in *To the Finland Station*, he cites Marx on the progress of "mechanical production and the accumulation of capital, rising out of the feudal world, wrecking it, and accelerating, reorganizing, reassembling in ever more ingenious complexity," bringing alien lands into its net "as it shapes the destinies of peoples, their bodies and minds and instincts and personalities, without their understanding of what is happening to them and independent of any individual's will." Seeking in Marx's psychology and background the source of the power behind the thought, in 1932 he already ascribed this to the Hebraic tradition.

When Wilson returned from the strife of Bell and Harlan counties, Kentucky, he found Margaret on the daybed in the arms of a classmate, the banker Bill Brown, "somebody," she said, "who likes me and makes a fuss over me." When asked whether she was "in love with Bill" she replied, "You know damn well I'm not!" But sometimes she'd claim Wilson "didn't need her, she was a luxury, something like Guerlain's perfume." In the jumbled maze of memories after her death, included by Leon Edel in *The Thirties*, he shows her waiting up when he worked late—"she'd lie there reading with a long glass of green alcohol gin fizz beside her, waiting for me to come to bed—then I'd stay up drinking, with my writing, and come to bed genial-drunk just as it was getting light, when she had no sleep." One night she burst out, "I'm a very gregarious person—Why don't you take me out and jazz me once in a while?—I like people!—you don't like people." They rented a two-room apartment on West Fifty-eighth from Ethel Hutchinson, the mistress of Colonel Ruppert, owner of Ruppert Breweries and the New York Yankees, who was a friend of Margaret's stepmother Daisy. The place was dark and for Wilson "embarrassingly chichi," the bedroom "done in a subaqueous green" with "the elegant white bed of a kept woman's boudoir." Adelaide Walker, the wife of his friend Charley, recalled Margaret "learning to live on sandwiches." She had a rare chance to share in Wilson's life when in the spring of 1932 Dos and he gave a party, serving bootleg gin, to rally support for William Z. Foster. Margaret was their hostess.

He had married her partly to free Frances and himself of one another, but they had no money to buy and fix up a home of their own and her custody arrangements condemned them to live for half the year on separate coasts. The onset of the Depression doomed the marriage. Margaret liked to say she had "champagne tastes," while Wilson (as she told Dawn Powell, who reported this to others) sometimes woke out of a nightmare "exclaiming that the revolution had to begin that morning!" Liquor, which had helped bring them together, deepened the strain. According to Harold Clurman, who shared an apartment immediately above them with his wife Stella Adler—Aaron Copland being next door—Margaret and Wilson "drank non-stop." When drunk she was maudlin, while he gave vent to anger. That he had a temper became clear to Clurman, who was promoting Wilson's talky drama of bourgeois collapse, *Beppo and Beth*, with his partner in the Group Theatre, Lee Strasberg. One day Clurman reported that Strasberg thought the play "disgusting," at which Wilson flew into a rage. Another time the director overheard a scene "that ended with his tearing the curtains from their rods, and with the frightened cries of his wife." This account is duplicated in Wilson's journal: "I had smashed

the card table, pulled the shades down—she had dreamed, she told me the next morning, that I was an ape climbing up the curtains."

New York had come to seem "so much darker at night"—the heart, he writes, "had been taken out of it" and "when the electric current is turned off, the filament looks pretty thready." People were "gaunt, grey, unsure of themselves, and gloomy." Margaret sometimes called him "old man Gloom himself," and when depressed would ask, "How can you worry about humanity and see someone who's so unhappy?" Citing his "complicated ideas," in these jumbled recollections she calls him a "ghoul" and "Frankenstein," and refers to herself as "your own suicide at home."

As June approached, she accepted the idea of a truce in their fractious life. They would spend the summer apart, "each with his own child." The night she caught the train, June 12, they had dinner with Dos, the Cummingses (now separated, each bringing a date), and Jean Gorman, who was traveling with Margaret. Wilson pressed his wife to go back to the apartment, all too obviously so they could make love before she left. They drank brandy in the compartment and he kissed her goodbye on the platform, she crying. Changing trains in Chicago, she sent a card—"Have survived very well so far—about to take the Santa Fe"; she'd "crashed into 12 hours sleep." Though she'd felt he was kicking her out and spoke of "going West and never coming back," in California Margaret got a grip on herself, writing, "It seems very quiet here without you and Rosalind, and I miss you terribly. Expect to get full of health, nothing doing—Merle is away with Douglas [possibly Oberon and Fairbanks Jr.], Reggie on the wagon, and no one knows where Ted is and the rest of the folk are dead anyway." It is the end of the twenties in Hollywood, but in a later letter, she has been "leading a very quiet life as to drinking and jazzing and feel fine."

Wilson "alternated between the apartment in New York and my mother's house in Red Bank. I worked on *Beppo and Beth*, drank gin, and played Beethoven on the phonograph." He had sublimated his love for Frances in his new social commitment. In "The Princess with the Golden Hair" the narrator's working-class mistress gives him "that life of the people which had before been but prices and wages, legislation and technical progress, that new Europe of the East Side and Brooklyn for which there was provided no guidebook." During the winter of 1931–32, however, Wilson had a disturbing dream in which Frances was working in a house where Margaret and he lived. She turned into a kitten that was bleeding and eventually became "a little round thing like a cell," which fell from his hand and

got lost on the floor while he "went on talking." He hadn't seen her since he married, but when Margaret had been gone a month he invited his former love over, and the journal records they had sex, on the couch. At the Cape in August with Rosalind and her nurse, Stella, he enjoyed the summer routine, becoming friends with Chauncey Hackett, a onetime lawyer who'd clerked for Justice Holmes, and the young woman for whom Chauncey had left a respectable marriage, herself later a painter. Working steadily, he completed half a dozen articles on men of letters for *The New Republic*, among them Michelet, historian of the French Revolution. It was satisfying to be without obligation except to Rosalind. But Frances wanted to reenter his life, and a letter thanking him for sending her some money urges him to see her in New York before his wife returns. A second letter, indicating they have met in Boston over the Labor Day weekend, closes, "Come home soon—I miss you. Love me? Oh! do hurry back."

On September 30 he returned with Rosalind to New York, to find Mary Blair waiting at the station with the news that Margaret was dead. Although *The New York Times* would report that she fell in front of a café, on the telephone a California neighbor explained that she had fractured her skull when she lost her footing on a flight of worn unevenly tiled stone stairs after a party at a Spanish colonial building. Only five feet tall, like Wilson's mother, Margaret habitually wore spiked heels and was always afraid of tripping—once she'd fallen down the steps in their apartment when answering the phone. That night she had been drinking. But Wilson, devastated, was afraid that she'd killed herself, since "she had talked so much about suicide." Rosalind, who'd just celebrated her ninth birthday, remembered well that awful evening not only because she'd lost someone she loved but because "my father spent the night in the guest room" and "I could hear him sobbing, the only time I ever heard him cry."

His willed obliviousness had broken down, and during the two-day flight to California he thought the low-flying plane might crash and he fall to his death—"not a bad thing if it did." On the road from Los Angeles to Santa Barbara he recalled Margaret's misery during her last months in New York. When welcomed by her mother, her sister, and her sister's clergyman husband, kindly conventional folk who made him comfortable in the rambling house hung with family portraits, he was reminded of her "natural smartness" and ease. Her mother—her voice sweet like Margaret's—urged him to believe in immortality, and at the funeral her brother-in-law the minister spoke vaguely but energetically of the soul rising again. The finality hit him at the mortuary viewing. "Her cheeks were

full of paraffin and hard, they had made them seem too big—lips cold and hard also, breasts—a look of pride, almost of scorn."

Feeling "like a murderer," he had himself driven around town obsessively questioning people about whether she could have killed herself. Ted told of finding "her and Jimmy making a meal on Corn Flakes." Mary McCarthy would speculate that it was Ted, jealous of Wilson and angered to see his Maggie neglected, who spread the story that she "threw herself" down the steps. Though Miggs did later kill herself, there is nothing to suggest Margaret did. Her son Jimmy Canby would recall to his daughters that it was a foggy night and the steps were slippery. Wilson wrote to the Dos Passoses it was "a turning staircase" and that "she had been in bed with the flu and had only just gotten up—was probably giddy and uncertain on her feet." Ten years later, however, he told his friend Helen Muchnic that Margaret was drinking because she was unsure of his love.

"I'll crash someday," she had sometimes told Wilson, the part of the eat, drink, and be merry attitude of the twenties that one didn't talk about. She had a premonition "she was doomed, would not live—she used to ask me what I'd do, who I'd notify, if she should die." A friend who was at the party remembered that, after she fell, "when they had carried her in and put her on the bed and asked her how she felt, she answered, 'Sleepy,' so low that they could hardly hear her." Her threat to go west and not return had been fulfilled in a way she hadn't intended.

In her letters from Santa Barbara that summer Margaret is glad she can help support herself, hopes to minimize their money problems the next winter. Lovingly, she urges Wilson to put her out of his mind financially, though "not in other ways, Darling." He wrote that he missed her and encouraged her to come back, but her last letter is depressed. With natural eloquence she reports that her usual sunny California "hasn't been Sun Kist at all here lately due to the mountains being all destroyed by fire and ashes falling like snow, a very impressive but gloomy sight, the sun being a red ball through the smoke, for a week now."

Wilson clung to these letters but burned his to her. The jottings that began to emerge on the plane, in Santa Barbara, and on the train trip home, which he'd expand over the years, are the most intense of his autobiographical writings, his feelings not displaced by description of sex, as in the journal they would sometimes later be. He recalls how hard she worked at life, making the most of the unpromising places they had rented just as she managed to dress elegantly on her limited budget, sometimes with the help of friends who gave her things. He remembers how she'd laugh when "she took off her dress and her underthings came with it so that she was naked: we both laughed—I'm one of those ready girls! she said." He tortures himself with the times he'd been neglectful and hears her saying, "I forgive you, dearr—I don't mind, dearr—" then reminds himself, "but now she was dead." He fell in love with Margaret as she'd so desperately wanted, but only when she was gone and he couldn't do anything about it, except feel guilty. Belatedly recognizing his incompetent, even duplicitous behavior, he sums it all up with "After she was dead, I loved her."

In Santa Barbara he began dreaming of Margaret, that she wasn't dead after all or could be rescued or had divorced him and they could marry again. Multiplying in the mid-1930s, these dreams persist in his journal into *The Sixties*. Variations on the Orpheus myth, in them Wilson thinks he can retrieve her from the land of shadows into which she vanishes, if only he wants her badly enough. Alternately, he blames himself for holding on to an existence she can no longer share. Eight months after her death, he wonders, "Were the possibilities of some other more congenial, more intellectually developed woman still able to tempt me?," then decides "that I did want her, yes, and I would have her, and persuade her to live." He wakes alone from this dream "among all the green foliage and lovely peace of a slightly overcast Sunday at Red Bank." The following December a dream that returns him to her beloved California in springtime gives way to "a dry fated sharp sickening feeling": "self-contempt and self-assertion, grim insolent will to go on living and awful sickening realizing of what had happened." He is trapped in a personal hell, the "hard, scared, self-acrid feeling I got in connection with her death beginning to grip me in its vise." It was suffering he couldn't have imagined during his youthful heartbreak over Millay. In his waking life too he punished himself, "sometimes passing on myself with sickening insight the verdict of suicide," avoiding open windows and exposed flights of steps, "glad of an excuse in Rosalind and Mother for staying alive."

In one of his dreams Margaret has registered as Mrs. Edmund Wilson at a seedy hotel where he knew she would have hated staying. Worried that another man is after her, he is about to get through on the phone when he wakes up. He believes her to be still alive and has to make himself face the truth: "I had to recall to myself that I had certainly seen her dead in the funeral parlor at Santa Barbara—that I had seen her pale and smooth and hard and rigid in death and now could never see her talking and affectionate, a little live human girl, again in New York, as I had thought I was going to in the dream. Shy and warm, inarticulate and lively."

12

314 East Fifty-third Street

Beginnings of To the Finland Station

On October 12, 1932, Wilson wrote to Ford Madox Ford that he couldn't contribute to a pamphlet in Pound's honor because of previous deadlines and of "the death of my wife." Gardner Jencks, an old friend at Cape Cod, believed that "the death of Margaret almost destroyed him." Hiding the depth of his grief, he moved his things across town to an old gray clapboard house between First and Second Avenues. 314 East Fifty-third Street was scheduled to be torn down and rented for fifty dollars a month. This musty-smelling place with "lumpy and rubbed yellow walls," amid the noise and grime of the slums—ironically, it would survive among the distinguished private homes on this street—was, until mid-decade, his base of operations. The radical Muriel Draper and her son Paul, a dancer, lived next door and were often seen in their garden. At one period, Wilson let friends camp out in the basement apartment and rented the bedrooms on the top floor, while at another time Frank and Edie Shay from Provincetown took over the main floor and he moved upstairs. He often ate at Rosa's, a working-man's cafe around the corner.

An old black woman from the South named Hattie brought a degree of order to his life during the next five years, through the first months of his marriage to Mary McCarthy, and again briefly after that ended. Hattie also took care of her grandchildren, saying her daughter was crazy. Rosalind describes Wilson as devoted to her, "patiently pleading her cause and painstakingly doing the endless paperwork" at relief agencies. The writer Nora Sayre, eleven when her family first employed Hattie in 1945, heard it was mutual—"She'd tried to lend him money when he was hard up, and balked when he offered her a raise." Hattie was agile and enterprising. When necessary she could acquire food, china, silver, even a bed or two from a neighbor, and once, for an honored guest, she borrowed a tablecloth someone on the block had lifted from the Yale Club. She and Wilson were prepared, at any time, to disappear when the sheriff came to throw them out for nonpayment of rent.

American society was fragmenting. On Election Night in 1932 at Rosa's a sallow-faced man with dead eyes sat drunkenly denouncing politicians— all were "swine, scavengers," as were Sacco and Vanzetti. As he spoke, sitting alone at a long table, he repeatedly struck his head with "the palm of a stiffened hand," whose fingers stuck out and bent back "like the prongs of a dying starfish." Entropy is the theme of the searing account of Chicago that winter called by Wilson "Hull House in 1932." He went there after Thanksgiving to write about Jane Addams and stayed at her establishment, which seemed a cross between a factory and a convent. At dinner the great lady presided like a mother superior, with someone playing Bach in the background. Classically educated and serious-minded, she had created her political community of women, and when her shame at being comfortable in the midst of misery was not alleviated, made a pilgrimage to discuss the problem with Tolstoy. Addams had defied American participation in World War I—Wilson had written to his mother that she was right to charge that French soldiers were filled with wine before each attack in the trenches—but in the current collapse of society she was helpless. Hull House was surrounded by streets where people barely survived.

He toured the neighborhood with a relief worker, quizzing immigrant families who grew poorer instead of assimilating into the American middle class. In the flophouses, he writes, the single men "eat their chicken-feed and slum amid the deafening clanking of trays and dump the slops in G.I. cans." They kill time "in big bare chambers smothered with smoke, strewn with newspapers like vacant lots, smeared like the pavements with phlegm." Sixty-seven black families huddled without any utilities in the seven-story Angelus Building, "caged in a dingy mesh of fire-escapes like mattress-springs on a junk-heap." In another neighborhood a woman fed herself and her son by picking through garbage, first removing her glasses so she couldn't see the maggots on the meat. The teenage boy, who could see perfectly well, weighed eighty-two pounds.

Back in New York people also went through garbage cans. When Rosalind came up from Red Bank and her father took her out to supper he sometimes said he wasn't hungry, because, she later realized, he couldn't afford a second meal. The business culture had been smashed, and the mediocre performances in lavish new Radio City Music Hall made no impression—Wilson heard a rival financier gloat at "that son of a bitch Rockefeller losing $100,000 a week!" Yet the town buzzed with revolutionary fervor. Matthew Josephson—no friend to the critic—described him as "*the* inspiring leader of the left literary movement," whose "burningly clear" depiction of socioeconomic injustice helped move the disenchanted middle class to the left. As the gulf widened between the Communists and their Trotskyist opponents (whom they invidiously called Trotskyites), people crossed the street to avoid someone of the other camp. Wilson tried to stay on reasonable terms with both. In 1934 he joined the editorial board of V. F. Calverton's radical *Modern Monthly*, and the Communists were sure he'd gone over to the enemy, since Max Eastman, whom Stalin called a Trotskyite conspirator, joined at the same time. Wilson saw that the magazine was edited more professionally and helped organize a symposium titled "Why I Am Not a Marxist" that included George Santayana.

In the *Monthly* he brought Malraux's *Man's Fate* to the attention of American readers—the dramatic juxtapositions with which the novel opens, the gallery of revolutionary characters, the murky blend of romantic individualism and Marxism. This review began a long friendship with Malraux, whose letter of thanks claimed he'd taken part in the insurrections in Vietnam "*et enfin à Canton*," though in fact he had not been in Canton at the time. Malraux always embellished his role, as Wilson would learn without ceasing to admire the man. In *The New Republic* he promoted two self-styled proletarian writers who were sometimes difficult to take: Mike Gold, author of *Jews Without Money*, went in for explosive diatribes against the very liberals Wilson urged to read him, and Edward Dahlberg, of *Bottom Dogs*, was given to descending on people at odd hours for long talks about his work—there is a story that once when Dahlberg visited, Wilson pretended not to be at home by hiding under the bed. In *The New Republic* he also reviewed Stein's *Autobiography of Alice B. Toklas* as an account of the heroic age of the Paris art world. He liked her quip about Pound—"He was a village explainer, excellent if you were a village, but if you were not, not"—and when Stein came to the States in 1934 she found "Bunny Wilson" stimulating; they agreed Fitzgerald had much more sense of form than Hemingway.

T.S. Eliot, whose "little evanescent poems" of these years, lyrics like

"Marina," Wilson thought "exquisite," also came over, spending the night of May 30, 1933, at East Fifty-third Street. Wilson invited Marianne Moore and Gilbert and Alice Seldes to tea, an occasion Moore described to her brother John as excruciatingly awkward. Eliot's acolyte, she was embarrassed that he had to listen to "much news of Shankar the Hindoo dancer" (the much older brother of Ravi Shankar) and a drummer, both staying in Wilson's house, the "drums disguised about the room as co-coanuts and cockatoos." The author who ended *The Waste Land*, with "Shantih Shantih Shantih" may not have minded as much as Moore, and he was amused when Wilson took him to Rosa's for supper, finding places at the long communal table. That evening they drank too much of Wilson's bootleg gin. Remembering Eliot as "the most highly refined and at-tuned and chiseled human being that I had ever met," fifteen years afterward Wilson said, "The next morning he had an awful hangover and said his joints creaked, and I felt as if I had wantonly broken some rare and exquisite vase."

Washington was still a provincial capital when he covered Franklin D. Roosevelt's inaugural for *The New Republic*. Following the military units, the parade turned into a three-hour processional of local bands, clubs, and drum majorettes, punctuated by political figures. "A very large loose old Negro in a purple and yellow-edged cloak [was] carrying the prong of an antler as if it were the Golden Bough," while overhead an auto-giro dragged the banner Re-tire with Lee's Tires. This strangely choreo-graphed spectacle before an apathetic crowd was "the ghost" the America of the boom "had given up." Wilson, echoing the Marxist line—two months before he had celebrated Trotsky in a two-part biographical sketch—paid more attention to the machine guns in their ominous "little cages" than to FDR's speech. The effete-seeming son of Harvard, the Hudson Valley pa-trician who brought Woodrow Wilson's "pulpit eloquence" together with Theodore Roosevelt's "pungent maxims," seemed a poor bet to lead an exhausted nation.

A year later there were successes to note: Roosevelt was pressing for a union election in the steel industry under the N.R.A., and John Collier had revamped the Bureau of Indian Affairs' policy of forced assimilation, while Eleanor Roosevelt and Frances Perkins—the latter not "one of those demon old maids" but attractive and smartly dressed—advanced other causes. Yet no coherent policy could be discerned in the lively talk that filled the Capital's "great brick and marble shell." Wilson didn't have much sense of practical politics. In a windowy room at a cheap Washington boarding house, he enjoyed the early Southern spring, looking over the newspapers and reading Edith Wharton's memoir, *A Backward Glance*.

Finding no answers in the American present, he turned to family history upstate in his memoir "The Old Stone House." The place was as solid and elegant as ever when he visited during the cold June of 1933. Like Hull House it had been the self-sufficient center of a community, even containing the village post office. Its bric-a-brac, busts, engravings, and books brought back the people he'd known in childhood as well as those of family legend: the shadowy Talcotts, the solider image of his Jacksonian great-grandfather Baker. Talcottville connected the critic with both the eighteenth-century republic and the frontier—"that brief period of freedom when we were independent men in a new country," he'd called it when naming Whitman the nation's greatest poet the year before. His essay is appreciative, nostalgic, but lacking sentimentality, crafted to give the reader an experience of such a "pocket of the past." Wilson's immediate family had long since been absorbed by what Thomas Baker might have called the "money power," and he had no illusion this agrarian life could be revived. "What is really needed here," he wrote to Louise Bogan, "is a thorough-going drinking party."

When he returned to the city, however, he learned that a milk strike had radicalized the countryside around Talcottville and rushed back to check it out. He called his report on a skirmish between the upstate farmers and the state police "The Second Battle of Oriskany," after an engagement during the Revolutionary War. Arthur Schlesinger, Jr., observes that, for Wilson, Charles A. Beard, and a few others in their generation—the last generation of whom that could be said—the American Revolution was "still a contemporary event." On the train back to New York, reading Herndon's *Lincoln* as his father had urged and full of thoughts of the frontier heritage, he offered his own apostrophe to the Great Commoner—"'Old Abe Lincoln came out of the wilderness, / Out of the wilderness, Out of the wilderness,'" he writes, the echo of the song in his mind inspiring him with "a kind of awe." He thinks of "the ungainly boorish boy from the settler's clearing" who yearned for the refinement and training of the East, and somehow made himself a vehicle for "the creative intelligence of the race," finding himself "the conscious focus of its terrible unconscious parturition." So Wilson first sounds the Hegelian theme of the hero in history: "His miseries burden his grandeur. At least they do for me at this moment." This image would lead to the wounded Promethean Marx who in *To the Finland Station* is the conscious focus of the struggle in which revolutionary socialism was born out of laissez-faire capitalism.

During a walk "somewhere in those East Fifties" he realized that no-body had ever presented the development of Marxism in "intelligible human terms." He "saw the possibilities of a narrative which would quite get away from the pedantic frame of theory," the endless arguments between the Marxist schools. His title came "at an early stage, and, as he wrote, "it did not occur to [me] till later that I was echoing it from *To the Lighthouse*." Contrasting the humble railroad station in Petrograd where Lenin took control of events in the name of Marx's vision to the imaginary castle where Axel found life inadequate to his refined ideas—as Wilson recalled his intention—he would celebrate the isolated individual's ability to identify his interest with the people, "to energize them with his own drive and to guide them to construct, not an aristocratic dream, but a workable human society." By 1934 he was planning another work of fiction derived from his journals, which he would have to put aside. The scope of the new project stirred him, and he found himself repeating Stephen Dedalus's words at the end of *Portrait of the Artist*, the apostrophe to life and art that concludes, "Old father, old artificer, stand me now and ever in good stead."

In a July 1934, letter to George Soule, a friend on *The New Republic*'s editorial board, he offered them a series on "the development of the modern conception of history" from the eighteenth century to the Russian Revolution. Since he had taken advances and owed the magazine money, he proposed to be paid "at half my old rates, the other half being charged against my debt," a formula previously suggested by Cowley; the old rates being "4 [cents] a word for regular stuff, 2 for book reviews." Hoping it would be shorter than the serial version of *Axel's Castle*, he began a work that would take seven years and be vastly expanded after the Moscow show trials, when he could no longer view the Russian Revolution as a model of something Americans might create on their own terms. "It is all too easy to idealize a social upheaval which takes place in some other country than one's own," Wilson stated when introducing a new edition of *To the Finland Station* in 1971. Begun in the belief that the strength of mind and will of Lenin and Trotsky had moved history ahead, the book would be completed in the certainty that Stalin had moved it back.

The first section on the French intellectual tradition remained unchanged. In the characteristically Wilsonian opening, the historian Jules

Michelet, when rummaging around in a secondhand bookstore, comes upon an obscure seventeenth-century treatise that persuades him the social world is not divinely ordained but *certainly the work of men*." Giambattista Vico's religious orthodoxy kept him from deducing that men could remake their world, but in the *Scienza Nuovo* he took classes and groups, nations and races, as interdependent and taught that one could reintegrate "through history the various forces and factors which actually compose human life." What Michelet made of this insight was Wilson's starting-point. Though the Frenchman had no grasp of economics or class structure (proposing to overcome the antagonisms in French society through fraternal love), he conveyed "the living complex" of the social being and "the peculiar shape and color of history as it must have seemed to the men who lived it," in a chronicle pointed toward a future of which they were unaware. Wilson had briefly carried a volume of the *History of France* in his knapsack in the army in 1918. In 1934 Louise Bogan wrote to a friend of counting eighty-six volumes of Michelet lined neatly on a long shelf in his study.

Michelet's vital force was in his images: "the Renaissance sawed in two like the prophet Isaiah," "the Revolution undermined by speculators like the termites in La Rochelle," "the unspoken words, congealed by fear, unfreezing in the air of the Convention," "the French language of the eighteenth-century travelling around the world like light." He brought the creative artist's skills to those of the scholar. In a passage evocative of much of Wilson's work from the thirties on, the critic writes, "He had the novelist's social interest and grasp of character, the poet's imagination and passion," which "instead of exercising itself freely on contemporary life, had been turned backward upon history and was united with a scientific appetite for facts which drove him into arduous researches." Michelet had "read all the books, been to look at all the monuments and pictures, interviewed personally all the authorities, and explored all the libraries and archives of Europe," and had "it all under his hat." This Frenchman made the ideal of Emerson's "American Scholar" real for Wilson. Learning languages and, on little money, traveling to explore his subjects firsthand, as Wilson's father and as Wilson did, Michelet was "simply a man going to the sources and trying to get down on record what can be learned from them; and this role, which claims for itself, on the one hand, no academic sanctions, involves, on the other hand, a more direct responsibility to the reader."

Taine now seemed too much the mechanist, his "immense sentences, vast paragraphs, solid sections, gigantic chapters" expressing the machine aesthetic and the materialism of the bourgeoisie. The sketches of Renan and Anatole France in *Finland Station* emphasize the enfeeblement of French intellectual life under the Second Empire. The relativism that had served Michelet's art corroded Renan's principles, keeping him from believing there were any values that could be clearly defended, and France, who called himself a socialist and fought for Dreyfus, gets short shrift here, no longer the broadly humane figure contrasted with the rarefied Paul Valéry in *Axel's Castle*. It was Gauss who had taught Wilson to lament the "palsying pessimism" that had entered French writing. When Gauss, ironically, accused him of scapegoating these historian-critics, Wilson explained that he aimed to "disarm" the liberal reader's objections to Marxism. He was also disarming his own objections by approaching Marx from this side rather than through German philosophy.

On the back of a real estate agent's letter threatening him with eviction in April 1934 he typed, "The true successor to Michelet's history was Marx's *Capital*." The Frenchman's personal identification with his story, warning, counseling, scolding the actors after the fact, anticipated Marx's revolutionary attempt to impose an idea through political agitation. From Marx and Engels, who saw clearly, as Michelet had not, that society improved only through changes in the means of production, Wilson looked in both directions: "Michelet, feeling, as he said, the force of humanity which creates itself, attempted to live his history; Lenin and Trotsky, analyzing this force, were able to make history live through them." Thus the writing and acting of history converged as Wilson's expanding literary skills made him believe he could import this tradition into the United States.

Yet his scheme imposed the logic of a three-act play on a century of radical endeavor, and the concluding section on the Russians wouldn't hold up after the Moscow trials. The Marx portrait would expand to dominate Wilson's canvas, for Marx's life and work were not defined by the October Revolution and could be gauged with the perspective of three-quarters of a century. While Michelet was his model as a historian, showing how to represent the revolutionary cause through those who gave it life, Taine's methods as a portraitist would color Wilson's Marx. In the conclusion of the *History of English Literature* once made vivid to him by Millay, a passage quoted in *Finland Station*, Taine states that Musset "suffered but invented": he "tore forth with despair from his entrails the idea which he had conceived, and held it up before the eyes of all, bloody and alive." This evocation of the romantic agony had helped Wilson envision Lincoln's inner struggle, and it spoke to his own ambition. Marx became his avatar of the wounded creator.

Lovers and Friends

The gulf between the page and his private life was deepening. In his loneliness, poverty, and guilt over Margaret, Wilson got so drunk one night that, coming home and unable, when he knocked on the door, to rouse his friends the Shays to let him in, he broke it down and "surged in carrying the frame of the front door on his back," then crawled up to his room and threw the furnishings around. "Pale and wan" when he arose the next afternoon, he asked if the Shays had heard him come in. Though Hattie's role in the house was stabilizing—among other wondrous abilities, she had hangover cures—a passage added to *The Thirties* calls this a "rather sordid period" in his life.

Nights on the town are satirized in "What to Do Till the Doctor Comes" (1934), an Eliotic sketch of people who might, when younger, have been at the macabre party in *Daisy*—the well-read Communist accountant with a good job falsifying the balance sheets of corporations, the bearded explorer who "had the idea of going to Komodo after the man-eating dinosaur lizards," the married couple who compensate for each other's failings: "what she lacks in taste and tact he makes up for by those overelaborate dinners, and for his queer deficiency in human feeling she compensates by her hearty howl." Resolved on a sober evening even as he downs his second cocktail, Wilson's narrator later hallucinates a wild animal springing from a bookcase into the center of the room, breaking cognac glasses. After working up a passion in a taxi with a woman who mildly interests him, he disastrously breaks his watch and his glasses when he finally stumbles into bed.

The ubiquitous Josephson relates a brawl at the Cape during the summer of 1934. Well into a bout of drinking, Wilson sat in an armchair at Mary Heaton Vorse's delivering "a long monologue on Emerson's *Essays*," while Margaret's friend Jean Gorman (now hotly pursuing Wilson) leaned forward muttering "affectionate obscenities." Josephson reports that "for the fun of it I ventured to interrupt him in a loud voice, declaring that I had long thought Emerson on 'Self-Reliance' and 'Individualism' a crashing bore," though his journals and his poetry were worth reading. Wilson, "flushed with anger" but unwilling to be drawn into a quarrel, stuttered, "I'm going." Jean cried, "Don't go," and seized his arm, until he thrust her roughly aside and went out to his bicycle. When she tried to keep him from getting on it, "he hauled off and gave her a tremendous slap in the face." She urged Josephson to get his old Chevrolet and "Stop him! Run him down!" and Wilson's fellow critic—in what he claims was low gear at about three miles an hour—"inched forward a bit, just snubbed his rear wheel, then stopped. At once bicycle and rider fell over with a crash." As Jean, "now all concern," bent over Wilson he slapped her again, picked up his bicycle, and rode away. That night, Josephson continues, Gorman spilled the gin in her bed at the hotel, and when she lit a cigarette the next morning she set her bed linen and mattress on fire, but laughed it off as she wrote out a check for the damages. The party of the twenties was still going on for her.

Frances was a refuge from this scene. "Come back from wherever you are," she had written when he was in California with Margaret's family, not knowing where he was or why, adding that she'd been expecting to hear from him every day and had "called the office"—a detail that gives her a status, among Wilson's associates, more like that of wife than mistress. She had none of Margaret's fear of being in the way. He didn't accept her offer to fix up the Fifty-third Street house, but she often came to see him there. She could stop him from drinking, something his wives struggled to do, in "her absolute and sober way of seeing things," simply saying, "You don't need it!" He admired her more when he saw her always giving money to her family, whose "food ticket," she told him, had been taken away because a cousin living with them was employed, although marginally. He wanted to get her away from Fatty's, for her stepfather told the Russian boarders Frances might be available, and the drunks he put up for the night sometimes threw up and even urinated on the cots where she or Adele had to sleep. Despite this environment she managed to keep her daughter clean and healthy, trying not to be overly severe with the child. She refused to move in with Wilson lest Adele think her a kept woman, but when he was at the Cape in the summer of 1933 they lived in his house and she kept him posted on the boarders. Perhaps this was when he angered Rosalind, then nearly ten, by trying to give her dollhouse to the younger girl. On August 24, picking up on her lover's moods,

Frances writes, "I feel something has gone wrong with you. Are you upset over your play and drinking again? What have you been doing with yourself? Do write darling, and let me know that you're all right."

A longhand passage written March 23, 1933, on what he thought might have been the anniversary of their meeting in bed six years before, reads, "It was delicious and peaceful. I was happy for three-quarters of an hour or so—for the first time in how long? Love that stayed on without revulsion or lessening after intercourse—tenderness that stayed warm with somnolent desire." After Wilson's death, his widow and his editor removed this and other tender moments with Frances. "Say something sweet to me!" he teases, and she replies, "Darling," and then, "I think it all inside. I can't say it." He loves her spontaneity, her ability to laugh "without any trace of harshness or irony, a laugh of pure merriment." One evening in the twilight she performs fellatio on him and then leaps up, claiming she's now strong enough to fight anybody for him. Such manifestations of their love may have threatened Elena Wilson, but Frances's wit survived the censorship. When he was cutting the pages of a book written in French she remarked, "Sometimes I think you're the smartest man in the world!" and when he asked how she knew he wasn't, replied, "If you were, you wouldn't be living on East 53rd Street."

He tried to do something for Adele, unsuccessfully asking Dorothy Elmhirst, the widow of the *New Republic* patron Willard Straight, who had since remarried and who had her own fortune, to underwrite the child's education. Having neglected Margaret, he vowed to Frances what the narrator of *Hecate County* calls "the devotion of a kind of cult." Sometimes she felt ill, her explanation usually being that she and her sister had been sickly children "because their mother had done her best to do away with them before they were born." He sent her to Dr. Helen Spencer, Rolfe Humphries's wife, who eventually recommended removal of an ovarian cyst. The surgery, which Wilson paid for, proved extensive, and afterward he sat by her bed "afraid she might actually be going to die." But with sleep and medical attention she soon looked better—"her skin, for the first time I had ever seen it, lost that tarnished look—it was humanly pink and creamy." Several times he went to see her in a new Brooklyn neighborhood of small pleasant houses near the ocean. Before long, however, she was again worn-looking. When she acquired a suitor named Jerry in the spring of 1935, Wilson stepped out of the way and Jerry ordered her not to see him, after which their attempts to end the relationship grew comical. She visited Wilson not once but twice, explaining "she couldn't get used to Jerry's face" and that he bored her—"he never took her to a movie, never bought her a drink—he couldn't drink himself, would pass right out"—and had done none of the things for her that he'd promised to do. When Jerry intercepted a telegram that showed she'd been with Wilson, she warned him and he got out of town.

One afternoon in Red Bank, "feeling morbid, appalled by the immediate," he dreamed that Frances had come to see him. They were about to make love when "in an excited, moved voice" she asked, "Why hadn't I done something about marrying her?" He took this dream as a sign that he needed to get another girl. He made the break final at a Childs restaurant where Frances was working, just as she'd been at a Childs when he said goodbye six years before. She still lived in poverty, but Jerry earned forty dollars a week and was paying off his debts so they could start fresh together. Wilson, who had reasoned himself into two unsuccessful marriages, had blocked off his love for this woman, or tried to do so. One evening he had sought to discourage Frances from coming by so he could take another woman to the train, but at home found her waiting and, tired though he was, discovered that making love to her cleared his mind of confusion. When Frances was in the hospital, the journal records that, returning home one night, he heard "what I thought was a triple knock (I have had the illusion before)." No one was outside the door and he "kept saying aloud, 'Oh darling!'"

These were also the years of his affair with Louise Fort Connor and close friendship with Louise Bogan. Connor was "temporary relief" from his "hard, scared, self-acrid feeling" after Margaret's death—"something gay, humane, hot—abundant, prodigal of life." He'd met her in 1926 at a birthday party for John Amen, determined, as she said, with only a few days in New York "to keep awake all the time." She and her twin sister Henrietta (Henri) are the flappers of the Sacco-Vanzetti story "The Men from Rumplemayer's," so charming when they sing "Forsaken":

> Forsaken—forsaken—forsaken I lie—
> Like a stone by the roadside, while men pass me by.

While engaged to the Chicago stockbroker Peter Connor, Louise had fallen for Dick Knight, an outrageous "bounder" from Dallas on the margins of the literary world, but she went ahead with the marriage anyway. Henri had also wedded a Chicagoan, and now they were young mothers, living not far apart, Louise on Lake Shore Drive. Wilson took refuge among them from the horrors around Hull House.

In his journal the Chicago bourgeoisie are almost as unhappy as the poor—"the future taken away from them, nothing to hope for, drinking and trying to stop drinking," "the men killing time in their offices and getting more and more nervous and uneasy," the women "bored and irritated by the gloominess and nervousness of their husbands, more on the loose than ever." Louise—who would confide a feeling that she "didn't fit into life"—was indeed on the loose. She and her husband drank, she said, and she spoke of having affairs. Though Wilson thought it too soon after Margaret's death, he didn't decline when this brainy, vital woman with abundant blue-black hair, a strong Irish nose, violet eyes, and full red lips he likened to rich strawberries offered herself as "a little treat." They made love under Jane Addams's nose in the dormitory at Hull House, then took a shabby room together. "I'd been too snobbish, limited, and unimaginative to have ever thought Halsted Street might be fun or exciting—the peppery Greek food in the cafés," Louise reflected in later years, recalling too "the broken tea set in [Robert Morss] Lovett's prim little flat. And the bedbugs later on Lasalle Street and the Maple Restaurant where you proudly showed me a letter from H. G. Wells." Wilson let light and air into her life, as she did into his.

Their affair unfolded from 1932 to 1937, in two- and three-day sexual bouts when he could get to Chicago or she to New York, or they met in Massachusetts or an Albany hotel. As he thought of someday using these experiences in a novel, he devised a primitive code to hide people's identities for the journal, moving their initials back one letter. Though Louise also appears under her own name, she is "K" in the sex scenes in *The Thirties* (Peter Connor being "O" and her sister Henri "G"). "O" wanted to get sex over quickly on their "twice a week" schedule. A drill officer in World War I, he liked to claim that if she'd been in his troop "he would make her behave herself," and she enjoyed defying him with Wilson. The next summer, rendezvousing at her parents' country home in Massachusetts, as she entered Wilson's room Louise joked, "I'm coming here partly out of habit and partly because I want to be a good hostess." Arriving in New York one day, she phoned that "the personal-service department" would be at his disposal after six thirty.

When she returned from Chicago for a four-day bacchanalian romp, however, they wore each other out, attraction and lust interrupted by quarrels, gossip about other lovers, and, on her side, spells of weeping. She wanted to intensify her sensations by being beaten, and he tried "slapping her in the face, always afraid I wasn't doing it hard enough." Rising to such occasions, Wilson also felt their tragic undertone, and he could be irritated by the disorder Louise's belief in the safety of making love during menstruation increased. He found himself reflecting that sex could be too long divorced from having children—"blocked by withdrawals and condoms," the drive to procreate had turned "into a desire to get more out of passion some other way." Sometimes, on the other hand, he felt that they were tending to think and feel close together, could "walk out on the street on Sunday afternoons almost like a married couple." Peter caught on to the affair when Wilson invited the twins to the annual *New Yorker* ball during the spring of 1935. Louise wrote, suggesting he take someone else, but misaddressed the letter, then thought she ought to come on anyway and was terribly rattled at the hotel, not explaining why till they stood by the return train to Chicago. About to go to Russia to see socialism in action, he offered to postpone the trip, but from home she conscientiously wrote, "It couldn't do either of us any good if you were here. If I am in it, I'll be in it and have to take it on the chin."

To Louise Bogan, when she was recovering from her 1931 breakdown at the White Plains sanitarium called Bloomingdale, Wilson had written, "The only thing that we can really make is our work, and deliberate work of the mind, imagination, and hand, done, as Nietzsche said, 'notwithstanding,' in the long run remakes the world." He urged her not to "let this sick society down." In a long, revealing letter about herself oddly omitted by her executor from *What the Woman Lived*, Louise gratefully replied she was "the last person to let society down, the very last." She added, "I have always vaguely suspected that you were the friend I liked best in the world. I love you like a brother." Born in Maine to an Irish family and brought up in a Massachusetts mill town, she was educated at Girls' Latin School in Boston, and when her first husband died at an army base in Panama she and her daughter, Maidie, went to New York. Tall, statuesque, and exuberant, she loved being a woman, bemoaned her inability to be "a female Dante." She came to count on what she called Wilson's "taste, sincerity, insight, and insistent passionate intellectual integrity." They discussed literature and read it aloud, played rhyming games, exchanged light verse. He entertained her group by belting out "topical songs, too, written at high speed and sung," she told a friend, "to a tune that borrows Kern's rhythm and Gershwin's melodic line."

More than one feminist critic has taken Bogan's account of "Women" complicit in their own defeat ("Content in the tight hot cell of their hearts / To eat dusty bread") as treachery, and her meditative, passionate lyric poetry has been neglected. Wilson admired her second book, *Dark Summer* (1929), and she sent him what turns out to be an alternate version of the lyric "Division," about the metaphysics of perception. In the book this concludes:

> Though broken, undone is the green
> Upon the wall and the sky,
> And time and the tree stand there.

Bogan's revised last line, "And tree and tree stand there," hasn't appeared in print, for the Holdens' country house burned down with all her papers a few weeks after she mailed the poem to Wilson.

They were closest during the thirties, between his marriages to Canby and McCarthy. Louise had her second breakdown in 1933, after her belief that her husband would betray her, as her father had her mother, proved a self-fulfilling prophecy. She was institutionalized for six months. For her release he formed the joint project of beginning German together, a pathway for her into Rilke, for him into the background of Marx. She gleefully reported to the critic Morton Dauwen Zabel, an interpreter of James among other things, that they met two nights a week and, each with a dictionary, read poetry with "absolutely no attention to verb forms or case endings." She and Maidie visited Wilson in Provincetown in the summer of 1934. She was now divorced from Raymond Holden, and on the boat from Boston began an affair with Zoltan Harajsti, who later managed the rare books department at the Boston Public Library, one of Wilson's Hungarian friends in *The Sixties*. The next winter Wilson spent many evenings in her apartment, where mother and daughter would "make me good little dinners and afterwards play piano duets." He was Uncle Ed or Uncle Bunny to Maidie, who listened in when he discussed his love life with her mother. Louise wrote to a friend, "I wouldn't marry Edmund if he were the last man on earth. Why should I? It's fine the way it is, except for the fact that he should have a Lithuanian to take up the slack in his love life. The Irish are no good at that."

When he spoke of his trip to the Soviet Union she teased that if they were "absolutely compatible, I could go to Russia with you, on my alimony. But you would continually growl at me." From shipboard he'd write, "I'm afraid that if I had a little more money, I'd decide to spend all the rest of my life drinking beer and stout with you." To Wilson in Moscow Louise wrote of being "made to bloom" by "the enormous love-making of a cross between a Brandenburger and a Pomeranian, one Theodore Roethke by name." They had been drinking and fornicating, and she hoped "one or two immortal lyrics will come out of all this tumbling about." Wilson never became as interested in Roethke as the latter would have liked. The poet would awkwardly seek the critic's opinion of his work at Princeton in 1952, and was furious when it was refused. As John Berryman told the story, upon being invited to a party by Wilson and his wife Elena he sent them masses of flowers, and when he arrived asked Wilson to go upstairs and counsel him:

> "I can't do that, I'm the host," Wilson very properly replied.
> Ted glowered at him. "You hate all contemporary poets, don't you?"
> Wilson began to protest angrily, and Ted reached over, seized Wilson's cheek, and said, "Why, you're all blubber."
> "Get out of here, you half-baked Bacchus!" Wilson cried.
> Ted got out.

Wilson was still trying to buck up the writers in his college circle. On its margins was Phelps Putnam, a dissipated Yale poet of whom Eliot had spoken well, now the private secretary and lover of Senator Bayard Cutting of New Mexico. To Phelps, Wilson writes in hopes that his example "will make you thoroughly ashamed of your own naysaying, malingering, Sicilian idling, false attitudes of ripe maturity, theosophy, easy living, narcissism and general hey-ho lackaday." John Bishop sometimes rebelled against this literary older brother, even to insulting him behind his back, but Wilson's friends took his view of John's situation. The Princeton group continued to blame Margaret, Alec McKaig reporting she'd "eaten up everything of John but the mustache," while Fitzgerald—who at one point called her "an awful woman"—told Wilson he had to fight her resistance whenever he tried to get John to his writing table. The couple and their three boys had settled at a château at Orgeval near Paris. Tate, who sometimes visited, thought John needed "sympathetic literary society," and Wilson kept urging him to return to the stimulation of the States. After he won the Scribner's fiction prize for a Southern novella and a book of mostly early poetry appeared in 1933, he finally came home and moved his family to the Cape, where they eventually built a grand house. On a summer picnic Wilson noted that he spoke of literature and art when Margaret was not around, though in her presence his conversation revolved around such subjects as getting French specialty foods sent by Macy's. But he had a career again, reviewing poetry and publishing occasional literary essays.

Dell, after nursing what he'd convinced himself was TB in the Southwest during the early twenties (and separating from Marion Cleveland), had been analyzed by Jung in Zurich and cured, Stanley thought, of the disease—apparently of the idea that he had it, as his mother had. Returning to the States during the thirties, he bought a farm near Wilson's old haunt of Washington, Connecticut, and they spent an evening together in 1935. In an effort to reroot himself in America he'd produced a Jungian reading of Uncle Remus.

Wilson visited the farm for several wintry days in 1936, and the account in his journal makes a revealing contrast to Dell's memories. His arrival in the snow was showily vigorous. He hitched a ride in a horse-drawn carriage driven by an athletic young New England woman whose figure he admired. They got lost and, as darkness came on, she left him at a nearby farmhouse, whence he set out through the drifts in his city shoes, towing his suitcase on a borrowed sled, the luggage continually falling off and overturning it. Stanley, he states, soon appeared on skis and "we ascended the hill, saying little, as I was too much out of breath with my efforts." Dell recollected having to tow Wilson partway "on top of his suitcase." Wilson admired the eighteenth-century country house with its wide floorboards and relished his gentlemanly friend's educated conversation, but he records silences at dinner, insisting that Stanley tried to fill them with accounts of the butler's complexes. The next day their daughters were introduced (Rosalind fetched from her nearby school, Wykeham Rise). When the girls spent a night elsewhere, Wilson wanted to invite the woman he'd gotten lost with for a party, or to ask over somebody's sister and try to get her "cockeyed," plans Dell disregarded. So Wilson thought, "he sabotaged my literary activity" by remarking that to work late was hard on the generator and removing the card table he'd been using from the room. Again Dell recalled it differently—though worried about the generator, he admired the way that Wilson "worked all night, and for several nights."

Wilson's relations with Fitzgerald remained uneven. He'd enjoyed the

\

lavish house party with which Scott celebrated his thirtieth birthday at Ellerslie, a handsome Greek revival house near Wilmington. When they met at election time Scott asked about the world situation and whether Wilson might be secretary of state, which the latter took as a mark of indifference to politics, though young Matthews, whom they'd stopped to chat with after an alcoholic lunch, later suggested "he was pulling your leg." Scott claimed to be abstaining when he was not—his "on the wagon" could mean any number of things, including drinking lots of beer. By this time, having generously helped Hemingway move to Scribner's, he was overwhelmed by a sense of inferiority to the writer who made himself a symbol of masculine courage. Intellectually, however, Fitzgerald had survived the wreck of the boom years. In response to "Hull House in 1932" and the first section of *Finland Station*, he assured Wilson "that one among many readers is absolutely alert to the implications and substrata of meaning in this new work," agreeing that "conditions irretrievably change men." He proposed that they were working along the same lines, though it had been "more fun" when they had all thought "that we were going to die together or live together, and none of us anticipated this great loneliness, where one has dedicated his remnants to imaginative fiction and another his slowly dissolving trunk to the Human Idea."

It wasn't fun but bizarre and sad when, going to New York in January 1933 "to get drunk and swinish," Scott arranged to have Wilson and Hemingway meet him in the dining room at the Plaza. Upon entering the room he fixed Wilson with a "cold eye," as if in appraisal. Later he had "his head down on the table between us like the dormouse at the Mad Tea Party—lay down on floor, went to can and puked—alternately made us hold his hand and asked us whether we liked him and insulted us." The other two reassured him about his writing, praising the story "Absolution." Grandiosely, Hemingway proclaimed it "a good thing to publish a lousy book once in a while," which must have amused Wilson, who'd complained to Fitzgerald that *Death in the Afternoon* was maudlin. Sharing male insecurities, Scott said "he was looking for a woman," Hemingway that "he was in no condition" for one, Scott that "perhaps he was really a fairy," to which Hemingway replied that "they used to kid like that but not to overdo it." Hemingway told him "he oughtn't to let Zelda's psychoanalysis ball him up about himself—he was yellow if he didn't write." Fitzgerald questioned Wilson, "Shall I hit him?" and when Scott lay down on the floor drunk, Hemingway reported the Paris conversation he'd make famous in the posthumous *A Moveable Feast*: "Scott thinks that his penis is too small. I explained to him that it only seemed to him small because he looked at it from above. You have to look at it in a mirror."

Wilson, noting that Fitzgerald shared this concern with everyone from Bishop to "the lady who sat next to him at dinner and who might be meeting him for the first time," in *The Thirties* hazards the idea of impotence was on everybody's mind because of the Depression, "the difficulty of getting things going." A few months after this meeting, though no lover of competitive sports, he challenged his friend with the metaphor of a footrace against Hemingway: "I have just read Hemingway's new short stories, and though the best of them are excellent, now is your time to creep up on him," Wilson wrote. Two weeks later he repeated, "Now is your time to creep up on Hemingway."

With Dos Passos he enjoyed a companionship free of the strains between men who had formed their ambitions together before they were twenty. Dos and he were peers, their interests close, and they were loyal to each other—Frances Steloff at the Gotham Book Mart remembered Wilson calling her to borrow two hundred dollars when Dos's mortgage was in jeopardy, money she didn't say that she'd saved for the rent. Their correspondence about literature and politics, which lasted almost forty years, is in its scope and dramatic interest second in American letters only to that of Jefferson and John Adams. In this conversation between craftsmen who are also men of the world, Wilson is characteristically optimistic and controlled, Dos Passos pungent and explosive.

In the mid-1930s their focus has shifted from the American Left to Russian communism. Dos Passos, the graduate of Choate, Harvard, and the gentlemanly Norton-Harjes ambulance service whom the Communists dubbed America's leading proletarian writer, judged the Soviet Union to be no longer a revolutionary state. In Moscow in 1928 he had heard a still terrified survivor describe the massacre, on Lenin's orders, of the mutinous Kronstadt sailors. Stalin's fearsome response to the assassination of Kirov in December 1934 (which at the time no Americans knew that Stalin apparently arranged) led him to ask Wilson what "us reds" would be saying if, after Joseph Zangara "took a pot shot at Franklin D., the U.S. Secret Service had massacred a hundred miscellaneous people, some because they were wops, others because they were anarchists, and others because they had stomach trouble?" Wilson argued that the brutality of the tsardom couldn't be expected to disappear overnight and shouldn't be considered a product of socialism, that an American socialism would differ significantly from the Russian version. Dos Passos, equally a patriot, agreed. Wilson saw the world now "profoundly permeated with Marxism— Washington as well as Moscow." He hoped to locate Marx and Lenin within "the humanistic tradition," saying, "You know that Marx said: 'As for me, I'm not a Marxist.'" Dos Passos declared that although the Revolution had accomplished "things that it will take the rest of the world a century to absorb," it "has gone into its Napoleonic stage and the progressive tendencies in the Soviet government have definitely gone under before the self-destructive tendencies." Unique on the American Left in this clarity of vision, Dos Passos was in 1935 ahead also of Silone, Malraux, Orwell, and Koestler. Echoing Lord Acton, he insisted that "the horrid law of human affairs by which any government must eventually become involved with power for itself, killing for the pleasure of it, self-perpetuation for its own sake, has gone into effect."

When the Trotskyists merged with Muste's American Workers Party, further involving the *Modern Monthly* in New York's sectarian warfare, Wilson wrote that, as someone to whom Stalin and Trotsky were irrelevant in connection with the politics of the United States, he was disaffiliating himself from all organizations and causes. The work he'd begun when bitterly protesting Dorothy Perkins's fate ten years before no longer compelled him; he had no heart for "writing up strikes and political meetings." One could do both agitational literature and "long-range writing"—Dante and Swift were effective partisan polemicists—yet the Dante "who wrote the *Divine Comedy* in exile" was "something quite different from the Dante who was so active in politics in Florence." In this distinction Wilson is equally far from the New Critics, for whom Dante's social and political commitments would be of no consequence, and from those leftist theorists who, at the tail end of the twentieth century, were to find aesthetic taste arbitrary, all writing political. To create lasting literature one had to step back from short-range goals, "to extricate oneself from the demands of the social complex to which one belongs" and—in Dante's words—"to make a party by himself." He was almost ready for such an effort of retreat and *"recueillement."**

Dos Passos, encouraged by Wilson to write a position paper for a literary congress, produced "a little preachment about liberty of conscience

*Recovery of perspective

or freedom of inwit" (Dedalus's "agenbite of inwit") with a title that suggests Thorstein Veblen's influence, "The Writer as Technician." He aligned the artist and "what used to be known as the humanities" with "the men, women, and children alive right now" who were subject to the daily exactions of the repressive managers of society, whether in Russia or the capitalist United States. He urged Wilson to take his time with *Finland Station*, saying, "One or two clearly thought out and clearly expressed paragraphs by a bird who knows what his words mean are worth more than all the debates in Cooper Union and Mecca Temple laid end to end."

When Wilson was awarded the then standard Guggenheim Fellowship of $2,000 to work in the Marx-Engels-Lenin Institute in Moscow, Dos helped out in numerous ways. When his visa was held up in New York—the *Herald Tribune* story about this had him a Trotskyist—Dos wrote airmail to Maxim Gorky "suggesting that he drop a note to the Foreign Office," and asked Dreiser to do the same. One couldn't, he said, let oneself be licked by the bureaucrats—"the little inkpissers"—for it made them "that much more powerful." He arranged for Wilson to collect rubles derived from the sale of his own novels, which would give him freedom within the tourist routine. Dos Passos also provided names and thumbnail sketches of Russian intellectuals, but warned that Moscow was full of lies and "hushdope"—"only the most independent people who are sure of their own positions dare talk freely to foreigners even about the most trivial things"—one should be careful quoting people's remarks or even "going round to see them." But he delighted in the rumor that Wilson might take his motorcycle along—the machine hitherto best known for landing its rider in Mrs. Wilson's shrubbery—and advised "the Motocyyklysteschki Critik" as to appropriate clothing. He wrote of informing Gorky that "the A 1 lit. critic etc." was coming. Maybe "the old walrus" would "have the Huzzar band out to meet Edmund Axel Wilson," in which case the latter should "present him with my most dissembled compliments."

13

The USSR in 1935

Wilson went to Russia as a supporter of the Revolution, an ideological pilgrim eager to believe, and returned trying to overcome his doubts. A flood of Western travelers had preceded him. The radicals cited seemingly well-run factories and collective farms, and if they criticized the bureaucracy, the secret police, or the rumored "liquidation" of kulaks and other "class enemies" they did so tactfully, pointing out, at the same time, the faults of capitalist societies. Literary relationships with the West seemed to be opening up in 1935, and the Russian classics were being revived. The American came with an image of Stalin as "a tough political boss with crude Marxist principles and considerable practical ability," and knew nothing of the great famines and the atrocious conditions of forced labor on the White Sea canal. Five months in the Soviet Union challenged his pieties and misconceptions. The Leningrad intelligentsia were in Stalin's sights, and there was fear among Wilson's acquaintances in Moscow. The show trials would begin only a year afterward. But he soft-pedaled the uneasier aspects of his experience in the account published on his return, wanting neither "to embarrass people and get them into trouble" nor "to put too much emphasis" on what might be a passing phase of the society he hoped his countrymen could learn from.

His struggle for perspective can be followed through three different texts. The first in diary form and published much later in *The Thirties*, is useful for its names and dates. In *Travels in Two Democracies* (1936) a kaleidoscopic impression of an arcane culture that is neither Marxism nor old Russia, though marked by both, is yoked to Wilson's incisive accounts of Chicago, the old stone house, and Washington during the early New

Deal. Despite his title, intended to link the United States and the USSR vis-à-vis Western Europe, he knows that Russia is no democracy, and this section of the book leads him back to the "permanent and absolute value" of republican institutions. Twenty years later in *Red, Black, Blond and Olive* he reprints this journal and, in bracketed interpolations, adds the hints of Russian acquaintances and his intuitions about the terror state of which Dos Passos warned him. *Red, Black* also incorporates memoirs of two Russians who befriended him in 1935. By 1955 the perhaps naive believer in progress through reason and will has had to confront the emergence of the age of the concentration camps and the gulag in the land he'd sympathetically observed.

The enthusiasm for Russian literature and history that long outlasted his belief in the Revolution goes back to Wilson's Russian tour. Like many Americans, he admired the devotion of this people to theater, literature, and the discussion of life, their warmth and moral seriousness that seemed the other side of a certain impracticality and inefficiency. He contrasted such traits with those of the English, whose social system he was coming to dislike as much as he loved their literature. On the boat train from Southampton to London the countryside was "lovely, familiar, and dear," but the Londoners, though enthusiastic consumers of American popular culture, condescended to the United States. His English fellow passengers on the Soviet steamer to Leningrad were stuffy, while the young Russian engineers in his cabin touched his heart when he came on them declaiming passages from Pushkin out of his Russian grammar.

Leningrad alternately pleased and puzzled Wilson. The victory of science over superstition was proclaimed at St. Isaac's Cathedral, where a pendulum hanging from the "remote dizzy dome" slowly shifted its arc above a map of the world to demonstrate to children of the Orthodox church that the Earth was not stationary. The bodies of a holy man and a tribal chief, displayed in glass cases, were seen to be in a similar state of decomposition. Yet the crowds in the imperial streets were "dingy and mute and monotonous." Soviet life was full of anomalies—mistaken identities, wrong telephone numbers supplied by Intourist, a phone call mysteriously cut off, evasiveness and equivocation on the part of the translator of Dos Passos's novels. The pressure of the regime was veiled in a constant propaganda against Hitler's Germany, but Wilson's capacity to believe in communism took its first blow at the theater, in a play about Peter the Great, whose mustache seemed to get more like Stalin's as the action proceeded. At one point Peter declared, "After all, you were my son—I loved you!," then, "Let him be executed!" In material Wilson added to *Red, Black* a companion whispers that the play is an attack on Kamenev and Zinoviev, recently arrested old Bolsheviks, and a warning to the writers sitting around them. Wilson notes that these people courageously refused to applaud.

A different sort of epitome of his days in Leningrad was Meyerhold's production of *The Queen of Spades*, Pushkin's fable of the aged countess's secret of winning at cards, which the desperate Hermann cannot master. After seeing this with Dmitri Shostakovich, Wilson went to bed "full of vodka and Pushkin," musing on the St. Petersburg of Russian literature. People stayed up all night, never stopped "talking and drinking, dancing and playing cards," while outside "the characters of Dostoevsky, uneasy, unable to relax in sleep, roam[ed] the bridges in the half-day of night: the dissipated, the lonely, the thoughtful, the poor." Russian artists were caught between the influence of Europe and the life of a vast land stretching in the opposite direction. "They had come back as we had done to a straggling provincial civilization among prairies and wild rivers and forests, bringing books and manners," and sometimes unsure what to do except—as Oblomov did—to go to bed; Wilson adds, "I had done the same thing myself." Echoing the image of Lincoln coming "out of the wilderness" in "The Old Stone House," he declares, "We never know what we have got in the forests and wastes of these countries; we never know what is going to come out of them." He is scarcely, however, thinking of Stalin, who will be characterized in *To the Finland Station* as a barbarian from the Caucasus.

It was old home week for American radicals in Leningrad and Moscow. He spent an evening with William Saroyan, who had unsuccessfully sought his roots in Soviet Armenia. He met a black professor who hoped to get the Russian Communists to override the American Party's abstract notion of "self-determination for the Black Belt," a construct of counties across the South where African Americans significantly outnumbered whites. When he took Muriel Draper, his next-door neighbor in New York, out in a droshky late one night, they spoke "about Lenin and Jesus, Communism and Christianity," Dr. Anti-Christ's tone more respectful than it would have been back in the States. As if to assure himself that he didn't—as Hemingway had put it—have to save his soul, the 1935 diary reports, "I hummed 'Smoke [Gets] in Your Eyes' all the way home."

In Moscow he found he wouldn't be allowed access to the materials in the Marx-Engels-Lenin Institute. He was suspect, since he wasn't a Communist and had Trotskyist friends in New York. Dos's rubles, however, got him outside the net of Intourist, and he had the use of the apartment of Walter Duranty, who was on vacation. Duranty, the *New York Times* reporter whose dispatches publicized the Five-Year Plans in the United States, would be embarrassed by the more critical observations in Wilson's *Travels*, but the apartment was a place to take Russian acquaintances. With it came an electric refrigerator, the hum of which always startled his visitors, and an elderly servant, who spoke the backstairs French of those who'd worked for the nobility. When this woman later came upon him in bed with a new Russian friend, Wilson assured himself she was an unlikely spy for the NKVD.

The status of literature in Russia at first marked for him what might happen when human imagination and will were no longer in thrall to the church. The theater was dazzling. The Russians did Shakespeare with a vitality, Chekhov and Ostrovsky with a sophistication and style, that shamed the New York stage, and he wrote to Bogan that he had "never seen such wonderful productions" as the Pushkin-Tchaikovsky operas. There were also propaganda plays—one featured a heroic young doctor who, after operating upon an official, falls dead as he declares, "The Commissar of the people will live!"—but these were sparsely attended. American writers were popular, among them Dreiser, Dos Passos, and Upton Sinclair, all three, ironically, newly out of favor with American Communists. Sergei Tretyakov, the government liaison, a genial literary leftist who had been the poet Mayakovsky's ally, arranged for Wilson to buy old editions of Russian writers (which, however, never reached him, being confiscated or stolen en route) in return for writing an essay on Hemingway for the Soviet journal *International Literature*. Done on his return to the States and reprinted in *The Shores of Light*, it charts Hemingway's unevenness while disputing the reduction of this to class issues.

Dos had provided an introduction to the futurist poet and songwriter Sergei Alymov, the source of Wilson's first impressions of the Russian intelligentsia. "A tall, shaved-headed middle-aged man" with "steely blue-grey eyes and a face that was completely impassive," Alymov (in *Travels* and *Red, Black* abbreviated to "S") had been exiled to Siberia under the tsar and fought for the Revolution. A patriot, late one night he proudly called attention to the coming of dawn over the Kremlin, not, Wilson thought, intrinsically a remarkable sight. After criticizing a government policy in public, he had "done time" on the White Sea canal. "Some people change," Alymov said, "but I *never* change," though his wife, Maria Fedorovna, had pledged to the authorities he'd be more careful.

The couple lived in one high-ceilinged room surrounded by their inherited antique furniture. Wilson loved the jolly evenings "around the big table in the crowded room, with the vodka, the cherries, and the herring," the Russians ringing the table shoulder to shoulder as they enjoyed one writer's tales of hilariously incompetent efforts to catch animals for the sparsely populated Moscow zoo (the refrain, after each disaster, was "Dey have to stuff"). Alymov would write to Wilson in the States how he appreciated the excerpts from *Finnegans Wake* and *The Waste Land* Wilson read to him. He and Maria Fedorovna introduced the American to his companion for the balance of his Moscow stay, the cosmopolitan lawyer Irina Grynberg, who, by one of those strange coincidences in life, would turn out to be the sister of Roman Grynberg, a very literary businessman and Wilson's friend in New York after World War II.

At the Grynbergs' dacha three or four families each had a room, rather like a crowded summer boardinghouse. The place was Chekhovian, people wandering in and out or briefly sitting down at the piano, an elusive world without emphasis or schedule. Wilson was careful not to talk politics—he confined himself to asking about aspects of the Russian language—but when he visited the dacha a second and third time the other families grew nervous to see the Grynbergs so often with a foreigner. One idyllic day, after everyone went swimming naked in a pretty little river and dried out in the sun, a woman asked, out of the hearing of others, if he were not a British agent. Not wanting to get his hosts in trouble, Wilson never went there again.

When soldiers at a railway station began to sing a melancholy marching song, Irina said that before the Revolution the Russians were *"tristes"* and now they were *"tristes."* The temptation to attribute what troubled him in this country to Russian history was reinforced by a day with his friends at the Troitsa-Sergeyeva Monastery. From a distance the fourteenth-century central building was a "rainbow delirium" out of the *Arabian Nights*—red and yellow and pink touches in "a grove of blue phallic spires painted with golden stars"—but inside it was nightmarish. "Church built by Ivan the Terrible to expiate the murder of his son—he had these alternations of piety with crime," Wilson noted, adding, "These six-winged angels give me the willies." Nor did he like the Greek Orthodox ikons, the early ones "so cramped and knotted, their gray eyes so anguished and so broken to anguish," the later ones "saccharine and sickly." He contrasted this religion of suffering that was bound up with the Russians' submission to tyrannical rulers to his sense of communion with Irina and the Alymovs over their picnic lunch. Through the window of their rented room they enjoyed a rare sunshiny day with blue sky and smallish white clouds. "A little foal with shaky legs came trotting down the sloping cobbled street in front of a horse and cart," followed by "a queer open carriage, very dirty and rickety-looking, driven by a little boy, and with a lot of other little boys in a long sequence of seats behind him." Against this pastoral backdrop, evocative of a Russian novel, his friends discussed the past as well as the future for which they "had worked so hard." Sergei recalled them to the present. "Come! We do have this little room, this vodka, this bread, this sausage, this view of the old monastery—these are *now!*" he said, an affirmation Wilson echoed in retitling the Greenwich Village play begun when he lived with Mary Blair *This Room and This Gin and These Sandwiches*.

The USSR was scarcely moving toward a classless society. He passed an evening at an exuberant banquet put on by the Red Army, one of the new elites. He became aware of the gulf between the elegant Sokolniki Gardens, once Ivan the Terrible's hunting park, now frequented by privileged groups, and the raw, dreary Park of Culture and Rest, where a sluggish populace gathered. In 1956 he admitted to having "purposefully soft-pedalled" a "class stratification that was already well-advanced," though it could be defended in Marx. He resented authoritarian government that issued its decrees in the name of the people—the masses demand better railway service, the masses demand the execution of the traitor so-and-so. On the other hand, there was "little, if any, destitution" in the parts of Moscow he explored—"no down-and-outers, no horrible diseases, no old people picking in garbage pails" as in Depression Chicago and New York. In the cheaper neighborhoods he sensed "a kind of assurance that doesn't exist with us. The certainty of work means a lot."

Why, then, was the city uneasy, full of suspicion? Though he realized that successful Soviet writers were politically correct, that the literary organizations fostered mediocrity just as in capitalist countries, he knew nothing of Ahkmatova, Mandelstam, and other dissidents already in a kind of underground limbo, waiting, as it were, to be demonized by the regime. *Travels* relates Wilson's surprise to find that he, too, suffers from "the Moscow tic," a compulsion to look over one's shoulder before discussing politics. In a passage added in *Red, Black, Blond and Olive*, when he asks Irina why the crowds out walking are so quiet, she replies, again speaking French for protection, "It's that everyone is terrified."

Alymov would survive the purges, dying at fifty-six in an auto accident, after which his wife married again. Wilson's friendship with D. S. Mirsky brought him closer than he then knew to the heart of the terror. Born a prince of the ancient Svyatopolks, Mirsky had fought with the Whites and gone into exile in England, where after the Crash he converted to Marxism. A critic of comparative literature whose work appeared in five languages, he was also a nationalist and chose Russia's historical grandeur over Western decadence, in 1932 returning to the Soviet Union under Gorky's protection. Reading Mirsky's book on Pushkin during his voyage across the Atlantic had suggested to Wilson the dimensions of Russian as a literary language and made him want to learn it. He tracked the writer down in a decrepit part of Moscow, a "tall, bearded, bald and bespectacled" figure with "large and glowing brown eyes," "a high intellectual forehead," and the hideously deteriorated teeth he would grow used to even in Americanized Russians. With his bed and the bathtub that doubled as a washstand in the background, they talked of *Paradise Lost*— Mirsky was updating an old translation—and of Wilson's experiences in the USSR. At the modest dinner the following night, Mirsky (once a gastronome in Paris) quoted poetry in several languages, and passionately declared that *The Waste Land* was a product of decadent capitalism and Eliot the greatest living poet. He voiced approval of Belinsky as the father of socialist realism. When reminded he'd once called Belinsky too poor a writer of Russian to have anything to say about art, he replied in German that that had been "*von einem anderem Standpunkt.*"*

The "Comrade Prince" is kept out of sight in *Travels*, appearing once or twice as "G," but a memoir added to *Red, Black, Blond and Olive*— strangely neglected in G. S. Smith's otherwise definitive biography of Mirsky—documents Wilson's summer friendship with this product of an aristocratic heritage and the most elite of educations, two years before his arrest and interrogation by the NKVD. When the men met for a drink or meal or to walk in the Sokolniki Gardens, Mirsky towered above others on the street, doubly conspicuous for his dilapidated British clothes. He

*From another standpoint

was sometimes accosted by strangers. One evening he asked what the Ford plant in Dearborn was like, and Wilson, responding that it was a prison full of spies, blurted (in this moment doubly naive), "In fact, it's rather like here." He was chastened when the Russian "got up from the bench and said, 'Shall we be moving?'" For several weeks Mirsky disappeared, afterward reporting that, traveling "hard" (in what would once have been a third-class carriage), he'd been sent out to lecture in the provinces, a mission, Wilson thought, that while perhaps designed to humiliate him, had the opposite effect, removing him from the politics of the capital and renewing his connection with the vast hinterland. Near the end of Wilson's stay he walked all the way across Moscow to seek the American out, and when Wilson explained he was departing and "thanked him for all his kindness," Mirsky answered, "No kindness on my part!" with "a beaming benevolent glow."

Two decades later Wilson reconstructed his fate. After criticizing a novel earlier in 1935, he had been attacked as elitist. Gorky came to his rescue by saying that "everybody knew" it was a poor book and that to have been born a prince wasn't Mirsky's fault, but an article denouncing him was simultaneously published in *Izvestia* and *Pravda*. When Gorky died a year later Mirsky was left unprotected. Wilson never learned when he was arrested—it was in June 1937—but through letters of prisoners made available to him by his wife Elena's connections in Paris, he established all that was known until after the collapse of the Soviet Union about Mirsky's death in the Siberian goldfields near the Arctic Circle. This portrait closes with a grim image of the collision between literature and the real world in one of its more ruthless phases. Mirsky is imagined "opening his door in his spectacles and dressing-gown, and being dragged from his inferior caviar and bad-smelling soap, from those almost Dostoevskian lodgings, in which he had had momentarily the illusion of serving the new Russia in lecturing to provincial officials and revising a translation of *Paradise Lost*."

The brilliant director Meyerhold, whose productions Wilson loved, and genial Tretyakov, who took him to an ancient bookshop and had his article on Hemingway published, were among the thousands who vanished during these years. Had Wilson any idea of what was happening, he could not have completed *Finland Station* as planned. In 1935 he took note of phenomena that he did not understand until long afterward. Stalin's likeness was "plastered all over the place," and he heard an intelligent Russian sigh when glimpsing "the inevitable cap and mustache" in the morning paper. The party line with Westerners was that Stalin did not personally enjoy this adulation, that a people under stress needed such an ikon. Yet one Russian acquaintance seemed afraid to use Stalin's name even to praise him, just as Mussolini, Wilson noted, was called by the Italians "*Lui.*" One day at the travel agency Wilson and the photographer Paul Strand, frustrated by red tape, indulged their American humor by saying, "Comrade Stalin has just stepped out to the toilet," "Comrade Stalin is at home with a severe headache," and a chill fell upon the office. At the Physcultúr Parade, where more than 100,000 people marched beside gigantic floats, passing in review before the dictator, Wilson sensed a bond between him and a populace descended from serfs, 80 percent of whom before the Revolution were illiterate. The soldiers bearing bayonets and bombers flying in formation, however, turned this celebration of sports and health into a demonstration of military preparedness. Since no one was allowed to sit while Stalin stood, Wilson left after four hours, but "thick round bare legs in shorts" marched on through his mind that evening.

Against this image of the Soviet Union less than two decades after the October Revolution he set another that reflected his own pieties. He too waited in the long line that continually looped back and forth across Red Square, to step down "past the walls of Ural marble, black and gray and sown with flakes of lapis lazuli like bits of blue butterflies' wings" and stare for a moment at Lenin's embalmed countenance. "Extraordinarily fine, intellectual, distinguished," he notes in *The Thirties*, projecting his literary idealism onto the Rorschach of the death mask—"square head, with high brow, bald forehead, gray hair, slanting eyes, features shrunken and sharpened by death, fine nose, square-tipped, effective fingers." Denied the use of the files (doubtless already cleansed of evidence of Lenin's less attractive side), when he met men and women who revered their memories of Lenin or his wife, Krupskaya, he did not allow for their need of an ikon, or his own. At the end of the Russian journal, Wilson deludes himself with his own secular ikon, returning to the leader's face and its value for his countrymen passing through the tomb under the Kremlin wall: they knew that Lenin "was theirs, that he was one of them, that he had summoned from their sluggish plasm all those triumphs to which life must rise and to which he thought himself but a guidepost." Wilson was perhaps projecting his own purpose as a critic.* To read this

---

*Cummings, the lyric poet, projected himself in a different way, seeing the dictator as a "silly unking of Un-," who merely says, "I Am Mortal. So Are You. Hello."

Darwinian affirmation of what an individual can do for the forward movement of the race on to what amounted to a state religion helped him postpone his rejection of Russian communism.

He wanted to visit Lenin's family home at Ulyanovsk for the portrait
in *To the Finland Station*, and after much foot-dragging, Intourist gave
him permission to catch a steamer down the Volga at the recently renamed city of Gorky. Ulyanovsk had been the distinguished provincial
city of Simbirsk, and was destined to flourish after World War II as a revolutionary shrine visited by as many as a dozen cruise ships a day. It was
shabby and abandoned in the August mud of 1935, but the restored
house strengthened his humanistic vision of Lenin. "Its sobriety and shining cleanness, its fine mahogany furniture, its maps and music and books"
recalled "the houses of cultivated New Englanders as I used to see them
in my youth." In *Finland Station* he sketches in the old-fashioned grand
piano with a score by Bellini in the music rack, the dining-room table
where Vladimir and his brother Alexander read, studied their lessons, and
played chess, the German, French, and Russian books on the shelves, a
magazine with an episode from *Tom Sawyer*.

While awaiting the next steamer Wilson spent the day with a "blondinka" who, along with her sister, made the beds in a flophouse. Clavdia
had reddish hair and rather weak blue-green eyes, a stout figure, and
muscular arms—she had him feel her muscle—but a delightful sensitivity, "a kind of sudden flurry of animation, volatile, emphatic, smiling" he
had observed in Russian women. He caressed her and was impassively re-
buffed. They played checkers, in confusion until he began to grasp the
Russian rules. "With the give and take of the moves" they seemed to be
"getting to understand one another intimately." He let himself flow with
the rhythms of a simpler world, at ease with ordinary people as he hadn't
been when trying to decipher the politics of Moscow acquaintances.
When the long awaited steamer unexpectedly arrived in the middle of
the night he had only time, as he ran for it, to shout out (we aren't told
whether in bad Russian or in the English of which they knew only a few
words) "what nice girls they were."

On the boat south he pondered documents he'd been given about the
arraignment of the old Bolsheviks, alleged to have plotted with Trotsky
against Stalin. Clearly "the charges and the evidence were frauds," but
there seemed to have been a plot by Mikhail Tukhachevsky and the other
officers, who "were not tried but simply shot in *camera*." Perhaps the next
time the Red Army would get rid of Stalin. The further Wilson moved

from the tensions of Moscow, the easier it was to believe in the Marxism of the Soviet Union. At Stalingrad former peasants were making tractors and the assembly line halted for lunch. Though this gave a false impression of the pace of Russian industrialization, it pleased the American writer. In Rostov the populace seemed taller and better-dressed, and in Kiev, while the crowds were quiet, they appeared happier.

He had begun trying to coordinate the anomalies and antique forms of Russian with the mental habits of those who spoke it. That their tenses didn't allow for the conception of a definite moment in the present explained to the rationalistic Westerner why people were routinely late for appointments and allowed long conversations to skew the schedule of the day or the evening. On the train to Odessa he had chills and a fever—Clavdia had had what she called a bad cold—and as he succumbed to illness, he wearied of the refrain of *"kak-kak"* and *"tak-tak"* and *"da da, da da da!"* among the passengers in his compartment. The all-purpose phrase *"Bolshoy skandal!"* was always spoken with a gleam of relish, whether the "big scandal" was the dismissal of a bureaucrat for forcing scores of female employees to have sex or to the reluctance of children to eat their dinner. Wilson bitterly reflected that the Russians kept closing the windows to repel the fresh air, that they served tea in hot glasses without handles, and their only liquor was a form of raw alcohol. Their meals were too heavy, the crumbs always swept onto the floor. The engaging variety of human expression loses its charm for him in the piece called "Word-Fetishism, or Sick in Four Languages in Odessa."

In Odessa he at last got medical attention—a cultivated doctor who was at first indifferent to his symptoms eventually muttered, "scarlet fever," and fled the room. In the vaudevillian sequence common to *Travels* and *Red, Black* Wilson is transported to the Hospital for Contagious Diseases and efficiently registered, showered, scrubbed, clothed again, and wrapped in a blanket like a mummy, only to be unwrapped for an inventory of the possessions in his pants. Bedbugs swarm when an infested mattress is treated with a kerosene torch, and during this operation a big wine bottle filled with gargle is knocked over and a medicine glass broken. When a new mattress arrives and more bedbugs emerge from it, an old woman sets out to kill them one at a time, then straps onto her foot an ancient floor polisher and begins dancing around the room. Falling into "my fever-dreams," he wakes with the thought "I mustn't let Russia get me."

His six weeks in the hospital afford the reader other entertainments.

He is "cupped" with heavy brass suction cups that are heated and applied to the small of his back (presumably part of the original eighteenth-century equipment of the hospital), and dosed regularly with valerian root (the effects of which, he'd learn from a medical dictionary in New York, were "mainly psychic"). Untrained nurses enter wrong figures in the temperature charts or lose records; instead of untieing the strings on the patients' nightgowns, they simply rip them off their necks. He is uncomfortably aware of garbage in the bathroom and the flies that fill the ward, breeding in the long grass outside the windows, these windows open but only one of them screened. Under Western eyes, as it were, such details serve Wilson's purpose as a Soviet sympathizer, for the backwardness of old Russia is an argument that the Revolution was needed, and at such an institution as the hospital the Communists were not, as in Moscow, oppressive politicos, but people who take responsibility. The Communist head nurse, whom he thinks of as the Ugly Duchess and admires for her devotion to duty, has a partner in the old doctor, Ilya Petrovitch, a stage character in his straw cap, spectacles, black coat, white vest, and striped trousers, an umbrella hooked over his arm. A former nobleman, he has a daughter in Paris but is in service to "the race of the new Russia." Endlessly wrangling over what to do about this or that, the nurse and he dramatize the cause of science and progress to which Wilson is committed.

Wilson read Marx and Engels during the daytime and Gibbon in the evening "beneath the all-clarifying naked bulb" in the operating room. In a talk for a literary group on the *Decline and Fall* fifteen years later, he believed "it was really Gibbon who pulled me through." The Englishman's "lofty, unperturbed and perfectly cool point-of-view" on human history enabled a reader to step back from the tensions of the present. Wilson— like Henry Adams before him—imagined the moment, on the steps of the Roman church that had once been a temple of Jupiter, when young Gibbon "conceived the idea of following step by step the process by which the civilization of Rome had broken down and been lost, of filling in the gap between the ruins of the Capitol among which he sat and the beginnings of the modern civilization which had produced himself sitting there, listening," as Wilson says, "without much sympathy to the bare-footed friars singing vespers." Setting out to tell the story of a thousand years that Gibbon recognized were as interesting as they were messy and distasteful, he turned out to be "a genius in presenting material." The writer who had begun *To the Finland Station* in response to the crisis of American society resumed his task with an enhanced perspective.

Children were among his fellow patients, and he translated a children's story in verse into English, yet was sick and grumpy enough (and sufficiently obtuse to the nervousness of the staff) to spank a commissar's charming but unruly son. When he suffered an acute kidney attack he was confined for an extra week, and when finally allowed to leave, his perceptions of the smells of the rugs and upholstery in the hotel where he spent a night and of "the perfumes" in its barbershop were "abnormally acute." From his hotel window "trees were shaking dark leaves in the darkening autumn light, and their shape and their shuddering movement both fascinated me and compelled me to turn away." The man whom Dos had christened Edmund Axel Wilson as he set out for the Soviet Union recovered from the hospital version of collective living by "declaiming aloud some old poems of my own composition."

He had intended to sail home via Istanbul, but the summer steamers were no longer operating. Wiring for an extra hundred dollars from Henry Allan Moe at the Guggenheim office in New York, he took the train back through a collapsing central Europe. The rise of Hitler, the Italian invasion of Ethiopia, and the decaying manners of the time seemed an extension of Gibbon's account of Rome's long collapse, and Russia appeared healthier as Wilson left it behind, a new world far from the old one, in this respect like the United States. His travelogue ends, "*Rigor mortis* has set in in Paris."

There he had two literary encounters, which go unmentioned in this journal. One was with Malraux, who had spoken with Trotsky and told the American he had a "King Lear side," "acting the tragic grandeur of his rejection by his own people." Malraux said the Soviets lied in blaming Trotsky for the plots against Stalin, a view he would be too politic to voice during a subsequent visit to the United States. The other meeting was a long awaited one with James Joyce, who had once written to thank Wilson for his review of *Ulysses* and, for *Axel's Castle,* had allowed him to use the outline made by Joyce's disciple Stuart Gilbert. It proved an anticlimax. As Wilson told the story to Edel many years later, he was warmly received at the house, but when the others left them and he gave the novelist "one of those very pointed looks" (Edel's phrase) as a prelude to what he hoped would be serious talk, Joyce fell silent. Wilson told another interviewer that, when he tried again by inviting the Joyces to dinner, Nora appeared alone saying that Joyce had a headache, but after a pleasant evening confessed the truth, that he hadn't wanted "to see that Wilson" or to be seen by him. To his wife Joyce had remarked of the critic, who was a few inches shorter, "All that he does is keep staring at my tie."

As often happens with travelers, this Russian tour renewed Wilson's awareness of his own country. His rediscovery of republican institutions further distanced him from American communism, the latter dominated during the late thirties by the notion (which the New Left revived during the 1960s) of "bourgeois democracy" as a sham. In 1935, however, Wilson could still have it both ways, as he no longer could once the public trials of the old Bolsheviks commenced. His Soviet journal closes with a romantic impression of Moscow as "the moral top of the world, where the light never really goes out," the short summer nights of the north a metaphor for the revolutionary enlightenment that, he ironically notes in *Red, Black*, was about to be firmly extinguished. He belatedly retrieves his balance in the Emersonian coda of *Travels*. "The states slip; the people cringe; all look after vanished suns," Wilson declares. "Yet still we refer to obsolete authorities decisions which must be made by ourselves, yet still we invoke from invisible forces the power we ourselves do not find. Still we think in terms of mythologies in this day when, if God cannot help us, the People or the Masses can do no better—when accuracy of insight, when courage of judgment, are worth all the names in all the books."

Through 1936 he worked away at Russian and began to study the literature. The next year the first of his essays on the Russian classics helped make Pushkin's *Eugene Onegin* accessible to English-speaking readers, and during the 1950s he'd produce fine portraits of Chekhov, Gogol, and Turgenev and his influential review of *Doctor Zhivago*. Wilson's account of Russian literature would be enriched by exchanges with Nabokov, with his Cape Cod friends Nina Chavchavadze and her husband Paul, with the teacher Helen Muchnic, the bibliophile Roman Grynberg, and by his marriage to Elena Mumm Thornton, who was of mixed Russian and German parentage.

He relied, too, on his only personal experience of this country. *Travels* angered the Soviets, and he was told he would never be granted another Russian visa, yet he had absorbed the spell of the landscape, "loose, untrimmed, running to wildness," dotted with "Corot-like birch trees, flimsy and tall and slim, stringing a loose lacy trim against the sky, still, so late, translucent, the so slowly waning light." He had seen and heard and felt the people and their history in the theaters of Leningrad and Moscow; in the Alymovs' intimate apartment, at the dacha, and the monastery; in Mirsky's austere lodgings and the streets where they talked; at the flophouse with Clavdia; and amid all the "old slowness and rubbish" of the Odessa hospital.

14

Trees and *The Triple Thinkers*

❧

"He has picked up a S. U. form of address, rough but chaste," Louise Bogan reported to Ted Roethke, poking gentle fun at Wilson's way of entertaining friends with his Soviet adventures. "He sits upright, talking diligently, and grasps you with his right arm, in a sort of bear hug." But when Wilson's account began appearing in *The New Yorker* and *The New Republic*, the representative of the news agency Tass gave him not a bear hug but the response of an angry dog, "sometimes barking and leaping at my throat in the way that I had come to recognize as one of the tricks for putting pressure on 'innocents' who show signs of resistance." Nor were most left-wing readers pleased by the account of Russia in *Travels in Two Democracies*. Dos Passos admired the storytelling chapters after Moscow had been left behind, their style making him "think of Thoreau and," he wrote, "for some reason, of Sterne—You hit a fine tone of eighteenth-centuryish equanimity." Yet Wilson's impressions of the USSR didn't work well with his essays on American subjects. He made a token effort to unify the book through the character called "the traveler," introduced in an opening scene of political paranoia, where everyone spies on everyone else, and returning in Wilson's speech on self-reliance at the curtain.

Louise wrote to Roethke that 314 East Fifty-third Street had been rented or sold out from under him "or something," and for a year he moved around, staying in furnished rooms in New York with long periods at Red Bank. In the fall of 1936 he acquired a haven for his *recueillement* from the cultivated locomotive heiress Margaret de Silver. Wilson had at some point proposed to Margaret, whom Rosalind describes as "beautiful and overweight, with tiny hands and feet and a sweet manner." She now lived in Manhattan with the Italian anti-Fascist leader Carlo Tresca, and

offered the critic the use of her country home, Trees, on the Mianus
River near Stamford, Connecticut. Trees was a modern stone house with
a cathedral ceiling in the main room and two wings, into one of which
Hattie moved with several grandchildren. In the journal Wilson recalls
the expressions of the old woman's "sensitive, very refined face," and the
"deep sympathy and affection" he came to feel for her at Trees. She could
fit a pipe as quickly as she could mend his evening clothes, and once a
visitor heard him shout for his underwear, "Hattie, where are my drawers?" Though the house was too isolated for teenaged Rosalind, "surrounded by spooky rocks and a nasty unswimmable little river running
below," Wilson loved its "absolute quiet." Working late and sometimes
through the night, he hurled an old tennis racket at the crows if they
woke him too early, collected moths in jars, and grew accustomed to the
sight of the playing card that, botching a magic trick, he'd managed to
stick to the main room's ceiling.

Soon after moving in, he invited Bogan for a four-day weekend, in October. She told Roethke that in an effort to save on household expenses
Wilson turned off the refrigerator at night, which made the food smell
bad, and "out of a desire for work and sobriety" bought gin "only one bottle at a time," cutting off their literary arguments at ten o'clock. Teasingly,
Wilson likened her loud snoring to the machinery that ran the fountains
at Versailles and kept the villagers awake, their anger included by
Michelet among the causes of the French Revolution. Bogan later signed
herself to him as "Waterworks Louise." By day she read on the living room
couch and watched "all the leaves in the world" fall outside the windows
while listening to the shallow river, the backdrop for "Song for a Lyre,"
"perhaps the only real love poem I ever wrote," she said, and one he admired:

> Soon fly the leaves in throngs;
> O love, though once I lay
> Far from its sound, to weep,
> When night divides my sleep,
> When stars, the autumn stream,
> Stillness, divide my dream,
> Night to your voice belongs.

The Sleeping Fury, with which these lines conclude, is dedicated "To
Edmund Wilson, in Gratitude." When Louise had a chance to be poetry

critic for *The New Yorker* he guided her reading and coached her on critical prose. A writer of lyrics who hadn't gone to college, she didn't think
she could manage it—"I remember, in the beginning, sitting at that desk
with the tears pouring down my face trying to write a notice. Edmund
Wilson would pace behind me and exhort me to go on." They relaxed in
their old literary games. In a spoof she signed with the name of one
"Pundit Acherya" at the Yoga Research Institute on Fifty-eighth Street,
she takes off on two poets whose work she adored. "W. Whew Oddun" is
said to be even more enthusiastic about "our head-standing routine, Lotus
and Karma positions, and patented Navel Exerciser" than such luminaries
as "Willie Yeats."

Since losing Frances, Wilson had been lonely, and he wanted to marry
again. One night he knocked on the door of the guest room at Trees and
got in bed with Louise, who had been content for Frances to have the
physical expression of his love. In the story he later told Mary McCarthy
and Louise told to a trusted friend (who, like McCarthy, was much amused
in the retelling), he had turned out the lights and was earnestly caressing
her when suddenly she asked, "Edmund, would you bring me a glass of
water, please?" He obligingly brought one and Louise, perhaps acciden-
tally on purpose, spilled it all over the bed. By contrast, there was nothing
lighthearted about his flirtation with his second cousin Helen Vinton Augur, who had had a crush on him in youth and was divorced in 1936.
Blond and blue-eyed, petite, Helen was sharp-tongued and could bicker
with Wilson, but her upbeat, clever letters usually address him as "Dearest" or "Darling," and at least once, early in 1937, they did make love.
Alluding to the "sheer pleasantness" of the evening with "brute tides underneath," Helen effuses that they've found each other at last. She recovers quickly, however, and by May signs herself "Your reformed character."

On his return from the USSR he had gone immediately to Chicago to
see Louise Connor, whom he'd left to face an angry husband alone, but
she wasn't permitted to see him. That fall, recovering and drying out in a
Massachusetts sanitarium after a breakdown, she wrote of being strangely
"detached" even from her children, "inert," "stupefied." Home by Christmas
and with hopes of a job, by their next meeting she was back to drinking,
and for over thirty-six hours their sex got "better and better." In a voyeuris-
tic journal scene Wilson, fusing the connoisseur pose of Casanova with
Titian's painterly perspective, describes them nude on a couch with
Louise's foot "held in my armpit," the thin gold wedding ring on her fin-

ger "resting on her opulent breast." By this time he was spanking her with a hairbrush, which she explained "would always bind us together." She might have wanted to bind them together, but she kept turning down his suggestions that she divorce Peter and marry him, proposals repeated—to Rosalind's dismay—over the upright phone in the living room at Trees. Their last tryst—after Peter sought him out and delivered him a blow on the chin—took place in "the saddest blankest sitting room" of a suite in an Albany hotel in September 1937. Louise had spent two and a half weeks on the beach, and when she pulled off her girdle, bra, and hat to wrap herself in an old bedcover, the straps of her bathing suit were "brought out by the burn as if they themselves had been burnt into her shoulders as scars." Wilson concludes, "She began to cry, and I knew that we loved each other still."

From the frustrations of this relationship he turned to a long flirtation with a woman as drawn to Wilson's mind as he was to her body, her coloring, and her "great round-lidded heavy-curtained eyes." With her husband Coulton, Elizabeth Waugh ran a hooked-rug shop at the west end of Provincetown, known as Waughsville. Coulton and his sister Gwyneth were painters (he was later the cartoonist for *Terry and the Pirates* and other features). Elizabeth was childless, had had a miscarriage after a pregnancy which, she told Wilson, had "spoiled" the look of one of her breasts. A stylish, highly intelligent woman with dyed red hair, she was embarrassed at being "in trade," bored with rugs, and had back problems when tugging them around. She painted and aspired to write. At a party in New York where she let Wilson kiss her she reminded him of "an old-fashioned American magazine cover-girl" with a tilted hat. She could also look "Isodesque, Guineveresque," and in a painting by her father-in-law, Frederick Waugh, is a Pre-Raphaelite version of a medieval heroine, beautiful, chilly, and removed. In the sensuous verse of Wilson's lyric "November Ride" Elizabeth is "soft as the goldsmith's chamois to the fingers." "D" in the journals, she would become the magnetic and cold "princess with the golden hair" of *Memoirs of Hecate County*.

Elizabeth destroyed almost all Wilson's letters lest they fall into her husband's hands, but hers have been collected and reveal the relationship. She thanks him for explaining to her "a little how you feel about Frances." She believes in Wilson's work, shrewdly observing that "the minds who serve humanity these days are for the most part very blunt or bigoted or tortured by inquisition, or war or starving," and that such a faculty as his "ought to be used positively." She sees herself as a Galatea to his Pygmalion: "It would be fun to let you educate my imagination—as you did for example in the case of 'Leda and the Swan,'" she says about Yeats's poem, but makes it clear that he is not her swan, her Zeus ("this, as our lives are to be arranged, can be done, I suppose, only by means of the printed word"). Apropos an essay on Lytton Strachey in *The New Republic* she writes, "if you were just prose I'd be mad about you." This letter declares, "You are a guileful lover and a straight thinker, which makes it bad for all of us."

He wanted her to have an affair with him and, if it worked out, to divorce Coulton and get married. Elizabeth, however, was almost forty when the flirtation began, ten years older than she let on. She believed that her health was poor and feared getting pregnant again—she likened the pain when Wilson bit her lip while kissing her to that of bearing "a still-born child." When he shared with her, as he did with all his friends, his struggles as a playwright, she said, "Even your damned plays get into my fallopian tubes." For two years following his trip to Russia she both retreated and encouraged his pursuit, closing almost all her letters to Wilson with what she called "Pink Love." She advised him to "lie out on the dunes, and know that I wish I was there too."

In February 1937 he persuaded her to an assignation—he thought "she half hoped that I would get her pregnant, that that would decide the thing for her"—but their meeting at the Concord Inn disappointed both. Registering under the name Mr. and Mrs. Edgar Watson, Jr., he was embarrassed when a "silent but prying" young man beside the cloak rack said, "Don't you know your wife's coat, Mr. Watson?" Though Elizabeth's body was perfection, her climax was private, almost self-directed. In his brown bathrobe she likened him to "one of those monks in Boccaccio," and in the mirror he was fat-faced and debauched, with the bump on his chin where Peter Connor had hit him looking like an unpleasant growth. Instead of staying for a second night they separated after breakfast in the morning, and he spent the brisk, bright day wandering among the English-looking streets behind the Boston State House and immersing himself in a bookstore. As they put the affair behind them he gave her novel the careful reading she wanted, and from Mexico she sent him a well-informed account of Trotsky's testimony before the international commission investigating Stalin's charges. She wrote affectionately after he'd married McCarthy and had a son, and in the months before World War II Wilson, although against the war, helped her find a job writing publicity on behalf of the allies. In 1942, however, Elizabeth had an operation of which she told him only that it would not result in the loss of "my sexual organs." She died two years later, of colon cancer, just as he found a publisher for *Hecate County*, the book that drew on their relationship.

Rosalind was brought up at Red Bank until she went off to boarding school a few days before her twelfth birthday, and he tried to be a father to her on weekends. She was a child with a vein of fantasy, and at the Cape during their wonderful summer with Margaret, Mary Blair wrote to Wilson to watch out for her on the beach, for she'd acquired a sword and talked of swimming out to stab a shark. At nine and ten, she had a shaky sense of her identity. Telling different sets of people, "what they wanted to hear," she recalled having "developed five sets of fictions: one for my grandmother, one for my mother, one for my father, one for my Rumson relatives and one for the Red Bank ones." She thought herself "a mess," and he reassured her. After taking her to a party where they met Margaret Mead, on the train to Red Bank he said, "Miss Mead, who is very famous, was observing you and she thought you were fine." But he worried when in Russia, sharing his concern with Muriel Draper, who later told Rosalind, "He kept telling me you were troubled because you didn't understand when he read you *Pickwick Papers* what Mr. Pickwick did."

Mary had married again, to Constant Eakin, vice president of Frigidaire. Hoping to prove she could be a mother, she invited her daughter for visits during which "the actress who wasn't acting," as Rosalind calls her, would in her terrifying stage voice announce, "I am your mother, Rosalind." She called her daughter a "spoiled fat child" whom Mrs. Wilson was bringing up "to be a useless snob" and at two in the morning ordered her to scrub the kitchen floor. Mary was drinking again and a compulsive smoker, Connie a flagrant alcoholic. Cowley remembered him one evening in the living room of their New York duplex, with its large portrait of Blair in costume done by Djuna Barnes. Connie was drunk and playing the grand piano with his bare feet while directing an invisible orchestra with his hands. In the spring of 1933 he had a breakdown triggered by the financial collapse of Charles E. Mitchell, the supersalesman of the boom in whose bonds he had overinvested.

Liquor eventually cost him his job, and in 1935, when Rosalind started school at Wykeham Rise, Blair was diagnosed with TB. She retreated to a hospital in Pittsburgh, attended, to everyone's surprise, by Connie, and had surgery that winter. Wilson wrote to her regularly. The only letter not destroyed by her sister amuses her with his summer routine while working at night at the Cape, turning off all the lights downstairs to avoid visitors. He asks "how long the money I have sent you for the hospital will last," urging her to let him know "right away." When he and Rosalind visited the hospital, the latter writes, "we would take my mother, who weighed only 70 pounds, to our rooms at the hotel, where she would lie on the bed and order up a big meal which she never touched. My father said that's what she'd always done."

Father and daughter twice summered together at Provincetown in the mid-1930s. One year Rosalind's childhood nurse, Stella, stayed with them, while the next Jennie, her grandmother's housekeeper, came up from Red Bank. To Adelaide Walker, Wilson's friend for four decades, the girl seemed "like something out of an early Henry James novel"—she would wear a velvet dress with a lace collar to go skating and say things like "Father doesn't allow me to go to the movies." Yet she loved the bohemian freedom of the Cape, and Wilson liked having her around. He wrote to Mary that she was better-mannered, "her observations on the people she meets quite penetrating." One of her eyes turned outward, and after various doctors had failed to improve the situation he found a Boston oculist who did. Elizabeth Waugh told him that his love for Rosalind was "one of the things I like best about you," calling him "a very good father" and the girl "full of life and soulful spark, so unlike a lot of these bored children our friends seem to produce." Several years later Elizabeth (whom Rosalind in fact resented) described her as "better lined with guts" than the other young folk.

At this point in her life she could get around her father. When he slept off a night out, "my policy was to go into his room around eight in the morning and say, 'I need some money for today.' He would groan sleepily and say, 'Take what you need,' motioning toward his wallet on the bedside table next to his watch. I would take perhaps a crisp twenty and be off, the only kid in town with twenty dollars for Popsicles and movies per diem." What made Rosalind miserable were Wilson's attempts to take her in hand intellectually. He decided she should learn a poem a day, but "he was not a good teacher where one of his own was concerned and it was emotional, with a great deal of shouting and stubborn resistance from me." On the day she tried applying a lot of makeup, he wiped it off her with one of his linen handkerchiefs and sent her back to "William Blake and his damned tiger." When a pretty teacher at her school suggested to her father that he tutor her in grammar, Rosalind sighed, and he made her miserable until Betty Huling, the *New Republic*'s lively copy editor, "taught me in three hours what he hadn't been able to in three weeks."

His women friends helped out as they could. In 1936 Betty drove Wilson and Rosalind with Hattie and three of Hattie's grandchildren to the Cape in the old Stutz Bearcat that was her prize possession, even though it seemed always to be breaking down. Helen Augur sometimes let them use her penthouse apartment in Manhattan, and one summer Helen drove Rosalind all over the Cape in her convertible, continually buying her ice-cream cones. Katy and Dos, who had no children and were always entertaining, included Rosalind in their hospitality—when she was older Dos indulged her love for champagne, calling her "Champagne Rosie."

Trees would be Wilson's home until mid-1938, and if he was sometimes lovelorn, a passage in *Hecate County* shows what the house in the woods meant to him. Fleeing a drunken party, the narrator stands before the stone fireplace regarding the terrace above the little river, the corridor to his study, and the simple bedrooms. Again he is "my old solitary self, the self for which I really lived and which kept up its austere virtue, the self which had survived through these trashy years." The 1937 poem "Past Midnight" links this discipline with a commitment to style:

> After writing,
> Reading late,
> Too tired and tense
> To take the author's sense,
> My mind a metronome
> That keeps its proper beat,
> Always starting and alighting,
> I strive to mark as if it were my own
> The other's pulse too stuttering and slow,
> To pull his periods straight,
> To stretch them tighter than the vibrant bow
> That speeds the arrow home.

Early that year Wilson produced the brief section of *Finland Station* on utopian socialism. As in his opening chapters on Michelet and the French critics, he writes history by focusing on individuals. The Jacobin hero Babeuf maintained that political equality depended on economic equality and that land should be held in common. But the French Revolution was fading into the past, and Babeuf was guillotined. The unworldly aristocrat Saint-Simon, who'd suggested how industrial society might be organized scientifically through a hierarchy of merit, lived out his old age on the charity of a former valet. Enfantin, a Saint-Simonist, briefly attempted the role of secular messiah. "Beginning as the Son of God," Wilson cracks, "he had ended as a fairly able railroad director." Wilson intends such quixotic efforts to set off the systematic, researched socialism of Marx and Engels, though before finishing this book he'd conclude that Marx and Engels were more utopian than they or he had known.

He admires Charles Fourier and Robert Owen, early socialists who tried to cure the ills of the industrial system through reason and experiment. Sharing the Rousseauist assumption that humanity was good, they designed utopian communities to be underwritten by enlightened members of the propertied classes. Owen, a Welsh saddle-maker's son who like Babeuf held to an ideal of absolute equality, is a minor hero of *Finland Station*. He had risen to the apex of the cotton industry and for twenty-five years directed the model community at New Lanark, was consulted by "the prime ministers, the archbishops, the princes," but never, Wilson thought, understood why his disciples, lacking his personal force, couldn't match his accomplishments. He began to oppose religion, property, and the family, and in his last days fled the oppressions of the bourgeois age by conversing in his mind with the magnanimous souls he had known, from Shelley to Jefferson. Fourier was committed to universal suffrage and a common education, favored labor over capital, and also rewarded "talent." His experimentation had touched the critic in childhood, when on Sundays Edmund was sometimes taken to visit a "phalanstery" in the New Jersey woods where his grandfather Kimball had patients among descendants of the original members. In this "pastoral little world" the transcendentalists had given talks, and there the faithful from Brook Farm had migrated: "there they had hoped to lead the way for their age, through their resolute stand and pure example, toward an ideal of firm human fellowship, of planned production, happy labor, high culture—all those things from which the life of society seemed so strangely to be heading away."

Wilson points out that in nineteenth-century America as many as 100,000 people had practiced some form of communism, from Owenites and Fourierists to French Icarians and German religious sects. They showed courage against the odds—dissension within and pressure from without—and endured sweeping fires and epidemics. Some groups were supported by outside funds, others relied on their own industries. Some were dedicated to chastity and others to "free love." By ancestry affiliated with the initially communitarian Puritan settlement at Massachusetts Bay, the critic was also heir to the rationalism of Wells and Shaw, and liked to believe that a successful socialist state would improve the breed through eugenics. *Finland Station* turns aside to the Oneida Community in upstate New York, where the minister John Humphrey Noyes and his followers had emigrated from Vermont to practice what they called perfectionism, dissociating sex from the idea of sin and (with some use of bundling and contraceptive techniques) achieving an early version of Planned Parenthood. Couples were designated to procreate and locked into their rooms. Noyes—whose features a later observer detected in many of the children—called this "complex marriage." But unlike the founder of Mormonism, another upstate product, he didn't have a Brigham Young to maintain his system and it collapsed in the next generation, though the community prospered by selling preserved fruits and making animal traps, and was later celebrated for its table silver.

A list at the back of volume sixteen, Wilson's journal for 1935–1936, reads "Flaubert as Social Critic, Henry James and Freud, Chapman, Bernard Shaw, Dickens as Neurotic, Mr. More and the Mithraic Bull." In 1937–1938, as the Moscow trials declared the failure of revolutionary Marxism, he stepped back to offer new insights into these leaders of the intellectual middle class. *The Triple Thinkers*, the "wonderful book" that persuaded young Isaiah Berlin that Wilson was a great critic, includes most of the names on his journal list except Dickens, who would open *The Wound and the Bow*, completed after *Finland Station*. In the second edition of *The Triple Thinkers* he'd remove "The Satire of Samuel Butler" and add "The Historical Interpretation of Literature," the memoir of "Mr. Rolfe," and his post–World War II Freudian study of Ben Jonson. The book begins with his dramatic memoir of the Princeton Sunday afternoon with More and Gauss. "Is Verse a Dying Technique?" follows, arising from a note, on the journal end-pages, about poetic effects common to Virgil and Dante, Proust and Joyce. Wilson contrasts the narrowing scope of rhyme and meter and of poetry itself, now become largely lyrical, with the great prose epics of the modern world. This thesis, which he would polish in talks at Smith College in 1942 and, two decades later, in a seminar at Harvard, has been called an example of historicism gone wrong, although in the twenty-first century few poets are committed to the mechanics of verse.

He once confessed that he was never happier than when telling people about a work they were unfamiliar with in a language they didn't know, and his essay on Pushkin's *Eugene Onegin* is second only to his Proust among Wilson's popularizations of classics. He teaches himself the language and absorbs the culture while exploring this novel in verse. As a professor on the page, Wilson swiftly distinguishes Pushkin's compressed, rigorous style from that of Byron, Keats, and other Romantics and locates his irony vis-à-vis that of Stendhal and Jane Austen. He provides a vivid synopsis of the desiccated protagonist's fumbled chance for love with an innocent but profound countrywoman who then makes another life in the world where Onegin had lost his illusions. Pushkin extracted all the richness from this situation, and his account of Lensky's fate presaged his own, dead at thirty-seven from a duel. Setting the conflicting values represented by Tatyana and the two men within the frame of Russian history, Wilson begins his thirty-five-year devotion to interpreting Russian literature to the West.

He develops the 1932 magazine pieces about Flaubert and Shaw into major essays. Shaw's persona is seen to be part householder, part socialist reformer, part philosopher-poet in the clouds. The dramatist conveniently shifted from one plane to another, so that reading him was like "looking through a pair of field glasses of which the focus is always equally sharp and clear but the range may be changed without warning." To recognize this old hero's limits frees Wilson to savor Shaw's "music of ideas"—"or rather, perhaps," he writes, "it is a music of moralities." In contrast, Flaubert, once his model of artistic control, is credited with historical insight Marx lacked: in the character of Senecal, the policeman who kills the good republican Dussardier in *L'éducation sentimentale*, Flaubert anticipated the despotic potential of socialism. "What is the artist if he is not a triple thinker?" the novelist asked in the letter to Louise Colet that gave Wilson a title for this volume. Yet the bloody uprising of the Paris Commune in 1870 left Flaubert politically stranded—the misanthropic satire of *Bouvard and Pécuchet* was a product of finding no "non-bourgeois way out."

In the essay "Marxism and Literature" Wilson proposes "a sort of law of moral interchangeability" by which the artistic dedication of Proust's novelist Bergotte (in his favorite passage from *À la recherche du temps perdu*) can be translated "into terms of whatever we do or are ourselves." He takes art as a "revolutionary 'underground'" where the will to transform society can be nourished, while rejecting the view of art as a weapon fashionable during the Popular Front, one revived among English department theorists half a century later. A related assessment of "Communist Criticism," reprinted in *The Shores of Light*, sees "no sense in pursuing a literary career under the impression that one is operating a bombing-plane. On the one hand, imaginary bombs kill no actual enemies; and, on the other, the development of a war psychology prevents one's real work from having value." The suggestion that "ethical and aesthetic" standards be sacrificed in the interest of social justice seems to Wilson fuzzy. Unless one is "trying to function as an organizer or an active politician (and agitational literature is politics)," one should work in good faith by the best traditions of one's art. "A conviction that is genuine will always come through— that is, if one's work is sound."

Reviewing the *General Introduction to Psychoanalysis* in 1920, he had promoted Freud as a hero of reason, who explored the strange abysses represented in dreams as well as the multiplying neuroses of his patients. He had cited Freud when rescuing Sophocles from the New Humanists a decade later. Freudian psychology forwards literary criticism in *The Triple Thinkers* and *The Wound and the Bow*. Wilson's interpretation of the role of repression and sublimation in *The Turn of the Screw* would long stand in opposition to readings of the tale as a study of terror beyond reason, evil without motive. He believes that the ghosts, like the tower on which Quint appears and the lake by which Miss Jessel is seen, are hallucinations of the governess. The argument of "The Ambiguity of Henry James" was refined in 1948, when the publication of James's notebooks made known his intention to write a ghost story. Wilson ventures that the novelist's repression blinded him to the class aspect of his characters' timidity—he'd have turned the petit-bourgeois Frédéric Moreau of *L'éducation sentimentale* into a "quietly vibrating" young American of tragic dimensions. This essay closes with the patriotism of the international novels and the intuitive understanding of the United States in *The American Scene*. Though the gilded age drove James to Europe with others of small incomes and nonacquisitive tastes, "he had never lost the democratic idealism, the conviction of having scored a triumph and shown the old world a wonder." Cited are his early naming of the American hero "Newman" and a late magnificent phrase "about Lincoln's 'mold-smashing mask.'"

"The voice, sent forth, can never be recalled" is the English translation of Housman's Latin motto, set at the beginning of Wilson's partial portrait of a man of genius weighted by the anomalies of his personality. Wilson could assume readers' familiarity with the lament of *A Shropshire Lad* for lost innocence, the pathos of "rose-lipped maidens" and "lightfoot lads" whose dark destiny awaited them. The bitterness of Housman's classical scholarship seemed to him petty rather than philosophical. In an old-fashioned prose that reminded him of Pope's, Housman attacked German professors who had "committed the unpardonable sin of editing the Latin authors inadequately with sentences that coil and strike like rattlesnakes, or that wrap themselves around their victims and squeeze them to death like boa constrictors." He was evidently unable to be heartened by what his verses did for human knowledge and human happiness. This essay has remained a point of departure for the poet's interpreters. Without attributing his despair to homosexuality, in the closet or otherwise, Wilson sets Housman among those British monastic minds who had also created *Alice's Adventures in Wonderland* and *Marius the Epicurean*. They lack, he says, emotional resilience: their works are "among the jewels of English literature rather than among its great springs of life."

Thus he integrates art, psychology, and politics as he plays off his generation's experience against the writers on whom they grew up. In these portraits and those that would follow, Wilson compresses the whole of a major artist into a single narrative perspective. "Whenever he wanted to write about somebody, he read all their works and accumulated an enormous amount of information until some shape emerged, built itself in his head," says Isaiah Berlin. For Alfred Kazin, "he has to make a point each step of the way and to show a case all round; he has to do it solidly, in his own style, gathering up all the details into one finally compact and lucid argument, like a man whose life hangs on the rightness of each sentence."

The quasi-Marxist, neo-Freudian threads of *The Triple Thinkers* are interwoven in the fine portrayal of John Jay Chapman, which mirrors aspects of both Wilson and his father. He met this bearded worthy at the Coffee House with Crowninshield in 1920 and at the decade's end they corresponded, Chapman delighted to find so ideal a reader. Chapman's letters, published in 1937, revealed his youthful battle against the corruption of intellectual standards by wealth and by the conformist instinct of Americans. Wilson shows him trying to fight off his neurosis. As a law student at Harvard, when unable to recognize his passion for the woman with whom he was reading Dante until it led him to assault another suitor, Chapman plunged his hand into a coal fire and held it there, necessitating its amputation. He got married and threw himself into the battle against machine politics, bitterly rejecting the compromises of his ally Theodore Roosevelt. But in this attack on the world from which Wilson Sr. had retreated, Chapman wore himself out and collapsed at thirty-eight, for three years convinced he couldn't walk without crutches.

Citing the pressures on humanistically educated men of the 1880s in exactly the language he'd apply to his own father twenty years later, Wilson then describes Chapman's criticism as if it were his own. For Chapman, Shakespeare and other masters "were neither a pantheon nor a vested interest. He approached them openmindedly and boldly," with a "flashlighting and spotlighting method" that could always tell you "something that you have not heard before." Although Wilson considered himself a pragmatist, viewing literature as a way to give life meaning and point, he admired Chapman's critique of William James's pragmatism. To James, Chapman wrote that "a thing is not truth till it is so strongly believed in that the believer is convinced that its existence does not depend on him." His insights into capitalism resembled Marx's, yet he called socialism a religious reaction "in an age which thinks in terms of money," a perception that helped Wilson see communism as his own religious temptation.

Chapman spoke of "the joy of casting at the world the stone of an unknown world." Passionately Emersonian, he drew strength from the Puritanism that hobbled him. As history eroded the secular faith of *Finland Station*, Wilson would fall back on the same moral heritage, while sometimes grouching that a hereditary Calvinism thwarted his creative powers. On his deathbed Chapman, an amateur violinist, called to his wife to help him remove the mute, saying, "I want to play on the open strings." This literary critic and fierce civic patriot, missing one hand and believing that he needed crutches, is a patrician American version of the wounded artist of the Philoctetes myth.

PART FOUR

"E.W. and M. McC."

15

A Literary Marriage Begins

Wilson's education, like that of Henry Adams, sometimes registered in criticism of others for views he had discarded not long before. When the trials of January 1937 illumined the nature of the Soviet regime, he lambasted Cowley for trying to defend them. One could believe nothing in the official version of events. Anticipating *1984*, Wilson saw how control of information enabled the ruling bureaucrats "to pass the sponge every day over everything that has happened before." Like Koestler in *Darkness at Noon*, he took the old Bolsheviks' confessions of participating in supposed Trotskyite and fascist plots as a desperate effort to give meaning to their existences. By November 1938 Wilson was insisting to Muriel Draper, his onetime neighbor on East Fifty-third Street and companion in Leningrad, that the Russians "haven't even the beginnings of democratic institutions" and "have totalitarian domination by a political machine." Such views made him a heretic in literary New York, a bastion of Communist orthodoxy during the late thirties. Yet he didn't go over to the Right, as Dos Passos did after José Robles, the foreign minister of the Spanish republic and his translator, was shot by the Communists during their takeover.

To the Finland Station was not completed in *The New Republic*, as *Axel's Castle* had been. He had been haggling with the magazine about money and resisting efforts to shorten his articles, and it was difficult for him to deal with Bruce Bliven. He considered the managing editor a philistine, as did young Lionel Trilling. Bliven wasn't straightforward either—Cowley recalled that when you went in to hash something over, "Bruce would envelop you in jelly." In the fall of 1937 Wilson was courted by the young literary radicals at *Partisan Review*. The Communist Party had closed the magazine down, and Philip Rahv, Fred Dupee, Dwight Macdonald, and William Phillips were reshaping it. Irving Howe, their Trotskyist contemporary, would remember how important to the prestige of the magazine was their effort to recruit the critic they'd all looked up to since *Axel's Castle*.

He came in from Stamford to meet the editors for lunch near Washington Square. They discussed his submitting "Marxism and Literature" for the first issue of the new *PR*, then settled on "Flaubert's Politics." With the young men was Mary McCarthy, whom Rahv had invited to join the editorial board and who had heard Wilson lecture on Flaubert at Vassar in 1932. At that time, in the first of what would be a lifetime of contradictory statements about her feelings for Wilson, she declared her interest in him to her friend Muriel Rukeyser, while to herself she noted how he "floundered, mouth ajar, gasping for air," at the podium. Now four years out of college, she had a job at a publishing house. Beautiful and witty, Mary had been married once and was notorious for sleeping around. Roger Straus would ruefully recall his youthful feeling of being almost the only man he knew who didn't claim to have bedded her. She was living with Philip Rahv and surprised her colleagues by seeming very much in love with him, but she set out to make an impression on Wilson. "I had on my black dress and my silver fox fur," she recalled, in one version of the story mischievously adding, "I was waiting." Mary McCarthy was twenty-five years old, Wilson forty-two.

So began the relationship with a woman that would prove to be his most stimulating intellectually and most trying emotionally. In her memoirs and in interviews with, among others, two of her biographers, Carol Gelderman and Carol Brightman, she told how he asked Margaret Marshall, the *Nation*'s literary editor, to come to dinner and bring her along. Since he'd had nothing to drink at the lunch with the editors, Mary's friends thought he might be on the wagon and Fred Dupee fortified her beforehand with several daiquiris. Wilson ordered manhattans, wine, and B&B, and she said, "I became totally drunk and told him the story of my life." She passed out that night, waking the next morning in the Chelsea Hotel, relieved to find that the person in the twin bed beside her was Marshall. Wilson had taken a room for the two women, and Margaret and he had put Mary to bed. Several weeks later he asked her out to Trees, again with Margaret, the three taking a taxi the forty-some miles to Stamford, where the older woman fell asleep in the guest room. As before, Mary got drunk, but "it ended less platonically" when she followed Wilson into the study—

wanting only, she later insisted, to talk with him. They made love on the couch.

The next morning she asked Philip to come out and bring her home. Clueless about what had been going on, he accepted an invitation to stay for lunch, creating a situation for which, the correspondence shows, she later apologized to Wilson rather than to the man she was living with. In an interview in 1984 McCarthy said that Wilson "wrote me endless love letters." In fact she wrote much more often, at greater length, and more amorously. After their first sexual encounter she is "all shaken up," a state "pleasant but painful." A day later she is still "*distraite*," and after their next meeting, from which she returned to New York on the four a.m. milk train, she presents herself as alternately languid and racked by jealousy of any possible rival. She excused herself to Rahv for these nights away by saying she'd been to prizefights—one of her pleasures—or to see friends in the country. In her *Intellectual Memoirs* (1992) Mary asserts that the death of her beloved grandfather made her vulnerable to the portly, red-faced older man, but ten days before that death occurred she wrote to Wilson that their secret intimacy gave her pleasure, adding, "I think you're wonderful."

As alluring as her arch words were Mary's magnetic smile and what Elena Levin, Harry Levin's wife, called her "wonderful gray eyes—searching eyes." This beautiful young woman's interest in him seemed to promise an integration of mind and feeling similar to that he'd dreamed of with Millay. Though they met in a milieu dominated by politics, what was important to each was literature and one's own writing. Mary tried out her ideas on Wilson. Reading for a possible article on Byron, she proposes that "perhaps a poseur can be a more incisive social critic than such a desperately 'honest man' as Wordsworth, simply because the heart is not really involved, only the mind." She could have been speaking of the satiric fiction which, with Wilson's encouragement, she'd begin to write three or four months later. In January 1938 he nervously gave a lecture at Harvard—Levin, who was there with his colleague F. O. Matthiessen, recalled Wilson fortifying himself from a pint of whiskey behind a screen at the side of the stage, not knowing he was visible in silhouette. Filling Mary in back at Trees, he wrote that the talk had been "chiefly attended by young undergraduate intellectuals in spectacles from Harvard and Radcliffe and very old people from Cambridge with earphones." He arranged to spend the next Saturday with her, saying, "I've thought about you all the time—have thought constantly how I wanted to tell you things, talk over people with you, etc."

The romance progressed rapidly. He sent her "Love as ever," with asterisk kisses, "though you say they mean comparatively little to you," and she responded, "You are wrong about kisses. They mean a great deal to me, but I put them in the classification of hors d'oeuvres." In *How I Grew*, McCarthy states that as a young woman "sex and love and social conquest were inseparably wedded in my mind with men, even though the male organs were far from beauteous in my eyes." William Phillips believed her so well-defended against the men she slept with in New York that she lost all feeling for any of them. In Wilson's case, however, an intellectual excitement took sexual form. "You mean more and more to me," she wrote. As if awaiting his intentions, she reminded him that he had said "You will hear from me"—an ominous assertion with "very little security or comfort in it." Elizabeth Hardwick's introduction to *Intellectual Memoirs* reports that, despite her youthful promiscuity, "Mary was greatly attracted to marriage."

Wilson had unsuccessfully proposed to both Louise Connor and Elizabeth Waugh during the past months. He'd married Mary Blair when the alternative was an abortion, Margaret when his relationship with Frances became too intense and conflicted. Margaret "had always been perfect" with Rosalind, and he persuaded himself this Vassar intellectual would be an ideal stepmother, a sophisticated supportive guide for an adolescent outgrowing her grandmother's narrow Victorianism. When he proposed, McCarthy says she first demurred and offered to live with him as his mistress; Wilson replied "I've had that," insisting he needed a wife in "the worst way." In an interview McCarthy recalled that "Philip already had a wife" and couldn't afford a divorce, nor did he want to have children, as Wilson did. Though she had not expected to get married, this alliance made sense to her. When Helen Muchnic, the young scholar of Russian whom Wilson met when lecturing at Smith in 1942, inquired about the proposal, Mary said she initially put him off with the coy reply, "Mr. Wilson, this is so sudden." Muchnic asked Wilson whether it was hard to persuade McCarthy to say yes, and he replied, "I didn't have so much trouble."

The *Partisan Review*ers would half seriously blame themselves for her choice of Wilson over Rahv, since they had so talked him up. But she had achieved everything she could in that milieu, as Wilson pointed out. Pronouncing her "Theatre Chronicle" in the magazine too narrowly argumentative, he said of Rahv, "Not doing anything for you, that fellow." Mary would one day decide it was Rahv she had really loved, but when two of her brothers were in town and she didn't want them to know she was living with Philip, she passed on to Wilson a friend's suggestion that Philip be dressed up as the butler. She aspired to a more comfortable and gentrified life—"we were going to go fishing, ride horses [as Wilson more than once did in the countryside around Stamford], read Juvenal and Catullus." She didn't realize that Wilson would do nothing to maintain the kind of life she imagined sharing with him.

In *Intellectual Memoirs* McCarthy states that she never loved this "old" man, who was "fat, puffing" and had "popping" eyes and bad breath. He "bullied her" into marrying him, and, she writes, she agreed to "as my punishment for having gone to bed with him—this was certainly part of the truth." In her introduction Hardwick finds this "Jesuitical" explanation of her marriage endearingly characteristic of her friend's moral life. In person Hardwick observed, "Mary is very loyal to the truth, but she thinks she is always telling the truth, and sometimes she isn't." Adelaide Walker, who would come to Mary's aid in divorce court and told her biographers of Wilson's faults as a husband, said, speaking as Hardwick did when McCarthy was still alive, "Mary will say anything about herself no matter how derogatory, but she doesn't always see herself or others with the clarity she thinks she does." That is the theme of the compelling interchapters of her *Memoirs of a Catholic Girlhood*, which investigate whether what is related as fact is actually true. It may well be that, as McCarthy recalled half a century later, on her wedding day in February 1938 Wilson's tight-lipped expression told her she was making a mistake, that she was frightened when, drinking heavily with her brothers in a bar at their Manhattan hotel, he burst out that they were agents of Stalin. One sympathizes with the twenty-five-year-old who was getting more than she'd bargained for. But, so too was the critic. If he concealed from her his alcoholism, when Mary told him her life story she failed to include the beatings she had endured from her Great-Uncle Myers, a trauma that would scar their marriage.

In *Catholic Girlhood*, McCarthy tells how, after she and her brothers lost their father and mother on successive days to influenza, their grandparents boarded the children out to Myers and her Great-Aunt Margaret, who punished them "all the time, as a matter of course, with the hairbrush across the bare legs for ordinary occasions and with the razor strop across the bare bottom for special occasions," such as when she had won a school prize and might get "stuck-up." Wilson later recalled her as "under the impression she had been beaten every day." McCarthy's novel *A Charmed Life* evokes hated Uncle Myers through the Wilson character, whose name is Miles. On the night of their marriage Miles suddenly strikes the heroine, Martha, "for no reason," when she is "climbing into bed," and she looks up at him "in mute amazement, too startled even to cry." The account in *Intellectual Memoirs* of her actual wedding night seems indebted to the imagined scene written four decades before. McCarthy claims that, while she lay in bed assessing her situation and silently wept, Wilson "grunted some threats" though "he did not hit me."

She had also been unhappy on the night of her marriage, after graduating from college, to the playwright Harold Johnsrud. In the account of her early years, *How I Grew*, published before she died, McCarthy writes, "As we climbed into the big bed, I knew, too late, that I had done the wrong thing. To marry a man without loving him, which was what I had done, not really perceiving it, was a wicked action," and she claims to have lain there "stiff with remorse and terror." If she did not love Wilson when she married him, as she claims in *Intellectual Memoirs*, she had done the same thing again, yet she would transfer any guilt she felt to the husband she soon identified with her wicked uncle.

"I'm married to a girl named Mary McCarthy," Wilson wrote to Allen Tate, as if bemused how this had happened, but a tide of rejuvenation is seen in the journal entry headed "*Stamford February 1938 (just after coming back married)*": "It seemed to me about the only really attractive February I had ever known to occur; beautiful bright clear days, some of them cold, but not too cold—on one perfect afternoon, we walked into Stamford—and some of them so warm that the birds began to come out." On the last night of the month "a big wind like those of March came up, and it was pleasant to feel it blowing through the bedroom between the two open windows, after we had gone to bed—one felt that it was sweeping the mists and the damp and the grayness away." He "was extraordinarily content" during the next weeks, according to Harry Levin, who recalled that, though broke, Wilson reserved the central room in the Hotel Vendome for a party for Mary. The bride, too, seemed happy, and when Dwight and Nancy Macdonald visited, they were surprised to find "the Irish girl from Seattle" who could intimidate the *Partisan Review*ers deferring to her husband. "Mrs. Wilson is really a darling, and I hope everything lasts," Bogan reported of a weekend "in the connubial atmosphere of Trees." She added,

"There will be an heir." For by the end of March Mary was pregnant, a pleased Wilson boasting—as she recalled apropos his old-fashioned expressions—that he'd managed this "the first crack out of the box." He had also shepherded her, typewriter in her arms, into the little room where Bogan and Margaret Marshall stayed and, McCarthy says, "shut the door firmly," though she denies the legend that he locked her in. She spoke of his "generous, fatherly" concern for talent, "like some botanist wanting a plant to come on and develop and display its originality." Quickly she completed the clever "Cruel and Barbarous Treatment," based on an affair at the end of her first marriage.

Wilson proudly introduced her to his old friends. In a letter to Dos Passos, a hero of hers since college, he presented her as his intellectual partner. Explaining why he thought the characterization in *Adventures of a Young Man* not so successful as in *U.S.A.*, he added, "Mary sends love. She has written about your book for *Partisan Review*, so that if you don't know how to write the next one, it won't be our fault." Allen Tate was never really in the inner circle, but Wilson wrote to Bishop, "Old Massa Tate has just been here with his wife, daughter, and dachshund." When he took Mary to meet the Bishops at South Chatham on the Cape, Mary noted that in designing their mansion Margaret cut John's study in half in order to enlarge her luxurious bathroom, creating the effect of "a kept-woman's boudoir filling practically the whole of one wing, with a little narrow cell behind it containing a small cot and a tiny desk and room for just a few shelves of John's books." She shared Wilson's dislike of Margaret, though she didn't think John as talented as Wilson did or blame his wife for his relative failure as a writer. She had her husband's impression of Fitzgerald the recovering alcoholic. When Scott brought his Hollywood girl Sheilah Graham out to Stamford, Wilson told Christian Gauss it was something new for their friend to have to present a sober and practical face to the world, "and he seems mild, rather unsure of himself, and at moments almost banal." Mary thought Fitzgerald "boring," doubting his talk of writing a book about Lucrezia Borgia.

She loved Wilson's satirical "Omelet of A. MacLeish," telling the present writer that he read it to her and Scott during the visit. This cruel satire struck at someone who mimicked the manner of serious art without accepting the challenge and pain it required. In MacLeish he saw

. . . the mean tang of Cummings turned saltless and sleek on the tongue;

And a Dante gone limp: and a shimmer and musical sound
That gleamed in the void and evoked approbation and wonder
That the poet need not be a madman or even a bounder.

Isaiah Berlin recalled, "When the poem appeared in the *New Yorker*
MacLeish went to bed for a week." Many years later, when Berlin asked
why Wilson had done this to "poor old Archie," Wilson, unwilling to discuss it, said, "He's just an idiot, you know." McCarthy recalled MacLeish
with the same word.

In *The Fifties* Wilson says that "Mary had an uncanny instinct for
knowing how my mind was likely to work; she established, in a peculiar
way, very close intellectual and what may be called sensibility relationships—as when we used to have dreams that paralleled one another's."
Yet they were beginning to quarrel, the first ones sparked by his drinking.
She enjoyed a cocktail before dinner as well as wine on their elaborate
picnics. Once started, however, Wilson found it hard to stop. Mary told
the story of how "he decided to give me a little party. He bought six bottles of Liebfraumilch and tied red ribbons around their necks. I said, 'Let's
wait till tomorrow,' but in the morning he had drunk them all." She spoke
of binges in which he consumed everything in the house, "even the
vanilla." When drink made him irascible, she said, "I always fought back."
Arthur Schlesinger, Jr., who knew both from 1940 on, ventures that "Edmund was probably used, when he got angry, to immediate acquiescence,
but Mary liked to fight, and she could be very infuriating."

Their quarrels were complicated by the "seizures"—her word in 1938
and one Rosalind used in retrospect—which apparently began occurring
early in her pregnancy. Although no mention is made of these in her
memoirs and she seems to have kept them from her biographers, in an interview some forty years later McCarthy conceded, "As a young woman
I had temper tantrums and a hysterical tendency. I had almost fits, fits of
weeping. Don't have them now." In his deposition in divorce court Wilson
cited "outbursts of temper and fits of hysterical weeping." There he also
stated that he was alarmed, during a quarrel, "because her whole appearance and demeanor had changed from those of her normal personality:
she looked different and talked differently. As she afterwards confessed
to me, when I talked to her about this change: 'I talk like a guttersnipe.'
This was the first time I had seen the other side of her double personality." McCarthy's heroine, Meg, behaves just this way in the short story
"Ghostly Father, I Confess," in *The Company She Keeps*:

The first time she got angry with her husband and heard a torrent of abuse pour from her own lips, she had listened to herself in astonishment, feeling that there was something familiar about the hysterical declamatory tone, something she could not quite place. It happened again and again, and always there was this sense of recognition, this feeling that she was only repeating combinations of words she had memorized long ago. She had been married some time before she knew that she sounded exactly like Aunt Clara. Yet she could not stop, she was powerless to intervene when this alien personality would start on one of its tirades, or when it would weep or lie in bed in the morning, too wretched to get up.

The tantrums and crying also mark unhappiness with Wilson, and in a notorious episode with so many versions that the truth can only be approximately sorted out, her childhood trauma exploded in consequence of his drunken bullying. Tate and his wife, Caroline Gordon, had come for dinner on June 7, 1938, and to spend the night. Mary served spaghetti and, as the Chianti flowed, Wilson turned from intellectual jousts with Tate to declaiming passages out of Pushkin in Russian, a language that, even when sober, he couldn't pronounce very well. The party continued after the hostess, two and a half months pregnant, went off to bed. McCarthy recalled that he came to bed drunk, and seeing the bed made up with some "blue-gray percale sheets" which she'd found at the bottom of a trunk and told the maid to use, he ordered her to "take these off the bed," then "tore the sheets off the bed, with me in them," and went off to sleep by himself. Looking back, she wondered whether his behavior echoed "some old incident," and in fact it did: in *The Thirties* a sheet so described is identified as Margaret's and snatched off a bed shared with Louise Connor.

With an unrepentant smile Mary added that she "taxed him" with his behavior when he awoke the next morning, whereupon he attacked her, giving her a black eye, "a real shiner." To Carol Gelderman she said she "flew at him with 'How could you?'," whereupon "he punched her repeatedly in the breasts and slapped her again and again in the face." To Carol Brightman she said it happened later in the morning, after the Tates had left. Except for the time he slapped Jean Gorman when she had Matthew Josephson run him down, no one but McCarthy has claimed Wilson ever hit a woman. Though McCarthy says Rosalind witnessed such assaults, in *Near the Magician* Rosalind states, "I never saw him hit anyone, in-

cluding Mary McCarthy. He would occasionally raise his hand in an ineffectual way as if he were going to." Of what she calls Mary's "symptoms
of apprehension," Rosalind says, "her childhood trauma made her think
she was about to be beaten, when she wasn't. She would wake up scream-
ing 'Don't hit me' when my father wasn't in the room." This testimony by
the only intimate observer of the marriage other than the maid Hattie is
not to be found in Brightman's *Writing Dangerously*. However, Mc-
Carthy's subsequent biographer, Frances Kiernan, quotes from the passage, as well as from an interview in which Rosalind differentiates the
couple's drunken fights from Mary's "seizures."

In recounting the marriages and affairs of the *Partisan Review*ers,
David Laskin has tallied alternative explanations of what happened that
June morning that led Mary to spend three weeks in the Payne Whitney
psychiatric clinic in New York:

> Did McCarthy suffer a "nervous breakdown"? A brief psychotic
> episode? A fit of hysteria induced by the hormonal changes of
> early pregnancy? Was this a marital spat that got blown out of pro-
> portion—an argument that mushroomed due to circumstance,
> misguided medical intervention, and the theatrical bent of the
> participants? Or was it a case of spousal abuse—a young wife
> driven off the edge by her rampaging alcoholic husband? Who is
> to blame? Wilson the monster, bent on beating his new wife into
> submission? Or McCarthy the bitch, who unleashed her husband's
> rage by "flying at him" when he was hung over? Or was Wilson in
> fact trying to help her, to calm her down, and was McCarthy too
> hysterical to perceive this?

In his divorce deposition in 1945 Wilson, denying he physically mistreated his wife, stated that until he knew better, he "used to try to fight
with her and hold her down" during these episodes. He was strong
enough to have torn a door off its hinges. Mary, who "liked to fight" and
"could be very infuriating," resumed the battle that morning and then
went to pieces.

Either Hattie or Wilson summoned Dr. Walter Gage from Stamford
and, unable to calm her, he recommended she be taken to a hospital in
New York. McCarthy's narrative style converts the painful experience into
something of a lark. That evening the couple rode into Manhattan "in one
of Edmund's inevitable taxis," stopping at the Sixty-eighth Street entrance

of New York Hospital, which she'd chosen for its "atmosphere and the yellow curtains." When turned away because of the hour they walked around the corner to what, she said, they didn't know was the psychiatric wing and checked Mary in. "Edmund had been so miserable that he went on a toot," but the next day "blew in at four or five in the afternoon freshly shaved and amiable," explaining what had happened so she could be moved to another floor. In the divorce action McCarthy testified that the next morning she "was diagnosed not as a psychotic but possibly in need of private psychiatric treatment."

In *The Group*, published twenty-five years later, Kay is sent to a psychiatric hospital because her husband, Harald Petersen—whose name links him to Mary's first husband, Harold Johnsrud—has brutally beaten her up, and Harald has committed her without her knowledge. Wilson didn't object to Mary's fictionalizing the incident, but when Doris Grumbach, in the first book about McCarthy, *The Company She Kept* (1967), claimed that the novel represented "an exact statement of what happened between" the two of them, he wrote to the publishers, "This is not true. Miss Grumbach does not know what happened, and Mary, in the state she was in, did not know what was happening either." He sent a copy to McCarthy, wondering "if you have seen this book and approved it in its present form. If you haven't seen it, I think you should. The author is evidently an idiot." McCarthy supported Wilson—also pointing out differences between him and the Miles Murphy of *A Charmed Life*—and Coward-McCann made Grumbach retract her identifications. But during McCarthy's last years she credited Harald Petersen's villainy to Wilson, claiming to biographers and in *Intellectual Memoirs* that he had known Payne Whitney was a psychiatric hospital and she did not. By this time she'd been embittered by Wilson's posthumous account of her instability, deleted from the published version of his journal *The Forties*. Kiernan concludes her review of McCarthy's accounts of entering Payne Whitney, "Life can imitate art, particularly in retrospect, when a story is told so frequently it begins to impose itself on the original version."

The passage in Wilson's journal that, to protect Mary, was never published states that the Stamford doctor sent her to this hospital, and among the critic's papers is a note in a hand not his:

admitted June 8, 1938
discharged June 29, 1938
referred by Dr. Walter Gage

Diagnosis: without psychosis
Anxiety reaction

"Mary in Payne-Whitney" is added on the margin in Wilson's handwriting.
Her case was assigned to a young Dr. Ripley, whom she liked. Wilson,
afraid, as McCarthy said, "that our whole marriage was about to fall apart,"
persuaded Dr. Sándor Rado, a pupil of Freud who then headed the Psy-
choanalytic Institute, to look in on her. Rado suspected a pregnancy-
derived hormonal imbalance, and when this proved untrue prescribed
therapy. Dr. Gage, who had observed her wild behavior at the house,
thought she should have an abortion, and Rado said he'd have strongly
recommended this had her pregnancy been less advanced. Wilson believed in psychoanalysis and urged her to make that "the main thing": they
"had counted on having a child" but could always do so later on, and at
the moment it would distract her and be more than they could afford, he
said, reminding her that this question must be settled before Rado could
do anything for her. Dr. Ripley, however, supported Mary's wish "to have
Edmund's child," arguing that what she wanted would be better for her
physically and psychologically. Wilson, who had welcomed the pregnancy,
quickly came around. Margaret de Silver needed Trees back for her son,
and to Mary (in a letter that belies the charge that he was determined on
an abortion) he reported finding a place at Shippan Point in Stamford that
"ought to be perfect for the baby." Rado, who was about to spend the summer in Stamford, agreed to take Mary as a patient on a temporary basis.

The couple were eager to make a fresh start. Sending her the current
magazines with a note from Nancy Macdonald and a card from Bogan,
Wilson draws some asterisk kisses and encloses a pair of earrings, saying,
"I am beginning to yearn for you pretty painfully." Mary returns with, "My
dear, I absolutely adore you. I'm awfully happy that I'm married to you
and that we're going to have a baby." She adds, "I was so frightened at first;
I thought everything, my whole life, was going to pieces, and nothing
could ever be salvaged. I don't mean I thought I was going crazy: I mean
I thought I had (so quickly and so irrevocably) managed to ruin everything. Well! I hope I haven't." Wilson too is hopeful for the future, writing, "We are going to be happy in spite of the psychoanalysis, etc. I don't
think we've made such a false start." He admits he isn't easy to live with,
writing, "I love you as ever" and "want you back with me for as much of it
as you can stand."

Mary had been informed she couldn't leave Payne Whitney for thirty days, but because Rado turned out, as she hoped, to be "one of those fanatical Freudians" who looked down on sanitariums, she was released a week early, as strong-willed as Wilson had been when he insisted on leaving Clifton Springs. Hattie, who didn't much like Mary, remained with her grandchildren at Trees, and Mary was relieved to have the "strange old woman" off her hands. Rado, reassuringly for Wilson, lived just down the street from their new home, and he gave Mary a session a week for a nominal five dollars an hour. Her outbursts, however, continued. Rosalind, nearly fifteen, joined them for the summer and had a grim exposure to the stepmother her father had thought would be ideal. "Mary would begin to scream and yell and attack him—it had nothing to do with drink, it had nothing to do with anything he was doing—and she was a big girl and it was frightening," she says, and "unlike anything I've ever seen." She could only call these "seizures." In divorce court, Wilson testified that the "fits of weeping" generally occurred early in the morning, when Mary's sense of reality was blurred. "When I would go over to her to put my arm around her and try to reassure her, she would sometimes say 'Help!' and behave as if I was going to hit her. Then she would hit me in an effort, I felt, to make me retaliate." When Mary made such a scene during a family trip to Red Bank, Rosalind says that Mrs. Wilson, who'd had two doctor brothers and a hypochondriacal husband, "slapped her face and brought her out of it." She adds that her father "took me for a walk when we were at Red Bank and explained it to me. Because he *had* to explain it to me," telling about the deaths of Mary's parents and something of her suffering and humiliation at the hands of her great-aunt and -uncle.

The baby was due at the end of December, and Mary's last months of pregnancy were easier. Wilson agreed to take her to a Vassar classmate's wedding on the twenty-fourth. After a champagne breakfast the couple walked downtown to Brooks Brothers, and a false labor ensued, which sent her to New York Hospital. They took a taxi back to Stamford and another that night back to the hospital where, on Christmas Day, she gave birth to Reuel Kimball Wilson. A friend recalled the young mother as "ecstatic," and Wilson wrote to Bishop that Mary and Reuel were "in fine shape. We are down here surrounded by snow and deep in domesticity." His mother soon supplied a baby carriage, and Wilson geared up to support his expanding family. The $1,700 Harcourt had sent him toward *To the Finland Station* was long gone, as was an advance for *The Triple Thinkers*,

but *The Atlantic* now paid him special rates, and he planned his next series of studies, which would include Dickens and Kipling—proposing to
W. W. Norton a collection "to be hung on the Philoctetes myth," asking
for a $1,000 advance and getting $800. A letter to Perkins tries to embarrass this friend into giving him a better contract. Scribner's, he alleges,
have failed to correct inaccuracies in *Axel's Castle*; they have refused a request for "what was certainly the very moderate sum of $75" and declined
to sponsor him for a bank loan "at a time when you were handing out
money to Scott Fitzgerald like a drunken sailor—which he was spending
like a drunken sailor. Naturally you expected him to write you a novel
which would make you a great deal more money than my books seemed
likely to do. But," Wilson notes, "after *The American Jitters* came out, I
never got the faintest sign of interest from Scribner's until Harcourt offered to publish my books."

He went down to Red Bank to ask for the money needed to keep his
family going—"I should say she gave him a considerable handout at least
once a month," McCarthy said of Wilson's mother. "She might have made
sure of visits that way." The bride who had imagined this alliance putting
her on the level of well-off Vassar classmates had to keep track of every
nickel, and would tell biographers of fighting for a separate bank account.
In 1939, however, while Wilson cajoled editors and publishers for money,
she collected dividends from the McCarthy family grain elevator business
of $1,300, which she turned over to him, and two years later she donated
a bonus for signing with Simon and Schuster toward their household expenses. Wilson pressed Gauss about doing something at Princeton. Though
not, he said, a good lecturer, he could read essays as lectures and be useful
to students in small groups.

He confided to Mary about his relationships with his parents, including the "tremendous turnaround at the moment of his father's death,"
unknown to Wilson's readers until "The Author at Sixty." Mary was irritated that her husband was deemed beyond the reach of analysis, since
he'd had his own breakdown and recovery ten years before, but as soon as
she could she went into New York for therapy with Dr. Richard Frank.
She saw Dr. Frank regularly through the spring of 1939 and would return
to him from 1940 to 1942. He is the Dr. James of "Ghostly Father, I Confess," who points out the return of Meg's girlhood trauma within her marriages to older men. This story telescopes different phases of the analysis.
Meg's shocked recognition of her alien personality as Aunt Clara dates

from the time when Mary believed in Dr. Frank, while the satire on the well-intentioned plodder whose patient thinks rings around him, the substitute priest with "the hygienic pipeline that kept the boiler from exploding," is from the period when (as Meg thinks of Dr. James) "she'd admitted he could do nothing for her" but "had no one else to talk to." "Ghostly Father" concludes with an ironic prayer, "Preserve me in disunity," to the Christian God in whom Meg does not believe.

In the summer of 1939, Wilson took a job at the University of Chicago set up by *The New Republic*'s Robert Morss Lovett, now teaching there, and by Morton Zabel, at the time at Loyola University. He was offered $1,200 for two ten-week summer courses. In one he could work out his ideas on Dickens, while the other would be about the "social interpretation with Taine and some of the Marxist texts." On June 1, a hideously hot day, Mary and Wilson, the baby and the baby's nurse, arrived in the city by train and crammed themselves into the Hyde Park apartment of the Twain scholar Walter Blair, setting up a cot for the nurse in the dining room. A few weeks later Wilson wrote to Dos, "We've been having an awfully good time out here." It was a stimulating metropolitan campus, and though to run a modern university on Aquinas and Aristotle seemed "fantastic," he had students "of all races, religions, nationalities, and colors—including a German Catholic nun," some "very bright."

He introduced Mary to Sherwood Anderson as well as to Zabel, and Saul Bellow would remember the thrill of meeting Wilson on a street near the university, being invited to drop by, and attending one or two meetings of the Dickens course. The couple saw something of Gerry Allard, a union organizer who edited *The Socialist Call*, and his beautiful Finnish wife. The British classics scholar David Grene remembered merry times with Wilson, and the journal contains a happy recounting of a picnic on the shores of Lake Michigan. Mary and Wilson, however, fell to squabbling in the small apartment. Laskin speculates that Wilson likely began their fights "with some intellectual quibble and climaxed, many ounces of alcohol later, in bellowing. McCarthy jabbed and needled, slapped and cut, and refused ever to admit defeat or let her husband have the last word." Walter Blair's wife recalled that their neighbors twice called the police, while her husband cracked, "The maid got a black eye. She got between them, trying to save one of their lives." Rosalind's arrival toward the end of July didn't help, even though she stayed in a dormitory, for the chemistry between her and Mary was never what her father had hoped.

Since he paid more attention to his daughter between marriages, it was natural for her to be jealous of his wives, while Mary would confess, "It bored me to have this young creature always there, something almost inevitable with a young stepmother."

Instead of reading aloud finished essays or chapters, for the first, and apparently the last, time Wilson taught his material before writing it. At least one student in the Dickens class thought the professor ill at ease, but Wilson felt he pulled it off—"I got used to talking on my feet and could hold them all right through my double classes of an hour and a half at a stretch. I made it all more or less informal." Rosalind remembered her father as "the soul of patience" with a student who was "radiant" when he finally passed her paper, and at the end the class paid him "little tributes." The Dickens essay in *The Wound and the Bow* is dedicated to the students of English 354.

When Mary left with the baby for a month with her grandmother in Seattle, Rosalind moved in and Wilson, worried he hadn't been giving her "the kind of life she ought to have," entertained her by taking her swimming as well as to the circus and to movies. His and Mary's correspondence restored some needed balance. From Seattle Mary wired, "INFANT HERCULES AND I ARRIVED SAFELY," and a letter likens her son in his playpen to "a regular Telemachus," who yells whenever her male acquaintances drop by. "Don't let anything happen to you while I'm gone," she writes. "I love you so much I couldn't bear it if you got anything wrong. Have tears in my eyes now just thinking about it. A highly suggestible subject I am, as you and Dr. Frank know." Wilson reports a sore shoulder, sore throat, fever, and other signs of a "trauma" of his own, one "caused by your departure." A week or two later he is "getting back into my old nocturnal habits," among them "writing letters all night: it's now four in the morning." After having nothing to drink for a week he has drunk too much the night before, and adds, "Celibacy is beginning to tell on me." He complains that she hasn't, as she had promised, sent "a scenic postcard for Rosalind," and when she (whose friends recalled her love for elegant clothes and jewelry) cashes all the checks he had given her at once—instead of doing so one by one—he is "down to my last dollar."

In August his spirits were lifted by an excursion to Madison, Wisconsin, to see his older cousin Dorothy Mendenhall, a Victorian feminist who was a doctor as well as married and the mother of sons. He wrote to Mary, "I had long conversations with her on politics, academic affairs, Gertrude

Stein [her classmate in medical school], Auden and Co., marriage and child rearing, and the family [the various branches who had summered in Talcottville]—about whom she is more illuminating than anybody but myself. She is always worrying for fear the women aren't leading their own lives." He adds, "She keeps a marvellous house with marvellous meals—the most attractive house I have seen for ages—I wish we had one like it: big and rambling and all the downstairs rooms with doors that open onto gardens, sloping lawns, moonlight in the trees." This aspiration would be partially realized when, in 1941, he bought a handsome old house at Cape Cod, once owned by a horticulturalist and with a well-designed garden of trees and perennial shrubs. During Mary's later summers in Castine, Maine, she would live elegantly in a large Federal-style house built in 1805.

They had borrowed the Dos Passos place on the harbor in Provincetown for a night or two the previous summer, and thinking of his past on the Cape, "a past when I had actually been much less happy than I now was," he'd experienced "unexpected nostalgia." Bored by Chicago and academic gossip, he suggested they spend the fall with "real live air and water, instead of the flatness of the lake and the oppressive inland climate—and the Dos Passoses, Walkers, Bishops, instead of the English faculty." Polly Boyden, a wealthy Chicago radical, offered them her three-story summer home at Truro for the fall and winter. The exiles Nina and Paul Chavchavadze, she the daughter of a grand duke and a cousin of the last tsar, he the son of a Georgian prince, lived in Truro, and Nina—a Romanov wearing jeans, with her cigarette holder and completely American English—was soon helping Wilson learn Russian. He was congenial with Chauncey Hackett—whose wife, Mary ("Bubs"), would describe her husband as a blocked writer—and the composer-pianist Gardner Jencks. Wilson was disappointed when such friends didn't produce the work they were capable of, but he enjoyed them and could try out his ideas on them. Though McCarthy would satirize the artistic failures of the Cape in *A Charmed Life*, she too felt at ease in this bohemia, liking the mix of radicals and literary types, European exiles and people of old American stock, who ranged from penniless to moderately well off.

Wilson threw himself into the Dickens essay, and was so absorbed in the subject that three weeks after leaving Chicago he informed W. W. Norton, to whom he thought he'd sold *The Wound and the Bow*, that he'd written twenty-five thousand words with a point of view on the novelist "more or less new" and "partly based on materials unknown to the general reader." The next spring "Dickens and the Marshalsea Prison" and "Dickens: The Two Scrooges" were published in *The Atlantic Monthly* and *The New Republic* respectively, and he would put them together along with new material in his collection of essays. In November he went to New York "for the purpose," he wrote to Zabel, "of shaking down editors and publishers," an effort that failed, he said because (a diagnosis revealing Wilson's premises) "they have ceased to make any pretense of being interested in publishing books, but talk wistfully about religion and the fate of the human race."

Charles Walker and his beautiful wife, Adelaide, lived nearby in Wellfleet. Wilson's old friend was no longer an orthodox Communist— "Charley and Adelaide were Trotskyists—it was adorable!" McCarthy lightly recalled without mentioning this was true of many in their circle, herself included. Wilson now had his reservations about "the old man" (as Trotsky's adherents sometimes called him), but he and Mary collaborated on verses satirizing Stalin's devious attempt to ally Russia with the Vatican in Spain, published in *PR* and signed "E. W. and M. McC." They made a foursome with the Walkers. Charley was a great gentleman and Mary liked Adelaide, who had much common sense and was exotic on two grounds, for having been born in Laramie, Wyoming, and as the former love of Harry Crosby, the expatriate whose flamboyant suicide in the Hotel des Artistes in New York ends Cowley's *Exile's Return*. She had been chair of the American Trotskyist party in 1936. Wilson learned from them of the house less than a quarter of a mile away which he acquired the next year. To a correspondent he affably wrote, "We came right up here from the West and hope to stay here more or less permanently."

He was engaged in a defining intellectual struggle. The man who since college had determinedly immersed himself in the present now plumbed the past in pursuit of truth, equity, and artistic meaning—values that were interdependent in his mind, as they are in *The Triple Thinkers*, *The Wound and the Bow*, and *To the Finland Station*. The domestic routine of the two writers is sketched in his journal. At Truro, "if the weather was good enough, we went out for a walk with the baby and pushed the carriage up and down the hills." In a tone redolent of Hemingway he adds, "We had a drink every day at five and some nights we kept on drinking in the evening. At noon we went for the mail. We subscribed to a number of magazines and read them all very carefully and sent for things that were advertised in them." They went to the movies in Provincetown "whenever there promised to be anything a little better than Charley Chan."

He and McCarthy had each married an idealized image of the other. When angry they became polarized, but Adelaide remembered that "when we first knew them at Truro and Wellfleet, Mary was still loving to Edmund, though for her that would be erased by time." She came to this union fresh from the heady experience of establishing herself as a critic, and was already being recognized for her fiction. She had an independent professional competence, a delightful son whom they adored, and a famous husband whose work excited her more than she admitted later on. Wilson was determined to make their union succeed and to foster Mary's fiction. He told friends she might be "the woman Stendhal" and made plans to move her career ahead.

When the spring of 1940 came, and *To the Finland Station* was finished, he and Mary stood together on a blustery March night at an upstairs window in Truro regarding the moon, "the inky clouds driven rapidly across it, showing their silver hems as they passed, and then the bright complete white (blinding) moon showing through the dark gauze fringe and swimming clear, complete and bright again," with "the wind of March that meant, after all, that winter was over, blowing past us." For Wilson it was like the winds of March at Stamford after their wedding, "sweeping the mists and the damp and the grayness away." With an effort to do justice to the differences between himself and his young wife, he writes, "The moon remained fixed and supreme. Mary said she always thought it was moving—I always thought it was standing still."

16

The Writing and Acting of History:
Wilson on Karl Marx

To the Finland Station, published in September 1940, is the biography of an idea, the idea that society can be remade by men in accord with human aspiration. It is a history of the effort to do so between the end of the French Revolution and the October Revolution in Russia. Like the historians Michelet, Gibbon, and Macaulay, whom in other ways he resembles, Wilson is engaged in the cause he chronicles. The belief of his characters that the flow of events has direction and meaning is echoed as he re-creates their struggles. These people speak to us from memoirs, journals, letters, and their own histories and polemic, like those in *Patriotic Gore*, his study of the literature of the American Civil War. Often noble, *Finland Station*'s radicals are marked by their mortality—flawed or ill-fated, limited by the world they seek to change. The art historian Meyer Schapiro noted how Wilson seizes on a trait and heightens it: "the writer's costume, his manner of speech, his imagery, his room are all appropriated as expressive signs, and fitted into a larger pattern of the personality which emerges in the ideas and actions as well." Schapiro likens these portraits, rooted in fact and document, to "the great fictional characters of literature."

The portrait of Lenin is an idealization that lingered. From family memoirs and his visit to the cultivated home at Ulyanovsk, Wilson renders the future leader's boyhood as a charming idyll of the provinces. Yet he doesn't allow for the effect of the hanging of Lenin's idolized older brother, followed by his own banishment from society, his admission to the universities contingent on a humiliating surveillance. The interpreter of such scarred creators as Housman and Chapman notes Lenin's occasional spontaneous bitterness of speech without seeing how it mirrored these experiences. His victimization as a member of a former cultivated elite as well as the pain of his brother's fate was absorbed and sublimated with a masochistic vengeance through Marx's doctrine of class hatred.

Though Wilson no longer sees the man as a great humanist, registering "the repetitiousness of Lenin's political writing and his monotonous addiction to a vein of rather flat-footed Marxist invective," he will not judge a revolutionary statesman by his polemics. His Lenin is deeply practical, understanding what the people want and the fragility of the tsardom. He molds rebels who were long confined in prison cells or in the gloom of the Arctic Circle into the disciplined force that destroyed the old regime. It would be decades before the American knew that for every revolutionary for whom Lenin was a charismatic leader there was another who detested his contemptuous dismissal of opposition, or that he created the secret police, and telegrammed colleagues addressing a difficult situation that they should "SHOOT MORE PROFESSORS." When Stalin suppressed this source material, what was left were witnesses who wore rose-colored glasses. Krupskaya told how her husband loved the people, and Gorky of his comrade's regret at having to put aside Beethoven's *Appassionata* to write some letters in a world it was his duty to change. Gorky reported that Lenin admired the hunt scene in *War and Peace*, and Wilson adds that he once refused to shoot a fox because it was "beautiful." In a letter complimenting Wilson on his Marx portrait, Vladimir Nabokov, newly arrived in the United States, wryly noted of his Lenin, "Pity that Russia was homely."

In the early thirties Trotsky had seemed to Wilson the intellectual as man of action, but his personal flaws were more visible than Lenin's, and this is a balanced portrait. He follows the young revolutionary through the explosive events of 1905, when as de facto leader of the St. Petersburg Soviet, Trotsky challenged the tsar for fifty days, and recounts some of his great speeches. He relates Trotsky's brilliant role in the civil wars, a record Stalin did everything to expunge. The man who rallied the Red armies, however, displayed "the terrific force of a will to domination and regimentation with no evidence of any sympathy for the hardships of the dominated and regimented." Unable, as Lenin did, to identify himself with the dispossessed, Trotsky depended on a Byronic sense of self, on the role of "the aristocrat of revolution." At his expense rather than Lenin's, Wilson admits that the Bolsheviks' actions in 1917 contravened Marx and

Engels, who "had usually described the dictatorship of the proletariat as having the form, for the new dominant class, of a democratic republic, with universal suffrage and the popular recall of officials." He points out that "the slogan 'All power to the Soviets' had never really meant what it said and that it had soon been exchanged by Lenin for 'All power to the Bolshevik Party.'" When consigning Martov and the other Mensheviks to history's rubbish heap, Trotsky invoked the Marxist version of a religious Providence. Also rejected is the double standard with which, writing in exile, he endorsed for progressive purposes the lying and killing he condemned in conservatives.

Wilson's sense, by the decade's end, of the American Trotskyists as futile sectarians sharpened his perspective on their "old man," and the trials had undermined his account of the October Revolution before he got to it. His last pages follow Lenin from Germany through Finland to the shabby little "tarnished pink" railroad station in the city then called Petrograd where the Bolshevik leader took control of events in Marx's name. Completing the book as he had planned, Wilson tells us that writing and acting history have at last been unified, that "Western man at this moment can be seen to have made some definite progress in mastering the greeds and the fears, the bewilderments, in which he has lived." The affirmation of "some definite progress" is equivocal, Stalin's dark figure already seen in the wings. Yet the failure of the quest has enriched *To the Finland Station*. The final sentiment Wilson takes from Lenin's wife Krupskaya, "Everything was understood without words," for his readers acquires irony and depth. A grim age was opening for Russia but the human hope would persevere.

Marx and Engels are the heart of *To the Finland Station*. The psychological and moral insight as well as the dramatic coherence of this shared portrait gives the book an authority after the fall of communism equal to that when Ulyanovsk, the site of Lenin's family home, was a favorite destination of cruise ships. Marx, like Lenin, is seen through a passage from Hegel's *Philosophy of History* cited in these pages, defining the "world-historical men," leaders alert to "what was ripe for development," able to know "the necessary, directly sequent step in progress, which their world was to take; to make this their aim, and to expend their energy in promoting it." Wilson would still be wrestling with Lenin's failure to understand which way the world was going in the introduction to *Patriotic Gore* in 1962, but he can separate Marx the thinker and writer from the Russian Revolution made in his name almost four decades after his death.

"He who first saw and said that man advanced on his belly—he himself had risen upright," Wilson had expansively stated at the end of *Travels in Two Democracies*. In *Finland Station* he takes a discriminating look at Marx's heroic figure. The intellectual strengths and weaknesses, the sacrifices and the perversities of the Father of Communism make these 250 pages an emblem of the artist-thinker's role in humanity's halting progress.

Wilson doesn't reduce communism, as Emerson said of history, to "the lengthened shadow of a man." The Marx-Engels system fused "the philosophies of three great countries, the ideas of both the working-class and the cultured," the work of "all the agitators, the politicians, the newspaper writers; the pamphlets, the conversations," the implications of "half-unconscious thoughts" and "unthinking instincts." Yet Marx was its creator. In him Wilson sees the prophetic role of generations of rabbis crossed with an eighteenth-century rationalism and the romantic will. Through the dark images of Marx's student poetry to Jenny von Westphalen, passed over by other biographers as pedestrian romantic angst, he evokes a restless soul who would share the pain of his life with Jenny and Friedrich Engels.

Engels filled in "the blank face and figure of Marx's abstract proletarian." He is viewed as the ideal collaborator, with less drive and a less trenchant mind than Marx but "flexible, lively, and active." Wilson sympathizes with this urbane youth who "grew up in a cage of theology" and under his father's control, then became a manager in the Manchester mills and kept a working-class mistress while he documented the miseries of labor. Marx's moral conviction and intellectual strength helped Engels "to keep his compass straight in his relation to that contemporary society whose crimes he understood so well, but out of which he himself had grown and to which he was still organically bound." Their partnership was founded on the belief that history had a meaning and plot, that the suffering and injustice they described could be overcome by writing and action. Wilson shows what it felt like to share these convictions.

Wilson later confessed his difficulties with the Hegelian background, due both to impatience with theory and to his limited German. "The deicide principle in Marx rebelled against the Absolute Idea," he says, making Marx's divergence from Hegel too much like his own rejection of Christianity. As a democrat he doesn't like the way Marx went about his "historical task" of destroying the old utopian abstractions—his condescension to Wilhelm Weitling, the self-educated tailor who stirred up the populace in the name of Justice, Solidarity, and Brotherly Love; and his intolerant attack on the French socialist Proudhon. For Wilson, Marx is at his best when Engels's "candor and humanity" qualify his fierce abstraction. The statement of the theory of class struggle in *The Communist Manifesto* is such a collaboration. Both men took bold parts in the failed revolutions of 1848. Afterward Engels fled on foot through France to Switzerland, his appetite for life refreshed by encounters with villagers and farmers. His vivid notes on the trip are contrasted to Marx's somber letters at the start of his long, impoverished exile in London. "Doomed to suffer and to make others suffer, he must forge on against the happiness of those he loves, against the course of natural human activity, against the ebb-tide of history itself, toward a victory which is to be also a tragedy," Wilson writes, allowing for the fact that the hero's struggle will be in some sense futile and history turn out to have been flowing in the wrong channel.

Several generations of readers of *Finland Station* have been moved by the account of Karl and Jenny Marx and their family in Soho. There were Sunday outings on Hampstead Heath with good food when they could afford it and happy songs on the way home. The couple would take turns at Shakespeare, and Marx recited *Faust* and *The Divine Comedy*. His motto was "*Nihil humani a me alienem puto*," and his and Engels's aspiration to lead the lives of Renaissance men entered into communism. Yet the Marxes often lived on bread and potatoes, and the dirty, cluttered apartment where the patriarch played games with his daughters could be a painful place. After he entertained the youngest of these with a fantasy of a better world than they knew, "she seemed to go into a trance" and improvised a kind of poem about another life on the stars. Jenny mourned the ill health of their son, who "drank in from me so much secret sorrow and grief with the milk that he was constantly unwell, lay in violent pain night and day." Her nerves gave way when the boy died from one of the infections rampant in the neighborhood—she'd indeed tasted "the poisoned cup" that the lover in Marx's youthful verse presents to his beloved. Twenty years later Marx couldn't bear to walk through this part of London.

This tableau sets off the insights of *The Eighteenth Brumaire* and *The Class Struggles in France*, books that, when Wilson went Left, had revealed to him the clashing interests behind "the old sport of competition for office, the old game of political debate." Marx's precision and his eloquence could "turn the collapse of an incompetent parliament, divided between contradictory tendencies, into the downfall of a damned soul of Shakespeare." Like Swift, another satirist of human self-interest, he "could get a certain poetry out of money," regarding it as the greatest of those commodity fetishes that negated human relations. Wilson has been called brilliant on Marx's economic theory in *Das Kapital*, and he shows how the theoretical, sometimes mathematical chapters are fleshed out with graphic reports on the misery and filth of the working class, the stratagems of employers raising their profit margins while equating laissez-faire economics with moral law.

In 1938, however, Wilson repudiated the dialectic. The critic Paul Berman has stressed the importance for *To the Finland Station* of Max Eastman's debate with Sidney Hook about the philosophical difficulties of Marxism, Wilson coming down on Eastman's side. But like Eastman, he later ceased to believe that Marx's socialism was scientific, retreating into an Anglo-American skepticism. As other New York intellectuals did, Wilson grants Marx's thesis, antithesis, and synthesis their value as metaphors, suggesting how one era emerged from another and giving statesmen the confidence to act. Yet the dialectic became for him a religious myth, a secular Providence displacing "man's conscious creative will." A convert could be deluded that history guaranteed certain results: thus the German Social Democrats, sure of the socialist future, had taken their nation's side in the world war that postponed this, perhaps indefinitely; so too did the Communists acquiesce "in the despotism of Stalin while he was uprooting Russian Marxism itself." Appended to the first edition of *Finland Station* is a satiric little "Prolet-Play" in which a purge-mad Marx destroys his enemies with the dialectic, which turns out to be a revolver, dropping his mask to show Stalin's smiling face.

What enabled Wilson to discount these "Germanic" abstractions was the conviction that Marx's true authority was moral. Although Marx was an atheist who considered the Jews moneylenders and usury the essence of capitalism, Wilson saw him drawing on his heritage, reviving the fervid vision and righteous wrath of the Old Testament. This hardly Marxist interpretation relies on Taine's categories of the moment, the race, and the milieu. "Nobody but a Jew in that middle nineteenth century could have commanded the moral weapons to crack the fortress of bourgeois self-satisfaction," Wilson declares, relating Marx's prophetic leadership to the emergence of the rabbinical tradition from the ghetto. "Nobody but a Jew could have fought so uncompromisingly and obstinately for the victory of the dispossessed classes." Wilson could identify with Marx via his own preacher ancestors, who had thought themselves spiritual descendants of the children of Israel. The Father of Communism was "the great secular rabbi of the 19th-century." Such a characterization freed the American critic to observe the holes in Marx's doctrine, as he fills one with fury against the wickedness of capitalists who are doing what he calls history's work. Expecting the proletariat to act on behalf of the good of humanity, Marx turns them into a Chosen People who will emancipate society along with themselves, though the workers lacked Jewish intellectual and moral discipline much as they did the property and education of the bourgeoisie. The prophetic role is entwined with a delusive mythology.

Wilson interrupts Marx's story for those of two colorful individuals who embody political alternatives often faced on the Left. Ferdinand Lassalle was a radical working within the establishment. He had energy, versatility, shrewdness, as well as idealism (he too, Wilson notes, was of Jewish descent) and an eloquence capable of manipulating juries and public opinion. For a time his program, including state aid for workers' associations, fit well with Bismarck's forging of a strong Germany under Prussian leadership. Wilson sympathetically relates the disappointments of Lassalle's later years, which he spent trying to extract concessions for the working class from the "blood and iron" Germany that was emerging. Habitually proud, Lassalle often overplayed his hand, and when an amour led to a challenge that he could not honorably refuse he was shot in the stomach, dying four days later of peritonitis.

While Marx's jealous pride prevented a close alliance with Lassalle, who wanted to install him as editor of a large German newspaper, more profound differences separated him and Engels from Mikhail Bakunin. A Russian aristocrat with an exhilarating, compelling personality and a genius for popular oratory, Bakunin was sentenced to eight years in prison after impulsively joining, alongside Richard Wagner, in a German rebellion against the king of Saxony. Led out, like Dostoevsky, supposedly for execution, he was handed over to the Austrians and eventually, in his words, "buried alive" in the Peter-Paul Fortress in St. Petersburg. When exiled to Siberia, Wilson says, he "sped away like a genie let out of his bottle," returning to Europe via Japan, San Francisco, and New York. Bakunin concluded that any social transformation must be international to be effective, and set up underground organizations in the less industrialized countries of Italy and Spain. Eventually he argued for the eradication of the entire state through alliance with "recalcitrant" and criminal elements, in a revolutionary catechism that looked forward to more than one variety of late-twentieth and twenty-first-century terrorism. On his deathbed he repudiated politics along with the inertia of the masses, grandly declaring, "Everything will pass, and the world will perish, but the Ninth Symphony will remain."

In the evolutionary vision of *To the Finland Station* a series of self-chosen individuals receive from their predecessors the idea of re-creating the social world and project it onto the conditions around them, but it is two steps forward, one step back. At the heart of the portrait that dominates this book, Marx is seen to internalize the exploitative relations of his society even as he forwards a vision of fundamental human rights. The moralist who excoriates capitalists and grimly parades the afflictions of the poor draws on his family's sufferings and the guilt involved in his capacity to use people. In 1940 scholars didn't know that Marx fathered a child by his family's maid, Lenchen, as Wilson points out in the 1971 introduction to *Finland Station*, but he notes Marx's sacrifice of Jenny to his work, gentle and kind as he tried to be to her. Wilson's damning insight is into Marx's inability to face up to the nature of his relationship with Engels. Since Marx refused to write for money—declaring the writer's endeavors *"ends in themselves"*—Engels had to keep his father's business going in order to keep Marx going. Another source of income was the articles Engels wrote in Marx's name for a New York newspaper. Marx excused himself because he was uneasy writing in English, then nagged and directed like a man with more important things to do. Wilson stresses the bitter solipsism of his letters to Engels after the death of Engels's mistress, Mary Burns. He didn't go to the funeral, and his clumsy efforts to apologize and acknowledge his partner's loss soon returned to his own afflictions, to "reveries about what it would be like to be blind or mad."

Marx sometimes imagined himself as Job, plagued by illnesses though steadfast, and famously hoped the bourgeoisie would have cause to regret his carbuncles. Not limiting himself to Jewish martyrdom, he also saw himself a Satan who defiantly refused to submit, and his deepest identification was with Prometheus: "a Satan who suffers, a Job who never assents," but instead "brings liberation to mankind." Yet Wilson shows how "his outraged conviction of the indignity and injustice of his own fate" was bound up with "his bad conscience at having inflicted that fate on others." This reading of Marx's character is supported by an account of his sado-masochistic imagery. The brilliant Marx of the 1850s kept returning to "cruel discomfort, rape, repression, mutilation and massacre, premature burial, the stalking of corpses, the vampire that lives on another's blood, life in death and death in life," while the vast theoretical web of *Kapital* was "unrelievedly saturnine." On this level Marx loathed himself and hated his ugly life.

Wilson describes something more complex than sublimation. Marx "found in his personal experience the key to the larger experience of society" and identified himself "with that society." In a formulation recalling Lukács's argument that the proletariat are uniquely qualified to understand the industrial system because they experience and internalize it, the critic concludes, "Only so sore and angry a spirit, so ill at ease in the world, could have recognized and seen into the causes of the wholesale mutilation of humanity, the grim collisions, the uncomprehended convulsions, to which that age of great profits was doomed." Hegel's world-historical man who grasps the deeper movement of events is here seen through Taine's image of Musset the suffering artist, and the romantic agony transferred from the garret to the psyche via Freud.

The New Critics charged that biographical criticism can obscure and eclipse the text, and biographers have often proved them correct. As Wilson, however, states in this passage, "the importance of a book depends not merely on the breadth of the view and the amount of information that has gone into it, but on the depths from which it has been drawn." He too was in some respects a sore and angry spirit, beleaguered and ill at ease in the world. He too had thrilled to Prometheus's defiance, and in 1962, suffering what he believed to be a heart attack, he would stand behind a desk on the third floor at 12 Hilliard Street in Cambridge, Massachusetts, denouncing God for bringing him low before he finished his task. This sense of mission was set off against the failures of his personal life. His memories of his confused marriage with Mary Blair were guilty ones, and Margaret Canby, whom he'd fallen in love with after her death, haunted him in dreams, while the harmony Mary McCarthy and he tried to maintain could collapse at any time. His poverty, though scarcely comparable to Marx's, was galling (he unsuccessfully tried to sell the manuscript of *To the Finland Station* to the Yale Library for $300). He entered into Marx's dark inner life, much as Marx identified himself with the life of the industrial age. Reviewing *Finland Station*, Sidney Hook, author of a philosophical study of Marxism, declared that there was "nothing in any language which equals the insight, the eloquence, and the essential justice" of this characterization, an opinion Hook maintained four decades later, after several biographies of Marx and after taking a sharply different political position during the Cold War than Wilson's. So responsive was Wilson to Marx that when writing this book he broke out in boils like those that afflicted the Father of Communism.

Of *Kapital* Wilson states, "The great crucial books of human thought—outside what are called the exact sciences, and perhaps something of the sort is true even here—always render articulate the results of fundamental new experiences to which human beings have had to adjust themselves." This pragmatism is not the only respect in which *To the Finland Station*, even though its subject is European history, is a native product, as the British critic V. S. Pritchett pointed out: "Again and again its sudden queer asides, its touches of vernacular pugnacity, its minuteness, and—for that matter—its shrewdness, piety, and good will mark it as deeply American." It was the most significant imaginative work to come out of the thirties in the United States except for several of Faulkner's novels. In his plainspoken fashion Wilson dramatizes the will to establish a society in which privilege isn't paid for by the exploitation of others, "a society which will be homogeneous and cooperative as our commercial society is not, and directed, to the best of their ability, by the conscious creative minds of its members."

Nowhere on the continent of Europe did a humanistic social revolution seem remotely possible as he completed the work. To Cowley in 1938 he wrote, "Did you see the interview with Stalin in *Liberty*, in which he invokes Peter the Great, Napoleon, and even Napoleon III, washes his hands of Spain and China, and returns a non-committal answer to a question about an alliance with Hitler?" The nonaggression pact between Russia and Germany followed, and the two nations soon divided Poland. What had happened to the Russian Revolution owed something, Wilson realized, to Marx's doctrine of class hatred and his deification of history. Yet Marx had grasped the destructive effects of the Industrial Revolution, the explosive force of capitalism, "bringing the people of distant cultures, at diverse stages of civilization, into its system" and inexorably destroying the more primitive but less alienated arrangements of previous societies. By helping people to detect their economic and class interests, he made it easier for them to reject the suffering of their fellows. Wilson would hold to Marx's belief that the dream of a better world must be matched with diagnosis and plan.

Before Marx died he struggled from his daybed to sit down at his work table, just as Wilson would in 1972 on the morning of his death. Rounding out a portrait that would remain his most powerful, Wilson traces the ramifications in Marx's family of his dedication to the revolution, including the unhappy adjustments and eventual suicides of two of his daughters. He describes how loyal, brave-hearted Engels made little of a painful death of throat cancer, leaving his money to the Party and to Marx's children. In this fashion Wilson elevates his characters while seeking the truth about their lives, and his summations project something of his own effort. When beginning *Finland Station* he wrote of Michelet, "He worked at night and made the centuries of the dead keep him company and lend him their strength and faith that he might wake strength and faith in the living." When ending it he wrote of Marx, "Out of the brooding and laboring thought comes an instrument that is also a weapon in the actual world of men."

17

1940: Wilson's Middle of the Journey

Wilson rejects in *Finland Station* Marx's capacity to envision communism as "an exclusive and relentless class despotism directed by high-minded bigwigs" like Engels and himself and hopes the United States will work out a form of socialism with safeguards to prevent it from becoming authoritarian. He is pleased to discover again the resilience of his own country, where, despite vast inequalities of wealth, the money is always changing hands and "we have the class quarrel out as we go along." FDR's experimentation, of which he had been so skeptical, had won for the government the power to regulate public utilities and mitigate the business cycle. In periods when the economy was strong Americans could enjoy what in Soviet Russia and fascist Germany the state had engaged to provide—a home with technological conveniences; sports, movies, inexpensive travel; "social services—hospitals, libraries, roads," plus—a very big plus—they had free movement and free speech, which other people would learn to want and would one day get. Wilson understood that the sprawling state-controlled economies would eventually have to respond to the appetite for political freedom as well as for consumer goods. But he didn't point out that at the end of the 1930s (and of the New Deal) the unemployment rate was still 14 percent. It would take the war that a majority of his countrymen, until Pearl Harbor, resisted, a war during which more than 400,000 of them would be killed, to bring about full employment in the United States.

"The body of this book belongs to 1934, while the soul is struggling to be the soul of 1940," a reviewer wrote of *Finland Station*, published as Stalinist Communism was discredited among the intellectuals and the conflict in Europe pressed more heavily on American concerns. Cowley noted the book's contradictions, balancing them against Wilson's command of detail and quotation. Others questioned his approach by way of Michelet and the French critics or noted his lack of authority about German philosophy, but there was general praise for his insight into character and the force and grace of his prose, reviving the tradition of history as an imaginative art. Wallace Stevens, whom young Wilson had shallowly seen as the pure aesthete, recommended the book to a friend, and Auden, in a review, observed that the portraits drew on the author's sense of self, writing, "Mr. Wilson brings out time and again the moral passion of his heroes, and every line he writes bears witness to his own." Sales would be slow during the war, but in the 1950s a new generation committed to social progress, though unsympathetic to communism, discovered revolutionary history through the Anchor paperback, and the book did still better during the 1960s.

Relieved that the "interminable" project was done, Wilson turned to the essays of *The Wound and the Bow*, in various states of completion. It was an easy step from his Marx, and that portrait can be imagined anchoring a collection of his work on wounds and bows. It could be framed by the psychological studies of Housman and Chapman in *The Triple Thinkers* and by Dickens, Kipling, and Sophocles' *Philoctetes* from the new collection. Wilson does not propose, as some believe, that art originates in neurosis, but in all this work a Freudian awareness enters into his understanding of the relationship between the personal life and creation.

"Dickens: The Two Scrooges" is his most widely read literary essay. The critic who expounds the symbolism of Joyce and Proust and looks at capitalism through Marx's eyes gives Dickens a new vitality for modern tastes. He seizes on twelve-year-old Charles's abandonment in the blacking factory, at the time when his family lived in the Marshalsea debtors' prison. Showing how this introduction to despair and social humiliation darkened the novelist's plots, Wilson follows Dickens's work from a nostalgic re-creation of merry England to stringent parables in which an ideal of virtue is thrust to the margins of society. Dickens's laughter, though "never vulgar," he states, "discloses the vulgarity of the revered" and "represents, like the laughter of Aristophanes, a real escape from institutions." Yet from the beginning "it is an exhilaration tainted by hysteria. It leaps free of the prison of life; but gloom and soreness must always drag it back." The second half of this portrait explores a divided personality that sometimes approaches the manic-depressive. Wilson follows Dickens's double life between different women and households and shows how his sympathy with the rebel shifts to the criminal, how his protest against the world becomes a struggle with self in the unfinished *Mystery of Edwin Drood*.

Marriage to McCarthy had alerted Wilson to the possible role of childhood oppression in creativity. Mary's sense of abandonment when her grandparents rejected her after her parents' deaths is echoed in his account of young Dickens's feeling of desertion, while her sinister experience at the hands of Aunt Margaret and Uncle Myers helped him understand the "bitter animus" Rudyard Kipling incurred through the six years he and his sister spent with cruel foster parents. McCarthy particularly admired "The Kipling That Nobody Read," in the Plutarchan sense a parallel portrait to the Dickens. If, as she said, Wilson discussed all his work with her, they surely compared the Englishman's "Aunty" and his uncle to hers.

The two essays investigate the literary use of such psychic scars, and each is premised on the antagonism between serious art and established power. Wilson shows how Kipling's harsh childhood fueled his youthful rebellion as the bard of the ordinary British soldier and the India interpreted in *Kim*. Yet he turned out to lack the courage and social insight that made Dickens "the poet of that portiered and cloistered world who saw clearest through the coverings and the curtains." Wealth and fame deprived him of the ability to sympathize with those of differing race or station, and propelled by his nation's history, he became a voice of British imperialism. He came to think of Americans, whom he'd once idealized, as barbarians and denounced them for relinquishing their country to immigrant hordes. And as Kipling's hostility turned from the foster parents by whom "it was originally aroused" to scapegoats and outsiders, this gifted literary technician who influenced everyone from Joyce to Hemingway and Lardner grew less able to explore dramatic conflict; in the subjects of his fiction, Henry James observed, he progressed steadily "to the more simple." Wilson's portrait expands well beyond this thesis: with a few reviews of Kipling to draw upon, he explores little-known work and judges several later stories to be classics. The sense of what was lost in the writer's inablity to challenge his society is deepened.

During the 1920s, when Fitzgerald's insouciant manner had masked his emerging brilliance as a novelist, Wilson was a surer judge of Hemingway, and he surveys the development of the author of *In Our Time* and *The*

Sun Also Rises in the essay initially called "Ernest Hemingway: Bourdon Gauge of Morale." The extraordinary gulf between first- and second-rate Hemingway suggests to Wilson (what became an influential idea) that his ego and his personal emotions undermine his perfect control of line. Wilson cites the overwrought love scenes of *A Farewell to Arms*, the juvenile aspect of the Spanish play *The Fifth Column*, whose hero, when not with a Vassar girl in his tent, bags men he labels fascists, and Harry Morgan's unbelievable feats in *To Have and Have Not*—he calls Morgan a Popeye without the spinach. Hemingway unsuccessfully applied a sophisticated fictional technique to autobiography in *Death in the Afternoon*, and "the publicity Hemingway" took over in *Green Hills of Africa*. Meanwhile he produced such fine stories as the African tales. For Wilson "The Snows of Kilimanjaro" and "The Short Happy Life of Francis Macomber" caught a new tension in American sexual relations. Just as Edna ("Vincent") Millay and her lovers had underlined the truth of the portrait of Brett Ashley in *The Sun Also Rises*, so living with Mary, even in their better early years, made Margot Macomber as the bitch-wife from Hell more than a paranoid fantasy. Wilson sees that Hemingway's fear of women feeds an impulse to dominate.

This is not a biographical study like the Dickens and Kipling. While noting the terror, first confronted in "Big Two-Hearted River," of a world the protagonist cannot control, Wilson doesn't point out that Hemingway's father killed himself, a fact that had been widely reported. He had never taken Gauss's injunction to tell the truth no matter whom it hurt as applying to people's private lives. But to receive such a "combing"—a word Wilson sometimes used—from the man who'd called attention to the strength of his first work infuriated Hemingway, and when the novelist learned that this essay in *The Atlantic Monthly* was part of a volume now set to be published by Scribner's, he protested, and eventually threatened a libel suit. Robert Linscott, his editor, recalled that the novelist could find nothing to base it on except that Wilson spoke of him "wearing an open shirt and holding up a huge fish" in the same photograph, when two different photographs were in question. However, Scribner's, afraid they'd lose their star, asked Wilson to omit the essay and, when he refused, they broke their contract. Retaining a considerable advance, he sent the collection to Houghton Mifflin. When Hemingway threatened an injunction against Houghton Mifflin, minor factual issues were hashed out with a lawyer.

In letters to others Hemingway sneered at Wilson for not spelling out his wound, saying that his father had "shot himself" and "I did not care, overly, for my mother." Wilson could also have pointed out, he said, that he himself had been shot nine times. But this account of the career to 1940 has survived to correct a reductive biographical criticism Hemingway would have disliked a good deal more, some of it laboring the concern with homosexuality in the unfinished, posthumously published novels. Wilson reaffirmed the major fiction. In a postscript on *For Whom the Bell Tolls*—adapted from a brilliant, little-known review—he praises the book's political honesty but notes "an infusion of the operatic, that lends itself all too readily to the movies."

"Justice to Edith Wharton" is less ambitious than its title. Without going back to Wharton's important early novels, he comments on her bluestocking devotion to culture, her use of furnishings and settings, her Puritan insistence that one face ugly facts, and her resentment of the cultivated male characters who let her heroines down. Yet he lacks information to understand the wound that others have sensed in Wharton but no one has convincingly defined. During the 1950s Wilson would be persuaded by the rumor, endorsed by her closest friend, that she was illegitimate, an explanation that has been replaced, in the twenty-first century, by the otherwise unsupported allegation, on the basis of the fragment "Beatrice Palmato," that she was a victim of paternal sexual abuse. Wilson links Wharton's escape to France from an unhappy marriage and a husband who eventually went insane to the decline of her steely prose and intelligence after *The Age of Innocence*. It has been noted that a similar falling off occurred in the later fiction of Mary McCarthy, after such an easing of emotional stress. McCarthy was, however, more the critic than the creator and continued to write excellent nonfiction.

Of the other essays in *The Wound and the Bow*, "Uncomfortable Casanova" is a neglected account of a figure of the Enlightenment against whom Wilson implicitly measures himself. He sees Casanova the intellectual undermined by the philanderer's cheap and servile side, yet admires the honesty and realism of Casanova's journals, which were among his models for recording his own sex life. "The Dream of H. C. Earwicker," about *Finnegans Wake*, has much in common with Wilson's paraphrases of Proust and of Pushkin's *Eugene Onegin*. He recounts the structure, indebted to Vico, of Joyce's grand attempt to derive the history of the race from the impulses, conscious and dormant, the unrealized potentialities of a single human being. Loyal to the author of *Ulysses* and distressed when its successor was read only by a clerisy of interpreters in graduate seminars, Wilson would keep coming back to the *Wake* and puzzling it out.

The myth of a wounded archer with a miraculous bow developed in the *Philoctetes* essay is flexible enough to apply to all the subjects of this book, including Joyce's dream novel. Harry Levin remembered reading the play aloud with Wilson and Robert Fitzgerald, translator of *The Odyssey* and of Sophocles. Fitzgerald was Philoctetes, Wilson Neoptolemus, while Levin took the part of Ulysses, who suggests they simply steal the bow. Wilson's identification with Neoptolemus went back to his hunger for a relationship with the father he'd liked to have rescued from behind the felt-lined door, and mirrored his insight into literary personalities. "Edmund penetrated beneath the surface in an extraordinary way," Isaiah Berlin said, and "had great emotional understanding of the writers he wrote about." He saw criticism forging the human connection with the artist-hero that, in the *Philoctetes* myth, must exist in order for society to acquire the bow. But his rationalistic assumption that one can read back to the painful experience from which a work springs does not accord with Freud's concepts of masking and repression. "I never meant to imply that all art was the result of disease or deformity," he told Lionel Trilling some years afterward, and did not "mean to limit to artists the phenomenon of a wound coexisting with a bow," though he happened "to have seen a good deal of the wound and bow combination." Implicit is the relationship of his own power to his personal confusions, to anger, pain, and loss. While Trilling, a stricter Freudian, in the essay "Art and Neurosis" points out that many people need therapy rather than the illusion that their wounds can make them artists, Wilson studies individuals whose neuroses are bound up with work of consequence and thus of practical use. Behind the romantic image of the artist's agony can at times be discerned the classical archetype of suffering and wisdom.

He finished the book in Truro during the summer of 1940, in a rented studio "half a mile through the woods on a narrow dirt path" where, Rosalind recalls, "either Mary or I took his lunch every day, prepared with perfection and trauma by Mary." That fall, as it went to press and *Finland Station* appeared, he moved with Mary and Reuel from the Cape to Stamford, commuting into New York for a stint at *The New Republic*. In three months that must be unique in the annals of the literary editors of political magazines, Wilson published a long poem by Auden, lyrics by Bogan and Louis MacNeice, a fine critical essay by Dos Passos, Richard Wright's review of Langston Hughes's autobiography, and several reviews apiece by

Tate, Randall Jarrell, Harry Levin, and one V. Nabokov, as well as pieces by Mary McCarthy, Dawn Powell, and others of his circle.

His own contribution was the series about California writers that became *The Boys in the Back Room*, which McCarthy later speculated was the result of a publisher's advance. "The boys" included John O'Hara, master of the *New Yorker* story, James M. Cain, one of the "poets of the tabloid murder" (a fan of *Finland Station*, Cain liked Wilson's account of his work), and Saroyan, whose writing gave one "the illusion of friendliness and muzzy elation and gentle sentimentality" people felt after a couple of drinks at their favorite bar. Steinbeck's characters in *The Grapes of Wrath*, Wilson shrewdly noted, "are animated and put through their paces rather than brought to life; they are like excellent character actors giving very conscientious performances in a fairly well-written play. Their dialect is well-managed, but they always sound a little stagy." What interested him in Steinbeck was the substratum of biology, the dimension of animal and vegetative life in human beings.

More impressive to Wilson artistically was the surrealist fantasy Nathanael West had moved from New York to California in *The Day of the Locust*. He had known West when the writer managed the Sutton Hotel in Manhattan during the 1930s, the background of *Miss Lonelyhearts*, which the critic considered his best novel. That was when Lillian Hellman—as she recalls to Wilson in *The Sixties*—used to help West "steam open the letters of the guests by means of a kettle which he kept in his rooms. He said that he was a novelist and that he had to find out about people." In *The Boys in the Back Room* Wilson calls *The Day of the Locust* the first novel to document the emptiness of Hollywood as "horrible," though West couldn't get to the cause of the malaise through his educated protagonist, who was "swirling around in the same aimless eddies as the others."

The New Republic had been caught up in the political currents stirred by the advance of Hitler in Europe and of the Japanese in Asia. Archibald MacLeish, the new Librarian of Congress, declared in a speech printed in the magazine that the United States could no longer afford the stance of the antiwar novels of Dos Passos and Hemingway, whose words disarmed democracy in the face of fascism. Wilson's stinging rejoinder noted that MacLeish had once said artists were not required "to bear arms" and "strictly forbidden to mix in maneuvers," and had written yearningly of the purity of "Dos" and "Ernest." Wondering how their skepticism of the war "to make the world safe for democracy" had been mistaken, Wilson smelled "a new set of political slogans, of 'declarations of moral purposes,' to be let loose from the same sort of sources which launched the publicity of World War I." He was ignorant that Roosevelt, while swearing there were no secret treaties, was now supplying British ships in the North Atlantic and was desperately trying to prepare the country to enter the war against Germany, aware that an incident could make it happen. But remembering how Woodrow Wilson, after pledging to keep the country out, had immediately "plunged us in," he wasn't reassured when the president campaigned for reelection on a platform of neutrality while his administration and its friends in the media kept up a drumbeat against the German menace.

Then came what Wilson always considered the betrayal of *The New Republic* by its owners. The editors had been guaranteed autonomy, but after FDR's November victory Leonard Elmhirst, the Englishman who, as Dorothy Straight's second husband, controlled the foundation that supported the magazine, arrived and imposed on the divided board a position favoring an alliance with the British empire. Bruce Bliven, the managing editor, who feared the loss of the foundation's subsidy, became his instrument. Wilson had hoped to persuade Elmhirst that the magazine needed to be reorganized under the leadership of "a more intelligent and competent person than Bruce," suggesting Soule, the economist. "I was heartily backed by everyone connected with the paper, with the exception, of course, of Bruce himself," he'd tell Trilling. To Kazin, however, he explained "I'm a terrible conspirator," for when Elmhirst met with Wilson the Englishman announced that Bliven was formally promoted to editor-in-chief, while Soule and Cowley were deprived of authority. They remained contributors, but a financial columnist named John T. Flynn, an Irish American who detested the British, was let go and Elmhirst published unsigned editorials, lightly revised by Bliven, proposing that the United States and Great Britain "jointly assume responsibility and leadership for the whole world, except that part of it at present under the heel of the totalitarians," a political line and tone so at variance with *The New Republic*'s usual ones as to make readers suspicious.

Wilson did not yet know his own position on the war. Some months before Pearl Harbor, in a long handwritten memo when *The New Republic* urged a declaration of war against the Axis, he noted that "whichever way we are going to decide" about this, the magazine's management was not disinterested. There is a legend that he tried to force his boss to register as the agent of a foreign power and was foiled by President Roosevelt, something quite possible given the old friendship of Eleanor with Elmhirst's wife, Dorothy. Recounting the takeover, in this memo he characterizes "Mr. E." as one of those "annoying Englishmen of good intentions but limited intelligence, who can see nothing improper in, etc," yet tells himself that "my natural sympathy with the English has survived the affair of the *NR*." The affair is sketched in *A Piece of My Mind* (1956). Upon Wilson's death in 1972 Bliven wrote to Leon Edel, "Neither of the Elmhirsts ever exerted any pressure whatever on the editors on any subject," asserting that he and George Soule "decided to advocate American entrance into the war." *After Long Silence* (1981), the autobiography of Michael Straight, Elmhirst's stepson, whom, on returning to England, he left in informal charge of the magazine, inclines to Wilson's version of events. Despite the pact "not to interfere in the management of *The New Republic*," Elmhirst had urged Bliven (and shocked Soule by so doing) to discard an approach to the war that "was both callous and timid."

Arthur Schlesinger, resisting the easy label of isolationist, groups Wilson with progressive Senator William Borah, conservative Colonel McCormick of the *Chicago Tribune*, publisher Oswald Garrison Villard, conservationist Amos Pinchot, Alice Roosevelt Longworth, the historian Charles A. Beard, the journalist Quincy Howe, "even perhaps Norman Thomas," perennial socialist candidate for president, as "twentieth-century nationalists." All these "old Americans," Schlesinger says—and George Kennan in some respects—maintained the stance of John Quincy Adams, who, in the line of the eighteenth-century revolutionaries, urged that the young Republic—though in "her heart" always on liberty's side—go "not abroad in search of monsters to destroy." Knowing no more about the millions of Russians already killed or sent to Siberia than about Germany's incipient destruction of the Jews, Wilson judged Stalin and Hitler equally monstrous. He was enough of a maverick on the Left to reject the preference of the White House for one dictator over the other, Soviet Russia over Nazi Germany.

When Hitler, discarding the Nazi-Soviet Pact, invaded the Soviet Union in June 1941, the Communist-influenced liberals, including many in Hollywood, began endorsing intervention. To Wilson *The New Republic* now spoke for a Stalinist-British alliance. Straight's revelation, in *After Long Silence* (1983), that he'd been recruited at Cambridge by the NKVD— the fifth man in the notorious group including Guy Burgess, Donald

MacLean, and Kim Philby, as well as Anthony Blunt—gives this charge a certain plausibility. Since 1938 his Soviet handler had been coming down from Brooklyn, Straight stringing the man along while he left the State Department for a position as a speechwriter for the president and others, where he was glad to have no secret information to provide to Michael Green. Opening a small D.C. office of *The New Republic* in 1941, he published long analyses of the issues involved in armaments production by onetime New Dealers, thereby, he would recall "pushing America toward war."* By this time, Wilson was back at the Cape. He doubted the Germans would conquer Russia, in a letter to a Russian friend four months after the invasion predicting, "Hitler will have to go home, like Napoleon." Yet he saw "the ebb-tide of history" sucking the United States from its prospects for a humane socialism into another world conflict. No economic determinist even during his Marxist phase, as he looked back on his experience in World War I he began to think that an "inveterate and irrational instinct" like that of animals in groups drove the aggressive expansion of national power units.

Wilson's personal world darkened when, several days before Christmas 1940, Fitzgerald died of a heart attack in Hollywood. Scott had saluted *Finland Station*'s beginnings six years before, and in October wrote that the book was "magnificent." Toiling over *The Last Tycoon*, he returned to the thought that the two were working along parallel lines. A month later he wrote that he believed his novel good, was struggling "to be exact and honest emotionally," in a P.S. noting the "horrible paucity of time." He was the only professional writer to have shared what, in Goethe's words, Wilson looked back on as the *"frohe tage"* of their youth. To Zelda, who had been institutionalized in North Carolina but was living in Montgomery with her mother when Scott died, Wilson wrote that he felt "suddenly robbed of some part of my own personality." In a letter to Bishop he said, "Men who start out writing together write for one another more than they realize till somebody dies."

---

*Straight first revealed this phase of his life in 1963, when considered for a post advising on the arts in the Kennedy administration. Rather than have his past as a Communist agent become an embarrassment to the president, he withdrew his name and took Arthur Schlesinger's advice to confess the facts to Attorney General Robert Kennedy. This led, via the FBI and MI5, to the unmasking of Blunt, the till then unknown fourth man in the spy ring. Blunt, who had become the Queen's curator of painting and been knighted for his work (the knighthood was later withdrawn by Margaret Thatcher), admitted everything when offered immunity from prosecution. Straight served as deputy chairman of the National Endowment for the Arts under President Nixon. He died in 2004.

Nathanael West died in a car crash the day after Fitzgerald did, and Sherwood Anderson, who had become a small-town newspaper editor and seemed to be recovering his literary form, died a few weeks later. "Come! Somebody's got to survive and write!" Wilson urged Bishop. Still owing *The New Republic* a literary supplement, he collected tributes to Fitzgerald by Dos, Glenway Wescott, John O'Hara, and the young Hollywood writer Budd Schulberg, and oversaw their publication in the February and March issues. This memorial and the volume that would follow, *The Crack-Up*, were distinguished by Bishop's moving elegy, "The Hours," set at the splendid house on the marshes at South Chatham, with a sea view that seconded the theme of mortality.

Bishop, whose health had been weakened by rheumatic fever as a child, was losing his appetite for life. As his poems turned macabre, his friends thought Margaret added to his gloom. She soon was commissioned in the Women's Army Corps, and John told Wilson she had him doing all the work at home while she attended to her official duties. One day, picking up John at Wellfleet in what appeared to be her major general's uniform, Margaret practically dragged him out of the house. When John confided he didn't want to spend another winter at South Chatham, Wilson asked Allen Tate to rescue him by getting him "a little job in Washington," which was soon arranged by MacLeish at the Library of Congress. He arrived in Washington in November 1943, but had a heart attack two weeks later and had to return to Massachusetts. He would die at the Hyannis hospital April 4, 1944, of what Wilson calls "a leaking heart." As with other literary comrades whose deaths took him by surprise, Wilson found it hard to realize the end was at hand. The difficulty that anyone has imagining the deaths of friends was magnified by his role as mentor and his stubborn expectation that he and his dwindling circle would keep producing. Introducing a memorial volume of John's prose (Tate did the poetry), Wilson wrote, "Even through these last days, when his life was running low, he continued to work on his unfinished poems."

While he arranged Fitzgerald's commemoration in *The New Republic*, Perkins let him have the drafts of Scott's unfinished novel and hired him to edit it, Wilson turning over the $500 payment to Fitzgerald's daughter, Scottie. He framed the episodes in chapters according to Scott's outline and rounded out the book with his notes on the ending, titling it *The Last Tycoon*. As Matthew Bruccoli has pointed out, Wilson's editing suggested the novel was closer to completion than it was, allowing him to claim that, though Fitzgerald hadn't "brought it finally into focus," this was his "most mature piece of work." Monroe Stahr was both "created from within" and located in business and social relationships more solidly realized than those of Jay Gatsby or Dick Diver in *Tender Is the Night*. The publication of *Tycoon* in October 1941, in a volume that included *The Great Gatsby* and five stories, caused Stephen Vincent Benét, in an influential review, to claim that Fizgerald was "not a legend" but a "secure reputation." Wilson next assembled *The Crack-Up*, where the wry, observant voice of Scott's letters to friends and to Scottie, his essays, notebooks, and best autobiographical pieces is complemented by his fellow writers—for example, Dos Passos ringingly predicts that his style will "raise the level of American fiction to follow in some such way as Marlowe's blank verse line raised the whole level of Elizabethan verse." After negotiations with Scott's executor, John Biggs, and a long tug-of-war with the publisher James Laughlin, New Directions brought out *The Crack-Up* at the end of World War II. Again Wilson took nothing for his efforts. Establishing the novelist as something more than a shadowy romantic figure hovering somewhere between Gatsby and Diver, the two books laid the groundwork for the Fitzgerald revival that began in 1950.

Wilson prefaced *The Crack-Up* with "On Editing Scott Fitzgerald's Papers," his most sustained and (thanks largely to Bishop's critique of a draft) most polished serious verse. Dated February 1942, it is written in iambic pentameter couplets and achieves a narrative and elegiac eloquence once associated with this form. As he contemplates his friend's "last fragments," he recalls correcting the spelling and punctuation of the college story "Shadow Laurels," Fitz's prophetic account of an artist "who loved applause but had his life alone / Who fed on drink for weeks; forgot to eat / 'Worked feverishly' . . . / Betrayed, but self-betrayed by stealthy sins / And faded to the sound of violins." Linking the loss of Fitzgerald to the moral darkness of the war, Wilson seeks to recover the color and feeling of the jazz age in a world whose artists are part of the general demoralization:

> Scott, the bright hotels turn bleak;
> The pace limps or stamps; the wines are weak;
> The horns and violins come faint tonight.
> A rim of darkness that devours light
> Runs like the wall of flame that eats the land;
> Blood, brain, and labor pour into the sand;

And here, among our comrades of the trade,
Some buzz, like husks, some stammer, much afraid,
Some mellowly give tongue and join the drag
Like hounds that bay the bounding anise-bag,
Some swallow darkness and sit hunched and dull,
The stunned beast's stupor in the monkey skull.

Wilson affirms the old humanist distinction between man and beast even as it collapses for him. Recalling his first glimpse of Fitz in college, he associates the glitter of those hard green eyes with an array of precious stones, among them "two emeralds, green and lucid, one half-cut, / One cut consummately"—*Gatsby* and either *Tender* or *Tycoon*. He pictures his friend's end—

Those eyes struck dark, dissolving in a wrecked
And darkened world, the gleam of intellect
That spilled into the spectrum of tune, taste,
Scent, color, living speech, is gone, is lost—

and is left to

. . . dwell among the ragged stumps,
With owls digesting mice to dismal lumps
Of skin and gristle, monkeys scared by thunder,
Great buzzards that descend to grab the plunder.

At Fitzgerald's death, Wilson was forty-five, a decade into the second half of what he called his threescore and ten, now "on the home stretch." He'd accomplished a mountain of work during the twenty years since he'd cared for the wounded and stacked dead bodies in France, and, usually on the move, lived hard. The cultural movements with which he identified himself were coming to an end, and his sense of purpose flagged. In these months when Scott and the others died so did their great predecessors—"Yeats, Freud, Trotsky, and Joyce have all gone in so short a time, it is almost like the death of one's father," he reflected in a letter of January 1941. Now Wilson entered upon several years without a regular job or salary, adrift in a nation at war, where intellectual life was on the back burner.

"Here at the top of the house I lie alone," he writes in a plaintive mood at Truro. He is "glad to hear only the wind in the window frame—or silence, silence—of the dullness of neighbors who do not know one another—of friends who have slid away down the other side of the mountain while still, if a little estranged, we seemed within calling distance—of death, of a person who never again can reach one, that one never again can reach— you cannot hear her voice because it is no longer there." Margaret has become the emblem of all that is irretrievable, and he concludes, "If I cannot hear or hold that person, I would rather have silence alone." McCarthy, the young wife downstairs, would recall, "He had a pair of Margaret's gloves," somewhat contemptuously adding, "he used to sit up there and weep over them." She also remembered "he'd be playing the phonograph— Beethoven, Mussorgsky—'The Great Gate of Kiev' from *Pictures at an Exhibition*—Schönberg's *Pierrot Lunaire*, Prokofiev, walking around up there, waiting till everybody'd gone to bed to play the phonograph. He would read his own works aloud to himself, would read old journals, sometimes write in them." So began the flood of retrospection that included portraits of teachers, family, and close literary friends, the prose and verse of *Notebooks of Night* and *Night Thoughts*, the stories in *Memoirs of Hecate County*.

By day he was upbeat. In April 1941, for $4,000—$1,500 borrowed from his mother, with a mortgage for the rest—he bought the old house on Money Hill near the Walkers in Wellfleet, a place built for a large family whose wealth came from shipping and banking, between the Atlantic beach and the saltwater ponds. After considerable renovation he moved his family in during the summer, and that fall put another $1,000 borrowed from the bank toward the heating. In his and Mary's letters their relationship seems on track. While she's in the city undergoing intensive sessions with Dr. Frank, he writes from Wellfleet sending money and her mail; he lists his engagements, explains he's hanging pictures and struggling with the furnace, that Reuel is fine. He wants her "to make use of these last days while Edna [the maid] is with us to get as far as possible with your book"—she needn't worry about his lunch and breakfast or "about the household" until the afternoon, and they can go out to dinner often. When their locations are reversed and "Dearest Edmund" is sweltering while teaching in New York, Mary reviews for him the bills and other domestic details as well as her social life—the Artist's Ball, to which Dr. Rado has taken her, a beach picnic, two afternoon occasions. After mentioning Reuel and her writing, she says, "I feel that I rattle around in this house without you. Your absence gives me a sort of castration complex"—their shared joke on Rado's Freudian specialty, the castration complex in women.

PR had just published "The Man in the Brooks Brothers Shirt," the comedy of a sexual encounter with a salesman in a Pullman car, and it was a succès de scandale, establishing McCarthy's reputation for honesty and daring as the era's avatar of feminism. Delmore Schwartz, still bitter at her treatment of Rahv, spoke of the story as "Tidings from the Whore," but in her letter to Wilson from the Cape she kids him that he'll be "luminous in a Brooks Brothers summer suit" when he comes home that weekend. Over the next years, however, as she began to struggle against the older husband who doggedly held on to her, their marriage fell apart. There is a German phrase, *lasten wie ein Alp*, that Marx repeats and Wilson considered a key to the man's psychology, translating it "weighs like an incubus." In her writing of these years Mary several times uses this phrase. The couple forgot their genial, loving beginnings as they were borne down by such a weight, and it would be 1945 before McCarthy felt strong enough to leave him.

Until he acquired a new platform as a journalist at *The New Yorker* in 1944, Wilson was at loose ends in his career, and in the isolation of the Cape he resembled the Philoctetes of Sophocles' play, the alienated possessor of a magical instrument. To his young admirer Kazin, who encountered him on his bicycle in Provincetown, he remarked that the Wellfleet house "made him shiver," that he was lonely there but too poor to live anywhere else. The war and the propaganda that accompanied it, dehumanizing the enemy, battered the faith in man and in his own country and its culture that had sustained Wilson's work. The failure of his marriage accentuated his political disillusionment.

In a letter after Paul Rosenfeld's death in 1946, he reflects that artists and writers in America "tend to die prematurely, to go to pieces with drink, or to sell out to the popular market. It has been harder in this country than in others to swim against the current: people either give out and expire or allow themselves to be carried in the other direction." A strong constitution and a gift of determined affirmation would enable Wilson to defy the pattern. A new job at *The New Yorker* and his marriage to Elena Mumm Thornton helped him recover his élan. Some journal notes from a walk beside the ponds in *The Forties* emphasize "the clear round lens of self" and promise much material "not yet brought to light."

18

Wilson and McCarthy, 1942–1945

The Minotaur and Mary

Wilson acknowledged that his irascibility, drinking, and single-minded focus on his work made him a difficult husband. He was physically restless, and moved from place to place during his seven years with Mary McCarthy, usually writing at home. McCarthy was amazed when, after drinking in his study late into the night, he emerged "in his snowy-white B.V.D.'s in the morning," freshly bathed and shaved and ready to go back to work. "It was as if he'd harrowed Hell," she thought. But this "spirited termagant of a wife" (as Meg calls herself in McCarthy's short story "Ghostly Father, I Confess") had a sharp tongue. Their English friend at the University of Chicago, David Grene, recalled how, when he spent six weeks with them at Truro in 1940, Mary used his drinking against Wilson: "She would rather snippily say, 'Edmund, *of course* you don't remember. How *would* you?' Jolly comments like that." Her friends would testify to his sexual jealousy, his that she sometimes set out to make him jealous. David Chavchavadze, the son of Paul and Nina, remembered his father saying, as they went off to a party, "Mary will give me a sexy kiss." David Laskin interprets their disputes as those of "two tyrants under a single roof, always amazed that they had failed to cow or convince the other." Adelaide Walker noted that when each reported on a quarrel their visions of reality were as mutually exclusive as those of the characters in *Rashomon*. She thought it would have been better if, after shining together in company, they could have retired to separate houses.

The house at Money Hill was always run-down. When Wilson was lecturing in New York, Mary wrote that the gas for the stove had been turned off—presumably an unpaid bill—and that a leak in the roof over the living room had stained the ceiling wallpaper. She generously offered her hundred-dollar advance from Simon and Schuster toward these disasters. Wilson's finances were as usual confused, with bills to be juggled, checks in danger of bouncing. For a time they had no telephone because, having failed to pay the bill on time, he refused to give the company the ten dollar deposit required to get it reconnected. He paid for McCarthy's psychoanalysis and the maid so she could write, but never gave her any cash. Yet he might spend all he had on a beautiful book, and would send whatever money he had to Mary Blair if she phoned for help. He kept taking long trips by taxi since he didn't intend to learn how to drive. *The Truro Tattler*, a paper David Chavchavadze typed out as a teenager, contained a notice that Edmund Wilson was seen passing through this Massachusetts town in a taxi with a Washington, D.C., license plate. Eventually Mary lucked into a car on a raffle ticket that cost him a quarter. Their neighbor Ruth Jencks taught her how to drive, easing subsequent escapes to New York.

As they looked back on their marriage long after it dissolved, McCarthy politely volunteered, "I was too young," to which Wilson replied "I was too old." The age gap doesn't appear to trouble them in the well-known 1942 photograph in which she is seated, radiantly smiling, and he stands close behind, right arm circling her, intently regarding the camera. Nor is it dominant in a photo accompanying a review of *To the Finland Station* in *PM*. While Gauss kiddingly dubbed this picture *New England: Indian Summer*, after Van Wyck Brooks's latest volume, the unposed shots taken by her brother Kevin at Wellfleet and included in *The Forties* might be called *Tobacco Road*, for weeds rise in front of the porch and the paint on the shutters is peeling, signs of the couple's poverty. Here they appear to be decades apart. The middle-aged man in a nondescript, mismatched jacket, tie, and soft trousers sits flat-footed in the rocking chair with a Sunday paper on his knee, chewing a blade of beach grass—he thought he looked as if he were taking snuff. In one shot he dotingly regards his alert young wife, who wears a frilly low-cut pinafore and sandals, in the other he is glancing down and she away. Here is the improbable pair whom young Arthur Schlesinger, on meeting them together, saw as a "terribly attractive girl married to an old man." Bowden Broadwater, Mary's next husband, referred to Wilson as "my father-in-law."

The story line fades in and out of the record of these turbulent years. After their separation, Broadwater said, Mary burned a pile of Wilson's letters, but those that survive, on both sides, show them struggling with their problems. "I am rather depressed because the last week has been so disastrous in every way, but perhaps your trip will break the pattern," she writes. He says, "I was rather in a bad state of mind myself when I came back from Bennington, and probably made your situation worse." After listing the household catastrophes (to cap these off, the maid has decamped for Boston), Mary wishes he'd "come back and share our harum-scarum bohemian life." He replies from New York that it is hot and muggy, and that his audience at the Columbia summer session is small and unresponsive. As always, they fill each other in on their social engagements and close lovingly, but by the late fall of 1941 their marriage was in trouble.

Describing the eruption of an "alien personality" within her marriage, one given, as she was not, to "tantrums and tears," the Meg of "Ghostly Father" adds that when this person began "to have love affairs, to go up to strange hotel rooms, and try to avoid the floor clerk, she could only stand by, horrified." During the divorce, in an effort to counter the charge that he was overly jealous, Wilson testified that Mary "went to New York by herself, slept with a young man she knew, and presently announced to me that she was pregnant, but did not know whether by him or by me. She discussed the matter with her analyst, Dr. Frank, and he arranged to have an abortion performed on her." The man would have been the translator Ralph Manheim, whom McCarthy met at the Cape (she writes to Wilson of talking with him about "The Man in the Brooks Brothers Shirt") and who Rosalind reports had an affair with Mary. A note from Wilson to Mary in the city on January 15, 1942, may date the operation, for he is waiting for news "by the noon mail" and closes, "I hope things are all right, my dear." The procedure "was not a success," he'd testify, "and she had to go to the hospital and was ill over a long period of time." Although she never denied Wilson's story, it goes unmentioned in the McCarthy biographies.

Wilson, who had cuckolded or tried to cuckold a number of husbands, was now in that role himself, and his suspicious outbursts alienated friends like Adelaide without affecting Mary's behavior. He thought his love might save the situation. A homemade valentine with a huge heart, presented to her along with anemones, apparently not long after her return from the operation in New York, appeals to her not to reject him:

> Dearest, do not blench or start!
> This big red thing is my heart.

When the heating system's numb,
This will make you warm as rum;

However, in the second quatrain the intellectual who in his work aspired
to a Promethean fire jocularly proposes to warm up his wife:

When the pipes are all congealed,
This will make the Winter yield;
When your own heart's cold and dark,
This will try to strike the spark.

This oppressive plea is not entirely indicative of their sex life. A journal
passage dated May 21, 1942, describes one of Mary's elaborate picnics at
the ponds, occasions when they sometimes made love. "We cleared a
space under the low branches of the pines so that we could get a little
shade, and the light openwork shadows rippled on Mary's white skin," he
writes, and erotically evokes "the little white violets with their lower lips
finely lined as if with beards," their long slim stalks and "faint slightly acrid
pansy smell," the "thready roots in the damp sand."

That spring or summer, however, Mary began running away. She
would leave Reuel with Rosalind if Wilson's daughter, who was devoted to
the boy, was around, or with his nurse or a woman friend. We do not know
how she felt about abandoning her adored child, but there is no evidence to
support the rumor that she once took him as far as California, Wilson
doggedly following. She usually went to the New Weston or the Little
Hotel in Manhattan, having, she recalled, no idea what to do when she
got there. Once she decided to take a job as a cook or maid ("the servant
girl fantasy"), though Rado advised against it on practical grounds. The
Wilson who came to get her in New York was never, she said, the drunken
brute she left behind. This was the Princeton gentleman, reassuringly re-
pentant, "clear-minded, reasonable, his urbanity mixed with awkwardness." Wilson had acquired for Mary the same double personality she had
for him.

One of McCarthy's best pieces of fiction, "The Weeds," a tale of a once
beglamored relationship that has soured, emerged from such an episode,
as if in illustration of his essays coordinating neurosis with creative power.
The unnamed heroine resolves to "leave him as soon as the petunias had
bloomed." The garden is her marriage, and she remembers when it had

not been menaced by spring weeds, "when her borders had been gay with simple clear colors, pink and scarlet, lemon yellow and cornflower blue, when her husband had stood by in admiration, saying, 'You have green thumbs, my dear.'" She wonders when the change took place and tells herself that "a marriage made out of loneliness and despair will be lonely and desperate." For a moment she wishes her husband dead; then, child-like, fearing the strength of her feeling may have killed him, she steals a glimpse through the window at the "man in a brown suit [recognizable as Wilson's regulation attire] slumped over some papers."

When the unhappy woman catches herself planning next year's expansion of the garden she knows she must flee, but there is is no one in the city to help her get a job and she spends aimless, unsatisfying days in her hotel room, breaking her only engagement because she can't decide what to wear. Her husband phones on the fourth morning, but she refuses to meet him and when he calls her that evening, drunk, she hangs up. On the sixth day, finally ready for the world, she finds him waiting in the lobby. Her only satisfaction upon returning home is that the crabgrass has taken over the garden. Her sense of imprisonment deepens as she observes her husband privately struggling to recover what is lost, but she pretends to accept his love when he brings in a weedy bouquet and with masculine pathos declares, "I've always loved your flowers." She cannot leave him "on her own initiative," for "the courage, the more attractive alternative, whatever it was that might separate them, was lacking."

In the summer of 1942, before McCarthy wrote this anatomy of the plight of dependent women, she became pregnant again, this time by Wilson. Hoping their love would be renewed, as it had been after the birth of Reuel, he ponderously ends a note to her, "Love (not hate) my dear." A few weeks later McCarthy lost the baby. In his memoir, "Growing Up with Edmund Wilson and Mary McCarthy," Reuel recalls a nightmare of being confined to his room, which "must have been tied with my parents' early-hours departure to the hospital in Hyannis, where MM had a miscarriage." She had been on a ladder washing windows, then with Adelaide had called on Sándor Rado, who had urged an abortion when she was pregnant with Reuel, and, at Rado's house she started to bleed. Instead of going home with Adelaide, she stayed across the street at the Dos Passoses', where she began to miscarry. Wilson later accused her of bringing this on, an allegation Adelaide thought "quite unjust." The Dos Passoses were, however, apparently convinced "she'd planned it." To Carol Brightman, Mary recalled the "fatal mistake" of washing windows that day. In a detached tone that sowed doubts with this biographer, she said, "I was disappointed by the miscarriage, as I should have liked to have another child."

"Analysis became a way of patching things over," McCarthy recalled. Rado now sent her to Dr. Abraham Kardiner. Kardiner had been trained by the father of psychiatry, but his memoir, *My Analysis with Freud*, reveals he was no stereotypical representative of Freudian thought. Sensitive to the plight of abused women (his mother and sister having been victims), he went on to write authoritative works on trauma and the effects of economic powerlessness, factors in Mary's depression. From New York she let Wilson know that she liked Dr. Kardiner, though his estimate of her case was harsh. Dr. Frank and she had "made a mess of everything by dissipating the analysis," and to correct this she'd have to live in or near the city and see Kardiner four times a week for a year. She asks "what am I going to do?" In an allusion to the miscarriage as well as their quarreling and, if Wilson is right about it, to the abortion a few months before, Mary says, "Dear Edmund, I have thought about you a lot. In fact, I have done nothing but think. Let us try not to rasp so much when I get back. I feel very sad about everything. It's as if this year had been a thousand years long, like a hangover."

He didn't want to live year-round in the city and couldn't afford to, but encouraged Mary to move to Manhattan and begin the analysis. A few weeks later she wrote, "Dr. Kardiner is well, and promised me that in six months I wouldn't recognize myself." Wilson held the fort with Reuel and the couple saw each other on occasional weekends, once for a tryst he called "wonderful"—this may be when they sexually experimented in a journal passage omitted on her account from *The Forties*—and once when she came home so he could go off to lecture at Smith College. In New York she enjoyed her old friends, talking with Rahv about *PR* and meeting Elizabeth Bishop for lunch. She had the satisfaction of being invited by Samuel Goldwyn, over lunch in his suite at the Waldorf Towers, to go to Hollywood, which she declined on grounds that "I had a husband and family." At Christmas 1942 Wilson and Reuel joined her for the winter in an apartment she had been sharing with Polly Boyden. They were in somebody else's place on East Eighty-sixth Street late in May, then back at the Cape for the summer, with Mary spending long periods in the city.

Through her later life McCarthy maintained the ridicule of psychiatry in "Ghostly Father," reflecting both her Catholic training and a fear of mental illness and its stigma. She represented her psychoanalysts as

Wilson's three stooges. In fact, her first months with Rado and the interrupted years with Frank fed the honesty about herself that gives this story and "The Weeds" places in her enduring fiction. We have no idea whether or how she profited from her analysis with Dr. Kardiner, other than by being able to live in New York without her husband. She came to object to the "cardinal doctrine" of psychoanalysis that one couldn't change one's life situation while under treatment, for this would condemn her to remain Mrs. Edmund Wilson. Seeing these sessions with Kardiner as Wilson's tool of control, she began to use them to frustrate him. As the analysis stretched on into 1943 he grew impatient, and a letter from her charges him with blaming every domestic difficulty on "my absence," his quarrelsomeness leading her "to anticipate the attack by an offensive of my own." She is surer of herself than when grieving over their quarrels a few months before. "I know it is hard on you and lonely for you, but what other solution was there or is there?" Mary asks. "If you want to put an end to the whole business, for God's sake do so. Suggest some arrangement. If you don't, you might try to forgive me my trespass of going to the analyst, and start from there."

Although her therapy offered freedom from the identification of Wilson with her Uncle Myers, in the short run it may have reinforced this, as his determination to hold on to her evidently did. The return of her childhood trauma, acted out within the marriage, must have been frightening. In her rages Mary more than once built a fire of papers against Wilson's locked study door and tried to push them underneath, explaining later to Elizabeth Hardwick and others that after beating her up he always hid there. To view their quarrels through the memory of her uncle's whippings had its uses, giving her leverage against Wilson with their friends and eventually in court. While he promoted her work at *PR*, the *Southern Review*, and *The New Yorker* (Katharine White was fiction editor when "The Weeds" was accepted) as well as to Nabokov, Mary told Adelaide that he beat her, and Adelaide, though she had no evidence of this, knew Mary "felt beaten anyway."

"He casts a long shadow," Martha says of Miles, the Wilson figure in *A Charmed Life*, by whose very existence she feels "depreciated . . . , like a worm, like a white grub in the ground." For almost two years, instead of leaving Wilson Mary, in her own mind, brought him down to size. She was bored by his categorizing of people and experiences—"Once something got into the authorized version," she recalled, "you could never get it out." When he let her look over his journals she judged his notes of the early 1920s, written at her age, more vital than the big books of 1938–1941: "he had become magisterial and practical, he was doing valuable, solid, sometimes penetrating work, but his early talent had turned to embers." Her criticism of *Finland Station* was shrewd. "It was a mistake for Edmund to like Lenin," McCarthy said, "but that was the only way he could believe in the Russian Revolution." She called the "Princess" story for *Memoirs of Hecate County*, which he wrote in 1943, "terrible," its erotica "nauseating," language that seems to indicate a sexual distaste for her husband. In a letter to Dos after the separation in 1945, Katy Dos Passos picked up on Wilson's view that Mary tried to undermine his writing— "she kept telling him it was worthless and getting worse."

Alfred Kazin records a glimpse of the couple when he came to their apartment to get Wilson's opinion of his history of modern American prose, *On Native Grounds*. Over the years Wilson would try to cool down the younger man's rhetoric. There is a story that, propped in bed with a bad cold and his head wrapped in a towel in the Plaza Hotel, he said of some writing Kazin had brought to him—adopting his British tone—"It won't wash, Alfie." That evening in 1942 he was politely noncommittal about Kazin's first book, but McCarthy jumped in and called it "terrible." She shifted her fire to her husband, and when their guest got up to leave, Wilson walked him across the street in the rain to the Third Avenue El, with a grin advising, "Write about *her* some time!" Then he was talking about Joyce, "about the cabman's shelter scene in *Ulysses*," repeating the word "shelter" while the rain bounced "off the tracks right on our heads." Completing his thought in "that extraordinary half-stutter," a voice that embodied the self in its "enormous effort to reach the world," Wilson "looked up at the rain dropping down his face, gave me a friendly pat on the shoulder, and trudged back."

In *Seeing Mary Plain*, Frances Kiernan describes a scene in which Mary's confidence and sexual independence have made her immune to Wilson's jealousy. His new job as *The New Yorker*'s book reviewer enabled them to take an apartment on Gramercy Park and enroll Reuel in kindergarten nearby, and they celebrated New Year's Eve in 1943 with a party, the guests including Dawn Powell, Philip Rahv (now married to the heiress Nathalie Swan), and Clement Greenberg, whose essay "Avant-Garde and Kitsch" had begun his ascent as an arbiter of taste in modern painting. Margaret Miller, a class behind Mary at Vassar, recalled to Kiernan that as midnight approached Mary was "sitting on the floor with her back against the wall and her legs straight out in front of her. She had her eyes closed and Philip Rahv's head in her lap." Greenberg's turn was to come: they began an affair later that winter. She now referred to Wilson as the Minotaur—alternately "the beast of Picasso"—herself implicitly an Ariadne waiting for a rescuer. Wilson even drew himself as a rather sensitive-looking and unhappy bull, with a Picasso-ish devil at his side.

She also called him "the Minotaur in a maze." The poet Conrad Aiken—famous for suggesting someone do a cartoon of the couple face-to-face, captioned "The Shock of Recognition"—versified his impression of "The Minotaur and Mary." Joking of the labyrinth and the bull-hero, Aiken adds:

> But as for the Minotaur's doxie
> Although you mix gin with her moxie
> I'm afraid she's too subtle
> For mortal rebuttal.

Her "maze" was "beyond orthodoxy," and she'd "have to be done in by proxy." For Hardwick their marriage itself was the maze. "Wilson was helpless in the man-woman situation with someone like Mary," Hardwick recalled in conversation. On the other hand, "she couldn't dominate him—he was too big."

The End of the Marriage

The Wilsons' household had its happy times, despite all these tensions. When Roman Grynberg, the Russian who collected books and published émigré journals out of his New York apartment, brought presents on a visit to the Cape, Reuel, nearly five and housebound with a cold, dictated a thank-you letter, which his mother sent on. Describing running the steam shovel around the house and experimenting with blocks, he writes, "Dada has been picking apples—he has picked all the apples," and adds, "I've learned to row. I mostly row backwards." Not surprisingly, his parents brought him up to love books. Mary read aloud the stories of King Arthur as well as Grimm's fairy tales, and went on to *A Tale of Two Cities*. When she read Henry James aloud to the five-year-old, Wilson thought this was too much, but he recited "The Owl and the Pussycat" and the rest of Edward Lear, and as Reuel grew older provided "gripping, almost daily after-dinner readings" of *Oliver Twist, Uncle Tom's Cabin*, and other classics.

Reuel recalled his mother as "uncomfortable in the presence of small children," saying hers was "a willed adjustment." Eileen Simpson, the poet John Berryman's wife, thought Mary nervous and indulgent, "not a natural mother," yet someone always eager "to do things right," while Adelaide approved of her enthusiasm. She arranged for playmates and admired the boy's every achievement. David Grene, who visited them at the Cape, thought Wilson "wonderful with Reuel": "he could do magic tricks in a way that would ravish any child's heart. He could produce rabbits out of hats; he could make the most fantastic shadows on the wall with his hands." Reuel would remember the mouse his father worked up for him "out of an old brown necktie," the magic drawer in a box in his bedroom where "some benign spirit" would from time to time leave "a roll of Necco wafers or another sweet." Wilson also taught him "a fondness for animals" and to observe nature in the woods—"the ways of aromatic fern and bread-and-butter plants with their tender, edible leaves," the intricate orange-and-black underside of a turtle.

His rages at Mary, however, revealed Reuel's father "in a very different and terrifying light" than the benign magician and puppeteer. "He had a fear-inspiring temper and a stentorian voice," the son recalls in his memoir. A vivid memory was of "crawling upon his hard brown cordovan shoes, perhaps in a vain attempt to stop the loud and ugly confrontation with MM that was taking place by the study doorstep." Reuel's subsequent stepfather, Bowden Broadwater, believed his father frightened him. He seems also to have quailed before his father's exacting standard. In a note dictated to Mary and incorporated into a letter of hers, he fills Wilson in on what he has been doing, saying, "I gave you some new things for your show, some new paper for ghosts." Running out of steam, he adds, "I can't think of anything else that you won't be disgusted about." That this detail is not an embittered wife's invention is clear when Mary adds, "He has really been very good in spite of that sublime last sentence."

Wilson's cards and letters from Europe the next year may have oppressed the six-year-old. He tells the story of Romulus and Remus as he'd learned it at thirteen. He touches on the ruins of Pompeii, showing "how people lived a thousand and a half years ago," and on the Delphic oracle and her powers. Promoting his own hobby, he buys Reuel marionettes as gifts "so we will have a lot of new characters for the theater," hopes he "will soon be old enough to give plays yourself to amuse Ebbie Given [Reuel's playmate]." He sketches the devastation of the war, with families living in cellars or tents and children who attend bombed-out schools in shifts and play with unexploded shells and in old tanks. Another letter explains that "the United States at the present time must be the best country in the whole world, because everywhere else has been ruined by the war, and you are lucky to be living there." When visiting Kemp Smith at Edinburgh he writes to Reuel on the child's level, evoking "old gloomy houses" in one of which is a ghost "who helps you on with your coat when you leave." In London, overdoing this, he describes a pantomime in which a wicked yellow dwarf captures a girl and drags her off to the Weird Wood, where the trees have eyes that light up and bears wait to devour her would-be rescuers.

Rosalind describes "Mary and my Father" as "two supersurvivors who left emotional destruction in their wake," and they fought over Reuel in the divorce. The brawl from which the breakup inexorably followed took place in 1944. They'd been arguing about who should take out the garbage after a dinner party at which too much liquor had been consumed— Wilson "was drunk and I wasn't sober," Mary recalled. When he replied, "You empty it yourself," she slapped his face and, she said, he pursued her into Reuel's room, saying, "You think you're unhappy with me. Well, I'll give you something to be unhappy about." This is perhaps the "one exception" Wilson made in denying, under oath, that he physically mistreated his wife. Rosalind says she was in Reuel's room while they fought upstairs, that she came up and separated them by persuading Mary to go swimming—Wilson, pursuing the women, apparently ran his hand through the window of the front door. The next morning he was hungover and, his daughter reported to Mary, who had fled to New York, was "full of dim suspicions" that they had joined forces against him.

McCarthy recalled the aftermath of the fight in the same breezy style in which she related their taxi ride from Stamford to Payne Whitney six years before. In the morning Reuel's nurse, Miss Forbes, saw blood on the kitchen floor and, as Mary put it, "followed the trail upstairs to Edmund's lair" (again the Minotaur). Before fleeing, Mary persuaded him to let her bandage the wound and call a doctor, something she said he always resisted, as much not to interfere with nature as to save money. She "somehow persuaded him to have a tetanus shot" and left Miss Forbes in charge, a situation with comic dimensions at that time, since Adelaide was also away and the proper Scottish nurse couldn't be expected to spend the night in either their house or the Walkers' with a man alone. In the confusion there arrived "a Gaspé salmon, packed in ice," a gift from a friend deep-sea fishing. "Edmund had to cope with this salmon. He had to get someone to cut it up and distribute it to all the ladies of that part of the Cape," McCarthy chuckled.

Wilson's letter to her in New York shows his strong feeling for her, momentarily heightened by the need to repair relations and, perhaps, by her incipient departure. "I have really loved you more than any other woman and have felt closer to you than to any other human being," he writes. "Sometimes I have been happier and more exalted with you than I have ever been with anybody." It is what he could never tell Margaret, and the word "exalted" claims something more than his love for Frances. He regrets they've come "to antagonize each other in bed," as yet unaware of Greenberg's shadow there. Reluctant to admit that Mary and he are "psychologically impossible" for each other, he urges her to come back for the rest of the summer "on a purely friendly basis." Mary returned to Wellfleet, and she said he kept his promise not to "touch another drop that summer," rather sadly adding, "That was our last summer."

For the next year she consented to share a house on Henderson Place in Manhattan's East Eighties, a few blocks from St. Bernard's, where Reuel began school, but was soon campaigning for a separation agreement, which she persuaded herself Wilson had promised. Her liaison with Greenberg continued. He was brilliant, and has been said to have had a "seedy sexual appeal" many women found "irresistible." Yet he was "gaining a reputation for settling arguments with his fists," Kiernan informs us, and Brightman says he "used to volunteer to come around and "spank Reuel" after she had left Edmund." Did this affair, in a revealing phrase of McCarthy's, come to seem too much "like sleeping with your wicked uncle"? She showed a strangely bitter animosity when it ended. Greenberg had retreated. "For one week I thought I wanted to marry Mary. When she was in between men. I didn't know enough to listen to my entrails," he remembered. "But I didn't pursue it." Though fun to be with she was too abrasive, and he was convinced that she would not marry him because he was Jewish.

It was Helen Muchnic to whom Wilson observed that Mary, instead of writing a novel, was making one out of her life. He'd enjoyed Muchnic's warmhearted, quick-witted conversation when lecturing at Smith, and she gave him companionship during the breakup. Born in Odessa, the daughter of a Russian-Jewish businessman, she graduated from Vassar in 1929 and studied with Mirsky when he was in London. In her dissertation, "Dostoyevsky's English Reputation," she had quoted from the monologue on literature incorporated at the dark center of *I Thought of Daisy*, which was published as "Meditations on Dostoevsky" in *The New Republic*. She loved Wilson's sympathetic treatment of literary characters as she did the life-giving spiritual intensity of the Russian writers. He tried out his ideas on her. Muchnic was grounded and sober and delightful. In the throaty voice that was part of her charm, she recalled the drive with which he attacked his subjects, "He really dug in." When she proposed writing a book about Russian literature, Wilson said, "Oh, wonderful! And I'll help you sell it!" He counseled her how to stand up to publishers, urged her not to dedicate the book to him so he could more persuasively review it, and did just that in *The New Yorker*.

Promoting her among Russian expatriate writers, he took Helen to dinner at the Princeton Club with Nabokov. The novelist did not have an American translator and, at Wilson's suggestion, tested Muchnic's Russian, pronouncing it excellent, with what, having lived in Russia as long as he, she thought a fatuous arrogance. Wilson also introduced her to the Grynbergs. "If Edmund wants you to meet the Grynbergs, you will meet the Grynbergs," Mary had declared, so they went together. Helen added that she and Mary "just didn't get along, though Edmund wasn't aware of this. When they were living on Gramercy Park, he sent me off to a Chekhov play with Mary, which was not much fun." He discussed his marriages and affairs with his protégée, without dwelling on Mary's failings. Helen learned how happy he'd been with Frances—interpreting this as the relief of "getting away from his own mind"—and how he loved Margaret, a love bound up with guilt. Louise Bogan told her Millay was the love of Wilson's life, but she doubted it. Wondering if there was any affection involved in such a variety of affairs, Muchnic decided, "Yes, there was." More than one observer had the impression she wanted Wilson to fall for her. Trying to fan the flames, Rosalind, who was fond of Helen and vice versa, wrote to her father in London in 1945—when he was passionately pursuing someone else—"You should hear her talk about you. Next to Dostoyevsky, she is obviously in love with you."

Wilson didn't see much of Louise Bogan during his marriage to Mary, though their literary correspondence continued for the rest of their lives.

In addition to Muchnic, the caricaturist and poet Peggy Bacon—known for wearing Victorian dress—and the novelist Dawn Powell kept him company. Bacon captured Wilson's strength in a drawing of him at the Cape during the mid-1930s, but she also knew his weaknesses. At a party at Henderson Place during the fall of 1944, when "Edmund was in a perfectly terrible humor," Helen recalled Peggy briskly saying, "Look, Edmund, why don't you go in another room and play by yourself?"

His relationship with Dawn was a product of the old Greenwich Village, involving shared friendships with Dos Passos and Margaret de Silver. "Plump, pink, and pretty," as Rosalind writes, Dawn was always "the first person" her father and Dos called up in New York, "supplanting even girlfriends." The light but warm correspondence Wilson established with her recalls that with Wylie and some of the letters between him and Bogan. He took the role of a down-at-heels literary man named Ernest Wigmore and Dawn that of the novelist Mrs. Humphrey Ward, otherwise Mrs. Humph. In the fall of 1943 Wigmore is "enchanted" by Mrs. Humph's latest novel, yet his letter teasingly promises a critique of her fiction which Wilson delivered in person before Wigmore wrote again. Six months later Powell's journal finds his company bracing: "curious effect a day with Bunny Wilson had on me—it balanced me so that I remembered again the natural pleasures of the mind—reading, thinking, and working—all of which are canceled by drinking." He would almost destroy their friendship with a frank review of her next book, *My Home Is Far Away*, finding its insight and delicious satire marred by writing errors and melodramatic plot devices Powell was characteristically too impatient to correct. A few months later, however, she sent to him an entertaining letter headed "HEADQUARTERS FOR MOBILIZATION OF THE DEAD PELVIS." It describes their friend Esther Murphy, Gerald's sister, wearing no underpants and exhibiting "a Blue Grotto, where something was winking away like a Buddha's orb."

After Christmas 1944, Wilson came up with a plan that would get him out of the household on Henderson Place and give Mary a taste of freedom while deferring the separation issue. With the war in Europe winding down, he asked *The New Yorker* to send him to report on what was left of the Old World. A letter outlines financial arrangements so she can remain in the house if she likes and says he'll provide for her and Reuel in a new will of which she'll be executor. The magazine has offered him $1,000 for an article every other week, so for a change, they'll have plenty of money—"I've left checks on my table upstairs," he says. He calls it foolish to work on a separation agreement when they're living in the same house, but (telling her he's sharing this letter with his lawyer) will sign a commitment either to separate or to divorce as she decides, and promises not to try to deprive her of Reuel. Dr. Kardiner, he adds, is holding a place for her, of which Mary did not avail herself. "The end of the analysis was the end of the marriage," she stated.

Six weeks before Wilson sailed, after nursing Rosalind through a case of chicken pox she'd caught from the boy, Mary took off with Reuel to a hotel and then the apartment of her brother Kevin. The couple had had another vicious battle. The famous "note in the pincushion" with which she exited—composed of tiny pieces of paper jammed into a pincushion with a hat pin—doesn't scapegoat him as do her later narratives. "Perhaps the fighting is mostly my own fault," she says, but it can't continue, for "Reuel had the wits scared out of him last night." She offers to "go 50-50 with you on him; you can have him in the summer and I in the winter or vice versa. If you want to make it legal it's all right with me." She sadly concludes, "The only way I can ever break off anything is to run away." She and Greenberg had parted—she told her brother Kevin it was the only time in her life she left a man with "no other man in the picture."

Not trusting Wilson to let her go, she served him papers. They tried to stay out of court by finding an arbitrator in John Biggs, Fitzgerald's executor, now a judge at the U.S. Court of Appeals in Wilmington. "Each had a separate room in a New York hotel," Biggs's son recalled, "and father shuttled between rooms," getting nowhere. When Mary sued for separation as a prelude to divorce she retracted her offer to give up Reuel for six months of the year, telling Adelaide her lawyer advised her to seek sole custody. It became a test of power, Wilson's stature in the literary world versus her stories of him as a monster. Mary stated that from the beginning of their marriage he'd proved to be an alcoholic wife-beater, and that she was "in mortal fear for my life and body." In an initial affadavit, hastily drafted as he left for Europe in March, Wilson, used to dismissing her complaints as neurotic and reminding people she was in analysis, accused her of "hysterical delusions and a persecution complex." She replied that these were exactly his symptoms. In sworn statements the three analysts then distinguished her "psychoneurosis" from an incapacitating mental disease, Dr. Frank specifying it as "hysteria."

Some at the Cape took Wilson's side—Harry and Elena Levin remembered Reuel crying himself to sleep because of the way Mary spoke to him of his father. Her supporters testified that Wilson was hard on her. Adelaide, risking an old friendship, went to Boston to give an affidavit that he was obsessively jealous. He was bitter she didn't let him tell her about Mary's affairs before testifying, and it would be three years before she felt able to clear the air, explaining that she'd never pretended to know the ultimate truth in trying to resolve their impasse. She believed the couple and their child "were being destroyed" by continuing to live together in rancor, and she was clearly right that Reuel depended on his mother.

In Europe Wilson, after holding on so stubbornly, found that he, too, was eager to end the marriage, but he was determined to share their son equally. He wanted authority over Reuel's education, with at least a year of this on the Continent. He detailed Mary's symptoms in a careful deposition back in the States, reporting she told him "that her hysterical weeping began at the time of her first marriage, and that she had once scared her husband to death by threatening him with a carving-knife." He painted her as too erratic to be a good parent, just as he'd once described himself to Adelaide. When the trial loomed in September 1945 each seems to have contemplated fleeing with the child. McCarthy turns out to have applied for a document that would enable her to enter Canada. Wilson, she recalled, took Reuel down to his mother's at Red Bank as he once had Rosalind, only to have Wilson's mother, now eighty, send the boy back.

Muchnic recalled how people sat on the two sides of the courtroom on September 24. On McCarthy's side were Rahv and his wife, Nathalie—who testified that Wilson humiliated Mary by criticizing her housekeeping before their friends—the Macdonalds, and half a dozen more *PR* people. Beside Wilson were Muchnic, Margaret de Silver, and Rosalind. Muchnic was disconcerted to observe Mary "making up to the judge"—though Wilson philosophically said, "Why shouldn't she?"—and surprised at how angry Mary was to see Rosalind seated by her father. Rosalind didn't accept her tales of Wilson's brutality ("It wasn't till I got to the trial that I realized Mary was claiming that I'd seen my father kick her in the stomach, which I hadn't"), but out of loyalty to Reuel refused Wilson's lawyer's request to testify about McCarthy's violent outbursts. The judge, scolding the couple as he saved them from airing more assertions and counterassertions, had the suit settled out of court. In the final divorce judgment a year later she was granted custody of Reuel for the school year, while Wilson had custody during summers, and the right to choose his schools. Holidays were shared. Alimony was established by the court at sixty dollars a week.

Each emotionally rebounded, immediately seeking other partners, and within two years had remarried. In Elena Thornton, a gentle, intelligent, cultivated European eleven years younger than he, Wilson at last found a helpmeet, while Bowden Broadwater, a Harvard aesthete who'd been a copy editor at *The New Yorker*, kept house for Mary and devoted himself to her career. Both new mates would be long suffering, for Wilson was set in his ways and this time around Mary married someone she could dominate. Reuel, in Adelaide's view the "waif of two brilliant people," was lucky in his stepparents. Bowden, a loving stepfather, tried to make Wilson interesting and funny rather than fearful, substituting "Monstro," out of H. P. Lovecraft's horror stories, for the Minotaur. Elena, who had a son six years older than Reuel, became a devoted second mother during the summers.

McCarthy recalled that they handled their relations reasonably "after the first bad period of shouting into the phone." She credited Wilson (who may well have been cued by Elena) with showing her how to behave as a divorced parent. "He was always so good about me to Reuel," she explained. "He refrained from any caviling and criticism. He gave me a sort of code about this, and I reciprocated." She eventually stopped belittling him to their son. "One day when Reuel was about nine," she told the present writer, "I began talking about Edmund and his work, with high esteem. Reuel said, 'Mommy, you mean my father is a great critic?'—and he smiled—'I always thought he was just a two-bit book reviewer.'" She was pleased that he called her on the way she had conditioned him to think of his distinguished father, glad to believe he'd grow up unburdened by her resentment. Though his parents' expectations wouldn't be easy on Reuel, the concerns about him expressed in their letters helped them become friends again.

As the radicalism of the 1930s faded they remained leaders of literary and liberal opinion, but had they remained married, their egos would have continued to collide. "When Edmund and Mary differed about American literature and politics, it was about something each thought he was an expert on," said Arthur Schlesinger, and Broadwater noted "a sense of rivalry between them" when he met them in 1945. One can compare the two on Conrad, whose "amount of control," Mary writes to Wilson of *Lord Jim*, "is wonderful," but whom Wilson, in a letter to Morton Zabel about *Under Western Eyes*, finds pedantic in his use of nonparticipant observers. Mary: "the theme is pursued with such absolute relentlessness—nothing is accidental or irrelevant; it is like a play of Racine's worked out in the romantic tradition, that is, nature, atmosphere, picturesque anecdote, etc. are used to promote a classical effect." Wilson: "he keeps going back and telling you what is behind scenes from which you have drawn the correct inferences, and these returns upon himself simply drive me crazy. You know from the moment that Razumov shows up in Geneva that he is going to be moved by Miss Haldin to perform some act of contrition and that is precisely what he does, in a way that occasions little surprise." Broadwater thought they had different kinds of intelligence. "Mary's mind was brilliant, but not fine, not subtle, not profound, as Edmund was, in his denatured way."

In a curious episode eight years after the divorce, Mary and Bowden spent a year at Wellfleet near Money Hill, buying a house that was later owned by the painter and writer Mary Meigs. McCarthy's congenial encounters with Wilson delighted Adelaide, who'd previously seen them "either at a high pitch of intellectual excitement or tearing each other apart." Elena found all this somewhat difficult, and Nina Chavchavadze kept others from encouraging Mary socially. In the satirical novel *A Charmed Life*, begun in Wellfleet and finished a year after she left, Mary pillories this bohemia, being particularly savage with Mary Meigs, to whom, many years later, she apologized. Wilson becomes the oafish critic Miles while his new wife—"a handmaiden made to serve," Mary privately declared of Elena—rushes around saying, "Dearest, Dearest, Dearest." In the rickety plot, Martha, the ex-wife, now married again, is half-seduced, half-raped on a horsehair sofa by Miles when her young husband leaves for the weekend. She finds herself pregnant, doesn't know who the father is, must have an abortion. Thus McCarthy's private history is fictionalized at Wilson's expense, from their initial meeting on the couch at Stamford, when she followed him into the study, through the consequences of her fling with the youth who may have been Ralph Manheim. On the way to the abortion Martha conveniently dies in a car wreck. It is not likely that all this was of much therapeutic value. Two years later, however, McCarthy directly engaged her past in *Memories of a Catholic Girlhood*, recounting the desolate years with Uncle Myers and Aunt Margaret.

Her rapprochement with Wilson as Reuel's father evolved into a reciprocal tolerance that they maintained until Wilson's death, despite Mary's travesty of him as Miles and his share in the Harald Petersen composite of *The Group*. In 1962 she wrote to him, "In case you saw the horrible thing about me in *Esquire*, I trust you gathered that I'm not responsible for unpleasant passages about you in it. The author must have dredged them out of the old court files." In 1971 she joined James Baldwin in lobbying for Wilson to be awarded a literary prize in France. She wrote to her ailing ex that it was worth "about $5545," and entertained him with the literary politics among the judges—"a very deaf Portuguese writer—the pivotal figure in the vote—thought he was being lobbied to vote for Angus Wilson." Urging Edmund to get more of his books translated into French, she happily reported that "Jimmy Baldwin told the audience (and the jury) that the only American writers who had influenced him when young were Henry James and you." Six years after Wilson's death, McCarthy plugged the selection of Wilson's letters that Elena had edited in the London *Observer*: "He sounds like a man of leisure with all the time in the world to advise, reprove, and comment on his writer friends, when in fact he was in a constant bustle of literary production, turning out goods and services of the highest quality in a variety of fields: journalism, editing, fiction, verse, on-the-spot reporting, talent-scouting, scholarship, spoofs, serious criticism." She had come into her powers in this workshop. Without Wilson's pressure and support she wouldn't, she often said, have written fiction, and in the best of her criticism, memoir, and travel writing she is his peer.

Wilson made a character of her once, in *The Little Blue Light*, published in 1950, produced in Cambridge that year and New York the next. In this play Frank, a liberal editor, struggles against the dark forces of monopolistic corporations and political cabals, assisted by his well-meaning but cynical and erratic wife, who has affairs. "A handsome brunette, in her early thirties," Judith "is tense, with a habitual tensity that never completely relaxes." At one point, trying to comfort her, Frank puts his arms around her, prompting her to cry out, "Don't hit me!" and then, "You want to kill me!" Jessica Tandy, who played the part, rendered this so convincingly that Rosalind says Wilson found it difficult to watch. Though he praised Tandy's skillful English acting, he was "much more comfortable," his daughter reports, with Arlene Francis's performance in the (brief) New York run. Perhaps Wilson's marriage had taught him something, for the little blue light, a mysterious electric ray, a sort of flashlight, with which the conspiratorial elite maintains its sway (it derived from a nightmare of his) is triggered by the destructive personal impulses of the forces of good. When Frank and Judith and their allies discover the blue light planted on the mantelpiece and begin arguing about whose emotions have turned it on, they are blown up.

A decade after Wilson's death and seven years before McCarthy's, in 1982, Leon Edel set off an equivalent explosion, which ended her hard-won tolerance of Wilson. In editing *The Forties* Edel sent her a page-and-a-half account of their marriage that Wilson had inserted into his journal. Explaining his near abandonment of journal writing from 1941 to 1945, he says he "could not bear to write about" these years, for "our life— though we had also a great deal of fun—was sometimes absolutely night-marish." Mary's dignity and sense of duty made her collapses "tragic," and covering them up was a strain. He admits to having "reacted neurotically too, as I usually do with women I live with," but adds that Mary found it hard to take responsibility and "except in the use of her intellect had al-ways remained a child." The passage has the smug paternalism of the self-styled rational man with an erratic wife, and it omits his explosions when drinking, yet is accurate about McCarthy's seizures. Four decades had passed, however, since "Ghostly Father" and "The Weeds," and in *Memoirs of a Catholic Girlhood* she hadn't conceded that the brutality of Myers and Margaret had any long-term effects on her behavior or her psy-che. "I don't mean I thought I was crazy," she had written to Wilson from Payne Whitney, and she took this journal entry as an attack from the grave upon her sanity. In leaving it out—as he would certainly have wished dur-ing her lifetime—Edel did not note that Wilson had anything to say on his own behalf. He was exposed to McCarthy's revenge, the attribution to him, for her biographers and in *Intellectual Memoirs*, of the behavior of the Wilson-Myers figure of her fiction. Her attack on Wilson as a batterer, in the vein of her first affadavit when seeking custody of Reuel, blackened his reputation until Kiernan collected evidence from all sides about Mc-Carthy's life.

That Wilson said so little about their marriage afterward was not only because at times it had been nightmarish. He hadn't been able to hold this "beautiful and brilliant girl," as he addressed her in a flattering letter. At last enjoying intellectual equality in a marriage, he learned that it could come with a price. After the window-breaking fight with Mary in

1944 he'd acknowledged that she had things she wanted to do in which he was no longer interested, that she couldn't be expected to "sympathize with the miseries—like the death of old friends, bad habits and diseases of one's own, and a certain inevitable disillusionment with the world that has to be struggled against—that hit you when you get on in your forties." Until defeated over the custody issue, however, he had tried to maintain control. "I am a very quarrelsome man," he admitted to Anaïs Nin when seeking sympathy for his wounds after the judge's decision. Yet over the years his remarks, in the journal and to more than one friend, indicate that he "never ceased to care for Mary." American letters has not seen another alliance so flawed and so distinguished.

19

Memoir and Fiction, by Night and by Day

In popular American history World War II is a crusade against evil, its barbarity justified by Pearl Harbor and the revelation of the Nazi death camps. McCarthy and Wilson both opposed the entry of the United States into the war. But in 1942 or 1943, when the evidence of Nazi atrocities registered with her Jewish friends at *Partisan Review*, Mary began to support the war effort. Wilson remained skeptical. He had affirmed the intellectual and moral tradition of Judaism through Marx, yet when Kazin urged that this was a war to save the Jews, he pointed out that FDR was quite willing to send the Jews back to Germany, that the United States had entered the European war because Hitler held to his Japanese alliance. He didn't—as Kazin asserts—consider Pearl Harbor a plot by the president as did Charles A. Beard, whom Wilson thought "too purposive and flint-like himself to understand the basic porousness of Roosevelt." Nor would he take the account in Secretary of War Stimson's diary of a White House meeting on November 26, 1941, about maneuvering the Japanese "into the position of firing the first shot without allowing too much danger to ourselves" (it was not known that they could bomb Pearl Harbor) as the president's intent. Roosevelt was, however, Wilson noted, relieved politically when the Japanese did strike first, and with his speech to the nation had "thrown on the switch," at once releasing "all the usual passions of war-time."

The propaganda on the home front came to sicken him. In 1943–1944 the journal records newsreels denouncing the Japanese as *"animals"* to be fought and killed—"precisely the same kind of thing that Goebbels used to instill into the Germans the idea that they could exterminate the Poles: the Poles were an inferior race—the blacks were not people but animals."

Documenting "the spiral of our society going, as Dos says, down the drain," he has a nightmare vision of his countrymen in thrall to push-button warfare. He sees how a euphemism like "softening up" the enemy works, and in the ability "to blow up whole cities from the air without getting hit or burnt oneself, and while soaring serenely above them" detects an element of illicit pleasure the Germans must also have felt when they "were bombing London before we had begun bombing them." Removed from one's object by a mathematical process and "the mechanical bomb-sight," one could put aside the "constraints of the conventions and codes that we live under" and gratify "the destructive spirit, as it were, in a pure abstract form." Wilson bitterly objected to the bombing of cultural monuments in Germany, the firestorm with which the RAF killed hundreds of thousands in Dresden. In essays of the 1950s, he reminded readers that the professedly Christian nations had gone in for "large-scale murder, for suffocating, burning, and blowing up one's enemies" as heartily as "the Odin-worshipping Nazis, the Emperor-worshipping Japanese or the officially atheist Russians," and denounced the American decision "to go the Nazis one better by destroying whole Japanese towns—killing or crippling for life all ages and sexes of noncombatants—through the effects of radioactivity."

This is the political background of *Memoirs of Hecate County*, the nominally interconnected tales of an intellectual suburbia where hopes and standards turn to dust. Singly and together, these stories, written through the early 1940s, are dark, as if Wilson were stalking through an imagined underworld presided over by the triple-headed goddess, a photo of whose statue graced the first edition alongside a quotation from Gogol's fearsome *Viy*. He called *Hecate County* "my favorite among my books," but it was only part of what he was producing in these years. Two sunny memoirs preceded it—the Lakewood scene of his Kimball grandparents in 1939 and "Mr. Rolfe" in 1942. His memoir of Paul Rosenfeld in 1947 would be followed by those of Millay and Gauss five years later. Together with "The Old Stone House" and the portrait of his father in "The Author at Sixty," these affirmations of the past might be brought together in a book of their own, which would have room for the autobiographical fragments of *A Prelude* and *A Piece of My Mind*. They suggest a Wilson quite apart from the man, grim and bleak and solitary, who wrote *Hecate County*. We have two Wilsons here, and the one who wrote fiction pursued the truth as he imagined it just as, in his nonfiction, the other attempted to reach and preserve the essence of people he'd lost.

Hecate County was written after a fiction project he did not complete. *The Story of the Three Wishes* was to take a man through successive destinies as a broker in Manhattan, a bureaucrat in Soviet Moscow, and an independent writer on the Cape. Wilson wrote only the first section, which took a different direction than he had planned. Published three decades after his death and named by Neale Reinitz, its editor, *The Higher Jazz*, this short novel returns to the mid-1920s, when people met at Paul Rosenfeld's to talk of American music. Wilson's German-American protagonist, Fritz Dietrich, aspires to compose in an idiom somewhere between jazz, the Americana of Charles Ives, and the European modernism of Schönberg and Stravinsky. Dietrich speaks for the author when he says, "Schoenberg had always gotten me and he still did. It was partly the Wagner that was still behind it, though all reduced to moonlight and blackness, discolored and flattened out—the old thrill of the Germanic musical theater, the shiver and the shudder and the longing ache." The harsh speech-song *Pierrot Lunaire* points this man's way when he sets it opposite the music of a burlesque show.

The Higher Jazz evokes the nervous energy and complicated harmonies of a decade with which Wilson identified as it receded into the past. He re-creates the raw, clever talk of evenings at parties and speakeasies and derives characters and incidents from his journals. The protagonist's wife, Caroline, is modeled on Margaret Canby; another character is in the image of Dorothy Parker, whose Benchley-like companion gives way to a lover drawn from those of Parker's later years. They play a game in which they take on different identities, and the game grows ever more destructive. The Parker figure's life begins to implode; she even tries to kill herself. Yet Wilson can't integrate his plot with the search for a musical synthesis. Not wanting to repeat the struggle of *I Thought of Daisy*, he put this work aside and began the stories of *Hecate County*.

"Ellen Terhune," about a major female composer blocked in her work, is one of the book's successes. A psychological ghost story with a flavor of Poe and of James's *Turn of the Screw*, it draws on the excitement and unease that Edna Millay and her poetry continued to stir in him. It reaches behind the twenties into his Victorian childhood. Ellen's home, Vallombrosa, is a magnified version of 12 Wallace Street, her forebears cultivated turn-of-the-century gentry, aloof from business yet vulnerable to Wall Street's cycles. Her large head, she says, damaged her mother at birth, and she wonders if her parents should have married. During several visits to her house the narrator is progressively taken into Ellen's past, and though the machinery of going back in time occasionally creaks, the tale is compelling, its ending uncanny. A conversation with a young woman who turns out to be Ellen's mother before marriage is superimposed upon Ellen's endless reiteration of a piano passage, heard as if it were in the next room, at just the time, it seems, that she pounded out on a piano the identical chords over and over in a New York hotel before dying of a heart attack. The description of her music (suggestive also of sexual failure) conveys the cry of her soul—music she was never able to complete, which now reaches the world in Wilson's characterization.

Offering *Hecate County* to Maxwell Perkins, he wrote that all six of these tales "have an element of fantasy and a kind of odor of damnation." Several are also briskly satirical. "The Man Who Shot Snapping Turtles" is Wilson's version of the Protestant-Puritan role in the rise of capitalism, a parable colored by the betrayal of Marxist ideals in the Soviet Union and his fear—as in his 1942 poem about Fitzgerald—that the species is deteriorating. A retired chemistry professor named Stryker, unable to protect the beautiful ducks in his pond from their ugly hereditary enemies, the snapping turtles, is persuaded by a sardonic ad-man neighbor to raise the snappers for soup, and himself becomes the capitalistic equivalent of a snapping turtle. "How do we know that some of His lowest creatures aren't beginning to get out of hand and clean up on the higher ones?" the advertising man asks in the vein of the introduction to *Patriotic Gore*, where Wilson would liken warring nations to sea slugs. "Glimpses of Wilbur Flick" caricatures rich dilettantes whom he had known. An effete outsider at college, and later the host of edgy parties in New York, Wilbur tries Catholicism after the Crash (when this fails, the chapel in his mansion is converted to a badminton court); he then hazards a vaguely Nietzschean aesthetic elitism, and is later enthralled by the secret brotherhood of the Communist Party. His only success is at sleight of hand, which he develops into a dazzling nightclub act, but he grows disillusioned with magic because of the dimension of fakery that it—and any art, Wilson suggests—contains.

"The Milhollands and Their Damned Soul" is a gossipy spoof of book clubs and the book business, driven by impatience with the cultivated Van Doren family, whose sunny salesmanship Wilson blamed for lowering standards. A decade before, in the verse satire "The Three Limperary Cripples" he'd laughed off their promotion of their own books alongside such treasures as *Elizabeth and [Es]Sex—A Farewell to Farms* by Mark van Dorman, *Black Majesty* by Dark Van Moron, *The Life of Joseph Wood*

Peacock by his uncle Doc van Doren, and *Training the Giant Panda* by "quaint old Trader van Horen." In *Hecate County* the once foolish Bunk of the Bunch Club has turned into a menacing monopoly called The Reader's Circle, which dumps thousands of books from second- to fourth-rate on the market, advertising the product through pretend-reviews in *The Booklover*. This is Devil's work, Wilson thinks, and his two kibitzing characters speculate that the Milhollands have a compact with Old Nick in which one after another of their associates is sold to him—the *âme damnée*, or fall guy, who'll make a fool of himself and be exposed as a crook while the racket continues to prosper.

Proposing that a new young Milholland just out of Yale will be cast in the sacrificial role, Wilson eerily anticipated Charles Van Doren's self-destruction on the rigged game show *Twenty-One* thirteen years after this book appeared. When Van Doren—himself a fine teacher—was trapped and corrupted, he rationalized that his staged successes would help Americans take learning seriously. In the 1994 film *Quiz Show*, which contrasts a genteel professoriat to the dark ways of NBC and Madison Avenue, Wilson is implausibly shown (and several times called "Bunny") at a family dinner on Mark Van Doren's birthday, a bizarre detail given the gulf between this family and everything that Wilson represented. Several years after the quiz show scandal, he observed to the author that the chickens of salesmanship and self-promotion had come home to roost.

Nearly half this 400-plus-page book is given to "The Princess with the Golden Hair," which embodies Wilson's wish that "literature could be reality, as natural as conversation, yet as deep as life itself." His excitement on reading over the journal passages about Frances Minihan was the story's source. He told Dawn Powell (revealing his limits as a fiction writer) that these 100 typewritten pages were better than a novel, for "an invented character would have to be so consistent it could not be described in constantly varying lights" and shifting perspective. Giving Frances the name Anna, and compressing their affair into two years, from before the Crash through the first months of the Depression, he contrasts her not to Margaret but to the partly invented character drawn from Elizabeth Waugh. As Imogen Loomis, Elizabeth becomes a blonde, and Wilson complements her classic beauty and arty romanticism with a Tudor country house (its "wainscoted and tapestried smell, like everything about the Loomises, several degrees too rich"), a social schedule in New York, and a tolerant public relations man for a husband.

The narrator tells himself he sympathizes with working people, that

Anna is "the real world, the base on which everything rested." Yet he is modeled on petit-bourgeois Frédéric Moreau in Flaubert's *L'éducation sentimentale*, and introduces himself with the thought that there may be "nothing more demoralizing than a small but adequate income." Imogen's exotic costumes and talk of faraway places and past eras enhance her role as the lure of the chase, the dream of female sexual perfection. Wilson's broadly Marxist perspective also depends on the dilemma of man's alleged desire for both female purity and great sex. The conventional values attached to the dance-hall girl and the upper-middle-class married woman are, however, reversed: the sexually eager Anna is characterized as pure, while the always retreating Imogen proves corrupt.

Imogen's surgical corset was not his invention. Mary McCarthy remembered that Elizabeth wore one for her "sciatica." Claiming a spinal injury from Pott's disease, Imogen uses hers to defend herself from men, knowing it increases their desire. If "all the women" in *Hecate County* "except Anna are witches," as Wilson wrote to an admirer of the book, Imogen is a witch out of Freud. A medical dictionary eventually informs the narrator of the neuromimetic version of her malady. "Delivered" of his dream of the princess, he cares for his mistress through a surgery, then, just as Wilson did, steps aside so she can marry another man, and is left with the damning sense of failure in this relationship that Wilson tried to dodge when he gave up Frances in 1929 and again in 1935. The story concludes, "I was back now in Hecate County and we should never make love again."

"My long story is probably the best damn thing I ever wrote," he boasted to Morton Zabel when it was done, qualifying this to "it has given me more satisfaction, as far as I can remember, than anything else." He thought he had come to terms with his class limitations, the bourgeois psychology and false romanticism that caused him to lose Frances. And the anatomy of sex, including the scene with Imogen drawn from his meeting with Elizabeth at the Concord Inn, would, until *Hecate County* was repressed, make it a bestseller. There is, however, an absence of joy in Wilson's realism, as Anaïs Nin points out—"a heaviness throughout, and a prosaic quality." Nabokov informed his friend that the effect was "remarkably chaste, despite the frankness," and two generations after *Lolita*— three after Henry Miller's *Tropics*—these passages seem marked by the Puritan heritage. Remote from what Wilson, momentarily looking back to his pursuit of Millay, calls "heartbreak, the love that faded out or that one had to lose," they affect us less than certain domestic and painterly evocations of sensuality ("I opened the window and we stood by it and felt on

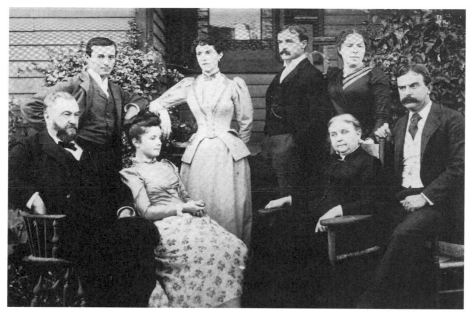

Kimball family group, including the grandparents, uncles, and aunts Wilson was closest to in his youth. His mother is third from left; Aunt Laura fourth from left; Uncle Reuel on right.

Wilson's paternal grandparents. Charlotte Ann Wilson, a more severe Calvinist than her minister husband, amused herself by studying mathematics and brought her son, Edmund Wilson, Sr., up on a hellfire catechism.

Edmund Wilson as Attorney General of New Jersey. A lifelong Republican, he broke up the Republican racket that controlled Atlantic City and sent more than one hundred men to jail.

Helen Mather Kimball Wilson in later life, after she told her son that brilliant men always have "something wrong with them"

Young Edmund with his mother

Sandy and Edmund, inseparable companions

Alfred Grosvenor Rolfe, whom at fourteen Wilson found a daunting figure, but in whose classroom there turned out to be "something human, heroic, and shining"

The boy looking settled in at Hill, already an acolyte of literature

Leader of the literary group at Princeton, named by his classmates most likely bachelor

An austere Christian Gauss

Stanley Dell in 1916. He didn't replace his Christian faith with a faith in literature, though he eventually found Jung.

John Peale Bishop, the romantic poet who would start out life with Wilson in New York, but never achieve what his friend hoped

The non-soldier in his mother's garden

Edna St. Vincent Millay. "For my time," Wilson recalled, "the word *love* had meant heartbreak, the love that faded out or that one had to lose."

Mary Blair in *The Crime in the Whistler Room*

Elinor Wylie, for a time Wilson's "spiritual sister" and his "mental mother"

F. Scott Fitzgerald in 1922

Ernest Hemingway in the twenties

Wilson at the end of the twenties

Margaret Canby, after whose death Wilson was long haunted by regret for their failed relationship

John Dos Passos commenting on his investigation of the West Virginia coal miners in 1931, six months after Wilson's trip

Louise Bogan, photographed by Ford Madox Ford in France in 1933. She loved Wilson "like a brother."

Elizabeth Waugh, the redheaded woman who became the Princess with the Golden Hair, painted by her father-in-law "Wizard" Waugh

Louise Fort Connor, Wilson's love for five years, who had him write to her doctor that she was not the Princess

Isaiah Berlin in conversation

"E.W. and M. McC.," 1942

Vladimir Nabokov during his
Wellesley years

Dawn Powell, dear friend and companion

Helen Muchnic, not long after she and Wilson met

Mamaine Paget, with whom Wilson fell in love in 1945, and whom he cherished as a friend until her untimely death

Anaïs Nin, who did not return Wilson's feeling, but wanted his praise for her work

The house on Money Hill Road in Wellfleet

Elena at Gull Pond

Reuel and his father, two years after his
parents divorced and remarried

The family, reconstituted by Elena, on the terrace she had made at Wellfleet. Reuel is on the left; Rosalind in the center, next to Edmund; Elena's son Henry Thornton on the right; and Helen Miranda in her mother's arms.

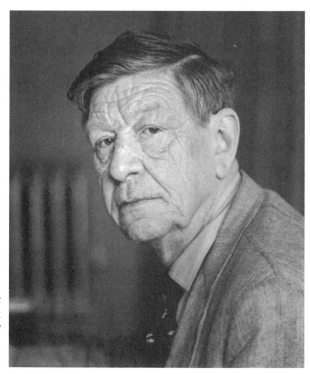

W. H. Auden, whose face Wilson likened to "some sort of technical map"

Wilson with the owl that became an emblem of its owner

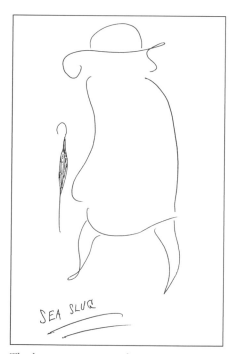

SEA SLUG

The bureaucrat as sea slug

Old New York literary club man
of the '90's

A devilish persona of EW

Mary Meigs, Marie-Claire Blais, and
Barbara Deming at Wellfleet in 1965

The old stone house

Mary Pcolar

Reuel and his mother in Paris, early sixties

Elena on the terrace at Wellfleet

Wilson at *The New Yorker*

Rosalind at the Cape in 1968

Helen Miranda, several years after her father's death

our sweaty cheeks the delicious fresh ice-cold air, and afterwards we went into the garden, where the rosebushes held drops of rain and the spare towering locust trees were stirring their fronds in a little wind, and we breathed in the rich August air that had a smell, as we said, like chestnuts"). The story Wilson tells pales beside his life in the years of Frances and Margaret and his first struggles on the Left. What *Hecate County* preserves, as Louis Menand has said, is "the seedy, desperate, hollow, and, somehow, hopeful world of New York" from Prohibition through the Depression. Wilson's shallow suburbanites coming into town to work in the arts or to shop or have assignations set off the Frances character with her Ukrainian background and gruesome home life, a figure of the city, grainy and vital.

The book ends with the phantasmagorical "Mr. and Mrs. Blackburn at Home." A vision of the Eastern Seaboard as a charming landscape with houses and boats amid lawns and woods sets off this dark tale, which stars the Devil, Blackburn, in a ten-page monologue in French about the difficulty of his job under modern conditions. Introduced as one of those cosmopolitan European refugees who've resettled in this country during the war years, the Devil is a wit of the age of Voltaire and a stand-in for Wilson, who, like Marx, could see himself contending with God (when Wilson visited his friends the Chavchavadzes he signed their guest book "N. N. Chernokhvostov," the Devil's Russian nickname). The Soviets and the Nazis give evil a bad name, are boorish and banal, Blackburn complains. They lack proper respect for the personage he calls "My Opposite Number." Explaining that during the Inquisition he'd sided with the strong-minded heretics who were its victims, he now understands that their liberating gestures had to be squashed. He credits his decision to settle in the United States to the survival of the sense of sin through the work of good men like Jonathan Edwards.

At the party where Blackburn holds forth in this fashion, the narrator momentarily thinks he can learn to like Hecate County—get a dog, a boat, be a good neighbor. But when he turns to kiss Jo Gates, a pleasant woman drawn from Margaret, her teeth are transformed to protruding fangs, and in the book's last scene his cherished house in the woods cannot protect him from a world where humans must confront terror and delusion at every turn. The flicker of hellfire throughout *Hecate County* echoes the old Manichaean theme of Mark Twain and Hawthorne and of Edwards's Enfield sermon, the fear that the world is "going to Hell in a handbasket."

At the opposite pole in the writing of Wilson's middle years are the memoirs of people and places of his youth that embody his personal values. This series had begun with his return to the old stone house at Talcottville during the Depression. "At Laurelwood" (1939)—first drafted at a café in Vittel twenty years before—is a Victorian idyll on which the world impinges through the millionaire Finch establishment, the autocratic young baron quick to instruct servants in "their duty." Wilson has learned that the real James Finch proved too frivolous to hang on to his railroad empire—"victim to a rival capitalistic brontosaurus who had just hatched out of the swamp and was still in the aggressive phase." This is said with a perceptible curl of the lip, but where Edmund the boy was sure his people were different, Wilson the student of Marx and Dickens knows that his Kimball uncles (and his mother) had "fallen into the orbit of the power" represented by his playmate. "The tides of society can give a new configuration to all but the strongest personalities, if they do not sweep them away."

In "Mr. Rolfe" he doesn't use the word "humanist," with its ideological burden after Babbitt and More, but recalls the "human, heroic, and shining" nimbus of his Greek teacher's classroom, invokes the "nobility and naiveté" of this language, the discipline required to learn it. Rolfe's Yankee accent and expression lead Wilson back to the Concord of Emerson and Thoreau, the moment when "a rough-hewn country stock" had acquired "the freedom to smile and to play, to work at belles-lettres for their own sake." He omits the limericks informing the boys about American presidents, the doggerel and pep songs that kept up their spirits, but amuses us with "Weeping Bob" and the other imported preachers, with Mrs. John earnestly quizzing potential sinners in the "Sky Parlor." These delicious vignettes of boys dragooned and exhorted reveal the pressures he had resisted when learning to think for himself, and he concludes by setting the ideals and discipline of Hellenism against "the political creeds, with their secular evangelism, that are taking the Church's place."

The portrait of Rosenfeld pays tribute to a friend whose career had been sidetracked. Paul had done much for the cross-fertilization of music with literature and painting during the 1920s. His writing was impressionistic, and its metaphoric density sometimes seemed overdone—at *Vanity Fair* Wilson had once performed (as he put it to Bishop) "a great phlebotomy" on one of Paul's essays, "letting off several quarts of surplus metaphor, prophesy, Pythian rhapsody, outpourings about Stieglitz and nameless lymphatic humors." His judgment was, however, as fine as Wilson asserts, and his responsiveness, his cultivated conversation, had been an oasis amid the confusion and waste of bohemia. He had lost his avant-garde readers as well as his small private income after the Crash, and hadn't lived to see his criticism reprinted in the new attention to American music after World War II. Wilson savors an evening of talk, not long before his friend's death, when they'd almost seen the night through together, "so exhilarated, abounding so, as Henry James would say, in our own old sense." The piece ends with his equivalent of a benediction. The kind of work Paul did "pays for itself," affording "elevation and liberation of spirit." On behalf of the priesthood of literature Wilson states that "Paul's best writing bears on every page his triumph and his justification."

The personal memoirs are for most readers more satisfying than *Memoirs of Hecate County,* for Wilson was never quite at ease with "invented" characters and the satirical stories lack Swift's gift for hate. He rounds out the reconsideration of his youth—to be expanded during the 1950s—with "Thoughts on Being Bibliographed," written to accompany a comprehensive list of his writings prepared by Arthur Mizener. Here he looks back on the 1920s and '30s as if summarizing ancient history—the overinflation of the literary marketplace as the boom progressed and the sobering up after the Crash, the revolutionary dream of "the first truly human culture," one then flattened beneath Hitler's and Stalin's tanks. With World War II, American writers retreated either into the debilitating embrace of Hollywood and Henry Luce or into the universities. Though Wilson disliked the symbol-myth criticism that took over the quarterlies as well as the English departments, and in this essay foresees the sublimated Marxist politics later to be in fashion there, he respects the young men and women who can find "no decent work" elsewhere and in teaching, he assumes, "are at least in a position to keep in touch with the great work of the past instead of degrading the taste of the present." He denounces *Time* and *Life* not, as liberals of the 1950s and '60s would, for their Republican bias, but for pretending that facts speak for themselves and dictate their own importance. It is the individual voice that must "give life some value and point."

He cites his debt to the journalism of De Quincey and Poe as well as Shaw and Mencken, critics who had actively contributed to their national literatures. Poe in particular had been able to do fine work in units suitable for the magazines and "by getting the editors, in some cases, to print pieces that had been published before but of which he had prepared new versions," scored the triumph of "making them pay him for the gratuitous labor of rewriting demanded by his artistic conscience." Much of Wilson's later work will use this strategy. He outlines the practice of developing subjects in reviews that will turn into articles to be thoroughly rewritten as a book, enabling him to refine his ideas and absorb criticism. Wilson's methodology as a literary journalist, along with his awkwardness at the podium and an impatience that made it hard to be a good classroom teacher, separated him from those who, like Allen Tate and Robert Penn Warren and the *Partisan Reviewers*, in these years began supporting themselves in academe.

He looked back to the shared aspirations of his youth, when "you read Shakespeare, Shelley, George Meredith, Dostoyevsky, Ibsen, and you wanted, however imperfectly and on however infinitesimal a scale, to learn their trade and have the freedom of their company." Sustained by this desire, he had arrived, he said, "at middle age under the illusion that I had not really begun to write." To examine the list of his hundreds of reviews and essays persuaded Wilson that he was "past the age for this kind of activity." However, by the time "Thoughts on Being Bibliographed" appeared he had a new platform at *The New Yorker* and, in Pip's phrase from *Great Expectations*, "had begun the world again."

20

At *The New Yorker* and in England and Italy:
Waugh, Silone, Santayana

Wilson placed poems as well as sections of his Russian journal and the memoir "At Laurelwood" in *The New Yorker*. Katharine White, previously Katharine Angell, who has been credited with making the magazine more literary, had cultivated him since 1928. Accepting the satire on Princeton, "Disloyal Lines to an Alumnus," she teasingly wondered whether it could be made less disrespectful of religion, then asked if he might someday be "open to the suggestion of a book reviewer job." Harold Ross also admired Wilson, and on the two or three occasions when he'd rejected something of his had managed to imply it was too good for the magazine—once Ross cracked that a piece made him resolve to be a better person, "but it's not for us."

Wilson sometimes dreamed of an organ of American literature like the *Nouvelle revue française*, and in April 1942—when he was broke enough to allow Tate to promote him with far-off Louisiana State University—he urged Ross to start such a journal and put him in charge of it. When Ross was unable to locate the necessary financial backing, Wilson mentioned that he could "handle a department" at *The New Yorker*. The following fall, after James Thurber explained the critic's principles to Ross and in a five-page letter to Wilson (written with a magic marker because he was going blind) touted the editor's "snarling and glorious independence of the business office, advertizers, publishers, and other influences," Ross offered him the post of weekly book reviewer, which had been held by Clifton Fadiman. Wilson wanted an office, a secretary who could make "a comprehensive list at the beginning of every publishing season of the books with their dates of publication," the authority to review books that led him into other fields, and leeway to consider reprints of work he thought important. He requested and received a one-year contract for $10,000 plus $3,000 for expenses.

Just as *The New Republic* of Herbert Croly and Walter Lippmann, with its aspiration for America, fostered his assimilation of a European avant-garde in art and politics, so *The New Yorker* of Ross and William Shawn would become a podium for his eclectic exploration of books and milieux after World War II. He lacked *The New Yorker*'s then characteristic tone, was never a member of the club, yet the editors' commitment to culture as opposed to commerce was his own and the magazine's sleek advertising, paradoxically, would help support his long articles. On its side, *The New Yorker* was enhanced by Wilson's intellectual and moral authority.

The criticism collected in his first literary chronicle, *Classics and Commercials*, addresses a much larger, more diffuse group of readers than he had before, and the range of these reviews, from British satire to the American bestsellers he famously attacked, reflects this. Sometimes books are paired off by comparison and contrast, as he'd done at *Vanity Fair*. Wilson's commentary is direct, yet fluent and conversational. He enables a reader to pick up bits of information much as a good teacher does, a skill more visible here than in his tightly focused critical essays. To go with him from book to book in *Classics and Commercials*, each a window upon a different scene, is to see the literary culture of the decade through the prism of Wilson's mind.

Omitted here, in addition to works with a topical bearing on the war, are several pieces launching new writers: Anaïs Nin's stories in *Under a Glass Bell* (called to Wilson's attention by Frances Steloff at the Gotham Book Mart) were dream fiction combining "a sometimes exquisite poetry with a homely realistic observation"; Saul Bellow's novel *Dangling Man* was an impressively honest account of the psychology of those who'd graduated in the Depression to confront the war. Also absent is Wilson's 1944 critique of Dawn Powell for leaving her "in many ways excellent" books in the state of "all-but-final-drafts," without "the sculptural rehandling" of the material "which is to bring out its self-consistent contours and set it in a permanent pose." He is at his most professional in this appraisal of *My Home Is Far Away*, one less well-known than the more generous 1962 assessment of Powell in *The Bit Between My Teeth*. Her biographer says she was "devastated" by his "astute" observations, for no equally powerful favorable review appeared to balance them. While tactfully leaving this piece out of *Classics*, he included "A Toast and a Tear for Dorothy Parker." The Viking *Portable Parker* revealed his old friend's authority as a voice of her time, though her lasting work seemed to end "somewhere in the early thirties." Hollywood, which Fitzgerald had survived as a writer, destroyed Parker. "Absolute Hollywood corrupts absolutely" was now one of Anti-Christ's sayings.*

The end of the American movements of his youth left English literature as the focus of Wilson's weightier pieces. He urged the virtues of Joseph Campbell's guide to *Finnegans Wake*, explained why Dr. Johnson impressed him more than Boswell, used new editions to take up Shakespeare and Jane Austen. Evelyn Waugh he deemed "the only first-rate comic genius that has appeared in English since Bernard Shaw." In Waugh's early novels a satirist's convention combined "the outrageous with the plausible without offending our sense of truth." Wilson loved the scene in *A Handful of Dust* in which the Englishman is captured by a tribal chief and must spend the rest of his life reading Dickens aloud to him in the jungles of the Amazon. Summing up Waugh, the critic declares that as an outsider, a climber, an artist, "the savagery he is afraid of is somehow the same thing as the audacity that so delights him."

This British standard is set against commercial, middlebrow work manufactured for the American mass market. Taking up the current formula of fiction by women for women, Wilson reports on a novel that allows its heroine to "have every possible cake and manage to eat it, too," predicting it will be a hit, and in a wry postscript noting its sales have just hit 900,000. *The Robe* had already sold 7.5 million copies. Though he protests against the "five-and-ten-cent store" prose of Lloyd Douglas's version of the Roman empire at the birth of Christ (the review is called "'You Can't Do This to Me!' Shrilled Celia"), he credits the book with a refreshing earnestness: it shows "that the ordinary reader, even in our ghastly time, does long for moral light, that he cannot live by bilge alone."

Wilson interprets the market for tales of horror as a longing for the supernatural characteristic of "periods of social confusion," "an instinct to inoculate ourselves against panic at the real horrors loose on the earth." So a decade later he would view the "awful orcs" of Tolkien, for whom his friend Auden had a passion. His famous attack on detective fiction—

---

*When Scott died, Parker was saddened by Hollywood's complete disinterest in his death. Standing over his coffin, she famously echoed the *Gatsby* character "Owl-eyes," murmuring, "The poor son of a bitch." Not recognizing the reference, the film industry took this as part of a pithy eulogy.

another vice for which he would tease Auden—sees these stories leading in well-rehearsed stages to the reassuring separation of the murderer from people "like you or me." Examining the favorites recommended to him by readers made him feel as though he had "to unpack large crates by swallowing the excelsior in order to find at the bottom a few bent and rusty nails." Dorothy Sayers's device of shutting up a man in an English belfry to be done in by the heavy ringing of the bells was "not a bad idea for a murder," he said in a follow-up article, one Conan Doyle could have realized "in an entertaining tale of thirty pages." Sayers padded it out to three hundred fifty via "one of those hackneyed cock-and-bull stories about a woman who commits bigamy without knowing it."

He was ready for a break when Shawn sent him to Europe at the beginning of 1945. While writing for *The New Yorker* every week for a year, he had completed "The Princess with the Golden Hair" and the concluding dark stories in *Memoirs of Hecate County*. The book was turned down by Scribner's and Houghton Mifflin, but Doubleday, newly managed by the lawyer Douglas Black, contracted to publish it and gave him a $2,000 advance. When McCarthy served papers on him, Nin provided sympathy. He'd admired her beauty at their first meeting several years before, making Mary momentarily jealous, and Anaïs was grateful for his review ("Being a writer, you must know what a joy it is when one is so accurately perceived," she wrote) and for including her book in his recommendations for Christmas reading. They had lunch before he sailed. "He is lonely and lost," Nin solemnly wrote in her diary after helping Wilson buy the clothing and sleeping bag required of a war correspondent. "He portrays himself as a man who has suffered because he loves clever women and 'clever women are impossibly neurotic.'" Travel, however, always picked Wilson up, and lonely and lost as he appeared to Nin, he went off to Europe on a high, singing, as he packed, the song "What's the Use of Wonderin'" from the new musical *Carousel*—"Something made him the way he is, / whether he's false or true."

When his Norwegian steamer docked in April 1945 he rediscovered London—the parks in their spring freshness, the statues, artists among them, mirroring a history of human accomplishment. The theater had apparently thrived on rocket attacks and the threat of instant annihilation. The literati were broadly educated, and if they condescended to things American, it was in opposition to the same easing of standards Wilson resisted. Initially taken around by the publisher Hamish Hamilton, he met

Elizabeth Bowen, Graham Greene, Stephen Spender, George Orwell, Henry Green, Peter Quennell, Evelyn Waugh, and Cyril Connolly, whose journal, *Horizon*, he'd been promoting. *Horizon* had stood apart from wartime rant and encouraged a variety of good writing. It reflected the personality of the polished dilettante and epicure who, though otherwise gleefully irresponsible, shared Wilson's passion for literature. Connolly gave a dinner party for him and the two enjoyed each other's gossip.

Wilson also met a beautiful and serious-minded Englishwoman of twenty-seven in the *Horizon* circle, who freed him from the grim fidelity of his struggle with Mary. Arthur Schlesinger recalled Mamaine Paget as someone "everyone adored," and Stephen Spender identified her with "the best of England." She and her twin sister, Celia, orphaned granddaughters of a clergyman, had been debutantes presented at court and featured in glossy magazines. Mamaine loved books and languages and was an accomplished pianist. Her manner was matter-of-fact and droll. She had an hourglass figure, an oval face with small, pouting, for Wilson eminently kissable lips, as well as "little diamond-bright blue eyes that might almost be used to cut glass or as points for Johanssen gauges." Her job was with the Ministry of Economic Warfare. She took him around the city, and he had enough of the perennial American fascination with English society to enjoy the chance to observe it with an insider.

Although Mamaine was devoted to Arthur Koestler, then in Israel, she responded to Wilson's interest in her, and as he flew on to Italy, all thought of restoring relations with Mary gone, he urged her not to "fall in love with anyone else before I see you again." "I miss you a lot," she wrote back, and reported that she was beginning to read *Finland Station* and that his "American propaganda" had made her eager "to go to the States, at the risk of being imprisoned for life in a Steel Town and lectured by everybody I meet [as he was evidently lecturing her] about British Imperialism." In another letter she is preparing to read Dante and says Wilson "is educating her by remote control!" She read the proofs of *Hecate County*, which were circulating among his acquaintances (Graham Greene enthusiastically promoting it, as he would *Lolita*), and liked the character of Anna. She proposed to join Wilson on a working vacation in Italy, and he shared his impressions of Rome with her, hoping she'd soon be there. When Mamaine voiced frustration at not being able to come, he fired off a letter bearing a formal proposal, a reasoned account of why, despite an age gap of over twenty years, she should marry him. Anticipating defeat, he didn't "suppose you could care about me as much as I do about you" and (Mary's experience being fresh) noted the disadvantages for her of having stepchildren, but hoped to persuade her he'd be a good husband.

He flew to England to press his case, and in a later journal recalls the "terrible attack of gout" that caused him to limp "up and down the front steps" of the Hyde Park Hotel in his military correspondent's uniform. To Mamaine he bore a cornucopia of gifts: "an antique veil for the hair and an antique black lace fan, two pairs of earrings," silk stockings, "the new book by Silone," whom she admired, as well as a magazine story criticizing British officials by the young novelist Alberto Moravia. But though she relished Wilson's company, he didn't appeal to her physically (as her sister Celia remembers), and she could no more have been happy living in the United States than he in England. Her relationship with Koestler made it easy to refuse. Mamaine's first letter after Wilson returned to Italy closes not, as before, with "love," but "your devoted friend," and she subsequently wrote, "I don't think I can marry you or indeed do anything to make our relationship fit any conventional pattern, if it doesn't do so anyway."

She would be embarrassed by the account of her as "G" in *Europe Without Baedeker*, the book that resulted from Wilson's five months abroad. To her sister she wrote, "he very clearly hints that I was his mistress, which God forbid!" All the pages in question actually reveal is his infatuation with a beautiful woman who held her own with men intellectually yet didn't have to fight with them as Mary did. To his pal Betty Huling Wilson humorously rationalized defeat: though "one of the brightest" women he had known, Mamaine was—"need I say?—rather neurotic," a diagnosis leading to the sensible conclusion that, "after my experience with Mary, I've been a lunatic to think of getting married to an even younger girl." In an unsuccessful effort to put the infatuation behind him he picked up a nice-looking French prostitute, who is described in *The Forties* and in a passage from *Europe Without Baedeker* that recalls Boswell's *London Journal*. Odette conducted "her commerce with men" somewhat as she might "have run her own shop." She had a daytime job with the Red Cross and was knitting a sweater for the director.

The snobbery of the London writers was getting on his nerves. He had resented British condescension on the Russian steamer and in the Soviet Union in 1935. During an argument he mediated in the letters column of *The New Republic* in 1929, Virginia Woolf had asserted that Americans could not write the literary English of a native and should content themselves with the rich resources of their own language, citing such words as "boob," "graft," "hobo," and "cinch." Elinor Wylie had told him that, when the Woolfs had her to dinner in London (after which Virginia characterized her as a "thick legged American") Virginia asked why she didn't write poetry in the language of Ring Lardner's baseball stories. In the *New Yorker* article that would become *Europe Without Baedeker*'s opening chapter Wilson reports that a novelist (Henry Green, whose work he liked) had pretended Vermont was a town in Florida, pronouncing the name "as if it had the same root as vermiform." A don (C. M. Bowra) "who quoted lyrics in Portuguese and had the Russian poets all at his fingertips" remarked that he hadn't read Whitman but believed him well regarded in South America. "When I said that *Leaves of Grass* was probably the greatest American book, he asked me whether I thought it even more important than the writings of Whyte-Melville," promoting a minor British Victorian at the expense of Whitman and, it seemed, Melville as well. The names of the authors of these remarks are tactfully omitted, as are those of Connolly and Orwell, who expatiated about their years at Eton, leading Wilson to contrast the pretensions of the public school as well as Bloomsbury to the larger horizon of Shaw and Wells, whom he'd devoured before World War I.

Orwell was the twentieth-century English writer with whom Wilson had most in common, a social critic who'd digested Marxism, a satirist and autobiographer, until *1984* better known as a man of letters than for his fiction. Orwell had praised the Dickens essay in *The Wound and the Bow*, as Wilson would Orwell's in *Dickens, Dalí, and Others*. When they met, Orwell's wife had just died during an operation. Remembering losing Margaret, Wilson was deeply sympathetic. Yet he was irritated when the Englishman, already preoccupied with the decay of his language, attributed this to Americans, giving an example Wilson thought absurd. Orwell would, however, write with apologies when the same example appeared in a book ("that dreadful little 'English People' book was written before I had that conversation with you about the American vocabulary"). In a review the next year Wilson called *Animal Farm* "absolutely first-rate," ranking its author with Swift and Voltaire. The political allegory didn't initially make much of an impression in England, where an early reviewer took *Animal Farm* as a sequel to *The Wind in the Willows*, but he helped sell many thousands of copies in the United States. Saluting Orwell's emergence as a major talent, Wilson later wrote to Mamaine of a feeling that the man was part of an England that was fading away. He was distressed by Orwell's death of tuberculosis after *1984*.

Evelyn Waugh proved as audacious, as savage, in person as the critic had pronounced his work. The details of their run-in at Connolly's party in April 1945 are not widely known, and this meeting is mixed up with a later one in the journal's scrambled retrospect (not straightened out by Edel in *The Forties*). When the two men met, Waugh, in the "lovely" voice that Wilson later said redeemed his ugliness, speculated that the American was somebody from Boise, Idaho, "alternatively that I was a Rhodes Scholar preoccupied with Henry James." According to Spender's memoirs, when Wilson briefly left the room a young woman (whom Spender one day identified as Mamaine) tactfully warned the assembled not to inquire about *Hecate County*. British customs officers had examined and apparently "stopped just short of seizing" the galleys as Wilson entered the country, and on the day of this party the book was apparently rejected on grounds of its sexual content by the publishers Secker and Warburg. As Spender tells it, Waugh mischievously elicited from the author that his book had not been turned down because of the paper shortage:

> WAUGH: Then what possible reason can there be for your publisher not letting us read it?
> WILSON: They say that it would be banned under the laws relating to pornography.
> WAUGH (after a long pause): Mr. Wilson, in cases like yours, I always advise publication in Cairo.

When queried by the author about Waugh's rudeness, the British satirist Angus Wilson, Edmund's friend of the 1950s and '60s, suggested this was a lesson in "how we do things." In his notes the critic struggles to recover. He reports that in a taxi en route to the Hyde Park Hotel, where the two men were staying, Waugh remarked, "The Americans are politer than anyone else," and he retorted, "Only than the British." Invited by Waugh to his rooms, "I talked about the antagonism to Americans, and he acknowledged it with a wicked gleeful grin in his bright little hard eyes, but went on to say that it was really based on jealousy"—the Americans were arriving like vultures, buying up old silver and antiques cheap. Waugh's diary the next day notes he'd "chucked appointment to show London to insignificant Yank named Edmund Wilson."

Isaiah Berlin, recalling that Waugh was once ejected from his club for throwing something at a waiter because he thought that indicated a gentleman's status, believed Wilson overlooked the man's nastiness because he was "a minor genius." Spender, on the other hand, thought Waugh's Cairo remark enraged Wilson and distorted his view of England, and Spender may have been right. Philip Hamburger, with whom Wilson became friends that summer in Rome (he had encountered the young reporter in the *New Yorker* offices), had an impression that the critic had been insulted, and in London ten years later Wilson told Nora Sayre "that English writers had developed the insult till it was an art." A dictum of *Europe Without Baedeker* is that "British rudeness" is "their form of good manners": in England "good breeding is something you exhibit by snubbing and scoring off people."

When Waugh and he met again in June, however, Wilson was invigorated by being back in England. Electioneering in the suburbs with Harold Laski, now Labour Party chairman, he was glad to see what, at *New Republic* lunches, he'd considered the man's abstract radicalism brought to life and forcefully meeting the needs of his audience, responding to the hunger for something better Wilson saw in the face of a woman there. He had been reading Auden, the best, he was sure now, of the Oxford poets. He was stirred by Benjamin Britten's opera *Peter Grimes* ("GREATEST MUSICAL DRAMATIC EVENT IN DECADES," he wired to Shawn as prelude to an article). Frederic Warburg had contracted with him for a British edition of *Hecate County* after all, and he obtained a $500 advance. However, because Wilson wouldn't cut any of the sexual passages, the proper British printers would refuse to set the book, delaying its appearance until 1951, when it was published by W. H. Allen.

Round two with Waugh began when the novelist took him for a drink at White's. In his renewed enthusiasm for the mother country, Wilson suggested they'd have to "put up an annex for the overflow from Westminster Abbey," but Waugh, as if aware of England's incipient decline, gloomily sniffed that "he didn't think there were going to be any more distinguished men." Wilson permitted himself to doubt that *Brideshead Revisited*, which had just appeared, added to his companion's distinction: "I said some derogatory things" about the book, "and this really rocked him. When I quoted some absurd sentence, he said, 'That doesn't sound like me, does it?' He handed me the book and said, 'Find it.'" The desire to score wouldn't, however, keep Wilson either from commenting favorably on Waugh's later work—he'd call *The Ordeal of Gilbert Pinfold* "the greatest Protestant allegory since *Pilgrim's Progress*"—or from extravagantly praising the first half of *Brideshead* in a *New Yorker* review. What irritated him in this novel was the blurring of religious piety with social climbing. It culminated on the last page, when Waugh's hero falls on his knees in deference not, quite possibly, the American suggests, to "the sign of the cross but the prestige, in the person of Lord Marchmain, of one of the oldest families in England."

The British establishment is caricatured throughout *Europe Without Baedeker*. Wilson mocks Sir Ronald Storrs, the "story-book" Englishman who'd supported T. E. Lawrence from Cairo. In the Italian chapters (in episodes reported to Wilson by others) Brigadier Storrs parades his knowledge of the classics and asks an Italian professor to arrange for him to lecture on Dante. He lectures about Lawrence to his soldiers on VE Day and, miffed when only fourteen show up, restages the event the day after. The rivalry of England and the United States during the last months of World War II, when Montgomery, Patton, and other generals competed, is mirrored in Wilson's vision of Britain's imperial politics. Elmhirst's takeover of *The New Republic* had revealed the empire in action. Yet to emulate the "British rudeness" from which he was smarting threw the critic off his stride. The vein of Anglophobia in *Europe Without Baedecker*— subtitled *Sketches in the Ruins of Italy, Greece, and England*—made it a "a bad book" to Mamaine, who drily wrote to Celia, "my immortality is not assured." Fredric Warburg, Wilson's publisher, saying the British public delight "to have rude remarks made about them" which they can attribute "to the malice and ignorance of the 'bloody foreigner,'" correctly predicted this animus would boost sales. Spender's review politely disputed his view of England, while Connolly wrote, "the most charitable put it down to your being on the wagon."

His experience in Italy in 1945 is the heart of the book. Naples was devastated and squalid, Milan grim, seemingly stunned by the indiscriminate allied bombardment and a civil conflict that led to Mussolini's and his mistress's brutal execution three days before Wilson toured the city. Rome, on the other hand, hadn't been bombed, and the handsome women were well dressed, the bookstores and newsstands lively, the streets full of political posters. As the responsibility of the U.S. Army's public relations section, Wilson was transported on American trains and planes, given American food and magazines and the New York papers, yet he felt close to the European literary world in his room at the top of a hotel on the Via Sistina near the Spanish Steps, with a splendid view of the Basilica of St. Peter's from his balcony, the same view, he noted, Stendhal had enjoyed from only a block away. A chapter called "Sketches for a New Piranesi" surveys the weedy, neglected Roman ruins, played in during the day by scrawny boys and home to prostitutes in the evening: the Temple of Faustina with its huge brick steps and stupefyingly grand façade, the "shapeless agglomeration" of the palaces of the Caesars, in their midst a still thriving garden with a maze that presently functioned as a latrine. Wilson's favorite corner of the Borghese Gardens, near a vine-covered wall "which just revealed sculptured griffins and the flank of an embedded sarcophagus," contained a café where he read his mail and longed to share the pageant of the churches and the museums with Mamaine.

The conversations in *The Forties* mark the variety of his encounters. An American professor has been asked to look after works of art, a Princeton businessman who lives in Rome explains the black market, while journalists chime in with their stories. Roi Ottley, African American correspondent for the daily newspaper *PM*, tells how a seemingly respectable Italian family offered to let him bed their eighteen-year-old daughter for twenty dollars. When Ottley rebuked them they assumed he was bargaining and lowered the price to fifteen. The Italian poet who gives Wilson language lessons has left-wing views, while Alberto Moravia, weary after hiding out in a barn near the fighting, is gloomy about Europe's future, and Count Morra—the illegitimate son of King Umberto— invokes Italian history. Wilson becomes friendly with "the erudite and slightly eccentric Mario Praz," author of *The Romantic Agony*, and with Ignazio Silone, who instructs him in Italian politics.

Silone (christened not Secondo but Secondino Tranquilli, his wife Darina insisted) was a hero of the antitotalitarian Left. A Communist leader in the underground at the end of the twenties, he'd grown disillusioned with the Party after witnessing Stalin, at a meeting of the Comintern, condemn Trotsky on the basis of evidence the delegates were not allowed to see. His books of the thirties did more to discredit Fascism than perhaps any other European literature of the time. *Fontamara* reveals the injustice and misery experienced by the peasants of his native Abruzzi, while in *Bread and Wine* a revolutionary activism is infused by a Catholicism outside the church. Wilson read these novels with a dictionary on a bench in the Borghese Gardens. He likened the adventures of Pietro Spina, in his clerical guise Paolo Spada, and the "procession of Italian characters" in *Bread and Wine* to "the great panoramas like *Huckleberry Finn* and *Dead Souls*." Silone's Christian play, *And He Hid Himself*, was, Wilson thought, brilliant in the way it nailed the likeness of revolutionary work to the power of a drug. Calling Silone "a queer mixture of priest and Communist underground worker," Wilson could not know how he anticipated the worker-priests of Latin America fifty years later. Wilson and he had to communicate in French—neither spoke the other's language—and he sometimes excused himself, leaving the other to converse with beautiful young Irish Darina.

Observers have called Silone "a haunted man," whose pain at the suffering caused by an earthquake in Africa was so intense he would withdraw for a day. Wilson perceived guilt to be one of his themes. *Europe Without Baedeker* cites a passage from a paper in which Silone defines himself as not like the ex-socialist Russian "God-seekers," but one of "those of whom St. Bernard speaks, those whom God pursues, and whom, when He overtakes them, He tears to pieces and chews and swallows." At the beginning of the twenty-first century, letters unearthed by revisionist historians and first published in a right-wing magazine, revealed that during his last years as a Communist, Silone was a double agent, giving information to the Fascists. How long this went on is not clear, nor whether it began before his efforts to mitigate the treatment of his younger brother, who was tortured in the Fascist prison where he died. One man testified that Silone was acting on Communist Party instructions. What he allegedly disclosed to his police contact and the value of this information are unknown. Darina, while encouraging the investigation, said, "All those who knew the truth have died."

Vibrations of this personal history of which Wilson had no idea can be detected in his account of Silone's conversation. "Silent and seemed *abattu*," he notes: "would allow remarks to pass without comment, but came to life occasionally to say something rather brilliant: Thomas Mann had perfected his literary instrument so that he could say, 'I will do this or that'"; but "an artist could not choose in that way: he did what he had to do." Silone had done what he had to do in the moral crisis that accompanied his break with the Party. Death being the alternative, he had turned to literature to save his soul from equivocation, so he explained to a police official named Bellone, an acquaintance, in the one letter of importance to which his signature has been authenticated. Another of Silone's observations to Wilson was that in Germany "an official was an official first and a man afterward." The Italian novelist believed the reverse: after persuading Bellone to let him break with the Fascists, he had asked the man to join him in prayer that his life be renewed on behalf of "the workers and of Italy." Such a request implies the radical faith in human solidarity of *Bread and Wine*.

The Sixties contains Silone's "gruesome stories" about the Communists and the Jesuits a generation later. A Jesuit studying communism for the Vatican has leaked to the Communist paper news about the Vatican that "could only have been derived from an inside source." Converted to communism, he is ruined when the Party line shifts to favor good relations with the church. In a second anecdote some Jesuits are "brainwashed" in Communist China and sent back to Italy as missionaries, then sent to a monastery and brainwashed "the other way." What Wilson took as the antics of these opposed brotherhoods had to be darkly ironic for the creator of the revolutionary Spina who is also the priest Spada. The porous aspect of Italian Fascism was beyond the American's ken, nor did he correlate the competing allegiances of *Bread and Wine* with the divided pieties of a country where communism and Catholicism contended on equal terms for several decades after World War II.

The Italy of 1945, however, robbed Wilson of a certain innocence. He was invited to luncheon at a country estate at Ninfa on the edge of the Pontine marshes by his friend Katherine Biddle's half-sister, publisher of the literary magazine *Bottege Oscure*, and her husband, Prince Raffredo Caetani. He enjoyed meeting the prince, whose grandfather had made the authoritative map of Dante's journey and who with dignity excused himself from the occasion to manage his estates. Silone later told Wilson how, when everyone was starving, the local stationmaster had, in his presence, asked Prince Caetani for corn for his wife and children. The princess pled his case but was turned down by the prince on the ground that soon people would work for practically nothing. A trip into Silone's world of the Abruzzi, recounted by Wilson to Mamaine, led through towns "absolutely demolished by shellfire and bombing, where we could see families visiting around in half rooms, the other half having been completely destroyed." He sketched the landscape, such churches as had survived, the sober people whose roads were "still planted with mines, which the young men are getting killed digging up for 20 lire (20 cents) a day—miles and miles of this." To Nabokov Wilson wrote, "The ruined parts of Italy affect me with more repugnance than anything else, I think, that I have ever seen."

Rome, in May astonishingly brilliant and clean, wore on him in the July heat, but after Mamaine's rejection talented Italian women distracted him. The surrealist painter Leonor Fini was voluptuous and elegant and talked brilliantly "about people and pictures and books." Her work contained an element of fairy tale and the commedia dell'arte that seemed quite natural in the context of the hippogriffs, sea horses, and sensual monsters of both sexes in the Vatican Museum. He was also intoxicated by Anna Magnani in the revue *Cantachiaro*, where she alternately impersonated a gamine of the streets and, in the manner of Beatrice Lillie, a duchess, taking off the allied occupation. It was the moment when Magnani and her friends were creating *Open City* on black market film and without studio lights. Philip Hamburger, on assignment in Italy for *The New Yorker*, saw Wilson follow her performances as the revue moved from one rather isolated section of the city built on seven hills to another. "It was as if he'd been struck by lightning by Magnani and Fini more or less concurrently."

Hamburger, whom Wilson liked to pump for anecdotes, contributes a revealing one about him. Having one night successfully persuaded a guard to show them St. Peter's in Vatican City by identifying another man in their car (the Washington lawyer Paul Porter) as vice president of the United States, the young reporter urged Wilson to accompany him to the Vatican, where weekdays at noon the Pope gave audiences for soldiers, moving around the room and blessing them. Very reluctantly this descendant of Puritan preachers, who in college had appreciatively come upon the sequence of popes in Dante's Hell, agreed to observe Pius XII at work. Leaving their horse-drawn carriage at the door of the enormous building, they walked up a series of staircases joined by long corridors and past the ornate Swiss Guards into a chamber the size of Grand Central Terminal. It was hot and crowded, and when Pius XII was five, ten, fifteen, and then twenty minutes late, Wilson "boomed out, 'Where is that goddamned pope?'" This outburst, Hamburger says, "brought to his side more Swiss Guards than had probably been seen in action since the Reformation, with their pikes extended toward him." At the same moment the Pope entered on a litter, and to Hamburger Wilson "said, in an equally loud tone, 'Let's get out of here, for God's sake.'"* And they did.

By contrast, Wilson would regard the reformer Pope John XXIII as a true holy man. Rosalind recalled that, in the catacombs of Rome in 1964, "when we were coming up a long flight of stairs, and my father wavered,

---

*After telling this story, Hamburger added that it was most definitely capital-G God whom Wilson, the secularized Protestant, had in mind.

the priest told him 'Pope John was just here,'" that he was walking in the Pope's footsteps. "Father was so heartened by this thought that he almost vaulted up the rest of the way." Wilson once spoke of being susceptible through his Protestant background "to the assertion of moral authority, the affirmation of the power of the spirit, in indifference to, if not in defiance of, what may be called the worldly situation—that is, of the *mise en scène*, the conditions of life, the amenities." The homage he denied to Pius XII, encased in worldly splendor and surrounded by his retinue, he gave to George Santayana, whom he found in a simple room at the Convent of the Blue Nuns. A volume of *Persons and Places*, the first book of Santayana's autobiography, had arrived in New York inscribed to Wilson, sent, it turned out, on the philosopher's behalf by an American soldier. In a review he compared it to Yeats's *Autobiographies* and *The Education of Henry Adams*. Writing of the next volume in an issue of *The New Yorker* dated the day of this interview, Wilson calls Santayana an exemplary supranational thinker. In *The Forties* he jots down the man's conversational critique of Socrates and the idealist position. To Shawn, however, he wired, "FASCINATING BUT CANNOT QUOTE MUCH OF WHAT HE SAID," and in *Europe Without Baedecker* this portrait is generalized as that of a secular saint or sage. Wrapped in a plain brown dressing gown "with a cord like a Franciscan friar's," "a table at his right, with papers and books, and, at his left, a small bed, concealed by a screen," Santayana embodies the priesthood of literature, as Mirsky does in his Dostoevskian lodgings in Moscow.

Characteristic is Wilson's judgment that when Santayana no longer "had to play the specialized philosopher," he came into his own as a poet in prose. He had evidently done a lot of writing in the convent. To encounter such an aloof and luminous mind at the center of the chaos and brute force of the war helped the critic, who would turn fifty in less than a week, accept growing older. At eighty-one Santayana was not "really alone in the sense that the ordinary person would be," was "still in the world of men, conversing with them through reading and writing, a section of the human plasm that, insulated by convent walls and by exceptional resistances of character, still registers the remotest tremors." It is James's idea of being someone on whom nothing is lost. Turning to this primary model, and to Liebnitz for a metaphor, Wilson states that Santayana "has made it his business to extend himself into every kind of human consciousness with which he can establish contact" and reposes on his shabby chaise lounge "like a monad in the universal mind."

Voicing hope to Dos Passos for a European confederation, "with England as the Massachusetts and Italy as the Louisiana," the Europe that would emerge a half-century later, Wilson moved on from Rome to Greece, much as, a decade before, he'd left Moscow for a simpler Russia in the south. The Greek countryside was "paler, purer, soberer" than Italy's, seeming "both wild and old and quite distinct from anything further west." He savored the brilliant light and indeterminate, fading colors of the little trees and the earth itself during the August dry season. In Athens he found the literary world full of Henry Miller's *Colossus of Maroussi*, as he'd write to the author on his return. He enthusiastically flirted with Eve Siphraios, a married woman who'd be a friend over the years. Talking to sympathizers of the Communist-controlled National Liberation Front, he pilloried British support of the Greek royalists, not anticipating that, as the Cold War began and the empire disappeared, the United States would step into England's place to defend the political status quo.

In Crete he saw how the Greeks had suffered. He was touched by the sincerity of the grizzled participants in a commemorative ceremony on the site of a remote, rugged mountain village, reached only by donkey, which the Germans had burned to the ground after the British used it as a base. A tourist at the ruins of Knossos, he likened "the Cretan ladies with their curled black coiffures" in "the piquant simplicity of their outlines" to drawings by Matisse. The frescoes of the naked priest-king with "his triple-plumed diadem" and "the cupbearers and saffron gatherers," the blue monkeys and brown partridges, their throats a vivid white, evoked the "liveliness, frivolity, and charm" of a civilization remote from both Egyptian stiffness and the chastity of ancient Greece. Thus indirectly reminding us of the mortality of our own civilization, as *Europe Without Baedeker* nears its conclusion Wilson reasserts the idea, which he'd stated in *Finland Station*, that America is the place where socialism can be achieved democratically. Noting the careerism and materialism to which democratic states are vulnerable, he turns to eugenics in a Shavian lecture on the need to produce better human beings.

The trip was more worthwhile than suggested by this potpourri of a book, which contains a little of everything, including contemporary history, literary criticism, sketches of people of various nationalities, a short story, and gossip. His visit to Santayana and the literary associations of the part of Rome where he was billeted renewed Wilson's ambition—to Nabokov he noted he hadn't "as yet written anything here that is as good as *Dead Souls* or the best of Keats." The Silones and Mario Praz became longtime friends. *Europe Without Baedeker* ends with a bracing visit to Norman Kemp Smith, in retirement at Edinburgh. In high-ceilinged rooms so cold at night that, though it was August, they went off to bed with warming pans, he shared his concerns for the future with his philosophy teacher of three decades before. "People's complacency shaken," the interpreter of Kant and Hume laconically observed, believing a constructive age might ensue. Wilson equated Kemp Smith's faith in God with "a vigorous physical persistence, a rectitude in relation to others and to one's own work in the world, and a faith in the endurance of the human mind."

PART FIVE

A Second Flowering

21

False Hopes and True:
Enter Elena Mumm Thornton

Home again, Wilson told friends about the "marvelous English girl" he'd fallen for. He hadn't given up his dream of marrying Mamaine. She had moved with Koestler to a remote Welsh cottage, but he wrote urging her to visit the States, at one point trying to persuade her to accept passage money and pay him back by helping out with paperwork. Mamaine said she was tempted to come, and when a letter from her revealed that her charismatic lover did not want to have children, and that this made her doubt the value of such a marriage, Wilson again urged his love. She'd given him her dimensions when he offered to send clothes from America ("height: 5'3"; waist: 24"; bust: 32""), and he promised, if she would visit him, to outfit her at Saks Fifth Avenue, but she decided not to come. At Thanksgiving he was still writing with appeals, her polite response being, "I am living with K. and hope to go on doing so." Although with Koestler she inhabited a brilliant cosmopolitan terrain, including Camus and other glamorous French intellectuals, for long periods she would sacrifice herself to his work, and he turned out to be a more difficult mate than Wilson, sometimes violent when drunk. She loved him deeply, however, and told Wilson with finality, "I was carried away by the idea of going to New York and seeing you, but I am afraid it would come under the heading 'having one's cake and eating it' and believe this is wrong."

The legal battle with Mary over custody of Reuel continued. He was consoled by Dawn Powell's company, recalling that after the separation they "became somewhat warmer and closer. She would get me dinner in her apartment, which she had never done before, and conceived a dislike of Mary, which she had never felt before." Rosalind was living with Wilson at the house on Henderson Place. She'd left Bennington College before graduating, which distressed him, but had won the *Mademoiselle* fiction prize with a story that was published there and spoke of becoming a novelist. Muchnic remembered her as "relaxed and delightful and humorous in her father's presence." When he was in a bad mood at a party she gaily observed, "The conversational ball does not seem to be rolling." Hattie was again taking care of Wilson, providing the dinners which that year he twice shared with Auden, whom he'd made friends with on returning from England. Living across the street, eleven-year-old Nora Sayre, the daughter of a *New Yorker* colleague, was drawn to him by his unaffected interest in the zoo in her Yorkville bedroom. On the night they met, he inspected the cages where a variety of creatures lived and (too often) died. When her mother summoned him back to the party he was busy improving the drainage of the terrariums with some wire clippers.

His review of *Under a Glass Bell* had established Anaïs Nin "as a serious writer of some importance," and another review praised her insight into the father-daughter relationship in *Winter of Artifice*. In October Wilson took her out for the evening, at dinner talking so much of Mamaine that, decades later, he apologized. He showed her the house, which Mary had left almost denuded of furniture, and, as they sat on rocking chairs beneath his Hogarth prints, which lined the walls, explained that "with Mary it was war. Even sex was a belligerent affair." Plaintively he asked, "You are a friend of man's, aren't you? You don't demolish him?," to which Anaïs's cheery reply was "If you demolish a man, you lose a lover." *The Diary of Anaïs Nin* states that he wanted her "to help him reconstruct his life, to help him choose a couch," and she may have been the one "of his ladies" who at this time, says Rosalind, "picked out a lot of ghastly imitation antique furniture with some horrible modern purple chairs."

Nin created alternate versions of this first date. In the published *Diary* she "wanted to leave" and ran out into the night, Wilson following to get her a taxi and shouting, "Don't desert me. Don't leave me alone." The next day she came down with a cold. He sent flowers and what she remembered as a complete Emily Brontë (Wilson corrected this to Jane Austen for Nin, before the volume of her diary covering 1944–1947 went to press, and in his own diary noted there was no such thing as a set of Brontë). "But I am not an imitator of past styles," she pronounced of his gift, somewhat menacingly adding, "Wilson, if he ever tastes of me, will be eating a substance not good for him." In her unpublished diary Nin says he tasted the forbidden fruit that very night. Once would be it, she'd thought, but several days later, lacking the attentions of her young lover, she returned to succumb to Wilson's "worship, desire, ardor, madness." For all his urbanity and intellectual control, she deemed him a sensualist, "irrational, lustful, violent."

Wilson, too, recalled their lovemaking, giving Nin false initials and likening their nights to "an affair with a nymph—too lovely while it was going on, unreal after it was over." She seemed "at once too perfect and too little fleshly to be a woman. For example, she had no smell." What drew him to her was the impulse to assist and teach that marked his relations with many women, but his advice to Anaïs to seek objectivity and form was oppressive to someone who rejected the patriarchal heritage of "libraries, formulas, and classical scholarship." Reliving her rebellion against a father who'd abused her sexually, she saw in Wilson "the full tyranny of the father, the wall of misunderstanding and lack of intuition of the father." Unlike Mary, Anaïs realized this was "not Wilson but my image of reality I see in him." According to the *Diary* he one day said, "I would love to be married to you, and I would teach you to write." She was already married to Hugo Guiler—she would later have another husband on the West Coast, commuting by plane between them—and her interest in Wilson (something he didn't know) faded in her fascination with the young Gore Vidal. But she wanted his help in her career, and she complained of the reservations in his review of *This Hunger*, though he praised her as "one of those women writers who have lately been trying to put into words a new feminine point of view, who deal with the conflicts created for women by living half in a man-controlled world against which they cannot help rebelling, half in a world which they have made for themselves but which they cannot find completely satisfactory." He'd be in Nin's corner over the years, setting up publishers' interviews and more than one contract for her, yet in her mind remained a threatening paternal presence.

This encounter between literary egos, his fatuous and yearning, hers uninhibited and professionally exploitative, had bizarre moments, as when she dreamt of Wilson as "a Roman emperor, wearing purple hair." They would have a rapprochement in the 1960s, after the aging critic sentimentally wrote and sent a photograph of himself. Anaïs replied that she'd matured—where once she'd expected him to keep praising her novels, she had realized the value of his careful criticism, something one didn't find in reviews anymore. They met again when her publishers told her to clear the portraits in her *Diary* with their subjects, and she was prepared for trouble when she eventually produced her rather unpleasant account of Wilson. She reports that he chuckled as he read "parts I thought would anger him." To his journal Wilson confided that it was odd to have been resented not merely as a father figure, but as a type of the bourgeois respectability "her whole life was pitted against." Nin's books (he elsewhere noted) were "stories about exquisite women told by an exquisite woman."

In a letter to him of the 1950s Nin recalls another woman novelist as "my true rival in your affection" at that time. This was the author of the work with the Keatsian title *Do I Wake or Sleep?*, whom in *The New Yorker* he gushingly celebrated for having "cut to roundness and smoothed to convexity a little crystal of literary form that concentrates the light like a burning glass," and whom he classified as of "the school of Henry James." Isabel Bolton, as she now called herself, was a journeyman novelist born Mary Miller in 1883. Wilson apparently never met her, but Vidal, reviewing a volume of her works and recalling the critic's enthusiasm, has amusingly pictured him knocking on a door and being greeted by a young goddess whose beauty causes "the cluster of violets" in his hand to fall to the floor, whose high instep causes his heart to flutter, only to have the white-haired lady in the background, whom he takes to be her mother, introduce herself as the author of the book he has praised. She presents the golden girl, with whom her relationship is evidently quite physical, as "my ward, Cherry."

Wilson's disappointing romance with Nin and misplaced ardor for Bolton's work were preludes to a real love affair, which began when he and Elena Mumm Thornton kissed passionately in a taxi at the beginning of April 1946. The day after that kiss, and again three days later, they met and made love. From *The New Yorker* he wrote to her, "I came to the office here full of joy." Matching his enthusiasm, she replied that she missed him "very definitely"—"have done so very many things since I left you but everything seems easy and pleasurable."

He'd first seen Elena swimming at Gull Pond in Wellfleet two summers before, when she was helping out her childhood friend Nina Chavchavadze in return for room and board. She moved with confidence in the water, he recalled in the love poem "The White Sand":

> loping a lazy crawl,
> Lifting lithe angular arms, as her slow easy-reaching strokes fell.
> Touched with delight, I looked, suddenly calmed and charmed.

Nina, who would encourage the match, and their friend Sofka Winklehorn—a descendant of the Kutuzov who defeated Napoleon—had called on him with Elena that afternoon.

In appearance Elena was Teutonic, with sparkling blue eyes and bobbed wavy light brown hair that streaked blonde in the summer. Hers was "a sensitive nose with flared nostrils and a generous mouth, slightly puckered as though she were about to laugh [or] cry," writes Dorothea Straus, her voice high and rather musical but husky from smoking. The wife of Roger Straus, who met Elena when he became Wilson's publisher five years later, Dorothea likens this slender, tall, and slightly stooped woman to "a stem, flexible but resilient." She seemed to Wilson shy, but during the winter of 1945–46 he encountered her as an assistant to the editor of *Town and Country*, where he'd submitted the satire "Glimpses of Wilbur Flick" from *Hecate County*. He was impressed enough to write of her to Mamaine, who replied, "What a pity she is married or you could perhaps have married her?"

Christened Helene-Marthe and the eldest of four children, Elena was the child of a German father who made Mumm's champagne and a Russian mother descended from a line of astronomers, the Struves, the first of whom had come from Germany to run a new observatory for Peter the Great. Her Russian grandfather was a diplomat, the tsar's ambassador to Japan, the United States, and Holland. She was born in 1906 in Rheims, France, the capital of the province of Champagne, and grew up there, in Paris, and in a town house in Frankfurt, with regular stays at Biarritz and the family seat at Johannisberg on the Rhine, where the family also made wine. Wilson thought she had a "quick German kindness," but was Russian in her responsiveness and humor. Though her Russian was "a little stumbling sometimes," David Chavchavadze could speak it with her when he didn't want others to know what he was saying. She was fluent in English, French, and German. In German she was formidably literate, and she had studied painting with Fernand Léger in a Paris still flavored by the belle époque. Elena's English, initially learned from a governess, could be laconic and eloquent—on seeing her old friend Henri Cartier-Bresson again after many years, she observed, "He is exactly the same only a little harder in the right way."

Though at one point Elena is said to have been named one of the World's Ten Most Glamorous Women, her life had been no fairy-tale romance. Her father, whom she adored and who was pro-French, was sent to a French concentration camp during World War I, emerging in 1918 to enlist in the German Army. She told Wilson that her parents' relationship never recovered from their years apart. In 1931, while on the rebound from a previous relationship, Elena met and, at their urging, married James Thornton, son of Sir Henry Thornton, president of the Canadian National Railway, then working in Frankfurt. Like young Wilson, Elena was genteel and democratic—as a child she'd been equally uncomfortable when a manservant's daughters curtsied to her at her grandmother's house in Frankfurt and when she had to curtsy to the Kaiser's sisters. She had a Parisian image of America as the country of the Marx Brothers, "of *le jazz hot* and the vertiginous *gratte-ciels* (skyscrapers). When Wilson was in Canada in 1962 he'd imagine her landing in English-speaking Montreal "at its stuffiest." The newlyweds were there, however, only two months, according to her son Henry Thornton, for his grandfather, Sir Henry, had lost his fortune in the Crash and been sacked when the Conservatives came to power in 1930. He moved to New York, and soon died. James—who was no more adept with money than Wilson—and Elena settled in Manhattan, where Henry, Elena's great joy in this marriage, was born in 1932.

Isaiah Berlin felt a sadness in Elena that he did not understand. The rise of the Nazis to power first burdened and eventually compromised her family. Her father spoke out when Jews were expelled from his Frankfurt club, and during the mid-1930s the younger of her brothers, Kyril ("Kiki"), then twenty-three, was framed after, Henry Thornton says, he jilted a girlfriend whose father was a Nazi functionary—arrested for stealing the evening bag that she asked him to hold for her at a dance, and disgraced in the newspapers. Despite all Elena's moral support Kiki was killed in a car crash, apparently a suicide. On a subsequent summer visit to Johannisberg she left her son with her family for a few days, only to learn from her sister, Olga, "how fine Henry had looked heiling Hitler." After this Elena became an American citizen. To friends she met through Wilson she would seem rather anti-German, and on a visit to Johannisberg after the war she would be called "*une sale renégate.*"* Harry Levin recalled that her Russian relatives in France were "also falling apart at the seams, and the effort of keeping the two families together, maintaining the pretense that they loved each other, all fell on her shoulders."

---

*A dirty renegade

Now forty, Elena was ready to commit herself to someone in most ways the opposite of her first husband. She later told Wilson that Jimmy "was morbidly conventional and afraid of not doing the right thing," with no interest in art or books. She developed her own intellectual interests, among them the philosopher-theologian Teilhard de Chardin. She admired intelligence in men, and her authority as a European complemented Wilson's as an American. He found her elegantly feminine and was delighted by "her frank and uninhibited animal appetite contrasted with her formal and gracious aristocratic manners." That such a woman could accept his sagging bulk and eagerly encourage his lovemaking seemed miraculous. Wilson fell in love at least as thoroughly as he had with Mamaine the spring before, this time with someone ready to reciprocate.

Elizabeth Waugh had said she'd be mad about him "if he were just prose" rather than a man in hot pursuit, and that spring and summer he courted Elena through letters. It was a different kind of epistolary courtship than he and McCarthy had, he now writing more often and in more detail, a cumulative record that at other important moments of his life took form in the journal. On April 13, in a long letter from Charlottesville, where he was visiting his cousin Susan, he wrote, "I went to sleep thinking about you and woke up thinking about you in the morning. I am going to write in my notebook some more descriptions of you [as he then did] so that I can never lose the images of how you looked at certain times."

This letter invokes the American past with a formal eloquence and a passion Elena "adored." At night, he says, "the great 'Rotunda' and colonnaded quadrangle imposes itself as a realized Jeffersonian dream of liberal learning and classical republicanism, and I was enchanted to go into Poe's old room and into the house" where "I had used to go in my childhood. Nothing I have seen in this country has moved me so much for years." Wryly, he suggests that his response may have been colored by the old-fashioneds they've been giving him. Lamenting that the Jeffersonian Enlightenment was gone, he adds that, though fond of Susan Wilson and interested in his Minor connections, he is wearied by the Southern "combination of wooliness and slackness with unshakable self-complacency." These "original Virginians," who had sold most of their land and fine houses to rich people from the North, went in for endless drinking, yet had "developed a sort of middle-class morality" that was "extremely depressing" on Saturday night at the country club—"a big house designed by Jefferson and so beautiful that it seemed to have been meant for a different race of

beings than those I met there, who, including the descendant of the original owner, were hardly different from any community of New Jersey or
Connecticut commuters."

Elena decided to end her fifteen-year marriage and help sustain the
artistic and intellectual life he embodied for her. "You have taken full possession of me I believe, and if that is really what you want everything will
be alright and just fall in line," she wrote to Wilson, though she put off
telling her husband, waiting for him to take a trip to Europe she hoped
would lead to a new job, a wait that lasted several months. Telephone
calls were awkward for her both at work and in the family's apartment,
but she and Wilson exchanged a steady stream of letters through the six
months until they went to Reno for their divorces in October. At one
point she flatters him she hasn't written twice to the same man in one day
since being engaged at twenty. Once he warns her against confusing a
wish to be kind to Thornton with trying to get him to do a financial errand
for her in Switzerland, but he is generally content to assert his passionate
longing and to chronicle his ups and downs as he tries to refurbish the
house at Money Hill with a series of helpers who promise much but soon
fade away, as do the caregivers needed when seven-year-old Reuel comes
for the summer.

He shares his worries over his boy, who was at first out of sorts and
disobedient, causing Phyllis Duganne, the mother of Reuel's best friend,
to pronounce him a bad influence. Wilson tells Elena of having "disciplined" him and fearing he'd inherited Mary's *"méchant"* disposition and
would acquire "her point of view of being an outlaw." The willing step-
mother-to-be advises him not to "worry one moment about Reuel," who is
adjusting to his parents' separation and a new household at what, in her
son Henry's case, had been a difficult age: "Just try and always be very
consistent with him, if one does say no it has to be so very definitely but
I do not believe one should be too strict except for 'sins' which remain
sins when you are grown up. Try and put him to bed sometimes at 6:30
and give him his supper in bed as very often being naughty is being tired."
Elena adds, "I sound like a Pollyanna but really one of the things I am
looking forward to is his being with you often as I am miserable without
little boys. My life has been geared to them for so many years now."

Trysts with her during these months were exhilarating. "She thought
it was degrading to make love in the dark—used to look me right in the
eyes with a sort of fierce expression," Wilson writes in *The Fifties*. "She al-

ways jumped with both feet after making love." He admired her ankles and feet, used to lie beside her and kiss her toes, loved "her crystal ice earrings and her blue ones—her pearls that she wore when she was nude." The then rough, unfinished room over his study at the Cape, which she'd remember fondly, was the scene of a meeting relieved, when he was unable to perform, by his telling Nabokov's funny Russian stories. At a subsequent encounter over tuna sandwiches and white wine he read to her "the German sex book" (shades of Ted Paramore above the furrier's on Lexington Avenue) until she exclaimed, "Enough theory!" That afternoon the grand duchess Nina, nominally Elena's hostess for the weekend, came in and, with them upstairs out of sight, poured herself a drink. Congratulating herself on having helped bring about this union, she progressed to planning the wedding and how the bride might improve the house. At a subsequent meeting in New York Wilson registered under the name of Edgar Watson. When writing afterward to her "dear, dear Mr. Watson," Elena fortunately didn't know this was his old alias with Elizabeth Waugh at the Concord Inn.

Although when they were apart the thought of committing adultery made her uncomfortable, she was at ease about their night in the hotel, urging him not to "worry about anything now and consider me already 'in the bag.' It might make it less exciting but this is the way it should be." Despite vague prospects in Switzerland and Germany (she was still a shareholder in the Mumm wine-making business near Frankfurt), she hadn't, she teased, one single penny. She was glad he had a house near the sea, which she claimed gave her energy, and jocularly promised to "swear allegiance to you and become very handy," as indeed she would, turning the old house into a well-organized, comfortable home, creating a fine office for his work. According to Rosalind, at Wellfleet her father had the habit of moving restlessly from one bed to another, often with a glass of Scotch, but in June 1946 he wrote to Elena, "I'm incredibly improved in health—due, I suppose, to cutting out my quart of whisky a night." Apropos some confusing changes of plan she assures him, "Please do not worry my dear. I am being straight." Her other close friend, Sofka Winklehorn, worried it might be a mistake to attach herself to such a demanding man, but Elena was sure of her decision. When she writes, "I love you, I will marry you, God bless you," she has found, she believes, an appropriate mate and will not change her mind. Wilson, who despite his three marriages still had traits of a congenital bachelor, had been blessed by fate. "It was incredible that I should find so late in life anybody I liked so much. But perhaps love gets better as you get older," he writes to her. "I made a mess of it when I was young."

His literary life continued. From New York in June Eliot wrote that he might visit, kidding Wilson that he preferred to eat "possibly at a different place" than Rosa's Cafe, "in spite of my very pleasant memories of that evening." The trip never came off. Rosenfeld's death in July threw Wilson back to a time when his circle, like other promising literary generations, assured one another they would stay the course. To Elena he wrote that Paul was "the fourth of my close friends who of recent years has died in middle age, with work unfinished and leaving the impression that they had never completely fulfilled themselves. You think that people are just on the point of producing their best work, and then suddenly they are dead and it appears that their work has been done." These sentences in the longest of a burst of five letters, when he was still courting her, invite her to help him complete his own work, though he neither expected nor wanted an intellectual prop. After a visit to Cambridge to see Nabokov, he reported on Volodya's relationship with Vera, "an extraordinary literary wife" who "writes all his lectures, types his manuscripts, and handles all his pub- lishing arrangements. She also echoes all his opinions—something which would end by making me rather uncomfortable but which seems to suit Nabokov perfectly."

Wilson was suddenly making more money than he ever had. Though the reviews of *Memoirs of Hecate County* weren't very complimentary and more than one acquaintance was put off by his description of sex— two women pronouncing that his narrator wasn't in love, two men that the documentation was boring—from the first the book did well, and on May 1, 1946, he wrote to Mamaine it was a bestseller. The White House had apparently bought a copy, and he preferred not to imagine President and Mrs. Truman reading "The Princess with the Golden Hair" aloud in the evening. Later that month he cheerfully told Elena, "I am afraid that the supply of prurient-minded readers is rapidly running out, and that I am not going to be able to afford for the place all the new things I had hoped." In July, when 50,000 copies had been sold, the New York police interfered with supply and demand. Responding to a complaint from William Sumner of the Anti-Vice Society, who was prompted by Cardinal Spellman and cheered on by the Hearst press, they seized some 130 copies in four Manhattan bookstores. Doubleday got the action temporarily stayed

in court, and Dos Passos organized a committee to support freedom of expression. In September Wilson told Mamaine, "In the meantime it has
been selling madly." A month later he called on Louise Bogan late one
night "shouting 'for the v. finest brandy'" since "I am so rich and have the
gout," explaining he expected to lose in court and be poor in a short time.

His fears were borne out, for the Manhattan district attorney, a respected Catholic named Frank Hogan, knew "filth" when he saw it. Liberal opinion in the nation had yet to put description of sexual experience
in the legally protected category of political dissent. When the case came
to trial October 29—Lionel Trilling testified for the defense on the book's
serious intentions—the district court ruled for the prosecution, banned
sales in New York and fined Doubleday $1,000. A month later the deci-
sion was upheld 2–1 by the state appellate court, with the two Catholic
judges not issuing an opinion, which was rare, and the dissenting Jewish
judge emphasizing Wilson's "concern with the complex influences of sex
and class consciousness on man's relentless search for happiness." *Hecate
County* was also banned in Boston and Los Angeles. When the case was
heard in San Francisco, where the church's influence was not so strong,
his side was represented by a liberal leader of the bar and the trial led to
a hung jury; the case was to be retried. Several years later the Supreme
Court would uphold the bans of the lower courts in a 4–4 tie, Justice
Frankfurter recusing himself on grounds of his acquaintance with Wilson,
who would be angered, assuming that on the merits Frankfurter would
this time have joined the liberals on the court. It angered him no less after he realized that Frankfurter would probably have voted against him.

Summer at the Cape had turned out better than expected. He'd found
competent help, gotten some work done, read *Uncle Tom's Cabin* aloud to
Reuel at the boy's bedtime, impersonating the characters with their varied personalities and accents as, he wrote to Elena, "you have to do." The
Dos Passoses regularly had him to dinner and he relayed the gossip to
Elena, amused when the head of Macmillan asked him to write a statement championing the risqué bestseller *Forever Amber*, which was being
prosecuted in Massachusetts. He negotiated by phone with McCarthy,
who at first said he could have a divorce whenever he liked and stop paying alimony, then tried to change the custody agreement in return for her
cooperation, ultimately turning the arrangements over to her lawyer. When
Elena's home situation grew tense, she visited old friends in Montreal
and took Henry to see Washington, D.C. We don't know what eighty-

year-old Mrs. Wilson thought of Elena, but when her son arrived in Red Bank with his latest wife-to-be, her devoted companion Jennie judged that "nobody could be that nice all the time."

After a last assignation in New York before she left for Nevada, Elena telegraphed from the train, "HAD A WONDERFUL TWO HOURS MISS YOU." The next day Wilson wired ahead to her in Nevada, "HAVE REACHED CHICAGO AND AM STEADILY MOVING WEST LOVE EDMUND." While others defended *Hecate County* in court, the couple spent a "not unpleasant, rather purgatorial" six weeks in separate rooms at an inn at Minden, near Reno, until their divorces became legal. Trying to interest himself in the local scene, Wilson thought the exotic mountain landscape too remote and "prehistoric" to have human meaning, and he was disappointed by the Nevada chapters of Twain's *Roughing It*. He sketched people living off gambling and the divorce trade, boasting in a letter to Nabokov that he could resist the addiction, in Russian novels, to cards and dice, for as a magician he saw through the clever manipulation of the pretty girls dealing the one and shaking the other at the tables. When exploring Virginia City and Lake Tahoe near the end of their stay he and Elena found places to spend the night together. He was moved to write: "she has always that beauty that shines like a light—the intelligence you can't get a grip on or wrestle with in an exchange of wisecracks."

From Nevada he arranged for them to honeymoon in San Francisco, where the second trial of *Hecate County* took place. Married in a civil ceremony in Virginia City on December 10, 1946, the next day the newlyweds were ambushed by reporters when they rushed for the San Francisco train. On the twelfth the *San Francisco Chronicle* reported that Wilson swung ineptly at a newsman and tried to grab a camera pointed at "his six-foot bride" (Elena was five foot nine, which made her taller than he). That same day, however, a jury took but a few minutes to decide that *Hecate County* was neither lewd nor salacious. At the victory party thrown by Wilson's lawyer, the young prosecutor confessed he hadn't thought the book indecent, though it seemed "rather silly." The two trial judges asked Wilson to autograph their copies. Staying at the St. Francis, where his parents and he had spent several days in 1915, he remembered his desire then to be a famous writer, noting this wasn't quite the fame he'd had in mind. He resolved to bring what the Wilsons and Kimballs represented "into my writing, make my writing exemplify their virtues."

The couple went back to Wellfleet, he to resume *Europe Without*

Baedeker, she to start remaking the house at Money Hill, a transformation complete when it absorbed his mother's furnishings five years later. In 1946 *Hecate County* had earned him $35,000, which paid for their separate divorces and the honeymoon plus work on the place. He was personally happy and fulfilled, financially successful, but the pull of the past was still there, at least on one level. Not long after the couple's return from California, he once again dreamed that Margaret was alive on the Coast. He'd married someone else, not Elena, someone he thought he "liked very much," but before he woke up realized he hadn't needed to marry again.

Wilson's fourth and most successful marriage would be not an idyll but "a lasting domestic accord," as Malcolm Cowley put it. The newlyweds' compatibility matched their ardor, and the Cape was a perfect place to be happy. He told Mamaine it was "one of the most marvellous places in the world: a mixture of woodland and dunes: with any sort of swimming—ocean, bay and little fresh-water lakes—and a climate that is never too hot and only in midwinter too cold." At Gull Pond, where he had first seen Elena, he wrote to her, before they left for Reno, "We have gone on having beautiful days. I feel that you and I have never yet been able to spend the whole of one of these days—in the sense of getting out of it all that it is worth—the way it ought to be spent." Wilson had found someone with whom to make the most of the twenty-five years that remained to him.

22

Old Commitments and New

In "Thoughts on Being Bibliographed" Wilson had looked to a new generation who would return from military service to "demand and provide
better work." First-rate war novels soon appeared, followed by a second
wave of American moderns. They could build on a rich tradition, and had
allies of sorts in the New Critics, who taught a student population expanded by the G.I. Bill how to read more deeply. The post–World War II
writers were diverse, including Southerners, Jews, and African Americans. There were distinguished women writers of fiction, as in the time of
Wharton and Cather. Yet this group lacked certain advantages of the major novelists and poets of the early twentieth century, who incorporated
the experimentation of Europe in a fresh view of their native land, emerging from the Victorian age and writing for a still cohesive educated class.
The advent of television is registered in Wilson's papers by a drawing of a
simple box, and by conversations in which editors foresee that this invention will threaten imaginative literature. The younger generation were
disappointed that he failed to recycle himself as their spokesman and interpreter, though he promoted some of them—Robert Lowell, John Berryman, and Elizabeth Bishop among the poets, James Baldwin and J. D.
Salinger in fiction. Ostensibly content to speak of himself, in the language of magazines, as "a back number," after World War II Wilson continued to sift the British tradition, while taking note of avant-garde
European fashions. He reported on the Zuni pueblo, Haiti, and Israel, a
travel writer verging on anthropology, and took up nineteenth-century
American figures behind whom loomed the Civil War.

One unfamiliar with *Europe Without Baedeker* might believe the author of a dozen or so reviews in the second half of *Classics and Commercials* to be a fervent Anglophile, so saturated are these pieces in England's literary and social history. He writes twice of Thackeray and Victorian Britain, takes up the aspect of "perversity" in Wilde's wit and in his tragic career, returns to Max Beerbohm and to the outrageous and serene decadence of Ronald Firbank, which unlike Waugh didn't depend on a celebration of orthodoxy. He characterizes the exquisite effects of Thomas Love Peacock's comic novels, turning to Mozart to locate this "delicious music, at the same time sober and gay, in which the words fall like notes from a flute, like progressions on an old-fashioned pianoforte, lighted by slim white candles." In response to the fashion of *explication de texte* in academia, he promotes the impressionist George Saintsbury, a late Victorian critic with a fine palate and omnivorous appetite, who like Wilson made others want to read what he admired.

The polished, worldly tradition of British satire—"distinguished, unscrupulous, hard; carved, gilded, and decorative; planned logically and executed deliberately; of good quality, designed for long wear"—had evolved from Jonson and Congreve. In what became an influential account of Ben Jonson, Wilson brought Freud's theory of the anal-erotic to the playwright's obsessive concerns. He gave weight to this essay by distinguishing the "ideal of feminine sweetness and purity" in Jonson's verse from its parallels in Gogol and in the triumphant bird-girl of Joyce's *Portrait of the Artist*. Endorsing an edition of Swift's savage *Journal to Stella*, as a book lover he regretted the absence of "a most remarkable folded facsimile of all four pages of one" of the letters, "which reproduced the color of the faded ink and the color and texture and watermark of the paper." He observed the effects of Swift's "intellectual rigor and strength," given "the darkness of his pessimism and the rigidity of his moral nature." This review defines a significant aspect of Wilson's own work: where Dante, he says, "got his whole career, personal, political and moral, inside his imaginary picture, Swift, though he, too, got his story told, scattered it in pamphlets and poems, in historical and political essays, in prayers and practical jokes, in epigrams and lampoons, in his correspondence with public men and in his personal letters to Stella."

Wilson's "Dissenting Opinion on Kafka" in 1947 has been said to mark the limits of his sensibility. He was reacting against the Kafka cult, which during the late 1940s seemed to take this writer as a theologian or a saint who could justify to the intellectuals—or, Wilson said, "help them

to accept without justification—the ways of a banal, bureaucratic, and incomprehensible God to sensitive and anxious men." It has been noted
that—unlike the artist's more solemn admirers—"Kafka would probably
not have disputed Wilson's assessment." The Kafka hero's helplessness,
"the half-expressed gasp of a self-doubting soul trampled under," was
remote from Wilson's Protestant heritage and—though anticipated in
Melville's "Bartleby the Scrivener"—not in the American grain.

He made fun of the nostrums and escapes of the literati in the raucous verse of "The Mass in the Parking Lot":

> . . . And whom should we meet there, on the loose,
> But Andre Gide in a big burnoose.
> What were his words of wisdom? Dammit,
> He was whooping it up for Dashiell Hammett.

Eliot and Auden, Waugh and Graham Greene are among the lost souls
gathered on a smoggy night in suburbia to seek their salvation, "All are
agreed they must hold a mass / To bring some poignant epihka to pass,"
an epihka being a conflation of epiphany with the pathos of the Kafka
cult. High church trendiness is Wilson's other target. In this vein, he
wrote to Cowley that "even Cummings, in the winter of 1945–'46, had a
phase of Christian piety and turning the other cheek which made him so
disagreeable that I have never looked him up since." When Tate, who had
converted to Catholicism, took note of Wilson's respect for Jesus' teach-
ings, he defended himself against the "slanderous" imputation that at
heart he was a Christian, stating, "It doesn't imply Christian tendencies
that one tries to cultivate kindness and respect for the rights of others,"
something he admitted he wasn't always good at. A few years later, issuing a Shavian statement on religion in A Piece of My Mind, he calls belief
in Jesus as a supernatural being no longer plausible and Christian ethics,
although appropriate for saints, impractical for humanity at large.

He discovered a religion he could admire when The New Yorker, yield-
ing to a repeated request, sent him to New Mexico to view the Zuni festival of renewal at the winter solstice in 1947. He grew interested in Haiti
through reviewing a novel about its peasant life and religion by two half-
brothers named Thoby-Marcelin. He arranged to meet Phito Marcelin
(in his journal, Wilson drops the Thoby), also a poet, who became a close
friend. To Elena, Wilson wrote, "Though a mulatto, he is pretty dark and

absolutely African in appearance, with intense and piercing black eyes," continuing, "He says that the position of the mulattos among the blacks in Haiti is like that of the Jews in a community that discriminates against them." As a writer and social critic Marcelin felt doubly out of place in a country whose social system was premised on exploitation of the peasantry. He lived in Washington but met Wilson in Greenwich Village and took him to call on a Russian-Jewish girl who had "a black canary in a very large cage named after the voodoo god of death, whom the owner had made her patron divinity, and," Wilson adds, "a lot of Haitian drums." At later meetings he quizzed Phito about a country run by former slaves where an artistic elite literate in French were trying to diminish the gulf between themselves and the masses, much as the Russian intellectuals had. Wilson was soon asking magazines to send him to Haiti.

He had begun digging into the American literary past with the anthology of memoirs, reviews, letters, and criticism called *The Shock of Recognition* (1943). McCarthy claimed this resonant title out of Melville was her idea, but the book's Wilsonian premise is that the responses of writers to one another move literature ahead. He made accessible Melville's view of Hawthorne and Emerson's and Whitman's of each other, Howells on Mark Twain, Twain on Cooper's literary offenses, Mencken on Dreiser's awkward truth-telling about American life, as well as the effusive vision of Lawrence's *Studies in Classic American Literature*. He focused the influence of Hawthorne on James and James on Eliot. The opening contrast of James Russell Lowell on Poe to one hundred pages of Poe's criticism shows how Wilson's characters comment on one another even as, in his brief introductions, he comments on them. The method anticipates *Patriotic Gore*, where a small anthology of quoted material will be shaped into the voices of dramatis personae who articulate the cultural and moral conflicts of the Civil War.

When he signed a contract with Oxford University Press in 1947, Wilson had in mind a book on turn-of-the-century writers he thought were wrongly eclipsed by Twain and James. He expected to draw on his accounts of Wharton, Chapman, and Santayana and to take up such regional figures as Harold Frederic and Henry B. Fuller. Instead he became absorbed in the writings of Ambrose Bierce, J. W. De Forest, and Sidney Lanier, soldiers whose experience during and after the war focused "a general shrinking and chill on the part of American idealism." Reviewing Van Wyck Brooks's literary chronicles helped focus his own ambitions.

Though Brooks did not give the major writers their weight, he skillfully digested vast masses of print and transmuted the lead of second- and third-rate literature into gold. *The Flowering of New England* showed what revolutionary New England had meant as "cultural spokesman for the new humanity to be built in the United States," and "the old virtue" could be seen passing out of Boston in *New England: Indian Summer.* These volumes joined *U.S.A.* and the Beards' *Rise of American Civilization* as "light-diffusing" studies of American society, and in two others Brooks reconstructed the New York tradition. Yet to view the Civil War through these regional and time frames led him to miss its centrality in American history, "breaking and embittering the South, inflating and corrupting the North," and dislocating those "whose training had prepared them for a different world from that with which they were later confronted." The literature that came out of the war conveyed "the stress of the period," "the moment of bankruptcies and wounds, of miscarriages, distortions, frustrations," and "the element of strain and waste," Wilson wrote, invoking the crisis of his father's generation in the central metaphor of his literary portraiture.

These new emphases were born in a period when his old emotional connections were dying. A decade after the end of their affair, Louise Connor's "strawberry-and-cream" complexion was gone, her face "leathery," with lines that "might have been cut with knives." Clearly she'd suffered, but she kept a wall between them as she talked of her success as a nurse's aide, her father's tales of retirement in some sort of Boston club, the quarrelsome turn her relationship with her twin, Henri, had taken. In the evenings she drank, and Wilson wondered whether she might also be taking drugs, from Rosalind learning it was sleeping pills. Life had turned bitter for his old lover. He wondered, "What had happened to Louise and Henrietta, Ted Paramore, the Fitzgeralds, the Amens, Phelps Putnam, John Bishop, Edna, Jean Gorman, Berenice Dewey (Cummings is tougher), all the 'glamorous' personalities of that period?" In "Riverton," the poem begun long ago with Margaret by his side, he'd said, "They flicker now who frightfully did burn," likening their beauty to "water in its flight."

At Millay's home, Steepletop, in 1948 Edna embodied for him "the tendency of the writers of my generation to burn themselves out or break down." Age had caught up with her and her addictions had destroyed her health even as her reputation, cresting for many with *Fatal Interview*

(1931), shrank following the victory of modernist tastes. She was now apparently a serious nervous case. As she and Wilson and their spouses made conversation he felt "sucked into her narrow and noble world, where all that mattered was herself and her poetry." Her presence was a "pressure as if to gouge me out, extirpate me, from my present personality and point of view and all that, during the intervening years, had made it." Their meeting threatened to resemble "one of my recurrent dreams about her"—"old images exaggerated, deformed, swollen with longing and horror." Philip Hamburger, whom the Wilsons ran into later that day at the Berkshire Music Festival in western Massachusetts, remembered how unnerved he seemed.

Mary Blair was another casualty. In 1935, when she entered the TB sanitarium in Pittsburgh, she had been told that time and rest would heal her lungs. Instead, Rosalind records that "they took out portions of her ribs, leaving her hunchbacked, and she spent months lying with sandbags around her." When nothing more could be done and she was discharged, she lived on beer and cigarettes in two small rooms of an apartment-hotel crowded with her and Connie Eakin's massive furnishings. She would berate him mercilessly, he sitting there saying, "Mary, oh Mary darling." When she died in her sleep in 1947, the obituaries, as she'd predicted, described her as the white actress who had kissed a Negro's hand onstage. Wilson paid for the funeral. Her loyal husband insisted to him that, even when "nothing but skin and bones, Mary was a person with sympathy and understanding that few will ever reach." Ten years later, in 1956, Constant Eakin's son wrote to Wilson that his father had disappeared. The family knew he'd gone to Greenwich Village and had the name of an old girlfriend, asking if Wilson had any suggestions for finding him, but Connie was never heard from again.

Blair's death occurred a week after the car crash in which Dos Passos, who was driving and momentarily blinded by sunset, lost the use of one eye and his wife, Katy, was killed. An undemonstrative person, Dos was effusively grateful for the visits of Wilson and Charley Walker to Massachusetts General Hospital, where he was hospitalized through the funeral. At Katy's grave on the hill that September afternoon, "so light, clean, and dry and yet human up there among the old four-square churches," Wilson went back in his mind over the life of the artists' colony on the Cape where they had settled. Two months later, touching on his guilt when Margaret "was killed," he offered Dos a formal expression of sympathy. He noted how the weather cleared up for the funeral, "the bay all silver in the four o'clock light and the bright waterway winding in-between the sands and the marshes." Thinking of his lost years with McCarthy, he wrote, "We had all been getting old together, and it was already, I say, a whole life behind us, with many things that we could never have again."

No other old friend had such literary range, political seriousness, or experience of the world, and when Dos married again in 1949 and recovered his father's estate on the Potomac, an eighteenth-century house with 1,800 acres, it was a loss for Wilson. They had shared the brilliant boozy republic of letters of the 1920s and the radicalism of the early Depression. Dos's art seemed incomplete—"it is always the milieux he impersonates, trying to tell the story in language appropriate to the different ones; he is not very good at impersonating his characters," Wilson thought. But he'd written admiringly to the novelist of those moments in *U. S. A.* when the people "are at loose ends or drifting or up against a blank wall—such as a passage in the first volume which stands out in curious relief in my mind, when Moorehouse has washed up in Pittsburgh and simply lies on the bed for several days, not knowing what he is going to do next—moments when the social currents, taking advantage of the set of the character, will sweep the individual in." Dos was then swept to the Right. After reading *The Head and Heart of Thomas Jefferson*, Wilson wrote satirically to Dawn Powell from Charlottesville that "a Mr. Dos Passos has been here inquiring about buying Monticello and that he has been asking around among the colored population to find out whether there are any who would like to go back to slavery in the service of a kind master." Dos Passos's later politics involved what the critic deemed the delusion that one could radically shrink the government while expanding its powers against the Russians. His article about Goldwater at the Republican convention in 1964 led Wilson to send Dos a postcard likening him to "a teen-ager squealing over the Beatles." Dos sometimes held his own—for instance, he would call his review of Wilson's polemic, *The Cold War and the Income Tax*, "Please, Mr. Rip Van Winkle, Wake Up Some More."

He missed Dos less because of a new intellectual companion and sounding board. A decade before his friend remarried and left the Cape, in the year Fitzgerald died, Vladimir Nabokov introduced himself to Wilson at *The New Republic*. He already had a brilliant career in his own language. The forties and early fifties were the great period of this friendship. The novelist's biographer Brian Boyd pictures "the lean, intense

Nabokov, with his full-vowelled Russian version of a Cambridge accent, and short, plump, puffy-faced Wilson, with his loud, curiously high-pitched voice," overwhelming and exhilarating each other with their energy. McCarthy recalled that "Edmund was always in a state of *joy* when Vladimir appeared," and they were soon exchanging long letters about everything from Russian politics to Pushkin's verse form as well as the American and English writers Wilson promoted. Nabokov would say, "I miss you a lot" or "You are one of the very few people in the world whom I keenly miss when I do not see them." Such a renewal of brotherhood meant more to Wilson as he lost literary contemporaries and grew discouraged with the state of the world, while his marriage to Mary disintegrated. Elena had known Nabokov's family in the Russian émigré milieu, and he saluted her arrival, coining for her the phrase "a salad of racial genes," which he would use for Humbert Humbert's father. He was pleased to see *Hecate County* on the bestseller list, then puzzled by the censorship of this "chaste" book. Soon afterward he returned to the idea of a story "about a man who liked little girls," planning, he told Wilson, to call it—after Poe's poem—"The Kingdom by the Sea."

Always generous with his influence, Wilson smoothed Nabokov's way with publishers and magazines from *The Atlantic Monthly* to *The New Yorker*, wrote a reference for his first Guggenheim, and promoted him for academic posts. When the novelist reported that at *The New Yorker* Katharine White was irritatingly fiddling with an episode from *Speak, Memory*, Wilson intervened in a note to Katharine blasting her as the victim of "a truly alarming condition of editor's daze." He didn't have to ride to the rescue against her boss. Nabokov reported, "Unfortunately, a man called Ross started to 'edit'" one of his stories ("odds and ends inserted in order to 'link up' ideas and make them clear to the average reader")—he'd been "on the point of calling the deal off when they suddenly yielded."

Wilson had a similar problem with William Shawn. After Wilson's death, Shawn said to the present writer that his prose was one of the half-dozen best expository and critical styles in the history of English, but he was not above trying to improve it. In 1947 they quarreled over the editor's powers. Backing up Shawn, Harold Ross said they were arguing about "a sentence three or four hundred words long that we proposed clarifying with punctuation." To Katharine White he called Wilson "by far the biggest problem we ever had around here," a man who "fights like a tiger, or holds the line like an elephant, rather." At *The New Republic* Wilson had been able to revise extensively through page proof, and he admitted to Ross that when working on his books he'd habitually turned in reviews not yet in shape and improved them afterward; he offered "to keep a deadline and eliminate telephone conversations" as part of a new contract with *The New Yorker*. He was "of course prepared to consider all your suggestions once and to accept those that seemed to me sound," but refused to be "badgered and made to engage in long arguments about questions that I [the operative word] had already decided."

He would confide to Shawn he was "tired of reviewing books, stale at it," and in a fan letter, Eudora Welty told Wilson he wasted his powers "on some book of the week." When offered hostile-seeming terms, he resigned his post. He agreed to do articles on an ad hoc basis, and over the next decades would take up longer projects on a looser schedule. Shawn was enthusiastic about his wide-ranging explorations and paid him by the word, a thirty-page article on the almost forgotten Southern fantasist James Branch Cabell, whom Wilson met in Richmond in 1953, earning him as much as a major piece of equal length on the correspondence of Justice Holmes and Harold Laski. Shawn retained authority over his punctuation—a letter from Wilson implores him not to "take out the semicolons."

All Wilson really needed was a copy editor to point out an occasional awkward construction or tell him he'd used the same expression twice within three or four pages. John Peck at Farrar, Straus and Giroux suited him perfectly. The publication of *Classics and Commercials* in 1950 began his association with that recently formed house. The connection was brought about by Robert Linscott, who phoned from Random House to ask Roger Straus if he was interested in this collection of reviews, saying that Bennett Cerf, long at odds with Wilson, wouldn't let him buy it. Eagerly Straus arranged to meet Wilson and get a copy of the manuscript, an occasion when, he recalled, "I couldn't have been more uneasy," for though he'd read *Axel's Castle* in college he was otherwise "flying blind." He made an offer of $1,500 or $2,000, which the critic persuaded him to raise by $500, setting the pattern of future bargaining sessions. When presenting the contract Straus, remarking that Wilson was "said to be death on publishers" and wouldn't stay with the firm unless they liked working together, struck the clause that gave him an option on future books. In fact, FSG would bring out all Wilson's subsequent work except *Patriotic Gore* (contracted for with Oxford), *The Scrolls from the Dead Sea* (which Oxford was willing to do in a fashion he preferred), and *Red,*

Black, Blond and Olive, published by Oxford in the United States and W. H. Allen in England. There were also the several reprints in Jason Epstein's paperback Doubleday Anchor series, which enhanced Wilson's reputation during the 1950s. Straus hazarded that the Anchor format contributed to Wilson's distinctive uniform design for his books at FSG, a squat shape roughly five by seven-and-a-half inches, which he deemed a good size to hold and read, conveying the solidity and ease for which he aimed in prose.

To find a publisher he could count on was a stroke of great good fortune, giving Wilson's life a new stability. Straus became a friend—they kept in touch through phone calls and notes as well as over lunch—and visited him at Wellfleet and, later, Talcottville. He made advances and loans to Wilson, who writes to Elena in a family emergency, "I'm going to try to get Roger Straus to let me have $2000," and three days later writes, "Roger Straus is putting $3000 in the bank." Thinking Wilson "a great writer," Straus recalled, "Of the various authors that I've published, he was not only the man I admired the most but the man who gave me the most pleasure to be with over a long period of time." After lunch or dickering about his next book, they'd cruise the secondhand bookshops, Wilson "buying this book or being given that book in a way that I admired. He was studious about the whole thing. It was absolutely great." As Straus looked back on all the "jokes, literary gossip, business talks" and "the excitement of his enthusiasm for other writers present and past," he said, "What I loved most about him was that he gave and expected candor. There was nothing you could not say to him about his work." This was a rare virtue, "especially when combined with a big heart. And nobody could deny the size of Edmund's heart."

Isaiah Berlin had long wanted to meet Wilson, but during the war Wilson shied away from anyone posted at the British embassy. In the spring of 1946 he invited Berlin to lunch in New York, the beginning of a friendship important to each. Sir Isaiah was taken aback when a "thickset, red-faced, pot-bellied figure not unlike President Hoover" appeared, then captivated as Wilson "spoke in a moving and imaginative fashion about the American writers of his generation, about Dante, and about what the Russian poet Pushkin had meant to him." Stirred as Berlin had been by meeting Pasternak and Akhmatova a year before, he thought that this American "talked about Russian literature in general, and particularly about Chekhov and Gogol, as well as I have ever heard anyone talk on any literary topic." Wilson had "a curiously strangled voice, with gaps between his sentences, as if ideas jostled and thrashed about inside him, getting in each other's way as they struggled to emerge, which made for short bursts, emitted staccato, interspersed with gentle, low-voiced, legato passages." Sir Isaiah's deep, soft voice also came in bursts, trailing off at the end of a breath and emphatically resuming. Each was hard to interrupt. When Berlin returned to the United States to teach at Harvard in 1949 he visited Edmund and Elena at Wellfleet. To Mamaine, Wilson sketched this "extraordinary Oxford don, who left Russia at the age of eight and has a sort of double Russian-and-English personality. The combination is uncanny but fascinating." Wilson confessed, "I unloaded on him all the best stories, bon mots, and stimulating ideas of virtually my whole life as if they were new and spontaneous," adding "he may have been doing the same thing with me."

Elena brought a casual glamour to Wilson's life, and he remained grateful that such a woman could care for him. His women friends were glad to see him matched to a dedicated wife. In her journal Dawn Powell writes, "Bunny and I had a very amusing lunch and he looked fine. Elena's prime achievement" (apart from being a good mother) had "been in de-irascibilizing as well as rejuvenating the Bard." In contrast to Wilson's capacity to slide from enthusiastic bursts of energy into depression, Elena was gifted with a good temper and the ability to enjoy daily life. Except for Margaret, who had often been away on the West Coast, she was the first of his wives who didn't also have a career to manage, and she wouldn't return to her painting during their marriage. When they first knew each other she sometimes drank a good deal, but she'd recall that for several years after marrying him she "didn't drink at all." Wilson sometimes went for days without liquor, though he continued to decompress from hard work on binges. Their sex life could be undermined by everyday reality— "after longing for one another and, as she said, idealizing one another, we began to fall out the next day"—but the romance survived.

As it turned out, in marrying Wilson she had also taken on Reuel and Rosalind. Her benign influence on Wilson's son would be lasting, although, perhaps in loyalty to his own mother, Reuel limited this. It was late for Elena to be very helpful to Rosalind, who as she entered adult life found it difficult to steer a steady course. Witty and a bon vivant, with interesting friends and used to spending time with her father, whom she resembled, she had a gift with words, and for a time Wilson believed in her future as a writer. But she wasn't able to work on her stories as she had planned, while living in a rented room, nor did she like newspaper work. She grew used to the bohemian milieu of the Cape and to not doing very much among celebrities and would-be celebrities. Elena made her comfortable at Money Hill until her father insisted she "go out on her own."

Rosalind most wanted to be desirable and have beaux. Her relationship with Wilson became part of her instability. Maintaining a Victorian paternal standard, Wilson left the dog in the front hall so that he'd let them know when she came in at night. He infuriated her by boobytrapping the back door with garbage cans stacked on top of each other so she would make a racket when returning home in the small hours after fishing expeditions with the romantic Prince George Chavchavadze. But, when her father advised against it, she declined the proposal of an Englishman who wanted to marry her and take her to Calcutta.

At the age of forty-one Elena became pregnant. Although the pregnancy was unplanned, they immediately decided to have the child. The picture of Wilson and his baby daughter, Helen Miranda, in the garden at Wellfleet a year later makes them look-alikes. Helen explains that her name was a compromise. "I wasn't christened, so Ma wanted to name me Christine; Pa Charlotte; Henry and Reuel (the older seventeen, the younger eleven) Orlando." But both families had many Helens. Elena had been christened Helene-Marthe, and Helen was also the cognomen of her favorite Russian aunt, as well as Wilson's mother's name and that of his Kimball grandmother. "The Miranda," Helen adds, "was for Shakespeare."

Wilson wasn't, however, so sure of his powers as is Shakespeare's benign magician. At a picnic with Cape friends not long afterward, when the subject of ticks in the grass came up he was glad they weren't Rocky Mountain ticks. "Wouldn't it be terrible," he asked Elena, "if I got Rocky Mountain spotted fever and died after I've gotten my life all straightened out?"

23

American Criticism and Portraiture
at Wellfleet, Princeton, and Talcottville

∞

For Wilson the 1950s opened with a whirl of exploration. He was reading
Chekhov in Russian, reading Sartre on Baudelaire and the new installments of Sartre's novel, as well as investigating documents about Dickens
and Wilde. Promoting Gilbert Highet's *The Classical Tradition* in *The New
Yorker,* in an act of scholarly one-upmanship he sent the author a 2,500-
word letter about everyone from "Hrotswitha, the German tenth-century
nun, who wrote Latin plays in imitation of Terence" to D'Annunzio.
When the middlebrow *Saturday Review of Literature* attacked the award of
the Bollingen Prize to Pound's *Pisan Cantos* on the grounds of their ob-
scurity (their real objection being to Pound's pro-Fascist broadcasts during World War II) and argued that Stevens's poetry was easier to understand,
Wilson, in a letter to the editor, urged that he familiarize himself "with the
works of these two admirable writers before sounding off about them in a
journal supposedly devoted to literature." As the Cold War began, he
sought the perspective of the *Decline and Fall,* which had rescued him in
the Odessa hospital. Gibbon's long view of history, he told a reading group
on the Cape, was "both calming and stimulating."

In August 1950 he went to Boston for the last rehearsals and the pre-
miere of *The Little Blue Light,* which for a fortnight filled Cambridge's
Brattle Theater almost to capacity. Hume Cronyn, who played the sermonizing gardener Gansvoort von Gandersheim (also called the Wandering
Jew) believed in the play, as did Jessica Tandy, the Mary McCarthy character. It needed cutting, and they unsuccessfully tried to persuade the
"likeable but frighteningly erudite" author that in plays "lots of things
didn't need to be on the page." Wilson was a nervous wreck at the open-

ing—Cronyn recalled that after the show he sat on the floor in his white linen suit with a drink in his hand and his back against the wall, "entirely compos mentis but drunk." When ANTA produced *The Little Blue Light* in New York, Tandy had committed to another role and Cronyn was passed over. The play was cut over Wilson's protest, and closed after eight days. He had begun *Cyprian's Prayer*, a less gloomy play based on his boyhood reading of Frank Stockton's story "The Magician's Daughter and the High-Born Boy." He was bringing the Devil onstage as a genial Promethean named "Mr. B." and hoped to cast Tandy and Cronyn as the magician's daughter and the young magician.

He'd become curious about race and the South. From his friend Roi Ottley's *Black Odyssey* he learned of Jefferson's mulatto children. Documenting how well treated and how loyal were Jefferson's slaves, Ottley believed that his body servant slept in "that curious bunk" above his bed at Monticello. Was there "something rather interesting that has been kept out of sight about Jefferson's relations with Negroes?" Wilson queried Dos Passos. "Did he have close and unpublicized relations with them that made up to some extent for his lack of close relations with white people?" Wilson sees as natural, even benign within its social frame, an intimacy that, half a century later, would entice his countrymen as guiltily sexual.

This subject would have interested him in William Faulkner's gothic triumph, *Absalom, Absalom!*, a novel that had appeared in 1936 while the fate of Russian communism engrossed Wilson. He didn't return to *Absalom*, but he reread *The Sound and the Fury* and *Light in August*, recommending them to Nabokov in the winter of 1948–1949, at the time of his judicious review of the less important *Intruder in the Dust*. Writing before Faulkner's Nobel Prize—though after Cowley's Viking Portable popularized Yoknapatawpha County—Wilson found his command of English lyric verse and romantic prose matched to a Shakespearean gift of dramatic articulation. He set Faulkner in "the full-dress post-Flaubert group of Conrad, Joyce, and Proust," and credited the novelist's vitality to the concreteness of his world, his seeming immunity, as a Mississippian, to the "abstract assumptions" that invaded the work of other modern novelists of his stature.

In *Intruder*, however, Faulkner was past his peak. Where once he'd justified his liberties with spelling, punctuation, and diction, now he was "not merely coining" words "but groping." The muddy rhetoric of the chivalric lawyer Gavin Stevens made Wilson miss the prose of the great

novels, "so steady and clear as well as so tense and so telling." Modern fiction was a by-product of an industrial society, and Faulkner's provinciality,
in other respects his strength, allowed him to become "slipshod." Eudora
Welty wittily protested this reasoning in *The New Yorker*. Calling Wilson
the only good writer "who counts for the city vs. the country," she asked
readers to picture "Mr. Faulkner in a striped cloth cap, with badge and
lunchbox, marching in to match efficiency with the rest only to have Boss
Man Wilson dock him—as an example, too—for slipshod bolt-and-nut
performance caused by unsatisfactory home address." But Faulkner wrote
to Wilson accepting the critique of his later prose ("The points you made
are good"), adding that Stevens was not just the author's voice and did not
stand alone: his opinions represented those of "the 'best' Southerner, the
one with culture and sensitivity, and some power in his land, and a belief
in human rights and justice." Faulkner called it his own fault that neither
Wilson nor Cowley had picked up on this.

The revival of interest in the twenties, beginning with Cowley's profile of Hemingway in *Life* in 1948 and that of Lillian Ross in 1950, gathered momentum with Arthur Mizener's biography of Fitzgerald and Budd
Schulberg's novel about Fitzgerald, *The Disenchanted*, which became a
Broadway play. Wilson's intervention made the biography better. He was
distressed to find anecdotes distorted in the draft, jokes and nonsense
mythologized or misinterpreted. Mizener hadn't caught the brilliance of
Scott and Zelda in their heyday, and by unsuccessfully playing the confusions of the life against the work he undermined Fitzgerald's character.
While voicing these concerns to Gauss, Wilson cajoled Mizener into a
second effort, insisting as well on Zelda's abilities—her conversation was
"full of felicitous phrases," and "even when her mind was going," her writing and painting had her "imaginative iridescence and showed something
of real talent." In the role of "Elder Biographer" proffering advice that may
not be accepted (though he makes it hard for the recipient to do otherwise), he recommends calculating the tone of each sentence as a novelist
must while weighing "what constitutes evidence," keeping in mind that
"anecdotes grow rapidly into legends"—he cites his difficulties in ascer-
taining the facts about Lenin. Mizener should check the several versions
of an incident with Dos Passos, who "was there and is an accurate observer" and, Wilson carefully adds, "is likely to tell you the truth."

In a letter to Lionel Trilling Wilson offered his perspective on the
friend whom he had once warned "I believe you might become a very

popular trashy novelist without much difficulty." Fitzgerald didn't "get enough of the right kind of education to sustain him in his absolutely first-rate ambitions," "could never quite get over the idea that serious literature did not provide a real, or a sufficient, career," yet "his serious vocation was inescapable: he could never really get away from it to do anything else successfully; and you have to compare him to the great wits and poets that he wanted to emulate, not with the half-baked naturalists or the moderately distinguished popular writers that are so much commoner here." An English literary standard had sustained him, as it did Wilson. Talking up the good sense of Scott's Hollywood girl Sheilah Graham, Wilson told Dawn Powell that she was "the kind of girl you imagine would never have done for Scott, who was not, I think, easily seduced by sex and who was extremely susceptible to boredom." But he contributes to the romance of the 1920s in "A Weekend at Ellerslie," reconstructing the house party Scott threw for his birthday in 1928. Wilson, who liked to hold forth to a captive audience, had been surprised to find that Thornton Wilder knew Proust as well as he did. They played the English game diabolo on the darkening lawn, where Zelda remarked that Galsworthy's writing was "a shade of blue for which I do not care." The next morning, sitting in his bathrobe, Scott had read aloud a Riviera scene from *Tender Is the Night* in which a group of attractive women "were floating and glowing in the richest Fitzgerald glamor." Wilson was sorry not to find it in the published novel.

This memoir is included in *The Shores of Light*, which he described to Nabokov as "a gigantic book containing ninety-two of my articles, mostly written in the twenties and thirties, which has been turning into a sort of volume of literary memoirs." A cornerstone of his reputation during the later years, it includes dialogues, sketches, and correspondence, and he retrospectively fills in gaps much as when reworking his journals for *The Twenties*. "I've rewritten almost to the point of forging my own early works," he told Bogan, and in the preface explained that he had "revised almost everything, sometimes trimming and toning down what I originally wrote and sometimes expanding it with material taken from my old notes." His review of *In Our Time*, for example, is enriched by the letters he and Hemingway exchanged at the time. Hemingway, who since *The Wound and the Bow* had denounced Wilson's judgments and made fun of his writing about sex, gave him permission to publish and gloomily extended an olive branch. "Now everyone is dead or to be dead," the novelist declared, "I think we might try to resolve our misunderstandings and see what good, if any, there is in all of us along with the bad." He was at this time, in a mood of elegaic affirmation, writing *The Old Man and the Sea*.

The Shores of Light takes its title from the phrase found in Virgil and Lucretius—about souls in the underworld yearning for the vivid life they will not know again, yet the book captures the living spirit of the 1920s. His reviews are framed in vivid opening and closing portraits of Gauss and Millay. Gauss had died suddenly of a heart attack on November 3, 1951. Wilson's tribute is intellectually more intense, more personal than "Mr. Rolfe" yet pictorially less vivid than that of his prep school Greek teacher, for he had begun to know the professor only as an upperclassman. "Christian Gauss as a Teacher of Literature" describes the influence of the courses in Dante and French writers on him and his friends. Gauss's wide learning, neoclassical aesthetic, and interest in literary personalities were complemented by a moral authority to which students who went into other fields could look back for guidance. Wilson portrays the kind of teacher who, rather than promoting a theory or ideology, "starts trains of thought" that are left "in the hands of his students to be carried on by themselves."

The memoir of Millay recollects emotion in a carefully maintained tranquillity. On the morning of October 18, 1950, he writes, he'd dreamed of her, first as the woman who initiated him and whose image dominated his early years in New York, then in conversation about John Bishop's truncated career. She died the very next day, and he confesses to an intuition of this—not anything "supernatural," he quickly says, "but the kind of sympathetic sense of the rhythms of another's life that may sometimes persist in absence." His reprise of his pursuit of her alongside Bishop in 1920 is discreet and tender. Omitting his love scene with Edna and desperate letters when rejected, he takes their story from the weekend at the Cape to Paris and, after her marriage, to the tiny house on Bedford Street and the Boissevains' New York State farm. He documents the poignant missed connections of their correspondence and, from the draft of a letter to him seen only after her death, quotes the poet's cherished touchstones, stanzas from "The Scholar-Gypsy," "The Eve of St. Agnes," and "Lamia," as well as some Catullus—poems she'd memorized after her collapse at Doctor's Hospital in 1946. The painful visit with Elena to Steepletop in 1948 had been a shock, for he had imagined her sometimes as "faded and shrunken, never ruddy and overblown as I saw her now."

Though to Floyd Dell, another of Edna's old lovers, Wilson said it was "important that she should eventually be shown as she was," he did not know the whole truth about her life or death. He believed she died on the stairs with a glass of wine. However, on National Public Radio in 2001, Nancy Milford testified she had mixed alcohol and barbiturates and was found lying at the foot of the stairs with a broken neck. Wilson assured her sister Norma that the poetry would "always be there to make the casualties of her life seem unimportant," and he recalls us to Millay's serious purposes; he sets her in the Romantic tradition that she renewed and brings to her work his rhetorical training and a love of the music of words. This essay continues to protect her reputation in a period when a careful review of Milford's and Epstein's biographies in *The New Yorker* was introduced with the heading, "Millay the dainty, best-selling rhapsodic poet was also a drunk, a drug addict, and a prodigious bisexual erotomane." Although unconvincing when grouping her with Eliot, Auden, and Yeats as major poets in an age of prose, Wilson conveys Millay's lyric affirmation with a clarity that has made the memoir a favorite of readers.

Wilson's mother died in February 1951. During her later years, not wanting to hear his requests for money, she might say, "He makes me sick," or "I won't send the car for him" when he proposed to visit. When Rosalind was there and the three sat together at dinner—Wilson never in his father's chair—father and daughter couldn't maintain a conversation on either side of the deaf old lady. Despite the flasks of brandy in the Cadillac, he did not drink when in her home, which made him more tense, yet Helen Muchnic noted his distress as his mother grew weaker. An unsuccessful cataract operation left her blind as well as deaf, and he wrote to Nabokov that she was "so arthritic she couldn't stand up." On the day of her death she displayed her usual lack of enthusiasm for Wilson's life's work, warning Rosalind (who'd pass this on) not to marry a writer "or you'll never have any money!" She died with her loyal granddaughter lifting her head so she could smell the kind of coffee she liked. Wilson was glad to see her face freed of the humiliation of having grown too old, a face that bespoke the determination that was part of her character and her son's.

Rosalind was left a small trust, Wilson the income from one that on his death would pass to Rosalind and Reuel, worth what was then the substantial sum of $200,000. He inherited the New Jersey and Talcottville homes. When the house on Vista Place in Red Bank was sold the following fall, he and Elena moved everything out, and his mother's fine furniture was digested room by room at Wellfleet as if, he reflected, the old place extending back from the road were an anaconda. He was irritated by the upheaval caused by Elena's scraping walls and painting and moving things around, yet so proud of the eventual results that he sent a drawing of the house to Mamaine, calling attention to his wonderful study and drawing arrows to the garden off at the side. Writing to the poet May Sarton, Bogan speaks of the front parlor with Edmund's mother's Federal furnishings, "a dining-room with more mahogany against blue walls" and "middle room" with blue walls and blue chintz, "and Edmund's magnificent study, with a bathroom attached." She reports that "for the first time poor E."—who'd had "a v. scrappy kind of life, down the years"—had "attention, space, and effectively arranged paraphernalia of all kinds." Now all moved smoothly, "with good meals at appropriate intervals." Elena, Louise adds, "really *loves* him," and "the little girl, Helen, is delightful."

Reuel's boyhood comrade Mike Macdonald sketches the new ambience at Money Hill. At lunchtime he'd hear the critic shout from his study that he was ready for his tray or see him come to get it—perhaps "a minute steak, a salad, buttered Portuguese bread warmed in the oven"—then retreat down the hallway past the black-bound ledgers containing his journals and a complete set of the Delphine classics to the room that resembled a library at a gentleman's club. The boys were interested in the collections of opera, pop, and vaudeville records, which they were allowed to take away and listen to while playing games on the floor of the front parlor—the only room that, for Mike, still had a flavor of McCarthy's time. He recalled that Wilson admired Bing Crosby's suavity, and one afternoon in 1955 he and Reuel were invited in to hear the Sinatra album *In the Wee Small Hours.* Reuel would remember his father singing to him, and later to his son Jay, in an enthusiastic tenor. "Enthroned on the settee in his study, and with a few drinks under his belt," he rendered "A Bicycle Built for Two" or paged through an old Princeton songbook. In their college years Elena took the youths into what she called her "blue room," where the chairs and sofas and cushions were costumed in many shades of that color. Ensconced on the couch, she talked with them about politics, an Adlai Stevenson liberal who detested Joseph McCarthy and Richard Nixon, just as Wilson did, and would be a staunch supporter of the Kennedys.

Wilson was an independent radical who opposed his country's expansionist tendencies, yet his writing on American subjects during the 1950s reflects the confidence of a society newly important in the world, one in which he was an actor, not a spectator. Mass culture was not yet its primary export. Eliot, Faulkner, and Hemingway were awarded the Nobel Prize for Literature in 1948, '50, and '54, respectively. Stevenson dignified politics as a presidential candidate, while historians like Arthur Schlesinger and Richard Hofstadter explored the foundations of liberalism in the American past. Wilson praised the first installment of Theodore Roosevelt's letters. "The pre-Presidential T. R." had not yet become the cartoon character of "the big stick" and the strenuous life, the imperialistic warmonger. He took ideas seriously and wrote well, a product of privilege who rejected the ideal of the businessman, the "unadulterated huckster" and could punch it out "with the sordid political boss, the arrogant millionaire, the bought senator, the exploiter of tenements, the Spanish War profiteer—all those types from whom so many of his stratum shrank, with whom they refused to contend." In this phase Roosevelt lived up to an idea of America that included "a rigorous abstention from prejudice, in dealing with race, color, nationality, religion, or social status."

As Wilson worked back from the turn of the century to the Civil War, Princeton asked him to give one of the Gauss seminars, constituting—as each of these did—half a dozen talks, for which a generous foundation paid each lecturer $5,000. Settled off Nassau Street in the fall of 1952 and scheduled "to perform" starting in December, he made light of his nervousness, telling Cyril Connolly that "a seminar consists of sitting at a table with an audience of thirty people and reading or speaking for an hour, after which a discussion takes place." You had also to attend six such talks by someone else, but "the rest of the time you do as you please, and parties are given for you." According to one participant, he wasn't adept at managing the discussions that followed his performances, but the drafts of the Lincoln, Grant, and Stowe portraits in *Patriotic Gore* profited by being rehearsed for a group that were far from the "mediocrities" with whom, he'd predicted to Cyril, the Princeton professoriat would "feel more at home." They included the theologian Paul Tillich, Saul Bellow, then writing *The Adventures of Augie March*, John Berryman, engaged in "Homage to Mistress Bradstreet," and Leon Edel, who recalled that Berryman's poem was "the talk of Princeton that winter."

"Let us begin with *Uncle Tom's Cabin*," the matter-of-fact and compelling phrase that would open Wilson's Civil War epic and from which everything flows outward in expanding waves, came to him later, but the review drawn on for his paper on Stowe begins dramatically enough: "Out of a background of undistinguished narrative, carelessly written and not even quite literate, the characters spring to life, arguing and struggling like real people who cannot be quiet." The Selbys and George and Eliza and Aunt Chloe and Uncle Tom were living beings who broke the dams of discretion behind which the subject of slavery had been contained, dramatizing how the institution corrupted republican democracy. Confederate Vice President Alexander Stephens's statement that with Lincoln the Union "rose to the sublimity of a religious mysticism" cued Wilson's portrayal of Lincoln. Updating William Herndon's account of the "hard distinction," the precision and clarity of Lincoln's mind, he noted the skill with language and sensitivity to word sounds in Lincoln's verse and "the art of incantation" in the great compressed speeches that imposed on the nation an evolving vision of events. Wilson's Grant emerged from his discovery of the *Personal Memoirs*. These sober and precise volumes written to save Grant's family from poverty as he was dying of throat cancer conveyed his force as the commander who made Lincoln's cause prevail. At Princeton Wilson also drew on reviews in which he praised Ambrose Bierce's "clear, flexible, and sharp-edged style, like the steel ribbon of a wound-up tape measure," and the intellect of J. W. De Forest, which combined "moral stoutness with open-eyed curiosity" in a fashion that "can only be called classical."

Thus he would be able to give the national epic its heroes, though he already saw the Civil War less as a crusade against slavery than as a crux in the history of American consolidation and expansion. That spring, along with the Lincoln and Grant portraits to be enlarged in *Patriotic Gore*, *The New Yorker* published his study of the Holmes-Laski correspondence, which points in one direction to the portrait that concludes *Patriotic Gore*, in another to Judaism and the Jews. As often, Wilson's curiosity was stimulated by an anomaly. Prompted by a biography of Harold Laski, who had died, he found in his old acquaintance's letters to Justice Oliver Wendell Holmes what turned out to be fabrications about everything from book buying to conversations with famous people. He noted that Holmes had also enjoyed the stimulation of the young Louis Brandeis and Felix Frankfurter, as well as that of the philosopher Morris Cohen. Had the fanciful Laski sought "a Jewish father" in the dry old justice, the product of a New England "discipline of life" originally modeled on the Old Testament? Did the Englishman's letters reawaken in Holmes "a flush of that fervor for the destiny of human society which had been blighted on the battlefields of the Civil War"?

Wilson's sense of Stowe's, Lincoln's, and even Holmes's prophetic dimension was stimulated by a Hebrew course that he took at the Princeton Theological Seminary, from which his grandfather had graduated a century before. Thaddeus Wilson's Hebrew Bible had turned up in the attic at his mother's house, and the critic set out to satisfy his curiosity about the language of the Old Testament. Edel was present when he had the seminarians and their instructor in for tea and cakes—the "neat, washed and scrubbed youths encircling Edmund and the instructor," Wilson, glass of scotch in hand, firing "question after question, about the absence of vowels, the need for gutturals, the packed-in nuances, as if he were at a Jewish parochial school in the basement or antechamber of some synagogue." Remembering Max Beerbohm's drawing of Robert Browning taking tea with the Browning Society, Edel thought Beerbohm might have entitled this scene "Mr. Edmund Wilson learning to read Genesis." Later in the year Wilson would set down his impressions in the essay on *Genesis* that led to his going to Israel.

Returning from Princeton to the well-ordered Wellfleet study, he was soon laying out different projects on different desks. His earlier work had developed from literary modernism through Marxism, sequential concerns of an intellectual avant-garde, but as that faded into the past he wove back and forth among a number of concerns and roles. In 1953 he had some of the early journals typed up and, happily surprised by "how much there was in them," considered how "to get some kind of book out of them"—he deemed it "rather cheap" of André Gide simply to publish his in unedited installments. Wilson next cut and shaped *The Twenties*, using the bracketed interpolations with which he expanded the Russian diaries and, during the 1960s, would turn jottings made on his first trip to Europe in 1908, at college, and during World War I into *A Prelude*. He begins *The Twenties* with a retrospect about Sandy's collapse and the New York scene in 1920–1922: *Vanity Fair* and Crowninshield, the Algonquinites and the Coffee House lunch club, his Yale apartment-mates. Explaining that he'd dropped the journal when "demoralized" by his passion for Millay, he inserts bad romantic verse about her and two short passages left out of his memoir. As the decade unfolds, he tells us what we need to know about the Fitzgeralds, Ted Paramore, Dos Passos, and various women friends, some of them protected by false names. He steps out of the journal to include essential information about his breakdown and recovery in 1929. The alternation between young Wilson and a Wilson thirty years older, who knows how it has all turned out, adds to the novelistic dimension of *The Twenties*.

This was the first of five journals that would be published after he and most of the people in them were dead. Initially a writer's notebooks, intended as a source for fiction, in his later years they stand as a record of his life and times. Before resuming this series, he collected his early reporting in *The American Earthquake*, where his kaleidoscope of the arts during the jazz age sets up a more polished version of "a year of the slump" in *The American Jitters*. Wilson shows what it was like when the whole structure of American society actually seemed to be going to pieces. "The Jumping-Off Place" leaves us in the exhaustion of the westward movement, facing the endless Pacific at the San Diego naval base, and his grisly evocation of the Chicago slums in the winter of 1932 ends with the contradictory injunction on a wall VOTE RED. THE PEOPLE ARE GOOFY. Joan Didion has spoken of her admiration for *Earthquake*, and of consulting this when warming up for her reportage. A postscript on FDR and Pearl Harbor anticipates Wilson's preface to *Patriotic Gore*. The nation's eventual willingness to accept the targeting of civilian populations underscores for him the ease with which an appetite for war can be created and wrapped in moral justifications, individual thought surrendered to a corporate bureaucratic machine. The United States was not exempt from the "primitive animal instinct to challenge, to subdue and, if possible to exploit other groupings of human beings," from "the irresistible instinct of power to expand itself, of well-organized human aggregations to absorb or impose themselves on other groups."

The old stone house in upstate New York became for Wilson the symbol of another America. It had been the site of his youthful revelation that he was, if not a poet, "something of the kind." For years he'd wanted his mother to give him the place, which, although she sometimes spent summers there, had meant more to his father than to her. As her death approached he had Mr. Peck, described by Mike Macdonald as "a gentle, reserved Yankee" with "a bow tie, white shirt, and Sam Snead straw hat" who drove the Wellfleet taxi, take him and Rosalind and Reuel over to Talcottville. This was a long trek each way, a full day or two half days, before the interstate highways. The lofty countryside once again stirred him, as did the colors of the fields and flowers and the sky at sunset, the way the light poured in the summer on the dewy morning. He returned with Elena, and though the country didn't excite her and the flame from the kerosene stove "went up half a yard," at first she recollected thinking, "I was so fond of him that I could take any place." In the summer of 1952 they went twice. He and Reuel dragged junk from the closets and the attic into the kitchen or out onto the lawn, where Elena read in a steamer chair, and she painted the bathroom while he threw out the Franklin stoves and arranged for the chimneys to be rebuilt so the fireplaces could work again. On a night when it was too cold to sleep, they wrapped themselves in blankets and he read aloud the whole of *The Old Man and the Sea*. To Dos he wrote that "the personal note of self-regard and self-pity" limited the tale and that Hemingway had "already congratulated himself so warmly that there is no point in anyone else's doing it," yet he was delighted to see their colleague back in form.

More than fifty people were said to have died in the old house, and at first Wilson felt lurking presences and found it caused him bad dreams to sleep in certain rooms. Each year, however, he brought the place back to life and made it more his own, making it "express at last my own personality and interests, filling it with my own imagination," yet feeling a continuity with everybody who had lived there, "basing myself, in some sense, on them." The only child relished reviving connections with his extended family, rural cousins who struggled to hang on to remnants of large farms and the Talcott heirs around the United States. Some of the latter—like Dorothy Mendenhall—still agitated the subject of his grandfather Baker's acquisition of the house by marriage and his father's purchase of the place from Baker heirs. Wilson lured one or two of these relatives back to town for part of the summer. From his study on the third floor with large windows looking out over the lawn, he imagined another batch of children playing croquet there.

This inheritance, which he loved, soon strained his marriage. Wilson often felt more creative in upstate New York: "As soon as I started out with Bill Peck, driving to Talcottville, my head became thronged with ideas for books." But Elena missed the sea and the salt air, believed she had less energy in the foothills of the Adirondacks, and didn't enjoy the omnipresent smell of cows or being chased by a bull, in her red dress, down the bank and across the Sugar River. She lacked her husband's romantic vision of this "kingdom of asbestos shingle and patched and mended asbestos shingle," as she would write in a thirty-four-page retrospect, "My View from the Other Window," the title echoing the feminism of *A Room of One's Own*, to which she was exposed by her daughter. Downstairs one morning she saw what she was sure was a ghost, a woman in nineteenth-century dress whose head was not visible as she went around a corner. Another day she saw an old man looking in through the vines of the low kitchen window, not a ghost, but no one she wanted spying on them. She worried about the drinking water, felt she had to bury the garbage rather than let it be thrown away and end up, as garbage sometimes did, on the banks of the little river where the children swam. She was concerned when five-year-old Helen, unable to play at home without disturbing her father during working hours, endlessly watched TV at the general store. The first time that, at seven, Helen rode her bicycle to a friend's farm, her mother walked the two miles to return with her in the evening. Helen Augur, the cousin who'd once made love with Wilson, had told Elena that, at Talcottville, she'd "been raped by an old man when she was seven and had never gotten over it."

These stresses color Elena's references to the "shallow, dark water and slimy, slippery rocks" of the rivers and ponds where she was urged to swim, the "pus substance" that oozed out of old trees afflicted with Dutch elm disease. So does the fact that Wilson came to drink more upstate, was harder for his family to be around. The 1955 season was happier for her. He noted that she made new friends, acquired an electric stove, and painted the dining room and small sitting room a shade of blue like her bedroom at Wellfleet. Elena, however, recalls that on the day when she re-hung two oval Hudson River–type landscapes—which looked, Wilson thought, "for the first time quite handsome"—she returned from town to find him repositioning the pictures and claiming for the phonograph records the table where she'd placed her typewriter. "At that moment," she writes, "I gave up trying to adapt myself." In 1957 she grieved when he left Wellfleet in June, but would not come to Talcottville until August.

While in Talcottville Wilson brought his journals up to date, and *Upstate*, the publishing triumph of his last years, would set the record of twenty New York summers against a backdrop of family and regional history. *A Piece of My Mind*, a loosely organized assemblage of thoughts and minor essays, was started at the stone house in August 1955 and finished there the following June. This book is not of much consequence except for vivid bits of autobiography. He holds forth on such topics as "Religion," "Europe," "Russia," "The Jews," "Education," "Science," and "Sex," but his only trenchant generalizations are about "The United States." He affirms the cardinal role of the serious republicans who put the nation above either art or science or, on the other hand, making money. He doesn't mean "to exalt this republican sense as the touchstone of American merit," for, "many people have had it to a greater or less degree, yet some have not had it at all. Justice Holmes felt a stake in the United States of a kind that his friend Henry James did not feel." James was a concerned patriot, yet his devotion was to "the art of imaginative literature, which was for him international." In this fashion Wilson defines the double allegiance that is a source of vitality in his own work. He combines James's religion of art with Holmes's special stake in his country.

The concluding essay, "The Author at Sixty," lifts this collection to another level. Wilson's memoir of his father preserves the lineaments of a once familiar American type, the leading citizen in countless small communities. Often a lawyer or a doctor, such men were individualists with the authority of their abilities and a strong belief in the republic. The critic enjoys remembering his father's place in the life of his New Jersey town and county, including odd acts of beneficence in which he engaged— sponsoring a writer of Victorian verse (which Edmund had politely called insipid) and the successful effort of a sign painter to go on stage as a stand- up comedian. His mother's death has freed their son to reveal the blight- ing hypochondria of the lawyer and semipublic figure. Wilson notes that his father, retreating from the transformation of the Jersey shore during the gilded age, was at home and able to relax in the tiny community of Talcottville, and these first summers after he inherited the house brought his father back to him. On a walk "over to Flat Rock across the fields, try- ing to find Father's slender cane, one of those he had whittled himself, which I had forgotten there," the wildflowers in the rainy weather seemed wonderfully "to burn in the grass."

In this memoir the old stone house—singular, isolated, enduring— affords a serene perspective on a society in which, Wilson writes, as to Elena after Paul Rosenfeld's death, life "is much subject to disruptions and frustrations, catastrophic collapses and gradual peterings-out." Admitting he'd sometimes believed himself vulnerable to such a fate, he likes being surrounded by the things from his past and proclaims that "old-fogeyism is comfortably closing in." The house had been an outpost of civilization in country Washington Irving found wild to the point of being unlivable. At the end of the essay Wilson imagines "its excellent proportions, its ele- gance of windows and doorways, its carved fireplaces and branching columns, crystallizing in the forests that the traveler describes." In this fashion he evokes the enterprise of American culture.

The Puritans had spoken of this as the errand into the wilderness. To contemplate the bland consumerism represented in *Life* magazine made Wilson feel "that I do not belong to the country depicted there, that I do not even live in that country." He asked himself, "Am I then in a pocket of the past?" and, with his ability to engage us in a drama and its outcome, answered, "I do not necessarily believe it." Reaching out to the reader as Whitman does when he tells us "What I assume you shall assume," he concluded, "I may find myself here at the center of things—since the center can be only in one's head—and my feelings and thoughts may be shared by many."

24

In the Old World

Delmore Schwartz, the poet and *Partisan Reviewer*, likened Wilson to a son of one of Henry James's heroes, who has his moral experience among the modernists of *Axel's Castle* and Marxists of *Finland Station* rather than in the London, Paris, and Italy where James's American characters define themselves. Wilson too was anchored to his native soil. Even when submerged in Proust and Joyce, he had focused on their relevance to the United States, and when Marx and Lenin replaced them during the Depression, his aim was to help transform his own society. Twenty years later, his detachment from the consumerist America of the 1950s was matched to a new enjoyment of Europe, accentuated when he went abroad with a European wife. He reminded himself that an American had no place lingering in the Old World, yet his tastes clashed with his principles. Once a victim of "British rudeness," he was warmed by the network of friendship and gossip in the close-knit British literary community, and on the Continent Elena had interesting friends, as well as relatives whose well-being she felt responsible for. Sailing on the *Île de France* in January 1954, they returned in 1956, and wintered in Paris in 1963–1964 while Helen spent the year in a Swiss school. The journals expand under the stimulation of these experiences and the memories that accompany them.

On the voyage over in 1954, the Wilsons saw something of Jason and Barbara Epstein, who were traveling first class on the *Île de France* courtesy of Doubleday. Jason, creator of the quality paperback that transformed American publishing, had contracted for four books by Wilson at the beginning of his Anchor series. *To the Finland Station, The American Earthquake, Eight Essays*, and *A Literary Chronicle* brought their author both money and fan letters and made him feel, he told Betty Huling, his old friend from *The New Republic*, "a little, for the first time in my life, as if I were a real success." At a festive New Year's Eve dinner in the dining room with its two-story descending staircase the two couples shared a table with the comedian Buster Keaton and his wife. Keaton was going to perform in the Cirque Midrano in Paris. When Wilson complimented him on his recent appearance in Chaplin's *Limelight* Keaton said he hadn't seen it, in a tone suggesting disappointment with this minor role. The party drank five bottles of champagne, and it was Epstein, not Wilson, who recalled how Wilson and Keaton were juggling the colored cotton balls that were to be thrown at midnight, one man adding one and the other one more. When Wilson asked him to do another act, "Keaton, cupping his hands around his mouth, whispered, 'No Props!' Edmund said, 'The ship is a prop.' It was a windy night, we were sliding from side to side and the water was splashing on the windows. The next thing we knew, Keaton was outside, in his dinner jacket, wiping the windows between waves with his napkin."

Arriving in London, while Elena and Helen and he settled into a comfortable hotel, he remembered the Maskelyne Temple of Magic, "the Dickensian waiter who amused my father at the Metropole Hotel" in 1908, and his bicycle tour with friends six years later, the crowds celebrating the incipient Great War. Wilson's British affinities were deep. His father's language had self-consciously English touches—he even liked to use the word "Zounds!"—and Wilson invoked "bounder" for objectionable characters from Dick Knight to Condé Nast, and to describe himself in his behavior with Margaret Canby. Yet he realized that his memories of the London of his youth were no longer part of "any present functioning consciousness." Though each could be "made to present itself as immediate," he wryly observed that they seemed "to topple over at the end of the curve of the lengthened span of my life, even to be lost as actual."

He was glad to see Mamaine again. She had been sometimes ill, and her life with Koestler was wearing. To Wilson she had written, "he has a violent and emotional temperament which carries him to extremes" but "is never mean or selfish" and "looks after me wonderfully." After she married him in 1950, however, Koestler became involved with his devoted secretary, Cynthia. She would be his second wife and, though more than twenty years younger, at fifty-five and in good health would commit suicide with him when he was worn out by cancer and Parkinson's disease. Mamaine and he separated, and she acquired a small house of her own and a job in publishing. Wilson had entertained her with newsy letters about his life and his reading. Enthusiastic about his articulate Civil War personalities in *Patriotic Gore*, in one letter he characteristically rehearsed the introduction in what he called "a little blurb." Mamaine's are the letters of a kindred spirit. She too has attempted Hebrew, she writes when he is doing so. She regards Greek, in which she is being tutored by "a charming, very ancient, toothless, bewigged schoolmaster," as "an oasis" in her life.

Mamaine gave a party for the Wilsons, as did Cyril Connolly, with whom he'd corresponded off and on during the last decade. *Horizon* was long gone, but Connolly remained a gatekeeper and talent scout for English letters. He worked at his craft, the American knew, yet allowed himself to be distracted from his own productions, as during World War II:

> Cyril Connolly
> Behaves rather fonnily:
> Whether folks are at peace or at fighting,
> He complains that it keeps him from writing.

Wilson saw Connolly through his gossip and his eccentricities. At a later meeting he told an endless, farcical story of his relations with Barbara Skelton, who'd divorced him when having an affair with the publisher George Weidenfeld, then returned to Cyril (though she married Weidenfeld that same year). She'd told Cyril she was converting her diary about him into a novel—the novel never appeared, but her diary was presumably the origin of her admirable autobiography *Tears Before Bedtime*.

Wilson and Elena sometimes stayed with Sylvester Gates and his wife, Pauline, in one of their two elegant homes in London. Gates, who in 1926–27 had been Wilson's rival for Magda Johann, was now chairman of a bank and a director of several, but Isaiah Berlin remembered him always with a classic in his hand, "some book you never had time to read and wished you did—Chaucer? Montaigne?" Wilson set down his host's salacious anecdotes as eagerly as once he had Frances Minihan's racy ones. Gates passed on the news that C. M. Bowra—who in 1945 had remarked on Whitman's popularity in South America—had received the Légion d'Honneur and in boasting of this to Jean Cocteau said, *"Et à la fin, j'ai été baisé par le président de la République."* The don's French was weak—he had meant to say "baisse" for kissed, but had pronounced the word for "fucked." With young women, however, Wilson was still a Victorian, and

Gates's talk of their bachelor youth one day caused him ponderously to warn Nora Sayre, now twenty-two, against this "wolf."

On this visit to London he often found his hosts charming. John Betjeman, one day to be poet laureate, stood up to the aristocracy, making fun of them in an essay on "Dim Earls." Wilson, who liked light verse, deemed Betjeman the best poet in the United Kingdom after Auden's removal to the States and Dylan Thomas's death. From his wheelchair, John Hayward, Eliot's sometime apartment-mate, described him as "a Henry James character, full of old-fashioned formalities." In the din of a literary party Wilson records a pleasant encounter with E. M. Forster, a slight man with spectacles and the "small slightly sagged mustache" of an older generation. "I said at once that I shared his enthusiasm for his three favorite books: *The Divine Comedy*, Gibbon, and *War and Peace.* —You would, of course. —But, I thought that *Das Kapital* almost belonged in the same category." Perhaps not wanting to dispute this, Forster shifted the subject to Jane Austen. He said, "Your essays have thrown a good deal of light for me on Kipling and other things."

Wilson's relish for British comedy persisted, and like everyone else he enjoyed the "male Cinderella" tale *Lucky Jim. That Uncertain Feeling*, Kingsley Amis's next novel, was, he said in a *New Yorker* review, a darker product of a "world that, even imitating America," still carried, "in an eroded and degraded form, the skeleton of its class-stratification." Angus Wilson's account of the pinched remnants of the upper-middle class was closer to Edmund's experience. These two became acquainted, and the satirist was glad to come to dinner. He felt indebted to the critic's Proust and Dickens essays. A social democrat and a Labour man, Angus Wilson would one day state that Dickens was in some sense "the great subject of my life." In the journal they are seen discussing the various English accents, the snobbery of bowler hats and rolled umbrellas, the habit of ending a discourse with the rather portentous "Hm" (Auden's version being "Um—ah"), and the resemblance of the accent of the royal family to something Edmund thought he'd heard in the East End in 1914 and that Angus called cockney—or, as he qualified Wilson's account in retrospect, "half-cockney, quasi-cockney."

In an editorial intrusion in *The Fifties* Leon Edel insists on Wilson's dislike of the British and their class-bound culture. Though Edel is wrong on the first score, at Oxford, except when Wilson sentimentally recalled reading English poetry as an undergraduate, "on a bench in Magdalene Walk," he assumed the familiar role of irreverent American. It was partly his dislike for the pedantry of universities. Berlin recalled that before meeting his colleagues Wilson launched "a sweeping attack on academic life and academics" as "murderers of all that was living and real in literature and art." In Sir Isaiah's memoir of this visit, Wilson remarks that the Bodleian Library (not yet fortified by Rockefeller money) is about to collapse, embodying the "decayed, conservative English academic life in its death throes." In *The Fifties* the Bodleian is "shabby and crumbling, scrofulous and leprous," and Wilson's room at All Souls excessively monastic. The servants named "scouts" are "obviously disaffected"—approvingly he noted that dinner in Hall was shortened by "the class-contemptuous waiters," who would "whisk the courses away before we had had a chance to eat them." Berlin invited David Cecil, Lord Salisbury's younger son, to dinner, but to Wilson the Englishman seemed a dilettante, while Cecil thought the American's view of literature too utilitarian. Also present were John Bayley and his wife, Iris Murdoch—"disaster, disaster," Berlin murmured thirty-odd years later, for Wilson was "bored" by the conversation, Berlin himself recalling it as "forced and dull." Wilson drank enough to confuse Bayley with the Dickens scholar Humphrey House, someone, his host thought, he'd have enjoyed more. He wanted to meet only two men: Cecil Roth, a Jewish antiquarian associated with the effort to date the Dead Sea Scrolls very late, thus nearer to the Christian era, and the historian A.J.P. Taylor, whose manners weren't at all donnish. When gruffly declaring Taylor to be "my kind of man," Wilson didn't know that he'd just attacked Berlin's account of Tolstoy in print.

Edel asserts that Wilson's "anglophobic malice extend[ed] even to Sir Isaiah," a statement belied by the meetings and correspondence of twenty years. But Wilson liked to bait his friend, as when describing Churchill, with his trans-Atlantic parentage, as "a romantic American journalist." In this vein he had written a whimsical letter signed Edmund MacArthur Wilson, which proposed that following the United States' takeover of England, Isaiah in the "Department of Colonial Culture" would supervise translating American writers into Russian and Russians into "the archaic dialect of American still spoken in the British isles," for which his compensation would be the opportunity to flood England with Russian idioms in limericks dropped from planes. Berlin himself said Wilson, not paying much attention to his work as a political philosopher, "saw me as a bridge between Russia and the West. Sort of an interpreter, a good interpreter."

At Edinburgh Wilson called on Compton Mackenzie, a Scot with an

American mother, who, rather like the critic, had a place in British literary life without being of it. Mackenzie had been a young man when Wilson read *Sinister Street* in college, before leaving that to Scott Fitzgerald and going on to Plato and Dante. Over seventy in 1954, he conveyed the flavor of a hearty Edwardian culture that Berlin knew Wilson would have relished more than Bloomsbury—"a jolly fellow [Sir Isaiah said] who drank and womanized and had adventures and had wonderful times in Greece, and wrote books which had to be censored, none of this trembling aesthetic." Mackenzie talked freely of his career and life, modestly classing himself a mere entertainer. He shared Wilson's prejudice against Somerset Maugham, whom he had silenced by saying, "Look here, Maugham: if you're going to be rude, I can be ruder than you—and when I'm rude, my rudeness is unforgivable." On a second visit a few years later, after investigating the New York State Iroquois, Wilson would be taken with Mackenzie's Scottish nationalism. Here was a fellow supporter of "the rights of small nations and cultural minorities, as against all the forces which are driving us in the direction of centralized power that tries to process or crush them." One imagines him pressing the point, over Scotch whisky, to the author of the book that became the movie *Tight Little Island*, about a bunch of bibulous Scots who are rebelling because they've run out of their national drink.

His first impression of France since 1935 was the landscape at Calais, still littered by World War II bombings a decade after the war ended. In the cold railroad car, with a damp mist outside over graying snow (as this is described in *A Piece of My Mind*), he relived the arrival of his unit in the Vosges so long before. In Paris Elena and he had bad colds. Her German brother Brat and sister Olga appeared on the scene, bringing with them the grim flavor of life at Johannisberg. Badly bombed during World War II, the place had now an odor of scandal, for Brat's wife Madeleine, a French woman who'd believed thoroughly in the Third Reich, had acquired a live-in lover, a decorated American veteran who admired Hitler. Brat and Olga, whom Elena was still close to, sometimes sided with Madeleine, the one who had called Elena a dirty renegade.

While Elena was occupied with the Mumms as well as her Russian relatives, Wilson saw a good deal of Mamaine, who was staying in the same Paris hotel. Her divorce had finally come through and she was depressed, having had to repudiate the man she adored in court, so Wilson cheered her up. After a day or two of this Elena got jealous, making him "rather surprised and also touched" that his beloved could think that at this point in his life he "could have that much interest in another woman." He would be glad to have spent time with Mamaine, for they wouldn't meet again. She too had a cold, and afterward he heard from her that the infection "had gone to her lung." Hospitalized for acute asthma several times in April and May, in her letters she courageously represents herself as on the mend and eager for his news, and when back in New York he filled her in at length. However, she never recovered between attacks and the drugs became ineffective. She died that June, a few days after receiving a query from Wilson about her condition. Her sister Celia had just married, and it was painful for him to think of Mamaine "shriveling up, losing her breath, alone in the hospital there" with Celia "gone to her husband in the country."

Mamaine's death darkened England for Wilson. When John Wain made a pilgrimage to Talcottville to interview him for the *Observer* three years later, Wilson characteristically had his own questions, among them "Do you ever have a feeling that English literature is rapidly shriveling up and that there will soon be nothing turned out that anybody is likely to remember except an occasional poem by John Betjeman and an occasional story by Angus Wilson?" A return visit to London in 1956 would confirm this impression. As always, he found the city relaxing and reasonable after New York, but the literary scene was discouraging. Except for Angus Wilson's study of Zola and Isaiah Berlin's of Tolstoy, in the weeklies the masters were neglected in favor of minor figures. Angus reported that the generation of Amis and Wain did little reading—even those who taught in the universities knew no poetry but Eliot and the metaphysicals, had no Continental culture, and "would discover Nietzsche with astonished enthusiasm." Wilson seized on these details in his sense of loss after Mamaine's death, when it was "almost as if there were no more London for me."

In France he realized that Europe had become provincial—this was "the great shift that has taken place during my time." Developing this perspective in *A Piece of My Mind*, the sometime sympathizer with the rights of small nations distrusts the revival of Gaelic as he does Yugoslavia's competing languages and cultures, marks of the "*passion* for fragmentation" of Europeans who might better organize in a federation to protect themselves against an imperial United States and USSR. But in January 1954 he found Paris stimulating despite his cold. It was the moment when Americans were fascinated by Camus and Sartre, but Genet, an immoralist with an outsider's contempt for respectability, had for some time seemed to Wilson the most vital contemporary French writer. Sending

Notre Dame des Fleurs to his faithful correspondent Nabokov, he had pointed out that "Huysmans, who could only do it synthetically, would have been crazy about Genet," whose language combined "argot, ordinary colloquialisms, very fancy literary vocabulary and precise technical terms," and who, like Faulkner, created words. In Paris the Wilsons were impressed and depressed by Genet's *The Maids*, a play about class and sexual self-contempt. Two sisters who are servants and, in the absence of their kind young mistress, mockingly enact her role are unable when she returns to kill her with a drugged tea, but one of the sisters decides to drink it herself. Two years later, Wilson encouraged Nicholas Nabokov, the novelist's roguish cousin, to arrange a meeting with Genet, who proved uninterested when it turned out the American wasn't planning to give him any money. On learning that he had been invited to a reception at the Academy and was seated beside the queen of Belgium, Wilson observed, "With all admiration for Genet, I do think it indicates a rottenness of Europe that he should be nowadays one of its great writers."

In February 1954 he interpreted American culture to Europeans at the Salzburg Seminar in Austria. Founded by Harvard students after the war and serially funded by several foundations, it was then centered on literature but included sociology and law. It was held at the Schloss Leopold-skron, a baroque castle that once belonged to Max Reinhardt, which featured chandeliers, painted panels and mirrors, cupids, large bearded black busts of Romans with gilded trimmings, and "enormous and terrible paintings of Archbishop Firmian willing the schloss to his nephew, with his favorite dog in the foreground." At nine in the cold mornings he trudged up the dark, spiral servants' staircase, a folder of notes in his hand. In order to "give them the American Civil War," he had to sketch in the whole intellectual and political background. His class, which turned into a seminar, included journalists, linguists, one or two teachers, serious-minded men and women in their thirties and forties from throughout Western Europe, and from Yugoslavia, which sent students struggling to see past the blinders of their Marxism. His colleagues included Lawrance Thompson of the Princeton English department, Isaac Rosenfeld, a philosophy professor who wrote fiction, and Roy Harvey Pearce, a historian of ideas who taught early American literature and would one day edit Hawthorne's stories for the Library of America. Wilson told himself that to teach a literary subject well required a "more extensive knowledge and permanent mastery" than to write about it for readers, but his attempted tolerance of academe broke down when he had to listen to Pearce on

American poetry—"a drop-dropping of little lead pellets of thought the meaning of which appeared to be nil—a kind of double-talk in a mushy California accent." Yet it would be Pearce who remembered that amid the toasts to the faculty and staff at the farewell dinner Wilson, who'd drunk even more than his usual quantity of wine, pulled himself out of his chair to toast the students.

His only exposure to Germany after being posted to Trier at the end of World War I was that winter. On weekends and after his course was finished, he visited some of Elena's relatives, including the Grunilius family at Frankfurt, cultivated civic bankers like those in Thomas Mann's novels. From what he had heard, Johannisberg, about forty miles by car south of Frankfurt, was a caricature of inbred aristocracy compromised by Nazism, but Elena regarded the place as her home and wanted Wilson with her for this visit. Olga, her sister, a nurse in Germany during World War II, drove them over "at a terrible rate of speed," and the introductions didn't go easily, not helped along by tea or drinks. At dinner, trying to establish good relations with Brat Mumm, Wilson spoke of the friendship between Americans and Germans at the end of the first war and reiterated his opinion that the United States had made a mistake in joining that conflict.

Conversation was in French, and Joe Bazata, the American "guest"—who slipped into the room of Brat's wife, Madeleine, at night (as the old beloved family servant whispered to Elena)—at first merely said, "*oui, oui,*" in affected fashion. At some point, however, Bazata insinuated that "Hitler would have been 'fine' if he had succeeded." After dinner he sat on the couch with his hand in Brat's young daughter's hair, and in passing seemed to Wilson to boast of cruelty to animals. Unable to throw the man out of someone else's house, Wilson attempted, in the British manner, to put him down: when Bazata spoke of American officials in Europe as clowns, of John Foster Dulles (whose policies Wilson detested) as sexually inadequate, he said, "You're not the person to talk, old top: you're a clown yourself," and goaded the ex-sergeant to the verge of a fistfight. Back in his and Elena's room, Wilson, deflated, realized that Bazata could hardly have squared off against a family connection almost sixty and in poor physical shape. Having "never insulted a guest in any decent house I had visited," he departed the next day, though he wrote to a friend that he hated leaving Elena to cope with this scene.

In 1956 in Paris, Elena and he enjoyed a second honeymoon, and pleasant meetings with his old friend Esther Murphy and others led him to imagine the easy life he might have had among the expatriates, holding forth on America and on comparative literature. When working on *Patriotic Gore* in Cambridge during the next years, which were difficult ones for the family, he had another idea for a novel, and envisioned writing it in Paris, where even the street signs showed respect for writers. After his Civil War book appeared, in an "interview" conducted with himself Wilson would write, "I feel sometimes that I'm getting to the proverbial point when good Americans die and go to Paris," reminded, however, by the student riots that "if one went there alive, one might be killed by a plastic bomb."

We see Helen from time to time in these journals, traveling with her parents. Though she and her father, who was old enough to be her grandfather, didn't actually spend much time together, in his thoughts he doted on "the little girl" born of this love match. He was proud that at five she could sit "quite formally" and talk with Stephen Spender at luncheon, and the kindly poet found her delightful. In London Wilson had also taken Helen to the Tower, the Christmas Pantomime, and a magical performance such as he'd enjoyed at thirteen. As she grew up his controlling instinct became clearer, but her mother, she says, ran interference for her, and in *The Sixties* she holds her own with her "Pa." A teenager, she lies in bed in Paris "writing endless letters to friends, which she illustrates with little drawings." Wilson adds, "When I said something about her handwriting, she explained that she had five different styles of writing, which she used for different purposes."

He grew fond of Elena's Russian connections, who were expansive and dramatic, the women earning such money as there was and in charge. Elena's fragile Auntie Elinka, whom she resembled and who was an important person in her life, died before this 1963 visit, but Auntie Maroussia, who lived with her daughter and grandson in an outlying working-class district, seemed indestructible. She liked telling how her great-grandmother danced with Pushkin and what he said to her. As a young woman she had never gotten dressed without the help of a lady's maid, but at this point she had a hard life, and Elena sent them money. Smart and determined, Auntie Maroussia also felt things deeply, was given to weeping over the fate of the monarchy and scandalized by Nina Chavchavadze's politics—"the cousin . . . of His Imperial Majesty a liberal!" Wilson found her entertaining. "One could not serve both God and *Maman*," she said, punning in French on the name of the god of the Philistines.

That spring both Helen and Rosalind joined them for an interlude in

Rome, a city he hadn't visited for almost twenty years. He alternated visits to the museums and the ruins with the social round. Two Italian professors of English are caricatured in the journal, one "a good old boy, who has just translated the whole of Shakespeare into prose. Beard, spectacles, the reddest nose I have ever seen," the other hardly able, at seventy, to speak English. In their homes, however, he took in the literary news: Moravia had succeeded in getting his girlfriend a prize for a book no one but he had read, while Lampedusa's brilliant novel of Sicily, *Il gattopardo*, had at first been rejected by the publishers because he was an amateur. It had been written on a dare, after a cousin won a prize for what Lampedusa deemed mediocre verse. Wilson decided that Lampedusa's last effort, the long story "Lighea," was his masterpiece, and one sees why this tale moved the aging romantic. A scholar divulges to a young friend the memory of a youthful affair on the beach with a Siren who had risen from the sea on hearing him declaim ancient Greek, a language akin to her own. After their three weeks, during which he was filled with a pagan intuition of life's deeper rhythms, she had left him saying she would respond if he ever needed her. At the end of Lampedusa's story, en route to a classical congress in Portugal, the elderly scholar inexplicably disappears from the ship.

In 1964 in Rome Wilson saw a good deal of Mario Praz, whom he'd met at the end of the war. Praz had a clubfoot and walked with a limp, though it hadn't keep him from being, like Byron, "a beautiful swimmer" when he visited the Wilsons at Wellfleet. Another time he went around Washington with Wilson and, an acerbic person, took note when a guide spoke of a stream called the Tiber running below the city on old maps, making D.C. the new Rome. Wilson admired the museum of precious furnishings and pieces of art Praz maintained in his home, everything from antique bidets to delightful figurines that danced. For Elena the place was too cluttered, but for the critic, no longer very mobile, his objets d'art defined this scholar-artist in his milieu. Wilson relished the genius of the city of literature, painting, food, attractive women, and the great structures and statues of the past. At the end of *The Bit Between My Teeth*, his last literary chronicle, Praz's collection is a metaphor for what Poe had called the grandeur that was Rome—"its cosmopolitan culture, its accumulations of the ages, its happy freedom from narrow prejudices, its conviction of being at the center of the world."

25

European Artists: Malraux, Beerbohm, and Stravinsky; Auden in America

Wilson had long since intellectually absorbed the great figures of his youth, and they were gone, Joyce, Yeats, Freud, and Trotsky all dying when Fitzgerald did, as he'd written to Bishop. Nabokov and Auden, important figures of his later years, were his peers rather than his masters. While welcoming the enrichment of American culture by such noteworthy European artists, when traveling abroad he sought out others who stayed in the Old World. In 1954 he spent the better part of two days with Max Beerbohm and another two with André Malraux. Between them these men illustrate the critic's eclectic intellectual life. Beerbohm, whose work had delighted him since college, was a prose stylist who also created caricatures in pen and ink, and Wilson, who never ceased his own Beardsleyan drawings and doodles, admired his skill. Malraux had survived the collapse of Marxist radicalism to reflect on human destiny in the World War II novel, *The Struggle with the Angel*, which contained "passages of sinewy and searching thought" and "strokes of dramatic imagination," though it was unevenly written. He reaffirmed man's will to remake the world in *The Psychology of Art*, for Wilson one of the triumphs of the postwar period. Beerbohm was the artist as craftsman, Malraux as philosopher.

In *Classics and Commercials* he ventures that a blend of British common sense with European aestheticism carried Beerbohm from the extravagances of *The Yellow Book* into his brisk journalism in the British *Saturday Review*, which honed his literary style, and on to the parodies of James, Shaw, and George Meredith in *A Christmas Garland* (1912). That year he left England, and four decades later Wilson called on him with *The New Yorker* writer S. N. Berhman at Rappallo, where he had settled. It is as though, during their talks and when writing them up for publication, Wilson stepped back into Edwardian London. Beerbohm had gently ridiculed the terse but mannered style of *The Wings of the Dove*, and he could still recite James's last lines, in which Merton Densher and Kate Croy detect the tragic fate they've made for themselves. Wilson recalled the amusing sonnet Beerbohm and Gosse, doing alternate lines, had written about James, and the Englishman recited it, again savoring the words. Wilson mentioned the theory that the ghosts in *The Turn of the Screw* were hallucinations of the governess, and when Beerbohm denounced this as the figment of "some morbid pedant, prig, and fool," he identified himself as that person and politely explained why he thought so. They discussed Shaw. Enough of a radical to have praised the dramatist, on his Tory side Beerbohm disapproved both of Shaw's politics and of his self-promotion, Wilson urging that such egotism was "a disability like any disability." Beerbohm also seemed to resent the stature of Virginia Woolf, whose novels such a consummate stylist should have admired, and Wilson defended her late novel *Between the Acts*.

At eighty-two the caricaturist was more imposing than his drawings of himself allowed one to expect, taller, with a large head and Germanic features. His hands were "quite astonishing—they seemed quite unlike any others I had ever seen. Instead of being slender with tapering fingers, the fingers were long and of uniform thickness, almost like the legs of a spider-crab." Resembling "very large engraver's tools," they were craftsman's instruments. Wilson considered Beerbohm's drawings imaginatively superior to his stories, essays, and parodies. Beerbohm himself deferred to the wonderful evocation of bodies and personalities in Sem's album *Tout Paris*, for Sem, he said, could draw people on the spot while he himself had to see a lot of his subjects and have a sense of understanding their minds. In his article Wilson notes that Sem lacked Beerbohm's historical sense and intellectual insight, and that James Gillray, whose imagination was as powerful as his, was crude by comparison. As a committed journal writer Wilson could appreciate what Beerbohm called his credo for drawing, to be "an impassioned eye, that sets down what he sees, or thinks he sees." Beerbohm said he had stopped caricaturing when (as Wilson phrased this to Elena) "he came to the time of life at which he realized what he was producing were simply painstaking likenesses that showed pity for their subjects instead of making them amusing." Wilson reversed this process. In his memoirs of dead friends and his father he is deeply respectful, while in the journals of the 1950s and '60s his sketches may be affectionate but are often also satirical.

During the thirties he had promoted *Man's Fate*, though its blend of Byronic Romanticism with Marxism hadn't deeply appealed to him. *The Imaginary Museum*, the first volume of the *The Psychology of Art*, for Wilson was Malraux's best book, conveying the premise that everything that had ever been done anywhere in the arts was now available to view, from "Alaskan totem poles glaring above the Pacific" through the treasures of Europe, Egypt and the East—"all the show paintings of all the palaces and all the places of worship, all the professional gallery pictures" and "the engravings and drawings and the preliminary sketches for paintings . . . , all the movie stills and other photographs." Malraux admitted that the great religious art was partly drained of meaning for modernity; he saw—though perhaps minimized—cultural decay in contemporary works. The reproductions were subordinated to a text that, especially in the second volume, *The Artistic Act,* Wilson thought hard going. Elliptical, sometimes turgid or overwritten, it nevertheless contained illuminating juxtapositions and occasional brilliant aperçus. At this time art historians, coming out of German academic or English connoisseurship traditions, tended to downplay Malraux's endeavor as that of a belle-lettristic outsider, but the condensed version of *The Psychology of Art* called *The Voices of Silence* would be popular in the United States. The author of *To the Finland Station* saw Malraux taking modern art as "a deliberate declaration" of the will to re-create the world that for the two men once had a radical political form. Like Wilson, Malraux hoped that humanity would be able to find in its own nature "what would formerly have been called its divine powers."

French literature was Wilson's second culture, and his talks with Malraux stretched over three decades, from their discussion of Trotsky in 1935 to a State Department lunch during the Kennedy administration. One of the two conversations related in *The Fifties* is lengthy. Now living far from central Paris with a younger wife (his brother's widow) and two sons, Malraux restlessly moved about the cold house making points and punctuating them with *"bon!"* and *"bien!"*—a "self-kindling, self-consuming force, whirling about without giving heat, but yet generating energy, in something almost like a vacuum: the room, the house, the quarter (extramural Paris, France, Europe)." Surrounded by remarkable objets d'art, he had the French pride of cultural mission, the drive to retain supremacy. He boasted of the Louvre and belittled the Metropolitan, claiming the

National Gallery in Washington had better paintings. When he praised U.S. foreign policy for lacking imperial intent, Wilson was reminded how hard it was for the French to understand the politics of a people whose parties didn't set forth logical positions and argue them. Yet in 1935 Malraux had grasped America's unique role: speaking of the provinciality of the Parisian press, he had said to Wilson, *"C'est parce que la France est en Europe, les États-Unis sont dans le monde."*

In 1954 Wilson hadn't discovered that the novelist embellished his biography, yet he thought it hard for Malraux to look one in the eye. He winked spasmodically and had a nervous tic halfway between "a clicking in the throat" and "a snort from the nose" that, when he became excited, was like a car exhaust. On some subjects he was dogmatic. When Wilson proposed that Genet was "the Sartre character which Sartre himself had not had the genius to invent," Malraux replied, *"Sartre n'a jamais inventé rien!"* *—though Genet "did not understand himself," he defined himself much better than did Sartre. Malraux's belief that Michelet's scandalous diaries should be censored surprised the American, for more than one reason: in the United States schoolchildren didn't get much of their history from a canonical text like the *History of France*, and Wilson wasn't to become his country's minister of culture. (About this time Faulkner, commenting on this division in American society, doubted that Secretary of Defense Charles E. Wilson "knows who Edmund Wilson is—ever heard of him.")

A few months later Malraux and Wilson touched on the implications of the Dead Sea Scrolls, T. E. Lawrence's psychology, the legends of Genet's thievery, gossip about publishers, and a film by Sacha Guitry about the court of Louis XV that systematically and vulgarly exploited all the personages of eighteenth-century France. Wilson had taken six-year-old Helen to see it, but after his wife's report Malraux refused to go. When Wilson spoke of Malraux's monograph on Goya, titled *Saturne*, the Frenchman said he'd been much struck by the "nightmarish and savage" murals Goya had painted in his house in Madrid. Wilson related Malraux's novels to these unflinching representations of the Inquisition's executions and the massacres during the Spanish war with the French. It turned out that Malraux took Stalin's Marxism more seriously than Wilson did, though thinking it too abstract. Offering a personal impression of the dictator— one not in his *Anti-Memoirs*—Malraux recalled that, in Stalin's presence,

*Sartre never invented anything.

Gorky reported Tolstoy's envy of a lizard, happy on its rock in the sun while human beings were making themselves miserable. The story had left Stalin cold.

Wilson's admiration for this brilliant generalist who worked on similar premises was scarcely uncritical. In a postscript on *The Voices of Silence*, written during the sixties, he restates his reservations about Malraux's allusive, "much obstructed" prose and raises questions implicit in the development of postmodern painting. How could the practitioners of abstract art, for Wilson "a void of floating color and line that has hardly been organized," clarify what Malraux called the human condition? How could "pop art" and "op art" resist the mass culture with which they represented a compromise? That Malraux, as minister of culture, was able to commission Chagall to do a new ceiling for the Paris Opéra couldn't restore to the pictorial arts a vitality bound up with all their lost functions in society. "If Manet cannot possibly be considered so great a painter as Titian," Wilson believed, "it is partly because, in his lifetime, there was so much less demand for his work."

Going to museums and concerts, though he did not write them up, as during the twenties, Wilson accumulated the opinions about the arts that are voiced in his late self-interview "Every Man His Own Eckermann." Music was as important to him as the visual arts, and a reception for Stravinsky recounted in *The Sixties* sets up a vignette of the composer he had considered a master since 1925. He catalogues the people at this get-together of the literary and artistic worlds, from Victoria Ocampo ("that splendid old girl"), who published Borges and others in the Argentine magazine *El Sur*, to the composer Virgil Thomson, who "sulked on the couch because he did not like opera singers and there was an important woman opera singer there." He exchanges words with the guests he knows. Assuming that Elena and he have been invited because she'd known Stravinsky's wife and the composer had been her mother's guest at Johannisberg, Wilson is pleasantly surprised to be welcomed with, "I read your lines," Stravinsky making lines in the air and repeating this in Russian ("'*vashi stroky*'"). Awkwardly he responds that Stravinsky's music "had been to me 'an inspiration'" ("*C'est réciproque*," the composer says). Wilson discovers "Str." to be "jolly, amusing, even bubbling—quite frank and accessible, I thought, as we find with delight that such masters may be." Stravinsky's wife says he must eat after conducting, even if it is "chicken à la king on an ashtray," and from time to time, as the two men talk, someone brings him cheese and brownies. At first he simply leans forward for the cheese and takes it on his tongue.

Stravinsky is "a little wisp of a man"—"in France they used to call him 'the insect'"—and to Elena resembles "a musical note: his legs and feet dwindle to tininess" (Wilson draws such a note at the top of his manuscript page), "but his opinions in conversation, like his music, are fearless and firm." He judges *Doctor Zhivago*—which Wilson thought a great work—"simply a collection of fragments." He has reservations about Schönberg. When Wilson says "that Schönberg came out of Wagner," he replies, "Mahler—and Wagner, yes." It is Anton Webern whom he really admires. Spender observed that this scene in the journal "is very dense and lively, what Henry James would have called 'bristling.'" When they part at the composer's car, Wilson on his way to an all-Stravinsky evening of ballet, which he says will be half over, the aged musician—like a wise clown in Shakespeare—instructs him, "'*Apploud!*' first making the motion of clapping, then throwing out his hands."

Wilson's friendship with T. S. Eliot had never ripened. During the 1950s, Eliot embodied the ideal of the New Criticism, while Wilson wrote for the general reader about personalities, cultures, and history. Reviewing the takeoff called *The Sweeniad* by a Cambridge professor who purported to be the shopgirl Myra Buttle (My Rebuttal), Wilson listed the poet's personae—"the genteel Bostonian, the Anglican clergyman, Dr. Johnson" and so on. He was unimpressed by Eliot the English gentleman. After the poet's famous remark on the danger presented by too many "free-thinking Jews," it was amusing to find Disraeli included in the conservative pantheon—"one free-thinking Jew" was evidently all right working "for the interests of the Tories." Yet no one who'd ever known Eliot or followed his career as a publisher and editor "could regard him as genuinely intolerant," Wilson insists. He cared "much more about literature than about anything else," and his verses lodged "in one's head without one's ever having learned them," remaining there for life.

Wilson's enthusiasm for the Englishman who became American equaled his reservations about the American turned Englishman. He couples W. H. Auden with Eliot in "The Mass in the Parking Lot," the travesty of literary escapism that opens with "Andre Gide in a big burnoose":

> More correctly garbed, we encountered later
> T. S. Eliot, the Great Dictator.

Having just awakened from troubled sleep,
He told us Charles Williams was terribly deep.
And Wystan Auden, with rigorous views,
But his necktie hanging around his shoes,
Expounded his taste for detective stories,
Which he reads to illumine the current mores.

Both poets are "Anglo-Caths, / Amateur clergymen, lean as laths, / Morally snobbish but madly self-humbling." Yet the stuffed shirt's disreputable sidekick is the more attractive. The most important literary friendship of Wilson's later years except with Nabokov, and one uncomplicated by rivalry, was with Auden, whose portrait he draws during a series of encounters in *The Fifties* and *The Sixties*.

He had first promoted Auden in a letter to Bogan in 1933, and a review of 1937 singles him out from the other "Oxford boys" for his original poetic language, absorbing "the emphatic alliteration of Anglo-Saxon . . . , the variety and ease of the Elizabethans . . . , the irony and bizarre imagination of the generation just before his own." The version of communism Auden shared with Spender, Isherwood, and MacNeice had for Wilson something of the fantasy of schoolboys defining themselves against their parents and teachers, but Auden's flight from a socially stratified England enlisted his sympathies. On the way back from China he had found that America wasn't class ridden, and he took satisfaction in being a citizen, was known to say, "I'm really a New Yorker." He envisioned the United States just as Wilson wanted to see it, saying, when they met in 1945, that it was "the only place where it is possible at present to be truly international." Wilson doesn't try to understand the relationship between Auden's dazzling early work and his later sobriety, one all too easily summed up by the English as a loss of poetic intensity. But he gives us the literary personality behind his subsequent writing.

"He is really extremely tough—cares nothing about property or money, popularity or social prestige—does everything on his own and alone," Wilson wrote to Mamaine of this new friend. The squalor in which Auden first lived in the United States was legendary—his shack at Fire Island shocked Spender, and in *The Fifties* Wilson notes that Stravinsky called him "the dirtiest man I have ever liked," perhaps because one evening the composer's wife, finding "a basin of dirty fluid on the floor" of his filthy bathroom in the East Village, threw out the chocolate pudding Auden's

partner Chester Kallman had intended for dessert. Auden was contemptuous of the bourgeoisie: "the only excuse for rich people" was to do
things like the reception for Stravinsky right, and they didn't do it right—
the ham was "too salt." For a while he had an unheated loft on Seventh
Avenue with a long curtainless window over the street and a guest room,
of which he was proud, likened by Wilson to "a doghouse built completely
inside the loft." Offering a bottle of hock, which he lifted from a case
amid the littered books and papers on the floor, he explained that he
hated living this way but he had to in order to be free for the work he
wanted to do. Though Wilson knew the value, for an artist, of asserting
one's independence, putting oneself to the test of living without the
amenities, he came to see such "sordid and grotesque lodgings" as part of
a Puritan effort to acquire merit.

Auden's character was full of paradox. He had a schoolmaster's impulse to discipline people of whom he disapproved. He was "always full
of moral indignation against Cyril Connolly," "would like to flog him, only
way to get him to work. Later, he was in favor of executing him, would like
to perform the execution himself." He was savage about Genet, who combined homosexuality with glorification of the thief and the murderer—
"when I mentioned Genet, he declared that he would like to see him
guillotined." Yet Auden saw homosexuals everywhere, making the best defense a strong offense. Wilson notes that he encouraged a rumor that
General Eisenhower was homosexual, and after listening to a broadcast
by Stalin, said to Nicholas Nabokov, "He's just an old queer!" He was
frank about his own sexual habits, confiding that he was too prudish to be
"good at flagellation: 'When they say, "Stop, stop!" I always stop, when what
they really want is to have you go on. And I don't like to say abusive things
unless I'm angry.'" A sense of humor was, Auden noted, inhibiting. It was
"significant that in one of Sade's books, when some *partouze* is being
arranged, that the parties are forbidden to laugh. To laugh would make
the whole thing impossible."

Wilson sometimes caricatures the poet as Beerbohm might have in a
drawing. "His hair now looks like a yellow wig, and he has become rather
portly and old-man-of-the-world, like somebody in an 18th-century coffeehouse." At another point his face is "crisscrossed with creases; it looks
squarer than when I saw him last and like some kind of technical map."
The Sixties contains a unique record of the eccentricities of Auden's readings, as at Harvard's Sanders Theater:

He was evidently a little tight but articulated perfectly distinctly and now puts on a much better performance than he used to. But he had brought the whole galleys of his forthcoming book (*Homage to Clio*) and did not seem to have picked out beforehand the poems that he wanted to read. The proofs would slip out of his grasp and fall on the floor as he fumbled with them, and then he would have to plunge down after them. It was a little like one of those comic paperhanger acts. At one point, when there seemed to be an inter-mission, we came down from the top tier in order to get better seats and found that in the meantime he had started again and was sitting at the table with his hat on. This also gave a comic effect, and I thought he had put it on in order to indicate a change of mood—something informal, a little droll. But he explained to us, when he came here to lunch [the] next day, that the poem had two alternating elements, one of which he printed in italics, and that for the passages that were italicized he put his hat on and took it off for the non-italicized passages. We had missed this explanation as we came downstairs.

Auden threw away correspondence, but a characteristically severe yet supportive 1947 letter from the critic at *The New Yorker* survives in car-bon to mark the discourse of these two. Wilson enumerates his recent sins, from contributing a poor title to a book of Betjeman's and offering "blasphemous strictures on Yeats" to "your mangling of the *Duchess of Malfi*, eliminating the last act so as to spoil the whole curve of the drama," and "your regurgitation, in *The Age of Anxiety*, in the girl's speech over the sleeping boy, of the last pages of *Finnegans Wake*." But *The Age of Anxiety* was in other respects "wonderful—as an exploit in language and imagery, it really rivals *Finnegans Wake*," he writes, adding, "Don't let anyone tell you your recent work isn't your best." Auden once went so far as to say he wrote for Wilson alone. In *The Sixties* he tells his friend of having reacted against Yeats and Rilke after being overly influenced by them, and learn-ing something from the later William Carlos Williams. "I said I couldn't see any influence. 'It's there.' 'What do you mean?' 'Technically.' 'How?' 'Length of lines.' I still don't know what he meant." They discuss the writ-ing of reversed rhymes, and Wilson notes that Auden has been reading Pope with enthusiasm—"didn't like the excremental book of the *Dunciad* but admired the last book. Resorted much to Pope and Horace these days." When Wilson says he doesn't much like the *Midsummer Night's Dream* of the poet's dear friend Benjamin Britten, Auden calls it "quite impossible to write music for the *Dream*. Shakespeare had already written it."

Their friendship was based on more than shared standards and abilities. For both, the love of literature was collegial. When Wilson asked poets to carve their lines into the windows of the old stone house or on panes of glass he traveled with, using a diamond-point pencil Elena had given him for Christmas, Auden's "Make This Night Loveable" austerely presided in the guest room, asking the moon to "Bless me, One especial / And friends everywhere":

> With a cloudless brightness
> Surround our absences;
> Innocent be our sleeps,
> Watched by great still spaces,
> White hills, glittering deeps.
>
> Parted by circumstance,
> Grant each your indulgence
> That we may meet in dreams
> For talk, for dalliance,
> By warm hearths, by cool streams.

Until the dark last stanza, at any rate, Auden's band of spirits—an echo of "the just" who "exchange their messages" and "show an affirming flame" in "September 1, 1939"—beautifully illustrates Wilson's view of the bonds of thought and creative instinct and fellowship.

Auden's British snobberies were never long in abeyance. "A peer and a prince," he announced to the American, were among those who elected him professor of poetry at Oxford, a boast that, with his remark to Elena that Kingsley Amis was *"dritten Klasse,"* suggested why he'd left England: if he'd stayed he wouldn't (as he agreed) have been able "to stand up to the temptation to become a member of the governing class, a public figure, clever and respected." Though Auden talked of the need to maintain the virtues of middle-class professionals, a loyalty Wilson shared, as a doctor's son he had sometimes felt inferior, and he'd regretted not going to Eton. When Masefield arranged for him to receive a medal from the king, he was "terrified and stammered" in the king's presence. As professor of poetry at Oxford, he planned to "give the 'Bronx cheer' on hearing something particularly silly." He successfully made waves there, and returned with his American patriotism renewed. Like Dickens and Kipling, however, he could be uncomfortable in the United States, telling Wilson he didn't enjoy seeing uncouth people in the restaurants where he ate.

Wilson, echoing his last sentence in "The Author at Sixty," suggests that Auden's move to New York gave him one of the assets Americans "can hope to have: a mind that feels itself at the center of things." From this city he could comprehend "the whole English-speaking industrial-ugly democratic-levelling-oppressive, urban and suburban world," the critic writes in *The Fifties*. His subject was "the problem of how to live in it, to get out of it what it can give, to avoid being paralyzed or bought by it," Wilson adds in "W. H. Auden in America." He had integrated American speech, customs, and allusions with a mixture of "Oxford gossip" and "country talk of leats and eagres," as well as "his technical vocabulary of botany, psychology, and metallurgy" in a brilliant international English that achieved a metrical variety unmatched since Tennyson, Browning, and Swinburne. Wilson stresses the first American poems. He finds the "strange *depayses* sonnets" of *The Quest* "unique and enchanting— their fairy-like phantoms that alternate with commonplace, down-to-earth phrases, their images that dilate or wobble, the mysterious concluding poem with its blur of beginnings and endings." *New Year Letter* invoked the task of "building the Just City" within conditions dictated by the machine age. It conveyed "the poet's exhilaration in moving about the world and the conviction of solidarity with companions in anxiety everywhere":

> O every day in sleep and labour
> Our life and death are with our neighbor,
> And love illuminates again
> The city and the lion's den,
> The world's great rage, the travel of young men.

The author of such passages absorbed modernity as "a great English poet who is also—in the not *mondain* sense—one of the great English men of the world."

Wilson was touched and heartened by Auden's understanding of the struggle of the "determined resistant minority" of serious American artists and writers, not a group with an ideology or cultural center but individuals "functioning in the crevices of cities, in the faculties of provincial colleges or scattered all over the country in the solitude of ranches and farms." He quotes a quatrain that he missed in the collected short poems, later learning it "had been sacrificed to a numerological mania: he didn't want to have more than 300":

> Some think they're strong, some think they're smart,
> Like butterflies they're pulled apart,
> America can break your heart.
> *You don't know all, sir, you don't know all.*

Auden reminded Wilson of his own commitment. When the poet returned from Oxford, Wilson greeted him with "a tirade about how horrible America was now, said that I had been working in it all my life and was now extremely fatigued. He said that of course it was 'hell,' that things were 'always wrong,' but that 'the dream' was always there," Wilson countering "that the 'American dream' was a sickening propaganda phrase." Auden concluded, "You must remember we depend on you," then specified, "I do. You have to go on even if you die with everything just as bad." For once, Wilson had the good fortune to receive the kind of loyal advice that he gave others in full measure. When he informed the author of "You don't know all" that he'd spent several weeks in a sanitarium after a breakdown, Auden said "That was very naughty: an Auden doesn't do that, a Wilson doesn't do that."

26

Nabokov and Russian Literature

In 1952 Wilson wrote that he was trying "to concentrate synoptically, as they say of the Gospels, to bring into one system the literatures of several cultures which have not always been in close communication, which in some cases have been hardly aware of one another." Russian literature had been somewhat isolated from the others, and he hadn't seen the Soviet Union since 1935, but warm relationships with Russian émigrés refreshed his enthusiasm. "Wonderful people, wonderful literature," he said. Elena seemed to him Russian in her "sensitivity, humor, human sympathy." Roman Grynberg brought the Russian intensity to books, while the Chavchavadzes breathed Russian history. His meetings with Nabokov and their continuing exchange of long letters contributed to his portraiture of Gogol, Chekhov, and Turgenev, the only group of essays of Wilson's later years that (with his review of *Doctor Zhivago*) rank alongside *The Triple Thinkers* and *The Wound and the Bow*. Nabokov must have been in Wilson's mind when, apropos of Turgenev, he wrote that "those Russians who are properly civilized are immeasurably more versatile and brilliant and learned than the intelligentsia of any other nation." When, after twenty-five years of friendship, their egos led them into a bitter public quarrel, each recognized their likeness to the feuding landowners in Gogol's story familiarly called *The Quarrel of the Two Ivans*, one of whom has called the other a goose. They would replicate the tragedy in Pushkin's *Eugene Onegin*, when neither Onegin nor Lensky can find it in himself to stop the duel.

Nabokov was at first a good deal more impressed with Wilson's русский язык* than were the acquaintances with whom he practiced it. Nina

*Russian (language)

Chavchavadze pronounced him "hopeless in his pronunciation and speech," though he "could read it all as well as I can." When her son David visited the Wilsons' house with a pretty girl, he remembered Edmund remarking, "'your female acquaintance is very attractive,' in the language of an 1850 novel." These limitations did not, of course, appear when he discussed Russian in English. When Wilson ventured that "these Russian verbs which mask and unmask themselves with prefixes" and "transform themselves, also (the verbs), through various internal changes, behaved differently from non-Slavic verbs and had something uncanny about them," Nabokov replied that he had always been delighted by the "magic world of Russian verbs." Having learned English in childhood, he could mediate between the Russian world he knew so well and Wilson, who liked to fire questions.

Wilson had an ear for Pushkin's verse, and Nabokov thought well enough of his translation of *The Bronze Horseman* to joke of pretending to students it was his own. They collaborated in translating one or two Pushkin poems, the only time Nabokov collaborated with anyone except his son Dmitri. The novelist went so far as to ask Wilson to be his translator, the critic demurring that "my Russian is so uncertain that going over my work would probably be nearly as much trouble for you as translating the book yourself." From the first they wrangled about versification, Nabokov expounding his theory of the difference between English and Russian verse in a ten-page treatise with diagrams, Wilson countering with passages from *The Winter's Tale* and *The Waste Land*. But Nabokov liked "enormously" the "Notes on Pushkin" in which Wilson, pursuing the linguistic impressionism of his essay on *Eugene Onegin*, sets the poet within the international Romantic movement and in relation to Mozart, whose mastery of form was similar. He catches the quality of Pushkin's melodic quatrains and soliloquies, use of balladry and jingling. Developing a hint from Nabokov, he conveys the linguistic drama of the verse tale *Count Nulin*, showing how the noun for "slap," the "swinging slap" of a Russian lady defending herself against the advances of an admirer, echoes through a dozen lines and a series of words, "thus referring by their meaning to Nulin's injured feelings and by their sound to his tingling cheek."

Pushkin "came through to the world via the Russian novel," Wilson wrote as he set out to explore major works of the prose masters in Russian, hoping the fresh insight of a foreigner would compensate for any amateurishness. "Seeing Chekhov Plain" usefully dissipates the dramatist's misty, soulful image in the English-speaking countries by focusing on his origins as a humorist, his analysis of social types and classes. "Gogol: The Demon in the Overgrown Garden" is an ambitious effort in comparative criticism. Fascinated by this writer's enormous vocabulary, including Ukrainian words not found in dictionaries, and by "the rhapsodies, the inventories, the interpolated anecdotes, and the huge Homeric similes that are whole short stories in themselves," he takes Gogol's style as a variety of the "viscous prose" common to Scott, Balzac, Charles Lamb, and early-nineteenth-century Americans. Compared to Gogol, however, Poe seemed "cerebral" and "such fancies of Hawthorne's as the Minister's Black Veil and the Black Sabbath of Young Goodman Brown mere phantoms of woven words." Wilson told himself that this was the attraction of the exotic—recalling "a remark that Jean Cocteau once made to me: 'Maupassant is a great writer in Russian'"—but the novelist was an addictive enthusiasm.

The prophetic tradition to which Gogol belonged was foreign to the American. Though Wilson saw the undercurrent "of sadness, of disgust, of chagrin" within the humor of *Dead Souls*, he couldn't understand why on his deathbed Gogol destroyed the long-awaited second part of his book. It was the act of a moralist desolate at having failed to renew the souls of his countrymen. On the other hand, Wilson's Freudian reading of the *Mirgorod* stories has been fruitful for scholars, who have pursued the varied rejections of love in these tales, from childhood dependency in "Old-World Landowners" to sexual love that fails in *Taras Bulba* and brings death in "Viy," the horrific vampire tale invoked in *Hecate County*. He suggests that for Gogol, who was threatened by women and apparently a virgin at his death, the Devil took female form.

Ivan Sergeyevich Turgenev, who lived in France and Germany and was thought a traitorous dilettante both by Dostoevsky and by left-wing ideologues, is the subject of Wilson's masterful literary portrait, "Turgenev and the Life-Giving Drop." He demonstrates that the darkness of this urbane, affluent writer's books, which surprised such friends as James and Mérimée, derived from personal experience and involved a level-headed appraisal of his nation's institutions and habits of mind. The theme of an "evil force" in Turgenev's fiction even anticipated Stalin, for he showed that the slavery of the people had bred a habit of lying and of abasement to an iron man expected to fix everything, someone who, in the end, would break the innocent on principle. Through Turgenev's personal ups and downs, "through his professions of belief in reforms from above and his secret contributions to radical papers; through his sometimes hysterical encounters with Tolstoy and Dostoevsky, his glowing amours and his slumps of gloom," Wilson writes, affirming his own intellectual ideal, "he sticks to his objective judgment, his line of realistic criticism, his resolve to stand free of movements, to rise above personalities, to recognize all points of view that have any sincerity or dignity, to show Russia how to know herself."

As Wilson does with Dickens and Kipling, he discovers a wound of youth, the novelist's tyrannical mother's oppression of her family and household. Varvara Petrovna Turgeneva, who played the tsar to five thousand serfs in the twenty villages she owned, is introduced with the information that her mother, Ivan Sergeyevich's grandmother, had knocked a serf boy unconscious and, irritated by the sight this presented, suffocated him with a pillow. Varvara Petrovna's viciousness to her servants, which she extended to her sons, had the same effect as the blacking factory on Dickens, permanently impressing upon the future writer the cruel side of the society he dramatized. Wilson's relations with his own parents alerted him to two resonant passages from the records. In a conversation overheard by a member of the household, Ivan begged his mother to accept his love and stop torturing his brother and him with the promise of gifts of property she didn't intend to fulfill. Also on record was a story that the novelist liked to tell to children, of a boy who must acquire the "life-giving" drop of water that yearly fell from the roof of a serpent-filled cave, in order to cure his father and mother of disease. Overcoming his fear of the hideous hissing reptiles, he caught the drop between his lips and got away.

Turgenev didn't, Wilson noted, "much care to revisit the cave." He could never spend a very long time in Russia, and Spasskoye, his estate, weighed on his spirit long after his mother's death and the publication of his *Sportsman's Sketches*, which contributed to the abolition of serfdom. Nor was he very happy personally, tethered to a married woman for whom he had a life-long passion, the opera singer Pauline Viardot. Yet Turgenev created major work. Wilson places the novelist among his peers: if not "one of the great inventors," he is steadily engaging and won't "betray our belief with extravagances" or "combine poetic vision with rubbish." In his tighter and more deliberate craft "he is perhaps the most satisfactory of the company to which he belongs, for he never oppresses, as Flaubert does, by his monotony and his flattening of human feeling, or fatigues, as Henry James sometimes does when his wheels of abstraction are grinding, or makes us nervous, as Conrad may do, through his effortfulness and occasional awkwardness in working in a language not native to him with materials that are sometimes alien." This literary essay contains no *explication de texte*, but in a ten-page appendix Wilson compares different translations of Turgenev's descriptions of nature and country life, the prose poetry for which he was famed.

While Wilson read and reread Turgenev's work between 1955 and 1957, Ivan Sergeyevich came to seem "a personal friend," and as we might expect, the survey of the fiction incorporates insights into the man's character. Wilson notes that this atheist "was a good deal more successful at practicing the Christian virtues" than either Dostoevsky or Tolstoy. Amusedly he charts Turgenev's attempted friendship with Tolstoy, whom he went to see at Yasnaya Polyana, which wasn't far from Spasskoye. Tolstoy held forth about his conversion, and Turgenev judged his host to be making progress in Christian humility when he was finally allowed to get a word in edgewise. Turgenev was nervous when "he beat the new saint at chess," while Tolstoy disapproved of him for dancing with a twelve-year-old girl at a birthday party. In his diary Tolstoy wrote, "Turgenev—the cancan. Sad."

It is interesting that in his letters to Wilson, Nabokov, who had praised *The Triple Thinkers* and *The Wound and the Bow* as well as Wilson's work on Pushkin, never acknowledges this essay. "Turgenev and the Life-Giving Drop" is much more confident than Wilson's piece on Gogol, which makes use of his friend's study of the novelist. Nabokov had a proprietary attitude toward Russian fiction, and he ranked Turgenev behind the other Russian greats.* He didn't admire the novelist's prose as much as Wilson did, and Wilson's stress on Turgenev's anticipation of Stalinism in the old Russia of serfdom may not have pleased Nabokov either, passing over the late-nineteenth-century industrial and social progress to which his father, a reformer and constitutionalist, contributed.

Meanwhile the two exchanged opinions about everything else in the voluminous correspondence that Nabokov likened to keeping up a diary. Their shared enthusiasm for "Pushkin, Flaubert, Proust, Joyce, etc.," sets off passionate disagreements about other writers, Freudian psychology, politics. These are men who know the world yet are not of it, uncompromising in their standards and ambitions though they market their work to

---

*Tolstoy topped his list. He praised the moralist and realist but detoured around *War and Peace*, and his brilliant study of *Anna Karenina* is relentlessly technical. He affected to think Dostoevsky "third-rate," converting *Notes from Underground* to *Memoirs from a Mousehole*.

magazines and publishers for fifty dollars here and five hundred there. Simon Karlinsky, who brought out the letters after their deaths with an expanded volume in 2001, notes their similar backgrounds. Both were sons of lawyers, Nabokov's father briefly minister of justice in Kerensky's transitional Russian government, Wilson's considered for an appointment to the Supreme Court. Not surprisingly, twentieth-century events affected the child of the Russian aristocracy and of the American gentry differently: Nabokov once said to Wilson that the October Revolution had made his life "a fool's," politically and morally irrelevant, while the end of the Age of Reform in America during World War I, mirrored in Wilson Sr.'s retreat from politics, hadn't kept the son from challenging capitalism after the Crash. Neither writer understood the other's view of the Russian Revolution. Coming to the United States in 1940, Nabokov failed to see how the collapse of American society during the Depression enhanced the appeal of the Soviet model. Though Wilson wrote to Gauss that Nabokov's family were "landowning liberals," he didn't always distinguish his friend's hatred of the Revolution from the way it was hated by reactionary White Russians (he hadn't read Nabokov's *The Gift*, which had not been translated). The novelist, detesting the Soviet politicization of art, a by-product of the moralizing Russian tradition, saw literature and politics as enemies, while for the critic, the idealism of which literature was an essential expression could also take political form.

In his letters Wilson promotes English and American books, Nabokov often initially questioning his enthusiasms. When Nabokov pronounces *What Maisie Knew* "terrible," Wilson urges him "before giving up Henry James, try the long novel called *The Princess Casamassima* and the first volume of his autobiography, *A Small Boy and Others*." He sends *Light in August* to his friend, declaring himself "spellbound" by the writing of Faulkner, "the most remarkable contemporary American novelist," an opinion not then widely held. Nabokov shrugs off "these puffs of stale romanticism," "the plot and those extravagant 'deep' conversations," and Wilson replies, "Your failure to see his genius is a mystery to me—except that you do not, in general, like tragedy. Have you tried *The Sound and the Fury*?" Asked to advise about English novels for a fiction course, he recommends "the later Dickens of *Bleak House* and *Little Dorrit*" and all of Jane Austen—"even her fragments are remarkable." Nabokov disdained women writers of fiction, their contribution in old Russia having been slight, and breezily rejected "Jane," only to have Wilson set him straight.

"Jane Austen approaches her material in a very objective way," Wilson declared. "Each of her books is a study of a different type of woman, whom Jane Austen can see all around. She wants, not to express her longings, but to make something perfect that will stand." Calling Austen "one of the half-dozen greatest English writers (the others being Shakespeare, Milton, Swift, Keats and Dickens)" he persuaded Nabokov to read *Mansfield Park*, which the Russian later included in his courses. Some of these exchanges are included in *Dear Bunny, Dear Volodya*, the witty dramatic dialogue that Terry Quinn excerpted from Simon Karlinsky's edition of the correspondence, which features their quarrel over translating Pushkin. This has been widely performed in Europe and the United States, Dmitri Nabokov sometimes reading his father's lines and Wilson played by, among others, William F. Buckley, George Plimpton, Terry Quinn, and the present writer.

Few readers, however, know what Wilson contributed to *Lolita* or how his distaste for the novel set the stage for their bitter dispute. *Hecate County*'s success, with the limitations of its account of sex, as Nabokov judged this, had stimulated his ambition. He states that his interest in writing *Lolita* was rekindled "around 1949" without mentioning Wilson's role in providing him a model for his protagonist. In a 1948 letter Wilson mentioned a confession by a Russian, attached as an appendix to Havelock Ellis's *Studies in the Psychology of Sex*. Writing in French, the man—actually Ukrainian—describes his encounters with nymphets and child prostitutes who turn out to be sexually more experienced than he, and despairs of his ability to control his appetite for them. Wilson's next letter enclosed the 106-page case study, which Nabokov immediately read and "enjoyed hugely." In *Speak, Memory* it is described as "especially lascivious."

He advertised *Lolita* to Wilson as an "amazing book" and "my best thing in English," saying "though the theme and situation are decidedly sensuous, its art is pure and its fun riotous." In another letter he is "very anxious for you to read" what he calls "*by far* my best English work." The anxiety was real, for he feared *Lolita* might not be publishable, and the first publishers to whom he submitted it turned it down. Wilson, who had been brought up in a Victorian culture that held on much longer in the United States, and who now had a young daughter, was put off by the book. Hurriedly looking it over, in a letter in which conventional aesthetic objections second conventional moral ones he declared, "I like it less than anything else of yours I have read. Nasty subjects [as opposed to the anatomy of sex between consenting adults in *Hecate County*?] may make fine books, but I don't feel you have got away with this." The short story that it grew out of was "interesting" but the characters and situation couldn't stand "this very extended treatment," not merely because they were so ugly, but because "presented on this scale, they seem quite unreal"—"the various goings on and the climax at the end" were "too absurd to be horrible or tragic" yet "too unpleasant to be funny."

The giggling cynicism that is part of the novel's brilliance evidently kept Wilson from crediting it with a serious moral intent. Joyce had affirmed the human family, while Proust overcame the decadence of his life in a heroic retrieval of his will. Wilson found no such justification in *Lolita*, disregarding Quilty's role as someone even Humbert Humbert can despise, and unconvinced by Humbert's last-minute moralizing. He had always told writers just what he thought of their work, but before sending this letter to Nabokov he solicited the views of Elena and Mary McCarthy. Mary hedged, while Elena, in an accompanying note that scarcely compensated for her husband's response, called the girl's "attractiveness and seductiveness absolutely plausible" and the novel important. Wilson didn't try to stand in his friend's way. He encouraged Elena to recommend the book to Roger Straus, who, though "somewhat ambivalent," agreed to publish it until Nabokov, who was afraid to lose his job at Cornell, stipulated it appear under an assumed name, which would make the prospective legal defense impossible. Wilson then gave it—minus his recommendation—to Jason Epstein, who thought *Lolita* wonderful but whose boss, Douglas Black, having fought his battle over *Hecate County*, turned the novel down.

Wilson knew he might "not have done justice" to *Lolita*. He expected Nabokov to accept his wish that he "could like the book better" and move on, and in the correspondence Nabokov tries to do so. To Roman Grynberg the next year, however, Wilson reported, "He makes a great grievance of my not liking it." His pride as an artist was hurt, his respect for Wilson's judgment weakened. Having likened *Hecate County* to "a block of ice in a surgical laboratory," he suspected the American of jealousy. He could not have been pleased when Wilson jested that *Lolita* would make his fortune "as a study of amorous paternity and delinquent girlhood," proposing a sequel in which "you can get her married to Pnin in Alaska and bring them home to life tenure and the American way of life in some comfortable Middle Western university," thereby earning a role "lecturing on young people's problems from Bangor to San Diego."

The commercial success of which the censorship had deprived Wilson then became Nabokov's. *Lolita* was first published by the Olympia Press in Paris, but excerpts from and commentary on the novel appeared in the United States. The Catholic Church and the Hearst newspapers were no longer so strong a force as ten years before, and in 1957 the Supreme Court in an important opinion by Justice William Brennan extended the reach of freedom of speech. After Graham Greene recommended *Lolita* as one of the year's best, G. P. Putnam put out an edition that went unchallenged in the courts and sold 100,000 copies in three weeks. The novel and the Hollywood film made Nabokov rich and a celebrity, while Wilson continued to work up nineteenth-century statesmen, generals, and second-line writers, as well as to attack big-power imperialism.

To Grynberg after a 1956 visit to Nabokov in Ithaca, New York, Wilson wrote that though *Lolita* "rather put me off him," he was glad to have had "an opportunity to get to like him again." A year later he spent another weekend in Ithaca, and they resumed their old jousts. Wilson used Dahl's authoritative dictionary to argue the meanings of Russian words, while Nabokov asserted "that Mérimée knew no Russian and that Turgenev knew only enough English to enable him to read a paper," thereby, thought Wilson, protecting his own status as a writer uniquely proficient in Russian, French, and English. Nabokov claimed Pushkin's verse was less regular, more flexible than Shakespeare's, insisting that Lear's "Never, never, never, never, never" is a regular iambic line. The man whose Russian was known for its captivating sound had Wilson try to read *Eugene Onegin* aloud, which, in Nabokov's genially partisan recollection, he accomplished "with great gusto, garbling every second word and turning Pushkin's iambic line into a kind of spastic anapest with a lot of jaw-twisting haws and rather endearing little barks that utterly jumbled the rhythm and soon had us both in stitches." All this set the stage for their estrangement, and in another respect the visit was unfortunate. Wilson had come without Elena and felt a certain tension with Vera, who resented his bringing pornography (*L'histoire d'O*), which the men, she charged, pored over like schoolboys. She was closely solicitous of her husband—as Stacy Schiff's biography shows—but when their guest had an attack of gout Vera did not seem to enjoy having to carry his food to him, extra work for which he apologized in a thank-you note from home. Wilson's sense of her attitude, magnified in his mind after the falling out over *Onegin*, would color the account of this weekend in *Upstate*.

The next year the men differed about *Doctor Zhivago*, which had been smuggled out of the Soviet Union and published by the Italian leftist Feltrinelli. That "a contemporary and peer of Faulkner, Malraux, Auden" had survived the reign of Stalin to defy the totalitarian state as a witness to the Revolutionary period was for Wilson a heartening event in "man's literary and moral history." He passionately affirmed the book in *The New Yorker*, hoping its characters would be remembered like Pierre, Prince Andrey, and Natasha in *War and Peace*. Karlinsky lists this review with his best work in the field of Russian literature. Titling it "Doctor Life and His Guardian Angel"—an allusion to the mysterious reappearances of Evgraf, Yury's half-brother—Wilson embraced the prophetic Russian tradition he usually shied away from. The Russian Christianity of Pasternak (who, he noted, had been born a Jew) affirmed the freedom of the individual soul. That the novel's plot is a series of coincidences, that the corrupt bourgeois lawyer, the doctor who represents the intelligentsia, and the murderous, desperate young commissar are all in love with the same woman and constantly being brought together in events scattered across thousands of miles, he ascribed to the influence of the Russian fairy tale. Pasternak's romanticism, like his faith, had, Wilson thought, helped him maintain his integrity through the terrible experience of his generation in Russia.

In a second article Wilson overreached, trying to find in *Zhivago*'s religious references a linguistic density like that of *Finnegans Wake*. He relied on the help of two women friends, Russian-speaking Eugenia Lehovitch, director of the School of American Ballet, and the poet Barbara Deming, future peace marcher and feminist leader, who had written an article on *Hamlet* in the *Tulane Drama Review*. Neither was a textual critic, and Isaiah Berlin wasn't impressed by their discovery of puns in *Zhivago* ("little ham" equalling "Ham-let"). Elena thought this enterprise a game— once she pointedly asked David Chavchavadze to come over and "play *Doctor Zhivago*" with Edmund. Pasternak politely repudiated their reading in a letter to his German publisher and an interview in *The Nation*.

Meanwhile Nabokov was dismissing Pasternak's novel as "a piece of pulp fiction, regrettably written by a poet he admired." His introduction to the Russian version of *Lolita* patronizes *Doctor Zhivago* as a book about a "lyrical doctor with penny-awful mystical urges and philistine turns of speech, and an enchantress straight out of Charskaya" (a reference to Lydia Charskaya's books for and about teenaged girls in pre-Revolutionary Russia). Competition entered into the novelist's tone: David Chavchavadze remembered him as "a bad sport" when *Lolita* and *Doctor Zhivago* were neck and neck in sales, and Nabokov's son Dmitri does not deny the story that Vera visited bookstores in Ithaca in order to reposition *Lolita* to advantage on the shelves. That *Doctor Zhivago* won Pasternak the Nobel Prize (which he refused, lest he be driven into exile) must have been galling. Yet Nabokov's harsh judgment was more than professional jealousy. There were others—like Stravinsky—who found the book neither coherent nor convincing, and fifty years later *Zhivago* would be considered a poet's experiment, important for its conversations about subjects then taboo in the Soviet Union. To read such literature smuggled from abroad was punishable, if one were a student, by immediate expulsion from the university and might get anyone a year or two of imprisonment. Nabokov, however, couldn't respect a work that, although subversively, allowed a certain humanity to Soviet culture.

Lolita's success enabled Nabokov to give up his job at Cornell—"getting sick of teaching," he'd complain—and move to Switzerland, ending the regular meetings where he and Wilson exuberantly mauled each other. Their intellectual correspondence fell away, and Wilson wrote no more about Russian literature except for a few pieces in a minor key at the end of his life. The last meeting of the two took place in January 1964, when Edmund and Elena drove from Paris to take Helen back to her Swiss school. The Wilsons and Nabokovs had dinner with Nabokov's German publisher, and Wilson hosted a gala lunch the next day, but he was somewhat put off by the ambience of the Montreux Palace Hotel, where they found Volodya living, Elena said, "like a prince of the old regime." Later that year Nicholas Nabokov's ex-wife Natasha told Wilson with amusement that when she'd visited, Volodya "wore a pince-nez with a ribbon *à la* Chekhov." They discussed the "bad manners and arrogance" with which, preparing the way for his own word-for-word translation of *Onegin*, in *The New York Review of Books* Nabokov had savaged the verse rendering for which Walter Arndt had just won the Bollingen Prize. In Wilson's view, he treated Arndt, as "an oaf and an ignoramus, incompetent as a linguist and scholar." Natasha attributed this to personal insecurity, Wilson to a too long frustrated sense of entitlement.

Nabokov's was a theory of word-for-word translation, and when shown a sample of his *Onegin* in Harry Levin's presence, Wilson had complained, "Volodya, there's no continuity from sentence to sentence." When its four volumes reached him in 1965 he wrote to Barbara Epstein at the *Review* that they were "almost as open to objection as Arndt's," be-

ing "full of flat writing, outlandish words, and awkward phrases." His review charged that Pushkin's elegance and clarity were sacrificed to something like "the products of those computers which are supposed to
translate Russian into English," quoting such passages as

> You will agree, my reader,
> That very nicely did our pal
> act toward melancholy Tatiana . . .

and

> Farewell, pacific sites!
> Farewell, secluded refuge!
> Shall I see you?

Having striven to make the great moderns more accessible, Wilson
ridiculed the use of archaic, pretentious words like "rememorating," "pro-
ducement," "curvate," "habitude," "rummers," "familistic," "gloam," "dit,"
"shippon," and "scrab," all found in the O.E.D. but useless, he said, to the
student for whom this text was to be a handbook to accompany the Russian. For a word that could mean either voluptuous languor or simple enjoyment Nabokov proposed "mollitude" and "dulcitude." Wilson wondered
how he'd end the famous lyric in which Pushkin sought "a faraway haven
of work and pure"—would it be "pure mollitudes"? "dulcitudes"?

Nabokov regarded these judgments, delivered in a magisterial manner, as a betrayal, and resented Wilson no less because the professional
Slavicists said the same thing: that the translation was Nabokese rather
than English, the "theory" behind it "shallow and spurious." Alexander
Gerschenkron, a Harvard economist and luminary in the world of Russian
letters, accused his compatriot of "a desire to be original at all costs," of
"confused theorizing, spiteful pedantry, unrestrained egotism," qualities,
he said, almost designed to annoy readers. The same critical consensus that
finds *Doctor Zhivago* flawed declares Nabokov's *Onegin* a failure, most
useful for the ninety-two-page commentary that was perhaps his real object, on which he lavished a verbal artistry he denied to Pushkin's text. Wilson liked the commentary, though thinking it long; he praised the
accounts of Pushkin's poetic effects and of his relationships with the De-
cembrist conspirators as well as "the excellent little essays—on Derzhavin,

on Baratynsky, on Zhukovsky, on Karamzin." He was skeptical of the appendix expounding a prosody supposed to work for both English and Russian. Rejecting—correctly, Karlinsky says—the novelist's claim that Pushkin knew almost no English, he called the real drama of Nabokov's *Onegin* its author's effort "to correlate his English and his Russian sides," which "continue to elude one another."

To the Russian, convinced that he alone could represent the literal truth of the national poet in English, Wilson was talking through his hat. Nabokov had been hurt by Wilson's response to *Lolita*, then vindicated, and he regarded his translation of *Onegin* as perhaps his greatest work. Wilson further offended him by linking what Sartre had called his "sado-masochistic Dostoevskian tendencies" to the creation of an unreadable translation (that is, he was compelled to make readers suffer). Writing in the scrappy New York tradition, the aging critic was stimulated by public dispute and willing to carry their argument into letters to the editor. To psychologize Nabokov in a review and link him with writers he disliked was, however, to bait him as Nabokov had Arndt.

Unfortunately for Wilson, when decrying Nabokov's misuse of English he challenged the novelist's Russian, as he'd sometimes done with dictionaries and grammars during their meetings. The Chavchavadzes begged him not to risk this in print, but he had his way and pretended to know much more of the language than he did. Nabokov jumped on his errors in a mocking letter to the *New York Review*. In reply Wilson, admitting a mistake or two and arguing other points, was apologetic for the tone of his review, which "sounded more damaging than I had meant it to be." Nabokov, asserting it had only "damaged" Wilson, transferred the quarrel to *Encounter*, where he venomously denounced Wilson's "ludicrous display of pseudo-scholarship" and "old-fashioned, naive, and musty method of human-interest criticism." Again in Montreux a prince of the old regime, he patronized the American who wrote for, among others, the general reader.

Their exchange continued in the *New Statesman* and was later resumed in *The New York Times Book Review*. Friends were sad to see these two who had relished one another's company and agreed to disagree about so much tear each other apart for the entertainment of readers. People who talked with both parties, including Barbara Epstein and Harry Levin (whose wife, Elena, was Russian), regarded the controversy as a game that got out of hand, each misunderstanding "the point at which the other would turn from playful to aggressive." Though McCarthy characteristically wanted Wilson to keep the dispute going, Berlin persuaded him to stop. He wrote Wilson that Nabokov's translation was "a curiosity of literature," with "all the faults of a self-intoxicated virtuoso with a vast narcissistic talent and no capacity for conveying other works of art, which needs the negative capability of which he is totally devoid."

When sending Nabokov his verse "Christmas Greetings" in 1966, the critic wrote, "I'm sorry our controversy has come to an end. I have rarely enjoyed anything so much." The novelist drily replied, "I did not relish quite as much as you tell me you did your *New York Review* piece." Wilson was the thicker-skinned, Nabokov more easily offended, yet these were more than differences of individual character. Wilson proposed to judge the translation with the objectivity to which Western criticism aspires, while for the Russian, the issue was personal, the conflict of literary egos an affair of honor. During these exchanges, Nabokov posted to his antagonist the rhyme *"Cet animal est très méchant, Quand on l'attaque, il se défend."** Long before, in a letter praising the *Onegin* essay in the revised *Triple Thinkers*, he'd told the American it was naive to envision duels in Russia as gentlemanly affairs in which men started back-to-back, marched in opposite directions, then turned and fired, not necessarily to kill. The Russian duel was the fierce *"duel à volonté"* of the Napoleonic code. Leaving a no-man's-land of "say ten paces" between them, the combatants marched toward each other and fired at will.

*This animal is very wicked. When attacked, he defends himself.

27

The Skeptic's Pilgrimage:
Israel and the Dead Sea Scrolls

❧

From the mid-1940s until the mid-1960s, when his battle with Nabokov occurred, Wilson explored non-Christian faiths as well as minority cultures. Recognizing that Marxism had had for him a religious dimension made him more aware of the advantages of faith for the believer. A symbiosis of sorts was involved in his relationship with Jewish writers and thinkers who, during the fifties, articulated the movement of their immigrant culture into the mainstream Wilson represented to them. He had long admired the Jewish intellectual and moral tradition. He identified the strengths of both Freud and Proust with Jewish ancestry, had been alternately irritated, amused, and impressed by Jewish Communists of different sorts, had taken Marx as a Hebrew prophet. While rejecting Christianity he could identify with the People of the Book through his Protestant training, and when he studied Hebrew at Princeton in 1953 he felt he was reverting to the type of his Puritan ancestors, who had thought themselves another chosen people, wearing skullcaps and talking of the Covenant they'd made with God. In their sermons they shaped the American sense of mission that came down in the Gettysburg Address and his father's wish to serve the republic.

His grandmother Wilson had read to him the patriarchal chronicles in the King James version that molded the English writers he absorbed in school and college. But the Bible stories had a fresh taste when approached with "a smattering" of Hebrew. Retelling them in his essay on Genesis, he observes the relationship of the ancient Hebrews to their God. His people can negotiate with Him—as Abraham saves his relatives but no one else in Sodom—and Abraham's trust that He will "provide the lamb" in Isaac's place is rewarded. From the dictionary of Gesenius, a nineteenth-century German humanist, Wilson learns that the mysterious presence with whom Jacob wrestles all night is not, in Hebrew, the angel but simply a "man," possibly God Himself. Lamed and finally blessed by Him, he is called Israel, a word meaning "striver with God," which for Wilson makes this a variant of the Prometheus story. Jacob's people gave themselves a name that suggested "they had conquered, at a maiming cost," some share in God's power. Entering into this power as a writer, one day at Wellfleet Wilson boasted to Adelaide, "You know that I always become my characters. Well, guess who I am now. I'm God!"

To learn the alphabet, the twenty-two signs that Moses supposedly brought back from Egypt, involved coordinating the dots and dashes of vowels with the consonants. The latter were often used alone, and he liked writing them out as they marched from right to left across the page. In printed Hebrew they were blocklike—"austere in their vowelless terseness" and "compact in form as in meaning, stamped on the page like a woodcut, solid verse linked to solid verse with the ever recurrent 'and,' the sound of which," Wilson observes, "is modulated by changes of vowel," while above and below them "a dance of accents shows the pattern of the metrical structure and the rise and fall of the chanting, and, above and below, inside and out, the vowel pointings hang like motes, as if they were the molecules the consonants breathed." Hebrew was emphatic and repetitive, onomatopoetic in its effects, the vehement, passionate verb forms hard to master. As in other Semitic languages, there were conjugations for perfect and imperfect but no allowance for an action completed in the present. Even Russian was more inflected than the language of Genesis, and when, recalling his impressions in the Soviet Union, Wilson correlates the Russians' verbs with their lacking any sense of schedule, the reader may wonder how the Old Testament Jews—or, indeed, their God—ever got anywhere on the appointed day. Yet the lack of a true system of tenses suited the message of a timeless and eternal deity. He links this biblical "aspect of eternity" to the survival of the Jews and the search for a higher justice in their sacred books, the utopian thrust of all the religions to which they contributed. Judaism, Christianity, Mohammedanism, and "the half-religion Marxism"—each had also its aspect of oppressive intolerance. Redefining Arnold's Hebraism and Hellenism, he states that "this sense of transcendent principle has always had to be corrected by the realistic observation, the practical worldliness of the Graeco-Roman tradition."

"On First Reading Genesis," which took its title from Keats's "On First Looking into Chapman's Homer," was an instant success. *The New Yorker* reprinted thousands of copies at the request of theological seminaries and linguistic institutions. Wilson began to tease such acquaintances as Isaiah Berlin, Alfred Kazin, and Jason Epstein that he knew their ancient tongue better than they did. They were not always persuaded by his vision of the Jews—Berlin thought he romanticized Judaism just as he had Lenin, while Epstein reminded him that this culture too had its non-heroic dimensions. But at parties where others were engaged in argument or gossip, Wilson was often seen in a corner parsing some newspaper article in Hebrew with whomever he could get to help him out. At one point he persuaded Elena he was going to have a very orthodox Jew come to Wellfleet for an indefinite period to teach him the language. Convinced she'd have to cook kosher meals, she was agonizing about making a mistake when he told her it was a joke.

He pictured the "perdurable" Hebrew letters reassembling in Israel. The Jewish state had been in existence since 1948, when the Western world, at the expense of Arabs living in Palestine, paid its debt to a people whose history of persecution climaxed in the Holocaust. In the spring of 1954, leaving Elena and Helen in Germany, Wilson went to Israel for *The New Yorker*. He arrived at Haifa on a ship from the Piraeus, saw people on the dock cheering Zionist immigrants and heard the short staccato Hebrew as a spoken language of everyday life. Stirred by the building of a modern state on ancient religious foundations, in his long *New Yorker* essay he contrasts this excitement to the discouragement, during the midfifties, of Western Europe, where the intellectuals had little stake in the life around them, and to the American preoccupation with "the McCarthy hearings, Indo-China [already there was talk of intervention] and the hydrogen bomb." He wasn't indifferent to the status of Israeli Arabs, in this article likening them to marginalized Navajos in the Southwest. A letter to a Jewish writer in America after his return states that "the real unconfessed preoccupation in Israel which I did not touch upon is a kind of imperialistic drive to expand in a territorial way and become a power in the Middle East." Wilson did not, however, correlate this with what he called "the great thing to grasp about Israel," that there the Jews no longer had to be different from other people. And in 1954 no one knew that the outcome of the Six-Day War would enable a small, cohesive society with an Arab minority to settle the occupied territories, eventually creating a political impasse.

The Jewish community had its own minorities, in whom he became engrossed. Meeting cosmopolitan immigrants at a kibbutz, Wilson was aware that the Christian allegorical reading of their Scriptures must seem strange to them. At the other extreme from such folk were the fundamentalists who called themselves Guardians of the City and cut their beards with blunt scissors so as not to violate a prohibition in *Leviticus*. Their costumes were picturesque, but their treatment of women was repulsive, and they spied on their own community and everyone else. On a windy hillside above Jerusalem he attended the Passover celebration of the tiny, inbred, Samaritan sect, who carried out a ritual slaughter of sheep according to Moses' directions in *Exodus*. "Independent worshippers of Jehovah" rather as the American was, their nighttime ceremonial was a tourist occasion like the Zuni dances he saw in 1947 but with a different moral. Instead of summoning the strength to continue, the Samaritans accepted their doom—they now numbered only 304, and their law forbade intermarriage.

These impressions of the culture were admired by people around Ben-Gurion, including Moshe Pearlman, an intellectual and a government spokesman, Harry Zinder, later Director of Israeli Radio, and Teddy Kollek, scholar, book collector, Mayor of Jerusalem and, for twenty-eight years, its peace-keeper. Wilson's *New Yorker* essay promoted S. Y. Agnon, whose merits he would urge on the Swedish Nobel committee. Agnon's humor, fantasy, and pathos, transplanted from a folk culture in a homely ghetto environment in Poland or Galicia, put this storyteller in the line of the authors of *Genesis*. His elegiac charm recalled that of Chagall's paintings, his moral and theological preoccupations those of Kafka, another product of central European Jewry, who spoke to a larger situation and audience than Agnon but might be said to confuse his relationships with God and with the collective. "In Kafka, the irony of the French Flaubert has tinctured with a certain contempt the abstraction of Jewish analysis," Wilson observes, bringing this one-time model into the comparison. Agnon's was a much older irony, based on the gulf between God's promises to his Chosen and what He allowed to happen to them.

Meanwhile Wilson pursued one of his great journalistic firsts, the story of the Dead Sea Scrolls. This extraordinary cache of manuscripts was discovered in a cave near the Dead Sea in 1947, and more kept turning up, all apparently the work of a sect of the first or second century B.C.E. Although they might challenge the uniqueness of Christianity, they were being pieced together by scholars supported by the various Christian churches, a circumstance that Paolo Milano, an Italian scholar of Dante, found disturbing in a letter to Wilson. The critic was soon crawling through caves and following the archaeologist, Dominican Father de Vaux, along narrow walls fifteen feet above the ruin that had been excavated at the Qumran wadi in Jordan. In this "monotonous, subduing and dreadful" land, the sect to whom the Scrolls belonged had tried to escape a wicked world and preserve a purer faith than that of the Temple in Jerusalem. At the Rockefeller Museum in East Jerusalem he observed the Polish priest J. T. Milik, by common consent the most brilliant of the original editors, at work on the fragments. He admired the green copper scroll, its Hebrew words incised with a stylus and readable from the other side.

Though able to follow a translation of Hebrew into ancient Greek better than many American biblical scholars, he didn't pretend to interpret these texts for himself, yet *The Scrolls from the Dead Sea*, published in *The New Yorker* in May 1955 and by Oxford in October, brought their importance to the common reader and those in other fields of scholarship. Setting the pattern for future tellers of this story, he began when a shepherd boy threw a rock into a cave and heard the unexpected sound made by hitting a jar. He carried the tale to the moment when, as the first Arab-Israeli war began, three scrolls were acquired by the son of the Israeli archaeologist Sukenik and three by a Syrian archbishop. Correctly taking the Scrolls to be a library, Wilson accepted the suggestion of the renowned archaeologist W. F. Albright that the sect who possessed them were the Essenes, whom the Roman Pliny the Elder placed at Qumran. An important text had long been in circulation—the Damascus Document, accessible in medieval copies that turned up at Cairo in 1897. One new text, *The War of the Children of Light with the Children of Darkness*, invoked an apocryphal struggle, perhaps figuring that of the Jews with the Romans. The Habbakuk Commentary spoke of the Teacher of Righteousness and the Wicked Priest who persecuted the Teacher, for which he would answer at the Judgment.

Eager as Wilson was to link the Teacher to Jesus, he saw that the Frenchman Dupont-Sommer, Renan's successor at the Sorbonne, did so only by inverting constructions, supplying words, or taking advantage of their different meanings. That this sect inhabited the desert where John the Baptist preached two or three generations later, however, underscored the echoes of the Scrolls in the New Testament. The *Manual of Discipline* or *Community Rule* described a daily meal with a sacramental dimension, apparently anticipating the Last Supper, and there were parallels between the Greek New Testament and newly published texts of the *Community Rule* and the Qumran Hymns. In fragments from Cave 4, discovered after Wilson's time, the Messiah was to work miracles like those in the Gospel of John. The Jewish scholar David Flusser told Wilson that the sect practiced ritual immersion, an anticipation of baptism, and had a doctrine of the Elect that seemed to imply predestination, though nothing like the idea of salvation through Christ. Unlike Jesus, who preached love, they hated their enemies. Wilson concluded that the Scrolls and the New Testament marked "successive phases of a movement," somewhat as would those radical American scholars who, after the belated publication of the Cave 4 documents in 1991, posited that the Essenes were pre-Pauline Christians.

Wilson assumed that faith in Jesus as the Son of God, performer of miracles and redeemer of the world, was waning and that the Scrolls would forward a historical view of Christianity. To his Princeton classmate John Wyeth back in New York he spoke of following in the steps of Voltaire and Renan. Although his *New Yorker* monograph and the book were a triumph, the Christian churches were untroubled. Catholic scholars took notice— an intelligent review was balanced by an editorial warning the faithful against him—but the connections with the Dead Sea sect weren't urgent for liberal students of the New Testament, who saw Jesus' messianic status being awarded to him posthumously by his following. At leading Protestant seminaries Jesus was already beginning to be placed in a series of messiahs and his divinity accepted only in a "symbolic" sense. Paradoxically, it was the evangelical and millenarian faith that in Wilson's time seemed on the wane that would make the Scrolls important to Christians fifty years later. An ancient Jewish community awaiting a messianic apocalypse became relevant to American fundamentalists maintaining their beliefs in a secular world, many of whom politically aligned themselves with Israel against its enemies. Their religion being beyond argument, they would not be threatened by the anticipation of the messiah-God in Judaism, and could turn the history against the liberal scholars.

Another issue was posed by Wilson's work as a generalist among specialists quick to question his expertise. James Sanders, who edited the Psalms from Cave 11 (published by Oxford University Press in 1965), recalled thinking Wilson's commentary "sometimes slanted according to who he was quoting or with whom he had conversations." When Sanders reread the book in 1995 it seemed "engrossing and enthralling but also amazingly balanced and fair." Wilson was for him a "grand explainer" who "better understands and expresses what the reader thinks," a "mirror" insofar as one's experience is refracted "through his sharper mind." The need for such interpreters was manifest, this scholar believed, in the gulf between well-educated graduates of divinity schools, absorbed in what they'd learned of the ancient languages and history, and their congregations, to whom this knowledge would never be made real the way a social or civic issue or a financial need would be.

Various Israeli scholars valued Wilson's work. Yigael Yadin, the archaeologist Sukenik's son, who in Wilson's narrative purchases three of the Scrolls after seeing an ad in *The Wall Street Journal*, noted the vital contribution of this "very scholarly amateur." Yadin, "tall, goodlooking and cosmopolitan," speaking English "incredibly well," was also his country's chief of staff during the Six-Day War. He would take account of the Jews' ancient wars in his plans and, after victory, acquire the Temple Scroll by presenting himself, with soldiers, at the door of the dealer who'd hidden it under the floor. On the other hand, David Flusser (as Wilson enjoyed reporting to Isaiah Berlin) declared that *"Israel est un tres petit pays, et je ne suis pas patriot."** A Czechoslovakian who had learned Hebrew as an adult and called medieval Latin his best language, with his "flaming hair brushed straight up and not parted, modestly Mephistophelian eyebrows, little cold green eyes, a dry and harsh laugh," Flusser seemed "the Devil's agent sent expressly to exploit the situation" created by the Scrolls. He explained that these ancient manuscripts also challenged the premises of orthodox Jews, threatening the authority of the Masoretic text. Flusser saw twentieth-century students of religion, overtaken by the crisis of their faith, pretending to a rigorous scholarly objectivity while they defended their bread and butter. Looking back in 1978 he stated that Wilson, though a rationalist in the eighteenth-century mold, was neither simplistic nor hostile to the "spiritual adventures of mankind," bringing to the subject of the Scrolls the "spiritual vivacity" it demanded. On the night when these two met they toasted the Holy Spirit of humanity.

Wilson began to update his book almost as soon as it appeared, reviewing an edition of the *Genesis Apocryphon* by Yadin and a colleague. In *The Dead Sea Scrolls: 1947–1969*, more than twice its predecessor's size,

---

*Israel is a very small country, and I am not a patriot.

he shares the general impatience with the slow progress of de Vaux's team and its proprietary attitudes, which became an academic scandal during the 1970s and '80s. What no one yet knew was the diversity of Judaism before the Bar Kochba revolt and the Roman destruction of the Temple. The availability of more Scrolls material has shown differences between the beliefs ascribed to the ancient Essenes and those of the Qumran sect, alternately called the Community of the New Covenant. Whoever they were, they resisted the pressures in Jerusalem for a reformed oral Torah, maintaining the truth of the Hebraic Scriptures and, insofar as they could, living like the people to whom Moses had brought the Commandments. It was clear that their library was much too large to have been written by the sect alone when the 15,000 fragments from Cave 4, comprising more than 500 documents, became widely available to scholars. This was not a library brought here for storage, for the Community adapted to their eccentric calendar everything they acquired from others. It has been speculated that the essential library was stored in jars in Cave 1 and the mass of Cave 4 fragments were the supporting documents, what was left over, hurriedly moved on the eve of the event that overwhelmed the settlement.

Wilson wouldn't have minded the irony that the Scrolls turned out to reveal more about intertestamental Judaism than Christianity. His passionate interest in these texts and in Hebrew fed each other. Through the 1950s and 1960s his many Bibles and his scholarly apparatus maintained a conspicuous place in the Wellfleet study and on a table by his desk when he set up shop at Talcottville. He found a fortifying motto in "מזק ונחמזק מזק," the three letters that conclude the Torah, variants on the root form of the word meaning "strong." Literally instructing the orthodox to begin reading all over again, they tell a Jew to reaffirm his Judaism and that of his community. To Wilson they meant be true to oneself and to one's best abilities as a writer. Through these Hebrew letters he was in touch with a moral force independent of the old "worry about being Elected" and "preoccupation with Hell," also of the "half-human figure" of the Saviour, with his residually anthropomorphic Heavenly Father. The words on the wall of the synagogue proclaimed "the power of the spirit, the authority of the moral sense." The source of this authority could be summoned up "only through thought and prayer." For the secular critic there was "only the conviction of its eternal reality and sometimes of its actual presence."

If Judaism stirred Wilson's piety, his skepticism was ascendant in those upstate New York hills where, from his point of view, "the word of God had not been spoken." This has been called "the burned-over district," and its religious sects had not been limited to the orthodox Christian denominations and to shaking Quakers and dour Mennonites. Joseph Smith's revelation at Palmyra incorporated "Greek and Hebrew letters, crosses and flourishes, Roman letters inverted or placed sideways," all "arranged in perpendicular columns" ending in "a circle divided into various compartments, decked with various strange marks, and evidently copied after the Mexican calendar by Humboldt, but copied in such a way as not to betray the source from which it was derived." When Wilson asked at Palmyra where the plates that had appeared from the skies were, he "was told that they had been taken back to Heaven." Brigham Young's organizing skills had, however, made something of the Mormon revelation, and Wilson speculated that, by incorporating polygamy, Mormonism usefully distributed the burdens of motherhood more widely at a time when men's first wives were worn out by bearing children, all mothers threatened by the terrible puerperal fever. He had a similar interest in the system of "complex marriage" employed by John Humphrey Noyes at Oneida. When the critic visited the place he had written about in *To the Finland Station*, he discovered that there were transoms above the doors that were big enough for people to leave their designated partners and "plan a different parenthood"—the escape hatch every religion needed. The New York faith Wilson took seriously was that of the Iroquois. The great feather dance, which he likened to a patriotic and religious hymn, revealed "the need of the human being, among spaces and wildernesses, between the so often indifferent earth which he still regards as his mother and the mysterious bowl of the heavens beyond which he cannot see, to declare, to create himself, to occupy the vacuum of the universe."

Wilson's need alternately to mythologize and demythologize has given us a lasting account of the paradox of faith in the essay "Jerusalem the Golden." As a tourist in the city sacred to three great religions he sets the intellectual and moral force invoked in them against the institutional forms people give to it. From a lingering Presbyterian perspective he registers "the bright, firm and even light" of Jerusalem, the barrenness of this "mild and monotonous" terrain where the Prophets had thundered and the savage wars of Scripture occurred. How remote it all was from the blazing color and teeming flesh of Renaissance paintings of these subjects, monuments to the beauty of the world, created for worldly folk—

"Pharaoh's daughter in her gorgeous silks," discovering Moses in the bulrushes; the "rippling and wistful Botticellian Judith, exhaling a delicate charm after cutting off the head of Holofernes; the beautiful blue madonnas, the heaven-cracking crucifixions," "all the Florentine miles of paint." From this "bright light," these "high bare hills," had come Jesus' injunction, "God is spirit and those who worship Him must worship in spirit and truth."

Wilson was unmoved by the holy places—the fragment of the Jewish Wailing Wall, the various sites that, without much historical evidence, Jesus' life was said to have touched—and oppressed by the huge, ersatz Church of the Holy Sepulchre, which incorporates churches of five different faiths with their individual stones and relics, their overlapping services. In 1954 it was approached through the barbed wire dividing Arab and Jewish in Jerusalem. At the "Tenebrae" (Easter) services he feared that "the whole stale and rickety place," smelling of urine and incense, supported by pillars with strips of glass that would break if a crack occurred, might, "fissured by some piercing note," at any moment "come down on our heads and bury us!" In Wilson's informed tourism this structure evokes Jerusalem's dark, explosive history of religious and ethnic conflict. He quotes Robert Curzon's account of a mob scene at the Tenebrae service in 1834, when the Christians got scared and trampled one another trying to get out the door, and the Mohammedan guards, thinking they were being attacked, joined in a fray that left five hundred people dead. Such were the suspicion, bigotry, and cruelty of competing cults, the fanaticism bound up with religion's promise, for the right people, of a particular version of eternal life and happiness.

He leaves us to consider the place of the religious instinct in thousands of years of "wars and rumors of wars." As he had catalogued the kinds and conditions of people killing themselves during the Depression in "The Jumping-Off Place," so at the end of "Jerusalem the Golden" Wilson lists a score of nations and their more notable rulers, a parade of triumphs and vicissitudes too large even for one soaked in history to grasp, all the nations and leaders seeming "to recompose, like the sequence of colors of the spectrum, in this tranquil luminous sky." The skeptical pilgrim balances faith as an instrument of human self-creation against its ability to unleash hatred. "The Jews," he concludes, "made Jerusalem the high place of God and thus gave it to the whole human race."

28

A Reporter in Minority Communities

The skeptic's fascination with Hebrew, the Jewish people, and the Dead Sea Scrolls was part of an interest in small cultures sustained by their religions on the margins of modernity. The old reporter liked the stimulus of travel, and through these decades he surveyed a series of societies from Haiti, the Zuni pueblo, and the Iroquois Reservations to French Canada and Hungary under the Russians. Wilson's critical methodology emphasized milieu and heritage. He had relished the vitality of immigrants in the army and in the streets of New York, and had rather innocently proposed that knowing Italian literature would ease the prejudice against Italian Americans that was evident in the Sacco-Vanzetti case. In later years a sense of increasing isolation in the United States helped make him, he thought, "obsessed with minorities." He allied himself with small communities in the face of the Big America of the Cold War and its Soviet antagonist.

Dos Passos and Dawn Powell had preceded him to Haiti, and Dawn gave him a witty list of traveler's tips—among other things, that the whiskey was poor but the native rum good and left no hangover. On the flight he read Aimée Cesaire's dramatic poem, *Cahier d'un retour au pays natal*,* which used a technique like Rimbaud's to voice "the rage, the love of race, the frustration, of the Negro of first-rate abilities growing up in a non-Negro world." His impressions of Haiti and of the Marcelin brothers interested Wilson in the literature of *négritude*, on which he became something of an authority. The South African critic Lewis Nkosi, who met him a decade later with Nadine Gordimer at Harvard, recalled his

---

*Notebook of a Return to My Native Land

command of this subject, and Richard Wright sought his advice when trying to build a literary bridge to Africa.

These weeks in Haiti also sensitized Wilson to the frustrations of African Americans. The Haitians had the satisfaction of having bloodily overthrown the whites and could take pride in the fantastic mountaintop fortress built by their tyrannical King Christophe, who, though he checked up on his workers with a spyglass and would even, legend had it, "pick off" slackers "with a cannon," had run the only solvent government in the island's history. His tomb had "the look of a clenched fist." In contrast, "our planters of the South were defeated, yet the Negroes did not win their freedom," still "living with their ruined masters" in the Southern decay and humiliation anatomized in Faulkner's *The Sound and the Fury*. During Wilson's youth as a Manhattanite he had been aware of the Harlem Renaissance only intermittently. On the Caribbean island he wondered whether segregation had prevented him "from knowing the best of American Negro life."

He explored Port-au-Prince with impressions and comparisons to other lands running through his head, and his extensive notes on Haiti, reprinted in *Red, Black, Blond and Olive*, retain their relevance after yet another American political intervention put Jean-Bertrand Aristide in power for ten years and then removed him. This was a mixed-blood community where everyone had some Negro ancestry and one's color and features were not necessarily a guide to social status. In an expedition to the south of the island, Wilson reported on a U.N.-sponsored experiment at Marbial, separated from the capital by a road that crossed the river some eighty times and sometimes ran along its bed. There crafts were taught alongside I. A. Richards's Basic English and phonetic Creole. The Methodist minister who ran the project unsuccessfully struggled against the influence of voodoo. Wilson was then instructed by Phito Marcelin's brother Pierre about the spiritual presences the Haitian peasants felt and saw around them, and met a third brother, Milo, who contributed to their research. Yet he didn't view a ceremony, unwilling to let himself be subjugated, in a hysterical frenzy, by a spirit who "mounted" one, as he read in Maya Deren's account of ecstatic possesson by the Grand Erzele.

The religious ceremonials of Native Americans appealed to him, and at the Zuni Shalako, the celebration of the winter solstice, he registered the energy, the internal beauty of unaffected animism, the unity of religion and art. On a bitterly cold night Sayatasha (or Longhorn) and Huututu, rain gods of the North and South, came down the distant hillside in their fantastic costumes and masks, followed by the Yamuhakto twins, whom Wilson calls wood carriers, and the Salimopia warriors, "a soft lively whistling" like birdcalls sounding their advance. As the procession passed "across the little dwindled river, where," Wilson writes, "a dead dog lies on the bank and old tin cans and paper boxes have been caught here and there on the mud flats," the song, "arising from no visible human source, scanning no human chant, yet filling the quiet air," seemed "the genuine voice of deities that are part of Nature." In the account of the Zuni that opens *Red, Black, Blond and Olive*, a scholarly literature about the creation myths and the Kachina written twenty to fifty years before Wilson's visit is absorbed into a pictographic record that is immediate and personal, carried by his appetite for magic and theater and the steady rhythm of his prose.

Wilson is anthropologist enough to note the difficulty of moving "from a community where people depend on print to a community in which everyone's relations with Nature and with his neighbor depend on direct perception," where "the handing on of history and the transmission of technical skills, as well as the spreading of news, are all oral and very limited"—such a world, "confined to a much smaller area" than ours, must, he thinks, "be much more searchingly seen and heard." He takes the Zuni as an autonomous unit with an organic culture not undermined by their ability to adapt to their American surroundings, just as they had to Spanish culture. After industriously building new houses with large rooms and high ceilings for the yearly arrival of the tribal gods, they put these, he learned, to a family's use. By the twenty-first century the Shalako was being sponsored by families who, although not rich, absorbed the expense of building several houses and slaughtering numerous sheep. If they chose to participate, they took as much as a year's time off work to learn the ritual.

One still has to observe these dances, as he did, from the back of the room or through a window, not approaching the altar near which the performance occurs. As a boy in Italy he'd seen the priests make the statue of Apollo talk by speaking through a tube, and he admired the Zuni performer who worked the mechanism of his enormous bird mask, pulling the cords that controlled the beak and the eyes but forbidden to look up "to watch the mystery in operation." The tenacity and discretion of this dancer enabled his people to create the phenomena in which they simultaneously believed. An unmasked dancer who accompanied the great bird ran in place with a trancelike concentration, as if "by his pounding, [he] were really generating energy for the Zunis; by his discipline, strengthening their fortitude; by his endurance, guaranteeing their permanence." Making the ceremony vivid to Americans for whom a dearth of electricity for air-conditioning and gasoline for automobiles constitutes an energy crisis, Wilson shows "human energy invoked and adored as a force that is at once conceived as a loan from the non-human natural forces and as a rival pitted against them." In terms closer to those of the Zuni, they had made "the life of the animal world and the power of the natural elements continuous with human vitality and endowed with semi-human form."

The Shalako—itself maintained by the medicine societies—is part of a yearly cycle of ritual art through which the survival of the pueblo is manifested. In Wilson's view, their intricate cults toughened the Zuni to resist the pressures that have smashed other Indian groups, and Dennis Tedlock, the anthropologist who has most closely studied them since Wilson's time, believes that he would not be disappointed if he could see the Shalako again. It can be crowded, for the Zuni like to display their culture, though they have occasionally closed this ceremony and do not allow any part of it to be filmed. Wilson can stop the motion of his account for background and analysis. His description eloquently captures the spectacular nature of the dances and the stamina required to enact them.

He observes a solitary dancer in another house, smoothly pavaning and pirouetting and gliding through the long room as the man balanced the cumbersome apparatus. "The great blue-and-white creature irresistibly took on an extra-human personality, became a thing you could not help watching, a principle of bounding and soaring life that you could not help venerating." Wilson combined the talent to write this fully and sympathetically with the ability to stand aside, noting that "it was hardly worthwhile for a Protestant to have stripped off the mummeries of Rome in order to fall victim to an agile young man in a ten-foot mask." Yet the middle-aged writer who'd said that in the United States one must be able to swim against the current was encouraged by this spectacle just as he had been by his encounter with Santayana at his desk in the Convent of the Blue Nuns.

At the heart of *Apologies to the Iroquois*, a more widely read study of an ethnic minority, are comparable rituals which he observed in a darkened room at the Seneca Nation and at Tonawanda, near Buffalo, New York. *Apologies* is also protest journalism, written as the cities of northern New York were spreading toward the Indian communities and huge engineering projects began to eat up their reservations. Wilson sympathized with these original Americans who had endured the paralyzing winters known to his ancestors and called the forested hills where he spent summers home. To forward their cause, through the late fifties he investigated court cases and the treaties cited by the tribes, hoping the engineers and bureaucrats could be as firmly checked as were the beavers building dams on a friend's trout stream. But the St. Lawrence Seaway had just been cut through the Mohawks' land at St. Regis on the U.S.–Canadian border. The Kinzua Dam, which flooded the central part of the Allegany Seneca Reservation on the New York–Pennsylvania border, could not be stopped when a newly elected President Kennedy read Wilson's account and looked into this. The site for the Seneca Long House decreed by Handsome Lake in 1804 was, by 1965, under a lake.

The Niagara controversy was the big issue when Wilson wrote. The autocratic planner Robert Moses wanted a significant part of the Tuscarora's 6,000 acres, which the tribe had owned since the eighteenth century, for his Niagara Falls power plant, their surviving lands to be separated from the plant by a forty-five-foot-high concrete wall. They resisted, led by an honorary or "pine tree" chief, Clinton Rickard. Wilson aroused Moses's enmity by recounting their near violent confrontation with employees of the State Power Authority, their surprising support among nearby whites, their lawyers' success in persuading the Federal Power Commission to keep the Power Authority from intruding on these lands without an act of Congress. His reporting didn't, however, affect the outcome. During the March 1960 week when *Apologies* appeared, the Supreme Court, with an eloquent dissent by Justice Hugo Black, upheld the state's right to condemn the land, ironically on the ground that, though tribally held, it was owned in fee simple rather than in trust by the government.

Such struggles would occur through the next half century, and in time the Iroquois, with powerful government support, began winning them. Wilson's contribution was to help create a new national interest in Eastern Indians, who were partly assimilated and lacked huge reservations in the picturesque landscapes of the West. Dawn Powell quotes him in her journal, telling her that "people are shocked by Indians going to college, living regular life, then coming back to tribal customs which he says is right—preserve them, translate them into modern terms. They use women for planting and agriculture, not through laziness but because they are fertile—traditional." In *Apologies*, he sketches the matrilineal clans of the Six Nations and the politics of hereditary chiefs versus elective chiefs and takes account of the mix of Iroquois of one or another Christian persuasion with a minority pledged "to follow the Longhouse Way," and of the varied racial stocks that continued to be absorbed. "He was not distracted by the common misconception among scholars that Indian cultures in transition are less valuable or valid than those encountered by the first colonists," recalled a Seneca woman who offered to make him a member of the tribe and later named her son for Wilson.

He met a number of impressive people. A Seneca chief with the stereotypical aquiline nose had been superintendent of construction for Bethlehem Steel, but thought he might have been happier if he hadn't been exposed to modern civilization—"I could have lived with the animals then." Chief Corbett Sundown at Tonawanda was foreman of a crew of gypsum miners as well as a guardian of ancient tradition. He spoke English "with a strong accent, giving an impression of formidable strength in reserve." At St. Regis Ernie Benedict—who would help bring to birth the Mohawk publication *Akwasasne Notes*—explained that he'd resisted the draft at the start of World War II because he didn't want to be classed as an American citizen. A historian interviewing Benedict as an old man would be invited to sit in "Edmund Wilson's chair," facing his by the St. Lawrence River. There was also Mad Bear, who has been called the first media Indian, who took over protests begun by others. He played checkers with Wilson at Talcottville and had a famous meeting with Fidel Castro.

At the reservations Wilson was sometimes guided by the ethnographer-historian William Fenton, an adopted Seneca who directed the state museum at Albany. Strange characters often came into the director's office, and at first Fenton thought the pudgy man stammering that he was Edmund Wilson, that he'd been to the Mohawk reservation at St. Regis, that "all the paths lead here," might be mad. Realizing it was indeed Wilson, Fenton gave him a bibliography of literature on the Iroquois and proposed they visit the Allegany Reservation after the winter solstice. On their trips he admired Wilson's questioning and his ability to listen, having "never seen anyone get into the confidence of informants so rapidly." As a reporter "he had schooled himself to retain whole conversations and to recall situations," rehearsing them in the letters and the journal from which his books emerged. He had an "uncanny ability to perceive the character of the person he interviewed and then to enliven this for his readers."

The reporter's prose achieves intensity when he comes to the renewal ceremonies. Reviewing *Apologies*, Auden distinguished between mere social customs and "genuine rites" in which, he presumed, "no Indian who was Christian, for example, or a freethinker, could conscientiously take part." Thus the whole Seneca tribe enthusiastically recharged themselves and their community in the spring dance of the Huskfaces. By contrast, the shamanism of the medicine societies depended on secrecy, something less important to the Zuni, whose communities are geographically isolated. The Dark Dance at the Seneca Reservation enacted a visit by the Little People, who live in rocky places and protect the Iroquois because a young hunter once generously gave them meat. To hear the music of these cave beings, which Wilson likened to an oratorio, gave him the illusion they had entered the unlit room. The songs grew simultaneously louder and higher in pitch, "as if something had opened out that was larger than those who released it, and that had some kind of independent existence," embodying "some projection of the human spirit which has survived through uncounted centuries, some collaboration of man with Nature—we have only this unsatisfactory word—which was now still alive in this shabby old house, rising up and renewing itself, taking over and animating the darkness."

The Little Water Ceremony at Tonawanda, also done without light, maintained the strength of a miraculous medicine that could revive the dying. The simplicity of the scene was powerful to this Protestant-trained observer—a kitchen containing a woodstove, a white sink, a washing machine, on the shelf a big box of cornflakes, ten men on benches against two walls that met at a right angle. In the legend as Wilson heard it enacted, the youths seeking the medicine are led by the whip-poor-will's voice to a mountaintop where a stalk of corn grows from a rock. When cut, it bleeds human blood but is immediately healed. There the animals tell them how to make the medicine. An old Christianized Indian had described the bird's song as a "flourish of the flute," and to the listener in the darkness it recalled "the bird in *Siegfried* that will guide the hero to the Ring." The songs then broke the pattern, beginning on unexpected notes and taking unfamiliar courses. "This is magic," Wilson declares, "a force beyond nature is tearing itself free." Like that of the Zuni, the ritual was "a builder of morale" and had "to be performed by a small group of men in a darkened room." He writes, "The members of this medicine society really constitute a kind of elite, and they are making an affirmation of the will of the Iroquois people, of their vitality, their force to persist. These adepts have mastered the principle of life, they can summon it by the ceremony itself."

In describing the Dark Dance and the Little Water Ceremony, Wilson was once again breaking cultural taboos, as he had those of his own society in *Hecate County*. He had received permission from Chief Sundown to try to make a better description of the Little Water Ceremony than did nineteenth-century anthropologists, but when *Apologies* appeared, a white protectress of the tribe accused Wilson's hosts of betraying their culture, and the book was for a time proscribed.* Paradoxically, *Apologies* has acquired a certain value for traditionalists in the twenty-first century world of TV and shopping malls, where reservations depend economically on legalized gambling and the selling of tax-free cigarettes and gasoline. Loyal though many Iroquois are to the Longhouse, fewer and fewer understand the languages on which the rituals depend. Only a handful of Seneca speakers remain. Wilson's translations of the Dark Dance and the Little Water Ceremony were checked and corrected by Fenton, his companion at these ceremonies.

There are no exalted scenes in *O Canada: An American's Notes on Canadian Culture*. Religion doesn't enter into Wilson's account of English Canada, nor is he sympathetic to the Jansenist Catholicism that had dominated New France (Quebec) since Montcalm's defeat by Wolfe. Canada, however, offered an alternative ethnic and political model to the United States. The English-speaking provinces hadn't been an independent country or produced writers like those who, before the Civil War, attempted "to give America an identity," and in the 1960s this country appeared resolutely unmelded. While English Canada experienced a patriotic resentment of the domination of American capital and American popular culture, rebellion stirred in Quebec, the province with the history most distinct from the others. Wilson explores a volatile situation while introducing the writing of his own country's vast northern neighbor. He limits himself to the Eastern Seaboard, ignoring the literature of the West that had been growing up in the bohemian neighborhoods of Winnipeg and Vancouver.

*No sanction extended to his guide. Fenton recorded how Chief Sundown came into his office and said, "We are having it again. You had better come."

He approached Canadian writing through Morley Callaghan, a link to the American twenties. Stopping in Toronto en route to the Six Nations Reserve, where Iroquois customs were being preserved, Wilson sought out the novelist, who told the story of his notorious boxing match with Hemingway in Paris, when Fitzgerald, the timekeeper, was so surprised to see Hemingway knocked down that he let the round go on too long. Encouraging Callaghan to write the memoir *That Summer in Paris*, Wilson made Callaghan's fiction the subject of a *New Yorker* essay reprinted in *O Canada* and there extended by a long postscript. His extravagant praise brought this contemporary attention, then, ironically, stimulated Canadians to reject him lest he get a swelled head. Hugh MacLennan, Wilson's other enthusiasm among contemporary novelists of English Canada, could invest with a kind of poetry the life of orphaned sisters in a slow-paced Ontario town or a strong-minded boy's escape from trouble alone in a stolen canoe. A Nova Scotian, he saw the United States somewhat as the critic did: MacLennan believed that American righteousness and technological aptitude came together during World War II, breaking the mood of the Depression and leading, unfortunately, to the use of atomic weapons at Hiroshima and Nagasaki.

While Wilson uncovered these storytellers and a few poets in the shadows of conservative English Canada, he looked into French-Canadian writers. The lawyer Malcolm Montgomery, who met him while working for the Iroquois at the Six Nations Reserve, noted in his diary a conversation in which "Callaghan interjected that Toronto was the heart of Canadian publishing and that more books were sold in Toronto than Montreal," but Wilson "said he felt more books were read in Montreal than Toronto." In *O Canada* he first looks, as in Haiti, at a poet in the tradition of Rimbaud. Filling in the background of Quebec through Parkman's multivolume *History of France and England in North America*, he refers the novelists' characteristic *"douleur"* and *"souffrance"* back to the Jansenist separation of spirit and flesh, the conflict between worshipping the Virgin and producing children to settle the wilderness. André Langévin's somber, well-told tales brought sexual energy to an anatomy of "souls at large," while Hector Saint-Denys Garneau and Anne Hébert (later to become a fine poet) expressed the frustrations of an inbred nobility. In *The Sixties* Wilson is told by Mavis Gallant that Hébert "had been kept at home and guarded by her father, who told her that she suffered from TB, up to the time when the doctor, who knew well that this was not true, threatened to take the matter into court. The mother had not left the manor for some incredible number of years."

Marie-Claire Blais, who at sixteen had written the grim rural fable *La belle bête* (translated as *Mad Shadows*), may have been the last imaginative writer to benefit by being the subject of Wilson's critical enthusiasm. The novels that followed this one, tales of dislocated love that were haunted by death, were the "most unrelievedly painful" he thought he'd ever read, a "desperate cry that emerges from the poverty, intellectual and material, the passionate self-punishing piety and the fierce defeated pride of Quebec." Dining with the young woman in Montreal, and a second time with Elena, Wilson admired Blais's fine features, her directness and self-possession, "the intensity of her personal responses to everything she sees or reads." She was then twenty-two. "She may possibly be a genius," he stated, and after supporting her successful application for a Guggenheim grant he was gratified by *Une saison dans la vie d'Emmanuel*, where "the turbid and swirling sediment of the actual French Canadian world" was "infused" by the fantasies, "the terrors and appetites, the starved and stifled aspirations" he too had known when young.

To Blais, Wilson was a dazzling and a daunting presence. Looking back as a successful novelist, she said he asked questions "penetrating your soul," and that her nervousness during their interviews perhaps reinforced for him the gloom of her writing. He and Elena, whom Marie-Claire at once adored, encouraged her to spend her fellowship year in Cambridge, Massachusetts, and after visits to Wellfleet she became part of the literary community there. With Wilson she sometimes talked about life's *"angoisse"* and suffering, and she eventually confided to Elena that she had been held captive for four months and raped by the priest and cultural impresario who had fostered her work, with whom, in *O Canada*, Wilson has an admiring interview. *"On ne se laisse pas violer pendant quatre mois,"** Elena drily commented in passing this story on to her husband, who set it down in his journal. When *The Sixties* appeared three decades later, Blais overcame her embarrassment and forgave Wilson, who, she said, "had to write about everything."

In calling this book *An American's Notes* Wilson admits that *O Canada* is not an integrated whole. It was published in 1965, when he was getting out his last literary chronicle and putting his best energies into the jour-

---

*One doesn't let oneself be raped for four months.

nals that would be *The Sixties*. Furthermore, he was "on the margin of it all" in Montreal and Toronto, meeting people "not under the same pressure" as Americans. They hadn't "had to save the republic, to justify the democratic experiment," hadn't been "through our crises and panics." The awakening of French Canada, like the Iroquois response to governmental "proddings and encroachments," was, for Wilson, salutary. He knew neither that the Canadian federation would be threatened nor how intolerant the French would become, and he saw firsthand how nationalism could stimulate art. He found himself "in a world which, though much more inbred and limited" than the States, offered writers "the stimulus of a common discontent, a common interest in preserving their language." So the writers of other "small nationalities, like Ireland and Hungary," had "provided an active ferment in the political life of the people."

His sojourn in Hungary in April–May 1964 was his last personal investigation of another society. It was stimulated when in 1960 he received a volume containing Hungarian translations of two of his plays, *Beppo and Beth* and *This Room and This Gin and These Sandwiches*. Though the translator presented them as accounts of capitalist decay, Wilson told himself "these Hungarians are capable of playing certain scenes ironically." Wintering that year in Cambridge, he began taking weekly language lessons from Zoltan Harajsti, his friend at the Boston Public Library—"they were invariably so tumultuous that Elena called them 'Hungarian rhapsodies.'" On a visit to upstate New York he found that the handsome woman who worked in the local drugstore and agreed to type and drive for him was Hungarian and could tutor him. Mary Pcolar's relationship with him began when she arrived for an interview at ten thirty in the morning to see "white hairless bare legs descending the staircase," followed to her immense relief by a bathrobe and Wilson with a drink in his hand. Her Hungarian lessons were soon complemented by those of another woman, Agatha Fasset, a Hungarian émigré in Cambridge, who said Pcolar made him sound like a peasant. When he set up his trip for the spring of 1964 he planned on meeting the lexicographer Laszlo Országh, whose dictionaries he used. He arranged to study the language with Charlotte Kretzoi, the literary wife of a professor in Budapest.

The tourist in Hungary in *The Sixties* knows the Hungarian names for a stork that flies up from a field carrying grass to its nest on a roof and for the long wool overcoat worn by a girl posing for photographs at a collective farm. Outside Budapest the Tisza is overflowing, "silvery, winding and quite lovely in the setting of the new green of the grass and trees, among which it was spreading its silver ponds." The city has a rough, coarse aspect, the "spiky and bristling" skyline with "the porcupine dome of the parliament house, the ubiquitous unendearing Cupids" contributing an "element of the goblinesque." There are "rearing" equestrian statues, poet-patriots with "erectile hair" and "long defiant mustaches." Visiting the galleries, Wilson judges the paintings, except for the El Grecos and Goyas, second-rate, unaware that the Nazis had stolen the best Hungarian work and various foreign treasures from the collections of Jewish millionaires, that they were then removed from Germany to Russia by the Soviets. He attends ballet and opera—Bartók in both cases—takes the Kretzois to the circus, and with Charlotte calls on the poet Gabor Devesceris, who had translated Homer and the Greek dramatists. The poet and the critic talk of Ovid's rhyming practices, of Wilson's experiments with elegiacs— a form Devesceris diagrams in "chiastic lines" that are reproduced in the journal—and of Keats and Shelley as rendered by the Hungarians, "a nation of translators." This scene in *The Sixties* suggests how the rhetorical tradition had once unified the intellectual class.

Wilson had denounced the Russian repression of the Hungarian revolt in the introduction to *Patriotic Gore*, published after *Apologies to the Iroquois* but before this tour. Such ex-Communists as Tibor Dery and Istvan Orkeny, who'd served prison terms after the 1956 revolt failed and were again at the forefront of the nation's art and life, would have gladly met him and been able to expand his understanding of the Hungarian situation. But Kretzoi, who was from the old professional class and called herself a bluestocking, was careful in her politics, though she recounted the barbarities of Russian soldiers in 1945. It was Devesceris who, the historian Istvan Deak believes, would have introduced him to the dissidents. Also at dinner that night at the poet's, however, was the translator of Wilson's plays, Peter Nagy. Nagy, editor in chief at the state publishing house Corvina, was someone with whom, Wilson belatedly realized, one couldn't be indiscreet.

It was ironic that the man whose interest in his work drew him to Hungary stood between him and a more than touristic experience. Fortunately, the scholar Országh enlightened Wilson about the political scene. Explaining that after his mother died he had managed to keep their second room by getting his library certified as a private museum, Országh took him home to an apartment in an old house built around a court, where one had to pay a woman to use the elevator and could only use it to go up. Upstairs, he warned it wasn't safe to write in one's journal and to be careful where one talked because of tape recorders.

On Wilson's last day Nagy put him on guard by rejecting what he called "bourgeois" sets in the theater, dismissing *Doctor Zhivago* as decadent, and variously rationalizing the regime. Országh then confirmed that Nagy was a "blood orange," red through and through, and back in the States, Deak let Wilson know that he was under suspicion of having "informed on a friend and got him executed." Wilson is discreet in the account of Hungary that is a postscript to the 1968 edition of *Europe Without Baedeker* giving much space to Hungarian grammars. But he left the country glad that the United States did not have this sort of empire to defend. Even the minority within the Party who believed in communism hated their Russian masters who directed everything from Moscow. He had gotten "a little the hang of things."

29

Patriotic Gore Reconsidered

Those who find the act of writing difficult can take comfort from the account of the creation of *Patriotic Gore* recorded by Lowell Edmunds, a Harvard senior who was Wilson's secretary. "Like most writers I have heard of, he will seize upon the slightest excuse not to write. He gets up to open and shut the window; goes down the hall to the men's room to fill his Old Fashioned glass with water; takes some candy from the jar Helen brought him from the South; sits back and stares into space or leans forward on his desk and groans." Yet there was a grim determination behind all these gestures, each leading Wilson "back to the long, legal-sized yellow page." At *The New Republic* in the mid-1920s Matthews had seen him bunching "his whole hand" around the pencil as he wrote and revised his articles straight through galleys and page proof. "When he writes," Edmunds observed in 1960, "he writes with a terrible intensity, as if all of his hundreds of pounds were quite literally behind the pencil. When the pages cross the desk to me to be typed, they are festooned with lines directing me into the margins where he has made additions, clarifications, revisions, even in the midst of the first writing; and with interlinear additions, sometimes impossible to read, and with cross-hatched lines where he has struck out whole paragraphs. He says that he can't write with dirty hands. That same feeling accounts for the cleanliness of style that comes out of all this."

After all the years with other cultures, with Proust and Joyce, Marx, Dickens, and Turgenev, Wilson returns to his own country, investigating American character and culture as they were dramatized by the Civil War. Moving through the nineteenth century and from the North to the South and back in an epic-like structure, he sifts the stories of statesmen

and soldiers, journalists, diarists, novelists, and poets, plays their perspectives off against one another, assesses their writing. Artfully deployed
quotations become the voices of characters who, he explains, "have written their own parts." Reading this book is a little like being set down in a
room packed with people, each one of whom wants your ear for however
long it takes to tell of himself or of others, of private struggles or of great
events. The "authorial commentator and curtain-puller" (as a critic called
him) also wants your ear, interpreting from the side of the stage. *Patriotic
Gore*, like *To the Finland Station* produced by one whose historical imagination works with and is faithful to the documentary record, has its own
leisurely rhythms and passionate commitments. In Wilson's words of a
minor figure whom he resurrects, "we feel that the experience has imposed itself on him, that a great moment in history has lived itself through
him." Robert Lowell and Alfred Kazin each called the book an American
Plutarch's *Lives*.

   "He was pulled in many directions," as Wilson had written of the
Michelet of the *History of France*, which "overflowed into a whole series
of smaller books which dealt more fully with special aspects of the subject." So with *Patriotic Gore* and its satellites, from *A Piece of My Mind* to
Apologies to the Iroquois to *The Cold War and the Income Tax* and *O
Canada*. Fifteen years went into this book, from his first accounts of
Stowe, De Forest, and Bierce to the controversial introduction written after the Bay of Pigs. His cast continued to expand. He added fresh material to the portraits drafted at Princeton in 1952, celebrating Lincoln's
imagination, mind, and will, Stowe's patriotic moral understanding,
Grant's strength of character and clear intelligence. Wilson's Lincoln has
the resonance of his long engagement with his father's hero. In one of his
epitaphs during World War I the hospital orderly echoed the Gettysburg
Address:

> Go, countryman of theirs: they bought you pride:
> Look to it the Republic leave not vain
> The deaths of those who knew not why they died.

In his Civil War book, as in these lines, Wilson wears the toga of the old
republic in Lincoln's place, but now he questions Lincoln's crusade. When
reading William Herndon's *Life* as his father had urged, during the Depression, he had been moved by the struggle of this "man of genius com

ing out of the crudeness and poverty of the frontier and perfecting himself," preparing for his role in the Republic's "terrible unconscious parturition." Yet Lincoln, "who saw so clearly into the historical moment, did not see into its depth," as Robert Penn Warren, echoing Wilson's Hegelian premise, phrased this in reviewing *Patriotic Gore*. The future of the Union sanctified in blood would be the technological capitalism that emerged from the business dealings Hawthorne observed at Willard's Hotel in Washington and from all the factories that assured the North's victory. Burdened by the conduct of the war, the president could no more anticipate this than Marx and Lenin could the future they strove to bring about. Wilson notes that when asked to speak on "Discoveries, Inventions, and Improvements," Lincoln paid tribute to the one that mattered to him, the art of writing.

His vocation was for statesmanship, his determination to prove to the world "the practicability of the principles of our revolutionary documents." Wilson believes that Lincoln grasped the ambiguity of his role as president in the early speech that warned against the coming of a "towering genius" who would impose himself on the Republic "whether at the expense of emancipating slaves or enslaving free men." He sympathized with slaves and grew more certain that slavery was wrong without ever claiming God had committed himself to the side of the North. As the slaughter of the war went on, however, the onetime freethinker fell back on providential history, invoking the unknown will of the Lord of Hosts. He veiled the horror of the Civil War in a religious myth validated for future generations by his martyrdom. Noting Lincoln's statement that Caesar and Brutus were created for each other, and the dreams and portents that foreshadowed his assassination, Wilson concludes, "It was dramatically and morally inevitable that this prophet who had crushed opposition and sent thousands of men to their deaths should finally attest his good faith by laying down his own life with theirs."

Mirroring Wilson's skeptical patriotism, this portrait has been influential, although it overlooks such political questions as how Andrew Jackson's acts in the 1832 nullification controversy limited Lincoln's options when confronting secession. The warmer account of the Grant of the *Personal Memoirs* has been a favorite of readers. "Humiliated, bankrupt and voiceless, on the very threshold of death, sleeping at night sitting up in a chair as if he were still in the field and could not risk losing touch with developments," the old soldier produced the two volumes that conveyed his dynamic force and capacity for inspiring confidence, qualities that, backed by Lincoln's moral direction, enabled him "to marshal men, to take cities, and to break down the enemy's strength." When the *Memoirs* were published by Mark Twain, 300,000 copies were sold and they were praised by everyone from Mathew Arnold to Gertrude Stein, then forgotten. Wilson enjoyed pointing out this modest American's distinction of style and feeling. Grant was too sensitive to suffering to face the agony of the soldiers—Wilson turns from the *Memoirs* to Horace Porter's description of the Wilderness and the "bloody angle"—and he escaped the burden of command in drinking bouts. Yet his description of accepting Lee's surrender and allowing the enemy army to keep their horses and mules for the spring plowing revealed the man in the unbuttoned blue-flannel shirt to be every bit as much a gentleman as the defeated aristocrat with his jewelled sword. The ideal of the powerful leader "who almost disclaims his official rank," one Grant shared with Lincoln, "was perhaps something new in the world."

Wilson didn't attempt to gloss over Grant's disastrous presidency, his role as a naive front man for industrial tycoons and crooks. The general admired by Charles Francis Adams is contrasted to the politician whom Charles Francis's brother Henry Adams deems so doltish as to refute the theory of evolution. Such a shifting perspective characterizes the method of *Patriotic Gore*. In our last glimpse of the general who, from youth, could not bear the sight of blood and hated to see people humiliated, Grant is comfortably conversing with Bismarck about the virtues of the death penalty. In a sentence Wilson, whom Marx had taught that conditions changed men, sums up the improbable career of "this man who had found himself, in his forties, the most conspicuous figure in what had been up to that time the most destructive war in history and afterwards at the head of the formidable state which this war had consolidated; the equal, the sympathetic colleague, of the master of that other great new state which had consolidated the German principalities."

The parallel portrait of William Tecumseh Sherman is a variation on this theme. "Uncle Billy," as his troops called him, became the Attila Sherman of Brady's 1865 photograph. Sherman disapproved of the abolitionists and always liked Southerners, had mixed feelings about slavery, talked of curtailing the suffrage—"Vox populi, vox humbug" was one of his maxims—and was not a religious man, yet set out to teach the wrath of God to the treacherous and devilish rebels, to "make Georgia howl!" Unlike Robert E. Lee (who thought it "good that war is so terrible. Otherwise we should grow to enjoy it"), Sherman acquired a relish for "the grand and beautiful game of war," an exhilaration of conquest, a lust to dominate and terrorize. But, like Grant, he was generous to the defeated, and he knew himself well enough to avoid Grant's postwar fate, famously telegraphing the Republicans "I WILL NOT ACCEPT IF NOMINATED AND WILL NOT SERVE IF ELECTED." With no more respect for military than political strutting, Sherman makes an attractive figure in his later years—a traveler, a diner out, a lover of the theater, a passionate spouse who cried out to his dying wife, Ellen, to wait for him to come with her. Three years later, after spending his seventy-first birthday in the room in which Ellen had died, he collapsed when "sitting in a rocking chair in front of the fire, rereading *Great Expectations*."

Ten pages on the tormented life of Sherman's son Tom round out this portrait, epitomizing the difficulties sometimes faced by children of distinguished Americans. Ellen was a pious Catholic and Tom Sherman, whose father wanted him to go to West Point, became a Jesuit priest, in which career he sought the satisfactions of a military man. He gave sermons like a commander addressing his troops, proclaimed that anarchists should be shot on sight, had a satisfying brush with combat in Puerto Rico, and eventually lost his faith and went insane, in his late years imagining himself a general. Was this, as one critic of *Patriotic Gore* thought, a psychological equivalent to the biblical injunction that the sins of the fathers are visited on the sons? As Wilson says in the introduction, the characters and careers must be their own moral.

Although he views Harriet Beecher Stowe's subsequent novels ("voluminous and about fifty percent terrible," he confided to a friend) as a commentary on New England clerical life, in *Uncle Tom's Cabin* she was "national, never regional." Stowe too was a patriot—on hearing the Declaration of Independence read aloud in her childhood she'd been "as ready as any of them to pledge my life, fortune, and sacred honor for such a cause," had longed "to do something, I knew not what: to fight for my country, or to make some declaration on my own account." This was one source of the novel that Harriet wrote as if in a trance and explained as one of God's mysteries, another being her anger at the hypocrisy of many professed Christians on the slavery issue. Wilson also sees in *Uncle Tom* the stress of living with her hypochondriacal husband, Calvin, who in his letters depends on his beloved to protect him against sexual temptation while complaining of her household management. The novel, "with its lowering threats and its harassing persecutions, its impotence of well-meaning people, its outbreaks of violence and its sudden bereavements," had been lived in Harriet's own home, "where the trials and tribulations, as they used to be called, of the small family world inside were involved with, were merged in, the travail of the nation to which it belonged." Here Wilson's theme of the wound and the bow supports what was a pioneering use of domestic history. *Uncle Tom*, projecting this "obscure personal anguish," drew as well on Harriet's "courage and faith, the conviction that God, after all, was just."

He lacks the same depth of background when sketching the Southerners. He describes a range of Southern ladies, from a lively young woman of the professional class, who defies the Yankees but will not insult them, to a dull paragon of Confederate orthodoxy, who, however, is morally relieved by slavery's demise. He investigates Mary Chesnut's diary when this was known in a corrupt and partial form, before C. Vann Woodward's definitive edition. Wilson shows how Mrs. Chesnut takes experience as metaphor, limning the fate of the Confederacy in her account of friends and family. She uses the failed romance of a socialite with a crippled war hero as an emblem of the South's lack of unity, and the gloomy family estate at Mulberry to dramatize race and gender issues. Every white woman, Chesnut writes, admits to knowing who has fathered the mulatto children in every household but her own. She reports what her husband heard a neighbor say at the end of the war: "They will have no Negroes now to lord it over! They can swell and peacock about and tyrannize now over only a small parcel of women and children, those only who are their very own family."

Vignettes of Southern soldiers set off Sherman and Grant. Through elegant Richard Taylor, Zachary Taylor's son, who is too sophisticated to believe the South will win, we observe Stonewall Jackson, that rare Virginian who, like the New Englanders, views himself as a vessel of God, his fatalism matched to a soaring ambition. Jackson is a refugee from Episcopalianism turned Calvinist. John Singleton Mosby, the storybook cavalryman whose mysterious ubiquity fascinated Melville in "The Scout Toward Aldie,'" sees the war as an extension of the classical, romantic, and historical reading he carries in his saddlebags and in his head, yet he discards the saber for the pistol and, like Jackson, is a ruthless fighter. The miniature of Lee carries weight in this gallery. Wilson takes satisfaction in a life that is "an exemplification of principles rarely expressed." As Robert Penn Warren said, what touches his heart most deeply "is some courageous manifestation of the old virtues," regardless of what their bearer stands for politically. Of Wilson's Lee, Warren writes, "With shrewd and economical strokes he has indicated the depth of personal struggle which could lead to such fortitude, such moral certainty, such self-control."

As a boy Wilson had encountered a different view of the war among Virginia cousins, and though in *Patriotic Gore* he sometimes thinks the secessionists romantic fools, ruined, as Twain said, by reading Walter Scott, he finds a literary ancestor of sorts in Alexander Stephens, the Confederate vice president whose 1,455-page testament defends state sovereignty through staged conversations with imagined Unionist opponents. The principled Stephens, who admired Lincoln's mystical vision of the Union, fought Jefferson Davis's attempts to follow Lincoln by instituting a military draft and suspending habeas corpus. In prison in 1865, Wilson writes, Stephens reads "Cicero, the Bible (the New Testament in Greek), Prescott's histories and Bacon's essays, Silvio Pellico's book on prisons, Burns and Coleridge and the first series of Matthew Arnold's *Essays*, just published and sent him by a lady in Boston, of which he found the morality dubious." He "offers to teach the orderly Latin and advises him to study law. He sings a hymn on arising every morning. He reflects on his relations with the bedbugs and mice," fond of "my mouse" but condemned to "an irrepressible conflict" with the bloodsuckers. Without analyzing Stephens's complex political career, Wilson uses his refusal to make terms with Lincoln at Hampton Roads in 1865 to contrast the individualist and "impossibilist" with the self-appointed leader who reflects the popular will, a "benevolent despot who wants to mold others for their own good, to assemble them in such a way as to produce a comprehensive unit" that realizes some larger vision. "The conflict between these two tendencies"—which on a large scale gave rise to the Civil War—may, Wilson says, "also break the harmony of families and cause a fissure in the individual."

The view of American history in *Patriotic Gore* mirrors Wilson's life and times. In Haiti he had judged that segregation kept him from knowing the best of American Negro life, and there are very few African American voices here. The journal of Charlotte Forten, who was on Georgia's Sea Islands for several years, yields a sympathetic portrait. But he doesn't tell the story of Frederick Douglass, who never got the commission Lincoln promised him, yet campaigned valiantly against black invisibility during the war and afterward. Harriet Jacobs is not included among Wilson's Southern women diarists. Harvard's Widener Library contained William Wells Brown's documentation of black troops serving with the Union, although Brown's book begins with the Revolutionary War and is titled *The Negro in the American Rebellion*. Otherwise blacks wrote little of the Civil War, and Wilson's studies of its literature, done during the 1950s, pre-date the civil rights movement. At one of the symposiums during his centenary year of 1995, Randall Kennedy declared the absence of "the voice of the slave, the fugitive slave," and "the free Negro" a fatal flaw in the book. From the audience Toni Morrison argued against an obligation of inclusiveness, saying she didn't want her work to be faulted fifty years later "because I had chosen to write principally about African-Americans' life experience, language, etcetera." She granted "the grand man of letters, the man of American letters" the freedom of an artist like herself.

White liberal opinion has not always been so scrupulous, given the diversity of voices, sources, and opinions Wilson explores. In an article on Jefferson's political debt to slavery in *The New York Review of Books* in October 2003, Garry Wills states that Wilson romanticizes the Ku Klux Klan. In the one account of the Klan in *Patriotic Gore*, it is romanticized by a Northerner who fought against it, Albion Tourgee, the carpetbagger-novelist-lawyer who later represented Homer Plessy of *Plessy v. Ferguson*. While Tourgee is extensively quoted on the organization through which a defeated ruling class reasserted its power, Wilson, in a passage unmentioned by Wills, specifies its "atrocities" and "crimes" as "blackmail, bullying, flogging, rape of women, castration of men, contemptuous violence to children, burning of Negro houses and shootings, stabbings, drownings, and hangings of anybody who offered serious resistance." He adds, "Thousands, both black and white—though less, of course, of the latter—were slaughtered by the Ku Klux Klan."* *Patriotic Gore* resists ideological orthodoxies. In the introduction, written in 1961, Wilson endorses African-American sit-ins in the South and rejects the methods of the segregationists even as he attacks the imperial state in a voice like that of Stephens.

The twentieth century's brutal wars, during which the United States became the most powerful nation in the world, color this book, as does the need of Americans to moralize their expansion. For Wilson, the apocalyptic light in which Lincoln came to see the Civil War serves to help his countrymen persuade themselves that theirs is always the just cause. Dismissing

---

*When a reviewer pointed out this misuse of evidence, in reply Wills quoted Wilson's statement, "The Klan was completely successful," as if it were approval. Wills added that for someone so opposed to the expansion of American power dictated by Washington, "The Klan riders had to be seen as freedom fighters."

the slogans that, in the modern age, rally the populace, the introduction to *Patriotic Gore* offers a sweeping, pseudo-scientific account of warring nations as sea slugs who ingurgitate one another at the bottom of the ocean. With a bitterness like that of the aging Mark Twain, Wilson proposes that "the difference in this respect between man and the other forms of life is that man has succeeded in cultivating enough of what he calls 'morality' and 'reason' to justify what he is doing in terms of what he calls 'virtue' and 'civilization.'" He attacks Soviet and American imperialism simultaneously, coupling the repression of the Hungarian revolt with a sketch of American history from the Mexican through the Civil Wars and the dispossession of the Indian tribes. On a visit to Talcottville, two friends urged Wilson not to burden the book with this "harangue," and some in the literary world wished he had not. While Warren admired his rejection of both Northern and Southern mythologies, and the Western rebel Edward Abbey welcomed his critique of centralization, Alfred Kazin would follow a celebratory review with an earnest letter to Wilson arguing the morality of the war to destroy the slave power, as he tried to convince him it had been wrong to resist American entry into the war against fascism. Wilson offended the Left by not distinguishing "good" or progressive wars from bad ones, and the Right by attacking manifest destiny. *Life* magazine denounced his analogies in an editorial called "Bismarck, Lenin, and Lincoln?"

He worried when churning these pages out, knowing he was at his best with individual people and their work, but thought he had a responsibility to say what he believed. That spring, Wilson signed the protest of Harvard faculty against the Bay of Pigs, and when he warns against the unreasoning unanimity of men at war, he intuits the disastrous adventure that would come not, as he feared, in Cuba but in Vietnam. The introduction to *Patriotic Gore* became cogent during the Vietnam years, and again after the collapse of the Soviet empire and the attacks of Al Qaeda on 9/11 made possible the invasion of Iraq. One need not blame the war policies of Lyndon Johnson or George W. Bush on Abraham Lincoln to observe the notable coincidence that, on an aircraft carrier named for Lincoln, a triumphant President Bush hailed the illusion of victory in Iraq ("Mission Accomplished"). Wilson makes the larger historical point efficiently: "Whenever we engage in a war or move in on some other country it is always to liberate somebody."

Paul Berman, collapsing this polemic into the 700 pages that follow, notes that Wilson has jettisoned the idea of progress, the expectation that human beings can re-create their world through state power. He calls *Patriotic Gore* "*Finland Station* upside down." Yet its very pluralism keeps this book from forwarding any single idea, including what Berman, in a fine general essay on Wilson, labels his "pacifist anti-statism and anti-centralism." There is no dominant figure like Marx or outstanding event toward which the book moves, like Lenin's arrival in Petrograd in 1917. Yankees and rebels, writers and men of action, reappear within one another's lives, and the hero of one account may be the villain of another. The main difference from *To the Finland Station* lies in the author's age and experience. While he had chronicled an unsuccessful effort to master history as he came into full possession of his powers, the seasoned Wilson sets off the sometimes heroic qualities of his characters against a backdrop of events and processes largely beyond their control. His two biographical epics complement one another. "The men of action make history, but the spectators make most of the histories, and these histories may influence the action," he writes when turning to Henry Adams and Henry James. "They also serve who only stand and watch." The adaptation of Milton's line is Wilson's signature in the corner of his vast canvas.

The book's unifying themes arise from the melding of his personality with his characters. From Stowe at the beginning to Justice Holmes at the end, those he most admires are imbued with a Hebraic Protestantism. That is the source of Lincoln's lofty voice, italicized as is nothing else in Wilson's text: "*Let us have faith that right makes might, and in that faith, let us, to the end, dare to do our duty as we understand it.*" Yet he is not so taken with Julia Ward Howe's lyrics for "The Battle Hymn of the Republic," though he responds to "the old rousing rhythm." Her climax, "As He died to make men holy / Let us die to make men free / While God is marching on," exemplifies what Wilson considers righteous naiveté. After *Patriotic Gore* appeared, he was pleased to learn that the last line of a version popular with Union troops was "And the God-damned war goes on." He rejects John Brown's declaration, in bleeding Kansas, that "without the shedding of blood, there is no remission of sins," for Wilson does not want to see religious ideals used to justify violence. He also does not want to lose their energizing current, as Andrew Delbanco has said. He takes the Protestant heritage as a fount of discipline and purpose, while blaming it for all that is too abstractly intellectual in American literature. In this book—as he did in conversation—the critic who had wanted to be a great

writer of fiction and drama strikes at John Calvin, somewhat as Ahab locates the cosmic enemy in Moby Dick.

Patriotic Gore is flawed not by abstraction, but by the excesses and
imperfections hard to avoid in books of a certain extended length, even to
the triad of his and E. M. Forster's shared enthusiasm, *War and Peace*, *À
la recherche du temps perdu*, and Gibbon's *Decline and Fall*. The postwar
literary history drags. An account of the poets that begins and ends with
Sidney Lanier manages to touch on everyone from Poe to Pound. Surveying the struggle of the ex-combatants to create realistic fiction, Wilson
sees only Ambrose Bierce confronting the magnitude and horror of the
killing. George Washington Cable, one of his minor heroes, is driven north
by intolerance and slowly suffocated as a writer by the romantic conventions of an increasingly feminine reading public, while Thomas Nelson
Page, author of *In Ole Virginia*, puts the sectional issues "to sleep with the
chloroform of magazine prose." The vignette of Kate Chopin and *The
Awakening*—beginning the revival of her work that feminist historians as-
sign to the late 1960s or early '70s—has been called one of Wilson's stunning achievements, showing his sensitivity to voices. But there follows a
seventy-five-page forced march through the novels of John De Forest,
which suffer, the critic concedes, from "a fundamental non-radiation."
We are far from the vital account, in an early chapter, of Francis Grierson,
the forgotten homosexual mystic whose poetic memoir, *The Valley of Shadows*, captured the Middle West of his childhood on the eve of the war.
Grierson, too, had tried to judge statesmen, like artists, "as creative forces."
Wilson observes the curve of his own development when he states, "The
appreciator of the modern French poets, the critic of Wagner and Nietzsche,
proves, after all, to feel himself closer to Lincoln than any of these."

As his editor at the Oxford University Press, Sheldon Meyer, tells it,
an "anxious and lugubrious" author finally delivered "two huge binders"
containing the typescript over drinks at the Princeton Club, saying "it
needed to be cut, with its long quotations and accounts of minor works,
but he didn't have the inclination or energy to do so." He asked for help,
and young Meyer, who had admired Wilson since college and soon discerned that *Patriotic Gore* was a classic, excitedly envisioned himself as
another Maxwell Perkins. He slashed "some two hundred pages" and returned the results, only to be ordered in Wilson's "high-pitched, furious
voice" on the phone, "Meyer, you've ruined it. Put back in everything
you've taken out." In fact, there were letters back and forth between April

and June, Meyer making corrections in the first half of the text and suggesting how it might be shortened, then proposing to remove some forty pages of quotations from the second—from Lanier and the poet Frederick Goddard Tuckerman, the Maryland novelist John Pendleton Kennedy, and De Forest, whose portrait was to lose fifteen pages. He suggested other passages to be omitted, including an account of the antislavery polemicist Hinton Helper's crazed racism. Wilson the editor had been "a concision-fetishist," but he was also "a hater of extracts and omissions," as he declares in the anthology *The Shock of Recognition*, there explaining, "I have printed the whole of everything." Though he later regretted not putting the De Forest portrait in an appendix, Meyer's only success appears to have been with the question "Do you really need to include Lanier's poem on mahogany furniture?"

The book recovers pace and focus in the dialectical tour de force "The Chastening of American Prose Style." Wilson sets the moral eloquence and speculative refinement of Hawthorne and Melville, rooted in the influence of the diary, the sermon, and the Romantic movement, alongside their lack of narrative momentum—"the close-knit blocks of *Moby Dick*," he states, "have to be surmounted one by one," and *Billy Budd*'s "huge units" put him to sleep when he tries reading it at night in bed. Through Edward Everett's high-flown, two-hour oration at Gettysburg he moves to Lincoln's lucidity and force, then relates the terseness of the Gettysburg Address to Mark Twain's prose, both reflecting the directness of the West and the need to address the "plain man," the effect of mechanization. The war forwarded a precise new "language of responsibility," the style of Lincoln and Grant and the soldier-officers from Bierce to Holmes, who had "to convince and direct," had no time to temporize or to waste words. It is no surprise that someone shaped by his World War I experience and committed to writing as action prefers this style to the ambiguity, prolixity, and irony of the American Renaissance of the 1850s and of Adams and James, who, escaping combat, fulfilled themselves at the century's end. Wilson had never much liked Henry Adams, whose sentences he'd called "weakbacked." In *Patriotic Gore* he states that the account of Grant's presidency in the *Education* wavers "between a mood of ironic malice" at the expense of this sordid era and "the consciousness of a personal inadequacy that he fears is his own fault." Adams undermined his favorite friends in describing them and seemed "sometimes to be undermining the Republic itself." Henry James fled the war's moral demands via the dubious injury he called his "obscure hurt," but courageously pursued his vocation, at the cost of fears of sexual incapacity and periods of debility during his later years. Admiring men of action and planning his career like a military campaign, he eventually worked his way back to a prose with the old embroidery and poetic eloquence.

In a lyrical passage in the chapter on Civil War verse, Wilson looks back to the fresh breezes of the early nineteenth century, when Americans were independent men in a new country. As entranced by Jefferson's architecture as Goethe was by the Palladian style in Italy, he notes how "the slight irregularity in the number and spacing of the pillars" in the colonnade at the University of Virginia "only make them blend more pleasantly with nature." He catches the colors and animation of Audubon's animal plates, "the red-bellied squirrels with their plum-like blend of rose-orange and purple-gray." He evokes the "brightness and freshness in the poems and notebooks of Emerson, in the liquidities and densities of *Walden*, in the vividness of Melville's voyages."

The transformation of the culture by the war is rendered in the concluding figure of four-times-wounded Justice Holmes. Experience killed Holmes's ardent support of the abolitionist cause and made him momentarily ready to accept Southern independence, given the size of "the butcher's bill." He learned that war was slavery's brother, indeed its parent, in barbarity, and doubted the army could achieve "the subjugation—for that is it—of a great civilized nation" (though at another time he doubted whether Southerners were very civilized). He brought out of the conflict a character "purposive, disciplined, and not a little hard," with a contempt for cant, seeing law as the expression of the dominant will of any considerable group and (a favorite aphorism) society "founded on the death of men." Wilson moves from young Wendell's letters to his parents, in one of which, underlining the phrase, he states that his conception of his duty has changed, to his record of the night when, apparently dying of a chest wound at Ball's Bluff, he preferred to risk Hell rather than recant his doubt that God existed. This portrait—one both echoed and qualified in the Holmes of Louis Menand's *The Metaphysical Club*—draws on Wilson's loss of Christianity in youth and of the Marxist faith at the end of the thirties.

Wilson's Holmes illustrates the process by which he animates and identifies with his subjects. He starts with quotations, noted his typist Edmunds, "and, getting them in order before him," adds "his very first thoughts, and builds and builds." Long talks with the justice's associates, law clerks, and secretaries, including Francis Biddle, FDR's attorney general, and Justice Frankfurter (their friendship having recovered from the *Hecate County* decision), helped Wilson perceive how a Brahmin's training insulated Holmes and entered into his philosophy of the law. Detached from the deterioration of public life during the gilded age—"I don't read the papers," Holmes noted as early as 1905, "or otherwise feel the pulse of the machine"—he brought to what he called a "jobbist"'s code the need "to assure one's ever-doubting soul" of having "touched the superlative" in his work, phrasing in which Wilson recognized the Calvinist idea of Election. Committed to "the great world of thought and art," Holmes was trying "to determine man's place, to define his satisfactions and duties, to understand what humanity is." Wilson mines his letters to Laski and particularly the British lawyer Frederick Pollock for a commentary on everyone from Jane Austen to Marx, while showing how Holmes's belief in a capitalist marketplace squared with his eloquent dissents over labor issues and governmental abridgment of free speech.

In *A Piece of My Mind* Wilson states that Holmes "*identified* his own interests with those of the American Republic." So did Wilson, and as if to remind us that a critic of his country's mythology may be the most orthodox of patriots, in the last paragraph of this portrait and the book he waves what, in his letters, he more than once calls Old Glory. He reports that two explanations have been proposed to him as to why the childless Justice left his money to the United States rather than to such an institution as Harvard Law School. One was that, walled off in a solitary egotism, he could think of nothing better to do with it. The possibility that Holmes knew exactly what he was doing sets up Wilson's measured conclusion: "He had fought for the Union; he had mastered its laws; he had served in its highest court through a period of three decades. The American Constitution was, as he came to declare, an experiment—what was to come of our democratic society it was impossible for a philosopher to tell—but he had taken responsibility for its working, he had subsisted and achieved his fame through his tenure of the place it had given him; and he returned to the treasury of the Union the little that he had to leave."

PART SIX

"My Books Live,
I Am Ceasing to Live"

30

Husband and Father

∞

Edmund and Elena

Patriotic Gore, an exception among Wilson's books, was a success immediately on publication. David Donald, who was to write a great biography of Lincoln, cited its "exhaustive, brilliant analysis" and "profound and disturbing reexamination of our intellectual history." C. Vann Woodward, dean of Southern historians, wrote that "no single work goes deeper into the meaning and the implications" of the war "for its more articulate participants," while Allan Nevins believed this "the best book ever done about the Civil War." With the exception of Perry Miller, the interpreter of the Puritans, who thought Wilson insufficiently credited his sources and should have paid more attention to major writers, the literary world was enthusiastic. Elizabeth Hardwick said that no other book could "make us feel our country so strongly." Three decades later, the art critic Jed Perl made the same point. Perl characterized the "density" of *Patrotic Gore*, its "way of going into people's lives, seeing people coping with their lives, day by day, all kinds of very specific tiny things in the lives of all kinds of people," and labeled it one of the greatest books "about the cultural experience of this country."

Wilson's personality was now more openly present in his work. Whether he wrote of the Civil War period, of writers of the 1920s or the Old World, or found his materials on the Indian reservations and in Israel and Jordan, he invested his subjects with an importance he could assume when writing of Joyce or Marx. The aging critic became something of a celebrity. Alfred Kazin describes him on the beach dubbed by the historian Stuart Hughes *"la plage des intellectuels"* at Wellfleet. In a stained old Panama hat, a large white dress shirt hanging down over his paunch and baggy tan bathing suit, a gold-topped cane that had been his father's planted in the sand, he held forth in his "high painfully distinct voice" about his current interests or reading, talking as if "reluctant to talk but too stubborn to stop," to the professors and the "television producers, government and U.N. advisors" who might be gathered around the "lonely proud face," the eccentric bulky man.

He continually received letters from people he didn't know, often requests for assistance, and usually having no secretary, he devised the engraved card "Edmund Wilson Regrets That It Is Impossible For Him To," with a list of twenty-one items from "Read Manuscripts" to "Supply Opinions on Literary or Other Subjects." It would be sent off with a check beside the line applicable. This card strengthened the impression of a difficult, irascible man made by his battle with Nabokov and by polemics against the IRS and the Modern Language Association. Yet Wilson did most of the things on this list for purposes he approved, from introducing a book on Dickens, a reissue of Aubrey's *Brief Lives* or Turgenev's *Literary Reminiscences*, to writing a hundred or so recommendations for Guggenheim fellowships, with a success rate of nearly 50 percent. As in youth, he maintained a huge correspondence. In the McCarthy years he had sometimes fallen into the old nocturnal habit of writing letters till four a.m., and they continued to flow in his more ordered life with Elena. The 70,000 or so of Wilson's letters at the Beinecke Library chart relationships with everyone from editors and publishers to the New Jersey liquor dealer who discussed Hebrew forms with him and sent him bottles of whiskey. Letters were not all Wilson sent through the mails—when his old acquaintance Conrad Aiken called his prose boring, he sent Aiken a mechanical bat in a box, which, the poet reported, "flew right into my face where it fluttered affectionately, then went to heel."

It was easier for Wilson to occupy his literary persona than to be without it, and his friends collaborated, for they were also admirers. They knew him, as it were, in costume—the Brooks Brothers suit, the paisley tie, the ancient well-kept brown shoes in which he greeted one at the bar in the Princeton Club and ordered half a dozen of their small martinis or Johnnie Walker Red Label. Jason Epstein, who on the night the two men met ordered several martinis of his own, would think Wilson "always inventing a scene, impersonating himself." Talcottville was to Epstein a literary creation. Though the highway seemed "right under the porch"—it would be more so when part of Wilson's lawn was taken to widen the road—and the traffic zipping by included those he called "the juvenile delinquents" on their motorcycles, as he stood by the front door "in his white linen suit and his panama hat, with his cane" and waved to acquaintances while he waited for a ride, he seemed to Epstein to enact the part of "some sort of patriarch or patroon." When upstate, Wilson also easily stepped back into the 1920s, singing a song of the vintage of Louise and Henrietta Fort's "Forsaken" in his "well-cadenced little tenor" as they rode down the highway:

> You can easily see she's not my sweetie,
> Cuz my sweetie's more refined.
> She's just a poor little kid, who don't know what she did.
> She's a personal friend of mine!

These lyrics took him back to the world of Margaret and Frances.

Dorothea Straus has pictured him against the backdrop of his "meandering book-lined workroom" at Wellfleet, with the stuffed owl that many noted looked remarkably like its owner. Mrs. Straus, herself a writer of literary memoirs, had been eager to meet this American Gibbon or Johnson, and he was as intimidating as she expected: "his snappish comments, his talent for utter silence that was even more disconcerting, his explosive laughter that sounded as though it were erupting over obstacles, like a dammed waterfall forcing its way between heavy boulders." Presiding at the table in his bathrobe and pajamas on mornings when there were guests, "he had round, protruding, claret-colored eyes under hooded lids—the eyes of the perpetual scholar most at ease when cast down upon the pages of a book. Yet when he raised them to the world about him, nothing escaped their reddish brown stare." This was the Wilson who categorized people in his journals and mined them fiercely if they had knowledge of subjects he was investigating. He told them what to read as well, and at a subsequent meeting was likely to inquire if they'd complied and what they made of the books.

Elena's spirit also reigned at the Wellfleet house. When Dorothea met her "she was wearing a faded checked gingham shirtwaist dress, her sunburned legs were scratched from berry picking and dotted with mosquito bites," and her feet "were bare. Yet there was about her an air of regality." A strong intuition or sixth sense enabled her to exclaim "Edmund is approaching!" when the car that was bringing him was perhaps forty minutes away. Despite her formidable intellect, Mrs. Straus pictured her against the backdrop of the *"hôtels splendides"* of her youth or on ski slopes with the aristocracy. Elena swam in the Atlantic late into the fall. When

Dorothea one summer day joined her in the buffeting waves and later washed off the salt and sand in a nearby freshwater pond, she remarked, as her friend's face emerged from the water with her hair slicked back, that she looked like Greta Garbo. Elena, however, scowled and said, "Oh, all that is finished."

To Marie-Claire Blais a decade later Elena said that the luxury of her youth was well lost, for it might have kept her from understanding "that true life lies in simplicity, that's where one's faith in God is hidden, and that true love lies there as well." The young woman—who in *The Sixties* Wilson sees given to a cult of "*angoisse*"—thought Elena "plagued by inner tensions, by some obscure duty of a seemingly religious nature," and noted she sometimes referred to people she admired as saints. When she spoke of a youth with the beauty of "a young God" who, fearing the rise of Nazism in his country, had mysteriously drowned in a lake during an outing with friends, the French-Canadian novelist took this as the symbol of a Germany forever gone. Yet Blais was not impressed when Elena said "that men must be placed above women and a woman must respect and obey her husband," a code she tried to fulfill, even when tempted by Helen's feminism. Wilson reported to Dawn Powell that his wife typed his memoir of Millay by day and listened to him read it to her by night— "'I think Elena is getting rather sick of it,' Bunny said with an embarrassed smile," and he found others to type his manuscripts.

Elena also made the house run smoothly, miraculously enabling a man without much money to lead, for the first time, the life of a literary gentleman. By three thirty or so, when he'd fulfilled his quota of six— later it was seven—legal-sized pages and perhaps also found time for letters or to write in his journal, she was ready for his jovial emergence from the study for a walk or an expedition. This was followed by listening to records or seeing friends, for whom she could work up a good meal on little notice, serving quality food and drink on what she saved in other ways, as by driving their own car, so they wouldn't have to go everywhere in a taxi. The Walkers, the Chavchavadzes, the Jenckses, or old college friends passing by might stop in; Peggy Bacon or Dawn Powell might be visiting the Wilsons. Edmund and Elena complemented each other in company. The balance of the American and European view made them a Jamesian couple, and Robert Lowell wrote to Wilson, "It's rare when both husband and wife are delightful and brilliant—always something goes wrong. I have so many old friends married to blocks. Then there are the great ladies, who charm the world and let their husbands crawl on hands and knees. Anyway, you both seem to have it right."

But, behind the scenes there were arguments, often provoked by his drinking. With Elena's help Wilson could stop for months, even a year, yet he always came back to it. Sometimes she hid the liquor, and Adelaide Walker once saw her hurl a bottle as far as she could out the kitchen door. When intoxicated he could fall into "bouts of unprovoked anger," and in an instance mentioned in the journal she lost her temper and kicked her shoe off at him, sending it to the ceiling. Half seriously, Elena would negotiate something for the house in terms of bottles of Scotch whiskey ("Come on, Edmund, let's have the lawn mower repaired; it's only ten bottles of Johnnie Walker"). Though he needed someone to look after him, Wilson rebelled against her managerial tendencies, saying about his wife the same thing he says of his mother in "The Author at Sixty," that she liked to have the people she loved "dependent on her." In the journal he recognizes "my frequent dreams of alienations and separations from Elena" as signs of the same need to assert his independence in which he'd let Margaret Canby "go off to Santa Barbara, where she died. Now in dreams I want her back. I have Elena but dream of leaving her." From the beginning of their marriage he left on reporting assignments, and by the mid-1950s they were separating for his trips back and forth to Talcottville. There, he could drink more freely, and he eventually found younger women to drive him around and keep him company when he wasn't working.

Elena and he had what turned out to be a second honeymoon in Paris in 1956, produced, as he said, by "the atmosphere of Paris, the freedom of being away from home." She wasn't keeping house and Wilson was in better physical shape, not drinking hard liquor, less on edge than when, at home, "the American drama" past and present preoccupied him. But in a restaurant mirror he contrasted "my big-bellied person and my red and swollen face, with a not too pleasant expression about the eyes and mouth," to Elena's "exquisite slimness and delicacy." In Paris she seemed "more than ever divine." It was her city, and her intelligence, initiative, character stood out among her Russian relatives. He liked "to hear her expounding America and crying up its merits," was reminded that "the unique person Elena" was "something she had created herself," through her capacity to love, that "love is creative as well as art." To contemplate her loving nature gave him, he says, "an erection as I write."

Back in the States their "erotic revival" had to compete with illnesses and dental problems, the argument about where to live (there was talk, which he didn't encourage, of finding a new place between Wellfleet and Talcottville), and the income tax mess that soon descended. However, he recounts a "delicious and wonderful" encounter on the blue divan in the middle room in November 1958 ("We loved each other afterwards") and the next year on the dune of a nominal island (they moved "back so we shouldn't fall over. Her blue clothes and white body made a harmony with the seascape. Afterwards I was thankful that love was lasting for me so long and remaining so satisfying").

Philip Hamburger believed that, in Elena, Wilson thought he had found the perfect woman, but that his restless Faustian spirit kept him searching. Rather fatuously noting that "irregular love affairs" were "a nuisance" and he was too closely tied to Elena "to be seriously tempted by other women," he was nonetheless tempted by Mary Meigs, who, with Barbara Deming, now owned a house at the Cape. Mary had silvery hair, was blue-eyed, *spirituelle*, but intent and directed, Barbara pale, fine-featured, with big brown eyes, straight dark hair and bangs, a plain face that had a Pre-Raphaelite beauty. Both were well born and cultivated, and the Meigses, as they were sometimes known, were popular at Wellfleet. He pronounced that Mary's painting showed great talent, and Barbara, who helped him with the second Pasternak article, in which he "played" *Doctor Zhivago*, was writing poetry. When he summoned them to his home, Mary, humorously embarrassed at the memory of their "doggy devotion," says "we fell under the spell of Edmund, triumphant," his face "pink and freshly-shaved" as he emerged from his music-filled study, "doing his card tricks, playing Authors, anagrams, Chinese checkers, *bouts rimés*." *The Fifties* contains samples of the end-rhyming sonnets the two women created alongside him in the lonely winter evenings when, as Meigs recalled, "good friends were scarce and life so austere that many Wellfleetians took to drink or escaped in other ways."

There was an intellectual current between him and Mary, and he was drawn to her physically somewhat as he'd been to virginal, refined Leonie Adams. Mary, fearful "of bodies, of kisses, of passion," was thrilled and wary when Wilson began saying he was in love with her. One evening he said, "You're really a sort of lesbian, aren't you?" and she left the house upset and spent a sleepless night, for she still, she says, "lived in the shadowy world of denial and pretense." The next morning he called to apologize. Drawn to the male power she feared but associated with artistic greatness, Mary accepted his kisses: "I did not want Edmund to be in love with me; I could not believe he really was, yet I was afraid he would cease to be, knowing the indifference that follows on the heels of love." Elena remained on good terms with her, saying "she was the only person since we've been married he's been seriously interested in" and "I don't make a fuss, because she's a lesbian. I do say, 'Let's see who will do what with whom.'" Mary then fell in love with Marie-Claire Blais, Wilson's French-Canadian protégée, and Marie-Claire moved in with the two women. For several years Mary and Barbara slept in one room, Marie-Claire in another; Mary was her lover, while Barbara said goodnight to her. In the Cape community Mary was missed more than Marie-Claire when these two departed, eventually settling in Montreal.

Through the late fifties and early sixties Elena had to cope with Wilson's tax delinquency, something impossible for him to do. Lucky to make ends meet while producing his books and articles, he had rarely earned enough money to have to pay taxes and was ignorant of the tax laws. At some point near the beginning of their marriage she discovered he had paid nothing as far back as 1940, a scary situation. He had made little during the war and tax was withheld from his salary at *The New Yorker*. Yet *Hecate County* earned him a good deal (he vaguely assumed it could be spread across the three years when the book was written) and the British edition eventually brought in $25,000, a later option on the film rights another substantial sum. Tax was withheld from the $5,000 paid him for the Gauss seminars, but in 1953 he'd begun receiving an annual income of $8,500 from his mother's trust fund. Two years later Elena took the situation to a lawyer recommended by John Biggs, but Wilson wanted it handled by his old friend John Amen. Before he and Elena left for Europe in 1956 he paid his taxes, having made more money than usual due to the popularity of *The Scrolls from the Dead Sea*. His $9,000 check to the IRS, however, bounced, and Amen never filed the $7,500 replacement check that Wilson left, nor did Amen file for 1956 or '57, or tell the couple they should file even if they couldn't pay the whole amount owed. Arthur Schlesinger largely attributed Wilson's tax troubles to "a drunken lawyer."

The IRS caught up with him in 1958. In "My View" Elena reports taking a suitcase filled with canceled checks to Talcottville, where she laid them out on tables and prepared the returns for two decades. That fall, as a New York State resident, Wilson was tried in Utica, his lawyer a local politician Elena distrusted, before the same judge he had attacked for a decision against the Iroquois. He pled guilty of failing to report $16,949 in income in 1957. The judge treated him, he thought, very fairly, dismissing the other criminal charges, fining him $7,500 for this failure to file, and lecturing him about leaving everything in Amen's hands. He borrowed the $7,500 from Roman Grynberg and Barbara Deming, but with penalties on the cumulative amounts unreported (50 percent for fraud, 25 percent for delinquency, 5 percent for failure to file, and 10 percent for allegedly underestimating his income) plus interest at 6 percent, he owed between $68,000 and $69,000. The IRS began seizing his royalties and his income from the trust fund. He had a windfall when Roger Straus was able to bring out an edition of *Hecate County* under the imprint of L.C. Page in Philadelphia. He made his initial deal with Straus on the journals, getting $5,000 apiece for them.

In the winters from 1957 to 1961 he worked on *Patriotic Gore* in Harvard's Widener Library, content with a sandwich and a bottle of ginger ale for lunch. Allergic to the dust from the musty books he brought back to his study from the stacks, he had sneezing fits and came to regard these as the scholar's malady. Among his more serious complaints was gout, and when the sulfa drugs didn't work they "made him crazy." Elena and Helen weren't happy in Cambridge. However, in 1959–1960, saddled with a large debt to the government, he accepted a year's appointment as Lowell Professor of English at Harvard. Arranged by Harry Levin, it was temporarily held up by Wilson's refusal to sign the Massachusetts loyalty oath, but by the fall of 1959 the family had moved into a semidetached house he liked more than his wife and daughter did, with a bay window on the second floor, a side porch, a small garden, and woodwork similar to that at 12 Wallace Street in Red Bank. This was when Mary Meigs gave them an old Plymouth and Elena learned to drive. Elena wasn't the only person who thought the English department treated the great journalist-critic shabbily, but stimulating writers and speakers passing through were glad to meet him—Isaac Bashevis Singer, dissident European intellectuals, Robert Oppenheimer and George Kennan, the last of whom shared Wilson's view that Stalin was responsible for the murder of Kirov. There were parties to accompany readings by Auden and Lowell. He found companionship among the historians Arthur Schlesinger, Stuart Hughes, and Richard Pipes, as well as with the writer Monroe Engel, who lived across the street.

Wilson taught two courses. In his comparative literature seminar, a throwback to the age before Great Books courses in translation, students had to know Latin and one modern language beside English. Though some dropped the course, Renata Adler—who "got in on German"—was excited by the contact with Wilson's circle. The subject was the representational and evocative use of language from the *Aeneid* to Proust and Joyce. He showed how Dante's Italian can vary from large and sonorous to swift and petty to serene, how Flaubert's irony is extended by his sound effects in the famous passage from *Madame Bovary* where the old peasant woman is given a medal for half a century of servitude. Wilson's lectures on the Civil War literature were, however, tense for him and awkward for his hundred students, the critic wheezing and stuttering and stopping to edit his text as he read, turning it around to add sentences in the margins. There were always papers to read, and after grading one batch, irritated by poor grammar and word usage, he astounded a student auditing the course by going down the class list "complimenting those by name who did well and mercilessly criticizing by name those who did not!" Meeting students outside class wasn't easy, for his reputation was intimidating and he had no small talk. There was a jar of sour balls on the desk, which he would offer in an effort to break the ice.

"I will really need a Vera Nabokov when I am teaching," he had written to Elena during the summer, contrary to what he'd once said. He complained that if she wasn't "willing to live where I have to live and to interest yourself in what I am doing," he didn't "know how we can see much of one another except by taking occasional vacations together." As he struggled to start both courses and get *Apologies to the Iroquois* into print, he thought she might at least help him leave the house with the right books in the morning. But he knew there was less for Elena in Cambridge than for him. She missed Wellfleet, where she found clarity in her routine beside the North Atlantic and had close neighbors. Wilson characteristically believed she'd be happier if she resumed her painting.

Elena wasn't threatened by Mary Meigs, but she was jealous when she had reason to be, and remarked to Rosalind that she wouldn't be "kicked out" of Wilson's bed "like the others," meaning Canby and Blair. In June 1960 he persuaded a Radcliffe undergraduate in his seminar to come and be his secretary at the Cape, and in less than a month Frances Nevada Swisher typed and indexed the whole proliferating text of *Patriotic Gore*. A serious quarrel with his wife ensued. Though Frances was engaged to, and then married, a graduate student whom she'd met in Wilson's sem-

inar (he gave them an Audubon print as a present), he praised her qualities in a way that caused Elena to feel "hurt, jealous, insulted." Afterward,
from Talcottville, he denied what may well have been an infatuation, saying that he'd been "accomplishing prodigies" with Swisher until Elena made
this impossible. When she said that people talked, he replied that they
talked about her when he was away from Wellfleet (which appears to have
been true), and that he had his jealous moments but was "fundamentally
sure that you and I loved each other." Humiliated by her loss of self-control,
she accused him of pushing her to the edge and likened him to a scorpion, then "had a kind of collapse." In retrospect Frances presented herself as oblivious of the situation, finding Wilson fun to work for and a
good family man, noting the walks the couple took every afternoon at the
Cape as indications of their closeness rather than as the tense exchanges
that must have been going on.

That upstate New York was the center of the tax struggle—though
Boston lawyers helped straighten things out—didn't make Elena more eager for her yearly two weeks there, weeks that confirmed her irritation
with this scene her mate romanticized. Her birthday fell during the August days that became her yearly commitment upstate, and Wilson celebrated this in verses meant to sell her on the place:

> My darling, I am trying still
> To make you not hate Talcottville.

One year his salesmanship turned testy:

> Elena de Mumm
>   Says, "This is a tomb!
>   Talcottville
>   Makes me ill."
> So here are some presents
> From Talcottville peasants
> Who fear she may languish in anguish and gloom.

For her part, Elena came to dislike what she saw as Wilson's feudal airs
in Talcottville. She thought him absurd to "walk through the village with
his cane nodding 'how do, how do'" to a populace mired in ignorance, the
women vulgar and "doughy," the mentally ill barely hidden in the back-

ground. At the Cape this sophisticated woman lived without snobbery among a population of equally low income people, friends with families neither affluent nor educated. But the pretensions of a modest upstate gentry turned her off as did the landscape, and the stone house seemed to her permeated by the quarrels it had known and bred, including hers with Edmund. She wished she could have it blessed by a Russian priest.

For Wilson this was an alternate household such as his mother's house had been, and he duplicated some of the Wellfleet accessories, buying a second croquet set, a second puppet theater. A source of resentment, it also served as a safety valve in their marriage, minimizing tensions elsewhere. Elena was enabled to compartmentalize, identifying what was most difficult for her with Wilson upstate. When at Talcottville, he usually reassured her that he was behaving himself: "I had some very good days of concentration and little eating and no drinking before Dawn and Margaret [de Silver] came," he writes; "I have now made myself a routine here and have accomplished a great deal—have got off since Nina [Chavchavadze] left the whole of the Seneca chapter and the revised *Hecate County*—and done very little drinking, usually two bottles of Molson's ale at dinner, which stops me automatically, because you can't possibly drink a third and I don't keep anything else in the house." But when Elena arrived in August 1962 he recalled that he was tense from not having had a drink—in Helen's recollection "he'd been drinking for a while when we arrived." After his wife said, "So-and-so sends you lots of love" for "about the fifth time," he rudely cut her off, upon which she burst into tears and asked whether he didn't want "to hear about anybody but these *govna* [Russian for shits] up here?"

Each recorded the quarrel on her birthday two days later, Wilson in his journal and Elena in "My View." At the Cape he'd bought a little painting she'd admired, but had forgotten to tell her to bring it along, and when he spoke of it she said, "Send it back to the dealers," then—because of their financial problems—"Sell it back." After the dinner guests, her friend Malcolm Sharp and his wife, Wilson's cousin Dorothy Furbish, left, he said she hadn't been to bed with him for a long time, that he was depressed and needed sympathy, something, she replied, that everybody needed. He threw at her an old copy of F. R. Leavis's magazine *Scrutiny*, which hit the wall by the door, and when she came in to make up, instead of going over to kiss her "threw at her another magazine, a larger and thinner one, which flapped and fell on the floor" (thus the aging Wilson renders his sense of ineffectuality). They realized that thirteen-year-old Helen was probably "hearing it all through the radiator pipe in the living-room ceiling." When they went upstairs Wilson records Elena saying "she didn't like my 'spongy body,'" which, he ruefully adds, "may well be true," and "she spat at me about Mary Pcolar," now typing his letters, teaching him Hungarian, and acting as his chauffeur.

Elena recalled the quarrel as provoked by her jealousy of Pcolar. She hadn't yet met Mary and wouldn't read about her until *Upstate*, at the end of Wilson's life, but recognized this as another one of his interests/infatuations. She must have tried to hit him, for she writes, "Hysteria on my part and it came to blows—degrading and ugly. Helen woke up and I got into bed with her. She was sobbing and kept saying: let's go home. She then quieted down and went to sleep. In the morning I packed our bags and told Edmund we were leaving." In his journal Wilson notes that she declared, "This is the abyss." On the way back she considered leaving him, according to Helen, but she was thinking, too, of Malcolm Sharp's advice that she should have stayed in Talcottville. The next day she reassured Wilson with a telegram from Wellfleet, "ARRIVED LAST NIGHT VERY SORRY HAVE WRITTEN LOVE." Before it came, however, he'd "had most of a pint of Scotch," and when Mary, after her late afternoon appointment to type for him, was leaving he tried to turn on the light on the porch but instead turned off the light in the hall, then kissed her on the neck in the dark.

Helen, Reuel, and Rosalind

Though their marriage was sometimes "stormy" and divorce more than once mentioned, Wilson's modus vivendi with Elena endured until the end of the 1960s, when failing health and morale caused him to drift away from her. He cared deeply about her, and her Parisian cousin Marina Schouvaloff remembered how, once on the beach, after a hot and difficult day and a swim, Elena read an article of his in *The New Yorker* and, as she got up, brushed the sand away and, smiling, said, "When I read his work I forgive him all his sins." He tried to care about his children, to believe in their abilities and foster them when he could. He wrote to a friend that "as they get older" they "become continually more interesting." Yet he was too caught up in himself and his interests and his alcoholism to be fully engaged as a father, telling his neighbor Mary Hackett (and doubtless others) that he "wasn't cut out for it." Mary Meigs, his loving admirer, wrote, "Personally I would not have liked to have him for a father and would have been frightened by his changes of mood." He was hard on the children—"strict and tough," in the words of his stepson Henry Thornton, who spoke of having "had the best of it." Two of his three children have confided in print their disappointments in and anger at him.

With Helen, whose mother, unlike Rosalind's or for that matter Reuel's, was a full-time functional presence, his relationship turned out better, because he stepped back, didn't interfere as much as he had with the others, and let Elena do the parenting. He loved "the little girl" and diligently read to her in the evenings. In an effort to ally Cape Cod with upstate New York he elaborated a bedtime story about a mermaid who lived in the Adirondacks. When Helen said, "This beautiful little white butterfly flies through the air with the greatest of ease," he was proud of her gift for words, and at about this age she wrote:

Dear, dear Father: I love you just as much as I love my Mummy.

Little dove
Fly away
Carry this note
To my father.

Wilson was, however, a terrible teacher of his own, and on her sixth birthday, at the Salzburg seminar, he tried to give her a lesson in Greek before she had her party and cake. Helen refused to appear at the party until her father left the room. At a later point she announced, "I am not Edmund Wilson's daughter. I am Elena Wilson's daughter." In a posed photograph at ten or twelve she resembles both parents, sitting between them, one hand in a hand of each. "Her expression, honest and penetrating, was her father's," Dorothea Straus thought, "her young lips molded in the shape of his eloquent severity."

Marie-Claire Blais recalls Helen, on her way to a career as a painter, as "a flamboyant flower-child," and Mrs. Straus remembers Wilson saying, "Bring in the 'hippies,'" when long-haired youths and maidens without bras entered the room. Helen studied Russian for a time at Barnard before going to art school. Afterward she continued to paint for years in her studio and began showing her work, while her mother helped to support her, aided by a legacy from Elena's sister Olga. Elena would never know the extent to which her faith in Helen's abilities was justified. Her small paintings are evocative, mysteriously erotic. Her landscapes and cloud studies have been said to "glow with a delicate and poetic light," and she has done a series of overlay paintings, like palimpsests, inspired in part by poems written on the windowpanes in the Wellfleet and Talcottville houses. She has had one-woman exhibitions mainly in New York City, and her work is included in public collections, among them the Hirshhorn Museum and the Metropolitan Museum of Art.

Helen told her mother she was "much luckier" than her siblings because her parents were married, and in "My View" Elena is pleased by the report that she has said, "*My* parents are happily married." In retrospect she took a hardheaded view of their partnership, stressing that each wanted to satisfy practical needs and believing her father made the better bargain. Her attitude toward Wilson, who died when she was twenty-four, is complex. Distressed by his flirtations, she saw him trying "to release the infantile part of himself" in his drinking and, when she read his journals, in the sometimes biting comments on people there. If introduced as Edmund Wilson's daughter Helen has remarked, "I'm not Edmund Wilson's daughter, I'm myself." She is clearly proud to be his daughter, yet hasn't, like Rosalind, confused her identity with her father's.

Reuel Wilson, as his stepfather Bowden Broadwater put it, has been "his own person." Until he went off to boarding school at eleven he lived with Mary and Bowden, spending vacations with Edmund and Elena. Bowden, whom he loved, recalled him as "witty, natural, and quite a good little observer." Bowden thought he'd eased the boy's fear of Wilson, and though Reuel didn't enjoy the approach of summer or its opening days, in retrospect he appreciated the books and nature walks and the dogs he and his father shared, calling Reckie (short for Rex) and Bambi "two of the best friends I had for many summers running." During the school year Wilson wrote to him conscientiously with the Wellfleet news, always including news of the dogs. Reuel had a special relationship with Elena, who helped his father and him get on easier terms while fostering him and his friends. In his recollection, this European woman even once swam nude with him at Gull Pond. His other three parents took Victorian attitudes toward his emerging sexual instinct, Mary and Bowden advising that some things were best kept to oneself, while Wilson, the old celebrator of pleasure, declared (as he believed) that the purpose of sex was to procreate.

Like his siblings, Reuel endured his father's ventures into home-schooling, in his case summer sessions in Latin and Greek prosody. He had to memorize "Catullus's moving poem on his brother's death" and "Tennyson's equally moving evocation of Catullus, inspired by the death of his brother Charles." By the time he complained to his mother, Wilson had added "Omar Khayyam," since Reuel, he told Mary, claimed an interest in Persian poetry. Good training for a future linguist, it came at a high psychic price. Remembering these "dreaded" hours, Reuel states that only "through my mother's gentle persuasion" did he learn "to call him Father, as he wished to be known."

Wilson had won legal authority over the boy's education, and with Mary and Bowden they visited boarding schools, four or five people piling out of the coupe in front of the headmaster's house. Wilson was pleased to see him mature at the Brooks School, yet chose his first year's courses when Reuel went on to Harvard. To Helen Sootin Smith, a graduate student whose prose style Wilson liked and who said that her father had taught her to write, he lamented that his son hadn't a better style. But over the years, Reuel would write intelligent, cordial letters to him. Elena believed that father and son had "a good adult relationship," and in the eyes of his roommate, Lowell Edmunds, who as Wilson's secretary saw much of the family, they got along well enough. Edmunds recalled Reuel's admiring account of Wilson at Talcottville, "sitting on the front porch with a drink in his hand after a night's work, watching the sun come up and unapproachable." When he told Mary that his father wasn't an intellectual but a literary man, she passed this on, knowing Wilson would like the distinction.

His use of the word "unapproachable" marks, however, the barrier Wilson had faced with his own father, who in childhood had frightened him. Though a portraitist of artist heroes, Wilson related more warmly to women than to men. He tried to be flexible with the boy. When Reuel didn't make much of a summer job Mary had arranged at the office of the Congress for Cultural Freedom in Paris, Wilson noted that he ended up "doing just what I thought he wanted to do: bumming around Italy on a motorcycle." Mary, who was always proud that Reuel was Edmund Wilson's son, said, "Edmund loved Reuel," though he expressed this awkwardly. Her love was extravagantly expressed. When Reuel was living in Warsaw to learn Polish and she visited her future husband, James West, there, she reported to Wilson that "he sailed into" a discussion of the movie *Hiroshima Mon Amour* "like an old *Partisan Review* contributor," that she "nearly kissed him and told him he was a true son of his parents." In London he had "stayed with the Spenders, saw Isaiah, Cyril, Stuart Hampshire, etc.," from whom she'd gotten "a shower of compliments for him." In such letters Mary seems entirely unaware that her pressure may be difficult.

Reuel's graduate education at Berkeley and Wisconsin wasn't always smooth sailing—it took him a while to get A's in his courses, he told his father—but each parent sent money and provided moral support. Wilson, less directive than Mary, admired him for finishing the Ph.D., with a dissertation on the travelogue in Russian literature. When he got a job at the University of Chicago, Wilson visited him there and found him enthusiastic about "the good that he thought might come from teaching foreign languages—the general understanding that might be prompted by exact comprehension of what other peoples were saying." The journal sketches Reuel's view of teaching versus research and other issues. In 1970 he got what became a permanent post as a professor at the University of Western Ontario. His parents would have rejoiced had he been a distinguished scholar, but as a linguist and translator of Russian he brought precision to a subject of which his father wrote sometimes inexactly, if with ease and passion. He corrected the proofs of *A Window on Russia* in 1971, at one point rather academically attempting to fortify Wilson's critique of Nabokov. Over the years he has also translated and reviewed Polish poetry.

While Reuel's correspondence with Wilson supports Elena's belief that he had overcome childhood resentments, that is not the impression made by the brief account of "Growing Up with Edmund Wilson and Mary McCarthy" (1999), written as a preface to a promised collection of their letters to him. Remembering the dreaded summer poetry lessons, he also reveals the scar that survived in the soul of the small boy who witnessed his father's "violent rages" at his mother. Though Reuel doesn't suggest that Wilson ever hit McCarthy—strong evidence that he did not—or that she wasn't equally responsible for their quarrels, he sees his father in the image of "the minotaur in a maze." Roger Straus believed that he had heard this language too often, and in what amounts to a p.s. to the account of his parents published about the same time, Reuel alludes to

Wilson's "sleeping lairs" about the house. The anger in "Growing Up" was perhaps deepened by Wilson's choice of Elena as his literary executor, not finding a role there for his son, and by a last-minute effort to deed the Wellfleet house, after Elena's life tenancy, to Helen rather than leave it to be shared. Yet Reuel shows no resentment of the mother who, Frances Kiernan informs us, failed to leave her only child a share of her estate. He was fortunate to inherit, under French law, half the proceeds from the sale of her valuable apartment in Paris, amounting to several hundred thousand dollars.

In "Growing Up" his parents are named EW and MM and his relationships with them evoked by photographs of himself with each, pictures by Cartier-Bresson that are included in the text. Leaning toward Mary with an arm around her shoulder, he smiles entertainingly, while with Wilson he looks as though he wants to bolt. "His hands rest heavily on my shoulders," Reuel writes. "My face is averted to one side and I am scowling." Has he chosen this photograph because of the story it tells, or does the picture shape what he says? At sixty-five, in person and on video, Reuel looks remarkably like his father, a Wilson with a little of McCarthy's smile but less intense than his parents. One wonders whether he was ever able to confront his father, and one recalls the message in which the child, at four or five, can think of nothing to add "that you won't be disgusted about."

Both Reuel and Helen maintained an independence beyond the capacities of Rosalind, who continued to look to Wilson for the inner balance she lacked. She was the first child, of whom much was expected, and her life was shadowed by her father's. Her happiest times with him had been the summers between his marriages with Margaret Canby and Mary McCarthy ("it was he and I alone during these months") and when she dropped out of Bennington and, with a friend, kept house for him in New York at the end of the McCarthy marriage. In 1948, when Rosalind was living at Wellfleet and Wilson eager for her to leave the nest, she wrote to him a charming April Fools' letter in which she pretends to be a rich and beautiful young widow who has just moved in across the street. She offers him a sound-proofed study, a wine cellar, a fine phonograph, and servants including a chauffeur, while promising to stay out of the way. An image fusing Wilson's bachelor days between marriages with his regular visits to her grandmother's home, this had, however, become irrelevant because of Elena. Its creator is the courtier who, in *Near the Magician*, competes with Elena while she complains that her father exploited her as his driver and his housekeeper. In the later years Rosalind wasn't as close to the magician as she wanted to be.

Wilson thought her "closer to me than either of my other children," and she looked like him, "short and fleshy, somewhat pugnacious of eye" and "imposingly eagle-like of brow." For a young woman who, as her father had, wanted lovers and romance, this was not a happy resemblance. She was clever and intellectually lazy, at any rate as she presents herself in her memoir, saying she didn't read Wilson's work, though she insists his mother had. Helen Muchnic accused him of insufficiently encouraging Rosalind's writing, but after a promising start she found it difficult to complete her various typescripts and manuscripts. His pressure that she get a job seemed vindicated when, not long after her April Fools' letter, she went to work as an editorial assistant at Houghton Mifflin in Boston. Soon she was "full of ideas" and had "a grasp of publishing problems," had "matured" astonishingly, pleasing the father who saw this as a second chance at a literary career. She got along well with his writer friends. Sent to the New York office for the summer of 1951, Rosalind found that Dawn Powell wanted a publisher for a collection of stories and would give whoever took it her next novel. *Sunday, Monday, and Always* (1952), *The Wicked Pavilion* (1954), and *A Cage for Lovers* (1957) were published by Houghton Mifflin when she was Dawn's editor there.

She had her first collapse when Wilson and Elena were abroad in 1956. "ROSALIND ILL AND SERIOUSLY DISTURBED EMOTIONALLY," her boss cabled. In his journal the next year Wilson cites "the awful blow" of a broken engagement, and is glad his daughter is again "doing well" and popular at Houghton Mifflin. She is in analysis and has schooled herself against romantic expectations, has supposedly detached herself from her father and stepmother. Elena remained loyal and kind, and Wilson, stern as he could be with her, burst into tears when recollecting a "weeping fit" that Rosalind had at their house on "vodka and an empty stomach." Several years later they tried to give her part of the trust fund from his mother, though this proved legally impractical.

In September 1963, when Elena had left for Europe and he was about to follow, Rosalind had a severe breakdown, triggered, she says in *Near the Magician*, by alcohol. To Elena he reported finding her "in a strangely exalted state, full of delusions," believing that "someone who was going to marry her was communicating with her—by means of some special wiring—through the music that was coming in over the radio." She had several times before "had the delusion" that somebody was "going to marry her." She said that for many weeks she'd been unable to "concentrate on reading manuscripts." At the hospital, she later told him, she was "off my head" for three days and put in a locked ward. She was released and prescribed lithium. Beginning to recover, she absorbed the news that she wouldn't get her job back, was cheered when Dawn was able to interest the *Saturday Evening Post* in one of her stories, and when it bought this and another piece she could afford to pay part of the hospital bill. Wilson spent two weeks with her at Wellfleet. He told Rosalind that in his own breakdown he'd had the sense she spoke of that the real world was unreal. The other side of his sympathy, however, was the assumption she could pull herself together as he had, and he wrote to Elena that she'd "straightened out" when she stopped taking tranquilizers. Soon after he joined Elena in Europe, Rosalind had to be readmitted to the hospital, where she spent, she said, "four weeks" that winter: "they kept trying to get me out, but I found it rather cozy."

She was well enough to meet the family the next spring in Rome, and for three years maintained an apartment on Louisburg Square in Boston Wilson perceived as "ill kept and dirty" and full of cats. After a Thanksgiving lunch with Rosalind in 1964 or '65, he had a severe attack of gout that kept him from going down the stairs—they are said to have been stuck for a couple of days in this one-bedroom flat. In these years she published two stories in *Ladies Home Journal*. She spent long periods at Money Hill, and in 1965 she was jailed for a night in Provincetown after being arrested for drunk driving. For the rest of her life Rosalind would suffer from a certain disconnectedness, evident in her memoir, where a roughly chronological organization collapses into gossip and personal association. She developed a paranoid streak, which he recalled as part of his own breakdown. Her problems were largely beyond her control—genes, or chemistry, perhaps, complicated by alcohol and her mother's absence, the pressure that put on her relationship with her father, the conflict between her grandmother and her father, and between their worlds. Having tried harder with her than he had to with Helen or Reuel, Wilson was susceptible to the feeling of failure, and to blaming it on her.

In two disconsolate pages of *The Sixties* he states that after all his mother tried to do for her and his hopes when she was young, she has "no ambition and no realistic plans, no one she is really close to," that her life has led her "into a blind alley." He'll go on giving her $5,000 a year, has told her "I'll also pay her doctor's bills." What he considered her self-indulgence made him impatient, and in this journal entry he admits to a "sharp peremptory tone" with Rosalind, while to Elena he once confessed to "roaring like a bull" at her, and Helen recalls him "flattening" her at the dinner table, saying she became "the family scapegoat." This was the other side of the sometimes intimate understanding between them. Wilson continued to send homemade Valentines, as his whole family did. In his last year a two-foot red card to Rosalind, with a goofy-looking white bear on the outside, opened to state, "Ours has been a strong and wonderful relationship."

Upstate New York partly saved Rosalind. After a summer in the stone house when she was able to diet and to control her drinking, she spent the winter of 1969–1970 there. Elena says in "My View" that their expenses in keeping the old place going were so large that she had to use her Social Security checks for food, but that Rosalind "sincerely loved the landscape and the house, which gave her a background without responsibility, and she got along well with the people." Her identification with her father's second home gave her the illusion, with the success of *Upstate* (1971), that the rest of his life and work were less important and that she understood him better than did Elena. Wilson decided to leave the house to her, though in his journal he predicted she would sell it, and she did.

Although he sometimes heard her "pounding her typewriter" or saw her at the writing table in her room, he didn't anticipate the effort of *Near the Magician* (1989), a freewheeling, witty, often bitter book that offers information not otherwise available about the man and his milieux. After Wilson's death, Rosalind told Helen he was "all I had," but she boasted to their friend Mary Hackett at the Cape that she'd told him off before he died, and both points of view are here. Rosalind is passionately possessive of her father and not averse to describing his hurtful, cruel behavior. She shows herself as arbitrary and high-handed as she says he was, reveals the torments and confusions as well as the satisfactions of her life in the shadow of Wilson.

That Wilson knew his limitations as a family man is evident from the Punch and Judy show he regularly put on at Wellfleet and at Talcottville. In this classic of defiant British humor, derived from the commedia dell'arte, Punch throws the baby out the window, beats his wife (as she does him), and gets away with a number of murders, including hanging the hangman, while cavorting and singing songs. He escapes the croco-diles and dragons and foils the devils who pursue him, in the end saved by Judy, who recovers the baby unscathed. Wilson Americanized the script. When Punch knocks his landlord on the head, an echo of Ophelia ("That's for remembrance!") is joined to Greenwich Village ("Down with the bour-geoisie! No more rent to pay!"), and when battering a policeman Punch declares, "That's the way to deal with the law," which the victim of the IRS may have found gratifying. Satan, retreating to Hell, remarks, "I haven't seen such insolence since Robert Moses tried to put his subway through here." But Wilson eventually replaced his crude American Punch with a brilliantly costumed and colored puppet made for him in London, who had "sharply carved features" and the smile Max Beerbohm had de-scribed as "frank" and "glad," that "of a great sinner well-knowing himself to be a great force for good." He found this a congenial self-image, and he was at any rate a force for good in the republic of letters.

He not only wrote this show but, Elena reports, "gave every character a different accent and sang the songs at the top of his voice," stripped to his underwear top behind the stage "because of the heat and the exer-tion." Rosalind's childhood had not included these festive occasions, but at Wilson's request Helen did some of the women and animal puppets. Reuel appreciated his father's "mastery of the quirky puppeteering art," contrasting it to "his mediocre attempts at conjuring." He thought Wil-son's favorite character the Devil, and in "Growing Up" the son judges his father much as the puppet devils do Punch when they tell him that his "real self" is "not a blustering, roistering lovable old rogue, but cruel, ma-lignant, ugly and very, very small." By contrast, Elena sympathized with her sometimes atheistic, sometimes agnostic partner thus captive to the Christian heritage, and she admired the strength Wilson projected as the jolly Punch: "Mr. Punch's sense of justice and outrageous bashing down of anything he disapproved of; Mr. Punch's gallivanting around with the hangman's daughter and his flirtations with Flora the Floosy, a degenerate pale puppet in seedy finery." She identified herself with Judy, "the good woman" who rode to the rescue; she thought this was perhaps "where I came in."

31

The Sixties and the Decade

Wilson and the Kennedys

Wilson's family life appears at the periphery of the vast social scene of *The Sixties*. One of his six or eight major works and, with *The Twenties*, the best of his journals, this book carries the reader from the last phase of a confident high culture through a man's losing struggle against a host of maladies to his death. Its place in Wilson's unwritten *Confession of a Child of the Century* is an essential one. There are really two parts, the first 650 or so pages to 1968 distinguishable from the significantly darker 150 pages that follow. In the last section the subject narrows and is more universal. Through the first eight years of the decade *The Sixties* usefully complements social histories of this transformative period.

The book's politics, more conspicuous in the first two or three hundred pages, reflect the last years of Eisenhower's presidency and the beginning of Kennedy's. There is concern about nuclear warfare. Three old friends, Thurber, Janet Flanner, and Morton Zabel, seem "all to have a kind of nuclear age jitters." Wilson sees this reflected in the "shouting" at cocktail parties, wondering whether it may be an unconscious effort "to glorify the Bomb? to rival the Bomb?" He identifies with the peace marchers through the radical minister A. J. Muste, whom he first knew as a labor organizer among the coal miners thirty years before, and through his friend Barbara Deming. On trial for trespassing at a peace demonstration, Barbara, like Joan of Arc before the judge in her white dress, pleads innocent (as Elena has advised) on grounds that her action was morally necessary. Though prepared to go to jail—she would later be jailed for twenty-eight days in a civil rights protest in Georgia—she is let off on a technicality, because, Wilson thinks, in the grungy scene of the criminal courts she is so visibly a lady.

Having written about the Iroquois, whose lands "the engineers" have been ruining, he attends a quiet, decorous church supper at which the Christianized ("salad-eating," as opposed to "corn-soup eating") members of the Six Nations are raising money for Indian education. In Cambridge he meets visiting Russian writers, including Leonid Leonov, whose fiction he'd called a talented expression of the party line. Leonov is discreet in the presence of their interpreter ("an old Russian-Jewish witch") and another man who seems a well-established Soviet hack, white-haired and tall, "shedding a smug Russian *poshlost* (mediocrity)." That a "blank-faced young" State Department man is also there to spy leads Wilson to declare that the Soviet Union and the United States are not the Communist and capitalist societies they pretend to be, each being "run by the army, the engineers and the *chinovniki* (petty bureaucrats)." But, when the interpreter is not present, Leonov opens up with Russian-speaking Elena, calling himself a "clever" survivor, advising her to understand his country through the eleventh-century aristocrat Vladimir Monomakh, saying goodbye with the traditional Russian "God be with you."

At the beginning of May 1962, in an episode vividly sketched in *The Sixties*, Elena and Wilson were invited to the White House for one of President and Mrs. Kennedy's dinners for artists and writers, occasions that encouraged Americans to take pride in a European-style cultural establishment. Wilson had voted for Kennedy but refused to attend the inauguration and protested the Bay of Pigs fiasco. He imagined that Kennedy's cultural allegiances were "worked up" by Schlesinger, who phoned to invite them to this occasion honoring André Malraux. Elena—herself very pro-Kennedy—was seated at a table between Adlai Stevenson and George Balanchine, while Wilson found himself with Malraux and his wife at the president's table. What followed might seem remarkable after the presidencies from Johnson through George W. Bush. *Patriotic Gore* had just appeared, and Kennedy asked about Wilson's title, words from the Confederate song "Maryland, My Maryland" that dramatized for him the effusion of blood and ink during the Civil War. Kennedy then inquired what conclusions he'd reached about the war. Wilson says he "answered that I couldn't very well tell him then and there and referred him to the Introduction. He said something about it being unusual for an author not to want to talk about his book." Wilson did not want to be rude and didn't expect the president to be interested in comparisons between the United States, the USSR, and Bismarck's Germany or in his critique of the psychology of nations at war. He did not want to dilute his anti-imperialist message.

He noted "how alert and intent" Kennedy was: "if you asked him a question, he crouched forward just as he does at his press conferences and pounces upon it with his answer the moment it has been asked." Introducing Malraux, Kennedy repeated his joke with his guests at a dinner for Nobel Prize winners, saying that there were more brains assembled that evening in the dining room "than at any time since Thomas Jefferson dined alone." When Malraux proposed that the United States was unique in acquiring imperial power without seeking it, Wilson said to Madame Malraux, across the table from him and seated by the president, "*Dites à Malraux que je n'en crois rien.*"* Kennedy, who turned out to have been taking French lessons, said "You don't tell us what you think," returning thus to *Patriotic Gore*. At the evening's end the president—who had wanted to do something for the Iroquois after *Apologies*—again referred to "my not wanting to tell him about my book: 'I suppose I'll have to buy it.' 'I'm afraid so,'" Wilson replied rather than point out that Oxford had sent him a copy. Among the other guests that evening, Saul Bellow, who didn't much like the introduction to *Patriotic Gore*, later drily observed that Wilson's "eccentricities deserved at least an imperial setting." Robert Lowell, by contrast, wrote that "of all the big names there, only you acted like yourself," everyone else seeming "addled with adulation" to have been invited. Lowell, who thought the intellectuals should be "windows, not window-dressing," was glad to see Wilson maintaining the "queer tense twist of principle" affirmed in his Civil War portraits.

At a State Department–sponsored lunch the next day Wilson taxed Malraux for having said that the United States had "the most powerful weapon in the world" and didn't want to use it ("After all, we had used it"). Thirty or so writers were sitting around in a circle when Robert Frost came in. Wilson introduced Phito Thoby-Marcelin to Malraux and Frost as Haiti's leading poet. Frost, he says, then went "into his act": in a "drawling" accent he explained the stages through which the poet created a public and was finally taken up by his government. His examples were Virgil and Augustus: "Virgil was a country boy who wanted to be a poet. Nobody encouraged Virgil. He had to do it for himself. Then Augustus took him up." Wilson, believing that Frost likened Kennedy to Augustus Caesar to suggest the parallel of himself with Virgil, would slap his thigh in laughter when recalling this.

*Tell Malraux I don't believe this at all.

Ironically, Wilson too was now taken up by Kennedy. The fight with the IRS had dragged on into the new administration, the agency never quite ready to compromise. In 1961 he mortgaged the stone house and sold his present and future papers to Yale for $30,000 (he could have gotten $75,000 at the University of Texas, but didn't like their agent or want his archive so far away). He paid back both Grynberg and Deming. When the IRS, wanting $40,000 in cash, threatened to put him in jail, Elena began appealing to Schlesinger at the White House. Commissioner Mortimer Caplin was asked to produce a settlement, and the government eventually agreed to $25,000, though continuing to insist on a $30,000 collateral agreement against future earnings. Wilson would die in debt to Straus for the money with which he paid this off, and Elena had to justify all the medical expenses of his last decade to auditors. She would be submitting detailed accounts in the year of her death, seven years after her husband's.

In June 1963 Wilson was sitting in his reading chair at Talcottville when Schlesinger phoned to say that he would be awarded one of the new Presidential Medals of Freedom. Kennedy had added his name to a list of nominees developed by Arthur Goldberg, then secretary of labor. I like to think that the Medal of Freedom meant more to him, with his devotion to the United States, than the Nobel Prize he at the end of his life hoped for but didn't get. Archibald MacLeish had been suggested as an alternative nominee, making Wilson happier that Kennedy chose him. He had just written *The Cold War and the Income Tax: A Protest*, welding an attack on his country's development of weapons of mass destruction, atomic, chemical, and biological, to a review of his tax delinquency and treatment by the government. He stipulated that the president had to be made aware of his pamphlet and sent the text to Schlesinger, who passed on a summary. When a man named Bacon from the IRS brought in a memorandum opposing the award—parts of it paralleling the ever expanding FBI file on Wilson—Schlesinger and Theodore Sorensen each remembered that Kennedy decisively stated, "This is not an award for good conduct but for literary merit."

Wilson failed to grasp the absurdity of his position in *The Cold War and the Income Tax*, the irony that a former socialist should attack the "bureaucracy" over this issue, the seeming effort to play the Thoreau of *Civil Disobedience* after evading taxes. Yet he eloquently protested the use to which his money was put, the fact that "what we do and what we make goes mostly not for life and enlightenment on this planet on which we have not yet found out how to get along decently with one another but for the propagation of darkness and death." He reviewed the case of Major Eatherly, conscience stricken after the bomber group he commanded killed 200,000 people at Hiroshima and Nagasaki, later held in a Veterans Administration mental hospital on orders of the Air Force and the State Department. He documented the American production of anthrax and other deadly chemical and biological agents, and the use already in Vietnam of poison gas and napalm. He was furthering the concerns voiced for that era in Eisenhower's Farewell Address, the general being the last American president willing—or perhaps politically able—to warn of "the total influence—economic, political, even spiritual" of "the military-industrial complex." Wilson concluded with a strategy for those who might not wish to pay taxes, and transferred the copyright for his protest to A. J. Muste's magazine *Liberation*.

This pamphlet occasioned an amusing, touching letter from Allen Ginsberg, who offered his new blend of spirituality, drugs, and pacifism to the man he addressed as "dear old heart," saying Wilson would find the world a more loving place if he embraced his postman. Also illustrative of the literary fraternity during that period is an evening in *The Sixties* with James Baldwin, whom Wilson called "not only one of the best Negro writers that we have ever had in this country" but "one of the best writers that we have." Baldwin comes for a drink and stays for dinner after a lecture at Brandeis University. They talk of Henry James—"I asked Baldwin why he thought that Strether had turned Mme. Vionnet down when she practically offered herself"—and the novelist (well known to be homosexual) says "that he knew men of his own generation" who "drew back from any serious relationship with a woman." They touch on "embittered Negro nationalism" and on Roi Ottley, who had resisted this ("He was a hero of mine," Baldwin says). The two men agree, in contrast with their president, that the United States is to blame for the trouble with Cuba. Wilson had, however, detected Kennedy's influence in Baldwin's response to questions after his lecture. He'd given "one of his rare broad-toothed grins" as he leaned forward to jump on a question in a way that, like Kennedy's, maintained the listener's sympathies. In Kennedy's spirit he spoke of evil as "the fear of taking chances, which amounted to choosing death."

Wilson wasn't surprised by Kennedy's dangerous stand during the Cuban missile crisis. He had written to Barbara Deming, "I don't believe it is possible to be President and not be willing to lead the country into a war.

Nobody can get to be President who has not himself a strong drive to power." He was heartened, however, by the diplomatic skill with which the president and his brother Robert extricated themselves and the world, and began working for "a peaceful settlement with Russia." The Wilsons were in Paris when Kennedy was assassinated. Wilson was sickened and humiliated for his country—"sordidness of the assassins, a schizoid boy who thought he was a Marxist rebel and a boastful crook who ran a small nightclub; ineptitude of the Dallas police." The catastrophe prefigured a collapse of society that he documents within his shrinking personal horizons.

He had written to Kennedy that he would be unable to be in Washington to receive the Medal of Freedom, and the American ambassador in Paris tried on behalf of Lyndon Johnson to deliver it, eventually sending it to him in Rome. He received a moving letter from Robert Kennedy, and in 1966 would be pleased to learn that the president's heir was seen carrying the new edition of *Europe Without Baedeker* when he went to the polls in his New York senatorial race.

The Last Journal: Autobiography and the Social Round

The Sixties opens with what growing older felt like: "*At my age*, I find that I alternate between spells of fatigue and indifference when I am almost ready to give up the struggle, and spells of expanding ambition, when I feel that I can do more than ever before." There is amusing talk about the Cambridge marriage of octogenarian William "Billy" James, whose bride has rescued him from "living alone on Irving St. and eating nothing but frankfurters and marinated herring." They have had to pass a Wassermann test and, in lieu of a clergyman, were married by the retired dean of the Harvard Divinity School, himself ninety years old. At one office Billy was told he "better hurry up." More "gossip in Cambridge" follows, an account of a friend who has died in a fire, and two sonorous rather Yeatsian poetic lines which, with the help of a decanter of "almost intolerably sour" white wine, Wilson has managed to retrieve from a dream "that at last I was going to write a wonderful poem."

In this way the author's life and the people he encounters create a drama savored and interpreted upon the page. His prose is matter-of-fact, authoritative, leavened by wit, and powered by a commitment to the unfolding scene in which he continuously seeks meaning. Determinedly he avoids generalization. As he states of Parkman's history in O *Canada*, "Each incident, each episode is different, each is particularized, each is presented, when possible, in sharply realistic detail, no matter how absurd or how homely, in terms of its human participants, its local background." Yet everyone, Isaiah Berlin noted, had a specific role on Wilson's stage: "Auden was a very good poet, Spender was a very nice man. Everybody had to be something." Wilson writes fondly that Isaiah himself behaves "like royalty," phoning ahead about his arrival and readjusting his plans in a series of telegrams, asking Edmund and Elena to let no one else in Cambridge know he's coming, while informing others of this "secret visit." With an eye for an individual's soft spots, Wilson represents their mutual friend Harry Levin as stuffily academic and (accurately, according to Berlin) as catty behind people's backs. A few years later, exaggerating in order to amuse, he reports that Cecil Lang, editor of the Swinburne letters and professor at the University of Virginia, teaches his classes at home and "apparently, only one hour a week," has never even "been around the Lawn," a picture Lang enjoyed when the journal appeared in 1993, recalling the author as "affable, amiable, charming," without a sign of the satirical detachment manifest in such notes.

His inner dramas occasionally surface. Ted Paramore had died in 1956, crushed under a repair hoist that collapsed beneath his car in a garage, but in Wilson's last recorded dream of struggling to recover Margaret he tries to persuade Ted to reveal where she is. Fifty pages along he notes that he has been "repeating with Elena the same 'pattern' of my behavior with Margaret." In April 1962—after drinking too much in a depression he attributes to maladies of aging (heart, teeth, and gout), the tax struggle, and another long winter in Cambridge—he has "a paroxysm of exasperation with Elena combined with an acute heart attack" (it turned out to be angina) and smashes "her filing cabinet, her typewriter and something else made of glass." That is all Wilson remembered of the night when, enacting a Promethean scene behind his desk, he cursed fate for prematurely bringing him down. Monroe Engel, whom Elena called over from across the street, described this scene in a memoir in the *Yale Review* and, in more detail, to acquaintances. They summoned Dr. Louis Zetzel, who "checked my pulse and my heart and gave me a shot in the arm to put me to sleep." The birthday quarrel with Elena in Talcottville followed. A few months later she met him at the Grand Bretagne Hotel in Montreal, where their estrangement was "completely healed" in bed. However, when they tried again a few days later his heart gave him trouble and he had to take a pill. "It is awful to be in such bad shape. I can't bear to have this spoiled— she is so divine," he writes. Several years afterward he notes, "Elena and I, I suppose, are really getting too old *pour l'amour*. Though we try it, at rather long intervals, it is likely to turn out that one of us comes but not the other."

Memories carry him into the past of his American generation. He thinks of Scott and Zelda when he sees Scott's Hollywood lover Sheilah Graham a decade after their first meeting, and again in Washington when lunching with Scottie Lanahan, who had written warmly of his help with the estate and admired Sheila as Wilson did. Touched that Scottie kisses him, he feels "pangs from far back"—how Fitzgerald, before introducing his bride, had said, "I wouldn't mind if she died, but I couldn't stand to have her marry somebody else"; how Zelda was embarrassed by the memory of the frilly white dress in which Wilson first saw her, saying "that her mother, in her Southern provincialism, had not known how to dress her for New York." A darker memory, sustained by the correspondence at the Beinecke Library, was that "Zelda, in her last more or less insane phase, became very religious and used to write to me letters begging me to become converted, telling me I had merits which oughtn't to allow me to be consigned to hell." At an elegant lunch with the Fitzgeralds' friends the Murphys, at Sneden's Landing north of Manhattan, Wilson has difficulty chewing because his bridge has fallen out, but is attentive to the talk of food, the antiquities of the town, and the Murphys' house, where a mayor of New York under the Dutch had lived. On meeting this couple a year or two before, Elena had said "she could understand Scott smashing their precious wineglasses." Wilson remembered "Scott's story about telling Hemingway that his book (*Tender Is the Night*) was based on the Murphys." Hemingway—who considered his own life heroic drama—had said, "I don't see how you could write a novel about them. I don't see how they could be anything more than subjects for a ballet."

A friend observed in July 1961 that Hemingway's suicide hit Wilson hard. In the journal he is shaken. "One of the foundation stones of my generation," Hemingway had urged writers "to last and get their work done," and to have him end his life in such a "panicky" way was "to have a prop knocked out." The news that he had been taking shock treatments at the Mayo Clinic and feared he was losing his mind made his suicide comprehensible, and his posthumous account, in *A Moveable Feast*, of the Paris version of the life Wilson had known only in Greenwich Village was exhilarating. Although malicious about many of his Paris acquaintances, Hemingway conveyed their personalities and mannerisms. He caught the voices of his fellow writers, re-creating "the tones and turns of speech" both of those he'd heard and of those he knew only on the page.

Deaths punctuate *The Sixties*, and the unexpected death of a genial, eccentric Harvard professor intensifies "the impression, which," Wilson writes, "so haunts me nowadays, of the flimsiness of human life: human relationships—our culture and history—a fabric of imaginary cobwebs hung about the habitable parts of the earth." Asserting the transitory nature even of one's intellectual concerns, this traditional memento mori turns upon itself in a way that is quintessential Wilson: "His death did brace me up a little. Though I am seven years older than he was—he was only 60—and though I suffer from various ailments, I am not yet so badly off as he was and may yet accomplish something," he asserts, the double "yet" sending him back to work.

Cape, Country, City, Europe

Wilson's life passes before us in a constantly changing scene—intellectuals in Cambridge, artists in New York City, politics in Washington. He is seen in his two homes. Kazin takes him as a remnant of a WASP establishment among technocrats and academics on the beach at the Cape, but in *The Sixties* the critic is nostalgic for "the old Jig Cook Provincetown or the old Dos Passos–Waugh Provincetown," composed of "writers and painters who were working and freely exchanging ideas." There were subjects one couldn't discuss with the new crowd, attached as they were to a university or the government. One summer all the congregating, eating, and drinking that Elena manages with the Hughes, Kazins, Edwin O'Connor, Schlesingers, Hofstadters, and Aarons drain Wilson's energies, and he is happiest doing magic tricks for a nine-year-old, "a Lolita, who had a pack of cards and was going to play solitaire as I used to do, in childhood, at parties." Reluctant now on account of his heart to go far into the cold water or struggle with the surf, he is eager for Talcottville.

He usually goes there at the beginning of June. Reading and writing intensively, he can work all day in his pajamas, as at Wellfleet. Otherwise, he enjoys the ordinary people around him. He gets to know Mary Pcolar's family and the local Hungarian community, and is introduced to its patriarch, with whom he discusses real estate and the man's coin collection. Mary tells long stories about complex semiromantic relationships with her bosses at the drugstores where she works, tales that would make her for Elena "the Madame Bovary of Boonville." "She wants something more, but she can't reach it," Mary's mother shrewdly remarks. Wilson tries to open doors for this determined woman, encourages her to take courses at a local college, gives her little lectures when she asks, "What is philosophy? What caused the French Revolution?" (She'd heard Marie Antoinette's "Why don't they eat cake?" attributed to the empress of Austria, by whom her forbears had been ruled.)

Between literary projects he takes breaks for visitors. One year it is Mary Meigs and Barbara Deming. With Marie-Claire not on the scene, Meigs recalls that Wilson comically propositioned her: "after drunkenly prowling the corridor, he tottered into my room in his dressing gown and seated himself on my bed," and when she refused—"calmly, loudly, to make him hear"—they went downstairs and discussed the obligations of marriage. When Dawn Powell visited, the couple had fun à la the 1920s. Rosalind writes, "I took Dawn and my father to town, where they bought some vodka, then we went for a drive. When I had a flat tire, they both disappeared in a cornfield with the vodka, supposedly seeking help. Dawn was tiny and my father short, and it was August, when the corn was at its highest. I soon hailed a passing farmer who fixed the tire. I waited two hours for them, and then, furious, went and took a swim, returning home to find them on the front porch. They'd stopped in the middle of the cornfield to kill the vodka, then staggered out into another county where a sheriff's patrol picked them up." A visiting academic friend from Cambridge remembered the time when Wilson "came down and proceeded to flout an alcohol-free regimen by drinking hard with us." The next morning he was "wandering around quite drunk"—he'd "been naughty," he said, "and tippled alone as the sun came up."

People come and go during Elena's August weeks at the stone house. There are yearly parties for the local people and the couples with summer homes upstate. In 1963 Morley Callaghan drove over from Toronto for a house party, and Phito and Eva Thoby-Marcelin joined them. Wilson's regular exchanges with Phito had been blurred by the gulf between the critic's French and Phito's Haitian dialect, then by Phito's insistence on practicing his English, but he became a drinking buddy when the Thoby-Marcelins settled not far away, in Cazenovia, New York. When Wilson told Eva, twenty years after their first meeting, that they'd finally had a really good talk, her explanation, quoted in *The Sixties*, is that they (for once) "were not full of whisky." The journal records the prejudice Phito encountered from the South African wife of one of his Canadian guests. This light-colored Haitian's situation showed how clumsy could be the categories of ethnicity and race.

The Fifties and *Upstate* include the lines of poets who, as Auden did, engraved them on window panes for Wilson. On the top floor were passages appropriate to views of the sky and the treetops: Marcelin's lines about a Haitian goddess, juxtaposed to lines from the prophet Isaiah that either Sir Isaiah or Wilson, who remembered this differently, carved for Berlin in a glass, as well as lines from Aeschylus's *Prometheus* set down by Charley Walker, and from *Vents* (*Winds*) by the Nobel Prize winner Saint-John Perse. On the second floor, in the various bedrooms, was verse about dreaming and sleep, including Bogan's "The Landscape Where I Lie," and in the glass of the door to the balcony Nabokov's

бывают ночи только ляту
в Россию поплывет кровать.* . . .

Spender's "I Think Continually of Those Who Were Truly Great" dramatically caught the late afternoon sun in the window at the top of the stairs. Perhaps half these writers had come to Talcottville. When Spender visited one June, Wilson took him for a picnic at Independence River, an occasion the Englishman called "very Huckleberry Finn."

As "a man of the twenties," Wilson writes in Talcottville, "I still expect something exciting: drinks, animated conversation, gaiety: an uninhibited exchange of ideas," and he seeks this on visits of anywhere from a weekend to ten or twelve days in Manhattan, rushing from one engagement to another. Elena is usually with him, and there are literary lunches, dinners, plays, movies and the opera, drinks and talk. He regularly sees his English friends in New York, and seventeen meetings with Auden are touched on in *The Sixties*. At one point the poet presents him "with bound sheets of his new collected poems," paying "extravagant compliments," as, Wilson notes, he often does "toward the end of the first bottle of wine." With Auden and the Spenders and Berlin the talk bridges books and politics. Wilson reads the same literary weeklies they do. They all know Stravin-

*There are nights when I lie in my bed, and my bed is swimming to Russia.

sky, an Anglophile, as well as Vladimir Nabokov's cousin Nicholas, whom Spender recalled as "a charming rogue" and whose gossip reached into the Kennedy White House.

Wilson tells Dawn and others that he dreams of flying. At lunch at the Algonquin the elderly blithe spirit confides that in these dreams "I flew to the ceiling." A companion that day recalled Wilson in a rather worn, ratty linen suit, an "ice cream suit," such as had been out of fashion for decades, extending his arms and swooping amongst the tables saying, "This is how I fly." His New York routine is not limited to the literati. Not long after the reception for Stravinsky, where he talks with Auden and others, he makes friends with young Mike Nichols and Elaine May, fascinated by their popular comedy act, their ability to command the stage and maintain so much dramatic tension. Nichols seems to be a brilliant man and "something of a writer." They discuss how artists can work, given the possibility of nuclear annihilation. Elaine is "emotional, imaginative, rather sombre," as an actress "perhaps something of a genius," the same judgment Wilson made of Marie-Claire Blais. He imagines having an affair with Elaine, tells himself he is "easy game for beautiful, gifted women," but the thought of Edna Millay and Mary McCarthy gives him pause, and he asks Mike "to tell Elaine that I was sorry not to be young enough to fall in love with her and ruin my life." Nichols replies, "I'll tell her exactly what you say."

With the end of Camelot, Wilson finds himself part of a cultural establishment that has re-formed in New York and in which, he thinks, Mike Nichols and Lillian Hellman as well as Lowell and Hardwick and Jason and Barbara Epstein figure. He interviews himself for the first issue of *The New York Review of Books*, founded by the two literary couples with the help of Robert Silvers. Jackie Kennedy is "somehow on the fringes" of this group. When Schlesinger takes him to a party to meet Mrs. Kennedy—who, however, turns out to be happily occupied with Tennessee Williams—Wilson observes that "she gave me a long interested look." But a year or two later this constellation of people is breaking up, and what with larger numbers of mentally ill people on the streets, and the threat of crime, the city becomes harder for his older friends to live in. He takes note of cheap sex films and an uglier popular culture, finds them paralleled, at Talcottville, in motorcycle gangs and the "delinquents" whom he tries to confront with his cane on the lawn.

In his account of the winter of 1963–64 in Paris, Wilson has aged. Paris wasn't what he'd expected. It rained a lot, the air was smoggy, and to

Dos Passos he wrote, "The women are no longer so chic, and everything seems more commonplace. The young people go crazy about new French singers with bogus American names, who hop around the stage with the tubes of loudspeakers that look like garden hoses and make their voices raucous and deafening." In the journal notes, when he goes to a striptease his heart is not in it, and he gives his hostess money and slips away. But he saw the Beatles at their concert at the Odeon that winter, and Gilles Couture, a French Canadian who had been his student at Harvard in 1960, remembered Wilson insisting he go, predicting their music would be important. Couture helped him get the books he wanted for his account of Canadian literature, and he discussed his ideas with the Canadian short story writer Mavis Gallant. His literary circle also included the incomparable Janet Flanner, *The New Yorker*'s Paris correspondent.

He revisits his World War I scene in the Vosges, and the raw climate and rural smells of Lorraine induce in him a Proustian sense of the past. Taking the road down the hill from the now collapsing château of St. Baslemont, where he and David Hamilton were given a Christmas glass of wine forty-five years before, as if at the bottom of the well of memory he finds the woman who'd owned the château, in a small cottage writing at a worktable. This strange person calls herself a man, then gradually admits to being female. "One struggles against a reluctance to be carried back into the past; one feels one ought to leave it behind," Wilson writes. "One is swimming back against the current."

Exploring the English village from which his Kimball ancestor departed en route to Massachusetts Bay on April 10, 1634, he considers spending a few days at the "Angel" in nearby Bury St. Edmunds, "where Mr. Pickwick got into the wrong room," but decides that "after three centuries," that would be "futile." In Isaiah Berlin's garden at Oxford he proudly contemplates the difference between the European and the American autumn. "Ours is so much more dramatic: sudden frosts, holocausts of foliage, clear cold stimulating days and blissful long interludes of Indian summer." In a line that reflects his own moment of Indian summer, Wilson concludes that to live in this dim atmosphere "would impose a different mood than ours, and I shall not be here long enough to adapt myself to it." His Paris notes contain a resolution to focus on the United States "in the limited time that is left me."

Wesleyan, 1964–1965

From their first meeting Paul Horgan, the director of Wesleyan's Center for Advanced Studies, knew that the man he viewed as a brilliant catch didn't want to come to the university even though he needed the money. In his bunched-up dark winter overcoat in the lobby of a Boston hotel Wilson resembled "a great bird in a chill, swollen with its feathers." When Horgan ran down the list of distinguished folk who would be Fellows at the Center and said how eager the college faculty were for him to come, Wilson—thinking of Harvard, where the usually mild-mannered Elena remarked that he'd "been served up like a roast beef"—said, "You don't know much about university people, do you?" Wilson then asked Horgan, "Are you a writer?" The director, himself published by Farrar, Straus, was quite willing to say goodbye to this difficult figure, who complained of "asthma, emphysema, bronchitis" and clearly found decision making hard. Horgan, however, flatteringly mentioned that he'd given Stravinsky a copy of *Patriotic Gore* the year before in Santa Fe and that, a week later, Stravinky, still reading it, had declared, "This book is a masterpiece." Wilson said, "How astonishing!" and immediately agreed to accept the fellowship, then turned into someone "jovial, solicitous, lightly gossipy," as the talk and the wine flowed.

When the account in *The Sixties* of his year at Wesleyan is matched to the memories of others, Wilson, turning seventy, can be seen in the round. At nine each morning he was at work in his glass-walled office at a desk usually covered with galley proofs. John Clendenning, a graduate student assigned to the Center, struck up an acquaintanceship with the modest man behind the gruff persona and intimidating reputation. When Clendenning was sitting in the lounge reading a magazine, Wilson "burst in and looked embarrassed, as if he had barged into my territory. He smiled and said, 'Hello, my name is Edmund Wilson,' and I thought that was the most incredibly self-effacing remark that he could have made, as if I wouldn't have known what his name was, and then he said, 'I'm just looking for a cookie.'" The Harvard logician Willard Quine, one of the Fellows, remembered Wilson's conversation as "vigorous, articulate, emphatic." But he'd have liked more contact with students. Other Fellows were asked by professors from their departments to chair a seminar or give a reading or a lecture or guide a student, yet the English department made little use of him.

Elena and he found their living quarters comfortable but Middletown "an odd little unit," its Main Street, where she shopped (except when they went to "madly metropolitan" Hartford), dismal—"the most primitive," Wilson noted, "I have ever seen in New England." He humorously called the booth at a Greek restaurant where he invited one for drinks "the Ritz bar," and called Paul Horgan's elegant Friday soirees, where one was served by Wesleyan students with bright red waistcoats and bow ties, after which one heard a talk, "the revels." Horgan he thought "an endearing and slightly ridiculous figure. A bachelor of the type who wants to be the beloved friend and is full of sympathetic consideration and all kinds of little services, he puts one off a little at first by his anxiety to please and to be in the know." Wilson could be a trial to the director. At a dinner that began at six, where he was offered one double martini after another, at nine he demanded to know when dinner would be ready. When told that it would be at ten and offered another drink, he roared, "Certainly not! I've been here for three hours. I am already drunk and starving. Good evening!—Elena," he called, "take me home!"

His host that evening was the director of the College of Letters, "an Egyptian named Hassan, married to a more or less succulent little piece of Danish pastry." One Friday night the dapper Ihab Hassan had given what Wilson found an irritating paper on "metacriticism": "he seemed to be saying that literature was finished, we shouldn't need it any more"—then "how much less should we need criticism?" Another night, John Cage, a past Fellow, alternated silences (for a number of seconds determined by drawing from a hat pieces of paper on which the audience had been asked to write numbers) with the reading of passages from "Emerson, Thoreau, John Cage and others," while a guitar string, a zither, and a humming sound on a tape recorder competed in the background. Wilson was usually half asleep in his corner, having drunk a good deal at the end of the working day. He thought that his snores were recorded as part of the accompaniment during this party game.

Controversy fueled his energy as his health failed, and cruelty to animals always set him off. Clendenning recalls that when a psychologist explained experiments that included giving infant rats alcohol and slapping them about (he was trying to prove that any stimulation of rats made them more intelligent), Wilson, who refused to poison the rats in his Wellfleet house, considering them family, "frightened" this researcher. The man observed that to give them measurable amounts of alcohol also produced intelligent rats, and "Wilson roared with laughter and applause. When he said you could even step on them, Wilson said, 'You know, if you just test these rats too much, they'll die.' The psychologist said, 'Yes, Mr. Wilson, they might die.' Wilson said, 'especially if you step on them!' and stormed out of the room." When sober he achieved a humorous perspective in a letter to the other Fellows from "A Worried Rat" whose mother has become an alcoholic and "lies around sodden with licker," "we children" being worn out with the effort it requires "to get a bottle of gin down without breaking it and to push it along the floor."

Missing the constant stimulation they'd had in Cambridge, Elena and he escaped when they could, usually to New York, sometimes driving back through a snowstorm or taking the wrong road. He had two or three close friends among the Fellows, including Father Martin D'Arcy, an adornment of the Jesuit order in England. John Clendenning understood this relationship better than did the worldly Horgan. "He had a strange sort of respect for people of religious convictions," the student observed. "He told me once that his Hebrew teacher at Princeton had begun each lesson with a prayer, and he said, 'Wonderful thing to do.' And D'Arcy seemed to feel a rather priestly concern for Edmund, who was getting old and drinking too much and unnecessarily abrasive toward people, even mean." Another friend was the writer Jean Stafford, with whom Wilson often visited at the end of the day. Horgan thought him very rude to her on the night when a drunken Jean was talking nonstop, an instance of the impressive monologuing she now produced in lieu of writing short stories. Wilson went to bed, and at nine emerged to insist she go home so he could get some sleep. Stafford also told Horgan of a night when, seeing her lights on late, he knocked at the glass door of her apartment. Saying "Jean, don't die! don't die!," he quickly walked away.

A Closing Horizon

In *The Sixties* Wilson records a dream at Wesleyan in which he is dead—he has committed suicide, he has no idea why. In the dream he asks Rosalind "whether I still seemed solid, whether she could see through me." She answers that, "even before, I had come to seem so faded that she couldn't notice much difference." In an aimless mood, with nothing else to do, his ghost decides to correct some proofs. But a dream is not reality. Dawn

Powell's death in 1965 leaves him feeling that "some part of my own life was gone," while Waldo Frank's a year afterward is depressing in a different way. Though gifted and widely read, his old radical friend, Wilson reflects, was intellectually lazy. Frank hadn't faced the gulf between his pretensions and his accomplishment—"he had no humility about his medium, never in fact taught himself to write." At the impressive Jewish service Wilson declines to speak, unable to "say what I honestly thought about Waldo and his work." He catches the Wellfleet undertaker looking at "some of us" appraisingly, with what Wilson wittily calls "a lecherous eye."

In a poem drafted in 1966 at the stone house and polished in *Upstate*, the family history is receding, the future grim:

> You fade, old presences, and leave me here
>   In dismal trickle of a dimming May,
> I play old records and lay solitaire
>   Through endless hours of Memorial Day.
>
> Cities I'll never visit, books that I'll never read,
>   Magic I'll never master. In a cage
> I stalk from room to room, lose heat and speed,
>   Now entering the dark defile of age.

In the final four years of his life a sense of hopelessness will enter *The Sixties* as the author struggles to recover from one manifestation after another of physical collapse. Till that point his partnership with Elena survives his failings as a husband, her jealousy, the arguments about where to live. He maintains his zest for life, and survives financially through Farrar, Straus and Giroux, Wesleyan, and with the help of literary prizes.

In an amusing episode, the gossip surrounding Norman Podhoretz's *Making It* (1967) helps Wilson strike a better deal for his journals with Roger Straus. As the young editor of *Commentary* Podhoretz told the critic he was "going to revolutionize" the magazine, then took it to the Right, a process that would be part of the conversion of one group of New York Jewish intellectuals into Washington neoconservatives. In *Making It* Podhoretz celebrated his acceptance (as Wilson puts it) by "Lillian [Hellman], ourselves, Jackie Kennedy, and everybody that everybody saw without anybody else's regarding it as a sign of having made it." Straus had given the author a $25,000 advance, only to refuse the book. Wilson learned about this from Jason Epstein, Podhoretz's college friend, who subsequently published it at Random House. Seeing an opening, he proposed to Straus "that if he bought a goldbrick from Podhoretz for $25,000, he ought to pay me more than the $5,000 a volume that had been agreed on for the pure gold" of these six volumes. He reports that the publisher, "after some squirming," agreed to $10,000 apiece. In 1967, $60,000 was a good deal of money, and the increase over their previous arrangement cleared part of his debt to the IRS. He had simultaneously prevailed over the publishing industry and been treated generously by a friend.

During his last decade Wilson won the Edward MacDowell Medal, the Emerson-Thoreau Medal, the Golden Eagle, the Jersualem Prize (which was eventually given to Borges, when Wilson was too ill to receive it in Jerusalem), and the National Medal for Literature. He insisted that he wanted these only for the money, though after the presentation of the Emerson-Thoreau Medal he forgot the check on Richard Pipes's couch. The Aspen Institute gave him $30,000, an unusually large award to an independent writer. Yet to be indebted to this organization was uncomfortable. It seemed the institute had been set up by corporations to offer two-week courses to their employees—"two days to Plato, two to the Gospel according to Saint Matthew," he was told, to which Elena satirically added "two to Scott Fitzgerald," and Schlesinger, when Wilson briefed him on the occasion, added "one to Allen Ginsberg." Of the forty-eight people at the black-tie presentation dinner at the Waldorf—moved for Wilson's sake to New York, since he couldn't strain his heart by going to Aspen, Colorado—he had something in common with only three, Straus, Henry Allen Moe of the John Simon Guggenheim Foundation, and Paul Horgan, whose introduction of him resembled a eulogy. Wilson drank too much, nervous about his acceptance speech and irritated by the ignorance of the oil millionaires who had contributed the prize and their wives, who passed *Who's Who* back and forth at the table in order to find out who he was. "You wrote *Finlandia*, didn't you?" asked the wife of the president of the institute, seated on his right, to which he replied, "No, that was written by a Finn."

He was having it both ways, feeling superior to people whose money he was glad to take. In Horgan's memoirs, which emphasize Wilson's grouchy egotism, he cries out "Tax free!" as he grasps the check "in a hawk-like swoop." But in the *New York Times* account of the award and his acceptance speech, Wilson is grateful that the money is tax free because he will not be supporting the "disgraceful" Vietnam War. He defines himself in his speech as a humanist devoted to liberal learning rather than specialization, urges artists and writers to be informed about science, and is pleased that the award has previously been given to persons in city planning and anthropology. He returns to his debt to Taine for an approach to criticism that brings narrative and drama to the literatures of different cultures. Yet, the opportunity to promote these values and attack the war in a conspicuous forum scarcely made this descendant of a gentry displaced by big money gracious with his well-intentioned patrons. While trying to maintain the very culture to which Wilson was dedicated, they reminded him how marginal it could become in the United States. "You felt," he writes, that they "were perfectly self-confident, that they could never have any misgivings, with those mountains of money behind them. The whole thing was slightly humiliating."

He was angered by the spectacle of American expansionism, and sometimes talked of leaving the country. At a dinner party at the Strauses, during an argument with a Columbia law professor who'd been assistant secretary of state, he said that he might move to Switzerland, and his antagonist called him a coward for not wanting to back his country. Elena, "echoing Thomas Mann" when Mann left Germany during the 1930s, told the man "there'd be America anywhere where I was." After the fake report of a North Vietnamese attack and the Gulf of Tonkin Resolution enabled President Johnson to escalate the war, the president, trying to repair relations with the intellectuals, invited Wilson and others to a White House dinner. Lowell accepted, then declined, which became a front-page story in *The New York Times* and angered Johnson. Wilson declined with a "brusqueness" that Eric Goldman, the president's assistant in cultural matters, "never experienced before or after in the case of an invitation in the name of the President and First Lady." His note was evidently thrown away. In the journal Wilson cracks that a law should be passed forbidding a Texan to be president.

By 1968, however, the public world is receding. He notes the assassination of Martin Luther King only in passing, while that of Robert Kennedy, two months later, goes unmentioned, as are Johnson's decision not to seek reelection and the clubbing of radical demonstrators by Chicago police at the Democratic convention. The journal becomes a record of life against death.

32

The Last Ten Years:
Criticism, Travel Writing, *Upstate*

Of his books, early in *The Sixties* Wilson observes, "They live, I am ceasing to live." For one "ceasing to live" he was productive, updating old interests and filling in the corners of his literary world. He moved among "Books and tables, all one asks, / Rotating interesting tasks," in the words of the verse credo "A Message You'll Expect, My Friends," and sometimes felt as though he had multiple personalities. The dialogue with himself called "An interview with Edmund Wilson" informs us that, once "a drummer boy at Gettysburg," he deserted and fled to upstate New York, where "I became what is called a Copperhead," opposing the war to keep the South in the Union. Now he is in London, having crossed the Atlantic to buy a set of Ackermann's *London* and dine for a last time at the Café Royal. He then confesses that he isn't really there and isn't "really in America either"—"there's hardly a house in New York where I ever lived or went in my youth that is still even standing now!" He locates himself in a garret in Cambridge, Massachusetts, at work on an essay on Swinburne, himself "a little unreal." Around the room are "the complete works of Swinburne and the six volumes of his correspondence and a lot of books about him on my desk, on the windowsill, on the bureau and on the empty bed next to mine. I sleep with them, work with them, eat with them. It's a possible mode of escape."

Swinburne was the subject of Wilson's last major portrait, reprinted from *The New Yorker* in *The Bit Between My Teeth*. As when turning from Housman's poetry to his classical scholarship, he looks behind the familiar sonorous verse of *Atalanta in Calydon* and "The Forsaken Garden" to six volumes of letters and some little-known, sexually charged fiction. This is a happier essay than the Housman, for Swinburne's letters evince "a life lived entirely for literature, in which nothing else is really important—and since literature is inexhaustible, a life that is immensely enjoyed." The poet, of a French-connected aristocratic family, is seen to have the heart of an impish schoolboy. He dances "like a fairy-maenad, round and round the dining-table" in an alcoholic trance, and is "dropped from his only club for stamping one night, in his cups, on all the hats that he found in the coat-room." A novelist manqué, in *Love's Crosscurrents* Swinburne re-created an emotionally inbred boyhood in great houses, while an erotic scene between brother and sister in *Lesbia Brandon* mirrored his disappointed love for a first cousin. Wilson, projecting himself, laments Swinburne's failure to make "his full contribution to English fiction." Though this was by the poet's choice, it is blamed on a schoolboylike deference to his friend Theodore Watts-Dunton, so determined to repress *Lesbia Brandon* he wouldn't give back parts of the text.

Wilson played Swinburne off in his mind against the Marquis de Sade, part of that libertine eighteenth-century France familiar to him from Casanova and others. He sympathized with a rebel whose vitality was eroded during decades of imprisonment, but didn't think Sade had written anything as good as Laclos's *Dangerous Liaisons*, and believed that the vogue of Sade mirrored a moral slippage brought about by World War II. He noted Sade's use of whips and knives and poisoned aphrodisiacs on women who were his social inferiors, an acknowledgment not *de rigueur* in the Sade cult of Barthes, Foucault, and others. By contrast, Swinburne didn't oppress women, but was ineffective with them. When his fellow poet Rossetti set him up with an "international charmer from New Orleans," six weeks later she reported being unable to "get him up to the scratch" or "make him understand that biting's no use." The old Etonian found a happy image of his schooldays in the flogging block. Wilson refers such public-school homosexuality to a social structure in which corporal punishment had been the norm and to the upper-class Englishman's extravagant need to prove himself. When denied parental permission to enlist in the cavalry at seventeen, Swinburne set off to scale an unscalable cliff by the sea and successfully flung himself across a crevasse. "At the top, he fainted; when consciousness returned, he was looking into the nose of a sheep and burst into 'a shout of laughter.'"

At this time Wilson was also pushing his idea for a uniform series of affordable high-quality reprints of American classics, on the model of the French Pléiade. He had proposed that Jason Epstein publish this and Epstein agreed to do so, noting that a substantial subsidy would be needed. In the spring of 1963 President Kennedy wrote a letter supporting the project. For the better part of two decades Epstein would unsuccessfully approach a number of foundations, beginning with the Bollingen Foundation. In 1965 Wilson thought he'd found a source of funds in the newly chartered National Endowment for the Arts and Humanities, the board of which included his old ally Henry Allen Moe. The trade association of English professors, however, acquired the potential subsidy for its Center for the Editions of American Authors. Malcolm Cowley recalled, "The M.L.A. editions had more political strength to muster," involving "a number of universities in different sections of the country," most of which could offer matching funds.

When the first of these books appeared, Lewis Mumford attacked the hedging in of Emerson behind the "barbed wire" of over twenty different editorial abbreviations, and Wilson satirized scholars reading Howells's and Mark Twain's lesser books backward in their search for variant readings. "I propose to disapprove," he says of these "Approved Texts" in "The Fruits of the M.L.A." He ridicules the reprinting of Howells's "tepid" first novel *Their Wedding Journey* (1871), with thirty-five pages of variants and a textual commentary that laboriously traces the book's emergence from travel articles and diaries. Recalling that in his boyhood it had been a popular wedding present, with a sequel, *Their Silver Wedding Journey*, that illustrated the aging of a happy marriage, he testified to reading both these wedding journeys "with a mild, rather cozy interest of tranquility recollected in tranquility." They were scarcely worth "ten dollars apiece as the cost of hyphen-hunting and regularizing the spelling." The "masterpiece of M.L.A. bad book-making" was *The Marble Faun*, where 467 pages of Hawthorne were burdened by 89 of textual introduction and 143 of textual notes, as well as 44 of historical introduction. This book, Wilson noted, was the work of the University of Virginia's Fredson Bowers, whose endless scrutiny of variants seemed without justification. When editing *Leaves of Grass*, Bowers was said to have "done everything for it but read it." Thus Wilson called the MLA to account, in what has been described as "the most important academic act of the post-war years," reminding "the scholars that their duty was to literature."

Though he thought he'd lost out to pedantry, seven years after his death a *New York Times* editorial would greet the founding of the Library of America as "Edmund Wilson's Five-Foot Shelf." The crucial event in the Library's origins would be $500,000 from the Ford Foundation, a farewell gift that its outgoing president McGeorge Bundy solicited to launch the project, conditional on a matching amount from the National Endowment. Bundy turned the money over to a group including Epstein and professors Daniel Aaron and Richard Poirier. The first books to appear, in 1982, were a complete Whitman, Melville's Polynesian novels, Hawthorne's *Tales*, and three novels of Harriet Beecher Stowe, among them *Uncle Tom's Cabin*. Reviewing these editions, Cowley noted that "the Library of America has signed a treaty of peace after Edmund Wilson's war against M.L.A.; wherever possible, it uses the practical results of collaborative scholarship."

Through his friend Morley Callahan's "That Summer in Paris" Wilson had returned to the twenties, the revival of which he'd assisted in after World War II. Dawn Powell recalls him advising Callaghan not to go to an *Esquire* literary event because "all those people are ones Scott and Hemingway hated," yet when promoting Callahan's fiction he allows us to see that his own role in relation to these two stars had sometimes galled him. The Canadian's "powers of observation, so quiet but so alert," were, Wilson states, "never blinded by the dazzling performances that these two great actors of the twenties spent so much of their time putting on": in "his less brilliantly imagined" scene the "self-assertive self-conscious ego" did not "force the world to come to terms with it and, whether in success or failure, to recognize its incomparable importance." It is that rare instance when Wilson the critic falls into solipsism. Proposing that Callaghan's "unobtrusive art is more subtle and his intelligence more mature than those of either of the others," he merely reveals his own wish to have exceeded them in a lifetime of nonfictional prose.

Among his addenda for *The New Yorker* and *The New York Review of Books*, he uses a biography of Mencken to sum up this mentor of his youth, "a poet in prose and a humorist, and in his time, in certain departments, one of the bringers of light to 'the Republic.'" He reviews the original typescript of *The Waste Land* as edited by Pound, judging that Pound's "selection of what is to be kept has been made with unerring taste" and concentrates "an intensity of image and feeling which is not to be found in these drafts." Of Hemingway's *Islands in the Stream*, he shrewdly observes that when the novelist set out to fulfill two familiar American ambitions, "that of becoming an accomplished outdoorsman and that of making a great deal of money," he lost "part of an ideal self that had partly been realized." Wilson had always thought Hemingway not hard-boiled but precarious and tragic. At the Plaza in 1933, Hemingway had recalled how, driving with his young son through what he called "the Faulkner country," he had sat up in their hotel room all night with his gun on the table before him, apparently convinced "that Mississippi was inhabited by Faulkner characters" and that Faulkner "might well send some of these characters to do him violence."

Wilson's farewell to comparative studies was "My Fifty Years with Dictionaries and Grammars," which has (in his words about Dahl's Russian dictionary) "the attractiveness, the personal flavor, of the man with a passion for his subject who has explored the whole field for himself." He looks back to his love of Greek in college and tells how Liddell and Scott's lexicon opened up the brilliance of that long buried world, linking a provincial American student to British poets and prose writers brought up on Greek. Gesenius's Hebrew lexicon illustrates the barrier between Christian and Jewish learning. "All that is unreliable, that is superfluous or now unintelligible in the Masoretic Bible" has "become so distilled to holiness" that a Gentile can hardly ever know what an orthodox Jew experienced in this text." Wilson has fun with Hungarian grammars that are oddly contrived to illustrate linguistic principles through the few words or forms the reader has learned, or that grind an ideological axe. Having set out to learn this language with "a slightly uneasy memory of the senile Baron Hulot in Balzac tottering up to the attic to embark on his last liaison," he reports that it is orderly and condensed. He offers impressions of Petofi and Ady, poets who helped to keep the national consciousness alive. Russian he considers a tissue of idioms, the grammar intractable, the verb forms resistant to Western reasoning. Beginning with Pushkin, however, "the great flow of Russian song and talk, now withdrawing and hushed, now hissing and pushing the shore, was made to pour itself at last into well-blown transparent containers that would make its volatility portable."

His last significant reporting trip was to Israel. On the way he satisfied his curiosity about the Bomarzo monsters near Rome, and an article left incomplete at his death sets down the darkly boastful morals and warnings of the inscriptions that interpret these winged beasts, ogres, and horrid evocations of sexual appetite that were carved in the Italian tufa (a very soft rock-face) as a monument to the bitterness of a sixteenth-century Orsini duke—supposedly a hunchback—whose wife had betrayed him with his brother. The written caricature of Wilson's journals reminds us that he admired Hogarth and others who depicted the grotesque. In *The Sixties*, Truman Capote is first described as "a not unpleasant little monster, like a fetus with a big head." When Capote visited them at the Cape with Newton Arvin—whom Wilson hadn't admired as a literary communist in the 1930s, but was loyal to during Arvin's homosexual scandal—"he seemed more birdlike, as if his head had shrunk." The challenge of getting to the Bomarzo monsters was now, however, almost beyond Wilson. Darina Silone, his companion that day, recalled that "it had been raining and the steep descents there were all muddy," that he was still "half-seas over" from the free liquor on the first-class flight from New York. He wrote to a friend that the hillside was "hard, at my age, to climb, with its dirt paths and worn-down steps." He guarded Darina's handbag while she scouted the lower-level walks and reported back. The power of the place lay in its mystery, and Wilson never believed he had the answers.

From Israel, Teddy Kollek had urged him, as "god-father of the Scrolls," to come see the new Shrine of the Book, which exhibited them with an effect the critic found "a little bizarre but dramatically quite impressive." That May of 1967 Kollek took him to see Agnon, who had received the Nobel Prize a year before. "We drank לחיים, 'L'hayim,' 'to life' in cognac." He reviewed the status of the Scrolls with Flusser and Yadin, delighted also to encounter a border official who tried to argue their dates until told by his supervisor not to do so on government time. Isaiah Berlin recalled Wilson saying that "only in Israel would I find a passport officer who wished to question the date of the Scrolls." It was the eve of the Six-Day War. Flusser informed him that the Arabs were still thinking, as at the time of the Crusades, "in terms of a Holy War: every man or woman of Israel that they blew up with dynamite they regarded as a score for Islam." To Wilson the Israeli military tattoo in preparation for Independence Day was "a terrific demonstration: feverish, high-keyed, a little sinister," and in his journal someone detects "a little the note of Nuremberg." An expanding Zionism would weaken the authority in Israel of the Jewish intellectual and moral tradition he had been depending on, and the potential for disaster was clear. Wilson retells a folktale passed around at the time, in which a scorpion persuades a fearful frog to ferry him over a river they both want to get across. Midway across the scorpion stings the frog, who asks, "'Oh, why did you do that when you'd promised? Now I'll die and you'll drown!' Hisses the scorpion, 'This is the Middle East!'"

A friend recalled how Wilson regretted being unable to report on the war, but the day before he left was "one of my dim and unsteady days," and he'd been "further fatigued" by the feverish "hubbub" at the Tel Aviv airport. Over the next two years he finished constructing a second account of the Dead Sea Scrolls on top of the first, stimulated by discussions with Malachi Martin, a scholarly renegade Jesuit, and W. F. Albright, the archaeologist who had authenticated these documents and hypothesized that the Essenes wrote them. Doubling the size of his 1955 *Dead Sea Scrolls*, in the 1969 edition Wilson takes the position of an aficionado of the various scholars and likens his commentary to that of Hemingway, at the bullring, on the styles of the bullfighters. He maintains a skeptical interest in the claims of John Allegro, an Englishman who, disappointed in his academic career, first told the media that the four Gospels were disguised Essene documents and would later link them and Christianity to a fertility cult involving "the sacred mushroom." When Allegro decided that a list of treasures in the Copper Scroll was real, he angered his colleagues by organizing an expedition that dug up the sites. Though Wilson agreed with him that this list was "too terse and particularized—in its way, too businesslike—not to indicate genuine treasures," he shared Milik's view that the stated quantities of the treasure were too impossibly large to be real. This is exactly where, after four conflicting translations, the debate about the Copper Scroll stands as the twenty-first century begins. A scholar of the Copper Scroll finds the numbers too large but "the very dullness of the document" a sign "this was a real list of something."

Adding the stories of Bar Kochba and of the doomed defense of Masada against the Romans, in the expanded *Scrolls* Wilson notes the interrelationship of religion and charismatic leadership. Though he calls himself "an inveterate myth-shrinker," he is more accepting of the religious temperament than formerly, "the cult of 'reason'" having come to seem "a blind alley." The diffuse last chapter of this book ranges from the beginnings of Mormonism in the revelations of "a charlatan" to "the Jewish poet Boris Pasternak"'s poem about Christ as history's judge, with which *Doctor Zhivago* ends. Yoking two villains of political and religious history, Wilson likens Stalin, who killed communism, to the tyrant Herod, who slaughtered the innocents. In Jesus' "divine-human role" he sees mankind forgiving itself for its imperfections. This was an old idea for the critic, who in 1936 had written, "He who first said, 'Lord, forgive them!' it was he himself who had forgiven." At that time Wilson paralleled Jesus' role in empowering mankind to that of Marx: "So he who said that man advanced on his belly, enabled him to stand upright."

A friend believed that "hard work and hard drinking" had "weakened

Wilson and made him less capable of pursuing a line of thought." But with the scrolls "off my mind" he turned to the pieces that conclude *A Window on Russia* (1970), the new introduction to *To the Finland Station* (1971), and the "T'ville memoir" that would be *Upstate*. He reviewed the memoirs and novels of women witnesses to the purges, books hard for the old progressive to read, detailing "the hatefulness and unnecessary sadism" of this experiment in the arbitrary destruction of human beings. He promoted Stalin's daughter Svetlana Alliluyeva, whose escape to the West and ability to tell her story fit Wilson's view that strong individuals triumph over conditions that defeat others. Her first book, *Twenty Letters to a Friend*, wasn't properly translated, and alternate versions were peddled by the Russians in an effort to discredit her, but he admired the spiritual force of *Only One Year*, giving it a place "among the great Russian autobiographical works: Herzen, Kropotkin, Tolstoy's *Confession*." He suggested his neighbor Paul Chavchavadze as translator, and when the job was done Svetlana came up to Wellfleet to meet Paul. David Chavchavadze recalled the uniquely Russian fashion in which she broke the ice. She had been left at the house while Nina was out shopping, and when the hostess returned she found her guest scrubbing the kitchen floor. Both women had spent part of their childhoods in the Kremlin. Elena liked Svetlana, as did Wilson, who thought her "simple and well-bred—rather shy but with very firm opinions." At one point she kissed him on the cheek, and many years later she'd enjoy recollecting what Wilson, along with George Kennan, had done for her. But she had no tolerance either for Soviet writers whom she thought were compromised or for American liberals she deemed naive.

Wilson now called Stalin simply insane. But "the existence of a Stalin, after all, implies the existence of a nation that will stand for the horrors he inflicts," he asserts in summing up Solzhenitsyn at the end of this uneven collection. The Nobel Prize judges rightly honored Solzhenitsyn's great talent and extraordinary courage, and the truth about the gulag had to be confronted, yet to one who had objected to the moral passivity of the Kafka cult, the Russians seemed to love "the suffering which they denounce." Was it their faith that enabled the characters in *Cancer Ward* and *The First Circle* to endure but not fight back? At points Solzhenitsyn's vision seemed overdrawn. In youth Wilson had objected to Dos Passos's account of "our middle-class republic as a place where no birds sing, no flowers bloom, and where the air is practically unbreathable." He observes that the cat in *Matryona's House* is lame in one paw and can't catch mice, that when she succeeds in catching the cockroaches she eats them and they make her sick. "Of course, she eventually escapes, and gets killed, and Matryona is deeply grieved."

When reading Tolstoy's later fiction in Jamaica during the winter of 1969, the Protestant and Westerner similarly questioned "The Death of Ivan Ilyich," arguing that a smug provincial judge wouldn't have had such a vision of the futility of worldly life. Nabokov, in contrast, endorsed the lengthy sermonizing of this tale as "Old Russian Truth." Wilson was glad Tolstoy had stopped worrying about the souls of starving peasants in order to feed them, that he struggled to overcome the gulf between them and the educated. When faced with the misery of the Moscow poor, Tolstoy asked the same question Nikolay Chernyshevsky had and that Lenin would: "What is to be done?" In these notes Wilson takes up "Resurrection," a tale dramatizing Tolstoy's struggle to rescue from the legal system a young woman who'd been his mistress—the woman finds a more appropriate mate, even as her former lover embraces the New Testament. The little-known short novel *Hadji Murad*, about an episode in an unsuccessful Russian war against the Chechens, impresses him. When a Russian soldier's death both saddens and relieves his wife, now pregnant by a clerk, the American feels he is back in the profound reality of *War and Peace*.

He liked to remember his favorite scenes from reading that novel so long ago at Trees. His own driveway covered in winter snow, he'd relished the pride with which old Prince Bolkonsky, detesting the slick Muscovite who comes to sue for his daughter's hand, has the serfs, who've shoveled miles of snow off the road, shovel it back before their guest arrives. "Though I did not always know which syllable of a Russian word should be stressed and could not have read a page aloud correctly," Wilson recalls, "the voices of the characters, in my winter solitude, seemed to come right out of the pages and to animate my little house": Prince Andrey, Pierre, and Nicholas Rostov, among whom Tolstoy had split up his own personality rather than, as in his late phase as a convert, trying to ignore its contradictions; girlish Natasha "bending her curly head to her knees and filling the whole room with her ringing laugh" as her father pretends to be an eagle. These people had relieved the lonely nights while he wrote *The Triple Thinkers* and began the Marx portrait in *To the Finland Station*. His late "Notes on Tolstoy" recommends *War and Peace* to anyone learning Russian, for "the vocabulary and style are not difficult," and the formal French that Tolstoy so often associates with a false sophistication affords relief from "the old blunt Russian," the length of the novel guaranteeing one learns a good deal of both.

The new introduction to *To the Finland Station*, based on sources not controlled by the Soviets, concedes that to many comrades Lenin seemed harshly oppressive in his "coldness, contempt, and cruelty." Wilson quotes extensively from Richard Pipes's book on the socialist intellectual Pyotr Struve. To Pipes, whom he liked visiting when in Cambridge, he said that, about Lenin, "we have been had," though this staunch anti-communist had never been part of such a "we." Similarly, to Isaiah Berlin, who recalled how he'd "used to preach" about "the horrors" under Stalin while denying that Lenin had anything to do with them, "in the end Wilson said in a strangled voice 'Ah, you know those things you used to say about Lenin, and you thought I was too kind to him, didn't you? Yes, well, well, yes, too kind to him. Yes, well, maybe I was.'" The concession is qualified in his introduction—Lenin "did not show himself so benevolent as I perhaps tend to make him"—but the myth has finally been buried.

If Talcottville may, as Epstein says, be regarded as a literary creation, *Upstate*, in conjunction with his elegiac picture of "The Old Stone House" three decades before, recovers the historical identity of a region. Wilson saw himself a successor to the New York State novelist Harold Frederic. He liked the way that, in Frederic's tale *The Copperhead*, the kindness and sense of justice of a nonconformist farmer opposed to the Civil War gain the respect of neighbors in what is still a frontier democracy. In the fall of 1967 he'd helped stage a conference about Frederic, who is paired with the Chicagoan Henry Fuller in the posthumous collection *The Devils and Canon Barham*. Doubting that the behavior of the hero's temptors in *The Damnation of Theron Ware* is quite plausible, Wilson here notes the difficulty of writing "a great novel" around an attractive character "so abjectly humiliated." Nor had Frederic's lifestyle—consuming endless quantities of liquor and cigars, he was also for a time a successful bigamist—served his work. After his death, James, who had known him in London, regretted (rather like Wilson lamenting the collapse of a college chum) "what H.F. might have done if he had lived—and above all lived (and therefore worked) differently!"

Upstate joins regional and family history to the summer sections of the diaries in a whole that is more than the sum of its parts. There are nature descriptions, residents and summer people, expeditions. He includes his weekend at Ithaca with the Nabokovs, while deleting the 1962 quarrel with Elena and other personal material. One or two notes on the old house "made on whisky" are added, as is an account of his fellow New Yorker Van Wyck Brooks's weaknesses as a critic and virtues as a literary historian. Wilson plays Brooks's nationalism off against the internationalism of T. S. Eliot in the same way that, in *A Piece of My Mind*, he contrasts Holmes and Henry James. The old gentleman who takes up such themes while reporting on his summers and his summer place was nervous whether this book would work, but it was soon selling 1,000 copies a week and bringing him $1,000 a week.

In the prologue the lingering presences of Wilson's ancestors have "mostly evaporated" and he is alone among shelves of books and bric-a-brac. The curtain opens with a tableau dated 1802, featuring a New England Congregationalist's account of visiting cheerful slatternly folk in Lewis County, whose progress has been blocked by the local feudalism. Glimpses follow of the early inhabitants' religious cults. Through the subject of "hardships and dream-pockets" Wilson arrives at Talcottville, where his great-grandfather broke up "the feudal unit" by selling lots to mechanics. He tells how Thomas Baker's acquisition of the stone house by marriage to a spinster Talcott had entailed upon his descendants a nominal dispute with such cousins as formidable Dorothy Mendenhall. He creates a portrait of Cousin Dorothy she would have enjoyed much more than the bust that, we learn, in youth she'd had thrown into a pond.

Many of Wilson's books incorporate cycles of engagement and withdrawal, the enthusiasm of new interests and a certain disillusionment involved in gaining perspective. *Upstate* records the fulfillment of a dream of Talcottville in one decade and its erosion during the next. The journal excerpts taken from *The Fifties* mark his happiness at bringing the old house alive and gratitude to the villagers who, as Elena withdraws, seem almost magically adept at the various tasks that keep the place up and him going. His boyhood enchantment with the landscape is renewed, and he writes, "Nobler country here, which, I think, has made nobler people. It is a part of the whole moral foundation of my life." He conducts us to the spot where an underground river gushes out of the hillside, the creviced terrain and abandoned mill and farm, the artful unfolding of the glen, the stream and falls, making an eighteenth-century wildness and charm. But in the *Sixties* parts of the book this yields to an eighteenth-century vision of decline and fall and a pessimism like that of Twain's late years. Wilson is aware of local unemployment and delinquency, an agrarian community breaking down, and fights a losing battle against the highway builders snatching his lawn to widen a country road. His deteriorating health is embodied in the "vast gray capsizing barns" of the one-time village of Highmarket—"huge carcasses of prostrate buildings, with mixed bones sticking out of a heavy hide."

"Am I really anywhere?" he had asked in his self-interview a decade before, to which the answer now appears to be "Nowhere at all any longer," unless it is at Hyde-Clarke Hall. This pseudo-baronial house had been a wreck since the 1890s, when the floor of the room called the office gave way and the furniture collapsed into the basement. Exploring the place in the epilogue to *Upstate*, he comes on the "gruesome remains" of a grand piano that was never unpacked but "left out on a porch to rot." More than Wilson's own condition is evoked in such an image of the ruins of the American dream. The culture which he had helped to sustain in the United States had, during the late 1960s, reached its end, one the Vietnam War accelerated. Gardner Jencks, Wilson's composer friend at the Cape, recalled that "he was very sad in his last years, because he'd always thought that what he stood for in America would win out." Jason Epstein thought that America was coextensive with the religion of the Enlightenment for Wilson. *Upstate* leaves us with the fragility of the institutions of northern New York, "the swift transience of everything in the United States," the elimination of the old literate class "all over the world."

33

Life Against Death

Wilson had returned from the Middle East to find old age in wait. He wore himself out in New York at the end of October 1967, seeing people, "talking and drinking or going to the theater every night and sometimes having talkative lunches." Back at the Cape he collapsed for several days, then put in some good weeks of work on his notes on Israel and his early journals, in a routine described in *The Sixties* as less than living. His morning bathroom ritual involved "getting the yellow goo off my tongue with a washcloth or towel, hawking up blood-embrowned phlegm, perfunctorily brushing my largely artificial teeth." He didn't get to work until eleven or twelve o'clock. In midafternoon, he reports, "if it is fine and I feel up to it, [Elena] takes me for a little walk like a dog, or a short drive," while in the evening, after listening to records, nursing his drink, and "a modest supper, I read or play more solitaire or am so muggy and sleepy that I go to bed and take a Nembutal or a whisky and go right to sleep." Or, stimulated by another drink, he may lie awake mulling over attractive ideas for writing projects only to discover the next day that he does not have the energy to realize them. Wilson's determined optimism regularly reasserts itself, and when braced by ambition or accomplishment he accepts his waning powers, grateful for an ordered life in the care of Elena and others. But the direction is downward. In December 1968 he writes, "A definite point has now been passed in my life."

The record of his illnesses makes us marvel that he remained so vital. From World War II on he had attacks of gout, and they tortured him when he drank. At different times he suffered from emphysema, diabetes, arthritis, shingles, and a disease resembling malaria, dating from Haiti two decades before, as well as an angina that eventually led to heart attacks. After the bout of shingles in 1968, Dr. Zetzel's notes state that Wilson had lost twenty pounds. As his body deteriorated, each recovery was undermined by the next disaster. He grew hard of hearing and began losing teeth that, when replaced, did not fit properly. His sphincter and urinary muscles grew feeble. He was forced to break away from a conversation in which Lionel Trilling was expounding a theory about *Gulliver's Travels* to go to the men's room but didn't get there in time, returning to the party with a wet trouser leg.

An old Darwinian, he believed that nature would have its way. He distrusted hospitals, believing that he came out in worse condition than he went in, but from 1969 to 1971 he was in and out of them, more than once insisting on leaving before the doctors thought it wise. Six months after signing a release to leave the hospital in Hyannis, where he had spent three days after a coronary, Zetzel noted that his patient had stopped taking his medication because this made him weak and had therefore put on weight, which made him short of breath. Wilson rationalized to his physician that liquor relaxed him when upset, but alcohol contributed to his debility. As it became harder for him to get around, he could be limited to a pint a day, which he and Elena fetched on walks to the local liquor store. His encounters with doctors and hospitals caused him to drink less during his last year or two, giving him a clearer idea of his condition.

He was losing sexual vitality, yet his relations with women provided the incentive to live. He was most likely to feel "a strong passion" for his wife when at the stone house without her. On a day when Elena and he made love, she remarked that they'd had "almost twenty years of one another," a line he used in verses for their anniversary dinner:

> All this, my dearest love, and so much more
> Makes up the woman that I still adore,
> Surprised to find myself now old and slow,
> The man who loved you twenty years ago.

The next year Wilson notes, "Though I think still a great deal about sex, it has come to seem to shrink in dignity and intrinsic importance." Yet a few weeks later in Israel, when chronicling his experiences in long letters to Elena that momentarily take the journal's place, he writes, "I think of you every morning when I first wake up and wonder why, when I still had it, I didn't make love to you everyday."

Platonic relationships helped sustain him. Until the end of his life he regularly wrote to Mary Meigs and she to him. "I really love her and always shall," he states in *The Sixties*. He had got to know Clelia Carroll when they served with Edward Gorey on the board of a children's book series called the Looking Glass Library. Charmed by the way she blushed and "her frank direct way of talking," he conceived a "yearning" for this woman who, like Meigs, seemed a throwback to his own generation, reminding him of the debutantes his college friends had dated. One day Wilson, sticking his neck out, asked Elena why he was so fond of Clelia, to which Elena—knowing that Clelia's father was a Manhattan financier and perhaps teasing him about their current finances—replied by spelling out "m-o-n-e-y." Clelia, then living on an eighteenth-century estate near Baltimore and engrossed in the demands of motherhood, found Wilson enormously stimulating. Though they rarely saw each other, the two corresponded for eight years. His letters to her, collected in thirty-five pages of *The Man in Letters*, cover everything from his travels and his eating habits when shifting for himself at Talcottville (caviar for lunch and pork and beans out of a can at supper) to his favorite operas, *Tosca*, *La Traviata*, and *The Ring*.

Wilson related to cultivated women by wanting to go to bed with them, and in the journal he supposes that his poem "By Dark Cocytus' Shore" was inspired by desire for Clelia. He sent this to her without comment when it was published in a limited edition, with Mary Meigs's drawing of a Lucifer-like man about town and an adoring blonde. When he dreamed of Clelia she was less attractive than in person, which he took as repression or censorship: "I wanted her not to be so attractive because I couldn't have her." Never, she stated, did Wilson say a word to her about love. The most intimate moment between them is mentioned neither in the journal nor in their letters. They were in a taxi and he asked her, "Do you believe in God?" She answered, "No," and, she says, "he took my hand and held it."

As his sexual relationship with Elena faded, erotic friendships with Mary Pcolar, Anne Miller, and Penelope Gilliatt flavor the journal as they did his life. All were younger women who looked up to Wilson. Mary was awed when she typed a letter from him to President Kennedy. Wilson admired her energy and all-round competence—she had once delivered a baby in a snowstorm—writing to Clelia from Talcottville, "My Hungarian superwoman is still able to console my solitude." Though Mary was first and always his pupil, she could challenge him intellectually. When she read *Memoirs of Hecate County* and didn't like it, she told the Wilson enthusiast Frederick Exley she had gone so far as to remark, "This effort at fiction is just a silly attempt to keep your finger in every pie." In *The Sixties* she observes that during these summers they have grown together, yet he was uncomfortably aware of the relationship "not having been consummated and never to be consummated: I can't make love to her and there is no opportunity of my doing very much to educate her." For a while he paid her tuition at Utica College, but her hard-earned good grades brought her no more success than her efforts to teach poise and manners in classes for women at the Boonville drugstore or to the stewardesses for Mohawk Airlines.

Wilson wrote to Mary—at first practicing Hungarian—from Wellfleet, Cambridge, the *New Yorker* offices, and from abroad, and sent her homemade valentines as he did Elena and all the other women in his life. On a night after his return from Israel he gave her champagne cocktails and white wine at dinner, then asked her to stop at the side of the road and "we had a real kiss." There were cars behind them, and she wouldn't stop again—"Have to put you in the back seat!" she said. He was gratified to have had "a spontaneous reaction," something that hadn't "happened to me in a long time." Mary later said "she'd been as if in a dream" that evening, "and this," he adds, "somewhat embarrassed me." To a woman observer about this time they projected an air of intimacy. Two years later, after his first major hospitalization, they kissed in the car again, and, with the lights out, on the living room sofa. "I took out my cock, and she felt it. It was gratifying to be conscious that it was capable now of an erection." Mary gave him "little kisses" in the dark, murmuring remarks "so softly that, in my deafness, I could not understand and would have to put my ear to her mouth and ask her to repeat it." At the end of this rather maternal scene she said, "Thanks for trying," and the experience, he says, "bucked me up." When *Upstate* came out, minus these details that wouldn't appear until long after their deaths, Mary rejoiced in her local celebrity as his companion. "How can I thank you for all you've done for me?" she wrote, extravagantly calling him "the world's greatest man," in a second letter saying "*We* have bridged the generation gap and the sex barriers were not involved. It's love in the purest sense."

An easier relationship was with Anne Miller, who, like Mary, was married with children, but was middle-class and in something of an open marriage. Dr. Edgar (Ned) Miller in Lowville was the only dentist able to keep Wilson's teeth functioning, putting back "three of my old upper row of false teeth [that] came out" and making him a denture. He thought Wilson wonderful when he rose from two miserable hours in the dentist's chair to ask where he could get the best champagne in town. Miller had been radicalized by a grim experience with a combat team that burned villages and transferred populations during the Korean War, and he would later join an Indian religious sect. Anne was independent-minded, interested in literature and life, and she was eager to be instructed. The interchange of the educational with the erotic that eluded Wilson with Mary occurred with her.

When the Millers took him to their lakeside camp in the fall of 1969, Anne showed him her free verse and he resolved to give her some training, following up with a note to the effect that a poet had to create his or her own form. In the journal, he sees in her work "her constant longings for something beyond and better, though with a certain enjoyment of her current life and love for her husband." The next June she came to see him, first with Ned, then by herself for an afternoon that included Moselle wine, criticism of her poetry, and discreet gossip about what had been her affair with a minister in a neighboring town, as well as extensive kissing. "I am a very warm person," she explained, later saying, "Nothing illicit," that she was resolved not to "put the horns on" Ned. Wilson was glad she showed a certain "yen" for him before finding his name on *Esquire*'s list of "the hundred most important people in the world." A few days later Anne took him to one of his favorite spots on the Sugar River, helping him through the stones—she swam naked, and from the hillside he saw "her slim brownish figure from behind." That day they discussed their children, the nature of his marriages to Elena and Mary McCarthy, as well as the subjects of companionship, loneliness, extramarital relations, and jealousy, she recalled from a list made after Wilson's death. Another day, they ate what he calls "terrible" sausage sandwiches at a roadside stand and drank a double bottle of "a cheap kind of wine called Ripple."

Wilson could, he writes, "only get an erection at half-mast," so Anne remained loyal to her "principles" while letting him caress her when he came back to Talcottville for more dentistry that fall. She liked the way he touched her, and at a second meeting in September 1970 she "undressed almost completely" and he stroked and kissed her wherever he wished. He thought she missed the minister and was glad to try to compensate; when she said she was "underkissed," he "told her that if she would forgive my saying so, he thought she was not fucked enough." In the journal he feels back "in the twenties," and perhaps this was when they discussed Millay, whose sonnets he'd mentioned, as well as Anaïs Nin, whom Anne had read. Like Louise Connor in his youth, Anne is given a false initial ("Z") in a passage Wilson moved to the end of a section of *The Sixties*, nominally disguising the woman who shows the old man in garters the virtues of open-mouth kissing and lets him savor the feel of her "wet, gluey, reeking" parts.

Anne Miller and he were never so physically intimate again, but from that fall until his death two years later they wrote back and forth, he sending his regards to Ned or his love to both. The increasingly crippled Wilson was eager for her companionship in this form and urged her to "drop me a line—I don't insist on a sonnet." Anne's letters—sometimes including poems, once a photograph Ned took of her in front of the stone house—recount her activities, everything from reading to traveling to gardening; she confides details of her life and asks questions of him. He mentions a "delightful meeting" with Nin, whose diaries from 1944 to 1947 had just appeared. When the next volume appeared he told Anne, that, inscribing him a copy, Anaïs called him "so much a father figure to her that she did not really have a clear idea of me." Anne, looking back in 1992, on Wilson's "multifaceted personality, ongoing curiosity, his enthusiasm, his objectivity and wisdom," thought Nin's diaries revealed "at times a less-than-kind and a rather superficial, 'fey' female"—as much of a challenge to "direct, sincere, worldly Edmund" as the learning of a new language.

His last fling was with Penelope Gilliatt, a brilliant woman of an aristocratic English family who had entered Oxford at sixteen, had been married to the playwright John Osborne, and was now one of *The New Yorker*'s movie critics. Wilson described her to Clelia in 1968 as "terribly nice," "very goodlooking, with bright red hair that she says not even the beauty parlors can believe is real." When they met she was breaking up with Mike Nichols. She entertained him with stories about her former lover (parts of which she seems to have fabricated), and was in other ways a pleasure to have around, laughing at his jokes, whispering into his ear as he grew too deaf to follow the conversation. Penelope was willing to drink with him, a lot, as Elena would not, and he sometimes escorted her in New York, with which Elena was quite comfortable. At one point her affection toward Wilson in public mildly embarrassed him. While earnest Anne Miller had thought him wise when he belittled the pursuit of happiness, saying, "Why do you speak of it so often? Living is not happiness alone," Penelope was impressed by his courage, that although he was so debilitated he hadn't given up. When he did the "trick with a white hand-kerchief that he called the jumping mouse" for her daughter Nolan, he couldn't manage it "with arthritic hands." One Christmas at Wellfleet Wilson had a hemorrhage in his right eye, but still filled stockings for Penelope and Nolan. At the top of the child's there was "a huge stuffed tiger," which she had to struggle to carry through the snow back in Man-hattan. When she said, "I can manage, I can manage," Penelope heard an echo of Wilson's fortitude.

On a dull election day at the Princeton Club in the fall of 1970, he and Penelope, finding the bar closed, began kissing on the couch and moved upstairs to his room, where she disrobed, revealing a more attrac-tive body than he'd expected—"firm but not large breasts," her vagina "with a little fringe of red hair. Beautiful sheer ivory white skin, the kind that goes with her hair." (Since Gilliatt was living when *The Sixties* went to press—she died before the book appeared—the word "red" in the original journal was omitted by the editor and the publisher, to each of whom she denied that she was "O.") Afterward, perhaps flattering him, Penelope said, "I look like a woman who's been fucked," to which, given his own capaci-ties, he replied, "Not enough," and though "she disillusioned me about my conquest by telling me she had two other 'fucking friends,'" in subse-quent letters she said she'd enjoyed herself and spoke of a repeat. The fol-lowing spring Penelope wrote to say he shouldn't distress himself that their intimacy would hurt or anger Elena. Assuming she was trusted as a family friend, Penelope didn't take any chances, and added, "Perhaps you should destroy this note." But Wilson destroyed nothing.

In Jamaica in 1969 Elena and he read the Russian classics side by side. Wilson came to enjoy swimming again, without much liking this ocean. A jingle titled "Tristes Tropiques" describes "the wide and calm unquiet sea" much as does Claude Lévi-Strauss, who calls the tropical ocean cheerless and associates the calmness of the weather with evil. They flew to Kingston, where cultural events were arranged at the Amer-ican embassy. He became friends with John Hearne, a writer of mixed Irish and African descent, who would visit him at Talcottville. Elsewhere on the island Wilson met expatriated Montrealers through Elena. But on his first night on the island he threw up with what he thought was ackee poisoning (a pendant to a kind of fruit which is poisonous until it is ripe), and when he insisted on returning to Wellfleet to read proofs, he had another attack on getting home. Elena had a similar episode in Jamaica, but her symptoms vanished, while his recurrent chills and fevers became, for Dr. Zetzel, "indirect evidence" that he was carrying a tropical parasite. They spent ten days at Lillian Hellman's Fifth Avenue apartment, from which he was admitted to Doctor's Hospital for a throat condition. Difficult months at Wellfleet followed. His appetite was poor, and in Cambridge Dr. Zetzel noted "He apparently had a stroke involving his right hand, so he has trouble with writing and can do so only with difficulty." However, "he refused to get undressed so I could examine him totally." Among the loyal friends of his later years were Hellman, whom Mary McCarthy would so bitterly attack for not telling the truth about her Stalinist past, and Charley Walker, once with Adelaide a Trotskyist, now like her orthodox Episcopalian. Hellman's politics bothered Wilson less than her plays. He wished she'd written about Jews, instead of projecting Jewish family dramas onto Southerners whom he found unconvincing. But the two of them shared a commitment to facts rather than theory, and she'd recall him phoning to discuss a comic strip and its meaning. Though Charley translated Greek drama and wrote about labor relations, his career had not been what Wilson hoped. Yet the Walkers had lived a few hundred feet from the Wilsons since Edmund's marriage to Mary McCarthy, the adults enjoying regular drinks and dinners, the children complaining that when the talk got juicy they were always sent to the kitchen for more ice. He felt that Charley should have discouraged Adelaide's testimony in the McCarthy divorce, but the coolness between the two men disappeared when they shared old age and heart problems. Rosalind says "they were deeply and touchingly close."

In New York in May 1971 his left leg buckled at an O'Neill play and he fell down in the aisle. The next day, after he took Penelope, Nolan, and Nolan's nanny to the circus, Penelope helped him up to his room. He'd had nothing to eat since morning but part of a sandwich, and rapidly swallowed "three martinis." When she left, he tried to sit on the edge of the bed and missed, coming down hard on the floor and fracturing a vertebra. "Like a good angel" Elena rushed down from the Cape to his rescue. A brief effort to recuperate in Talcottville failed and he returned to Wellfleet. His final summer there was calming but monotonous, with at night "sterile fantasies" of Penelope and Anne.

Paul Chavchavadze also had a heart condition, and when Wilson learned that their old neighbor Dos Passos's heart had been weakened by recurrent rheumatic fever, he wrote Dos to recruit him for "the Cape Cod Cardiac Writers Association." These sufferers had organized to demand their rights—abolition of the unnecessary blood tests that weakened one, "the use of pornographic matter to be synchronized into the rhythm" of the heartbeat monitors. Offering a positive example at the letter's end, as was his wont, Wilson states that since his latest hospitalization his life has been most "enjoyable," that it is convenient to have a bed in his study and be able to "crawl" to his writing table. Dos wanted to live on—he told Crystal Ross, once his fiancée, that they should do so as long as they had their wits—but he would die of rheumatic fever in September 1970, less than six months after this letter and some eighteen months before Wilson's death.

The letter claims he doesn't know whether to relate Dos Passos's heart trouble to the novelist's expedition to Easter Island—"to your report on which," he says, "I am eagerly looking forward"—or to "the strain of your public statement that [Spiro] Agnew is 'the greatest Greek since Pericles.'" It had been thirty-five years since they were close allies, when he'd lent Dos his books and articles on Henry Ford for the biographical sketch in *The Big Money*, and Dos opened doors for him in Moscow while warning of its "hush-dope" politics. In *The Sixties* Wilson cites Dawn Powell's view that Dos's right-wing agenda was inspired, not just by recovering his Virginia estate, but "by a belatedly developed family sense, the result of having a daughter and a genuinely wifely wife, and by the desire 'to belong.'" Wilson agrees, adding, "He now wants to be an upstanding flourishing 100% American, the kind of character that he used to despise in his youth." *U.S.A.* would return to favor as the century ebbed, keeping its author before college classes, but Dos's later novels were little read. In conversation, Wilson thought their weakness wasn't that he attacked American culture from the Right rather than the Left, but that he was "now a farmer" and lacked time for serious work, having only "between six in the morning and quarter of nine to write." On his part Dos noted that when "the Talcottville Squire" visited "Spence's Point" he showed no interest in farming.

Upstate New York continued to absorb him. The reporter's last foray was to the spiritualist town of Lily Dale at the western end of the state on Lake Erie. It turned out to be a strange community "of sleazy fakers—uncomfortable and unreal." He sat through several seances and with one of his companions, an English professor at Hamilton College, made an appointment for a seance at which he intended to try to materialize Scott Fitzgerald. The medium didn't show up and he told himself she feared to be exposed by a writer, since he was going around making notes on his usual yellow legal pad. *Another* expedition to check out an imposture would have been amusing were it not for the image it gave him of his own condition. The Cardiff giant was a fake petrified man that had been first planted, then dug up, in an enterprising hoax a century before. A statue more than ten feet tall and carved in Chicago, the Onandaga Indians had believed it genuine, and the aged Emerson declared it "very wonderful and undoubtedly ancient." When Wilson's housekeeper drove him to see the statue in a pit near Syracuse, its legs had been broken off at the knees and its genitals and toes eroded. Having been dragged to a succession of county fairs and made to endure the terrible winters, the giant lay "as if stiffened by death, with its immense square skull and imposing penis, the product, it seems to me, of an overwhelming compulsion to create some superhuman being to walk those New York State hills, where the Word of God had not been spoken." Wilson comments, "Poor old giant! One can't help pitying him."

When Wilson broke the trip between Talcottville and Wellfleet at Helen Muchnic's home in Cummington, Massachusetts, in 1971, he was too weak to shave himself and "Elena was carrying a special mechanism, which helped him breathe in attacks of angina." Muchnic invited V. S. Pritchett, the British critic and story-writer, for lunch. Learning that the trip had been such a strain that he wasn't able to join them, Pritchett expected to see "a disastrous figure." He recalled, "Far from it: there he was lying on a couch with a tartan rug over him, and the moment we came into the room a bubble of conversation started, just like a fountain, as gay as anything! In two minutes he was laughing—not out loud; he never laughed very loudly, but seemed to laugh all over his body quietly. His chest began to shake, his stomach began to shake, his legs began to shake, laughter seemed to be absolutely pouring down him. He went from subject to subject, delighted by everything that was at all amusing. He appeared to me to be absolutely full of life." The Englishman was afraid of staying too long, but as he finally left, Wilson commanded Elena, "with a real imperial manner," to bring in some more friends. Yet this interval seems to have cost him, for the journal notes that "in some ways [Pritchett] makes rather heavy demands: laughs too much, and you have to laugh with him."

By this time, Nabokov had learned that Wilson had been ill, and he wrote that he'd long since ceased to bear a grudge "for your incomprehensible incomprehension of Pushkin's and Nabokov's *Onegin*." On rereading their letters he'd felt again "the warmth of your many kindnesses, the various thrills of our friendship, that constant excitement of art and intellectual discovery." In a line missing in Simon Karlinsky's collection of the correspondence—this edition was cleared by the two widows, and Vera apparently excised it—Nabokov provocatively adds, "I am sure you agree with me that Solzhenitzyn is basically a third-rate writer." Replying, Wilson disagreed and called Solzhenitzyn "remarkable, though somewhat monotonous." He let Nabokov know that he'd included "an account of my visit to you in a book that will be out this spring," hoping this "will not again impair our personal relations (it shouldn't)."

However, the pages about the 1958 Ithaca weekend in *Upstate*, which had just gone to press, made a rapprochement impossible. Wilson noted the issues of tact in publishing these accounts of the past, yet when writing of his old antagonist he sticks to his intention—stated to Leon Edel—not "to cut any corners." The two men are seen arguing about Russian and English versification, and Vera sides with Volodya when his authority is challenged, a slightly jealous protector who is perhaps "irked" at having to serve Wilson away from the table. In a summation Nabokov cannot have appreciated, Wilson relates the *schadenfreude* he dislikes in the novels to Nabokov's displacement from Russia and the "miseries, horrors, and handicaps" he had confronted in exile, which the artist had "overcome by his fortitude and his talent." Nabokov was "a strong character, a terrific worker, unwavering in his loyalty to his family, with a rigor in his devotion to his art which has something in common with Joyce." Thus Wilson the moralist comes to the critic's rescue, enabling him to link Nabokov to Joyce without putting their work on the same plane. Of this judgment Isaiah Berlin observed, "he was a moral being, Edmund was, whose approach to life was indelibly moral, as is that of the Russian writers." Nabokov, however, Berlin adds, "was purely aesthetic." He had no interest in being praised more than his work, and the references to Vera enabled him to take the whole passage as an insult.

In a letter to *The New York Times Book Review* when the book appeared, Nabokov purported to feel sorry for Wilson because of his health, but declared that "in the contest between compassion and honor, honor wins"—had he known his guest's disrespect for his wife, he'd have asked him to leave the house. Wilson's brief reply—he had less than a year to live—cites "What Whistler said of Degas, 'You behave as if you had no talent.'" Katharine White, who had edited both at *The New Yorker*, believed this a "perfect answer" to a letter that was "uncalled for and outrageous and just plain silly. His honor!" It saddened her "to see how an overwhelming ego like his and world-wide success can change a man's personality so shockingly." For the Russian, however, the duel had been resumed.

Upstate also jolted Elena, for Wilson was all too satisfied with his life in that world from which she had subtracted herself. Because he used only the parts of what would be *The Fifties* and *The Sixties* set in northern New York, she was deprived of passages about her importance to him and their lovemaking, the verses for their anniversary dinner, the account of their marriage as a love affair that continued. He left out the description of their birthday quarrel in 1962, but at one point it is recalled as "rather bitter." Although he censored his intimacies with Mary Pcolar, what Elena calls "the Upstate Book" made her feel betrayed. She was distressed at what local people would think of him for spending so much time with Pcolar, and told Rosalind she was disappointed that this woman, whom she'd met once in her "drip-dry drugstore uniform," wasn't "better quality." Rosalind stoked Elena's fears with the apparently false report that Mary had "a reputation of sleeping with old rich men" and aroused her maternal indignation by reporting that Mary had said Helen could profit by her instruction in charm.

Elena completed her memoir of Talcottville, "My View from the Other Window," in Florida, where they spent their last winter. So lacking in her characteristic resilient warmth, this reprise of bitter details was darkened by a desolate three months in Naples. The environment of condo retirement living, which they chose as preferable to flying to the Caribbean, oppressed them. Because of a construction project they had to switch apartments, and their car was smashed when Elena was run into at an intersection. Though a doctor said it was his gout, Wilson thought he had another stroke, which turned out to have been the case. "One ought perhaps to have died before reaching this point, when one still had the illusion of participating," he'd written not long before, and, of the life around him, "All that energy expended to peter out! One looks down on an empty arena." In the five journal pages devoted to Naples, he observes from a window rich old couples trying to enjoy themselves around a pool, makes conversation when he can, works up a character or two. It is "a sunlit hell of dullness (air-conditioned nightmare)."

Rallying as best he could from his illnesses, Wilson had continued to give his life meaning through his reading—he was marching through Balzac's novels—and in the journal, *The Sixties*. Throughout its last 150 pages, after the Aspen Institute dinner, he records illnesses and recoveries of enthusiasm. "The most beautiful fall here I have ever seen," he writes at Talcottville, where during her two weeks Elena and he "go for little walks every afternoon"—"foliage so wonderful that, at this time of life, I hardly try to describe it," though the paragraph contains brilliant evocations. "Sometimes a gold-soaked mist," he writes. Sharing this doesn't lead Elena to stay on upstate, and in a happy dream in the journal's later pages, he imports Frances to the old stone house, into the bed that had been moved downstairs for him. "When, with joy, I was just about to possess her, the nurse tapped my shoulder to wake me up and take the medicine."

If daily reminders of his coming demise were not enough, he was moved by the decline and death of others, both present and past. Several times he visited his old friend Betty Huling at the hospital in New York. This staunch woman had been reduced to "a state of helplessness" by cancer long before she knew it was fatal. "Too bossy, too independent" to have been married, she ended up entirely alone: "So abounding in good nature and affection and energy and humor, to be extinguished as a suffering withered wisp like this." The dedicated writer's luminous language was supported by his sense of his great predecessors. When he finished reading the *History of England* in the middle of the night Macaulay's example encouraged him: "Though he was dying, he more or less rounded it out by writing the deaths of James and William" before he'd reached the place of these in his narrative. "Quite fortifying to find him sustaining it, with the same high morality and thoroughness."

After his last coronary Wilson determinedly refused a pacemaker, convinced that nature should take its course, not wanting to end up on life support with diminished mental capacity. Elena and he returned from Naples to the Cape via Charlottesville, where he briefly visited his cousin, Susan, a strong-minded woman to whom, in the later years, he felt increasingly close. He outlined "the present state of my various books" in a letter to Roger Straus, and at Wellfleet in April planned the publication of *The Twenties*, having added, he thought, enough interpolated commentary and outlived everyone about whom, in this early installment of his memoirs, he'd written with any frankness. John Peck, his copy editor, absorbed into the text the entries on Frances that had been in a separate notebook. A sales conference was set for May 18, and there was to be talk about the jacket design. Early in May, however, Wilson had a severe stroke. While waiting for the ambulance, on the phone in a voice that was "a little thick" he reminded Straus of promising to publish the diaries without any cuts. He spent a week in the Hyannis hospital and when he got out was still unable to "talk distinctly," but he wrote to his soul mate Mary Meigs. His voice began to come back, though he had trouble moving around. On May 27 he wrote to Shawn at *The New Yorker* that he would be at his New York State address for a couple of weeks, saying "Roger Straus will send you a complete proof of my book on the twenties. Please send me your selections from it so that I can see what has been done." He added the postscript, "The writing of books is an endless matter. *Ecclesiastes* 12:12."

In 1971 Elena had done her best to prevent him from going to Talcottville, saying "it would kill him." But in 1972, in the letdown documented in "My View" and with Helen now at Wellfleet, Reuel and his family soon to arrive, she didn't insist on accompanying him when he was determined to go and he didn't coax her. Instead, recalled Helen Muchnic, "he made all kinds of plans for her benefit as to what he would do when he came back." Elena later said the airlines wouldn't have taken him if they'd known how sick he was, that Mary Pcolar encouraged him to come. But when Mary picked him up at the Syracuse airport—as she later told Exley—she was painfully aware of the difficulty with which he moved from what he called a "wheeled chair" to her car. For some time he had been using a walker. Rosalind, who now lived across the street in the house that had belonged to Wilson's Aunt Addie, had prepared the downstairs room with an emergency telephone and a green oxygen tank and engaged a neighbor, Elizabeth Stabb, who was a trained nurse. She was pleased that her father had returned to the turf they'd shared since 1969, and during the first week she spent several nights on the couch, relieving Mrs. Stabb. Glyn Morris drove him around and helped him pass the time, as did Anne Miller.

Wilson brought with him a piece of unfinished business. It had sobered him to grow sicker, and when recuperating from his stroke at Wellfleet he realized that he and Elena and Rosalind and Helen had pretty well gone through his advances for *A Window on Russia*, the new edition of *To the Finland Station*, the book of essays that would be *The Devils and Canon Barham*, as well as *The Twenties*. He still owed almost $25,000 to Farrar, Straus, with the contract for his journals held as collateral. His will gave the royalties for his work to Elena and then to Helen, but for some years all he was likely to leave them was debt, and he worried that Helen, setting out on the life of a full-time artist, had no trust fund such as Rosalind and Reuel would divide, by then worth almost $300,000. Having once mentioned to Helen that he was dubious about Reuel and her dividing the Wellfleet house, late in May he called her into the study and explained that he was leaving it to her alone, as the library was left to his son. Though Reuel had lived there for three or four years of his childhood and visited every summer, he could not practice his professon at the Cape, as Helen one day might, and since the two of them got along well, Reuel and his wife and child could continue to come and go in summers. Helen recounted this interview to her mother, and Wilson had sent from Boston a codicil to his will, which he took over to Talcottville, his legal residence, to sign and have witnessed. He apparently intended to explain all this to his son on return to the Cape, where Reuel was expected. Reuel, ironically, passed by south of Talcottville on the New York Thruway on the night of June 6.

The codicil was witnessed by Glyn Morris and Rosalind, but it was not signed by Wilson, for Rosalind became hysterical when she learned that he was leaving the house to Helen, saying she didn't want to take part in something that would hurt her brother. She had loved him since he was a baby, and the alliance had a place in her competition with Elena and Wellfleet. In her version of events in *Near the Magician* (1989), her father attributes the codicil to Elena's pressure and assures her she shouldn't worry because "Nothing will come of it." Rosalind presents his failure to sign as the magician's last trick, one played on his wife. Helen recalls that Wilson told Elena on the phone that Rosalind had made a scene, but that he had the document witnessed and sent it off to the lawyer. When Elena learned it had arrived unsigned, she assumed he'd forgotten to write in his own name while trying to reassure his daughter, and by this time Wilson was dead.

In his last days he went through the motions of drinking, pouring drinks as if for old time's sake and then leaving them covered by pieces of paper. "One day he got up and went all through the house, managing the two flights of stairs up to the top floor," Rosalind noted. When Mary came to do his letters, he sent her to Boonville for some hamburger steak and the newspapers. In the last letter she typed for him—her fingers, she recalled, almost paralyzed above the keys by the sound of his labored breathing—he congratulated Auden on being given a cottage at Oxford where he could finish out his life comfortably. In Wilson's final picture, taken by a photographer for Roger Straus three days before he died, he looks out stoically from his chair upon the world that he expected to leave like "a puff of smoke."

Among the journal's last undated passages are a comment on "Father's language," seven lines of humorous verse "for E." about the plight of old age, and Tennyson's line, "and white sails flying on the yellow sea," followed by Swinburne's comment on the beauty and truth of this poem. In a brief note done June 5 or 6, these first days in Talcottville are called "rather a desolate stay," marked by other people's maladies and misadventures. A second short paragraph begins "Millers and Glyn Morris madly working for McGovern." Wilson, who thought Nixon "an empty valise," sported a McGovern button when taken by Mary to *The Godfather* on the night of June 8 and by Anne to *The French Connection* on the night of the tenth. "Painful getting in and out of theatres," he writes, and sums up the two films, "Bang bang." His last note, apparently written Sunday morning the eleventh, is "Ned Miller harangued me about diet as if he had had a religious conversion." That day the Millers left off some pills, which Wilson ignored, pleasing Rosalind, who resented Anne. Dr. Miller thought doses of vitamin C might help him absorb all the ibuprofen he was taking for pain, potentially straining his digestion and his heart. Miller, however, knew Wilson "hated living now, had no great fear of death."

When Glyn took him for a country drive on Sunday afternoon and they passed a cemetery he seemed fascinated, saying "I'm going to be cremated." He signed his Social Security check and had Rosalind cash it at a store. He told Mary he was going back to the Cape Monday morning and didn't know when he'd see her again. After what Rosalind says was a good supper, he had her put him to bed, remarking, "Oh that I should have come to this." She got him up again when his farmer cousins the Munns called—he was apparently doing some fence-mending, after a tactless characterization in *Upstate*. The next day Rosalind was to drive him to Helen Muchnic's, there to be met by Elena for the return trip to Wellfleet. But she recalled saying not "Goodnight," but "Goodbye, Father," as she left him to go back to her house. Wilson was put back to bed by his nurse, Mrs. Stabb. He read over Housman's *Last Poems* in a copy that he'd given to an upstate aunt he loved, and had a glass of white wine.

Before Karl Marx died, Wilson describes him getting out of bed and sitting down at his work table. Mrs. Stabb said that on the morning of

June 12 Wilson got himself up and went to his chair in the front room behind the table with his papers, the pose of his last photograph. He had picked up a book and was reading it—found nearby was a dog-eared copy of *The Mystery of Edwin Drood*, with which Dickens had been struggling at his death. For some time, in the tradition of the nineteenth-century masters that he carried on, he had been considering what would be his last words, as he'd told Helen Muchnic, little knowing that it would come down to one. When Mrs. Stabb asked whether he'd like a bath or breakfast first, he answered, "Breakfast." Hearing a harsh rasping noise she returned. She hooked him up to the oxygen cylinder and phoned Rosalind, who hurried over in her nightclothes. Wilson had two convulsions and by 6:30 a.m. was dead of a coronary occlusion, which the doctor later said a pacemaker would have prevented. But he had died on his own terms in a place he loved, nowhere near doctors and hospitals. Rosalind called Elena, who "kept saying 'It's not true. It's not true.'" On the phone to Helen Muchnic, about seven o'clock, however, Elena said, "Well, he wanted it this way."

There were two services, one for the Talcottville people and another at Wellfleet. The Talcottville service was at home. Laid out in his pajamas and robe on the big brass bed in the library, Wilson looked to the local writer Walter Edmonds "more like a Roman bust than a dead body." He had told Glyn Morris, "I don't want any of these atheistic funerals," and Elena, as he requested, asked Glyn to read the Ninetieth Psalm and the twelfth chapter of Ecclesiastes, which he had cited to Shawn. Elena spent a moment with the body before it was placed in the coffin.

She returned with Wilson's ashes to Wellfleet, where his three children, close friends, and many others gathered at the gravesite. The service again consisted of Ecclesiastes and the Ninetieth Psalm. The Ecclesiastes reading seemed to Daniel Aaron "a posthumous lecture to his contemporaries and a bleak, hedonistic assertion from the Other Side: What can we know of the future, much less of the hereafter, or of justice on this earth where the wicked prosper? Nothing. Cling to this life, do your work well." Charley Walker—himself, Rosalind writes, "in the last stages of terminal heart trouble"—read a short eulogy. When he said that Wilson was "religious," Elena broke in with "That's absurd, Charley." She was loyal to Wilson and a committed Christian. But in some sense Walker too was right, for in Wilson an affirmation of mundane reality, the day and its expressive task, sustained the religion of art. Of the agnostic Flaubert he had written to Gauss, "Some of his books may resound a little bit like tombs, but say what you please, he had in him the real principle of spiritual life."

As Walker's reading ended, in Jason Epstein's account he "took a step toward the grave, flung his arms wide" and said, "*Shalom*, old friend." The three letters of Wilson's Hebrew motto, were cut on the white marble tombstone by Helen's companion Timothy Woodman, not many years later to be joined by ΑΘΑΝΟΤΟΣ Η ΨΥΧΗ on Elena's stone, the Greek for "Deathless the soul."

Elena wrote to his Red Bank acquaintance Margaret Edwards, who had known Wilson since childhood, "He had been very, very sick but he died quickly and easily and his mind was all there—all of it." Wilson's work of re-creating what he saw and thought continues to sustain us, through words that seem to effortlessly flow (as we know they did not). Some of the prose of his late observations upstate takes us into the appreciative heart and discerning mind of this American patriot, who, as the country's institutions seemed to fail, found through his art the balance of life and death in the very landscape. He had absorbed much in his long, strenuous life and had carried, among other things, the wonder of his early nature walks with an aunt into old age. At the Sugar River falls, he writes, "You find yourself in a high-walled chasm of stratified limestone rock which is feathered with green fern and lined in the cracks with green moss. Birds flit back and forth between the walls. The river runs shallow here with moderate rapids. The cliffs where they overhang are dripping with springs, and across the river, the farther one goes, the more densely they are plumed, grown with trees: ash, feathery hemlock, elm—bushes of sumac. A dead tree droops down over the stream. The cascade is white, rather crooked and ragged." The passage ends, "Above the chasm, against the blue, the coverlet of small dappling clouds crawls slowly below the sky."

Epilogue, 2005

∞

The world that Wilson created upstate did not long outlast him. Mary Pcolar divorced and married again, moved to Florida, and died there from carbon monoxide in a trailer fire. Anne Miller and her husband, Ned, divorced, though they remained close. Ned spent years with an Indian sect on the West Coast, returned to live in the backwoods near Lowville, and eventually developed Alzheimer's. He is still living. Anne married again. Although reluctant to embarrass her second husband, she loyally allowed the description of her encounters with Wilson in *The Sixties* to stand as written. Two acquaintances, Glyn Morris at nearby Lyons Falls and Richard Costa in Utica, wrote memoirs of their times with him, Costa's published and that of Morris deposited at Yale.

Rosalind lived on, enjoying her friends in New York's Lewis County and the role of Edmund Wilson's daughter, while continuing to resent him and, after his death, Elena, as *Near the Magician* shows. Thirteen years after its publication, in 2002, at seventy-seven, her father's age at his death, she died, leaving $35,000 in credit card debt. She had sold the stone house to a family based in New York City and in Washington, who had local roots and esteemed its former owner. After contracting for the sale, Rosalind removed the window panes with their etched verse and gave some of them away, apparently selling others. Those with Auden's "Make This Night Loveable" have come into the possession of the New York Public Library. The old house remains, now closer to and more quickly passed by cars on a more upscale, faster road.

Dorothea Straus has described the deserted feeling of the house at Wellfleet during the summer after Wilson's death, "the absence of a presence" in the library. But Elena had already brought her desk into the formal front parlor, and a year later the place had been transformed by her work as literary executor. On a drop-leaf table in the library Wilson's letters were arranged in folders by decades, a distillation of his evolving intellectual life. Working alongside the critic and historian Daniel Aaron, Elena evaluated the contents of thousands of letters, put aside the more intimate correspondence, and cut personal details as well as redundancies from the literary letters they considered best. The young art critic Sanford Schwartz and others helped her, she said, to group these both chronologically and by topic. She introduced the recipients of Wilson's letters and assembled the biographical summaries and most of the needed annotation in his own words, making *Letters on Literature and Politics* (1977), except for Aaron's fine introduction, "entirely Edmund's." Her collaboration with Leon Edel, named by Wilson the general editor of his papers, was not always so agreeable. Edel, who wanted a scholarly edition of the letters, observed to Rosalind that she presumed on her role, while Elena told Helen that dealing with him was enough to make her a feminist.

Elena died of an aneurysm only seven years after Wilson's death, and Helen became sole owner of the copyrights to her father's work, Roger Straus advising her, as he had her mother. The will and unsigned codicil, however, left the Wellfleet house in limbo. After Wilson's funeral Elena showed the codicil to Reuel, who refused to honor it. Helen remembers him abruptly departing with his wife and child, a moment from which she sadly dates the end of their good relations. In a 1994 letter to Wilson's first biographer, Reuel, not mentioning the codicil, says, "Elena and Helen were aggressively urging me to renounce my eventual half-interest" in the house. The debt Wilson left to Elena he calls "the ostensible reason they wanted to acquire the whole Wellfleet properly for Helen." Reuel sold Wilson's library, except for the Russian books, to the University of Tulsa, and he eventually traded his share of the house for the wing of a nineteenth-century house across the road that Elena had bought when the house was scheduled for demolition and moved to their side. Over the years Helen became friends with his son and daughter. In the meantime she and Timothy Woodman lived and worked in a loft in TriBeCa in lower Manhattan. She used the back of the house at Money Hill as a studio during the summers, and in 1999 moved to the Cape year round.

Wilson's *New York Times* obituary began front-page center and filled two interior pages of the paper, complete with a photograph taken three days before his death and long quotations from his writing. "If there is an American civilization," the *Times* stated, "Edmund Wilson has helped us to find it and is himself an important aspect of it." In the literary journals he was described as the most important critic of his era, perhaps the last great man of letters. His books continued appearing. While Straus, acting as agent, kept in print those published during Wilson's lifetime, sometimes subcontracting them to academic presses, his legacy to American letters unfolded in the posthumous writing.

The five journals published between 1975 and 1993 kept his figure before the public. Wilson's journals are a repository of twentieth-century social life, and in a sense they take the place of the great autobiographical novel he had once aspired to. He had edited *The Twenties*, adding bracketed materials, and Edel made his own interpolations and provided an opening biographical portrait. Edel believed that *The Thirties*, which details the collapse of society during the Depression, would prove the big book of the series. Wilson, however, hadn't lived to bring perspective in these pages to the melange of his efforts on the left, his marriage to Margaret, and his sexual adventuring. *The Thirties* contracts and dwindles with his strenuous intellectual work of 1937–1941 and his marriage to Mary McCarthy. *The Forties* detours around their bad years and is dressed out by 200 pages of notes for *Europe Without Baedeker* and the Zuni and Haiti sections of *Red, Black, Blond and Olive*. *The Fifties*, a substantial work and a more consistent portrait of its period, ends with 150 pages of notes for *Apologies to the Iroquois*. When Roger Straus died in 2004, he had in mind a one-volume edition that would represent the best of the three middle journals and of *The Twenties* and *The Sixties*, the two that stand most solidly on their own.

Wilson had stipulated to Straus that his journals not be censored, and Elena (and Helen after her) didn't censor his graphic scenes of their lovemaking. Edel was, however, sometimes troubled by what Wilson said about people and inclined to repress it, which Straus had suggested to the critic might be a problem (see "Remembering Edmund Wilson," in *Centennial Reflections*). *The Sixties*, Wilson's largest, most ambitious journal, was full of frank remarks about people still living when, in 1991, with Edel in his eighties, I agreed to edit it in accord with Wilson's wishes while checking his accounts against ascertainable fact and the memories of others. Wilson had apparently known he wouldn't be able to revise this book and its later pages are festooned with marginal additions of para-

graphs and sentences written as he composed. I organized the encom-
passing canvas in chapters and sub-chapters that register a kaleidoscope
of shifting interests as the author moves between Wellfleet, Cambridge,
upstate New York, and Manhattan, with forays to Canada, Europe, and
the Middle East.

Wilson's centenary in 1995 saw the publication of Jeffrey Meyers's biography and the first of the books reprinting materials the critic had put
aside. With his longing for success in fiction, he might have been pleased
by the publication of *The Higher Jazz* when this was discovered in the
files, and by a spritely new *I Thought of Daisy*, both edited by Neale
Reinitz. He probably wouldn't have enjoyed the resurrection of some of
the short pieces in *From the Uncollected Edmund Wilson*, but David Castronovo and Janet Groth created a volume useful to literary journalists as
well as scholars. These two have also brought out a second volume of Wilson's correspondence. *The Man in Letters* is an eclectic sampling rather
than the "more complete and scholarly edition" Edel had wanted and
Elena hoped would follow hers. Much of the literary correspondence remains unexplored, though at long last sorted in the Beinecke Library at
Yale. Simon Karlinsky opened the door with his edition of the Nabokov-
Wilson letters, recently expanded. This was Wilson's largest exchange with
a writer friend, but engrossing volumes might be made of the letters between him and other writers—there are scores of them to John Dos Passos, Allen Tate, Louise Bogan, and Morton Zabel.

Wilson has longed survived what Cyril Connolly jestingly referred to
as the test of the first ten years. He is regularly cited in the literary sup-
plements and general magazines. Readers respond to what Auden called
the unassertive elegance of his prose, with its vigorous narrative rhythm,
to his reserve of apt and forceful imagery, and his art of quotation. British
critics have been attached to the sometimes prickly American who carried on the best of their heritage, from the generation of Spender and
Pritchett to the Australian Clive James, who, three decades later, praised
his clarity and concreteness, his imposition of a dramatic narrative on the
world, his capacity for detached judgment. What Nabokov, during their
quarrel, contemptuously called Wilson's "human interest" criticism for
Isaiah Berlin were insights into books, writers, and social circumstances
deeper than those of the competition. Recalling that the shade of
Achilles, in the underworld, has to be "pumped with blood" from a sacrifice before he can talk to Odysseus, Berlin said Wilson "put his blood in
it," bringing his whole self to every word he wrote.

Wilson's influence is part of the rebirth of American critical journalism at the twentieth century's end. It is apparent in the work of Louis Menand, Paul Berman, and Jed Perl. Like Wilson, Menand makes the whole culture his subject. Admiring Wilson's ability to bring a story to life through its people, he says that he wrote his history, *The Metaphysical Club*, on the model of *To the Finland Station*. Berman, also indebted to *To the Finland Station*, has reversed what he considers the politics of *Patriotic Gore* in response to 9/11, interpreting American expansion in the Middle East as a Lincolnian project, a war for liberal ideals. Within the world of art criticism, Jed Perl's searching mind has created a chronicle like that in *The Shores of Light*. These and other working journalists with literary ambitions renew the role that Wilson took over from the Old World and Americanized. Such commentators are less belles-lettristic than he, less likely to survive as stylists. Yet they too bring keen artistic imagination and intellectual heft to the study of society and history, and they give substance to the role of public critic.

In these pages Wilson has been observed as a unifying force through fifty years of literary and intellectual culture in the United States, and his survival reflects the continuing authority of that vanished age as well as his ability to preserve its atmosphere and texture in his writing. He was acquainted with and wrote of most of the celebrated figures of the modern period, and with his solid artistic standard and broad-gauged interests, regenerated himself as their world faded. He did not need to learn self-trust from Emerson. Although a determinist à la Taine, Marx, and Freud, when he went left during the Depression it was by giving up his *New Republic* position to report on the labor front, rather than by constructing an ideological bridge or adopting a more tolerant artistic standard. After surveying the United States in 1930–1935, he went to see Russia for himself. The failure of Marxism there didn't drive him into defeatism or dogma, by virtue, Elizabeth Hardwick has said, "of his rampant curiosity and the intensity with which he pursued its objects one after another and often simultaneously." He progressed from Russian to Hebrew and Hungarian, and at the end lamented he was too old and weak to learn Chinese.

Arthur Schlesinger calls Wilson "a patriot of a certain generation and style," and a similar statement was made by David Levine's drawing of Wilson as an owl-like version of the American eagle. Like Dos Passos, he lambasted the bureaucracy (see, in the photographs, the drawing of a man with a briefcase titled "Sea Slug," vis-à-vis the gent called "Old Literary Clubman of the Nineties"). The tiny community of Talcottville engrossed him as much as the artistic world of New York City or President Kennedy's White House. He expressed his loyalty to the old idea of an anointed nation doing God's work in the world by attacking the corruption of this idea in moralistic cant. His commitments to the Republic and the republic of letters fed one another.

Wilson's theme of the man of letters as hero, most clearly articulated in *The Triple Thinkers* and *The Wound and the Bow*, was derived from the nineteenth century and in his later years reinforced by Judaism. It mirrored the strength and enthusiasm he brought to life. His friends admired his determination even when the circumstances were faintly ridiculous. Robert Linscott, who sketches him talking of Proust while raising and lowering the same spoonful of food to and from his mouth, leaves a glimpse, that weekend at the Cape, of Edmund floating through the surf on an inner tube, "majestic and unsmiling, and looking, with his imposing head, like a late Roman emperor." Malcolm Cowley described him removing his glasses before squaring off against a Stalinist. Absurdly awkward with his hammer and the shutters at O'Neill's place on the dunes, he was less so when, in middle age, bending over young Nora Sayre's terrariums with wire clippers. At sixty he crawled through caves and walked on narrow walls at the Dead Sea, and at Bomarzo at seventy, on "one of my tottery days," he sent Darina to report on monsters too far down the muddy hillside. But he kept pushing himself physically even when a wreck, getting to the movies with his female friends during his last nights in 1972, his green oxygen bottles by his side.

With whatever psychological limitations, Wilson lived life as Hemingway characters talk of doing, "all the way up." In a symbolic moment, he toasted "Life" with S. Y. Agnon after Agnon's Nobel Prize. He was always ready to have a party—think of Wilson and Dawn Powell drinking gin in the cornfield—but maintained an intense focus on the work that was his life's purpose. If future conditions allow the half-century in which he wrote to survive as a subject of study, Wilson may well be perceived, like Dr. Johnson, at the center of his age. In the meantime he and his writing, in a word that he took over from Emerson, are fortifying.

Notes

Abbreviations

Frequently cited author's interviews and correspondents of Wilson (EW):

ARB: Alfred Raymond Bellinger
AW: Adelaide Walker
Elena: Elena Mumm Wilson
FSF: F. Scott Fitzgerald
HM: Helen Muchnic
HMKW: Helen Mather Kimball Wilson (Mrs.)
HMW: Helen Miranda Wilson
JPB: John Peale Bishop
JDP: John Dos Passos
LB: Louise Bogan
MB: Mary Blair
MC: Margaret Canby
MMcC: Mary McCarthy
MP: Mamaine Paget (Koestler)
VN: Vladimir Nabokov
WSD: (William) Stanley Dell

Manuscripts

The Beinecke Rare Book and Manuscript Library, Yale University, is abbreviated Beinecke. *Notes without citations refer to the Edmund Wilson Archive there. Other manuscript collections are identified in the Notes.*

Frequently Cited Collections of Letters

Fourteenth Chronicle. *The Fourteenth Chronicle: Letters and Diaries of John Dos Passos*, ed. Townsend Ludington (Boston, Gambit Press, 1973).

Letters. Edmund Wilson, *Letters on Literature and Politics, 1912–1972*, ed. Elena Wilson (New York: Farrar, Straus and Giroux, 1977).

Letters of FSF. The Letters of F. Scott Fitzgerald, ed. Andrew Turnbull (New York: Scribners, 1963).

Man in Letters. Edmund Wilson, The Man in Letters, eds., David Castronovo and Janet Groth (Athens: Ohio University Press, 2001).

N-W Letters. Dear Bunny, Dear Volodya: The Nabokov-Wilson Letters, 1940–1971 (New York: Harper and Row, 1979); revised and expanded, Berkeley: University of California Press, 2001).

Woman Lived. What the Woman Lived: Selected Letters of Louise Bogan, 1920–1970, ed. Ruth Limmer (New York: Harcourt Brace Jovanovich, 1973).

Periodicals

Hill Record: Hill School Record
Nassau Lit: Nassau Literary Magazine
NR: The New Republic
NYT: The New York Times
NYRB: The New York Review of Books
NY: The New Yorker
VF: Vanity Fair
WQ: Wilson Quarterly

Books That Refer to Wilson

Centennial Reflections. Edmund Wilson: Centennial Reflections, ed. Lewis M. Dabney (Princeton: Princeton University Press, 1997).

Magician. Rosalind Baker Wilson, *Near the Magician: A Memoir of My Father, Edmund Wilson* (New York: Grove Weidenfeld, 1989).

"My View." Elena Wilson, "My View from the Other Window." Unpublished typescript.

Books by Wilson

Bit. The Bit Between My Teeth: A Literary Chronicle of 1950–1965 (New York: Farrar, Straus & Giroux, 1965).

Castle. Axel's Castle: A Study in The Imaginative Literature of 1870–1930 (New York: Scribner, 1950).

Classics. Classics and Commercials: A Literary Chronicle of the Forties (New York: Farrar, Straus and Co. 1951).

Daisy. I Thought of Daisy, with an afterward by Neale Reinitz (Iowa City: University of Iowa Press, 2001).

Devils. The Devils and Canon Barham: Ten Essays on Poets, Novelists and Monsters (New York: Farrar, Straus & Giroux, 1973).

Earthquake. The American Earthquake: A Documentary of the Twenties and Thirties (Garden City, N.Y.: Doubleday Anchor, 1951).

Europe. Europe Without Baedeker: Sketches Among the Ruins of Italy, Greece and England,

Together with Notes from a European Diary, 1963–1964 (New York: Farrar, Straus & Giroux, 1966).

Fifties. The Fifties: From Notebooks and Diaries of the Period, ed. Leon Edel (New York: Farrar, Straus & Giroux, 1986).

Finland Station. To the Finland Station: A Study in the Writing and Acting of History (New York: Farrar, Straus & Giroux, 1972).

Forties. The Forties: From Notebooks and Diaries of the Period, ed. Leon Edel (New York: Farrar, Straus & Giroux, 1983).

Hecate. Memoirs of Hecate County (New York: Ballantine Books, 1967).

Iroquois. Apologies to the Iroquois, with a study of the Mohawks in High Steel (Syracuse N.Y.: Syracuse University Press, 1991).

Israel/Scrolls. Israel and the Dead Sea Scrolls (New York: Farrar, Straus & Giroux, 1978).

Jazz. The Higher Jazz, ed. Neale Reinitz (Iowa City: University of Iowa Press, 1998).

Jitters: The American Jitters: A Year of the Slump (North Stratford, N.H.: Ayer Company Publishers, 1995).

Memoirs. Memoirs of Hecate County (New York: Ballantine Books, 1967).

Night Thoughts. Night Thoughts (New York: Farrar, Straus & Giroux, 1961).

Note-Books. Note-Books of Night (San Francisco: The Colt Press, 1942).

O Canada: O Canada: An American's Notes on Canadian Culture (New York: Noonday Press, 1966).

Patriotic Gore. Patriotic Gore: Studies in the Literature of the American Civil War (New York: Oxford University Press, 1962).

Piece: A Piece of My Mind: Reflections at Sixty (New York: Farrar, Straus and Cudahy, 1956).

Plays: Five Plays (London: W. H. Allen, 1954)

Prelude. A Prelude: Landscapes, Characters and Conversations from the Earlier Years of My Life (London: W. H. Allen, 1967).

Protest. The Cold War and the Income Tax: A Protest (New York: Farrar, Straus & Giroux, 1963).

Red, Black. Red, Black, Blond, and Olive: Studies in Four Civilizations: Zuñi, Haiti, Soviet Russia, Israel (New York: Oxford University Press, 1956).

Scrolls. The Dead Sea Scrolls, 1947–1969 (London: Collins, 1971).

Shores. The Shores of Light: A Literary Chronicle of the Twenties and Thirties (New York: Farrar, Straus & Giroux, 1952).

Sixties. The Sixties: The Last Journal, 1960–1972, ed. Lewis M. Dabney (New York: Farrar, Straus & Giroux, 1993).

Thinkers. The Triple Thinkers: Twelve Essays on Literary Subjects (Oxford: Oxford University Press, 1948; revised and enlarged edition).

Thirties. The Thirties: From Notebooks and Diaries of the Period, ed. Leon Edel (New York: Farrar, Straus & Giroux, 1984).

Travels. Travels in Two Democracies (New York: Harcourt, Brace and Company, 1936).

Twenties. The Twenties: From Notebooks and Diaries of the Period (New York: Farrar, Straus & Giroux, 1975).

Uncollected. From the Uncollected Edmund Wilson, eds. David Castronovo and Janet Groth (Athens: Ohio University Press, 1995).

Upstate. Upstate: Records and Recollections of Northern New York (New York: Farrar, Straus & Giroux, 1971).

Window. A Window on Russia: For the Use of Foreign Readers (New York: Farrar, Straus & Giroux, 1972).

Wound and Bow. The Wound and the Bow: Seven Studies in Literature (New York: Oxford University Press, 1947).

When reviews and essays have been collected they are cited from the books, where they are more accessible, even when Wilson slightly changed his phrasing from the original. In the rare instance where the change affects meaning, the original is cited in the notes.

Preface

xi "a British ship . . . James": Lionel Trilling, *A Gathering of Fugitives* (Boston: Beacon Press, 1956), 49.

xi "one . . . lost": James, "The Art of Fiction," *Selected Literary Criticism*, Morris Shapira, ed. (New York: Horizon Press, 1963), 57.

xii "You must . . . young men": Interviews with EW, 1963.

xii "that this . . . after me": "Thoughts on Being Bibliographed," *Classics*, 111.

xii "to thrust . . . eat him": Ibid., 109.

xii–xiii "You should . . . powers": Interviews with EW, 1963.

xiii "more or less . . . biography": *Centennial Reflections*, 16.

Introduction

3 "bowled over": EW related this in 1965 to John Clendenning. Interview with Clendenning 1991.

3 "simply one triumph after another": "The Poetry of Drought," *Dial*, Dec. 1922, 615.

3 "straining always . . . darkness": "Ulysses," *NR*, July 5, 1922, 164.

5 "by nature . . . about": *Centennial Reflections*, 138.

5 "to see what . . . next": Malcolm Cowley, *A Second Flowering* (New York: Viking, 1973), 241.

5 "searching for . . . writing": Paul Horgan, *Tracings* (New York: Farrar, Straus & Giroux, 1993), 231.

6 "characters who have . . . parts": *Patriotic Gore*, ix.

6 "disharmonious"; "He was always . . . genius": "Isaiah Berlin on Edmund Wilson: An Interview by Lewis M. Dabney," *WQ*, Winter 1999, 38–49.

6 "just intelligent sentences"; "everything . . . content": Ibid., 47.

7 "bold enough . . . world": "An interview with Edmund Wilson," *Bit*, 534.

1: 12 Wallace Street

11 "In the spring . . . swamps": *Magician*, 5.

11 "beautiful Irish . . . saint": Ibid., 37.

11 "just like a plum-bun": *Prelude*, 43.

12 "At Sea Bright . . . smooth": "Variations on a Landscape," *Night Thoughts*, 147.

12 "Thick-set . . . mustache": *Prelude*, 21.

12 "a terrific worker": Ibid., 20.

12 "I knew . . . interesting": Ibid., 28.

12 "a very moderate one"; "bleak and severe": "The Jews," *Piece*, 88.

12 "had scrapped . . . it": Ibid.

13 "a 'queer' and morbid side": "The Author at Sixty," *Piece*, 215.

13 "stood very . . . of": *Prelude*, 29.

13 "a bloody tyrant": Introduction to *Patriotic Gore*, xvii.

13 "with nothing . . . watch": *Prelude*, 29

13 "new America . . . move": "The Old Stone House," *Earthquake*, 497.

14 "so bloodless . . . mummy": Ibid., 499.

14 "pocket of the past": "The Author at Sixty," *Piece*, 239.

14 "the widening . . . feather-dusters": "The Old Stone House," *Earthquake*, 496.

14 "we fished . . . games": Ibid., 504.

14 "first the dedicated . . . orgy": *Upstate*, 251.

14 "with the first . . . kind": Ibid., 4.

14 "the son . . . railroads": "At Laurelwood," *Night Thoughts*, 166. Originally published in *NY*, Nov. 18, 1939, under the title "These Men Must Do Their Duty!"

15 "These men . . . servant": Ibid., 172.

15 "had been . . . Finches": Ibid., 174.

15 "the superior . . . wider": Ibid., 177.

16 "rusticated": *Prelude*, 119.

16 "learning, logic . . . suspended": "The Author at Sixty," *Piece*, 218.

16 "retained to . . . reared": Robert H. McCarter, "Proceedings on the Presentation of a Portrait of Edmund Wilson, Esq., Freehold, NJ, Sept. 28, 1926." Unpublished typescript.

16 "dominated by corporations": "The Author at Sixty," *Piece*, 221.

16 "The Republic . . . saved": "The United States," *Piece*, 23.

17 "You think . . . instrument": Story told by Thomas Knight, about the beginnings of his practice in Dallas, Texas. The elder lawyer was Lewis M. Dabney (grandfather of the author). Thomas Knight was the father of Dick Knight, elsewhere mentioned in this chronicle.

17 "a silvery quality of clearness": "The Problem of English," *Piece*, 160.

17 vindicated the national ideal: A Memorial Day address by Wilson's father, in the vein of "When Lilacs Last in the Dooryard Bloom'd," juxtaposes the "awful morality" of the Civil War and "stately gorgeous spring with all its flood of genial warmth and light," its "flowers without number, and manifold in figure, hue, and scent"—"these," the orator says, "we scatter on your sepulchre." Unpublished typescript.

17 "a casky vinous smell": "The Author at Sixty," *Piece*, 221.

18 "for desolating drives or walks": Ibid., 228.

18 "freeze us . . . something": *Daisy*, 123–24.

18 "going quite . . . people": *Magician*, 48.

18 "were lasting . . . years": "The Author at Sixty," *Piece*, 228.

18 "may partly . . . damnation": Ibid., 215.

18 "What does . . . condition?": Ibid., 233.

19 "mad": Ibid., 215.

19 "a three-foot . . . ear": *Magician*, 158.

19 "I would . . . wife": Ibid., 180.

19 "There's no . . . bank!": Ibid., 35.

19 "did not wash": "The Author at Sixty," *Piece*, 224.

19 "lively and gay": Ibid., 229.

19 "simply visited . . . legislatures": Ibid., 230.

19 "he began . . . cab": Ibid., 222.

20 "sunken out . . . baize": "A House of the 'Eighties," *Night Thoughts*, 103.

20 "I was . . . secrets": *Sixties*, 182.

20 "those long . . . things": "At Laurelwood," *Night Thoughts*, 160.

21 "he would . . . figures": Margaret Edwards Rullman quoted in Jane Foderaro, "Red Bank: Birthplace of Edmund Wilson," [Red Bank] *Daily Register*, April 18, 1967, 9.

21 "What I . . . story": Wilson papers.

21 "amazement, a . . . beauty": "Mr. More and the Mithraic Bull," *Thinkers*, 13.

21 "interesting" or "very interesting": *Prelude*, 15.

21 "a wheel . . . badly": Ibid., 23.

22 "what was really going on": EW to Margaret Edwards Rullman, March 11, 1966, Princeton University Library.

22 "one of his sprees": *Prelude*, 21.

22 "fetishistic": *Devils*, 3.

22 "the murders . . . them": Ibid.

22 "small, squat, much-used volumes": "The Library," *Hill Record*, June 1912, 274.

22 "Lasting depressions . . . childhood": "Dickens: The Two Scrooges," *Wound and Bow*, 6.

23 "From his mother . . . know": "Appendix," *Magician*, 286.

23 "my pretty . . . kiss": *Upstate*, 4.

23 "the versatile . . . class": *Prelude*, 42.

23 "a great success": "The Conjuring Shop," *Hill Record*, Mar. 1910, 154.

23 "hopeless hypochrondriac"; "lined with . . . deaths": "The Sane Tea Party," *Hill Record*, May 1912, 226.

23 "You're a great girl": Ibid., 238.

24 "this world . . . murder": "Below Stairs," *Nassau Lit*, Jan. 1926, 287.

24 "to imagine him answering": "The Author at Sixty," *Piece*, 229.

24 "a dream . . . mother": *Prelude*, 168.

24 "weltering . . . threaten me": "The Problem of English," *Piece*, 161.

24 "mostly consisted . . . him": Ibid., 159.

25 "no longer afraid": "The Author at Sixty," *Piece*, 225.

25 "made, automatically . . . Lincoln": Ibid., 226.

25 "When dead . . . for": "When All the Young Were Dying," *Night Thoughts*, 67.

25 "Now I'm . . . house!": "The Author at Sixty," *Piece*, 233.

26 "My methods . . . lectures": "The Problem of English," *Piece*, 160.

26 "a great . . . Republic": "The Author at Sixty," *Piece*, 227.

26 "You're a cold . . . Wilson": *Thirties*, 236.

27 "in the . . . doors": *Magician*, 46.

27 "a man . . . forehead": *Stephen Spender: Journals 1939–1983*, ed. John Goldsmith (London: Faber and Faber, 1985), 411.

27 "She . . . him"; "'Plenty good . . . expect": Interviews with MMcC, 1984.

27 "the silver umbilical cord": Interview with Edith Oliver, 1986.

27 "scenes": *Magician*, 57.

27 "supporting that house": Ibid., 164.

27 "what she'd . . . eat": Ibid., 39.

28 "Nobody will ever love you": *Thirties*, 446.

28 "he had a . . . anyone": *Magician*, 32.

28 "alone, at night . . . puppet-queen": *Fifties*, 351–52.

28 "the woman . . . father": Ibid., 352.

28–29 The victim . . . needs": *Wound*, 294.

29 "These brilliant . . . them": "The Author at Sixty," *Piece*, 234.

29 "In taking . . . as well": *Wound*, 295.

2: "School-Days and Early Influences"

30 "a slender . . . eyes": EW and E. E. Paramore, Jr., "Pistols for Two," *Hill School Bulletin*, Feb. 1926, 31.

30 "I didn't . . . week": EW to HMKW, Feb. 28, 1910.

30–31 "We had . . . exhortations": "Mr. Rolfe," *Thinkers*, 246–47.

31 "agonizing shyness . . . hysteria": "Things I Consider Overrated," *VF* 15, no. 2 (Oct. 1920), 65.

31 "from force of habit": EW to HMKW, Nov. 12, 1909.

31 "He drilled . . . language": "The Problem of English," *Piece*, 161.

31 formed by his father: Interview with John A. Lester's daughter, Wendy Lester, 1987.

31 "the Great . . . Ease": "The Problem of English," *Piece*, 161.

32 "dark and . . . nerves": EW to ARB, Feb. 4, 1913.

32 "better read . . . any good": Bellinger, *Hill School Bulletin*, Apr. 1960, 5.

32 a parody: Its full title was "The Decadence of Modern Literature by Brainard Spargo," *New York Evening Mail*, Sept. 8, 1911.

33 "in a handsome . . . career": "Adventures of a Gentleman," *Hill Record*, Feb. 1911, 133.

33 "a publisher of cheap novels": Ibid., 137.

33 "He saw . . . York": "The Successful Mr. Sterne," *Hill Record*, Apr. 1911, 219.

33 "a hair . . . room": "A Modest Self-Tribute," *Bit*, 1.

33 "He had . . . values": Ibid., 2.

34 "some qualities . . . Youthful Fragments": "Exchanges," *Hill Record*, Dec. 1911, 97–98.

34 "you knew . . . rhythm": "Mr. Rolfe," *Thinkers*, 241.

34 "Clearly the rest . . . Achaia": Ibid., 243.

34 "that there . . . shining": Ibid., 237.

34 "John Quincy Adams . . . foes": "The Presidents," *Mr. Rolfe of the Hill*, compiled and edited by Boyd Edwards and Isaac Thomas (Feroe Press, n.d. [before 1928]), 91.

34 "could rouse . . . levity": Isaac Thomas, "Alfred Grosvenor Rolfe," *Hill School Bulletin* Feb. 1943, 3.

34–35 "worked on . . . that writer": "Mr. Rolfe," *Thinkers*, 246–47.

35 "Under the . . . taste": Ibid., 250.

35 "John A. Leicestair . . . life": *Magician*, 64.

35 "mysterium tremendum": John A. Lester to EW, Jan. 10, 1957.

35 "a vividly . . . poem": "Bernard Shaw at the Metropolitan," *Earthquake*, 491.

35 "came to . . . before": "Mr. Rolfe," *Thinkers*, 250.

36 "ve-ery impo-ortant . . . yourself": Ibid., 252.

36 "the official . . . Hill": Ibid., 253.

36 "struggles, earnest labors, sleepless nights": Ibid., 251.

36 "on the edge of the abyss": Ibid., 248.

36 "Between the . . . light": "The Grass Brown, the Bushes Dry," *Night Thoughts*, 136.

36–37 "With Mother . . . *if we fail*": EW to ARB, Oct. 1912. The poem is titled "The Retrospective Matriculant: To Mr. A. R. Bellinger."

37 "in that . . . Influences'": EW to ARB, Oct. 1912.

3: Literature Among the Playboys

39 "Playing chemistry . . . face": *Prelude*, 80–81.

39 "meticulous": Anaïs Nin to EW, Sept. 27, 1967.

39 "the progress . . . our own": "Editorial: The Fog Lifts," *Nassau Lit*, Apr. 1915, 43.

39 "a soldier . . . head": "Thoughts on Being Bibliographed," *Classics*, 114.

39 "The Sleeping . . . birth": "The Sleeping College," *Nassau Lit*, Feb. 1916, 381.

39–40 "Dr. Johnson . . . *the World*": "Editorial: The Curriculum," *Nassau Lit*, Dec. 1915, 256.

40 "poor scholar . . . up": "A Modest Self-Tribute," *Bit*, 1.

40 "Scotch honesty . . . one": EW to ERB, Sept. 2, 1915, *Letters*, 23–24.

40 "scrupulous thoroughness . . . limitations": EW to ARB, July 2, 1916, Ibid., 26.

40 "England!" in "awed ecstasy": *Prelude*, 72.

41 "where half . . . written": Ibid., 74.

41 "riding on . . . holiday": "War," *Piece*, 40.

41 "working our . . . puddle": "T. K. Whipple," *Classics*, 74.

41 "passionless masterpiece": *Prelude*, 108.

41 "two masterpieces . . . *Frome*": EW to ARB, Mar. 29, 1913, *Letters*, 12.

41–42 "Born on . . . poetry": "T. K. Whipple," *Classics*, 74.

42 "At Oxford . . . posterity": "Editorial: The Need for a Nimbus," *Nassau Lit*, Apr. 1915, 45, 47.

42 "Swaying from . . . centuries": *Prelude*, 85.

42 "in literature . . . doing": *Europe*, 347.

42 "a favorite daughter": Ibid., 348.

42–43 "without looking . . . eyeglasses": "Christian Gauss as a Teacher of Literature," *Shores*, 8.

43 "no matter . . . hurt": EW quotes Harold Medina, a federal judge who had been Gauss's student, Ibid., 19.

43 "objectivity . . . reasoned morality": Ibid., 14.

43 "to write . . . effect": Ibid., 15.

43 "too artistic . . . civilization": "Joris Karl Huysmans," unpublished essay from EW's sophomore year, ix, xviii.

43 "dialogues, fables . . . criticism": George Steiner, *Three Honest Men: A Critical Mosaic*, ed. Philip French (Manchester, England: Carcanet New Press, 1980), 37.

44 "He was . . . different": Interview with WSD, 1963.

44 "Out of . . . correct": "Christian Gauss as a Teacher of Literature," *Shores*, 22.

44 "Without the belief . . . accomplishing": *The Papers of Christian Gauss*, eds. Katherine Gauss Jackson and Hiram Hayden (New York: Random House, 1957), 168.

44 "a last . . . stone": *Twenties*, 61.

44 "never-ending . . . civilization": "Christian Gauss as a Teacher of Literature," *Shores*, 20.

44 "that good . . . suburbanism": Ibid., 5.

44 "The shy . . . Court": F. Scott Fitzgerald, "My Lost City," *The Crack-Up*, ed. EW (New York: New Directions, 1945), 24.

44–45 "moonlight skating . . . Brook": "My Fifty Years with Dictionaries and Grammars," *Bit*, 604.

45 "Calvin . . . justified": EW to ARB, Jan. 7, 1916, *Letters*, 24.

45 "the semi-godlike . . . critic": "T. K. Whipple," *Classics*, 73.

45 "a procession . . . above it": "Editorial: The Age of Saturn," *Nassau Lit*, Mar. 1916, 429–30.

45 "arbitrary and . . . snobs": "Editorial: Catalogue of Crimes," Ibid., 431.

45 "the debonair . . . republicans": "The United States," *Piece*, 26.

45 "much distinction . . . words": EW to ARB, Jan. 17, 1913.

46 "the impression . . . cross-motive": "Henry James," *Nassau Lit*, Nov. 1914, 289; *Uncollected*, 27.

46 "fine Puritanism . . . the *Screw*": Ibid., 295; *Uncollected*, 34.

46 "came in . . . context": EW to ARB, Jan. 16, 1914, *Letters*, 14–15.

46 "I never . . . dance": *Prelude*, 147.

46–47 "a great future . . . the same": EW to ARB, n.d. [1915–1916].

47 "rather Spartan": *Prelude*, 54.

47 "Red-haired . . . handful": Christian Gauss, "Edmund Wilson, the Campus, and the 'Nassau Lit,'" *Princeton University Library Chronicle*, Feb. 1944, 50.

47 "largely futile and uninspired": "Editorial," *Nassau Lit*, March 1916, 431.

47 "had held . . . intimacy": WSD to EW, Sept. 19, 1916.

47 "thumb your . . . world": EW to LB, Dec. 12, 1933, *Letters*, 234.

48 "something immoral": *Prelude*, 82.

48 "I had . . . eclipse": Ibid., 133.

48 "I have never . . . literature": Ibid., 82.

49 "the courses . . . University": John Biggs, "A Few Early Years," *Princeton Tiger*, Jan. 1957, 21.

49 "hard green eyes": "On Editing Scott Fitzgerald's Papers," *Night Thoughts*, 120.

49 "the increasing . . . age": EW to FSF, Aug. 28, 1915, *Letters*, 24.

49 "go further . . . years": *Nassau Lit*, Jan. 1916, 318–19.

49 "Do you . . . I 21?": FSF to EW, n.d. [fall 1917], *FSF Letters*, 320.

49 "I want . . . he knew": "Thoughts on Being Bibliographed," *Classics*, 110.

50 "I can . . . too!": *Prelude*, 106.

50 the Devil: F. Scott Fitzgerald, *This Side of Paradise* (New York: Scribner's, 1953), 112.

50 "hookers . . . never done!": *Prelude*, 148.

50 "ghastly"; "when you . . . Renaissance": EW to FSF, Oct 7, 1917, *Letters*, 30.

50 "country-house social prestige": EW to Gauss, May 15, 1944, Ibid., 335.

50 "the blasted . . . my youth": Interview with EW, 1963.

51 "never got out of the nineties'": Interview with WSD, 1963.

51 "Scott, your . . . tonight": "On Editing Scott Fitzgerald's Papers," *Night Thoughts*, 119.

51 "You read . . . company": "Thoughts on Being Bibliographed," *Classics*, 110.

51 "more things . . . leaves": "Southampton," *Night Thoughts*, 3.

51 "sentimental emotions": *Prelude*, 180.

52 "I too . . . bonds": "Disloyal Lines to an Alumnus," *Night Thoughts*, 90.

52 "the keen . . . tea": Ibid.

52 "what is bad about it": EW to JDP, March 17, 1957, *Man in Letters*, 55.

4: World War I: "The Others Stayed with Their Class"

53 "Don't you . . . serious": "The Author at Sixty," *Piece*, 227.

53 "with her . . . of ether": *Twenties*, 62.

53 "so nervous . . . target": *Prelude*, 152.

53 "loathed . . . blood": "War," *Piece*, 49.

53–54 "places . . . dead": "A Weekend at Ellerslie," *Shores*, 378–79.

54 "brilliant" and "amiable": EW to ARB, July 29, 1916, *Letters*, 28.

54 "a kind of . . . snobbishness": Ibid.

54 "inevitable": F. Scott Fitzgerald, "My Lost City," *The Crack-Up*, ed. EW (New York: New Directions, 1945), 23.

54 "writing up . . . most of them": EW to ARB, Nov. 17, 1916, *Letters*, 29.

54 "I could . . . exciting": *Prelude*, 156.

55 "Some died . . . ask for": WSD to EW, Sept. 19, 1916.

55 "for recovering . . . danger": Quoted by EW to ARB, Nov. 17, 1916.

55 "profanity, obscenity, and pure stupidity": EW to HMKW, Sept. 2, 1917.

55 "the real . . . light": EW to WSD, Sept. 19, 1917, *Letters*, 31–32.

56 "with men . . . the top": "Soviet Russia," *Red, Black*, 150.

56 "40 men, 8 horses, lengthwise": EW to HMKW, Nov. 19, 1917.

56 "I had flopped . . . Europe": "Europe," *Piece*, 53.

57 "fine and sober smile": *Prelude*, 211.

57 "the worst . . . doctor": EW to HMKW, Jan. 17, 1918.

57 "on one . . . stand by": EW to Edmund Wilson, Sr., Mar. 1, 1919.

57 "soup, French-fried . . . apiece": EW to HMKW, Dec. 12, 1917.

57 "her black . . . oval face": *Prelude*, 208.

58 "decided to . . . war": EW to FSF, Dec. 3, 1917, *Letters*, 34.

58 "At first . . . sympathy": *Prelude*, 157.

58 "the hospital . . . political cause": EW to WSD, Dec. 29, 1917, *Letters*, 36–37.

58 "terrible . . . feeling": Reuel B. Kimball, Jr., to EW, Dec. 9, 1917.

58 "thyroid . . . advice": Reuel B. Kimball, Jr., to EW, Feb. 24, 1918.

58 "my self-imposed . . . sunlight": Reuel B. Kimball, Jr., to EW, March 24, 1918.

59 "the unseen, unrealized reality": EW to FSF, Dec. 3, 1917, *Letters*, 34.

59 "sober loveliness": *Prelude*, 238.

59 "a certain support": "Every Man His Own Eckermann," *Bit*, 582.

59 "Boom! . . . to do?": EW to HMKW, Mar. 13, 1918, *Man in Letters*, 24.

59 "*On se débarrassé . . . autre*": *Prelude*, 210.

60 "all over mud and blood": EW to HMKW, June 6, 1918.

60 "those tones . . . that bark": "New Ode to a Nightingale," *Night Thoughts*, 6.

60 "seemed unconscious . . . gesture": *Prelude*, 207.

60 "arsenic that damages the lungs": EW to HMKW, Aug. 1, 1918.

60 "my nights . . . burns": EW to ARB, Aug. 26, 1918, *Letters*, 41.

60 "One patient . . . died": *Prelude*, 225.

60–61 "patrolling . . . very short)": EW to Gilbert Troxell, Sept. 28, 1918, *Letters*, 40.

61 "no one . . . bacteria": "Reunion," *Earthquake*, 149.

61 "humanity was a raving madhouse": Ibid., 147.

61 "an elderly undertaker . . . ditches": *Prelude*, 276.

61 "indifferently or trivially again": "Reunion," *Earthquake*, 148.

61 "stand outside . . . Truth": "The Case of the Author," *Jitters*, 307.

62 "Holland came . . . Detroit": EW to HMKW, Oct. 19, 1918.

62 "in a state . . . dissolution": EW to HMKW, Nov. 14, 1918.

62 "enforce different . . . inevitable": EW to HMKW, Nov. 23, 1918.

62 "administered a filing cabinet": *Prelude*, 236.

63 "bitterness, grief . . . suffocating": EW to HMKW, Dec. 22, 1918.

63 "square-tipped mechanic's fingers": *Prelude*, 236.

63 "the death . . . at all!": Ibid., 245.

63 "strength of . . . vindictiveness": EW to Edmund Wilson, Sr., March 16, 1919.

63 "to the vast debate . . . future": EW to Edmund Wilson, Sr., March 1, 1919.

64 "there's only . . . leave!": *Prelude*, 265.

64 "the dry . . . train": "July 1919," Journals (typescript), vol. 3, 109–11.

64 "be surprised . . . anyone else": Reuel B. Kimball, Jr., to EW, April 6, 1919.

65 "a shock . . . absorbing": *Twenties*, 12.

65 "much worse . . . gloomy": EW to HMKW, Aug. 22, 1919.

65 "partly retained . . . king": *Twenties*, 13.

65 "for discipline"; "quite cheerful now": EW to HMKW, Aug. 22, 1919.

65 "passed into eclipse": *Twenties*, 13.

65 "amputation of a whole relation": Ibid., 12.

65 "felt as . . . trauma": Ibid., 13.

65 "old smile . . . away": *Fifties*, 19.

66 "who only yesterday . . . democrats": "The New Patriotism," *Night Thoughts*, 8–9.

66 "unexpectedly proud"; "The inefficiency . . . citizens": "The Author at Sixty," *Piece*, 225.

67 "these last . . . right": ARB to EW, Dec. 12, 1919.

67 "he not . . . infallible": ARB, "Preface," unpublished manuscript, n.d.

67 "the habits . . . prejudices": *Prelude*, 277.

67 "It enables . . . completely": EW to Edmund Wilson, Sr., March 1, 1919.

67 "for a young . . . cooperation": *Patriotic Gore*, 765.

68 "The others . . . class": Interviews with EW, 1963.

5: *Vanity Fair*, Mencken, and Edna St. Vincent Millay

71 "the Elevated . . . clothes": Marion Meade, *Dorothy Parker: What Fresh Hell Is This?* (New York: Villard Books, 1988), 43.

71 "a crazy . . . the time": Interview with Jeanne Ballot, 1986.

72 "was apparently not . . . acolyte": Frank Crowninshield, "Crowninshield in the Cubs' Den (Part 2)," *Vogue*, Nov. 1, 1944, 126.

72 "had a wonderful . . . educate me": Interview with Ballot, 1986.

72 "'Miss Ballot' . . . Bergson": Jeanne Ballot, "A Very Innocent Bystander," unpublished ms., 3.

72–73 "Mr. Bishop . . . panic-stricken": Ibid.

73 "paying her court": *Twenties*, 33.

73 "partly Irish"; "had a . . . sniffed": *Jazz*, 122.

73 "drank highballs . . . raptures": Ibid., 98.

73 "she was . . . Fitzgerald": *Twenties*, 48.

73 "a road . . . Supper": Dorothy Parker, quoted in Ibid.

74 "slight sandyheaded . . . somersault": John Dos Passos, *The Best Times* (New York: New American Library, 1966), 139.

74 "understood Europe . . . intelligence": "The Gulf in American Literature," *VF*, Sept. 1920, 65.

74 "the Freud . . . truth": "The Progress of Psychoanalysis," *VF*, Aug. 1920, 41.

74 "I am not . . . brooks": "Things I Consider Overrated," *VF*, Dec. 1920, 106; *Uncollected*, 124.

74 "underrated": "Things I Consider Underrated: Three Little Essays in Constructive Criticism," *VF*, March 1921, 38; *Uncollected*, 141.

74–75 "a genuine . . . him": "H. L. Mencken," *NR*, June 1, 1921, 12.

75 "No one . . . even me": Mencken to EW, quoted from memory to FSF, July 5, 1921, *Letters*, 65.

75 "the most . . . people": Walter Lippmann, "H. L. Mencken," *Saturday Review*, Dec. 11, 1926, 413.

75 "historical perspective . . . wrong": "Van Wyck Brooks' Second Phase," *Classics*, 11.

76 "come down": "The Delegate from Great Neck," *Shores*, 155. First published in EW, *Discordant Encounters*.

76 "who happened . . . novelist": Ibid., 148.

76 "souls buried in . . . light": "Shut Out the Square!," *Night Thoughts*, 28.

76 "to deal . . . dart": "Edna St. Vincent Millay," *Shores*, 748.

76–77 "She was dressed . . . muse": Ibid., 749.

77 "Edna ignited . . . my life": *Twenties*, 64.

77 "almost raffish": "Edna St. Vincent Millay," *Shores*, 760.

77 "I was . . . are": *Forties*, 224.

77 "running around . . . swinging": Phyllis Duganne quoted in "Edna St. Vincent Millay," *Shores*, 793.

77 "We were . . . ferry": Edna St. Vincent Millay, "Recuerdo," *Collected Poems* (New York: Harper and Row, 1958), 128.

78 "disarming impartiality": "Edna St. Vincent Millay," *Shores*, 755.

78 "the choirboys . . . her": *Twenties*, 65.

78 "lewd": quoted in Nancy Milford, *Savage Beauty: The Life of Edna St. Vincent Millay* (New York: Random House, 2001), 189.

78 "A large mouth . . . As any": Ibid.

78 "eyes meaningless . . . male": Unpublished, initialed JPB.

78 "He could . . . himself": Unpublished, initialed EW.

79 "demoralized": *Twenties*, 64.

79 "that your desire . . . process": JPB to Edna Millay, June 5, 1920, Library of Congress.

79 "divine": Jean Gould, *The Poet and Her Book* (New York: Dodd, Mead, 1969), 118.

79 "after all a weaker vessel": Millay to EW, June 15, 1920.

79 "innocent long . . . broken heart": *Twenties*, 15–16.

79 "when I had . . . it's gone!": *Sixties*, 168.

79 "I love you": EW to Millay, July 27, 1920, Millay papers, Library of Congress.

79 "please be . . . pretty flat": EW to Millay, July 28, 1920, Library of Congress.

79 "I suppose . . . you know": EW to Millay, Aug. 1, 1920, Library of Congress.

79 "stupidly . . . arguments": EW to Millay, Aug. 12, 1920, Library of Congress.

79 "false . . . with bitterness": Millay to EW, Aug. 3, 1920, Library of Congress.

80 "to the deepest . . . alone?": EW to Millay, Aug. 17, 1920, Library of Congress.

80 "through scrub-oak . . . night": "Edna St. Vincent Millay," *Shores*, 759.

80 "he never drank": Diary of Alec McKaig, quoted in Milford, *Savage Beauty*, 192.

80 "haunt . . . the solution": "Edna St. Vincent Millay," *Shores*, 764.

80 "By the time . . . already": *Forties*, 223–24.

80 "Modern Sappho . . . marrying her": Diary of Alec McKaig, quoted by Andre LeVot, *F. Scott Fitzgerald* (New York: Warner Books, 1984), 84.

81 "a wretched . . . room": *Twenties*, 28.

81 "depressing illnesses": "Edna St. Vincent Millay," *Shores*, 767.

81 "immortal page . . . mind": Millay, *Collected Poems*, 243.

81 "farcical mishaps . . . concerned": JPB to Millay, Dec. 8, 1920, Library of Congress.

81 "botched"; "bloody and weakened": Milford, *Savage Beauty*, 197.

81 "our old . . . basis": "Edna St. Vincent Millay," *Shores*, 769.

81 "After dinner . . . better share": *Twenties*, 64–65.

81 "the three . . . together": Daniel Epstein, *What Lips My Lips Have Kissed: The Loves and Love Poems of Edna St. Vincent Millay* (New York: Henry Holt, 2001), 148.

81 "*ménage-à-trois*": Ibid., 151.

82 "in a serious . . . manuscripts": EW to JPB, July 3, 1921, *Letters*, 68.

82 "breaking hearts and spreading havoc": Ibid., 67.

82 "would leave . . . attractive": *Twenties*, 92.

82 "When I . . . early years": EW to JPB, July 3, 1921, *Letters*, 67.

82 "on the occasion . . . steadfast love": Millay to EW, July 20, 1922.

82 "on her . . . see people": EW to JPB, Jan. 15, 1924, *Letters*, 118.

83 "This is just . . . Bunny": Millay to EW, March 4, 1926.

83 "Any great . . . kinds": *Daisy*, 74.

83 "Your verdict . . . to me": Millay to EW, Aug. 1946; "Edna St. Vincent Millay," *Shores*, 781.

83–84 "Love is not all . . . would": Millay, *Collected Poems*, 659.

84 "Oh, sleep . . . Moon!": Ibid., 681.

84 "a resplendent . . . and fame": Judith Thurman, "Siren Songs," *NY*, Sept. 3, 2001, 91.

84 "The whole . . . her now": "Edna St. Vincent Millay," *Shores*, 787.

84 "produced dreadful . . . bankruptcies later": *Forties*, 289.

84 "rushed phrases . . . wonder": *Daisy*, 12.

84 "groping back . . . underworld": "Edna St. Vincent Millay," *Shores*, 786.

6: Coming of Age

85 "strong physical passion": *Twenties*, 51.

85 "a prime . . . correctitude": EW to WSD, May 26, 1922, *Letters*, 83.

85 "lead John . . . balls": EW to FSF, June 26, 1922, Ibid., 85.

85 "Stanley is . . . volume": Marion Dell to EW, Nov. 28, 1920.

85–86 "zealous disciples . . . Dell": WSD to EW, Dec. 20, 1922.

86 "the gauzy . . . Italy": WSD to EW, Aug. 25, 1925.

86 "astonishing prettiness": EW to Arthur Mizener, March 3, 1950, Ibid., 478.

86 "excited her erotically": *Twenties*, 214.

86 "seize . . . something": EW to Christian Gauss, April 28, 1920, *Letters*, 53.

86 "Zelda rushed . . . a bath": *Twenties*, 55.

86 "wonderful form": EW to JPB, Sept. 22, 1922, *Letters*, 96.

86 "No *Saturday* . . . talent!": EW to FSF, Aug. 9, 1919, Ibid., 44.

86 "this history . . . form": EW to FSF, Nov. 21, 1919, Ibid., 46.

86 "make something really beautiful": Ibid.

86–87 "p. 10x . . . Ha-ha!": FSF to EW, Feb. 21, 1921, in *Correspondence of F. Scott Fitzgerald*, eds. Matthew J. Bruccoli and Margaret M. Duggan (New York: Random House, 1980), 81.

87 "I have . . . so reticent": FSF to EW, postmarked Jan. 24, 1922, *FSF Letters*, 329.

87 "intense and exceedingly intelligent": Caption in *VF*, April 21, 1924, 12.

87 "is determined . . . or no": "The Provincetown Players' Scrapbook: 1915–1924," New York Public Library for the Performing Arts, Lincoln Center), New York City.

87 "a pre-flapper . . . studies": Interview with Malcolm Cowley, 1985.

87 "they did . . . together": *Magician*, 30.

87 "It's all . . . lizard": *Twenties*, 220.

87–88 "all our . . . sight": MB to EW, n.d. [1921].

88 "in a Cinderella . . . each other": MB to EW, n.d. [1921].

88 "a tumor": MB to EW, n.d. [1921].

88 "a deluxe cathouse": *Twenties*, 39.

88 "serendipity": Geoffrey T. Hellman, *Mrs. De Peyster's Parties* (New York: Macmillan, 1963), 171.

89 "timid old . . . books": EW to WSD, Feb. 19, 1921, *Letters*, 56.

89 "occupied with . . . here": EW to WSD, Aug. 16, 1921, Ibid., 74.

89 "Through Walter . . . friends": Memo, Crowninshield to EW, June 3, 1921.

89 "Be simple, Ezra, be simple": *Twenties*, 86.

90 "Yours for . . . New York": EW to FSF, June 22, 1921, *Letters*, 63.

90 "of merely antiquarian interest": FSF to EW, May 1921, *FSF Letters*, 326.

90 "one of those . . . affairs": EW to JPB, July 3, 1921, *Letters*, 68.

90 "the intellectual . . . country!'": EW to FSF, July 5, 1921, *Letters*, 64.

91 "dear E.W. . . . small": Djuna Barnes to EW, July 22, 1922.

91 "I arrived . . . like this": EW to JPB, Sept. 5, 1922, *Letters*, 95.

91 "drift idle . . . dawn": "Boboli Gardens," *Night Thoughts*, 17–18. See also journal entry in *Twenties*, 102–3.

91 "the barbarity . . . against it": Night Thoughts in Paris," *NR*, March 15, 1922, 76.

91 "the machines . . . source": "The Aesthetic Upheaval in France," *VF*, Feb. 1922, 49.

92 "I shall not . . . punch-bowl!": "Night Thoughts in Paris," *NR*, March 15, 1922, 87.

92 "the old madhouse": EW to FSF, July 31, 1922, *Letters*, 88.

92 "a volume . . . edition": *Twenties*, 43.

92 "floral bombs . . . hearts": "From Maupassant to Mencken," *VF*, Dec. 1922, 26.

92 "has been given . . . express": "F. Scott Fitzgerald," *Shores*, 27.

92 "an instinct . . . envy": Ibid., 30.

93 "does not . . . life": Ibid., 29.

93 "like everything . . . approbation": FSF to EW, n.d. [Jan. 1922], *FSF Letters*, 330.

93 "The most . . . Zelda": FSF to EW, n.d. [Jan. 1922], Ibid., 331.

93 "a solid hunk . . . American": Virginia Woolf to Vita Sackville-West, July 15, 1926, *The Letters of Virginia Woolf*, vol. 3, *1923–1928*, eds. Nigel Nicolson and Joanne Trautmann (New York: Harcourt Brace Jovanovich, 1977), 280.

93 "almost skeletally . . . a peacock": *Twenties*, 78.

93–94 "Why, Milton . . . do you?": Ibid., 115.

94 "every little . . . blackbird's beak": "Wild Peaches," Elinor Wylie, *Collected Poems* (New York: Knopf, 1933), 12.

94 "need for romance . . . sexual expression": Judith Farr, *The Life and Art of Elinor Wylie* (Baton Rouge: Louisiana State University Press, 1983), 6.

94 "my spiritual . . . mother": EW to Wylie, Aug. 2, 1922, *Letters*, 90.

94 "among members . . . in N. Y.": Wylie to EW, Aug. 14 [1920s].

94 "which aimed . . . you liked": *Twenties*, 31.

94–95 "outfitted with . . . inferno": Arthur and Barbara Gelb, *O'Neill* (New York: Harper & Brothers, 1960), 495.

95 "Mary was . . . enough": Kenneth Macgowan, quoted in Ibid., 502.

95 "could vary . . . time": Louis Shaeffer, *O'Neill: Son and Artist* (Boston: Little, Brown, 1973), 42.

95 "to entertain our girls": *Twenties*, 29.

95 "I go . . . my soul!: EW to FSF, May 26, 1922, *Letters*, 85–86.

95 "to buy . . . alone": EW to JPB, Sept. 5, 1922, *Letters*, 95.

95 "into a . . . bath": EW to JPB, Nov. 29, 1922, *Letters*, 99.

95 "We *must* . . . purposes": *Twenties*, 136.

95   "hated abortions": Interview with HMW, 1984.

95   This one, however, did not occur: Wilson then borrowed Fitzgerald's house at Great
      Neck, where he and Zelda had not yet moved in, to talk the situation over with Mary.
      He assured his conventional friend they intended "to sleep in separate beds": EW to
      FSF, March 24, 1923, *Letters*, 105.

95   "any woman . . . completely": *Magician*, 32.

96   "Crowninshield . . . was alien": *Twenties*, 41–42.

96   "Mary is . . . sometimes": EW to JPB, June 30, 1923, *Letters*, 107.

96   "leaning at . . . degrees": *Twenties*, 141.

96   "the execrable . . . inhabitants": EW to H. L. Mencken, Aug. 17, 1923, *Letters*, 110.

96   "housewife"; "plant manager": *Magician*, 3.

96–97 "formal candidacy . . . grace": E. E. Paramore, Jr., to EW, n.d. [1923].

97   "but left . . . ages ago": EW to JPB, June 30, 1923, *Letters*, 107.

97   "Your father's . . . my case": EW to Burton Rascoe, Oct. 2, 1931, *Letters*, 215.

97   "melancholia . . . even the balance": EW to JPB, June 30, 1923, Ibid., 107.

7: Private Life

98   "preferred her . . . maternity": Interview with Hazel Hawthorne, 1984.

98   "At home . . . type": Interview with Mary Hackett, 1984.

99   "East vs. . . . vulgarity, etc.": Sherman Paul, *Edmund Wilson: A Study of Literary
      Vocation in Our Time* (Urbana: University of Illinois Press, 1965), 46.

99   "No knife . . . idiom": Review by Alexander Woollcott, *The* [New York] *Sun*, Oct. 10,
      1924.

99   "silken ties . . . broken": *This Room and This Gin and These Sandwiches, Five Plays*,
      299–300.

99   "for drawing . . . people": "Eugene O'Neill and the Naturalists," *Shores*, 100.

100 "piercing scream": Blair could "make our protesting blood run cold with her piercing
      scream at the curtain." Brooks Atkinson's 1929 *NYT* review of *Before Breakfast* is
      quoted in Gelbs's *O'Neill*, 55.

100 "Agnes O'Neill . . . husband": MB to EW, Jan. 21, 1926.

100 "I'll be . . . O'Neill moods": Ibid.

100 "I knew . . . ecstacies": "To an Actress," *Night Thoughts*, 42.

100 "a Do Not . . . door": *Magician*, 32.

100 "I'm sorry . . . worse": Undated, signed "E."

100 "in a howling . . . frock": Millay to EW, Jan. 8, 1924, Library of Congress.

100 "the man in the iron necktie": *Twenties*, 209.

100 "to talk . . . bed?": Ibid., 240.

100 "melting": Ibid., 194.

100–101 "I told her . . . drinking": Ibid., 195.

101 "overadmirous": Dawn Powell to Malcolm Cowley, April 4, 1962, *Selected Letters of
      Dawn Powell, 1913–1965*, ed. Tim Page (New York: Henry Holt, 1999), 300.

101 "Five days . . . poisons all": "Infection," *Night Thoughts*, 30.

101 "The dirty . . . below": *Twenties*, 256.

101 "simply threw . . . end of it": Ibid., 255.

101 "keyed down by the heat": Ibid., 310.

101–102 "I read . . . Arnold": Ibid., 318.

102 "MANAGEMENT . . . AS WELL": Telegram MB to EW, Sept. 15, 1926.

102 "a perfect . . . bulb": T.S. Matthews, *Angels Unawares: Twentieth Century Portraits* (New York: Ticknor & Fields, 1985), 183–84.

102 "felt secure . . . exist": *Magician*, 56.

102 "hated": Ibid., 55.

102 "never loved": Ibid., 149.

102 "taken from . . . my child": Ibid., 3.

102–103 "I am . . . for me": MB to EW, Aug. 21 [1926].

103 "Dear Bunny . . . Mary": MB to EW, n.d.

103 "the deep heart . . . by brine": "To an Actress," *Night Thoughts*, 42–43.

103 "Say that . . . lie to me!": *Thirties*, 260.

103 "well and normal again": *Twenties*, 417.

103 "When we kissed . . . taught me": Journals (typescript), vol. 3, 178–79.

103 "She was . . . unresponsive": *Twenties*, 349.

104 "as if . . . desired": Ibid., 359.

104 "all my adoration": Ibid., 334.

104 Wilson never knew: "Isaiah Berlin on Edmund Wilson," *WQ*, Winter 1999, 38–49.

104 "Daniel Webster . . . kind": *Twenties*, 340.

104 "she didn't . . . happy": Ibid., 339.

104 "for a limited . . . sheik role!": Ibid., 340.

104 "I wanted . . . cloth cases": Ibid., 190–91.

105 "a great . . . jazz band": EW to JPB, Jan. 15, 1924, *Letters*, 117.

106 "beat her . . . suicide": E. E. Paramore, Jr., to EW, Sept. 28, 1924.

106 "if a man . . . lover": *Twenties*, 202.

106 "headlong and demoniac": *Hecate*, 135.

106 "with gentle . . . flowers": Ibid., 137.

106 "deep husky city voice": *Twenties*, 411.

106–107 "If you come . . . it off": Ibid., 365.

107 "the snap . . . feel guilt": *Hecate*, 157–58.

107 "three quarts . . . toilet": Agnes O'Neill to EW, July 4, 1927.

107 "Her pale . . . stimulation—": *Twenties*, 410.

107 "the night . . . dark red": Ibid., 432.

107 "little narrow . . . anything else": Ibid., 413.

107 "personally to destroy . . . lifetime": EW's first will, 1927.

108 "vigorous and brilliant," "to decorate . . . worn": "Signs of Life: Lady Chatterley's Lover," *Shores*, 405.

108 "didja ever . . . the same": *Twenties*, 407.

108 "He that made . . . lost": W. B. Yeats, "Never Give All the Heart," *The Collected Poems of W.B. Yeats* (New York: Macmillan, 1956), 77.

108 "Like me . . . for instance": Journals (typescript), vol. 3, 178. Al is changed to Sam in *Twenties*, 417.

108 "Honestly it's . . . that!": *Twenties*, 402–3.

108 "'and oh . . . know'": Ibid., 440.

109 "his deferred manhood": John Updike, "Wilson's Fiction: A Personal Account," *Edmund Wilson: The Man and His Work*, ed. John Wain (New York: New York University Press, 1978), 167.

109 "after we . . . cock": *Twenties*, 437–38.

109 "had invested . . . killed himself": Ibid., 434.

109 "always beautifully turned out": Interview with Cowley, 1985.

109 "amorous adventures": *Thirties*, 260.

109 "hard pointed . . . (groaning)": *Twenties*, 440

109–110 "it had . . . Adonis": ibid., 441.

110 "felt that . . . company)": T. S. Matthews, *Angels Unawares*: Twentieth Century Portraits (New York: Ticknor and Fields, 1985), 183.

110 "was beginning . . . to go": *Twenties*, 441.

110 "My health is beyond worry": MC to EW, n.d. [1927].

110 "go and debauch . . . God": MC to EW, June 27, 1928.

110 "It will cheer . . . life with": MC to EW, July 9, 1928.

110 "a side car . . . yourself": MC to EW, July 28, 1928.

111 "seems . . . tradition": "The All-Star Literary Vaudeville," *Shores*, 243.

111 "touch of Spanish sensuality": *Twenties*, 442.

111 "the Great . . . house": LB Rolfe Humphries, Dec. 27, 1925, *Woman Lived*, 24.

111 "what the . . . about": Interview with Judith Farr, literary executor of Leonie Adams, 1986.

111 "I'm not . . . so dear": *Twenties*, 442.

111 "Edmund . . . flesh": Adams, quoted by Farr in interview, 1986.

111–112 "rebellion . . . death": Leonie Adams, "April Mortality," *The Best Poems of the English Language*, ed. Harold Bloom (New York: HarperCollins, 2004), 935–36.

112 "delivering a number of preachments": Adams to EW, July 21, 1928.

112 "My health . . . think": Adams to EW, July 21, 1928.

112 "my health . . . all right": Adams to EW, n.d. [Aug. 1928].

112 "The days . . . completely": *Twenties*, 445.

112 "I'm happy . . . Al": Journals (typescript), vol. 4, 35. Al is changed to Sam in *Twenties*, 456.

112 "I don't . . . you go": *Twenties*, 457.

112–113 "I didn't . . . to me!": Ibid., 458.

113 "Dearest Ed . . . you did": Frances Minihan to EW, Nov. 2, 1928.

113 "the dry . . . fireplace": *Twenties*, 474.

113 "all make . . . sand": Ibid., 465.

113 "earthly paradise"; "a little soft and cloying": Ibid., 467.

113 "isn't necessary . . . standing": EW to Maxwell Perkins, Nov. 19, 1928, *Letters*, 153.

113 "easier . . . nerves": Ibid., 152.

113 "he never . . . naked legs": *Twenties*, 482.

113 "all the . . . eyes": Ibid., 470.

114–115 "Stepped . . . her, etc.": Ibid., 471.

114 "feel like singing . . . Butterfly": MC to EW, Dec. 22, 1928.

114 "walking . . . strumpet": MC to EW, Jan. 4, 1929.

114 "I didn't care . . . so much": MC to EW, Dec. 22, 1928.

8: Literary and Cultural Criticism

115 "With each . . . joy": "The Historical Interpretation of Literature," *Thinkers*, 270.

115 "let out a whoop": "The Critic Who Does Not Exist," *Shores*, 372.

115 "piling up . . . another": "The Poetry of Drouth," *Dial*, Dec. 1922, 612.

115 "of strained . . . institutions": Ibid., 616.

115–116 "Eliot's own . . . surroundings": EW to JPB, Sept. 5, 1922, *Letters*, 94.

116 "Air for Vitriol and Demi-Virginal"; "Thou looks . . . hat": unpublished typescript.

116 "to write . . . reality": W. B. Yeats, "The Fisherman," *The Collected Poems of W. B. Yeats* (New York: Macmillan, 1956), 146.

116 "probably comparable . . . long life": "W. B. Yeats," *NR*, April 15, 1925, 10.

116 "the great . . . very sensitive": JPB to EW, n.d. [1922–1923].

116 "A NUD . . . OZ": "Anagrams on Eminent Authors," *Night Thoughts*, 199.

116 "melting music": "Wallace Stevens and E. E. Cummings," *Shores*, 50.

117 "into the full . . . imagination": "The Pilgrimage of Henry James," *Shores*, 219.

117 "Henry's bicycle": Ernest Hemingway, *The Sun Also Rises* (New York: Scribner's, 1954), 115.

117 "so he . . . or Lisette": "Representative Americans," *The New Masses* 1, Oct. 1926, 9.

117–118 "swift manipulation . . . dreams": "Mrs. Wharton in Eclipse," *VF*, Sept. 1922, 19.

118 "a bitter . . . conventions": "Things I Consider Underrated: Edith Wharton," *VF*, March 1923, 38.

118 "conscientious and sane": "A Guide to Gertrude Stein," *VF*, Sept. 1923, 60.

118 "why literature should not"; "inevitably founded on ideas": Ibid., 80.

118 "people and . . . justice": Gertrude Stein to EW, Oct. 3, 1923.

119 "I have come . . . and then": Sherwood Anderson to EW, n.d. [1921].

119 "soothed as . . . explorations": "Sherwood Anderson's *Many Marriages*," *Shores*, 93.

119 "gift for . . . universal significance": EW to Stanley Dell, Apr. 25, 1922, *Letters*, 79.

119 "a humorous . . . Southwestern": EW to Maxwell Geismar, n.d. [1942], Ibid., 130–31.

119 "anecdotes, adventures, queer characters": "All God's Chillun," *Earthquake*, 128.

119 "wonderful erotic . . . American life": EW to JPB, Sept. 22, 1922, *Letters*, 97.

119 "took pen in hand": EW to Geismar, n.d. [1942]. *Letters*, 131.

119 "gone to . . . he was": Ernest Hemingway to EW, Nov. 25, 1923, included in "Emergence of Ernest Hemingway," *Shores*, 117.

119 "in the States . . . for": Ibid.

120 "invaluable for . . . head": Ibid., 118.

120 "distinctively American development in prose": Ibid., 119–20.

120 "artistic dignity": Ibid., 121.

120 "one of . . . newspapermen": "That Summer in Paris," *Bit*, 522.

120 "the thugs . . . sophisticated": EW to Hemingway, May 4, 1927, *Letters*, 140.

120 "feel, behind . . . relation": "The Sportsman's Tragedy," *Shores*, 344.

120 "not a propagandist even for humanity": "Emergence of Ernest Hemingway," *Shores*, 121.

120–121 "a no-nonsense . . . sensibility": Morris Dickstein, "Edmund Wilson: Three Phases," *Centennial Reflections*, 17–18.

121 "three-dimensional ogres": "From Maupassant to Mencken," *VF*, Dec. 1922, 25.

121 "newspaper narrative . . . crimes": "The All-Star Literary Vaudeville," *Shores*, 246.

121 "independent one-man turns": Ibid., 247.

121 "ridden by adolescent resentments": Ibid., 232.

121 "snuffed out": "Dos Passos and the Social Revolution, *Shores*, 433.

121 "by what . . . actually did": *Twenties*, 323–24.

121 "From the point . . . encouraging": "Dahlberg, Dos Passos, and Wilder," *Shores*, 450.

121 "a lot . . . a year": "The Delegate from Great Neck," *Shores*, 151.

121 "deep blue patches"; "ruthlessly": *Twenties*, 186.

121–122 "accomplished something . . . dinners": Ibid., 185.

122 "Decision on . . . Europe": F. Scott Fitzgerald's ledger (Washington, D.C.: NCR/Micro-card Editions, 1972).

122 "I feel . . . now": FSF to Maxwell Perkins, n.d. [before April 16, 1924], *FSF Letters*, 163.

122 "I cannot . . . capable of ": *FSF Letters*, 162.

122 "about the best . . . written": FSF to Perkins, n.d. [before Aug. 27, 1924], *FSF Letters*, 166.

122 "wonderful": FSF to EW, n.d. [postmarked Oct. 7, 1924], *FSF Letters*, 341.

122 "It is very . . . beautiful": EW to FSF, Nov. 13, 1924, reproduced in *NYTBR*, Oct. 9, 1977, 1. This letter is not found in any collection of Fitzgerald's letters or in his papers at Princeton. The word "phrases" is partly covered by a penknife in the photograph.

122 "undoubtedly in . . . hyena cage": EW to FSF, April 11, 1925, *Letters*, 121.

122 "inspired imagination . . . brilliance": "The All Star Literary Vaudeville," *Shores*, 232.

123 "the vividness . . . that one": EW to Hamilton Basso, May 9, 1929, *Letters*, 173.

123 "might well have taxed Dostoevsky": "A Weekend at Ellerslie," *Shores*, 375.

123 "highschool (Princeton University) stuff": EW to FSF, Dec. 4, 1933, *Letters*, 233.

123 "a loose . . . impersonal one": "Christian Gauss as a Teacher of Literature," *Shores*, 15.

123 "originates all . . . wigs": "Alice Lloyd and Farfariello," *Earthquake*, 38.

124 "fantasy"; "harlequinade": "The Follies as an Institution," *Earthquake*, 51.

124 "*You've got . . . again!*": "The Finale at the Follies," *Earthquake*, 44.

124 "You'll find it . . . little gal!": Ibid., 46.

124 "The new woman . . . foot": "The Follies in New Quarters," *Earthquake*, 80.

124 "it speeds . . . Cantor": "Burt Savoy and Eddie Cantor of the Follies," *Earthquake*, 59.

124 "In the . . . green thigh": "Night Clubs," *Earthquake*, 32.

124 "wassup": "The National Winder Garden," *Shores*, 275.

125 "the free-est . . . style": "The Greatest Show on Earth," *Earthquake*, 42.

125 "short strong . . . aquiline-nosed": "Houdini," *Shores*, 174.

125 "scrupulous and serious-minded": "A Great Magician," *Shores*, 289.

125 "among the . . . chosen work": Ibid., 291–92.

125 "I often . . . pages": Gilbert Seldes to EW, August 11, 1963.

126 "the inequalities . . . coarse": *Twenties*, 159–60.

126 "of a feathery . . . marmoreal": "The Stieglitz Exhibition," *Earthquake*, 100–101.

126 "genuine sparkle": Alfred Stieglitz to EW, Sept. 27, 1925.

126 "ribbon of talk": Postscript, 1957 to "The Stieglitz Exhibition," *Earthquake*, 101.

126 "little bird refuge for artists": Ibid., 103.

126 "as bracing . . . had been": Ibid., 102.

126 "He almost . . . Matisse": Jed Perl, "Wilson's Eye," *Modern Painters* (Winter 1996), 78.

126 "old servant's . . . light": "It's Great to Be a New Yorker!" *Earthquake*, 29.

126 "the bespectacled . . . setting": "Paul Rosenfeld: Three Phases," *Classics*, 509.

127 "make something . . . Culture": EW in interview with Henry Brandon, *NR* (March 30, 1959); letter to the author on Copland's behalf by Ronald Caltabiano.

127 "transmuted by . . . Copland": "Paul Rosenfeld: Three Phases," *Classics*, 505.

127 "I'd never . . . today": "Everyman His Own Eckermann," *Bit.*, 580.

127 "upright rectangles . . . towers": "On This Site Will Be Erected," *Earthquake*, 17.

127 "huge coarse . . . refuge": "The Crushing of Washington Square," *Earthquake*, 94.

128 "the Stars . . . passionate life": "The People Against Dorothy Perkins," *Earthquake*, 24.

128 "women have . . . killing": Ibid., 28.

128 "those praisers . . . my day": "To a Young Girl Indicted for Murder," *Night Thoughts*, 31.

128 "iridescent": "On Editing Scott Fitzgerald's Papers," *Night Thoughts*, 120.

128 "sprees . . . universal": "The Lexicon of Prohibition," *Earthquake*, 91.

128 "about midnight . . . heads": EW to Allen Tate, May 20, 1929, *Letters*, 165.

129 "ordered all . . . others": EW to Lionel Trilling, May 3, 1957, *Man in Letters*, 72.

129 "pursuing a line . . . subjects": "Thoughts on Being Bibliographed, *Classics*, 112.

129 "into a rapid . . . aims": Ibid., 113.

130 "the impressionistic . . . categories": EW to R. P. Blackmur, Nov. 14, 1929, *Letters*, 170.

130 "at thirty . . . professor's": T. S. Matthews, *Name and Address* (New York: Simon & Schuster, 1960), 192.

130 "then, collecting . . . dart out": Ibid., 193.

130 "When he . . . left off": Ibid.

130 "peculiar way . . . the point": T. S. Matthews, *Angels Unawares: Twentieth-Century Portraits* (New York: Ticknor & Fields, 1985), 184.

130 "Anything . . . revisions": Ibid.

131 "a little casket . . . was kept": "A Preface to Persius," *Shores*, 267.

131 "Why, I've . . . subways up!": Ibid., 270.

131 "the mysterious . . . our hand": Ibid., 271.

131 "loud sour laughter"; "all pink . . . size": Ibid., 268.

131 "Europe heavily . . . gulf": Ibid., 233.

131 "rude collisions with reality": *Twenties*, 426–27.

132 "a certain . . . circulate": "The Critic Who Does Not Exist," *Shores*, 369.

132 "a free . . . of them": Matthew Arnold, "The Function of Criticism at the Present Time," in *Four Essays on Life and Letters*, ed. E. K. Brown (New York: Appleton-Century-Crofts, 1947), 16.

132 "had no doubt . . . this world": "Woodrow Wilson at Princeton," *Shores*, 317.

133 "the ghost . . . a mole": JPB to Tate, June 11, 1934, *The Republic of Letters in America: The Correspondence of John Peale Bishop and Allen Tate*, eds. Thomas Daniel Young and John J. Hindle (Lexington: University of Kentucky Press, 1981) 100.

133 "during the . . . form": EW to JPB, Oct. 22, 1928, *Letters*, 154.

134 "condemned clams": "The Men from Rumplemayer's," *Earthquake*, 155.

134 "FORSAKEN . . . summons": Ibid., 160.

134 "even under . . . New York": "Dos Passos and the Social Revolution," *Shores*, 432–33.

134 "a sort . . . nobility": "T. S. Eliot and the Church of England," *Shores,* 439.

134 "everybody's world": Ibid., 440.

134 "he seemed . . . in Paris": Lionel Trilling, *A Gathering of Fugitives* (Boston: Beacon Press, 1956), 50.

135 "unwritten and . . . heavens": "Notes on Babbitt and More," *Shores*, 451.

135 "in 'dealing . . . moderate": Ibid., 457.

135 "to a people . . . foot": "The Delegate from Great Neck," *Shores*, 143.

135 "often only semi-literate": "The All-Star Literary Vaudeville," *Shores*, 246.

135 "all that old stuff"; "burn it up": "Mr. More and the Mithraic Bull," *Thinkers*, 8.

136 "its throat . . . the earth: Ibid., 13.

9: Between the Acts: 1929

137 "doubtful human . . . violent": "The Death of Elinor Wylie," *Shores*, 396.

138 "very uneven . . . tremendously": Edna Millay to EW, Feb. 6, 1929.

138 "narrow . . . her then": *Twenties*, 491.

138 "some sort . . . Margaret": Ibid., 491–92.

138 "moped and . . . experience": Adams to EW, Dec. 28, 1928.

139 "torn membrane"; "healed"; "fiendish": Adams to EW, Jan. 22, 1929.

139 "worried": Adams to EW, Jan. 22, 1929.

139 "You mustn't . . . about August": Adams to EW, Feb. 15, 1929.

139 "on the whole . . . human contact": Adams to EW, Feb. 22, 1929.

139 "she sought . . . this": Frost made this comment to Judith Farr; interview with Farr, 1986.

139 "work at . . . my room": *Twenties*, 492.

139 "seized with . . . morphine": Ibid., 492–93.

140 "was going . . . Sandy": Ibid., 493.

140 "green slope . . . stand it": Ibid., 453.

140 "was not . . . of will": Ibid., 493.

140 "thought there . . . by itself": *Magician*, 31.

140 "couldn't get . . . illusion": Quoted by Glyn Morris, *Nights and Days with Edmund Wilson*, 78, in Jeffrey Meyers, *Edmund Wilson: A Biography* (Boston: Houghton Mifflin, 1995), 125.

140 "the panics . . . cannot describe": *Twenties*, 493.

140 "exhilarating relaxing effect": Ibid., 494.

141 "terrible"; "The moment . . . girlish diary": Millay to EW, March 5, 1929.

141 "book on modern literature": EW to Gauss, Feb. 16, 1929, *Letters*, 159.

141 "a central . . . symbolism": Gauss to EW, Feb. 25, 1930, *The Papers of Christian Gauss*, 260.

141 "the passage . . . symbolism": *Twenties*, 493.

141 "the geniuses": Interview with Irving Hubbard, 1984.

142 "psyched": EW to Phelps Putnam, March 3, 1937, *Letters*, 288.

142 "tried to . . . couch": *Magician*, 32.

142 "I hate . . . myself": *Twenties*, 494.

142 "sense of . . . companion": Ibid., 495.

142 "and it would . . . that now": Adams to EW, n.d. [1929].

142 "I AM . . . TO YOU": Adams to EW, March 2, 1929.

142 "I AM . . . UNDERSTAND": Adams to EW, March 16, 1929.

142 "harrowing interviews": *Twenties*, 495.

142 "the thing . . . possible": Interviews with MMcC, 1984.

142 "a beautiful . . . enough": Interview with Farr, 1986.

142–143 "warm gusts . . . themselves": *Twenties*, 506.

143 "get tied . . . my dear": MC to EW, Mar. 7, 1929.

143 "She was . . . hidden": *Twenties*, 497.

143 "though I . . . human being": Ibid., 495.

143 "I still loved . . . forever!": Ibid., 503–4.

143 "Her nose . . . tar soap": Ibid., 505.

143 "come and valet": MC to EW, Aug. 16, 1929.

143 "determined to marry": Ibid., 516.

143–144 "I think . . . house": Ibid., 518.

144 "aborted Wilson's . . . 1929": Meyers, 114.

144 "You must . . . a ticket": MC to EW, Sept. 12, 1929.

144 "the many . . . knowledge": MC to EW, Sept. 25, 1929.

144 "capable young . . . satisfaction": *Twenties*, 521.

144 "she put . . . relief": Ibid., 528.

144 "sober judgment . . . the end": Ibid., 423.

144 "I begin . . . country": EW to Allen Tate, May 20, 1929, *Letters*, 162.

145 "into a country . . . our own": "Dostoyevsky Abroad," *Shores*, 412.

145 "without the roller coaster": MB to EW, n.d. [June 1929].

145 "we can . . . foundation": MB to EW, Nov. 23, 1929.

145 "LITTLE BIRDIE . . . RSVP": Anne Barton Cummings to EW, March 29, 1929.

145 "the pure . . . the ghost": EW to Tate, Aug. 13, 1929, *Letters*, 168.

145 "Farewell, gay . . . glass": "Poets, Farewell!" *Night Thoughts*, 69.

146 "I leave . . . tongue": Ibid.

146 "exercised enough . . . to burst": "The Literary Consequences of the Crash," *Shores*, 496.

146 "exhilarated at . . . fraud": Ibid., 498.

146 "the gigantic . . . wall": "Enlightenment Through the Films," *Earthquake*, 76.

146 "a rending . . . Judgment": "The Literary Consequences of the Crash," *Shores*, 496.

146 "She didn't . . . my hands": *Twenties*, 534.

147 "So you . . . nine times": Ibid., 533.

147 "not to cheat on Margaret": Ibid., 534.

147 "Just take . . . won't mind": MC to EW, Sept. 12, 1929.

147 "bringing incongruously . . . Blues"; "brindled hair": *Twenties*, 542.

147 "I've come . . . some work": EW to JPB, Jan. 15, 1930, *Letters*, 191.

147 "They flicker . . . depart": "Riverton," *Night Thoughts*, 102.

147–148 "a look . . . counted on me": *Twenties*, 545.

148 "acting out . . . writing one": EW to HM, Feb. 14, 1945.

148 "in which . . . a way": "A Weekend at Ellerslie," *Shores*, 383.

148 "When all . . . begins": *Twenties*, 512.

10: From Whitehead and Proust to Marx: *I Thought of Daisy* and *Axel's Castle*

149 "pungent, pithy . . . charming": Marianne Moore to Kauffman, April 30, 1953.

149 "a certain . . . alcohol": E. E. Paramore, Jr., to EW, March 14, 1930.

149 "compounded of . . . proportions": "A. N. Whitehead: Physicist and Prophet," *NR*, June 15, 1927, *Uncollected*, 60.

150 "blowing ourselves . . . atom": "A. N. Whitehead and Bertrand Russell," *NR*, Dec. 30, 1925, *Uncollected*, 46.

150 "the poetry and fiction"; "concrete images": EW to Dorothy Walsh, Sept. 10, 1969, *Letters*, 703.

150–151 "As Edmund . . . to eat": Robert Linscott, "Edmund Wilson: Casual Recollections," American Heritage Center, University of Wyoming. Unpublished typescript.

151 "symphonic movements": "Foreword, 1953," *I Thought of Daisy* (New York: Farrar, Straus & Young, 1953), 2nd page.

151 "clear pink . . . bell hat": Quoted in Neale Reinitz, "Afterword," *Daisy*, 266.

151 "Resolutely": *Daisy*, 98.

151 "more or less real": EW to JPB, Oct. 4, 1929, *Letters*, 174.

152 "as to . . . Church": *Daisy*, 138.

152 "sober, even morose": Ibid., 137.

152 "an unending . . . snapping": Ibid., 78.

152 "cadaverously closed": Ibid., 159.

153 "a fortress . . . wisdom": Ibid., 155.

153 "Mr. Suburban . . . straw hat": Ibid., 245.

153 "the fluidity . . . position": Ibid., 255.

153 "new . . . half thrilling": Ibid., 246.

153 "hot, moist, mucilaginous and melting": Ibid., 260.

153 "from the . . . think": Ibid., 263.

153 "a gulf . . . experience!": Ibid., 156.

153 "Oh, it was you who bought it": Quoted by Cyril Connolly, "Edmund Wilson: An Appreciation," *The Sunday Times* (London), June 18, 1972, 40.

154 "very fine": EW to Perkins, n.d. [before Sept. 12, 1928], *Letters*, 150.

154 "warming their . . . forests": "Notes on Modern Literature," *NR*, March 4, 1925, 40.

154 "popular accounts . . . them": EW to Perkins, n.d. [before Sept. 12, 1928]; *Letters*, 150.

154 "life grown . . . windows": *Twenties*, 23.

154 "the horror . . . place": *Castle*, 105.

154 "a sort . . . lucid": Ibid., 115.

154 "luminous and noble": "Four Plays for Dancers," *The Freeman*, March 29, 1922, 68.

154 "one of the . . . magnitude": "W. B. Yeats," *NR*, April 5, 1925, 10.

155 "sustain a grand . . . heightening": *Castle*, 37.

155 "the product . . . machinery": Ibid., 45.

155 "He had . . . a year": Yeats, quoted in Ibid., 46.

155 "Joyce was . . . hearts": *Dial*, Nov. 1924, 435.

155 "Dublin, seen . . . remembered": *Castle*, 211.

155 "solid institutions . . . factors": Ibid., 222.

155 "of the river . . . syncopated": Ibid., 231–32.

155–156 "social episodes . . . scale": Ibid., 139.

156 "the shimmering . . . Hell": Ibid., 159.

156 "refusal to be neurotic": Sherman Paul, *Edmund Wilson* (Urbana: University of Illinois Press, 1965), 87.

156 "which seem . . . intelligence": *Castle*, 187.

157 "psychological . . . enormous": "Gertrude Stein," *NR*, April 23, 1927, 228.

157 "systematic comic nonsense": *Castle*, 253.

157 "the shift in *Axel's Castle*": Kenneth Burke, "Curriculum Criticum," *Counterstatement* (Berkeley: University of California Press, 1968), 213.

157 "going further . . . time": EW to Tate, May 28, 1930, *Letters,* 196.

157 "which constitutes . . . the people": "Dahlberg, Dos Passos, and Wilder," *Shores*, 449–50.

157 "to make . . . society": *Castle*, 293.

158 "a sedative for sick Americans": "The Economic Interpretation of Wilder," *Shores*, 503.

158 "of the Heartbreak . . . master": *Castle*, 190.

158 "I felt . . . Proust": Alfred Kazin, *Starting Out in the Thirties* (Boston: Little, Brown, 1965), 5.

158 "with Adolphe . . . Joyce": EW to LB, July 1, 1936, *Letters*, 277.

158 "an effect . . . *Wood*": Stanley Edgar Hyman, *The Armed Vision* (New York: Knopf, 1948), 19.

158–159 "passionate identification . . . response": Frank Kermode, "Edmund Wilson and Mario Praz," *Encounter* 16, no. 5 (1961), 70.

159 "the great . . . that word'": Donald Hall, letter to the author, July 28, 1987, elaborating on an interview.

159 "based on . . . language": *Castle*, 284.

160 "the whole . . . art": Ibid., 298.

11: With Margaret Canby: Political Commitment and Tragedy

163 "to the . . . island": *Thirties*, 4.

163 "stronger and . . . clothes": *Jazz*, 94.

164 "the sick . . . nations": Harry Kemp, "Wind of Change."

164 "strange, inept man": Interview with Hawthorne, 1984.

164 "Stay in me!"; "large pink prong": *Thirties*, 253.

164 "was always . . . me": *Magician*, 72.

165 "Never, after . . . screen": *Finland Station*, 236.

165 "nice little man": "Dwight Morrow in New Jersey," *Earthquake*, 173.

165 "the men . . . hardened": Ibid., 171.

165 "take Communism . . . Communists": "An Appeal to Progressives," *Shores*, 532.

165 "Money-making . . . humanity": Ibid., 525–26.

165 "Love-making . . . stain)": *Thirties*, 47.

165–166 "battle cry . . . obstacles": JDP to EW, Jan. 14, 1931, *Fourteenth Chronicle*, 396.

166 "on a white horse": Katharine Dos Passos to MC, Jan. 9, 1931.

166 "full of . . . ladies": MC to EW, Oct. 3, 1930.

166 "go in . . . yourself up": *Thirties*, 252.

166 "would smoke . . . distinctions": Ibid., 236–37.

166 "a broad-brimmed . . . hat": Matthew Josephson, "Encounters with Edmund Wilson," *Southern Review*, Autumn 1975, 743.

166 "forty-eight . . . sixth)": "May First: The Empire State Building: Life on the Passaic River," *Earthquake*, 293.

166 "a gigantic . . . erection": Ibid., 296.

167 "blown out . . . floor": Ibid., 300.

167 "brassy proscenium . . . settings": "The Metropolitan Opera House," *Earthquake*, 205.

167 "Now can't . . . fuck'": Interview with Cowley, 1985.

167 "to break . . . words": *Thirties*, 258.

167 "There were . . . sip?" Interview with Cowley, 1985. Adelaide Walker confirmed that Margaret liked to sip.

168 "off her head": EW to Perkins, n.d. [1930], *Letters*, 201.

168 "My God . . . hell": One of two stanzas enclosed with LB's letter to EW [April 1931] on stationery of the Neurological Institute.

168 "Everything is . . . flux": EW to LB, April 1931, *Letters*, 207.

168 "neither experience . . . whoopee": JDP to EW, Jan. 14, 1931, *Fourteenth Chronicle*, 398.

168 "talk the . . . worruker": "Detroit Motors," *Earthquake*, 230.

169 "from which . . . credit": JDP to EW, Nov. 2, 1934, *Fourteenth Chronicle*, 449.

169 "the Southern . . . society": Tate to EW, July 30, 1930, addressed from Clarksville, Tenn.

169 "the deadening . . . communities": "Tennessee Agrarians," *Earthquake*, 332.

169 "JITTERS UNDER PERFECT CONTROL": MC to EW, June 1, 1931.

169 "in bed . . . chubby": MC to EW, June 9, 1931.

170 "wanton promiscuity": "Indian Corn Dance," *Earthquake*, 361.

170 "FROM HEAD . . . LOVE": MC to EW, June 12, 1931.

170 "which was . . . mouth": *Thirties*, 243.

170 "the strain . . . relation": "Mr. and Mrs. Blackburn at Home," *Hecate County*, 411.

170 "All Virgil's . . . embrace": "The Voice: On a Friend in a Sanitarium," *Night Thoughts*, 104.

171 "You don't . . . like me": *Thirties*, 248–49.

171 "making the . . . capitalism": Ibid., 120.

171 "went to . . . she did": *Magician*, 73.

171 "very Californian"; "Of course . . . been called)": *Thirties*, 255–56.

171 "an American form of Communism"; "with a crash": John Howard Lawson, "A Calendar of Commitments: Another View of the Twenties and Thirties," Southern Illinois University Library, Carbondale, 231. Cited by David J. Snyder in a master's thesis for the American Studies Program, University of Wyoming, 1997.

171–172 "sour situation"; "wonderful country": EW to Gauss, July 31, 1931, *Letters*, 211.

172 "cultivated enervated people"; "mixturesque beauty": "The City of Our Lady the Queen of the Angels," *Earthquake*, 379.

172 "cheery little . . . mystic's fingers": Ibid., 380.

172 "July: family . . . drowning": *Thirties*, 130.

172 "the last . . . world": "The Jumping-Off Place," *Earthquake*, 416.

172 "solemnly reading . . . marching on!": Ibid., 417.

172–173 "throw themselves . . . Honolulu": Ibid., 420.

173 "half-dead in the kitchen": MC to EW, n.d. [1931].

173 "do a Miggs": *Thirties*, 259.

173 "only individuals on the make": "Mr. and Mrs. X," *Earthquake*, 433.

173 "insipid, fatuously . . . span": Ibid., 436.

174 "the life . . . profits": "The Case of the Author," *Jitters*, 306.

174 "classical reading . . . irresponsibility": Ibid., 308.

174 "seemed to be coming apart": Interview with Sidney Hook, 1987.

174 "an engineer's . . . forces": "Marxist History," *NR*, Oct. 12, 1932, 227.

174 "the creed . . . churches": "What I Believe," *Jitters*, 313.

174 "Bunny's book . . . soul": Hemingway to JDP, May 30, 1932, *Ernest Hemingway: Selected Letters, 1917–61*, ed. Carlos Baker (New York: Scribner's, 1981), 360.

174 "In the moment . . . up": "Hemingway: Gauge of Morale," *Wound and Bow*, 231–32.

174 "so completely . . . will": Elizabeth Spindler, *John Peale Bishop* (Morgantown: University of West Virginia Press, 1980), 167.

174 "ascended the . . . streetcar": Michael Gold, *The Hollow Men* (New York: International Publishers, 1941), 68.

175 "the bellwether . . . side": Interview with Cowley, 1985.

175 "in his high . . . like that": T. S. Matthews, *Name and Address* (New York: Simon & Schuster, 1960), 198.

175 "those desperate . . . worked": "Postscript of 1957," *Earthquake*, 574.

175 "then received . . . Communism": *Thirties*, 163.

175–176 "is going . . . general": Anecdote told by Daniel Aaron, *Centennial Reflections*, 207

176 "entering war zone": *Thirties*, 167.

176 "covered with . . . darkness": Ibid., 177.

176 "You can . . . lie": Frank, quoted in Ibid., 177.

176 "class-war exhibit": "Class War Exhibits," *The New Masses*, April 1932, 7.

176 "if the literati . . . suckers": EW to JDP, Feb. 29, 1932, *Letters*, 222.

176 "disappeared": Josephson, 745.

176 "it was logistically . . . time": Quoted by Edel in *Thirties*, 179.

176 "Bunny's behavior . . . part": Interview with Cowley, 1985.

177 "had kept a record": Interview with John Hammond, 1986.

177 "crucial symbol"; "new cultural order": "Manifesto," accompanying a letter to Theodore Dreiser, May 2, 1932, *Letters*, 222–23.

177 "What are . . . table?": JDP to EW, May 1932, *Fourteenth Chronicle*, 409.

177 "the famous fifty-three": Josephson, 745.

177 "outside the bourgeois psychology": "Critics of the Middle Class II: Gustave Flaubert," *New York Herald Tribune Book Review*, Feb. 21, 1932, 6.

177 "mechanical production . . . will": "Critics of the Middle Class I: Karl Marx," *New York Herald Tribune Book Review*, Feb. 14, 1932, 6.

177–178 "somebody . . . I'm not!": *Thirties*, 242.

178 "didn't need . . . perfume": Ibid., 237.

178 "she'd lie . . . no sleep": Ibid., 366–67.

178 "I'm a very . . . people": Ibid., 257.

178 "embarrassingly chichi . . . boudoir": Ibid., 141.

178 "learning to live on sandwiches": Interview with AW, 1984.

178 "champagne tastes": *Thirties*, 238.

178 "exclaiming that . . . morning!" Quoted by Josephson, 742.

178 "drank non-stop": Harold Clurman, *All People Are Famous* (New York: Harcourt Brace Jovanovich, 1974), 106.

178 "disgusting"; "that ended . . . wife": Ibid.

178–179 "I had . . . curtains": *Thirties*, 241–42.

179 "so much . . . thready": Ibid., 157.

179 "gaunt, grey . . . himself": Ibid., 156.

179 "How can . . . at home": Ibid., 235.

179 "each with his own child": Ibid., 192.

179 "Have survived . . . sleep": MC to EW, June 13, 1932.

179 "going West . . . back": *Thirties*, 235.

179 "It seems . . . anyway": MC to EW, June 18, 1932.

179 "leading a very . . . fine": MC to EW, June 19, 1932.

179 "alternated between . . . phonograph": *Thirties*, 193.

179 "that life . . . guidebook": *Memoirs*, 291.

179–180 "a little . . . talking": *Thirties*, 158.

180 "Come home . . . back": Minihan to EW, Sept. 9, 1932.

180 "she . . . suicide": *Thirties*, 261.

180 "my father . . . cry": *Magician*, 76.

180 "not a bad . . . did": *Thirties*, 229.

180 "natural smartness": Ibid., 235.

180–181 "Her cheeks . . . scorn": Ibid., 239.

181 "like a murderer": Ibid., 240.

181 "her and . . . Corn Flakes": Ibid., 262.

181 "threw herself": Interviews with MMcC, 1984.

181 "a turning . . . feet": EW to JDP, October 18, 1932.

181 "I'll crash someday": *Thirties*, 235.

181 "she was doomed . . . her": Ibid., 248.

181 "not in other ways, Darling": MC to EW, June 23, 1932.

181 "hasn't been . . . now": MC to EW, Sept. 14, 1932.

182 "she took off . . . said": *Thirties*, 252.

182 "I forgive . . . dead": Ibid., 260.

182 "After she . . . her": Ibid., 250.

182 "Were the . . . Red Bank": Ibid., 369.

182 "a dry fated . . . happened": Ibid., 407.

182 "hard, scared . . . vise": Ibid., 406.

182 "sometimes passing . . . suicide": Ibid., 407.

182 "glad of . . . alive": Ibid., 368.

182 "I had to . . . lively": Ibid., 654–55.

12: 314 East Fifty-third Street

183 "the death of my wife": EW to Ford Madox Ford, Oct. 13, 1932, *Letters*, 228.

183 "the death . . . him": Interview with Gardner Jencks, 1984.

183 "lumpy and rubbed yellow walls": "The Old Stone House," *Earthquake*, 510.

183 "patiently pleading . . . paperwork": *Magician*, 91.

183 "She'd tried . . . raise": Nora Sayre, *Previous Convictions* (New Brunswick, N.J.: Rutgers University Press, 1995), 64.

184 "swine, scavengers": *Thirties*, 264.

184 "the palm . . . starfish": "Election Night," *Earthquake*, 445.

184 "eat their . . . phlegm": "Hull-House in 1932," *Earthquake*, 457–58.

184 "caged . . . junk-heap": Ibid., 460–61.

185 "that son . . . week!": "A Great Dream Come True," *Earthquake*, 477.

185 *"the* inspiring . . . clear": Matthew Josephson, "Encounters with Edmund Wilson," *Southern Review*, Autumn 1975, 733.

185 *"et enfin à Canton"*: André Malraux to EW, Oct. 2, 1934, incorporated in *Shores*, 573.

185 "He was . . . not": "27, rue de Fleurus," *Shores*, 577.

185–186 "little evanescent poems"; "exquisite": EW to LB, Apr. 9, 1934, *Letters*, 235.

186 "much news . . . cockatoos": Marianne Moore to John Warner Moore, June 11, 1933, *Selected Letters of Marianne Moore*, ed. Bonnie Costello (New York: Knopf, 1997), 308.

186 "the most . . . vase": EW to Maxwell Geismar, May 27, 1942, *Letters*, 383.

186 "A very large . . . Bough": "Washington: Inaugural Parade," *Earthquake*, 481.

186 "the ghost"; "had given up": Ibid., 483.

186 "little cages": Ibid., 478.

186 "pulpit eloquence"; "pungent maxims": "The Hudson River Progressive," *NR*, April 5, 1933. See also untitled typescript on President Roosevelt.

186 "one of . . . maids": *Thirties*, 461.

186 "great brick and marble shell": "Washington: Glimpses of the New Deal," *Earthquake*, 535.

187 "that brief . . . country": "Brokers and Pioneers," *NR*, March 23, 1932, 145.

187 "pocket of the past": "The Author at Sixty," *Piece*, 239.

187 "money power": "The Old Stone House," *Earthquake*, 508.

187 "what is . . . party": EW to LB, July 19, 1933.

187 "still a contemporary event": Arthur M. Schlesinger, Jr., *Centennial Reflections*, 209.

187 "Old Abe . . . parturition": "The Old Stone House," *Earthquake*, 509–10.

188 "intelligible . . . theory": *Thirties*, 298.

188 "at an . . . *Lighthouse*": Ibid., 298–99.

188 "to energize . . . society": "Postscript," *Red, Black*, 498.

188 "the development . . . history"; "at half . . . reviews": EW to George Soule, July 11, 1934, *Letters*, 246.

188 "It is . . . one's own": Introduction to the 1971 edition, *Finland Station*, v.

189 *"certainly . . . men"*: Ibid., 5.

189 "through history . . . life": Ibid., 6.

189 "the peculiar . . . lived it": Ibid., 21.

189 "the Renaissance . . . light": Ibid., 56.

189 "He had . . . researches": Ibid., 15.

189 "read all . . . hat": Ibid., 17.

189 "simply a . . . reader,": Ibid., 18.

190 "immense sentences . . . chapters": Ibid., 54.

190 "palsying pessimism": "From Absolutism to Doubt," lecture delivered on Apr. 3, 1922, *The Papers of Christian Gauss*, eds. Katherine Gauss Jackson and Hiram Hayden (New York: Random House, 1957), 154.

190 "disarm": EW to Gauss, Oct. 21, 1934, *Letters*, 249.

190 "The true . . . through them": Typed note, April 1934.

191 "suffered but . . . alive": Taine quoted in *Finland Station*, 59.

191 "surged in . . . wan": Letter from Edie Shay to Katy Dos Passos, quoted in Virginia Spencer Carr, *John Dos Passos* (Garden City, N.Y.: Doubleday, 1984), 339.

191 "rather sordid period": *Thirties*, 296.

191 "had the . . . lizards": "What to Do Till the Doctor Comes," *Earthquake*, 529.

191 "what she . . . howl": Ibid., 528.

191–192 "a long . . . all concern": Josephson, 752–53.

192 for her: In *The Sixties* Wilson recalls Jean's second husband, Carl Van Doren, coming home to find "she had hanged herself" (108). This memory comes at a moment when, in his distaste for the present, he is tempted to gloss over the horrors of the past.

192 "Come back . . . are"; "called . . . office": Minihan to EW, Oct. 7, 1932.

192 "her absolute . . . need it": *Thirties*, 341.

192 "food ticket": Ibid., 392.

193 "I feel . . . all right": Minihan to EW, Aug. 24, 1933.

193 "It was . . . desire": Journals (holograph, vol. 13, 89; typescript version, 70).

193 "Say something . . . say it": Journals (typescript) vol. 13, 39.

193 "without any . . . merriment": Journals (typescript), vol. 14, 54–55.

193 "Sometimes I . . . 53rd Street": *Thirties*, 438.

193 "the devotion . . . cult": "The Princess with the Golden Hair," *Hecate*, 260.

193 "because their . . . born": *Thirties*, 392.

193 "afraid she . . . to die": Ibid., 426.

193 "her skin . . . creamy": Ibid., 431.

193–194 "she couldn't . . . out": Ibid., 501–2.

194 "feeling morbid . . . marrying her?": Ibid., 495.

194 "what I thought . . . darling!'": Ibid., 427.

194 "temporary relief": "hard, scared, self-acrid feeling"; "something . . . life": Ibid., 407.

194 "to keep awake all the time": *Twenties*, 329.

194 "Forsaken . . . me by": "The Men from Rumplemayer's," *Earthquake*, 156.

195 "the future . . . than ever": *Thirties*, 276.

195 "didn't fit into life"; "a little treat": Ibid., 296.

195 "I'd been . . . H.G. Wells": Louise Connor to EW, Sept. 4, 1962.

195 "twice a week": *Thirties*, 594.

195 "he would . . . herself": Ibid., 383.

195 "I'm coming . . . hostess": Ibid., 380.

195 "the personal-service department": Ibid., 439.

196 "slapping her . . . enough": Ibid., 595.

196 "blocked by . . . other way": Ibid., 597.

196 "walk out . . . couple": Ibid., 596.

196 "It couldn't . . . chin": Connor to EW, n.d. [1935].

196 "The only . . . society down": EW to LB, April 1931, *Letters*, 207.

196 "the last . . . brother": LB to EW, n.d. [April 1931].

196 "a female Dante": LB to Morton Dauwen Zabel, July 29, 1934, *Woman Lived*, 79.

196 "taste, sincerity . . . integrity": LB to EW, Oct. 11, 1929.

196 "topical songs . . . line": LB to Zabel, Feb. 14, 1933, *Woman Lived*, 72.

197 "Content in . . . bread": Louise Bogan, "Women," *The Blue Estuaries* (New York: Noonday Press, 1968), 19.

197 "Though broken, undone is the green . . . there": Bogan, untitled verse.

197 "absolutely no . . . endings": LB to Zabel, July 27, 1934, *Woman Lived*, 78.

197 "make me . . . duets": *Thirties*, 727.

197 "I wouldn't . . . at that": LB to Rolfe Humphries, Dec. 2, 1936, *Woman Lived*, 144.

197 "absolutely compatible . . . me": LB to EW, Aug. 22, 1934, Ibid., 81.

198 "I'm afraid . . . you": EW to LB, May 13, 1935, *Letters*, 271.

198 "made to . . . about": LB to EW, June 22, 1935, *Woman Lived*, 84–85.

198 "'I can't . . . got out": Allan Seager, *The Glass House: The Life of Theodore Roethke* (New York: McGraw-Hill, 1968), 207.

198 "will make . . . lackaday": EW to Putnam, March 24, 1936, *Letters*, 276.

198 "eaten up . . . mustache": *Twenties*, 208.

198 "an awful woman": FSF to EW [postmarked September 14, 1930]; deleted by EW from *FSF Letters* in 1963, when Margaret Bishop was still alive.

198 "sympathetic literary society": Introduction, "A Personal Memoir," Allen Tate, ed., *Collected Poems of John Peale Bishop* (New York: Scribner's, 1948), xiv.

199 "we ascended . . . efforts": *Thirties*, 609.

199 "on top of his suitcase": Interview with WSD, 1963.

199 "cockeyed": *Thirties*, 612.

199 "he sabotaged my literary activity": Ibid., 610.

199 "worked all . . . nights": Interview with WSD, 1963.

200 "he was pulling your leg": T. S. Matthews, *Name and Address* (New York: Simon & Schuster, 1960), 195.

200 "that one . . . Human Idea": FSF to EW, Sept. 7, 1934, *FSF Letters*, 347.

200 "to get drunk and swinish": FSF to EW, March 1933, Ibid., 345.

200 "cold eye": *Thirties*, 302.

200 "his head . . . us": Ibid., 301.

200 "a good . . . hit him?": Ibid., 302.

201 "Scott thinks . . . time": Hemingway, quoted in Ibid., 303.

201 "the difficulty . . . going": Ibid., 303.

201 "I have . . . up on him": EW to FSF, Oct. 21, 1933, *Letters*, 231.

201 "Now is . . . Hemingway": EW to FSF, Nov. 4, 1933, Ibid., 232.

201 "us reds"; "took a . . . trouble?": JDP to EW, Jan. 31, 1935, *Fourteenth Chronicle*, 461.

202 "profoundly permeated . . . Marxist": EW to JDP, Jan. 31, 1935, *Letters*, 257.

202 "things that . . . effect": JDP to EW, Dec. 29, 1934, *Fourteenth Chronicle*, 459.

202 "writing up . . . meetings": EW to JDP, May 9, 1935, *Letters*, 268.

202 "long-range writing": Ibid., 264.

202 "who wrote . . . Florence": Ibid., 266–67.

202 "to extricate . . . himself": Ibid., 264.

202–203 "a little preachment . . . right now": JDP to EW, March 27, 1935, *Fourteenth Chronicle*, 468.

203 "One or two . . . to end": Ibid.

203 "suggesting that . . . powerful": JDP to EW, May 7, 1935.

203 "hushdope . . . Critik": JDP to EW, April 2, 1935, *Fourteenth Chronicle*, 471.

203 "the A 1 lit. . . . compliments": JDP to EW, May 8, 1935, Ibid., 474–75.

13: The USSR in 1935

204 "a tough . . . ability": "Soviet Russia," *Red, Black*, 382.

204 "to embarrass . . . emphasis": Ibid., 148.

205 "permanent and absolute value": Ibid., 375.

205 "lovely, familiar, and dear": Ibid., 150.

205 "remote dizzy dome": Ibid., 169.

205 "dingy . . . monotonous": Ibid., 167.

206 "After all . . . executed!": Ibid., 179.

206 "full of vodka . . . of them": Ibid., 187–88.

206 "self-determination . . . Black-Belt": Ibid., 271.

206 "about Lenin . . . Christianity": Ibid., 222.

206 "I hummed—home": *Thirties*, 566.

207 "never seen such wonderful productions": EW to LB, n.d. [1935], *Letters*, 271.

207 "The Commissar . . . live!": "Soviet Russia," *Red, Black*, 270.

207 "A tall . . . impassive": Ibid., 234.

208 "done time": Ibid.

208 "Some people . . . change": Ibid., 235.

208 "around the . . . herring": Ibid., 232.

208 "Dey have to stuff": Ibid., 233.

208 *"tristes"*: Ibid., 258.

208 "rainbow delirium"; "a grove . . . stars": Ibid., 251.

208–209 "Church built . . . sickly": Ibid., 253.

209 "A little foal . . . are *now!"*: Ibid., 254.

209 "purposefully . . . well-advanced": Ibid., 223.

209 "little, if . . . means a lot": Ibid., 220.

210 "the Moscow tic": Ibid., 201.

210 "It's that everyone is terrified": Ibid., 219.

210 "tall, bearded . . . forehead": Ibid., 289.

210 *"von einem anderem Standpunkt"*: Ibid., 237.

210 "Comrade Prince": Mirsky was so called by a high-placed Soviet acquaintance of EW (Ibid., 291), giving him the title under which this memoir appeared in *Encounter*, July 1955, 10–20.

211 "In fact . . . moving?'": "Soviet Russia," *Red, Black*, 292.

211 "thanked him . . . glow": Ibid., 295.

211 "everybody knew": Ibid., 294.

211 "opening his . . . *Lost*": Ibid., 241.

211 "the inevitable cap and mustache": Ibid., 245.

212 *"Lui"*: Ibid., 244.

212 "Comrade Stalin . . . headache": Ibid., 247.

212 "thick round . . . in shorts": Ibid., 240.

212 "past the . . . wings": Ibid., 376.

212 "Extraordinarily fine . . . fingers": *Thirties*, 551.

212 "was theirs . . . guidepost": "Soviet Russia," *Red, Black*, 377.

212 "silly unking . . . Hello": E. E. Cummings, *Eimi* (New York: William Sloane and Associates, 1933), 243–44.

213 "Its sobriety . . . youth": "Soviet Russia," *Red, Black*, 310–11.

213 "blondinka": Ibid., 311.

213 "a kind . . . intimately": Ibid., 312.

213 "what nice girls they were" Ibid., 318.

213 "the charges . . . in *camera*": Ibid., 382–83.

214 *"kak-kak . . . skandal!"*: Ibid., 332.

214 "scarlet fever": Ibid., 336.

214 "my fever-dreams . . . get me": Ibid., 339.

215 "cupped"; "mainly psychic": Ibid., 342.

215 "the race of the new Russia": Ibid., 366.

215 "beneath the . . . bulb": Ibid., 356.

215 "it was . . . through": Unpublished typescript on Gibbon, 7.

215 "lofty, unperturbed . . . point-of-view": Ibid., 6.

215 "conceived the . . . vespers": Ibid., 3.

215 "a genius in presenting material": Ibid., 1.

216 "the perfumes"; "abnormally acute"; trees were . . . composition": "Soviet Russia," *Red, Black*, 367–68.

216 "*Rigor . . .* Paris": Ibid., 373.

216 "King Lear . . . people": *Fifties*, 163, where the first phrase is given in French (*le côte Lear*).

216 "one of . . . looks": Interview with Leon Edel, 1987.

216 "to see . . . my tie": Nathan Halper, "Conversations with Edmund Wilson," *Journal of Modern Literature*, September 1979, 548.

217 "the moral . . . out": "Soviet Russia," *Red, Black*, 375.

217 "The states . . . the books": *Travels*, 325.

217 "loose, untrimmed . . . light": "Soviet Russia," *Red, Black*, 248.

217 "old slowness and rubbish": Ibid., 356.

14: Trees and *The Triple Thinkers*

218 "He has picked . . . hug": LB to Theodore Roethke, Oct. 20, 1935, *Woman Lived*, 112.

218 "sometimes barking . . . resistance": "Soviet Russia," *Red, Black*, 381.

218 "think of . . . equanimity": JDP to EW, June 27, 1936, *Fourteenth Chronicle*, 485.

218 "or something": LB to Roethke, Oct. 16, 1936, *Woman Lived*, 111.

218 at some point proposed: Rosalind recalls him several times wistfully saying, "She was almost your step-mother." *Magician*, 92.

218 "beautiful and . . . manner": Ibid., 92.

219 "sensitive, very refined face"; "deep sympathy and affection": *Thirties*, 658.

219 "Hattie . . . drawers?": Herbert Solow, quoted by MMcC, *Intellectual Memoirs*, 100.

219 "surrounded by . . . below": *Magician*, 94.

219 "absolute quiet": EW to Zabel, Nov. 6, 1936, *Man in Letters*, 58.

219 "out of . . . time": LB to Roethke, Oct. 28, 1936, *Woman Lived*, 140.

219 "all the . . . world": Ibid., 139.

219 "perhaps the . . . wrote": LB to EW, Nov. 14, 1936, *Woman Lived*, 142.

219 "Soon fly . . . belongs": Louise Bogan, "Song for a Lyre," *The Blue Estuaries* (New York: Noonday Press, 1968), 90.

220 "I remember . . . go on": Ruth Limmer, *Journey Around My Room: The Autobiography of Louise Bogan: A Mosaic* (New York: Viking, 1980), 132.

220 "W. Whew . . . Willie Yeats": Pundit Acherya [LB] to EW, n.d.

220 "Edmund, would . . . please?": Interview with MMcC, 1984. Ruth Limmer, Bogan's literary executor, told the same story to the poet's biographer, Elizabeth Frank Interview with Frank, 1991.

220 "sheer pleasantness": "brute tides underneath": Helen Augur to EW, March 24, 1937.

220 "Your reformed character": Augur to EW, May 12, 1937.

220 "deatched"; "inert"; "stupefied": Connor to EW, n.d. [1935].

220 "better and better": *Thirties*, 593.

220–221 "held in . . . breast": Ibid., 599.

221 "would . . . together": Ibid., 595–96.

221 "the saddest . . . other still": Ibid., 692–93.

221 "great round . . . eyes": "November Ride," *Night Thoughts*, 135.

221 "spoiled": *Thirties*, 669.

221 "an old-fashioned . . . Guineveresque": Ibid., 402.

221 "Soft as . . . fingers": "November Ride," *Night Thoughts*, 135.

221 "a little . . . Frances": Elizabeth Waugh to EW, Oct. 6, 1934; in John Friedman and Kristen Figg, *The Princess with the Golden Hair*. (Madison, N.J.: Fairleigh Dickinson University Press, 2000), 89.

221–222 "the minds . . . positively": Waugh to EW, Sept. 30, 1937; Ibid., 139.

222 "It would . . . printed word": Waugh to EW, March 20, 1936; Ibid., 110.

222 "if you . . . of us": Waugh to EW, Dec. 7, 1933; Ibid., 83.

222 "a still-born child"; "Even your . . . tubes": Waugh to EW, Mar. 4, 1936; Ibid., 109.

222 "lie out . . . there too": Waugh to EW, Oct. 6, 1934; Ibid., 89.

222 "she half hoped . . . her": *Thirties*, 673.

222 "silent but . . . Boccaccio": Ibid., 671.

223 "my sexual organs": Waugh to EW, Dec. 11, 1942, Friedman and Figg, *The Princess*, 159.

223 "what they wanted to hear": *Magician*, 67.

223 "developed . . . ones": Ibid., 66–67.

223 "a mess"; "Miss Mead . . . fine": Ibid., 66.

223 "He kept . . . did": Ibid., 57–58.

223 "the actress who wasn't acting": Ibid., 71.

223 "I am your mother, Rosalind": Ibid., 70.

223 "spoiled fat . . . useless snob": Ibid., 69–70.

224 "how long . . . away": EW to MB, Sept. 19, 1936, included in Ibid., 83–85.

224 "we would . . . done": *Magician*, 71.

224 "like something . . . movies": Interview with AW, July 22, 1984.

224 "her observations . . . penetrating": EW to MB, Sept. 19, 1936, quoted in *Magician*, 85.

224 "one of the . . . to produce": Waugh to EW, July 4, 1936, Friedman and Figg, *The Princess*, 117.

224 "better lined with guts": Waugh to EW, Feb. 20, 1942, Ibid., 160.

224 "my policy . . . per diem": *Magician*, 87.

224 "he was not . . . from me": Ibid., 78.

225 "William Blake . . . tiger": Ibid., 80.

225 "taught me . . . weeks": Ibid., 95.

225 "my old . . . years": "Mr. and Mrs. Blackburn at Home," *Memoirs*, 403.

225 "After writing . . . home": "After Writing . . ." *Night Thoughts*, 109.

226 "Beginning as . . . director": *Finland Station*, 119.

226 "the prime . . princes": Ibid., 111.

226 "pastoral little . . . heading away": *Finland Station*, 130.

227 "Flaubert as . . . Bull": Handwritten at end of Journals, vol. 14 (typescript).

227 "wonderful book": Interview with Isaiah Berlin, 1991. Only part of this appeared in the *Wilson Quarterly*.

228 "looking through . . . warning": "Bernard Shaw at Eighty," *Thinkers*, 179.

228 "music of ideas . . . moralities": ibid., 183.

228 "What is . . . thinker?": Flaubert to Louise Colet quoted on title page of Ibid.

228 "non-bourgeois way out": Ibid., 87.
229 "a sort of . . . are ourselves": "Marxism and Literature," *Thinkers*, 205–6.
229 "revolutionary 'underground'": Ibid., 212.
229 "no sense . . . value": "Communist Criticism," *Shores*, 650.
229 "ethical and aesthetic": Ibid., 648.
229 "trying to . . . sound": Ibid., 650.
229 "quietly vibrating": "The Ambiguity of Henry James," *Thinkers*, 103.
229–230 "he had . . . mask'": Ibid., 118.
230 "committed . . . constrictors": "A. E. Housman": Ibid., 66.
230 "among the . . . life": Ibid., 70–71.
230 "Whenever he . . . head": "Isaiah Berlin on Edmund Wilson," *WQ*, Winter 1999, 45.
230 "he has to . . . sentence": Alfred Kazin, "The Critic and the Age," *The Inmost Leaf: A Selection of Essays* (New York: Noonday Press, 1959), 93–94.
231 "were neither . . . boldly": "Chapman," *Thinkers*, 156–57.
231 "flashlighting and . . . before": Ibid., 157.
231 "a thing . . . on him": Ibid., 155.
231 "in an age . . . money": Ibid., 144.
231 "the joy . . . world": Ibid., 155.
231 "I want . . . strings": Ibid., 164.

15: A Literary Marriage Begins
235 "to pass . . . before": EW to Cowley, April 15, 1937, *Letters*, 287.
235 "haven't even . . . machine": EW to Muriel Draper, Nov. 14, 1938, *Letters*, 331.
235 "Bruce would envelop you in jelly": Interview with Cowley, 1985.
236 "floundered, mouth . . . air": Carol Brightman, *Writing Dangerously: Mary McCarthy and Her World* (New York: Clarkson Potter, 1992), 152.
236 "I had on . . . waiting": Interviews with MMcC, 1984.
236 "I became . . . my life": Ibid.
236 "it ended less platonically": Ibid.
237 "wrote me endless love letters": Ibid.
237 "all shaken up"; "pleasant but painful": MMcC to EW, Nov. 30, 1937.
237 "*distraite*": MMcC to EW, Dec. 1, 1937.
237 "I think you're wonderful": MMcC to EW, Dec. 20, 1937.
237 "wonderful gray eyes—searching eyes": Interview with Elena Levin, 1984.
237 "perhaps a . . . mind": EW to MMcC, Dec. 1, 1937, McCarthy papers, Vassar.
237– 238 "chiefly attended . . . you, etc.": EW to MMcC, Jan. 26, 1938, Vassar.
238 "Love as . . . to you": EW to MMcC, Jan. 18, 1938, Vassar.
238 "You are . . . d'oeuvres": MMcC to EW, Jan. 19, 1938.
238 "sex and . . . eyes": Mary McCarthy, *How I Grew* (San Diego: Harcourt Brace Jovanovich, 1987), 153.
238 "You mean . . . in it": MMcC to EW, Jan. 24, 1938.
238 "Mary was greatly attracted to marriage": Elizabeth Hardwick, introduction, Mary McCarthy, *Intellectual Memoirs: New York 1936–1938* (San Diego: Harcourt Brace, 1992), xx.

238 "had always been perfect": Journals (typescript), vol. 16, 117.

238 "I've had . . . worst way": *Intellectual Memoirs*, 101, 100.

238 "Philip already had a wife": Interviews with MMcC, 1984.

238 "Mr. Wilson . . . trouble": Interview with HM, 1984.

239 "Not doing . . . fellow": Interviews with MMcC, 1984.

239 "we were . . . Catullus": Ibid.

239 "old"; "fat, puffing"; "popping": *Intellectual Memoirs*, chapter 3, passim.

239 "bullied her"; Interviews with MMcC, 1984.

239 "as my . . . truth": *Intellectual Memoirs*, 101.

239 "Jesuitical": Hardwick, Introduction, *Intellectual Memoirs*, xiii.

239 "Mary is . . . she isn't": Interview with Elizabeth Hardwick, 1984.

239 "Mary will . . . she does": Interview with AW, July 22, 1984.

239 a trauma: In *Intellectual Memoirs* (93), McCarthy fears that she included these details, but Wilson repeated to Rosalind "again and again that she'd never told him about this before they were married" (Frances Kiernan, *Seeing Mary Plain: A Life of Mary McCarthy* [New York: W.W. Norton, 2000], 155).

239– 240 "all the time . . . stuck-up": Mary McCarthy, *Memoirs of a Catholic Girlhood* (New York: Penguin, 1965), 57.

240 "under . . . every day": EW deposition, 4.

240 "for no . . . to cry": Mary McCarthy, *A Charmed Life* (New York: Harcourt Brace, 1992), 105–6.

240 "grunted some . . . hit me": *Intellectual Memoirs*, 113.

240 "As we climbed . . . terror": *How I Grew*, 267.

240 "I'm married . . . McCarthy": EW to Tate, April 13, 1938, *Letters*, 301.

240 "It seemed . . . grayness away": *Thirties*, 704–5.

240 "was extraordinarily content": Interview with Harry Levin, 1984.

240–241 "Mrs. Wilson . . . heir": LB to Zabel, May 19, 1938, *Woman Lived*, 170.

241 "the first . . . box": Interviews with MMcC, 1984.

241 "shut the door firmly": *Intellectual Memoirs*, 104.

241 "generous, fatherly"; "like some . . . originality": Interviews with MMcC, 1984.

241 "Mary sends . . . our fault": EW to JDP, July 16, 1939, *Letters*, 320.

241 "Old Massa Tate . . . dachshund": EW to JPB, Sept. 10, 1938, *Letters*, 308.

241 "a kept-woman's . . . books": EW's phrasing of McCarthy's impression of the Bishops' house, *Thirties*, 709.

241 "and he seems . . . banal": EW to Christian Gauss, Oct. 27, 1938, *Letters*, 314.

241 "boring": Quoted in Brightman, 182.

241–242 "the mean . . . bounder": "The Omelet A. MacLeish," *Night Thoughts*, 86.

242 "When the poem . . . you know": "Isaiah Berlin on Edmund Wilson," *WQ*, winter 1999, 48.

242 "Mary had . . . one another's": *Fifties*, 81.

242 "he decided . . . them all": Interviews with MMcC, 1984.

242 "even the vanilla": Ibid.

242 "I always fought back": Ibid.

242 "Edmund was . . . infuriating": Interview with Arthur Schlesinger, 1984.

242 "seizures": "What we will call for politeness' sake 'a seizure'"—MMcC to EW, n.d. [Thurs.] ("My Dear: How are you?")

242 "As a young . . . now": Interviews with MMcC, 1984.

242 "outbursts of . . . double personality": EW deposition, 1.

243 "the first time . . . get up": Mary McCarthy, "Ghostly Father, I Confess," *The Company She Keeps* (New York: Simon & Schuster, 1942), 293.

243 "blue-gray . . . old incident": Interviews with MMcC, 1984.

243 "taxed him"; "a real shiner": Interviews with MMcC, 1984.

243 "flew at him . . . the face": Carol Gelderman, *Mary McCarthy* (New York: St. Martin's, 1988), 91.

243–244 "I never . . . going to": *Magician*, 81.

244 "symptoms of apprehension": Ibid., 99.

244 "her childhood . . . the room": Ibid., 114.

244 "Did McCarthy . . . perceive this?": David Laskin, *Partisans* (New York: Simon & Schuster, 2000), 91.

244 "used to try . . . down": EW deposition, 1.

244 "liked to . . . infuriating": Interview with Schlesinger, 1984.

244–245 "in one of . . . amiable": Interviews with MMcC, 1984.

245 "was diagnosed . . . treatment": MMcC deposition, 3. Vassar.

245 "an exact . . . idiot": EW quoting Grumbach to John J. Geoghegan of Coward-McCann, Sept. 24, 1966, with comment to MMcC in margin, Vassar.

245 "Life can . . . version": Kiernan, 154.

246 "that our . . . fall apart": Interviews with MMcC, 1984.

246 "the main . . . child": EW to MMcC, June 17, 1938, Vassar.

246 "to have Edmund's child": Interviews with MMcC, 1984.

246 "ought to . . . baby": EW to MMcC, June 1938, Vassar.

246 "I am . . . painfully": EW to MMcC, June 22, 1938, Vassar.

246 "My dear . . . I haven't": MMcC to EW, n.d. [Thurs.] ("I am using your own enormous paper to write you").

246 "We are . . . can stand": EW to MMcC, June 17, 1938, Vassar.

247 "one of those fanatical Freudians": MMcC to EW, n.d. [Thurs.].

247 "strange old woman": Interviews with MMcC, 1984.

247 "Mary would . . . seizures": Rosalind Wilson quoted in Kiernan, 154.

247 "fits of weeping": EW deposition, 1.

247 "When I . . . retaliate": Ibid., 4.

247 "slapped her . . . of it": *Magician*, 100.

247 "took me . . . it to me": Rosalind Wilson quoted in Kiernan, 154.

247 "ecstatic": Interview with Mary Hackett, July 8, 1984.

247 "in fine . . . domesticity": EW to JPB, Feb. 1939, *Letters*, 315.

248 "to be . . . myth": EW to W. W. Norton, May 26, 1938, *Letters*, 304.

248 "what was . . . my books": EW to Perkins, Oct. 18, 1938, *Letters*, 312.

248 "I should say . . . way": Interviews with MMcC, 1984.

248 "tremendous turnaround . . . death": Interviews with MMcC, 1984.

249 "the hygienic . . . exploding": McCarthy, *The Company She Keeps*, 288.

249 "she'd admitted . . . talk to": Ibid., 287.

249 "Preserve me in disunity": Ibid., 304.

249 "social interpretation . . . texts": EW to Gauss, March 31, 1939, *Letters*, 317.

249 "We've been . . . very bright": EW to JDP, July 16, 1939, *Letters*, 320.

249 "with some . . . word": Laskin, 88.

249 "The maid . . . lives": Quoted in Kiernan, 161.

250 "It bored . . . stepmother": Interviews with MMcC, 1984.

250 "I got . . . informal": EW to Gauss, Nov. 29, 1939, *Letters*, 323.

250 "the soul of patience": *Magician*, 95.

250 "radiant": EW to MMcC, Aug. 19, 1939, Vassar.

250 "little tributes": EW to MMcC, Aug. 26, 1939, Vassar.

250 "the kind . . . have": EW to MMcC, Aug. 6, 1939, Vassar.

250 "INFANT HERCULES . . . SAFELY": MMcC to EW, Aug. 1, 1939.

250 "a regular Telemachus": MMcC to EW, n.d. [Fri. morning].

250 "Don't let . . . Dr. Frank know": MMcC to EW, n.d. [Thurs. morning].

250 "trauma . . . your departure": EW to MMcC, July 31, 1939, Vassar.

250 "getting back . . . tell on me": EW to MMcC, Aug. 14, 1939, Vassar.

250 "a scenic postcard for Rosalind": MMcC to EW, n.d. [Fri. morning].

250 "down to my last dollar": EW to MMcC, Aug. 19, 1939, Vassar.

250–251 "I had long . . . trees": EW to MMcC, Aug. 26, 1939, Vassar.

251 "a past . . . now was"; "unexpected nostalgia": *Thirties*, 707.

251 "real live . . . faculty": EW to MMcC, Aug. 14, 1939, Vassar.

252 "more or less . . . reader": EW to Norton, Sept. 14, 1939, *Letters*, 321.

252 "for the purpose . . . human race": EW to Zabel, Nov. 26, 1939, *Letters*, 322.

252 "Charley and . . . adorable!": Interviews with MMcC, 1984.

252 "E. W. and M. McC.": *Partisan Review*, Fall 1939, 102, reprinted *Night Thoughts*, 35.

252 "We came . . . permanently": EW to LB, Oct. 10, 1939, *Man in Letters*, 46.

252–253 "if the weather . . . Charley Chan": *Thirties*, 716.

253 "when we . . . by time": Interview with AW, 1984.

253 "the woman Stendhal": EW to Gauss, Sept. 8, 1941, *Letters*, 344.

253 "the inky . . . past us": *Thirties*, 724–25. Edel also includes this same passage in *Forties*, 8, where it more properly belongs.

253 "The moon . . . still": Ibid., 725.

16: The Writing and Acting of History: Wilson on Karl Marx

254 "the writer's . . . of literature": Meyer Schapiro, "The Revolutionary Personality," *Partisan Review*, Nov.–Dec. 1940, 467.

255 "the repetitiousness . . . invective": *Finland Station*, 449.

255 "SHOOT MORE PROFESSORS": Quoted by David Remnick, *Centennial Reflections*, 184.

255 "beautiful": *Finland Station*, 447.

255 "Pity that Russia was homely": VN to EW, Dec. 15, 1940, *N-W Letters*, 33. VN later wrote to EW (Feb. 23, 1948) that when his enthusiasm for the Revolution had yielded to "a more mature judgment and the pressure of inescapable facts," "you

somehow did not bother to check your preconceived notions in regard to old Russia, while, on the other hand, the glamour of Lenin's reign, retained for you the emotional iridescence which your optimism, idealism and youth had provided" (*N-W Letters*, 195).

255 "the terrific . . . regimented": *Finland Station*, 517.
255 "the aristocrat of revolution": Ibid., 503.
256 "had usually . . . Party'": Ibid., 511.
256 "tarnished pink": Ibid., 547.
256 "Western man . . . lived": Ibid., 547.
256 "Everything was . . . words": Ibid., 554.
256 "world-historical . . . promoting it": Ibid., 168.
257 "the philosophies . . . cultured": Ibid., 166.
257 "all the . . . instincts": Ibid., 167.
257 "the blank . . . proletarian": Ibid., 173.
257 "flexible, lively, and active": Ibid., 155.
257 "grew up . . . theology": Ibid., 154.
257 "The deicide . . . Absolute Idea": Ibid., 144.
258 "candor and humanity": Ibid., 185.
258 "Doomed to . . . tragedy": Ibid., 208.
258 "she seemed . . . trance": Ibid., 259.
258 "drank in . . . day": Ibid., 243.
258 "the poisoned cup": Ibid., 390.
258 "the old . . . debate": Ibid., 236.
258 "turn the . . . Shakespeare": Ibid., 237.
259 "could get . . . money": Ibid., 340.
259 "man's conscious creative will": Ibid., 220.
259 "in the despotism . . . itself": Ibid., 230–31.
259 "Nobody but . . . classes": Ibid., 359.
260 "buried alive"; "sped away . . . bottle": Ibid., 317.
260 "recalcitrant": Ibid., 324.
261 "Everything will . . . remain": Ibid., 332.
261 *"ends in themselves"*: Ibid., 246.
261 "reveries about . . . mad": Ibid., 303.
261 "a Satan . . . mankind" Ibid., 370.
261 "his outraged . . . others": Ibid., 361.
261–262 "cruel discomfort . . . life": Ibid., 366.
262 "unrelievedly saturnine": Ibid., 368.
262 "found in . . . was doomed": Ibid., 371.
262 "the importance . . . drawn": Ibid.
262 "nothing in . . . justice": Sidney Hook, "Thinkers Who Prepared for Revolution," *New York Herald Tribune*, Sept. 29, 1940, ix. Hook said he had not changed his mind when interviewed in 1987.
263 "The great crucial . . . themselves": *Finland Station*, 371.
263 "Again and . . . American": V. S. Pritchett, *NY*, Dec. 23, 1972, 78.

263 "a society . . . members": "Marxism at the End of the Thirties," *Shores*, 743.

263 "Did you . . . Hitler?" EW to Cowley, Oct. 20, 1938, *Letters*, 310.

263 "bringing the . . . its system": *Finland Station*, 339–40.

264 "He worked . . . living": Ibid., 32.

264 "Out of . . . men": Ibid., 384.

17: 1940: Wilson's Middle of the Journey

265 "an exclusive . . . bigwigs": *Finland Station*, 381.

265 "we have . . . libraries, roads": Ibid., 378.

265 "The body . . . 1940": John Chamberlain, "The New Books," Harper's Magazine, October 1940.

266 "Mr. Wilson . . . own": W. H. Auden, "Who Shall Plan the Planners?," *Common Sense*, Nov. 1940, 22.

266 "interminable": EW to Gauss, March 17, 1940, *Letters*, 358.

266 "never vulgar . . . back": "Dickens: The Two Scrooges," *Wound and Bow*, 13–14.

267 "bitter animus": "The Kipling That Nobody Read," *Wound and Bow,* 139.

267 "the poet . . . curtains": "Dickens: The Two Scrooges," *Wound and Bow,* 9.

267 "it was originally aroused": "The Kipling That Nobody Read," *Wound and Bow,* 139.

267 "to the more simple": James, quoted in Ibid., 153.

268 "wearing an . . . fish": Robert Linscott, "Authors on Publishers," unpublished typescript, 8, American Heritage Center, University of Wyoming.

269 "shot himself . . . mother": Hemingway to Arthur Mizener, May 12, 1950, in *Ernest Hemingway: Selected Letters, 1917–61*, ed. Carlos Baker (New York: Scribner's, 1981), 694.

269 "an infusion . . . movies": Postscript 1940 to Hemingway: Gauge of Morale," *Wound and Bow*, 242.

269 illegitimate: EW to Blake Nevius, July 31, 1953, and to Van Wyck Brooks, Oct. 6, 1957, *Letters*, 545–46, 547–48.

270 "Edmund penetrated . . . wrote about": "Isaiah Berlin on Edmund Wilson," *WQ*, Winter 1999, 47.

270 "I never . . . combination": EW to Trilling, Aug. 31, 1953, *Man in Letters*, 70.

270 "half a mile . . . Mary": *Magician*, 106.

271 "poets of the tabloid murder": "The Boys in the Back Room," *Classics*, 21.

271 "the illusion . . . sentimentality": Ibid., 27.

271 "are animated . . . stagy": Ibid., 42.

271 "steam open . . . people": *Sixties*, 44.

271 "horrible"; "swirling around . . . others": "The Boys in the Back Room," *Classics*, 54.

271 "to bear . . . maneuvers": "Archibald MacLeish and the Word," *Classics*, 6.

271 "Dos"; "Ernest": Ibid., 8.

272 "a new set . . . World War 1": Ibid.

272 "plunged us in": "The Author at Sixty," *Piece*, 220.

272 "a more . . . Bruce": Handwritten memo on Elmhirst and the *NR*.

272 "I was . . . himself": EW to Trilling, May 3, 1957, *Man in Letters*, 72.

272 "I'm a terrible conspirator": Alfred Kazin, *New York Jew* (New York: Knopf, 1978), 21.

272 "jointly assume . . . totalitarians": Editorial, *NR*, Dec. 1940, 7.

272–273 "whichever way . . . etc.": Handwritten memo by Wilson.

273 "my natural . . . *NR*": Ibid.

273 "Neither of . . . war": Bruce Bliven to Edel, Apr. 18, 1973.

273 "not to interfere . . . timid": Michael Straight *After Long Silence* (New York: W. W. Norton, 1983), 159.

273 "even perhaps . . . to destroy": Arthur M. Schlesinger, Jr., *Centennial Reflections*, 209.

274 "pushing America toward war": Straight, *After Long Silence*, 162.

274 "Hitler will . . . Napoleon": EW to Roman Grynberg, Oct. 9, 1941, Library of Congress.

274 "the ebb-tide of history": *Finland Station*, 208.

274 "inveterate and irrational instinct": "War," *Piece*, 43.

274 "magnificent": FSF to EW, Oct 21, 1940, *FSF Letters*, 349.

274 "horrible . . . time": FSF to EW, Nov. 25, 1940, Ibid.

274 *"frohe tage"*: EW to Gauss, May 15, 1944, *Letters*, 335.

274 "suddenly robbed . . . personality": EW to Zelda Fitzgerald, Dec. 27, 1940, Ibid., 327.

274 "Men who . . . somebody dies": EW to JPB, Jan. 2, 1941, Ibid., 328.

275 "Come! . . . write!": EW to JPB, Jan 14, 1941, Ibid., 329.

275 "a little job in Washington": EW to Tate, Sept. 28, 1943, *Letters*, 331.

275 "leaking . . . poems": Introduction, *Collected Essays of John Peale Bishop*, ed. EW (New York: Scribner's, 1948), xiii.

275–276 "brought it . . . from within": Introduction, *The Last Tycoon Together with The Great Gatsby and Selected Stories*, ed. EW (New York: Scribner's, 1941), ix–xi; *Uncollected*, 296.

276 "not a legend"; "secure reputation": Stephen Vincent Benét, *Saturday Review of Literature*, quoted in Matthew Bruccoli's introduction to *The Loves of the Last Tycoon* (New York: Simon & Schuster, 1993), lxxvi.

276 "raise the . . . verse": John Dos Passos, "A Note on Fitzgerald," F. Scott Fitzgerald, *The Crack-Up*, ed. EW (New York: New Directions, 1945), 339.

276–277 "last fragments . . . the plunder": "On Editing Scott Fitzgerald's Papers," *Night Thoughts*, 119–22.

277 "on the home stretch": "The Author at Sixty," *Piece*, 236.

277 "Yeats, Freud . . . father": EW to JPB, Jan. 14, 1941, *Letters*, 329.

278 "Here at . . . silence alone": *Forties*, 8.

278 "He had . . . in them": Interviews with MMcC, 1984.

278 "to make . . . household": EW to MMcC, Sept. 13, 1941, Vassar.

278–279 "Dearest Edmund . . . complex": MMcC to EW, n.d. [Mon.].

279 "Tidings from the Whore": Brightman, 206.

279 "luminous in . . . suit": MMcC to EW, n.d. [Thurs.]

279 "made him shiver": Kazin, *Centennial Reflections*, 148.

279 "tend to . . . direction": EW to Elena, July 31, 1946.

279 "the clear . . . light": *Forties*, 273.

18: Wilson and McCarthy, 1942–1945

280 "in his snowy-white . . . Hell": Interviews with MMcC, 1984. See also McCarthy, 93.

280 "spirited termagant of a wife": McCarthy, *The Company She Keeps*, 279.

280 "She would . . . like that": Quoted in Kiernan, 173.

280 "Mary will . . . kiss": Interview with David Chavchavadze, 2000.

280 "two tyrants . . . other": Laskin, *Partisans*, 88.

281 "I was . . . old": *Sixties*, 322.

281 "terribly . . . man": Interview with Schlesinger, 1984.

281 "my father-in-law": Interview with Broadwater, 1988.

282 "I am . . . pattern": MMcC to EW, n.d. [Sat. morning].

282 "I was . . . situation worse": EW to MMcC, Sept. 13, 1941, Vassar.

282 "come back . . . life": MMcC to EW, Aug. 12, 1942.

282 "alien personality . . . horrified": *The Company She Keeps*, 293.

282 "went to . . . performed on her": EW deposition, 6.

282 "by the . . . my dear": EW to MMcC, Jan. 15, 1942, Vassar.

282 "was not . . . period of time": EW deposition, 6.

282–283 "Dearest, do . . . the spark": Homemade Valentine, Vassar.

283 "We cleared . . . sand": *Forties*, 27–28.

283 "the servant girl . . . awkwardness": Interviews with MMcC, 1984.

283 "leave . . . bloomed": Mary McCarthy, "The Weeds," *Cast a Cold Eye* (New York: Harcourt Brace, 1950), 3.

284 "when her . . . my dear'": Ibid., 8.

284 "a marriage . . . desperate": Ibid., 9.

284 "man in . . . papers": Ibid., 12.

284 "I've always loved your flowers": Ibid., 41.

284 "on her own . . . lacking": Ibid., 40–41.

284 "Love (note hate) my dear": EW to MMcC, July 27, 1942, Vassar.

284 "must have . . . miscarriage": Reuel K. Wilson, "Growing Up with Edmund Wilson and Mary McCarthy," *Paris Review*, Winter 1999, 241.

284 "quite unjust": Interview with AW, 1987.

284 "she'd planned it": *Magician*, 111.

284 "fatal mistake . . . another child": McCarthy, quoted in Brightman, 236–37.

285 "Analysis became . . . over": Interviews with MMcC, 1984.

285 "made a mess . . . hangover": MMcC to EW, n.d. [Thurs.].

285 "Dr. Kardiner . . . myself": MMcC to EW, Nov. 18, 1942.

285 "wonderful": EW to MMcC, Nov. 9, 1942, Vassar.

285 "I had . . . family": MMcC to EW, Nov. 18, 1942.

286 "cardinal doctrine": Interviews with MMcC, 1984.

286 "my absence . . . start from there": MMcC to EW, n.d. [Thurs., 1943].

286 "felt beaten anyway": AW quoted in Kiernan, 191.

286 "He casts . . . ground": McCarthy, *A Charmed Life*, 112.

286–287 "Once something . . . it out": Interviews with MMcC, 1984.

287 "he had . . . embers": Interviews with MMcC, 1984.

287 "It was . . . Revolution": Interviews with MMcC, 1984.

287 "terrible"; "nauseating": Interviews with MMcC, 1984.

287 "she kept . . . worse": Katy Dos Passos to JDP, Nov. 8, 1945. JDP Papers, University of Virginia.

287 "terrible"; "Write about *her* some time!": Alfred Kazin, *New York Jew* (New York: Knopf, 1978), 67–68.

287 "about the cabman's . . . trudged back": Ibid., 68.

288 "sitting on . . . lap": Kiernan, 194.

288 "the beast of Picasso"; "the Minotaur in a maze": Interviews with MMcC, 1984.

288 "But as for . . . proxy": Conrad Aiken, unpublished limerick.

288 "Wilson was . . . too big": Interview with Hardwick, 1984.

288 "Dada has . . . backwards": Reuel K. Wilson to Roman Grynberg, included by MMcC in a letter to EW, n.d.

289 "gripping, almost . . . readings": Reuel K. Wilson, "Letters from Mary McCarthy to Reuel Wilson," *Provincetown Arts*, 2001, 38.

289 "uncomfortable in . . . adjustment": Reuel K. Wilson, videotaped lecture at Vassar College, Oct. 10, 2001.

289 "not a natural . . . right": Quoted in Kiernan, 189.

289 "wonderful with . . . hands": Ibid., 173.

289 "out of . . . another sweet": Reuel K. Wilson, "Growing Up," 241.

289 "a fondness . . . leaves": Ibid., 236.

289 "in a very . . . light": Ibid., 241.

289 "He had a . . . voice": Ibid., 249.

289 "crawling upon . . . study doorstep": Ibid., 241.

289 "I gave . . . about": Reuel K. Wilson to EW, part of MMcC's letter to EW, n.d. [Oct.–Nov. 1943].

289–290 "how people . . . Ebbie Given": EW to Reuel K. Wilson, June 7, 1945.

290 "the United . . . there": EW to Reuel K. Wilson, June 27, 1945.

290 "old gloomy . . . leave": EW to Reuel K. Wilson, April 7, 1945.

290 "Mary and . . . their wake": *Magician*, 115.

290 "was drunk . . . unhappy about": Interviews with MMcC, 1984. Her court deposition (Vassar) contains the same details.

290 "one exception": EW deposition, 4.

290 Rosalind says: Kiernan, 196–97.

290 "full of dim suspicions": Rosalind Wilson postcard to MMcC, Vassar.

290–291 "followed the . . . the Cape": Interviews with MMcC, 1984.

291 "I have . . . friendly basis": EW to MMcC, July 13, 1944, Vassar.

291 "touch another . . . last summer": Interviews with MMcC, 1984.

291 "seedy sexual appeal"; "irresistible": Adam Gopnik, "The Power Critic," NY, March 16, 1998, 77.

291 "gaining a reputation . . . fists": Kiernan, 215.

291 "used to . . . Edmund": Brightman, 259.

291 "For one . . . pursue it": Greenberg, quoted in Kiernan, 215.

292 "He really dug in": Interview with HM, 1984.

292 "Oh wonderful! . . . sell it!": Interview with HM, 1984.

292 "If Edmund . . . there was": Interview with HM, 1984.

292 "You should . . . you": Rosalind to EW, June 1945.

293 "Edmund was in . . . yourself then?": Interview with HM, 1984.

293 "Plump, pink . . . girlfriends": *Magician*, 199.

293 "enchanted": EW to Powell, Oct. 4, 1943, *Letters*, 397.

293 "curious effect . . . drinking": *The Diaries of Dawn Powell, 1931–1965*, ed. Tim Page (South Royalton, Vt.: Steerforth Press, 1995), 215.

293 "HEADQUARTERS . . . orb": Powell to EW, April 11, 1945, in *Selected Letters of Dawn Powell, 1913–1965*, ed. Tim Page (New York: Henry Holt, 1998), 123.

294 "I've left . . . upstairs": EW to MMcC, Jan. 17, 1945, Vassar.

294 "The end . . . marriage": Interviews with MMcC, 1984.

294 "Perhaps the fighting . . . run away": MMcC to EW, n.d. [Dec. 1944].

294 "no other man in the picture": MMcC, quoted in Kiernan, 214.

294 "Each had . . . rooms": John Biggs III quoted in Jeffrey Meyers, *Edmund Wilson: A Biography* (Boston: Houghton Mifflin, 1995), 210.

294 "in mortal . . . body": MMcC deposition.

294 "psychoneurosis": Affidavits of Drs. Rado, Frank, and Kardiner, Vassar.

294 "hysteria": Dr. Frank affidavit, Vassar.

295 "were being destroyed": Interview with AW, 1984.

295 "that her . . . carving-knife": EW deposition, 5–6.

295 "making up . . . shouldn't she?": Interview with HM, 1984.

295 "It wasn't . . . I hadn't": *Magician*, 114.

296 "waif . . . people": Interview with AW, 1987.

296 "Monstro": Interview with Broadwater, 1988.

296 "after the . . . phone": Interviews with MMcC, 1984.

296 "He was . . . reciprocated": Interviews with MMcC, 1984.

296 "One day . . . reviewer'": Interviews with MMcC, 1984.

296 "When Edmund . . . expert on": Interview with Schlesinger, 1984.

296 "a sense . . . them": Interview with Broadwater, 1988.

297 "amount of control"; "is wonderful"; "the theme . . . effect": MMcC to EW, n.d. [1943].

297 "he keeps . . . surprise": EW to Zabel, Oct. 31, 1938, *Letters*, 367.

297 "Mary's mind . . . way": Interview with Broadwater, 1988.

297 "either at . . . apart": Interview with AW, 1984.

297 "a handmaiden made to serve": Interviews with MMcC, 1984.

298 "In case . . . court files": MMcC to EW, July 27, 1962.

298 "about $5545 . . . and you": MMcC to EW, reprinted in Mary McCarthy, "A Memory of James Baldwin," *NYRB*, April 27, 1989, 49.

298 "He sounds . . . criticism": McCarthy, "Books of the Year," *The Observer* (London), Dec. 17, 1978.

298 "A handsome . . . relaxes": *The Little Blue Light, Plays*, 421–22.

298 "Don't hit . . . kill me!": Ibid., 480.

298 "much more comfortable": *Magician*, 115.

299 "could not . . . child": Journals (typescript), vol. 16, 116–17.

299 "beautiful and brilliant girl": EW to MMcC, Nov. 9, 1942, Vassar.

300 "sympathize with . . . forties": EW to MMcC, July 13, 1944, Vassar.

300 "I am . . . man": *The Diary of Anaïs Nin: 1944–1947*, ed. Gunther Stuhlmann (New York: Swallow Press, 1971), 92.

300 "never ceased . . . for Mary": Interview with HM, 1984.

19: Memoir and Fiction, by Night and by Day

301 "too purposive . . . Roosevelt": "Postscript of 1957," *Earthquake*, 568

301 "into the position . . . ourselves": Ibid., 567.

301 "thrown on . . . war-time": Ibid., 570.

301 *"animals . . . but animals"*: *Forties*, 47.

302 "the spiral . . . drain": Ibid., 44.

302 "softening up"; "to blow . . . abstract form": Ibid., 45.

302 "large-scale . . . Russians": "The Vogue of Marquis de Sade," *Bit*, 168.

302 "to go . . . radioactivity": "Postscript of 1957," *Earthquake*, 568.

302 "my favorite . . . books": Frontispiece, 1967 edition of *Memoirs of Hecate County* (Philadelphia: L. C. Page).

303 "Schoenberg had . . . ache": *Jazz*, 116.

304 "have an . . . damnation": EW to Perkins, Dec. 5, 1941, *Letters*, 433.

304 "How do . . . higher ones?": *Hecate*, 14.

305 "quaint old Trader van Horen": "The Three Limperary Cripples," *Note-Books*, 71–72.

305 rationalized that his staged successes: Charles Van Doren in conversation with the author at Columbia University.

305 "literature could . . . itself": *Daisy*, Reinitz ed., 33.

305 "an invented . . . lights": *The Diaries of Dawn Powell; 1931–1965*, ed. Tim Page (South Royalton, Vt.: Steerforth Press, 1995), 215.

305 "wainscoted and . . . rich": "The Princess with the Golden Hair," *Hecate*, 127.

306 "the real . . . rested": Ibid., 197.

306 "nothing more . . . income": Ibid., 130.

306 "sciatica": Interviews with MMcC, 1984.

306 "all the . . . witches": EW to John E. Austin, 1957, *Letters*, 440–41.

306 "Delivered": "The Princess with the Golden Hair," *Hecate*, 258.

306 "I was . . . again": Ibid., 292.

306 "My long . . . else": EW to Morton Zabel, Sept. 10, 1943, *Letters*, 436.

306 "a heaviness . . . quality": *The Diary of Anaïs Nin: 1944–1947*, ed. Gunther Stuhlmann (New York: Swallow Press, 1971), 95.

306 "remarkably chaste, despite the frankness": VN to EW, March 8, 1946, *N-W Letters*, 165.

306 "heartbreak, the . . . lose": "The Princess with the Golden Hair," *Hecate*, 169.

306–307 "I opened the . . . chestnuts": Ibid., 172.

307 "the seedy . . . New York": Louis Menand, "Edmund Wilson's Vanished World," *NYRB*, Sept. 23, 2004, 86.

307 "N. N. Chernokhvostov": Interview with David Chavchavadze, 2000.
307 "My Opposite Number": "Mr. and Mrs. Blackburn at Home," *Hecate*, 379.
308 "victim to . . . the power": "At Laurelwood," *Night Thoughts*, 174.
308 "The tides . . . away": Ibid., 177.
308 "nobility and naiveté": "Mr. Rolfe," *Thinkers*, 236.
308 "a rough-hewn . . . sake": Ibid., 243.
308 "the political . . . place": Ibid., 256.
308 "a great . . . humors": EW to JPB, Aug. 1, 1922, *Letters*, 92.
309 "so exhilarated . . . sense": "Paul Rosenfeld" Three Phases," *Classics*, 518.
309 "pays for . . . justification": Ibid., 519.
309 "no decent work": "Thoughts on Being Bibliographed," *Classics*, 116.
309 "are at least . . . present": Ibid., 108.
309 "give . . . point": Ibid., 120.
309–310 "by getting . . . conscience": Ibid., 113.
310 "you read . . . company": Ibid., 110.
310 "at middle . . . write": Ibid., 111.
310 "past the . . . activity": Ibid., 115.

20: At *The New Yorker* and in England and Italy: Waugh, Silone, Santayana

311 "open to . . . job": Katharine S. White to EW, Feb. 14, 1934, *New Yorker Archive*, New York Public Library.
311 "but it's not for us": Harold Ross to White, 1935. *New Yorker Archive*. EW had submitted the account of writing for magazines and editors called "The Literary Worker's Polonius."
311 "handle a department": EW to Ross, May 22, 1942, *Letters*, 403.
311 "snarling and . . . influences": James Thurber to EW, Oct. 22, 1943.
311 "a comprehensive . . . publication": EW to Ross, Oct. 17, 1943, *Letters*, 403.
312 "a sometimes . . . observation": "Under the Glass Bell," *NY*, April 1, 1944, 81.
312 "in many . . . pose": "A Novel by Dawn Powell—Monsignor Knox's New Testament," *NY*, Nov. 11, 1944, 87.
312 "devastated"; "astute": Tim Page, *Dawn Powell* (New York: Henry Holt, 1998), 198–99.
313 "somewhere in the early thirties": "A Toast and a Tear for Dorothy Parker," *Classics*, 171.
313 "Absolute Hollywood corrupts absolutely—Old Antichrist's Sayings," *Letters*, 302.
313 "the only . . . Shaw": "Never Apologize, Never Explain: 'The Art of Evelyn Waugh,'" *Classics*, 140.
313 "the outrageous . . . truth": Ibid., 142.
313 "the savagery . . . him": Ibid., 147.
313 "have every . . . too": "Ambushing a Best-Seller," *Classics*, 317.
313 "five-and-ten-cent . . . bilge alone": "'You Can't Do This to Me!' Shrilled Celia," *Classics*, 208.
313 "periods of . . . earth": "A Treatise on Tales of Horror," *Classics*, 173.

313 "awful orcs": "Oo, Those Awful Orcs!" *Bit*, 326–32.

314 "like you or me": "Why Do People Read Detective Stories?" *Classics*, 237.

314 "to unpack . . . nails": Ibid., 233.

314 "not a bad . . . knowing it": "Who Cares Who Killed Roger Ackroyd?," *Classics*, 259.

314 "Being a . . . perceived": Anaïs Nin to EW, Apr. 5, 1944.

314 "He is lonely and lost": Anaïs Nin, *Diary of Anaïs Nin: 1944–1947* (New York: Swallow Press, 1971), 41.

314 "He portrays . . . neurotic'": Ibid., 79.

315 "everyone adored": Interview with Schlesinger, 1984.

315 "the best of England": Interview with Stephen Spender, 1991.

315 "little diamond-bright . . . gauges": *Europe*, 183.

315 "fall in . . . you again": EW to MP, April 28, 1945, *Letters*, 418.

315 "I miss . . . Imperialism": MP to EW, May 6, 1945.

315 "is educating . . . control!": MP to EW, June 7, 1945.

315–316 "suppose you . . . about you": EW to MP, May 28, 1945.

316 "terrible attack . . . steps": *Sixties*, 255.

316 "an antique . . . Silone": *Europe*, 183.

316 "your devoted friend": MP to EW, July 6, 1945.

316 "I don't . . . anyway": MP to EW, July 26, 1945.

316 "he very . . . forbid!": MP to Celia Paget, May 27, 1947, in *Living with Koestler: Mamaine Koestler's Letters, 1945–1951*, ed. Celia Paget Goodman (London: Weidenfeld & Nicolson 1985), 62.

316 "one of the . . . girl": EW to Elizabeth Huling, July 4, 1945.

316 "her commerce . . . shop": *Europe*, 19.

317 "as if . . . vermiform": Ibid.

317 "who quoted . . . Whyte-Melville": "Notes on London at the End of the War," *NY*, June 2, 1945, 52.

317 "that dreadful . . . vocabulary": George Orwell to EW, Feb. 14, 1948.

317 "absolutely first-rate": "George Orwell's *Animal Farm*—Albert Cossery's *Men God Forgot*," *NY*, Sept. 30, 1946, 97.

318 "lovely": *Forties*, 157.

318 "alternatively that . . . James": Ibid., 151.

318 identified as Mamaine: Interview with Spender, 1991.

318 "stopped just short of seizing": Edward de Grazia, *Girls Lean Back Everywhere: The Law of Obscenity and the Assault on Genius* (New York: Random House, 1992), 220.

318 "Then what . . . Cairo": Christopher Sykes, *Evelyn Waugh* (Boston: Little, Brown, 1975), 284–85.

318 "how we do things": Interview with Angus Wilson, May 4, 1986.

318 "The Americans . . . British": *Forties*, 157.

318 "I talked . . . jealousy": Ibid., 151.

318 "chucked appointment . . . Wilson": *The Diaries of Evelyn Waugh*, ed. Michael Davie (Boston: Little, Brown, 1976), 625.

319 "a minor genius": "Isaiah Berlin on Edmund Wilson," *WQ*, Winter 1999, 43.

319 "that English . . . an art": Nora Sayre, *Previous Convictions* (New Brunswick, N.J.: Rutgers University Press, 1995), 67.

319 "British rudeness . . . people": *Europe*, 22.

319 "GREATEST MUSICAL . . . DECADES": EW to William Shawn, June 25, 1945, *Letters*, 427.

319 "put up . . . 'Find it'": *Forties*, 151.

319 "the greatest . . . *Progress*": "An Interview with Edmund Wilson," *Bit*, 537.

320 "the sign . . . England": "Splendors and Miseries of Evelyn Waugh," *Classics*, 300.

320 "a bad book . . . assured": MP to Celia Paget, May 27, 1947, *Living with Koestler*, 62.

320 "to have . . . foreigner'": Frederic Warburg to EW, May 14, 1947, in Meyers, *Edmund Wilson*, 278.

320 "the most . . . wagon": Cyril Connolly to EW, Jan. 18, 1949.

321 "shapeless agglomeration": *Europe*, 57.

321 "which just . . . sarcophagus": Ibid., 62.

321 "the erudite . . . Praz": EW to VN, May 31, 1945, *N-W Letters*, 151.

321 "procession of . . . *Souls*": "Two Survivors: Malraux and Silone," *Europe*, 92.

322 "A queer mixture . . . worker": EW to MP, June 1, 1945, *Letters*, 421.

322 "a haunted man": William Weaver, "The Mystery of Ignazio Silone." *NYRB*, March 14, 2002, 35.

322 "God-seekers . . . swallows": Quoted by EW in *Europe*, 95.

322 "All those . . . died": Interview with Darina Silone, 2002.

322 "Silent and . . . do'": *Forties*, 74.

323 "the workers and of Italy": Silone to Guido Bellone, quoted in Alexander Stille, "The Spy Who Failed," *NY*, May 15, 2000, 48.

323 "gruesome . . . inside source": *Sixties*, 333.

323 "brainwashed"; "the other way": Ibid., 334.

323 "absolutely demolished . . . destroyed": EW to MP, May 22, 1945, *Letters*, 419.

323 "still planted . . . this": EW to MP, May 28, 1945, Ibid., 421.

323 "The ruined . . . seen": EW to VN, May 31, 1945, *Letters*, 424.

324 "about people . . . books": *Europe*, 206.

324 "It was . . . concurrently": Interview with Philip Hamburger, 1984.

324 "boomed out . . . sake'" : Interview with Hamburger, 1984.

324–325 "when we . . . way": *Magician*, 228.

325 "to the assertion . . . amenities": Postscript, *Red, Black*, 496.

325 "FASCINATING BUT . . . SAID": EW to Shawn, May 14, 1945, *Letters*, 420.

325 "with a cord . . . screen": *Europe*, 43.

325 "had to . . . philosopher": Ibid., 55.

325 "really alone . . . tremors": Ibid., 54.

325 has made . . . universal mind": Ibid., 55.

325–326 "with England . . . Louisiana": EW to JDP, June 3, 1945, *Letters*, 425.

326 "paler, purer . . . west": *Europe*, 236.

326 "the Cretan . . . gatherers": Ibid., 309.

326 "liveliness, frivolity, and charm": Ibid., 310.

326 "as yet . . . Keats": EW to VN, May 31, 1945, *Letters*, 424.

327 "People's complacency shaken"; "a vigorous . . . mind": *Europe*, 349.

21: False Hopes and True: Enter Elena Mumm Thornton

331 "marvelous English girl": Interview with HM, 1984.

331 "I am living . . . wrong": MP to EW, Nov. 24, 1945.

331 "became somewhat . . . before": *Sixties*, 64.

332 "relaxed and . . . rolling": Interview with HM, 1984.

332 "as a serious . . . importance": Deirdre Bair, *Anaïs Nin* (New York: Putnam, 1995), 297.

332 "with Mary . . . a lover": *Diary of Anaïs Nin: 1944–1947*, 88.

332 "to help . . . couch": Ibid.

332 "of his . . . purple chairs": *Magician*, 120.

332 "wanted to . . . alone": *Diary of Anaïs Nin: 1944–1947*, 88.

332 "But I . . . him": Ibid., 84.

333 "worship, desire, ardor, madness": Quoted in Bair, 305.

333 "irrational, lustful, violent": *Diary of Anaïs Nin: 1944–1947*, 83.

333 "an affair . . . smell": *Forties*, 163.

333 "libraries, formulas . . . scholarship": *Diary of Anaïs Nin: 1944–1947*, 89.

333 "the full . . . father": Ibid.

333 "not Wilson . . . in him": Ibid., 93.

333 "I would . . . write": Ibid., 89.

333 "one of those . . . satisfactory": "Isherwood—Marquand—Anaïs Nin," *NY*, Nov. 10, 1945, 93–4, 96.

333 "a Roman . . . hair": *Diary of Anaïs Nin: 1944–1947*, 99.

334 "parts I . . . him": "Winter, 1970–71," *Diary of Anaïs Nin: 1966–1974* (New York: Harcourt Brace Jovanovich, 1980), 161.

334 "her whole . . . against": *Sixties*, 863.

334 "stories about . . . woman": Ibid., 504.

334 "my true . . . affection": Nin to EW, n.d. [early 1950s].

334 "cut to . . . Henry James": " 'Do I Wake or Sleep?': Drama and Reverie," *NY*, Oct. 26, 1946, 113.

334 "the cluster . . . Cherry": Gore Vidal, "A Lost World," *NYRB*, Dec. 18, 1997, 24.

334 "I came . . . joy": EW to Elena, April 11, 1946.

334 "very definitely . . . pleasurable": Elena to EW, April 12, 1946.

334 "loping a . . . charmed": "The White Sand," *Night Thoughts*, 266.

335 "a sensitive . . . cry": Dorothea Straus, *Palaces and Prisons* (Boston: Houghton Mifflin, 1976), 150.

335 "a stem . . . resilient": Ibid.

335 "What a pity . . . her?" MP to EW Nov. 24, 1945.

335 "quick German kindness": "The White Sand," *Night Thoughts*, 265.

335 "a little stumbling sometimes": Interview with David Chachavadze, 2000.

335 "He is . . . right way": Elena to EW, June 7, 1946.

336 "of *le jazz* . . . stuffiest": *Sixties*, 131.

336 "how fine . . . Hitler": *Fifties*, 191.

336 "*un sale renégate*": Ibid., 180.

336 "also . . . shoulders": Interview with Harry Levin, 1984.

337 "was morbidly . . . thing": *Sixties*, 133.

337 "her frank . . . manners": *Forties*, 162.

337 "I went . . . self-complacency": EW to Elena, Apr. 13, 1946.

337–338 "original Virginians . . . commuters": EW to Elena, Apr. 15, 1946.

338 "You have . . . in line": Elena to EW, May 18, 1946.

338 "disciplined": EW to Elena, June 15, 1946.

338 "*méchant*"; "her point . . . outlaw": EW to Elena, June 14, 1946.

338 "worry one . . . now": Elena to EW, June 17, 1946.

338–339 "She thought . . . expression"; "she always jumped . . . love": *Forties*, 174–75.

339 "the German . . . theory!" Ibid., 173.

339 "dear, dear Mr. Watson": Elena to EW, Aug. 14, 1946.

339 "worry about . . . should be": Elena to EW, Aug. 12, 1946.

339 "swear allegiance . . . handy": Elena to EW, June 18, 1946.

339 "I'm incredibly . . . night": EW to Elena, June 9, 1946.

339 "Please do not . . . straight": Elena to EW, Aug. 1, 1946.

339 "I love . . . bless you": Elena to EW, Aug. 1, 1946.

340 "It was . . . young": EW to Elena, July 1, 1946.

340 "possibly at . . . evening": T. S. Eliot to EW, June 6, 1946.

340 "the fourth . . . done": EW to Elena, July 31, 1946.

340 "an extraordinary . . . perfectly": EW to Elena, Oct. 4, 1946.

340 "I am afraid . . . hoped": EW to Elena, May 20, 1946.

341 "In the meantime . . . madly": EW to MP, Sept. 9, 1946, *Letters*, 439.

341 "shouting 'for . . . gout": LB to Zabel, Oct. 13, 1946.

341 "concern with . . . happiness": Justice Nathan Perlman quoted in Edward de Grazia, *Girls Lean Back Everywhere*, 225.

341 "you have to do": EW to Elena, Aug. 20, 1946.

342 "nobody could . . . time": *Magician*, 134.

342 "HAD A . . . MISS YOU": Elena to EW, Oct. 24, 1946.

342 "HAVE REACHED . . . EDMUND": EW to Elena, Oct. 26, 1946.

342 "not unpleasant . . . prehistoric": EW to VN, Dec. 1, 1946, *N-W Letters*, 179.

342 "she has . . . wisecracks": *Forties*, 189.

342 "his six-foot bride": *San Francisco Chronicle*, Dec. 12, 1946, 3.

342 "rather silly": *Forties*, 195.

342 "into my . . . virtues": Ibid., 199.

343 "liked very much": Ibid., 202.

343 "a lasting domestic accord": Interview with Cowley, June 13, 1985.

343 "one of the most . . . too cold": EW to MP, Sept. 9, 1946.

343 "We have . . . spent": EW to Elena, July 31, 1946.

22: Old Commitments and New

344 "demand . . . work": "Thoughts on Being Bibliographed," *Classics*, 120.

344 "a back number": Epstein, *Centennial Reflections*, 30.

345 "perversity": "One Must Always Seek What Is Most Tragic," *Classics*, 335

345 "delicious music . . . candles": "The Musical Glasses of Peacock," *Classics*, 407.

345 "distinguished, unscrupulous . . . wear": "A Revival of Ronald Firbank," *Classics*, 493.

345 "ideal of . . . purity:" "Morose Ben Jonson," *Thinkers*, 231.

345 "a most . . . paper": "The Most Unhappy Man on Earth," *Classics*, 454.

345 "intellectual rigor and strength": Ibid., 455.

345 "the darkness . . . nature": Ibid., 456.

345 "got his . . . Stella": Ibid., 455.

345–346 "help them . . . men": "A Dissenting Opinion on Kafka," *Classics*, 384.

346 "the half-expressed . . . under": Ibid., 392.

346 "Kafka . . . assessment": Frederick Crews, "Kafka Up Close," *NYRB*, Feb. 10, 2005.

346 "And whom . . . pass": "The Mass in the Parking Lot," *Night Thoughts*, 182–83.

346 "even Cummings . . . since": EW to Cowley, Jan. 5, 1951, *Letters*, 496.

346 "slanderous;" "It doesn't . . . of others": EW to Tate, Jan. 4, 1951, Ibid.

346–347 "Though a . . . them": EW to Elena, Sept. 28, 1948, *Man in Letters*, 160–61.

347 "a black canary . . . drums": EW to Elena, Sept. 30, 1948, Ibid., 162.

347 "a general . . . idealism": "Van Wyck Brooks and the Civil War Period," *Classics*, 427.

348 "cultural spokesman . . . virtue": "Van Wyck Brooks's Second Phase," *Classics*, 15–16.

348 "light-diffusing": Ibid., 18.

348 "breaking and . . . confronted": "Van Wyck Brooks and the Civil War Period," *Classics*, 426.

348 "the stress . . . waste": Ibid., 429.

348 "strawberry-and-cream . . . knives": *Forties*, 298.

348 "What had . . . period?": Ibid., 300.

348 "the tendency . . . down": Ibid., 289.

349 "sucked into . . . poetry": Ibid., 287.

349 "pressure as . . . made it": Ibid., 291.

349 "one of . . . horror": Ibid., 290–91.

349 "they took . . . around her": *Magician*, 148.

349 "Mary, oh Mary darling": Ibid., 149.

349 "nothing but . . . reach": Constant Eakin to EW, n.d. [1947].

349 "so light . . . churches": EW to JDP, Nov. 24, 1947, *Letters*, 449.

349 "was killed": Ibid., 448.

350 "the bay . . . have again": Ibid., 449.

350 "it is . . . characters": EW to Powell, Jan 5, 1952, *Man in Letters*, 77.

350 "are at . . . individual in": EW to JDP, July 22, 1936, *Letters*, 279.

350 "a Mr. . . . master": EW to Powell, April, 16, 1946 (signed Esmond Whitmore), on a large postcard of Monticello, *Man in Letters*, 75.

350 "a teen-ager . . . Beatles": EW to JDP, Sept. 15, 1964, *Letters*, 653.

350 "Please Mr. . . . More": John Dos Passos, *National Review*, Jan. 28., 1964, 71–74.

350–351 "the lean . . . voice": Brian Boyd, *Vladimir Nabokov: The American Years* (Princeton, N.J.: Princeton University Press, 1991), 26.

351 "Edmund was . . . appeared": MMcC quoted in Ibid.

351 "I miss you a lot": VN to EW, Mar. 7, 1943, *N-W Letters*, 96.

351 "You are . . . them": VN to EW, Nov. 1, 1948, Ibid., 210.

351 "a salad of racial genes": Quoted in Meyers, *Edmund Wilson*, 286.

351 "chaste": VN to EW, March 8, 1946, *N-W Letters*, 165.

351 "about a . . . girls": VN to EW, April 7, 1947, Ibid., 188.

351 "a truly . . . daze": EW to Katharine White, Nov. 12, 1947, Ibid., 410.

351 "Unfortunately, a . . . yielded": VN to EW, June 17, 1945, Ibid., 154.

351 problem with Shawn: Interview with William Shawn, 1988.

351 "a sentence . . . punctuation": Harold Ross to EW, Nov. 28, 1947.

351 "by far . . . rather": Ross to Katharine White, undated memo, in *Letters from the Editor: The New Yorker's Harold Ross*, ed. Thomas Kunkel (New York: Random House, 2000), 280.

352 "to keep . . . conversations": EW to Ross, Jan. 15, 1948.

352 "of course . . . decided": EW to Ross, Jan. 26, 1948.

352 "tired of . . . it": Shawn, on a conversation with EW, quoted by Ross in undated memo, *New Yorker Archive*, New York Public Library.

352 "on some . . . week": Eudora Welty to EW, Jan. 12, 1949.

352 "take out the semicolons": EW to Shawn, Dec. 9, 1947; *New Yorker* Archives.

352 "I couldn't . . . blind": Roger Straus, *Centennial Reflections*, 143.

352 "said to be death on publishers": Interview with Roger Straus, 1991.

353 "I'm going . . . bank": EW to Elena, Sept. 19 and Sept. 22, 1963; "Appendix A," *Sixties*, 891–892.

353 "a great . . . time": Straus, *Centennial Reflections*, 145.

353 "buying this . . . great": Ibid., 143.

353 "jokes, literary . . . past": Straus, quoted in de Grazia, *Girls Lean Back Everywhere*, 238.

353 "What I . . . heart": Interview with Straus, 1995.

353–354 "thickset, red-faced . . . topic": Isaiah Berlin, "Edmund Wilson at Oxford," *The Yale Review* 36, no. 2 (March 1987), 139–40.

354 "a curiously strangled . . . passages": Ibid., 139.

354 "extraordinary Oxford . . . me": EW to MP, June 6, 1949, *Letters*, 454.

354 "Bunny and I . . . Bard": *The Diaries of Dawn Powell*, 171.

354 "didn't drink at all": Elena Wilson, "My View," typescript, 14.

354 "after longing . . . day": *Fifties*, 248.

355 "go out on her own": Ibid., 407.

355 "I wasn't . . . Orlando": Note from HMW to the author, 2004.

355 "The Miranda . . . Shakespeare": Interview with HMW, 1984.

355 "Wouldn't it . . . out?": Interview with AW, 1987.

23: American Criticism and Portraiture at Wellfleet, Princeton, and Talcottville

356 "Hrotswitha, the . . . Terence": EW to Gilbert Highet, Nov. 7, 1949, *Letters*, 456. Amusingly, Wilson cites a paper on the obscure German nun in the *Bulletin of the Boston Public Library* without mentioning that it was given to him by the author, his friend Zoltan Harajsti. The meat of the letter, however, is his discussion of Virgil, Dante, Joyce, and Pushkin.

356 "with the . . . literature": EW to Harrison Smith, Apr. 27, 1959, *Letters*, 483.

356 "both calming and stimulating": EW to MP, Sept. 7, 1950, Ibid., 491.

356–357 "likeable but . . . drunk": Interview with Hume Cronyn, Aug. 14, 2000.

357 "that curious bunk"; "something rather . . . people": EW to JDP, Sept. 5, 1950, *Letters*, 491.

357 "the full-dress . . . Proust": "William Faulkner's Reply to the Civil Rights Program," *Classics*, 463.

357 "abstract assumptions"; "not merely coining . . . but groping": Ibid., 464.

358 "so steady . . . telling": Ibid., 463.

358 "slipshod": Ibid., 464.

358 "who counts . . . home address": Eudora Welty, letter to the Editors, *NY*, Jan. 1, 1949, 51.

358 "The points . . . justice": William Faulkner to EW, Oct. 29, 1948.

358 "full of . . . talent": EW to Arthur Mizener, March, 3, 1950, *Letters*, 478.

358 "what constitutes . . . legends": Ibid., 479.

358 "was there . . . truth": EW to Mizener, April 4, 1950, Ibid., 480.

358–359 "I believe . . . difficulty": EW to FSF, Nov. 21, 1919, Ibid., 44.

359 "get enough . . . commoner here": EW to Trilling, Aug. 31, 1953, *Man in Letters*, 70.

359 "the kind . . . boredom": EW to Powell, Jan 26, 1959, Ibid., 78.

359 "a shade . . . care": "A Weekend at Ellerslie," *Shores*, 380.

359 "were floating . . . glamor": Ibid., 381.

359 "a gigantic . . . memoirs": EW to VN, Jan. 18, 1951, *N-W Letters*, 255–56.

359 "I've rewritten . . . works": EW to LB, March 19, 1952, *Man in Letters*, 49.

359 "revised almost . . . notes": *Shores*, ix.

359–360 "Now everyone . . . bad": Hemingway to EW, Sept. 10, 1951, in *Ernest Hemingway: Selected Letters; 1917–61*, ed. Carlos Baker (New York: Scribner's, 1981), 733.

360 "starts trains . . . themselves": "Christian Gauss as a Teacher of Literature," *Shores*, 3–4.

360 "supernatural"; "but the . . . absence": "Edna St. Vincent Millay," *Shores*, 790.

360 "faded and . . . now": Ibid., 787.

361 "important that . . . she was": EW to Floyd Dell, June 19, 1952, *Letters*, 70.

361 "always be . . . unimportant": EW to Norma Millay, Jan. 31, 1952, quoted in Milford, *Savage Beauty*, 497.

361 "Millay the . . . erotomane": Judith Thurman, "Siren Songs," *NY*, Sept. 3, 2001, 87.

361 "He makes . . . for him": *Magician*, 159.

361 "so arthritic . . . stand up": EW to VN, Feb. 7, 1951, *N-W Letters*, 256.

361 "or you'll . . . money!": *Fifties*, 13.

362 "a dining-room . . . delightful": LB to May Sarton, June 14, 1954, *Woman Lived*, 288–89.

362 "a minute . . . oven": Michael Macdonald, *Centennial Reflections*, 162.

362 "Enthroned on . . . belt": Reuel K. Wilson, "Growing Up with Edmund Wilson and Mary McCarthy." *Paris Review*, Winter 1999, 238.

363 "unadulterated huckster": "The Pre-Presidential T. R.," *Bit*, 67.

363 "with the sordid . . . contend": Ibid., 74.

363 "a rigorous . . . status": Ibid., 71.

363 "to perform": EW to John Berryman, Aug. 2, 1952, *Letters*, 508.

363 "a seminar . . . for you": EW to Cyril Connolly, Dec. 6, 1952, *Man in Letters*, 93–94.

363 "mediocrities"; "feel more at home": EW to Connolly, Aug. 26, 1952, Ibid., 92.

363 "the talk . . . winter": Edel, interpolation in *Fifties*, 47.

363 "Let us begin . . . *Cabin*": *Patriotic Gore*, 3.

364 "Out of . . . quiet": "No! No! No! My Soul An't Yours, Mas'r!," *NY*, Nov. 27, 1948, 134.

364 "rose to . . . mysticism": *Patriotic Gore*, 97.

364 "hard distinction": "Abraham Lincoln: The Union as Religious Mysticism," *Eight Essays* (Garden City, N.Y.: Doubleday Anchor, 1954), 183.

364 "the art of incantation": Ibid., 188.

364 "clear, flexible . . . measure": "A New Presentation of Ambrose Bierce," *NY*, Jan. 18, 1947, 82.

364 "moral stoutness . . . classical": "John de Forest: A Roman of the Civil War," *NY*, Aug. 10, 1946, 67.

364 "a Jewish father": "The Holmes-Laski Correspondence," *Bit*, 91.

364 "discipline of life": Ibid., 98.

365 "a flush . . . War": Ibid., 100.

365 "neat, washed . . . Genesis": Edel, introduction to *Fifties*, xxvi–xxvii.

365 "demoralized": *Twenties*, 64.

366 VOTE RED . . . GOOFY: "Hull-House in 1932," *Earthquake*, 464.

366 her reportage: Interview with Joan Didion, 1991.

366 "primitive animal . . . beings": "Postscript, 1957," *Earthquake*, 570.

366 "the irresistible . . . groups": Ibid., 569.

366 "gentle, reserved . . . hat": Macdonald, *Centennial Reflections*, 161.

367 "went up . . . any place": Elena Wilson, "My View from the Other Window," unpublished typescript, 1.

367 "the personal . . . doing it": EW to JDP, Sept. 8, 1952, *Man in Letters*, 54.

367 "express at . . . on them": *Fifties*, 282.

367 "As soon . . . books": Ibid., 267.

367 "kingdom of . . . shingle": "My View," 5.

368 "been raped . . . over it": Ibid., 7.

368 "shallow, dark . . . substance": Ibid., 5.

368 "for the . . . handsome": *Upstate*, 119.

368 "At that moment . . . myself": "My View," 4.

369 "to exalt . . . him international": Ibid., 27–28.

369 "over to . . . the grass": *Upstate*, 89. Wilson has sharpened this description from the original in *Fifties*, 41.

369 "is much . . . peterings-out": "The Author at Sixty," *Piece*, 211.

369 "old-fogeyism . . . closing in": Ibid.

369 "its excellent . . . describes": Ibid., 239.

370 "that I . . . many": Ibid.

24: In the Old World

372 "a little . . . success": EW to Betty Huling, Nov. 8, 1953, *Letters*, 514.

372 "Keaton, cupping . . . napkin": Interview with Jason Epstein, 1984.

372 "the Dickensian . . . Hotel": *Fifties*, 108.

372 "Zounds!": "The Problem of English," *Piece*, 160–61.

372 "bounder": *Twenties*, 34; *Thirties*, 254.

372 "to topple . . . actual": Ibid., 109.

372 "he has . . . wonderfully": MP to EW, Feb. 17, 1946.

373 "a little blurb": EW to MP, Dec. 5, 1953, *Letters*, 611.

373 "a charming . . . oasis": MP to EW, Dec. 18, 1952.

373 "Cyril Connolly . . . writing": "Enemies of Promise," *Night Thoughts*, 195.

373 "some book . . . Montaigne?": Interview with Berlin, 1991.

373 "*Et à la fin . . . République*": *Fifties*, 372. Thirty pages later Gates elaborates on this
      story, told to him by a French professor to whom Bowra told it, who affected to be
      shocked that he was so treated "*devant toutes ces dames françaises*" (400).

374 "wolf": Nora Sayre, *Previous Convictions* (New Brunswick, N.J.: Rutgers University
      Press, 1995), 66.

374 "a Henry James . . . formalities": *Fifties*, 127.

374 "small slightly . . . things": Ibid., 117–18.

374 "male Cinderella": "Is it Possible to Pat Kingsley Amis?," *Bit*, 275.

374 "world that . . . class-stratification": Ibid, 280.

374 "the great . . . life": Interview with Angus Wilson, 1986.

374 "Um—ah": *Sixties*, 762.

374 "half-cockney, quasi-cockney": Interview with Angus Wilson, 1986.

374 "on a bench . . . Walk": *Fifties*, 140.

375 "a sweeping . . . throes": Isaiah Berlin, "Edmund Wilson at Oxford," *The Yale Review*,
      36, no. 2 (March 1987), 141.

375 "shabby and . . . leprous": *Fifties*, 134.

375 "scouts . . . eat them": Ibid., 135.

375 "disaster, disaster": "Isiah Berlin on Edmund Wilson," *WQ*, winter 1999, 44.

375 "bored"; "forced and dull": *Fifties*, 138.

375 "my kind of man": Interview with Berlin, 1991.

375 "anglophobic malice . . . Isaiah": *Fifties*, 99.

375 "Department of . . . British isles": EW to Berlin, June 5, 1949, *Man in Letters*, 97.

375 "saw me . . . interpreter": "Isiah Berlin on Edmund Wilson," *WQ*, Winter 1999, 40.

376 "a jolly . . . aesthetic": Interview with Berlin, 1991.

376 "Look here: . . . unforgivable": *Fifties*, 145.

376 "the rights . . . crush them": "An Interview with Edmund Wilson," *Bit*, 540.

376–377 "rather surprised . . . woman": *Fifties*, 154.

377 "had gone to her lung": Ibid., 155.

377 "shriveling up . . . country": Ibid., 278.

377 "Do you . . . Angus Wilson?": "Edmund Wilson Interviews John Wain," *Letters*, 550.

377 "would discover . . . enthusiasm": *Fifties*, 382.

377 "almost as . . . for me": Ibid., 266.

377 "the great . . . time": Ibid., 253.

377 *"passion* for fragmentation": "Europe," *Piece*, 57.

378 *Notre Dame des fleurs:* VN first dismissed "the homosexual burglar's book," but when he read it he wrote to EW that a particular description was "superb" and the transsexual character Divine "the *pièce de résistance.*" He noted that there were "no girls around—the only *jeune putain* [young whore] was sandwiched between two boys kissing each other, the idiots" (VN to EW, April, 17 and 19, 1950. *N-W Letters*, 236, 238).

378 "Huysmans, who . . . technical terms": EW to VN, April 27, 1950, *N-W Letters*, 238.

378 "With all . . . writers": *Fifties*, 383–84.

378 "enormous and . . . foreground": Ibid., 168.

378 "give them . . . War": EW to Roman Grynberg, Nov. 8, 1953, Library of Congress.

378 "more extensive . . . mastery": *Fifties*, 173.

379 "a drop-dropping . . . accent": Ibid., 168.

379 toast the students: Interview with Roy Harvey Pearce, 1988.

379 "at a terrible rate of speed": *Fifties*, 180.

379 *"oui, oui"*: Ibid., 182.

379 "Hitler would . . . succeeded": Ibid., 185.

379 "You're not . . . yourself": Ibid., 187–88.

379 "never insulted . . . visited": Ibid., 188.

380 "I feel sometimes . . . bomb": "An Interview with Edmund Wilson," *Bit*, 542.

380 "the little girl": EW to MMcC, March 10, 1948, *Man In Letters*, 223.

380 "quite formally": *Fifties*, 140.

380 "writing endless . . . purposes": *Sixties*, 268.

380 "the cousin . . . liberal!": *Fifties*, 266.

380 "One could . . . *Maman*": *Sixties*, 300 (a sentence rendered in French in the journal).

381 "a good . . . ever seen": Ibid., 327.

381 "a beautiful swimmer": Ibid., 325.

381 "its cosmopolitan . . . world": *Bit*, 668.

25: European Artists: Malraux, Beerbohm, and Stravinsky; Auden in America

382 "passages of . . . imagination": *Europe*, 88.

383 "some morbid . . . fool": "A Miscellany of Max Beerbohm," *Bit*, 47.

383 "a disability like any disability": Ibid., 48.

383 "quite astonishing . . . tools": Ibid., 43.

383 "an impassioned . . . sees": Ibid., 44–45.

383 "he came . . . amusing": EW to Elena, Mar. 15, 1954, *Letters*, 706.

384 "Alaskan totem . . . photographs": "André Malraux: The Museum Without Walls," *Bit*, 138.

384 "a deliberate declaration": Ibid., 139.

384 "what would . . . powers": Ibid., 144.

384 *"bon!* . . . Europe)": *Fifties*, 158–59.

385 *"C'est parce que . . . monde"*: Ibid., 160.

385 "a clicking in the throat": Ibid., 158.

385 "a snort from the nose": Ibid., 257.

385 "the Sartre . . . understand himself": Ibid., 162.

385 "knows who . . . of him": Frederick L. Gwyn and Joseph L. Blotner, eds. *Faulkner in the University* (New York: Vintage, 1959), 105.

385 "nightmarish and savage": "André Malraux: The Museum Without Walls," *Bit*, 143.

386 "much obstructed": Ibid., 147.

386 "a void . . . organized": Ibid., 145.

386 "If Manet . . . work": Ibid., 146.

386 "that splendid old girl": *Sixties*, 10.

386 "sulked on . . . there": Ibid.

386 "I read . . . may be": Ibid., 12–13.

386 "chicken . . . an ashtray": Ibid., 12.

387 "a little . . . fragments": Ibid., 12–13.

387 "that Schönberg . . . Wagner, yes": Ibid., 13.

387 "is very . . . 'bristling'": Letter from Spender to the author, April 19, 1991.

387 "'*Apploud!*' . . . his hands": *Sixties*, 14.

387 "free-thinking . . . Tories": "'Miss Buttle' and 'Mr. Eliot,'" *Bit*, 388.

387 "could regard . . . else": Ibid., 396.

387 "in one's . . . them": Ibid., 400.

387–388 "More correctly . . . self-humbling": "The Mass in the Parking Lot," *Night Thoughts*, 181–82.

388 "the emphatic . . . his own": "The Oxford Boys Becalmed," *Shores*, 671.

388 "I'm really a New Yorker": Orlan Fox, "Friday Nights," *W. H. Auden: A Tribute* (New York: Macmillan, 1975), 178.

388 "the only . . . international": EW quoting Auden to MP, Feb. 23, 1946, *Letters*, 431.

388 "He is . . . alone": EW to MP, Feb. 4, 1946, Ibid., 430.

388 "the dirtiest . . . liked": *Fifties*, 292.

388 "a basin . . . floor": Robert Craft's diary quoted in Charles Osborne, *W. H. Auden: The Life of a Poet* (New York: Harcourt Brace Jovanovich, 1979), 240.

389 "the only . . . people"; "too salt": *Sixties*, 12.

389 "a doghouse . . . loft": *Fifties*, 293.

389 "sordid and grotesque lodgings": Ibid., 292.

389 "always full . . . guillotined": Ibid., 349.

389 "He's just an old queer!": Ibid., 292.

389 "good at . . . thing impossible": Ibid., 604.

389 "His hair . . . coffeehouse": Ibid.

389 "crisscrossed . . . technical map": *Sixties*, 12.

390 "He was evidently . . . downstairs": Ibid., 18–19.

390 "blasphemous strictures . . . your best": EW to Auden, Oct. 9, 1947, *Letters*, 431.

390–391 "I said . . . days": *Sixties*, 762.

391 "quite impossible . . . written it": Ibid., 827.

391 "Bless me . . . streams": W. H. Auden, "Make This Night Loveable," *Collected Shorter Poems, 1927–1957* (London: Faber & Faber, 1969), 274–75.

391 "A peer and a prince": *Fifties*, 348.

391 *"dritten Klasse"*: Ibid., 348.

391–392 "to stand . . . silly": Ibid., 348.

392 "can hope . . . things": "W. H. Auden in America," *Bit*, 355.

392 "the whole . . . world": *Fifties*, 299.

392 "the problem . . . by it": "W. H. Auden in America," *Bit*, 359.

392 "Oxford gossip . . . metallurgy": Ibid., 360.

392 "strange *depayses* . . . endings": Ibid., 357.

392 "the poet's . . . everywhere": Ibid., 358.

392 "O every day . . . men": Auden, quoted in Ibid.

392 "a great . . . world": Ibid., 363.

392 "determined resistant minority": Ibid., 359.

393 "functioning in . . . farms": Ibid., 359–60.

393 "had been . . . 300": *Sixties*, 567.

393 "Some think . . . *know all*": Auden, quoted in *Bit*, 360.

393 "a tirade . . . propaganda phrase": *Fifties*, 526.

393 "You must . . . do that": Ibid., 527.

26: Nabokov and Russian Literature

394 "to concentrate . . . another": "A Modest Self-Tribute," *Bit*, 3.

394 "Wonderful people, wonderful literature": Quoted in "Isaiah Berlin on Edmund Wilson", *WQ*, Winter 1999, 41.

394 "sensitivity, humor, human sympathy": "Dearest Elena," letter of dedication in *Window*.

394 "those Russians . . . nation": "Turgenev and the Life-Giving Drop": *Window*, 112.

395 "hopeless in . . . 1850 novel": Interview with David Chachavadze, 2000, quoting Nina Chachavadze and EW, respectively.

395 "these Russian . . . Russian verbs": "My Fifty Years with Dictionaries and Grammars," *Bit*, 620.

395 "my Russian . . . yourself": EW to VN, April 20, 1942, *N-W Letters*, 59.

395 *"enormously"*: VN to EW, n.d. [early Nov. 1943], Ibid., 108.

395 "slap . . . tingling cheek": "Notes from the Forties: Pushkin," *Window*, 21.

395 "came through . . . Russian novel": "In Honor of Pushkin," *Thinkers*, 32.

396 "the rhapsodies . . . themselves": "Gogol: The Demon in the Overgrown Garden," *Window*, 42.

396 "viscous prose": Ibid., 41.

396 "cerebral"; "such fancies . . . words": Ibid., 42.

396 "a remark . . . Russian'": Ibid., 39.

396 "of sadness, of disgust, of chagrin": Ibid., 47.

396–397 "through his . . . know herself": "Turgenev and the Life-Giving Drop," *Window*, 99.

397 "life-giving": Ibid., 81.

397 "much care . . . cave": Ibid., 83.

397 "one of the great inventors": Ibid., 122.

397 "betray our . . . rubbish": Ibid., 120.

397–398 "he is perhaps . . . alien": Ibid., 122.

398 "a personal friend": EW to Lily Herzog, May 30, 1957, *Letters*, 581.

398 "was a good . . . virtues": "Turgenev and the Life-Giving Drop," *Window*, 117.

398 "he beat . . . chess": Ibid., 116.

398 "Turgenev—the cancan. Sad": Tolstoy's diary, quoted in Ibid. 117.

398 "Pushkin, Flaubert, Proust, Joyce, etc.": EW to VN, Dec. 1, 1946, Ibid., 179.

399 "a fool's": Interview with Harry Levin, with whom EW shared this conversation.

399 "landowning liberals": EW to Christian Gauss, Nov. 12, 1940, *The Papers of Christian Gauss*, eds. Katherine Gauss Jackson and Hiram Hayden (New York: Random House, 1957), 331.

399 "terrible": VN to EW, Jan. 25, 1947, *N-W Letters*, 182.

399 "before giving . . . *Others*": EW to VN, Jan. 30, 1947, Ibid., 184.

399 "spellbound"; "the most . . . novelist": EW to VN, Nov. 5, 1948, Ibid., 211.

399 "these puffs . . . conversations": VN to EW, Nov. 21, 1948, Ibid., 212–13.

399 "Your failure . . . *Fury*?": EW to VN, Sept. 28, 1949, Ibid., 230.

399 "the later . . . remarkable": EW to VN, Apr. 25, 1950, Ibid., 238.

399 "Jane": VN to EW, May 5, 1950, Ibid., 241.

400 "Jane Austen . . . Dickens)": EW to VN, May 9, 1950, Ibid., 243.

400 "around 1949": Nabokov, "On a "Book Entitled *Lolita*," *The Portable Nabokov*, ed. Page Stegner (New York: Viking, 1971), 232.

400 "enjoyed hugely": VN to EW, June 10, 1948, *N-W Letters*, 202.

400 "especially lascivious": Quoted by Karlinsky from the Russian version of *Speak, Memory*, in Ibid.

400 "amazing book": VN to EW, June 20, 1953, *N-W Letters*, 282.

400 "my best . . . riotous": VN to EW, June 30, 1954, Ibid., 285.

400 "very anxious . . . English work": VN to EW, Sept. 9, 1954, Ibid., 287.

400–401 "I like it . . . to be funny:" EW to VN, Nov. 30, 1954, Ibid., 288.

401 "attractiveness and . . . plausible": Elena to VN, Nov. 30, 1954, Ibid., 289.

401 "somewhat ambivalent": Quoted in de Grazia, *Girls Lean Back Everywhere*, 247.

401 "not have done justice": EW to V. S. Pritchett, Feb. 17, 1959, *Letters*, 306.

401 "could like the book better": EW to VN, Nov. 30, 1954, *N-W Letters*, 288.

401 "He makes . . . liking it": EW to Roman Grynberg, Dec. 8, 1955, Library of Congress.

401 "a block . . . laboratory": VN to EW, n.d. [late Sept. 1946], *N-W Letters*, 173.

401 "as a study . . . San Diego": EW to VN, June 12, 1957, ibid., 315.

402 "rather put . . . again": EW to Grynberg, Sept. 28, 1955, Library of Congress.

402 "that Mérimée . . . paper": *Fifties*, 424.

402 "with great . . . stitches": VN, letter to the *NYRB*, Aug. 26, 1965, 25.

403 "a contemporary . . . Auden": "Doctor Life and His Guardian Angel," *Bit*, 426.

403 "man's literary and moral history": Ibid., 446.

403 "little ham": "Isaiah Berlin on Edmund Wilson," *WQ*, Winter 1999, 41.

403 "play *Doctor Zhivago*": Interview with David Chavchavadze, 2000.

403 "a piece . . . Admired": Karlinsky, introduction to *N-W Letters*, 24.

403 "lyrical doctor . . . Charskaya": quoted by Karlinsky, 24.

403 "a bad sport": Interview with David Chavchavadze, 2000.

404 "getting sick of teaching": VN to EW, Oct. 22, 1956, *N-W Letters*, 304.

404 "like a prince . . . regime": *Sixties*, 295.

404 "wore a . . . arrogance": Ibid., 434.

404 "an oaf . . . scholar": "The Strange Case of Pushkin and Nabokov," *Window*, 209.

404 "Volodya, there's . . . sentence": Interview with Harry and Elena Levin, 1984.

404–405 "almost as . . . phrases": EW to Barbara Epstein, June 11, 1964, *N-W Letters*, 652.

405 "the products . . . English": "The Strange Case of Pushkin and Nabokov," *Window*, 213.

405 "You will . . . see you?": Nabokov's translation quoted in Ibid.

405 "mollitude . . . dulcitudes": Ibid., 211.

405 "theory"; "shallow and spurious": Edward Brown, "Round Two: Nabokov vs. Pushkin," *Slavic Review* (March 1977), 101.

405 "a desire . . . egotism": Alexander Gerschenkron, "A Manufactured Monument" *Modern Philology*, May 1966, 336.

405–406 "the excellent . . . Karamzin": "The Strange Case of Pushkin and Nabokov," *Window*, 227.

406 "to correlate . . . another": Ibid., 230.

406 "sado-masochistic Dostoevskian tendencies": Ibid., 210.

406 "sounded more . . . to be": "Edmund Wilson Replies," *NYRB*, Aug. 26, 1965, 26.

406 "damaged . . . criticism": Vladimir Nabokov, "Reply to My Critics," *Strong Opinions* (New York: McGraw-Hill, 1973), 262–3.

406 "the point . . . aggressive": Interview with Barbara Epstein, 1984.

406–407 "a curiosity . . . devoid": Berlin to EW, Jan. 25, 1966.

407 "I'm sorry . . . piece": Notes in the New York Public Library, included in neither of Karlinsky's collections of the correspondence.

407 "*duel à volonté*"; "say ten paces": VN to EW, Jan. 4, 1949, *N-W Letters*, 219.

27: The Skeptic's Pilgrimage: Israel and the Dead Sea Scrolls

408 "a smattering": "On First Reading Genesis," *Red, Black*, 387.

408–409 "provide the lamb": Ibid., 404.

409 "man": Ibid., 408.

409 "striver with God"; "they had . . . cost": Ibid., 409.

409 "You know . . . God!": Interview with AW, 1987.

409 "austere in . . . breathed": "Israel," *Red, Black*, 395.

409 "aspect of eternity"; "the half religion Marxism": Ibid., 425.

409 "this sense . . . tradition": Ibid., 426.

410 "the real . . . Middle East": EW to Waldo Frank, Dec. 14, 1954, *Letters*, 529.

410 "the great . . . Israel": *Israel/Scrolls*, 108.

411 "Independent worshippers of Jehovah": "Israel," *Red, Black*, 432.

411 "In Kafka . . . analysis": Ibid., 448.

412 "monotonous, subduing and dreadful": *Scrolls*, 42.

413 "successive phases of a movement": Ibid., 96.

413–414 "sometimes slanted . . . fair": James Sanders, *Centennial Reflections*, 169.

414 "grand explainer"; "better understands . . . mind": Interview with Sanders, 2000.

414 "very scholarly amateur": Quoted by Leon Edel, foreward to *Israel/Scrolls*, xi.

414 "tall, goodlooking . . . well": *Sixties*, 615.

414 "*Israel est . . . patriot*": "Isaiah Berlin on Edmund Wilson," *WQ*, Winter 1999, 46.

414 "flaming hair . . . the situation": *Fifties*, 234.

414 "spiritual adventures of mankind": David Flusser, "Not Obliged to Any Religion," *An
     Edmund Wilson Celebration*, ed. John Wain (Oxford: Phaidon Press, 1978), 111.

414 "spiritual vivacity": Ibid., 113.

415 "worry about . . . actual presence": "The Jews," *Piece*, 106–7.

416 "the word . . . spoken": "New York Religions," *Upstate*, 33.

416 "Greek and . . . to Heaven": *Israel/Scrolls*, 391.

416 "plan a different parenthood": *Sixties*, 98.

416 "the need . . . universe": *Iroquois*, 246.

416 "the bright . . . monotonous": "Israel," *Red, Black*, 482.

417 "Pharaoh's daughter . . . paint": Ibid., 469.

417 "bright light . . . and truth": Ibid., 482.

417 "the whole . . . bury us!": Ibid., 478.

417 "wars and . . . human race": Ibid., 483.

28: A Reporter in Minority Communities

418 "obsessed with minorities": *Fifties*, 471.

418 "the rage . . . world": "Haiti," *Red, Black*, 78.

419 "pick off"; "with a cannon": Ibid., 82.

419 "the look . . . fist": Ibid., 83.

419 "our planters . . . freedom": Ibid., 79.

419 "living with their ruined masters": Ibid., 144.

419 "from knowing . . . life": Ibid., 144.

420 "a soft . . . of Nature": "Zuni," *Red, Black*, 26.

420 "from a community . . . heard": Ibid., 15.

421 "to watch . . . operation": Ibid., 29.

421 "by his pounding . . . permanence": Ibid., 38.

421 "human energy . . . form": Ibid., 38.

421 "The great . . . venerating": Ibid., 41.

421 "it was . . . mask": Ibid., 42.

423 "people are . . . traditional": *The Diaries of Dawn Powell*, 400.

423 "to follow the Longhouse way": William N. Fenton, "Songs from the Iroquois Long-
     house: Program Notes for an Album of American Indian Music from the Eastern
     Woodlands," in *An Iroquois Source Book;* vol. 3, *Medicine Society Rituals*, ed. Eliza-
     beth Tooker (New York: Garland, 1986), 12.

423 "He was . . . colonists": Betty Crouse Mele, "Edmund Wilson and the Iroquois," *An
     Edmund Wilson Celebration*, ed. John Wain (Oxford: Phaidon Press, 1978), 38.

423 "I could . . . then": *Iroquois*, 218.

423 "with a strong . . . reserve": Ibid., 294.

423 "Edmund Wilson's chair": Interview with Laurence Hauptman, 2000.

423 "all the paths lead here": William N. Fenton, "Apologies to Edmund Wilson," introduction to *Iroquois*, xii.

423–424 "never seen . . . situations": Ibid., xvi.

424 "uncanny ability . . . readers": Ibid., xx.

424 "genuine rites . . . part": W. H. Auden, "Review of *Apologies to the Iroquois*," *Mid-Century* 9 (Feb. 1960), 9–10.

424 "as if . . . darkness": *Iroquois*, 208–9.

424 "flourish of the flute": Ibid., 188.

424 "the bird . . . itself free": Ibid., 306.

425 "a builder . . . ceremony itself": Ibid., 310.

425 "We are . . . come": William N. Fenton, "Apologies to Edmund Wilson," *Iroquois*, xxiv.

425 "to give America an identity": *O Canada*, 174.

426 "Callaghan interjected . . . Toronto": From a 1959 entry in the unpublished diary of Malcolm Montgomery.

426–247 "had been . . . years": *Sixties*, 309.

427 "most unrelievedly painful": *O Canada*, 149.

427 "desperate cry . . . Quebec": Ibid., 153–4.

427 "the intensity . . . reads": Ibid., 157.

427 "She may . . . genius": Ibid., 148.

427 "the turbid . . . aspirations": Foreword to Marie-Claire Blais, *Une saison dans la vie d'Emmanuel* (Montreal: Editions de Jour, 1965), vi–vii.

427 "penetrating your soul": Interview with Marie-Claire Blais, 2000.

427 "*On ne se . . . months*": *Sixties*, 407.

427 "had to write about everything": Interview with Blais, 2000.

428 "on the margin . . . panics": *Sixties*, 125.

428 "proddings and enchroacments": *O Canada*, 241.

428 "in a world . . . the people": Ibid., 175.

428 "these Hungarians . . . ironically": EW to Mary Meigs, Aug. 22, 1960, *Letters*, 599.

428 "they were . . . rhapsodies'": *Sixties*, 54.

428 "white hairless . . . staircase": Quoted by Frederick Exley, *Pages from a Cold Island* (New York: Random House, 1975), 153.

428–429 "silvery, winding . . . ponds": *Sixties*, 382.

429 "spiky and . . . mustaches": Ibid., 347–8.

429 "chiastic lines": Ibid., 356.

429 "a nation of translators": Ibid., 355.

430 "blood orange": Ibid., 386.

430 "informed on . . . executed": Ibid., 485.

430 "a little the hang of things": Ibid., 383.

29: *Patriotic Gore* Reconsidered

431 "Like most . . . all this": Lowell Edmunds, "Edmund Wilson and Others: The Literary Scene at Harvard in 1960," unpublished typescript, 2.

432 "have written their own parts": *Patriotic Gore*, ix.

432 "authorial commentator and curtain-puller": Daniel Aaron, "Edmund Wilson's War,"
     Massachusetts Review, Spring 1962, 536.

432 "we feel . . . him": *Patriotic Gore*, 80.

432 "He was . . . the subject": *Finland Station*, 30.

432 "Go, countryman . . . they died": "American Soldiers," *Night Thoughts*, 4.

433 "who saw . . . depth": Robert Penn Warren, *Commentary* 34 (August 1962), 153.

433 "towering genius . . . free men": *Patriotic Gore*, 107.

433 "It was . . . theirs": Ibid., 130.

433–434 "Humiliated, bankrupt . . . enemy's strength": Ibid., 144.

434 "who almost . . . world": Ibid., 148.

434 "this man . . . principalities": Ibid., 173.

434 "Vox populi, vox humbug": Ibid., 187.

434 "make Georgia howl!": Ibid., 185.

435 "the grand . . . of war": Ibid., 184.

435 "I WILL NOT . . . ELECTED": Ibid., 204.

435 "sitting in . . . *Great Expectations*": Ibid., 210.

435 "voluminous and . . . terrible": EW to Chauncey Hackett, Dec. 9, 1952, *Letters*, 509.

435 "national, never regional": *Patriotic Gore*, 8.

435 "as ready . . . own account": Ibid., 9.

435–436 "with its . . . was just": Ibid., 30.

436 "They will . . . family": Ibid., 298.

436 "an exemplification . . . expressed": Ibid., 330.

436 "is some . . . self-control": Warren, *Commentary*, 153.

437 "Cicero . . . morality dubious": *Patriotic Gore*, 393.

437 "offers to . . . irrepressible conflict": Ibid., 393–94.

437 "impossibilist": Ibid., 434.

437 "benevolent despot . . . the individual": Ibid., 435.

438 "the voice . . . free Negro": Randall Kennedy, *Centennial Reflections*, 224.

438 "because I . . . etcetera": Toni Morrison, Ibid., 231.

438 "the grand . . . letters": Ibid., 230–31.

438 "atrocities"; "crimes"; "blackmail, bullying . . . Klan": *Patriotic Gore*, 535.

438 "The klan . . . fighters": Garry Wills, letter to the editor of *The Wall Street Journal*,
     Nov. 24, 2003, contesting the review of Alan Pell Crawford (Nov. 5, 2003).

439 "the difference . . . 'civilization'": *Patriotic Gore*, xi–xii.

439 "harangue": "To Be a Pilgrim," unpublished memoir by Daniel Aaron, 1. Aaron's com-
     panion on this visit to Talcottville was the Harvard historian H. Stuart Hughes, a
     peace candidate for the U.S. Senate in 1962.

439 While . . . centralization: See Robert Penn Warren, *The Legacy of the Civil War* (New
     York: Random House, 1961), passim, and Edward Abbey, "A Writer's Credo," *One
     Life at a Time Please* (New York: Henry Holt, 1987), 173.

439 "Bismarck, Lenin, and Lincoln?": *Life*, May 18, 1962, 4.

439 "Whenever we . . . somebody": *Patriotic Gore*, xxiii.

440 "*Finland Station* . . . anti-centralism": Paul Berman, "Edmund's Castle," *NR*, June 3,
     1996, 38.

440 "The men . . . and watch": *Patriotic Gore*, 92.

440 "*Let us . . . understand it*": Ibid., 114.

440 "the old rousing rhythm": Ibid., 92.

440 "without the . . . sins": John Brown, cited on title page of Ibid.

441 "to sleep . . . prose": Ibid., 613.

441 "a fundamental non-radiation": Ibid., 671.

441 "as creative forces": Ibid., 75.

441 "The appreciator . . . these": Ibid., 81.

441 "anxious and . . . taken out": Meyer, *Centennial Reflections*, 215.

442 "a hater . . . everything": *The Shock of Recognition*, ed. EW (London: W. H. Allen, 1956), viii.

442 "Do you . . . furniture?": Meyer to EW, June 14, 1961.

442 "the close-knit . . . units": *Patriotic Gore*, 637.

442 "plain man": Quoted from T. W. Higginson, *American Orators and Oratory* in Ibid., 640.

442 "language of responsibility"; "to convince and direct": *Patriotic Gore*, 650.

442 "weakbacked": *Classics*, 13.

442 "between a . . . Republic itself": *Patriotic Gore*, 667.

443 "the slight . . . with nature": Ibid., 485.

443 "the red-bellied . . . purple gray": Ibid., 486.

443 "brightness and . . . Melville's voyages": Ibid., 487.

443 "the butcher's bill": Ibid., 751.

443 "the subjugation . . . nation": Ibid., 749.

443 "purposive, disciplined . . . hard": Ibid., 754.

443 "founded on the death of men": Ibid., 764.

443 "and, getting . . . builds": Edmunds, "Edmund Wilson and Others," 2.

444 "I don't . . . machine": *Patriotic Gore*, 790.

444 "to assure one's ever-doubting soul": Ibid., 788.

444 "touched the superlative": Ibid., 787.

444 "the great . . . humanity is": Ibid., 781.

444 "*identified* his . . . Republic": "The United States," *Piece*, 28.

444 "He had . . . leave": *Patriotic Gore*, 796.

30: Husband and Father

447 "exhaustive, brilliant . . . history": David Donald, "Blood and Ink, 1861–'65," *New York Herald Tribune Books*, April 29, 1962, 4.

447 "no single . . . participants": C. Vann Woodward, "A Stance of Moral Neutrality," *American Scholar* 31, Autumn 1962, 640.

447 "the best . . . Civil War": Nevins, quoted in Paul Horgan, *Tracings* (New York: Farrar, Straus & Giroux, 1993), 233.

447 "make us . . . strongly": Elizabeth Hardwick, "An American Royal Personage," *Harper's*, July 1962, 88.

447 "density"; "way of . . . this country": Jed Perl, *Centennial Reflections*, 227–28.

447 "*la plage des intellectuals*": Kazin, quoted in *Sixties*, 105.

448 "high . . . voice": Kazin, *New York Jew* (New York: Knopf, 1978), 238.

448 "reluctant to . . . stop": Ibid., 239.

448 "television . . . advisors": Ibid., 237.

448 "lonely proud face": Ibid., 238.

448 "Edmund Wilson Regrets . . . Subjects": A copy of this card is at the Beinecke.

448 "flew right . . . to heel": Conrad Aiken to EW, Aug. 13, 1969.

448 "always inventing . . . porch": Interview with Epstein, 1984.

448 "the juvenile delinquents": *Upstate*, 274.

448–449 "in his . . . of mine!": Interview with Epstein, 1984.

449 "meandering book-lined workroom": Dorothea Straus, *Palaces and Prisons* (Boston: Houghton Mifflin, 1976), 148.

449 "his snappish . . . stare": Ibid., 152.

449 "she was . . . regality": Ibid., 150.

449 "Edmund is approaching!": Elena, quoted in Ibid.

450 "Oh, all that is finished": Ibid., 161.

450 "that true . . . as well": Marie-Claire Blais, *American Notebooks: A Writer's Journey*, trans. Linda Gaboriau (Burnaby, B.C.: Talonbooks, 1996), 33.

450 "plagued by . . . nature": Ibid., 7.

450 "a young God"; "that men . . . husband": Ibid., 34.

450 "'I think . . . smile": *The Diaries of Dawn Powell*, 306.

450–451 "It's rare . . . right": Robert Lowell to EW, Nov. 15, 1957.

451 "bouts of unprovoked anger": Reuel K. Wilson, "Growing Up with Edmund Wilson and Mary McCarthy," *Paris Review*, Winter 1999, 240.

451 "Come on . . . Walker": Marina Shouvaloff to the author, Sept. 29, 1992.

451 "dependent on her": *Magician*, 133.

451 "my frequent . . . leaving her": *Fifties*, 231.

451 "the atmosphere . . . ever divine": Ibid., 378.

451 "to hear . . . I write": Ibid., 388.

451 "erotic revival": Ibid., 397.

452 "delicious and . . . afterwards": Ibid., 582.

452 "back so . . . satisfying": Ibid., 605.

452 "irregular love . . . women": Ibid., 551–52.

452 "doggy devotion . . . *bouts rimés*": Mary Meigs, *Lily Briscoe: A Self-Portrait* (Vancouver: Talonbooks, 1981), 13.

452 "good friends . . . ways": Ibid., 23.

452 "of bodies . . . passion": Ibid., 18.

452 "You're really . . . pretense": EW, quoted in Ibid., 14–15.

453 "I did . . . love": Ibid., 14.

453 "she was . . . with whom'": *Magician*, 223.

453 "a drunken lawyer": Interview with Schlesinger, 1984.

455 "got in on German": Interview with Renata Adler, 1984.

455 "complimenting those . . . not!": Eliot Stanley quoted in Meyers, *Edmund Wilson*, 389.

455 "I will . . . together": EW to Elena, June 2, 1959.

455 "kicked out . . . the others": *Magician*, 131.

456 "hurt, jealous, insulted": Elena to EW n.d. [late July 1960].

456 "accomplishing prodigies": EW to Elena, July 21, 1960.

456 "fundamentally sure . . . other": EW to Elena, July 21, 1960.

456 "had a kind of collapse": *Sixties*, 30.

456 "My darling . . . Talcottville": EW to Elena, n.d.

456 "Elena de Mumm . . . gloom": EW to Elena, n.d.

456 "walk . . . doughy": Elena Wilson, "My View," 6.

457 "I had . . . came: EW to Elena, June 30, 1959.

457 "I have . . . the house": EW to Elena, June 2, 1959.

457 "he'd been . . . arrived": HMW to the author, 2003.

457 "So-and-so . . . up here?": *Sixties*, 114.

457 "Send it . . . back": Ibid., 115–16.

457–458 "threw at . . . Mary Pcolar": Ibid., 117.

458 "Hysteria on . . . leaving": "My View," 17.

458 "This is the abyss": *Sixties*, 117.

458 "ARRIVED LAST . . . LOVE": Ibid., 118.

458 "had most . . . Scotch": Ibid., 117.

458 "stormy": Interview with David Chavchavadze, 2000.

458 "When I read . . . sins": Elena, quoted in Shouvaloff to the author, Sept. 29, 1992.

458 "as they . . . more interesting": EW to Zabel, Jan. 31, 1950, *Man in Letters*, 214.

459 "wasn't cut out for it": Interview with Mary Hackett, 1984.

459 "strict and tough"; "had the best of it": Interview with Henry Thornton, 2004.

459 "This beautiful . . . ease": Quoted in *Fifties*, 30.

459 "Dear, dear Father . . . father": Included in a letter from Elena to EW when he was abroad.

459 "I am not . . . daughter": Quoted in interview with AW, 1984.

459 "Her expression . . . severity": Straus, *Palaces and Prisons*, 156.

459 "a flamboyant flower-child": Blais, 34.

459 "Bring in the 'hippies'": Straus, *Palaces and Prisons*, 155.

460 "glow . . . light": Alan Singer, Bulletin Board for ASK/ART Home, 3/4/01.

460 "much luckier . . . married": "My View," 17.

460 "to release . . . himself": Interview with HMW, 1984.

460 "I'm not . . . myself"; Quoted in interview with Dorothea Straus, 2003.

460 "his own . . . observer": Interview with Broadwater, 1988.

460 "two of . . . running": Reuel K. Wilson, "Growing Up," 236.

461 "Catullus's moving . . . Charles": Ibid., 239.

461 "dreaded": Ibid., 238.

461 "through my . . . known": Ibid., 243.

461 "a good adult relationship": "My View," 14.

461 "sitting on . . . unapproachable": Lowell Edmunds, "Edmund Wilson and Others; The Literary Scene at Harvard in 1960," unpublished typescript, 5.

461 "doing just . . . motorcycle": *Fifties*, 639.

461 "Edmund loved Reuel": Interviews with MMcC, 1984.

462 "he sailed into . . . for him": MMcC to EW, March 30, 1961.

462 "the good . . . saying": *Sixties*, 707.

462 "violent rages": Reuel K. Wilson, "Growing Up," 241.

463 "sleeping lairs": Reuel K. Wilson, "Letters from Mary McCarthy to Reuel K. Wilson," *Provincetown Arts*, 2001, 38.

463 "His hands . . . scowling": Reuel K. Wilson, "Growing Up," 251.

463 "it was . . . months": *Magician*, 4.

464 "closer to . . . children": *Sixties*, 254.

464 "short and . . . brow": Frederick Exley, *Pages from a Cold Island* (New York: Random House, 1975), 190.

464 "full of . . . matured": EW to Elena, April 11, 1950, *Man in Letters*, 200.

464 "ROSALIND ILL . . . EMOTIONALLY": Paul Brooks to EW, n.d. [1956].

464 "the awful blow"; "doing well": *Fifties*, 407.

464 "weeping fit"; "vodka and an empty stomach": Ibid., 406.

464–465 "in a strangely . . . radio": *Sixties*, 252.

465 "had the . . . marry her": EW to Elena, Sept. 11, 1963, Appendix to *Sixties*, 887.

465 "concentrate on reading manuscripts": EW to Elena, Sept. 18, 1963, Ibid., 890.

465 "straightened out": *Sixties*, 252.

465 "four weeks . . . cozy": Rosalind Wilson to the author, June 21, 1994.

465 "ill kept and dirty": *Sixties*, 252.

465–466 "no ambition . . . blind alley"; "I'll also . . . bills": Ibid., 653.

466 "sharp peremptory tone": Ibid.

466 "roaring like a bull": EW to Elena, Sept. 30, 1948, *Man in Letters*, 199.

466 "flattening"; "the family scapegoat": Interview with HMW, 1984.

466 "ours . . . relationship": *Magician*, 10.

466 "sincerely loved . . . people": "My View," 30.

466 "pounding her typewriter": *Sixties*, 653.

466 "all I had": Interview with HMW, 1984.

467 "That's for . . . the law": EW, "Punch and Judy," unpublished typescript, 5.

467 "I haven't . . . here": Ibid., 14.

467 "sharply carved . . . good": *Europe*, 411.

467 "gave every . . . exertion": "My View," 25.

467 "mastery of . . . conjuring": Reuel K. Wilson, "Letters from Mary McCarthy," 38.

467 "real self . . . small": "Punch and Judy," 15.

467 "Mr. Punch's . . . came in": "My View," 25.

31: *The Sixties* and the Decade

468 "all to . . . jitters": Ibid., 50.

468 "shouting"; "to glorify . . . Bomb?": *Sixties*, 20.

469 "salad-eating"; "corn-soup eating": Ibid., 26.

469 "an old . . . blank-faced young": Ibid., 20.

469 "run by . . . bureaucrats": Ibid., 21.

469 "clever"; "God be with you": Ibid., 22.

469 "worked up": EW to Kazin, March 31, 1962, *Letters*, 626.

469 "answered that . . . book": *Sixties*, 76.

470 "how alert . . . asked": Ibid., 89.

470 "than at . . . alone": Ibid., 77.

470 *"Dites à Malraux . . .* you think": Ibid., 78.

470 "my not . . . so'": Ibid., 80.

470 "eccentricities deserved . . . setting": Saul Bellow, "White House and Artists," *Noble Savage* 5 (1962), 5.

470 "of all . . . principle": Lowell to EW, May 31, 1962.

470 "the most . . . used it": *Sixties*, 78.

470 "into his act"; "drawling": Ibid., 83.

470 "Virgil was . . . him up": Robert Frost, quoted in Ibid., 84.

471 "This is not . . . merit": Interview with Schlesinger, 1984; interview with Theodore Sorensen, 1986.

471–472 "what we . . . death": *Cold War*, 92.

472 napalm: Meyers points out that Wilson was one of the first to challenge the Pentagon's claim that the widely used defoliant, Agent Orange, was "no more harmful than a gardener's weed-killer" (*Edmund Wilson*, 383).

472 "the total . . . complex": Dwight D. Eisenhower, "Farewell Radio and Television Address to the American People," *Public Papers of the Presidents of the United States: Dwight D. Eisenhower* (Washington, D.C.: Government Printing Office, 1960–1961), 1038.

472 "dear old heart": Allen Ginsberg to EW, Oct. 28, 1963.

472 "not only . . . we have": "An Interview with Edmund Wilson," *Bit*, 546.

472 "I asked . . . broad-toothed grins": *Sixties*, 169.

472 "the fear . . . death": Ibid., 168.

472–473 "I don't believe . . . power": EW to Deming, April 11, 1962, *Letters*, 618.

473 "a peaceful settlement with Russia:" *Sixties*, 273.

473 "sordidness of . . . police": Ibid., 272.

473 *"At my age . . .* before": Ibid., 3.

473 "living alone . . . herring": Ibid., 4.

473 "better hurry up"; "gossip in Cambridge": Ibid., 4.

473 "almost intolerably sour"; "that at . . . poem": Ibid., 8.

474 "Each incident . . . background": *O Canada*, 51.

474 "Auden was . . . something": "Isaiah Berlin on Edmund Wilson," *WQ*, Winter 1999, 40.

474 "like royalty": *Sixties*, 5.

474 "secret visit": Ibid., 6.

474 "apparently, only . . . Lawn": Ibid., 691.

474 "affable, amiable, charming": Interview with Cecil Lang, 1991.

474 "repeating with . . . Margaret": *Sixties*, 60.

474 "a paroxysm . . . glass": Ibid., 71.

474 "checked my . . . sleep": Ibid., 71.

474–475 "completely healed"; "It is awful . . . divine": Ibid., 146.

475 "Elena and I . . . other": Ibid., 528.

475 "pangs from far back": Ibid., 90.

475 "I wouldn't mind . . . else": Fitzgerald, quoted in Ibid.

475 "that her . . . New York": Ibid.

475 "Zelda, in . . . to hell": EW to Anne Miller, Aug. 3, 1971.

475 "she could . . . wineglasses": *Sixties*, 127.

475 "Scott's story . . . a ballet": Ibid., 210.

475 "One of . . . knocked out": Ibid., 47.

476 "the tones and turns of speech": *Devils*, 109.

476 "the impression . . . earth": *Sixties*, 189.

476 "His death . . . something": Ibid., 190.

476 "a Lolita . . . parties": Ibid.

477 "the Madame Bovary of Boonville": "My View," 18.

477 "She wants . . . it": *Sixties*, 101.

477 "after drunkenly . . . hear": Mary Meigs, *Lily Briscoe: A Self-Portrait* (Vancouver: Talonbooks, 1981), 19.

477 "I took . . . up": *Magician*, 198–99.

477 "came down . . . came up": Aaron, "To Be a Pilgrim," unpublished typescript, 1.

478 "were not full of whisky": *Sixties*, 793.

478 "very Huckleberry Finn": Ibid., 30.

478 "a man . . . ideas": Ibid., 48.

478 "with bound . . . wine": Ibid., 555–56.

479 "a charming rogue": Interview with Spender, 1991.

479 "I flew to the ceiling": *Sixties*, 175.

479 "ice cream suit"; "This is how I fly": Interview with Philip Carroll, 1992.

479 "something of a writer": *Sixties*, 36.

479 "emotional, imaginative . . . genius": Ibid., 39.

479 "easy game . . . women": Ibid., 39.

479 "to tell . . . say": Ibid., 62.

479 "somehow on the fringes": Ibid., 497.

479 "she gave . . . look": Ibid., 439.

480 "The women . . . deafening": EW to JDP, n.d. [1964], *Man in Letters*, 57.

480 "One struggles . . . current": Ibid., 276.

480 "where Mr. Pickwick . . . futile": Ibid., 258.

480 "Ours is . . . it": Ibid., 264.

481 "a great . . . feathers": Paul Horgan, *Tracings* (New York: Farrar, Straus & Giroux, 1993), 211.

481 "been served . . . beef": Elena, quoted in interview with Richard Pipes, 1991.

481 "You don't . . . bronchitis": Horgan, *Tracings*, 214.

481 "This book . . . gossipy": Ibid., 215.

481 "burst in . . . cookie'": Interview with Clendenning, 1991.

481 "vigorous . . . emphatic": Meyers, 388.

482 "an odd . . . New England": *Sixties*, 419–20.

482 "the Ritz bar": Horgan, *Tracings*, 224.

482 "the revels": Interview with Clendenning, 1991.

482 "an endearing . . . the know": *Sixties*, 425.

482 "Certainly not! . . . home!": EW, quoted in Horgan, *Tracings*, 220.

482 "an Egyptian . . . pastry": *Sixties*, 431.

501 "I wanted . . . her": Ibid. 512.

501 "Do you . . . held it": Interview with Clelia Carroll, 2002.

501 "My Hungarian . . . solitude": EW to Carroll, June 3, 1965, *Man in Letters*, 239.

502 "This effort . . . pie": Frederick Exley, *Pages from a Cold Island* (New York: Random House, 1975), 179.

502 "not having . . . her": *Sixties*, 460.

502 "we had . . . long time": Ibid., 655–56.

502 "she'd . . . me": Ibid., 658.

502 "I took . . . me up": Ibid., 816.

502 "How can . . . man": Mary Pcolar to EW, Sept. 30, 1971.

502 "*We* have . . . sense": Pcolar to EW, Nov. 19, 1971.

502–503 "three of . . . out": *Sixties*, 847.

503 "her constant . . . husband": Ibid., 820.

503 "I am a very warm person": Ibid., 844.

503 "Nothing illicit": Ibid., 846.

503 "put the horns on": Ibid., 860.

503 "yen"; "the hundred . . . world": Ibid., 845.

503 "her slim . . . behind": Ibid., 843.

503 "terrible"; "a cheap . . . Ripple": Ibid., 846.

503 "only get an erection at half-mast": Ibid., 864–65.

503 "principles": Ibid., 860.

503 "undressed almost . . . enough": Ibid.,862.

504 "in the twenties"; "wet, gluey, reeking": Ibid., 863.

504 "drop me . . . sonnet": EW to Anne Miller, Dec. 3, 1970.

504 "delightful meeting": EW to Miller, Nov. 5, 1970.

504 "so much . . . me": EW to Miller, n.d. [January 1972].

504 "multifaceted personality . . . Edmund": Miller to the author, Jan. 3, 1992.

504 "terribly nice": EW to Carroll, Jan. 10, 1968, *Man in Letters*, 257.

504–505 "Why do . . . alone"; EW, quoted by Anne Miller in a list of subjects discussed with her.

505 "trick with . . . hands": Interview with Penelope Gilliat, 1992.

505 "firm but . . . hair": *Sixties*, 864.

505 "I look . . . friends'": Ibid., 864.

505 "Perhaps you should destroy this note": Gilliat to EW, April 12, 1971.

505 "the wide and calm unquiet sea": "Tristes Tropiques," *Holiday Greetings and Desolating Lyrics from Edmund Wilson* (privately printed, 1970), 6.

506 "indirect evidence": *Sixties*, 807.

506 "He apparently . . . totally": Dr. Louis Zetzel's notes on his examinations of EW from 1962 to 1971.

506 "they were . . . close": *Magician*, 143.

506 "Like a good angel": *Sixties*, 870.

507 "the Cape Cod . . . crawl": EW to JDP, April 19, 1970, *Letters*, 715.

507 "to your . . . Pericles'": Ibid.

507 "by a belatedly . . . his youth": *Sixties*, 400.

507 "now a . . . to write": Interviews with EW, 1963.

482 "metacriticism"; "he seemed . . . criticism?": Ibid., 449–50.

482 "Emerson, Thoreau . . . others": Ibid., 447.

482–483 "frightened"; "Wilson roared . . . room": Interview with Clendenning, 1991.

483 "lies around . . . the floor": Appendix B: The Rat Letters, *Sixties*, 896–97.

483 "He had . . . mean": Interview with Clendenning, 1991.

483 "Jean, don't die! don't die!": EW, quoted in Horgan, *Tracings*, 231.

483 "whether I . . . difference": *Sixties*, 418.

484 "some part . . . gone": Ibid., 490.

484 "he had . . . his work": Ibid., 565.

484 "some of us"; "a lecherous eye": Ibid., 564.

484 "You fade . . . age": *Upstate*, 294–95.

484 "going to revolutionize": *Sixties*, 10.

484–485 "Lillian, ourselves . . . it": Ibid., 568.

485 "that if . . . squirming": Ibid., 569.

485 "two days . . . Ginsberg": Ibid., 716.

485 "You wrote . . . Finn": Ibid.

485 "Tax free! . . . swoop": Horgan, *Tracings*, 235.

486 "disgraceful": "Edmund Wilson Criticizes War as He Accepts the Aspen Prize," *NYT*, June 13, 1968, 44.

486 "You felt . . . humiliating": *Sixties*, 718.

486 "echoing Thomas Mann"; "there'd be . . . was": Ibid., 203–4.

486 "brusqueness"; "never experienced . . . Lady": Eric Goldman, *The Tragedy of Lyndon Johnson* (New York: Knopf, 1969), 423.

32: The Last Ten Years: Criticism, Travel Writing, *Upstate*

487 "They live . . . to live": *Sixties*, 28.

487 "Books and . . . tasks": "A Message You'll Expect, My Friends," *Night Thoughts*, 213.

487 "a drummer . . . Copperhead": "An Interview with Edmund Wilson," *Bit*, 545.

487 "really in . . . escape": Ibid., 541.

487–488 "a life . . . enjoyed": "Swinburne's Letters and Novels," *Bit*, 235.

488 "like a . . . dining-table": Edmund Gosse quoted in Ibid., 237.

488 "dropped from . . . coat-room": Ibid., 238.

488 "his full . . . fiction": Ibid., 269.

488 "international charmer from New Orleans": Ibid., 260.

488 "get him . . . no use": Gosse quoted in Ibid., 260.

488 "At the top . . . laughter": Ibid., 265.

489 "The M.L.A. . . . the country": Malcolm Cowley, "American Pleiade," *New York Times Book Review*, April 25, 1982, 3.

489 "I propose to disapprove"; "Approved Texts": "The Fruits of the M.L.A.," *Devils*, 163.

489 "tepid": Ibid., 168.

489 "with a . . . tranquility": Ibid., 167.

489 "ten dollars . . . spelling": Ibid., 168.

489 "masterpiece of the M.L.A. bad book-making": Ibid., 170.

489 "done everything . . . it": Ibid., 170.

489 "the most . . . literature": Clive James, *As of This Writing* (New York: W. W. Norton, 2003), 381.

490 $500,000 from the Ford Foundation: My account of this is from Jason Epstein and Daniel Aaron.

490 "the Library . . . scholarship": Cowley, "American Pleiade," 18.

490 "all those . . . hated": Powell to JDP, March 19, 1963, in *Selected Letters of Dawn Powell*, 315.

490 "powers of . . . the others": "That Summer in Paris," *Bit*, 515–16.

490 "a poet . . . 'the Republic'": "The Aftermath of Mencken," *Devils*, 104.

490 "selection of . . . taste": "*The Waste Land* in Deshabille," *Devils*, 115.

490 "an intensity . . . drafts": Ibid., 117.

490 "that of . . . realized": Ibid., 111.

491 "the Faulkner country": Hemingway, quoted in "That Summer in Paris," *Bit*, 522.

491 "that Mississippi . . . violence": Ibid., 522–23.

491 "the attractiveness . . . himself": "My Fifty Years with Dictionaries and Grammars," *Bit*, 624.

491 "All that . . . text": Ibid., 610–11.

491 "a slightly . . . liaison": Ibid., 630.

491 "the great flow . . . portable": Ibid., 652.

491–492 "a not unpleasant . . . shrunk": *Sixties*, 438.

492 "it had been . . . over": Interview with Darina Silone, 2002.

492 "hard, at . . . steps": EW to Clelia Carroll, Sept. 26, 1968, *Man in Letters*, 262.

492 "god-father . . . Scrolls": Teddy Kollek to EW, Jan. 12, 1965.

492 "a little . . . impressive": *Israel/Scrolls*, 353.

492 "We drank . . . cognac": *Sixties*, 615.

492 "only in . . . Scrolls": "Isaiah Berlin on Edmund Wilson," WQ, Winter 1999, 46.

492 "in terms . . . Islam": *Israel/Scrolls*, 361.

492 "a terrific . . . sinister": Ibid., 333.

492 "a little . . . Nuremberg": *Sixties*, 618.

492 "'Oh, why . . . Middle East'": *Israel/Scrolls*, 348.

492 "one of . . . days": *Sixties*, 623.

492 "further fatigued"; "hubbub": Ibid., 630.

493 "too terse . . . treasures": *Israel/Scrolls*, 283.

493 "the very . . . something": P. Kyle McCarter, Jr., "The Mystery of the Copper Scroll," in *The Dead Sea Scrolls After Forty Years*, ed. Hershel Shanks, James C. Vanderkam, P. Kyle McCarter, Jr., and James A. Sanders (Washington, D.C.: Biblical Archaeology Society, 1992), 54.

493 "an inveterate myth-shrinker": *Israel/Scrolls*, 386.

493 "the cult . . . blind alley": Ibid., 387.

493 "a charlatan": Ibid., 389.

493 "the Jewish poet Boris Pasternak": Ibid., 401.

493 "divine-human role": Ibid., 397.

493 "He who . . . upright": *Travels*, 325.

493–494 "hard work . . . thought": Aaron, "To Be a Pilgrim," unpublished typescript, 4.

494 "off my mind"; "T'ville memoir": *Sixties*, 789.

494 "the hatefulness and unnecessary sadism": "Svetlana and Her Sisters," *Window*, 25

494 "among the . . . *Confession*": Ibid., 259.

494 "simple and . . . firm opinions": *Sixties*, 756.

494 "the existence . . . inflicts": "Solzhenitzyn," *Window*, 276.

494 "the suffering which they denounce": Ibid., 277.

494 "our middle-class . . . unbreathable": "Dos Passos and the Social Revolution," *Shore* 433.

495 "Of course . . . grieved": "Solzhenitzyn," *Window*, 278.

495 "Though I . . . laugh": "Notes on Tolstoy," *Window*, 166–67.

496 "the vocabulary . . . difficult": Ibid., 168.

496 "the old blunt Russian": Ibid., 167.

496 "coldness, contempt, and cruelty": *Finland Station*, ix.

496 "we have been had": Interview with Richard Pipes, 1991.

496 "used to . . . maybe I was": "Isaiah Berlin on Edmund Wilson," WQ, Winter 1999, 39.

496 "did not . . . him": *Finland Station*, xii.

496 "a great novel"; "so abjectly humiliated": *Devils*, 64.

496 "what H.F. . . . differently!": James, quoted in *Devils*, 75.

497 "made on whisky": *Upstate*, 120.

497 "mostly evaporated": Ibid., 6.

497 "hardships and dream-pockets": Ibid., 35.

497 "the feudal unit": Ibid., 50.

497 "Nobler country . . . life": Ibid., 189–90.

498 "vast gray . . . heavy hide": Ibid., 346.

498 "Am I really anywhere?": "An Interview with Edmund Wilson," *Bit*, 541.

498 "gruesome remains . . . to rot": *Upstate*, 383.

498 "he was very . . . out": Interview with Gardner Jencks, 1984.

498 "the swift . . . States": *Upstate*, 381.

498 "all over the world": Ibid., 380.

33: Life Against Death

499 "talking and . . . lunches": *Sixties*, 674–75.

499 "getting the . . . to sleep": Ibid., 675–76.

499 "A definite . . . life": Ibid., 751.

500 "a strong passion": Ibid., 528.

500 "almost twenty . . . another": Ibid., 528.

500 "All this . . . ago": Ibid., 651.

500 "Though I . . . importance": Ibid., 588.

500 "I think . . . everyday"; EW to Elena, May 23, 1967.

501 "I really . . . shall": *Sixties*, 432.

501 "her frank . . . talking": Ibid., 176.

501 "yearning": Ibid., 329.

501 "m-o-n-e-y": Ibid., 496.

507 "of sleazy . . . unreal": *Sixties*, 852.

508 "very . . . ancient": *Upstate*, 32–33.

508 "as if . . . him": Ibid., 33.

508 "Elena was . . . angina": Interview with HM, 1984.

508 "a disastrous . . . imperial manner": V. S. Pritchett, *Three Honest Men*, ed. Philip French (Manchester: Carcanet New Press, 1980), 36–37.

508 "in some ways . . . him": *Sixties*, 871.

509 "for your . . . discovery": VN to EW, March 2, 1971, *N-W Letters*, 332.

509 "I am sure . . . writer": VN to EW, March 2, 1971, full version in Wilson's papers.

509 "remarkable, though . . . shouldn't)": EW to VN, March 8, 1971, *N-W Letters*, 332–33.

509 "to cut any corners": Quoted in Edel, Editor's Foreword to *Twenties*, xiv.

509 "irked": *Upstate*, 161.

509 "miseries, horrors . . . talent"; "a strong . . . Joyce": *Upstate*, 162; *Fifties*, 427, 426.

509 "he was . . . Russian writers"; "was purely aesthetic": "Isaiah Berlin on Edmund Wilson," *WQ*, Winter 1999, 41.

509 "in the contest . . . honor wins": VN to *New York Times Book Review*, November 7, 1971, 49.

510 "What Whistler . . . no talent'": EW to *New York Times Book Review*, Ibid.

510 "perfect answer . . . so shockingly": Katharine White to EW, Dec. 22, 1971.

510 "rather bitter": *Upstate*, 241.

510 "the Upstate Book": "My View," 32.

510 "drip-dry drugstore uniform": Ibid.

510 "better quality": Ibid., 18.

510 "a reputation . . . men": Ibid.

510 "One ought . . . arena"; *Sixties*, 876–77.

510 "a sunlit . . . nightmare)": Ibid., 881.

511 "The most . . . mist": Ibid., 736.

511 "When, with . . . medicine": Ibid., 867.

511 "a state of helplessness": Ibid., 743.

511 "Too bossy, too independent"; "So abounding . . . like this": Ibid., 786.

511 "Though he . . . thoroughness"; Ibid., 818.

511 "the present . . . books": EW to Roger Straus, Jan. 16, 1971, *Letters*, 731.

512 "a little thick": Straus, *Centennial Reflections*, 144.

512 "talk distinctly": EW to Mary Meigs, May 18, 1972, *Letters*, 739.

512 "Roger Straus . . . *Ecclesiastes* 12:12": EW to Shawn, May 27, 1932, *Letters*, 740.

512 "it would kill him": *Magician*, 246.

512 "he made . . . came back": Interview with HM, 1984.

512 "wheeled chair": *Sixties*, 878.

513 "Nothing will . . . it": *Magician*, 259.

513 "One day . . . floor": Ibid., 258.

514 "a puff of smoke": *Sixties*, 234.

514 "Father's language"; "for E."; "and white . . . sea": Ibid., 882.

514 "rather a . . . McGovern": Ibid., 881.

514 "an empty valise": EW to Celia Paget Goodman, Spring 1969, *Letters*, 701.

514 "Painful getting . . . conversion": *Sixties*, 882.

514 "hated living . . . death": Interview with Dr. Edgar Miller, 1992.

514 "I'm going to be cremated": *Magician*, 261.

514 "Oh that . . . this": Quoted by Rosalind in Exley, *Pages from a Cold Island*, 189.

514 "Goodbye, Father": *Magician*, 261.

515 "Breakfast": Interview with Elizabeth Stabb in Jeffrey Meyers, *Edmund Wilson: A Biography* (Boston: Houghton Mifflin, 1995), 481.

515 "kept saying . . . 'not true'": *Magician*, 262.

515 "Well, he . . . this way": Interview with HM, 1984.

515 "more like . . . body": Meyers, *Edmund Wilson*, 482.

515 "I don't want . . . funerals": Quoted in *Magician*, 263.

515 "a posthumous lecture . . . well": Aaron, "To Be a Pilgrim," 9.

515 "in the . . . trouble": *Magician*, 265.

515 "religious"; "That's absurd, Charley": H. Stuart Hughes, quoted by Meyers, 483.

515–516 "Some of . . . life": EW to Gauss, Aug. 25, 1937, *Letters*, 294.

516 "took a step, . . . old friend": Jason Epstein, "E. W., 1895–1972," *NYRB*, July 20, 1972.

516 "He had been . . . of it": Elena to Margaret Edwards Rullman, June 22, 1972, *Man in Letters*, 341.

516 "You find . . . the sky": *Sixties*, 843–44.

Epilogue

517–518 "the absence . . . presence": Dorothea Straus, *Prisons and Palaces* (Boston: Houghton Mifflin, 1976), 149.

518 "entirely Edmund's": Elena Wilson, "Note to the Reader," *Letters*, xxxi.

518 "Elena . . . Helen": Quoted in Meyers, *Edmund Wilson*, 534.

519 "If there . . . of it": *NYT*, June 12, 1972, 47.

520 "more complete and scholarly edition," Elena Wilson, "Note to the Reader," *Letters*, xxxi.

520 "pumped with blood"; "put his blood in it": "Isaiah Berlin on Edmund Wilson," *WQ*, Winter 1999, 48.

521 "of his . . . simultaneously": Elizabeth Hardwick.

521 "a patriot . . . style": "*Patriotic Gore* and the Introduction," *Centennial Reflections*, 209.

522 "majestic . . . emperor": Linscott, "Edmund Wilson: Casual Recollections," American Heritage Center, University of Wyoming. Unpublished typescript.

522 "one of . . . days": *Sixties*, 596.

522 "Life," Ibid., 615.

Acknowledgments

637 "temper tantrums . . . tendency"; "fits of weeping": Interviews with MMcC, 1984.

Acknowledgments

People did not forget their encounters with Wilson, and this book is a testament to their impressions, anecdotes, and memories of all kinds. I want to specify my profound debt to a few among those who have died. During a long afternoon at the Athenaeum Club in London, Isaiah Berlin, the most modest of great men, reflected on the merits as well as the quirky nature of his friend. Malcolm Cowley described Wilson's vision of the republic of letters and located him within the scene of the old *New Republic* and on the Left during the 1930s. Mary McCarthy allowed me the use of her correspondence and the divorce records, and in three days of continuous interviews in Castine, Maine, she provided vital information about Wilson and herself. Despite what has appeared in her biographies, McCarthy confided—on the condition that I not publish this during her lifetime—that she did indeed, when young, have "temper tantrums and an hysterical tendency" including "fits of weeping," and that they continued into her years as Wilson's wife. Adelaide Walker, a source of useful detail in the book, spoke frankly of the critic in his marriages and his relations with his children. Helen Muchnic observed him from the early 1940s to the end of his life. She knew Wilson's limitations and loved his strength of mind and heart.

The generous and thoughtful contributions of many others in interviews or conversation over the years helped tell this story. Often they are mentioned in the text by name. For such details I am indebted to Daniel Aaron, Edward Abbey, Renata Adler, Svetlana Alliluyeva, Jeanne Ballot (Wyndham), Marie-Claire Blais, Austin Briggs, Margaret Briggs, Bowden Broadwater, Kenneth Burke, Joan Canby, Clelia Carroll Carey, Philip Carroll, David Chavchavadze, John Clendenning, Gilles Couture, Hume Cronyn, Istvan Deak, W. Stanley Dell, Vida Deming, Joan Didion, Leon

Edel, Lowell Edmunds, Monroe Engel, Barbara Epstein, Jason Epstein, Judith Farr, William Fenton, Penelope Gilliatt, Celia Paget Goodman, Mary Hackett, Donald Hall, Anna Hamburger, Philip Hamburger, John Hammond, Elizabeth Hardwick, Laurence Hauptmann, Hazel Hawthorne (Werner), Sidney Hook, Harold Hoskins, Irving Howe, Irving Hubbard, Gardner Jencks, Ruth Jencks, Simon Karlinsky, Alfred Kazin, Anne Miller Kellogg, Frank Kermode, Cecil Lang, Wendy Lester, Elena Levin, Harry Levin, Townsend Ludington, Michael Macdonald, Mary Meigs, Sheldon Meyer, Dr. Edgar Miller, Malcolm Montgomery, Dmitri Nabokov, Mike Nichols, Edith Oliver, Edward Pcolar, Roy Harvey Pearce, William Phillips, Richard Pipes, Lady V. S. Pritchett, Stacy Schiff, Arthur Schlesinger, Jr., William Shawn, Countess Marina Shouvaloff, Pavel Sigalov, Darina Silone, Helen Sootin Smith, Theodore Sorenson, Elizabeth Spencer, Stephen Spender, Dorothea Straus, Roger Straus, Frances Swisher, Katharine Peterkin Tate, Dennis Tedlock, Eva Thoby-Marcelin, Henry Thornton, John Wain, Christopher Walling, Robert Penn Warren, Angus Wilson, and John Wyeth. Not long before his death, Aaron Copland, through the composer Ronald Caltabiano, spoke to me of his debt, as a young man, to Wilson's belief in American culture. Through the kind offices of Monroe Engel, Dr. Louis Zetzel, Wilson's physician, with whom I was unable to meet, provided me his notes on his patient from 1962 to 1971.

As essential have been the literary materials in which Wilson and his contemporaries speak to us. The vast Wilson archive at the Beinecke Rare Book and Manuscript Library, Yale University, was made available to me by the estate, and unpublished pieces including passages from the manuscripts and typescripts of the journals are here cited. The archive includes copies of Wilson's letters gathered from around the world by his wife Elena. His letters are complemented by letters to him of wives and lovers, friends and acquaintances throughout the literary world. The papers of some are uncollected. Cited from the Wilson papers and apparently found only there are communications of which I am sending copies to the libraries that own the following collections: Leonie Adams (Judith Farr, Literary Executor), Conrad Aiken (Joseph D. Killorin), Sherwood Anderson (Estate of Sherwood Anderson), Djuna Barnes (Authors League, New York, Literary Executor, Estate of Djuna Barnes), John Peale Bishop (Jonathan Bishop), Bruce Bliven (Daniel Horowitz), Louise Bogan (Mary Kinzie, Executor, Literary Estate of Louise Bogan), Margaret Canby (Joan Canby), Cyril Connolly (Copyright 1949 Cyril Connolly; reproduced by permission of the author c/o Rogers, Coleridge, and White, Ltd., 20 Powis Mews, London W11 1JN), Louise Connor (Peter F. Connor), John Dos Passos (Lucy Dos Passos Coggin), T. S. Eliot (Faber & Faber, Ltd), William Faulkner (Jill Faulkner Summers), Allen Ginsberg (The Allen Ginsberg Trust), John A. Lester (Wendy Lester), Robert Linscott (Estate of Robert Linscott), Robert Lowell (Elizabeth Hardwick), Edna St. Vincent Millay (The Edna St. Vincent Millay Society, Elizabeth Barnett, Rights and Permissions), Vladimir Nabokov (Dmitri Nabokov), Anaïs Nin (The Anaïs Nin Trust, Author's Representative Barbara W. Stuhlmann), George Orwell (A. M. Heath & Co), Mamaine Paget (Celia Paget Goodman), George Bernard Shaw (Society of Authors, on behalf of the Bernard Shaw Estate), Gertrude Stein (Estate of Gertrude Stein, Literary Executor, Stanford Gann, Jr., of Levin & Gann, P.A.), Alfred Stieglitz (The Georgia O'Keeffe Foundation), Allen Tate (Helen H. Tate), and Elinor Wylie (James Benet). A letter of Marianne Moore about *I Thought of Daisy* is used by permission of Marianne Craig Moore (Executor, The Literary Estate of Marianne Moore). Letters to Wilson from Katherine White, James Thurber, and Harold Ross, a letter from Ross to White, and an undated memo by Ross are courtesy of *The New Yorker*/The Condé Nast Publications Inc., www.new yorker.com.

My accumulated debts to libraries and their staffs are too large to be listed here, and I ask the forgiveness of all who are not mentioned. I have used letters not available to Elena Wilson from collections like those of Lionel Trilling at Columbia University, Cyril Connolly at the University of Tulsa, and Roman Grynberg at the Library of Congress. The Library of Congress now contains the love letters from Wilson to Edna St. Vincent Millay that long lay in the back room of a New York lawyer. Alice Birney at the Manuscript Division there has given me good advice about various subjects. I am grateful to the Vassar College Library and Dean M. Rogers for help with the McCarthy papers, and to Margaret Rich at the Princeton University Rare Books and Special Collections Library, which houses Wilson's letters to John Peale Bishop, F. Scott Fitzgerald, and Helen Muchnic, as well as the papers of his lifelong Red Bank friend, Margaret Rullman. My thanks, too, to Eliza Roberston and her colleagues at the National Humanities Center in North Carolina and to the University of Wyoming's reference librarians. Steve Jones, in public services at the Beinecke Library, has helped me out for twenty years, and Karen Speicher, having expertly sorted the Wilson Papers, retrieved certain material that I needed.

This book has been supported by fellowships from the National Endowment for the Humanities and several sabbaticals from the University of Wyoming. A draft was finished at the National Humanities Center, on a fellowship endowed by the Glaxo-Smith-Kline corporation. I am indebted to Jonathan D'Amore, then completing his Ph.D. in English at the University of North Carolina at Chapel Hill, and to University of Wyoming students including Garry Alkire, Carollynn Wolff Bartosh, William Clark, Natalie Dykstra, Tony Magagna, Cinda Nofziger, and Kathryn Jane Flitner Wallop. Julia Stuble devotedly assisted in the final revisions.

Matthew Bruccoli, Gerald Early, Elizabeth Hardwick, James Sanders, Stacy Schiff, and Arthur Schlesinger, Jr., have commented on parts of the text. Jed Perl, John Raeburn, and Neale Reinitz have read most of it, and their suggestions have been vital, as was the patient wisdom of Joan Sutton-Straus, who read more than one draft. The book is marked by Sarah Dabney's steady contributions, her clarity and wit. Warm thanks are due to Helen Miranda Wilson for her integrity and her perception, and to Lorin Stein, Annie Wedekind, and JoAnna Kremer at Farrar, Straus and Giroux. I owe most to Roger Straus. Himself a sprinter in college, Mr. Straus called me his "distance runner" and loyally sustained the project to its end.

Index

ILLUSTRATION CREDITS

Kimball family group: Courtesy of Beinecke Rare Book and Manuscript Library, Yale University

Wilson's paternal grandparents: Courtesy of Beinecke Rare Book and Manuscript Library, Yale University

Edmund Wilson, Sr.: Courtesy of Red Bank Public Library Historical Photograph Collection

Helen Mather Kimball Wilson: Courtesy of Beinecke Rare Book and Manuscript Library, Yale University

Young Edmund with his mother: Courtesy of Beinecke Rare Book and Manuscript Library, Yale University

Sandy and Edmund: Courtesy of Beinecke Rare Book and Manuscript Library, Yale University

Alfred Grosvenor Rolfe: Courtesy of Hill School Archives

Wilson at Hill: Courtesy of Beinecke Rare Book and Manuscript Library, Yale University

Wilson at Princeton: Courtesy of Beinecke Rare Book and Manuscript Library, Yale University

Christian Gauss: Courtesy of Seeley G. Mudd Manuscript Library, Princeton University

Stanley Dell: Courtesy of Beinecke Rare Book and Manuscript Library, Yale University

John Peale Bishop: Courtesy of Seeley G. Mudd Manuscript Library, Princeton University

Wilson in uniform: Courtesy of Beinecke Rare Book and Manuscript Library, Yale University

Edna St. Vincent Millay: Courtesy of the Library of Congress

Mary Blair: Courtesy of the Billy Rose Theatre Collection, The New York Public Library for the Performing Arts, Astor, Lenox and Tilden Foundations

Elinor Wylie: Courtesy of Beinecke Rare Book and Manuscript Library, Yale University

F. Scott Fitzgerald: © Minnesota Historical Society/CORBIS

Ernest Hemingway: Courtesy of Helen Breaker/The Associated Press

Wilson in the twenties: Courtesy of Beinecke Rare Book and Manuscript Library, Yale University

Margaret Canby: Courtesy of Beinecke Rare Book and Manuscript Library, Yale University

John Dos Passos: Courtesy of Wide World Photo

Louise Bogan: By permission of the Trustees of Amherst College, Amherst College Archives and Special Collections

Elizabeth Waugh: Courtesy of the Ulrich Museum of Art, Wichita State University

Louise Fort Connor: Courtesy of Peter Connor

Isaiah Berlin: © British Broadcasting Corporation

Wilson and Mary McCarthy: Courtesy of Sylvia Salmi and Vassar College

Vladimir Nabokov: Courtesy of Wellesley College Archives

Dawn Powell: Courtesy of Tim Page

Helen Muchnic: Courtesy of Smith College Archives

Mamaine Paget: Courtesy of Beinecke Rare Book and Manuscript Library, Yale University

Anaïs Nin: Courtesy of Beinecke Rare Book and Manuscript Library, Yale University

The house on Money Hill Road: Courtesy of Beinecke Rare Book and Manuscript Library, Yale University

Elena Wilson: Courtesy of Beinecke Rare Book and Manuscript Library, Yale University

Wilson and Reuel: Photograph by Henri Cartier-Bresson

Wilson family group: Courtesy of Beinecke Rare Book and Manuscript Library, Yale University

W. H. Auden: Photograph by Rollie McKenna

Wilson with owl: Photograph by Rollie McKenna

Wilson sketches: Courtesy of Lewis M. Dabney

Mary Meigs, Marie-Claire Blais, and Barbara Deming: Courtesy of Marie-Claire Blais

The old stone house: Photograph by Carl E. La Tray

Mary Pcolar: Courtesy of Beinecke Rare Book and Manuscript Library, Yale University

Reuel and his mother: Courtesy of Vassar College

Elena on the terrace: Photograph by Joan Colebrook

Wilson at *The New Yorker*: Photograph by Henri Cartier-Bresson

Rosalind Wilson: Courtesy of Beinecke Rare Book and Manuscript Library, Yale University

Helen Miranda Wilson: Photograph by Matthew Spender